The Jewish People
in the First Century

VOLUME ONE

Compendia Rerum Iudaicarum ad Novum Testamentum

SECTION ONE

THE JEWISH PEOPLE IN THE FIRST CENTURY

IN TWO VOLUMES

I.   THE JEWISH PEOPLE IN THE FIRST CENTURY: Historical Geography, Political History, Social, Cultural and Religious Life and Institutions. Edited by S. Safrai and M. Stern in co-operation with D. Flusser and W. C. van Unnik. Second printing. 1974.

II. THE JEWISH PEOPLE IN THE FIRST CENTURY. Historical Geography, Political History, Social, Cultural and Religious Life and Institutions. Edited by S. Safrai and M. Stern in co-operation with D. Flusser and W. C. van Unnik. 1976.

SECTION TWO

THE LITERATURE OF THE JEWISH PEOPLE IN THE PERIOD OF THE SECOND TEMPLE AND THE TALMUD

IN THREE VOLUMES

I.   MIQRA. Reading, translation and interpretation of the Hebrew Bible in Ancient Judaism and Early Christianity,
Editor: M. J. Mulder

II. JEWISH WRITING OF THE SECOND TEMPLE PERIOD. Apocrypha, Pseudepigrapha, Qumran Sectarian Writings, Philo, Josephus, 1984.
Editor: M. E. Stone

III. THE LITERATURE OF THE SAGES. Midrash, Mishnah, Talmud.
Editor: S. Safrai

Advisory Editors:
D. Flusser, J. Goldin, Th. C. de Kruyf, R. Le Déaut, G. W. MacRae, K. Stendahl, S. Talmon, E. Tov.

Executive Editors:
W. J. Burgers, H. Sysling, P. J. Tomson.

Published under the Auspices of the Foundation Compendia Rerum Iudaicarum ad Novum Testamentum, Amsterdam.

The Jewish People in the First Century

Historical Geography, Political History, Social, Cultural
and Religious Life and Institutions

Volume One

Edited by S. Safrai and M. Stern
in co-operation with D. Flusser and W. C. van Unnik

second printing

1974
VAN GORCUM, ASSEN
FORTRESS PRESS, PHILADELPHIA

The publication of this book was made possible through a grant from the Prince Bernhard Fund of Amsterdam

ISBN 90 232 1070 0

Printed in The Netherlands by Van Gorcum, Assen.

Preface

In September, 1964, a working committee was created to produce a general handbook on the interrelation between Judaism and Christianity in the first two centuries. Aspects of this history had been explored previously by individual scholars, but this committee felt that this was an appropriate time to comprehensively gather together and evaluate the available information on the many sides of this question in a series of volumes. New discoveries, such as the Dead Sea Scrolls, and the reevaluation of known materials stimulate reexamination.

Many factors have encouraged this new examination of our histories. The shared suffering of Jews and Christians during World War II convinced many that they were persecuted for their faithfulness to the same God. Although begun earlier, Christian reflection upon the ways in which misguided Christians and some forms of Christian theology have contributed to anti-Semitism has been intensified by these experiences in the war. Christians as well as Jews today are searching out and exposing such ideas to promote good understanding of the historical relations of our two communities.

The World Council of Churches, the growing Jewish-Christian dialogue and Vatican II have all encouraged a new look at the early Christian Church and its place in the Jewish world of that time. Renewed interest among Jewish scholars in Early Christianity has stimulated the rediscovery of the two Jews, Jesus of Nazareth and Paul of Tarsus. In all this a new conception of our two communities seems to be arising in which they are no longer rival brothers, each claiming the whole birthright, but sisters carrying on the traditional heritage. Each is beginning to see not only the legitimate values in its own history but that which the other preserves as well.

In previous works on this subject attention has been given to one side or the other. Thus, attention has focussed either on Early Christianity and its Jewish background or on the history of the Jewish people with the Early Christian sources treated incidentally. In *Compendia* the focus is on both Judaism and Early Christianity with a concentration on their relations in history, literature and thought. It is surprising to see the relative lack of discussion between scholars in the fields of Early Christianity and Jewish studies in the Second Temple period. Christian scholars have tended to utilize those Jewish sources, preserved in the Church, such as the apocrypha and pseudepigrapha but to leave unexplored rabbinic sources. Rabbinic scholars have concentrated upon the sources, preserved in Hebrew or Aramaic in the Synagogue.

'There is nothing new under the sun.' There have been exceptional scholars in both fields, such as Lightfoot and Schürer or Ginzberg and Montefiore and others. *Compendia* attempts to bring together scholars of Early Christianity and Rabbinic studies and others in related fields to examine as comprehensively as possible the many sources for Judaism and Christianity in the first two centuries.

Thus, it was decided to publish a series which could form a bridge between Jewish and Christian theology. For Christians this was an ecumenical decision of the first order; for them the *oecumene* is incomplete without the Jews. For the Jews such a project could contribute to the battle against anti-semitism, practiced by groups and individuals in Christianity because of incorrect interpretations of the Gospel.

Much has happened between 1964 and 1973. The original plan of eight volumes has been expanded to ten, and the later history of the relationship between Jews and Christians until the present time has been included.

In the course of these years the working committee has met to discuss the outline and contents of this project on more than a hundred occasions. Among the initial workers we wish to thank Prof. C. A. Rijk, who was followed by Prof. Th. de Kruyff after his departure to Rome, Messrs. B. Folkertsma and W. A. C. Whitlau and Dr. M. H. König. Although their names do not appear in the list of collaborators, their pioneering activities has been of great importance to us. We also greatly appreciate the contribution of Mr. Kappelle, whose work as treasurer was continued after his death by his son, Mr. D. Kappelle.

Soon contacts were established with outstanding international scholars; they have offered their collaboration freely and spontaneously in nearly every instance. It was felt that one could not refuse to contribute to this scientific, scholarly project, aimed at eliminating age-old misunderstandings and their evil consequences.

Invitations were issued to international editors and authors; and in April, 1967, a number of scholars gathered at the Hoorneboeg conference centre in Hilversum to organize and allocate the work. The papers, presented at that conference, have been published as *Studies on the Jewish Background of the New Testament*, (Assen, 1969). The American Jewish Committee made this meeting possible through a generous gift. We thank especially its Director of Interreligious Affairs, Rabbi Tanenbaum, and the European Director, Dr. Schuster, who participated there. Its example has been followed by many institutions and individuals in the course of the years. We wish to note in this connection the donations of the Evangelische Kirche im Rheinland, the Secretariat for the Promotion of Christian Unity in Rome, the World Council of Churches, the Dutch Reformed Church's Council for the Relationship between the Church and Israel, the Gravin van Bijlandt Foundation of The Hague, several private donors in West Germany and the Leerhuis in Hilversum. Numerous other private donors have generously helped; we wish to recognize particularly the assistance of the late Mr. Dudok van Heel of Laren, Mrs. Koperberg of Zeist, Mr. Doodeheefver of Hilversum, Dr. H. D. Pierson, Prof. U. Lohmar, M.d.B., Bonn, and Präses Prof. J. Beckmann of Düsseldorf.

We also wish to mention with gratitude the moral support and help of Bundespräsident Dr. Gustav Heinemann and Dr. M. Klompé, former Minister for Cultural Affairs of the Netherlands. With appreciation we record the help of the Netherlands Organization for the Advancement of Pure Research (Z.W.O.) for editorial activities in this series and of the 'Prins Bernhard Fonds' for its contribution toward the publication.

It is impossible to mention in this preface all the names of those who have assisted in our project. We have not mentioned the names of editors and contributors here because they have made their place in the pages of this work through their contributions already. However, I should like to make an exception for Prof. O. Michel, Prof.

H. Kremers, Prof. J. van Goudoever, Prof. M. de Jonge, Rabbi Y.
Aschkenasy, Prof. S. Safrai, Prof. D. Flusser and Prof. S. Sandmel,
who have devoted extensively of their time and energy to make this
edition possible, far beyond their editorial activities.

Also for the following volumes we shall need the assistance of many
to see this project to its completion. It is with an appeal to all who
read this that I greet this first volume as a beginning step on the road
to a better understanding between our two religious communities
and to a deeper insight into Torah and Gospel. May God's blessing
rest on our further work.

H. VAN PRAAG
President,
Compendia Foundation

Members of the Compendia Foundation:

H. van Praag, President
J. van Goudoever, Secretary
J. Morreau, Treasurer
Y. Aschkenasy
H. de Bie
L. Dequeker
H. Kremers
A. C. Ramselaar
C. A. Rijk
J. C. Tupker

General Introduction

The *Compendia Rerum Iudaicarum ad Novum Testamentum* is designed as a historical work on the relationship of Judaism and Christianity. The work will concentrate on the history of Judaism in the first and second centuries C.E.—with a necessary retrospective view of the preceding period—and on the origin of Christianity within Judaism, the rupture of relations between the early church and Judaism and the subsequent separate history and development of the two communities. The history of the relationship between Judaism and Christianity after 200 C.E. will be sketched in general lines to illustrate the ways in which the decisive historical events of the first period have exercised lasting influence upon both groups until the present day.

It is the firm conviction of the editors that cooperative historical research, carried out in an unbiased way and concentrated upon the fundamental issues, has an important contribution to make in the effort to gain a better insight into the background of present-day relationships between Jews and Christians with different perspectives. Thus, although this series of handbooks is designed for the use of pastors, priests, rabbis, teachers and other non-specialists, it presupposes careful research and demands not only clarity of expression but also a truly scholarly approach from the contributing authors. The *Compendia*, therefore, is written not only to provide comprehensive summaries but also to make a real contribution to historical research in this field.

Since the publication of E. Schürer's *Geschichte des jüdischen Volkes im Zeitalter Jesu Christi*, (3 vols, 3rd-4th ed. 1901-11), and H. Strack and P. Billerbeck's *Kommentar zum Neuen Testament aus Talmud und Midrasch*, (4 vols, 1922-28) with its two volumes of indices, prepared by J. Jeremias (1956, 1961), much new material has been discovered. Many attempts have been made to provide surveys of research on the various aspects of Jewish life and literature at the beginning of our era and to contribute towards a better understanding of the origins and early history of Christianity against the background of developments within Judaism. Yet a comprehensive, up-to-date survey of all the material, available at the present time, and a thorough study of the many facets of this field has been lacking until now. (cf. O. Michel, 'Zur Methodik der Forschung', *Studies on the Jewish Background of the New Testament*, Assen, 1969).

Of course, there are many difficulties in the undertaking of a series of volumes, intended as a new survey of the material and a clear description of the manifold developments in Judaism and early Christianity in their many intricate interrelations with the Hellenistic and Roman world. The editors of the *Compendia* are fully cognizant of this. The available material is so vast and variegated that no single person can be expected to give a full survey of it. Thus, the cooperation of many scholars in various fields is necessary. Generally New Testament scholars have no firsthand knowledge of the Jewish material, especially of the rabbinical writings. Often specialists in rabbinic studies are not adequately familiar with material, preserved in the New Testament and early Christian writings, to use them critically and easily in their own research. Presently the early Christian documents are being studied along various lines and being analyzed according to as many different methods, some of which may well be useful in the study of rabbinic documents and their sources. Methods of rabbinic study may also prove valuable in the study of the New Testament and the early Christian literature. Only in close cooperation between New Testament scholars and specialists in rabbinics and in a thorough discussion of the methods involved, shall we gain new insight and a better understanding of the relations between Judaism and Christianity in the beginning of our era.

Hellenistic-Jewish and apocalyptic sources have traditionally received more attention from historians of early Christianity than have the rabbinic sources. But there, too, so many text-critical and exegetical problems arise that only specialists can adequately evaluate the results of this field of research for other studies. Again these specialists are not necessarily well-versed in rabbinics or the early Christian literature. To illustrate the kinds of material, not yet available in the time of Schürer, we need to mention only subsequent archeological discoveries; a survey of this material, written by experts, needs to be prepared for the scholars in related fields.

Collecting the various contributions of specialists in these many fields will reveal not only our present knowledge but the gaps in our comprehension as well. All scholars, working in the field, will be aware of the fact that much attention has been devoted to certain subjects whereas other areas have been neglected. Some might say that the fact, that there is so much we do not know and that has not been finally evaluated yet, should warn us against the production of a series such as the *Compendia* or should persuade us to postpone such a venture at least. If there is work yet to be done, we shall encourage young scholars to pursue the many subjects which await further investigation, but we must provide the provisional framework within which they will work.

When in 1968-69 the first plans for the *Compendia* were being drafted, discussions between scholars of various religious and cultural backgrounds and with different approaches were held; these discussions convinced the editors that much more is needed than a common desire to provide unbiased information on the basis of critical historical research. Of course, all the contributing authors have been and will be asked to work on this basis; but at the same time it will be necessary to question ceaselessly all points of departure, all approaches, all methods. The ostensibly self-evident may be the result of prejudice or misunderstanding. It is here that discussions between Jewish scholars of different backgrounds, Christian historians of various denominations and schools and scholars of no religious affiliation, meeting on the basis described, will be very necessary and extremely useful.

The first section, *The Jewish People in the First Century*, gives an over-view of our present knowledge concerning the Jewish people at that time; thus, historical geography, political history and social, cultural and religious life and institutions are discussed here. These topics were chosen because it was considered useful to open the series with a description of Jewish life in the period under consideration. One can use the two volumes of this section as a separate whole; however, they are designed as the first two volumes of the series of ten. Consequently, a number of subjects are treated here only insofar as they pertain to the subject matter of these volumes; they will return in a different context and perspective in subsequent sections. For example, the first chapter of volume one deals with the literary documents only as they can be used as sources for the history, described in the following chapters of this section. As literary documents they will be studied in a much wider context in section II; in that section the questions, related to their viewpoints on past and contemporary events and their historical reliability, will be raised anew.

The second section will treat *Oral and Literary Tradition in Judaism and Early Christianity*; it is divided into two headings: the first on the reading and interpretation of Scripture and the second on the various types and genres of religious and other writings. The third section will deal with the *Social and Religious History of Judaism and Early Christianity* within the context of the surrounding Oriental, Hellenistic and Roman world. In this world Christianity originated as a movement, consisting of various streams and groups who held differing attitudes, e.g. vis-à-vis the Jewish tradition from which Christianity had sprung and the Hellenistic-Roman world around it. To write the history of Judaism and early Christianity and of the interaction of the two movements in a highly complex cultural setting will be no easy task, but it is hoped that teamwork will bring us further than Schürer alone could come.

Section IV will be devoted to a *Comparative Study of Jewish and Early Christian Thought* and will show some resemblance to the excursses of Strack-Billerbeck's magnum opus in volumes IV/I and IV/2. It will examine the central topics of Jewish and early Christian religious thought with the intention of discovering where and how the two are related and where their ways separate. This examination presupposes the literary studies, carried out in section II, and the historical analyses, contained in section III. It will not result in an enumeration of parallel texts of certain New Testament paragraphs, but individual articles will treat the development of certain concepts in Judaism and Christianity.

Section V, finally, is entitled *The History of Jewish-Christian Relations from the Third Century to Modern Times*; it will attempt to show how the events, developments and decisions of the beginning of our era have constantly affected that history.

M. DE JONGE
S. SAFRAI
General Editors

Introduction

These two opening volumes of the *Compendia* are devoted to the political, cultural and religious *realia* of the Jewish people in the Land of Israel and the Diaspora in the first century. An effort has been made here to record the main elements which represent a picture of this people within the framework of its religious and social institutions and the world in which the people lived. The lack of space within only two volumes has prevented an exhaustive treatment of all sources and research literature, even in those areas which have been covered; other subjects had to be entirely disregarded. The authors and editors have attempted to consider all the sources and researches and have striven to present as faithful and complete a representation as possible. The subjects, dealt with in the chapter on literary sources, have been restricted to those materials which are most fruitful for the chapters in these two volumes. Thus, apocrypha and pseudepigrapha, the discoveries at Qumran and the Aramaic translations of the Bible (*Targumim*) have not been discussed. Their principal importance lies in their representation of the literary traditions and their witness to the history of religious and social thought. Because the authors of this section utilize these sources only incidentally, it would be inappropriate to discuss them in the introduction to the section. Again the talmudic literature and the New Testament have been described as historical sources for these chapters but not for their own sake. Such a detailed and extensive discussion will be devoted to them in its proper place in section II on *Oral and Literary Traditions*.

Surveys of private law according to the Jewish and Hellenistic systems have been presented. The first system was in effect among Jews in the Land of Israel, and the latter affected Jewish life in the Hellenistic Diaspora both when Jews had recourse to the courts of Hellenistic cities and as a source of influence upon the independent courts of the Jews in the Diaspora. Not every locality in the Diaspora possessed a Jewish court; nor did Jews always turn to their own courts; and even the Jewish courts acted within the framework of the Hellenistic judicial system, although the exact manner and extent is debatable. The chapter on law is schematic and gives no description of the history of either Jewish or Hellenistic law; as far as possible the known turning points and changes within the temporal limits of our period have been indicated. A complete survey of the history of Jewish and Hellenistic law would have been inappropriate for the programme of the present work. No survey of Roman private law is presented because this system did not affect the Jews in the Land of Israel nor those in the Diaspora. Nor is there a specific chapter on Jewish public law because this subject is incorporated into the relevant chapters.

The editors hope that the choice of subjects and mode of execution of these two volumes will promote the aim in the minds of the initiators of the *Compendia* project and of those who were partners in the creation of this section.

S. SAFRAI

M. STERN

Editorial note and acknowledgments

The contributions by S. Safrai and M. Stern, which were originally written in Hebrew, were translated into English by S. Applebaum (all contributions by M. Stern) and by J. Braude, I. H. Levin and Channah Schmorak. The entire manuscript was checked and stylistically revised by K. Smyth. The following translations have been used: Revised Standard Version for biblical quotations, Danby's translation of the Mishnah, and the translations of Josephus and Philo in the Loeb Classical Series.

We are pleased to see the appearance of the first volume in the revised translation of SCHÜRER, *Geschichte des jüdischen Volkes im Zeitalter Jesu Christi*. Although it was not available to the authors at the time of writing, references to SCHÜRER I from this new edition, SCHÜRER, VERMES, MILLAR, *The History of the Jewish People in the Age of Jesus Christ I*, 1973, were inserted in the final editorial stage.

Indices to the two volumes of this section will follow at the end of the second volume.

Contents

Abbreviations

AASOR	*Annual of the American Schools of Oriental Research*, 1919 ff.
AJA	*American Journal of Archaeology*, 1897 ff.
AJPH	*American Journal of Philology*, 1880 ff.
ASTI	*Annual of the Swedish Theological Institute*, 1962 ff.
BA	*The Biblical Archaeologist*, 1938 ff.
BASOR	*The Bulletin of the American Schools of Oriental Research*, 1919 ff.
BCH	*Bulletin de correspondance hellénique*, 1877 ff.
BGU	*Aegyptische Urkunden aus den königlichen Museen zu Berlin:. Griechische Urkunden*, 1895 ff.
BJPES	*Bulletin of the Jewish Palestine Exploration Society* (in Hebrew), 1933-50, continued as *Bull. Israel Ex. Soc.*, 1950 ff.
BJRL	*The Bulletin of the John Rylands Library*, 1913 ff.
BSAA	*Bulletin de la Société archéologique d'Alexandrie*, 1904 ff.
CAH	*Cambridge Ancient History*, 12 vols, 1923-39
CERP	A. H. M. Jones, *The Cities of the Eastern Roman Provinces*, 1937, ²1971.
CIG	A. Boeckh *et al.*, *Corpus Inscriptionum Graecarum*, 1828-77
CII	*Corpus Inscriptionum Iudaicarum*, ed. J. B. Frey, 1936-52
CIL	*Corpus Inscriptionum Latinarum*, 1863 ff.
CPJ	V. A. Tcherikover, A. Fuks, M. Stern, *Corpus Papyrorum Judaicarum*, 3 vols, 1957-64
DAC	*Dictionaire d'Archéologie Chrétienne et de Liturgie*, 1924-53
EB	*Encyclopaedia Biblica* (in Hebrew), 1950 ff.
FIRA	*Fontes iuris Romani antejustiniani*, 3 vols, 1940-3.
Gabba	E. Gabba, *Iscrizioni greche e latine per lo studio della Bibbia*, 1958
Hermes	*Hermes, Zeitschrift für klassische Philologie*, 1866 ff.
HTR	*The Harvard Theological Review*, 1908 ff.
HUCA	*Hebrew Union College Annual*, 1924 ff.
IEJ	*Israel Exploration Journal*, 1950 ff.
IG	*Inscriptiones Graecae, Königliche preussische Akademie der Wissenschaften in Berlin*, 1873 ff.

IGLS	*Inscriptions grecques et latines de la Syrie,* ed. by L. Jalabert R. Mouterde *et al.,* 1929 ff.
IGR	*Inscriptiones Graecae ad res Romanas pertinentes,* vols. I, II and IV, ed. R. Cagnat-Lafaye, 1906-27
ILS	H. Dessau, *Inscriptiones Latinae selectae,* 1892-1916
FGH	*Die Fragmente der griechischen Historiker,* ed. F. Jacoby, 1923 ff.
JAOS	*The Journal of the American Oriental Society,* 1843 ff.
JBL	*Journal of Biblical Literature,* 1881 ff.
JEA	*Journal of Egyptian Archaeology,* 1914 ff.
JJP	*The Journal of Juristic Papyrology,* 1946 ff.
JJS	*The Journal of Jewish Studies,* 1948.
JPOS	*Journal of the Palestine Oriental Society,* 1920-48
JNES	*Journal of Near Eastern Studies,* 1942 ff.
JQR	*The Jewish Quarterly Review,* 1888 ff.
JRS	*Journal of Roman Studies,* 1911 ff.
JTS	*Journal of Theological Studies,* 1899 ff.
M.	*Mishnah*
MAMA	*Monumenta Asiae Minoris Antiqua,* 8 vols, 1928-62
MGWJ	*Monatschrift für Geschichte und Wissenschaft des Judentums,* 1851 ff.
NNM	*Numismatic Notes and Monographs*
NTS	*New Testament Studies,* 1954 ff.
OGIS	W. Dittenberger, *Orientis Graeci inscriptiones selectae,* 2 vols, 1903-5
PAAJR	*Proceedings of the American Academy for Jewish Research,* 1928 ff.
P.Col.Zen.	W. L. Westermann, E. S. Hasenoehre, C. W. Keyes, and H. Liebesny, *Columbia Papyri* (Greek Series): *Zenon Papyri,* 1934-40
PEF	*Palestine Exploration Fund, Quarterly Statement,* 1869 ff.
PCZ	C. C. Edgar, *Catalogue général des antiquités égyptiennes du Musée du Caire: Zenon Papyri,* 4 vols, 1925-31
P.ELEPH.	O. Rubensohn, *Elephantine-Papyri,* 1907
PEQ	*Palestine Exploration Quarterly,* 1937 ff.
PG	*Patrologia Graeca*
P.Giess.	E. Kornemann and P. M. Meyer, *Griechische Papyri im Museum des oberhessischen geschichtsvereins zu Giessen,* 1910-12
P.Gur.	J. G. Smyly, *Greek Papyri from Gurob,* 1921

P.Hal.   *Dikaiomata, herausgegeben von der Graeca Halensis*, 1913

P.Hib.   B. P. Grenfell, A. S. Hunt, E. G. Turner, and M. Th. Lenger, *The Hibeh Papyri*, 1906-55

PIR   *Prosopographia Imperii Romani*, 2nd ed., 1933 ff.

PL   *Patrologia Latina*

P.Lond.   F. G. Kenyon and H. I. Bell, *Greek Papyri in the British Museum*, 1893-1917

P.Oxy.   *The Oxyrhynchus Papyri*, 1898 ff.

PSI   *Pubblicazioni della Società italiana per la Ricerca dei Papiri greci e latini in Egitto: Papiri greci e latini*, 1912 ff.

P.T.   *Palestinian Talmud*

P.Tebt.   B. P. Grenfell, A. S. Hunt, J. G. Smyly and E. J. Goodspeed, *The Tebtunis Papyri*, 1902-38

PW   Pauly-Wissowa, *Real-Encyclopädie der classischen Altertumswissenschaft*, 1893 ff.

QDAP   *Quarterly of the Department of Antiquities in Palestine*, 1932 ff.

RB   *Revue Biblique*, 1892 ff.

REG   *Revue des Études grecques*, 1888 ff.

REJ   *Revue des Études juives*, 1880 ff.

RHR   *Revue de l'histoire des religions*, 1880 ff.

RIDA   *Revue internationale des droits de l'antiquité*, 1948 ff.

SEG   *Supplementum Epigraphicum Graecum*, Leiden 1923 ff.

SIG   W. Dittenberger, *Sylloge Inscriptionum Graecarum*, 3rd ed., 1915-27

T.   *Tosefta*

T.B.   *Babylonian Talmud*

ZDPV   *Zeitschrift des Deutschen Palästina-Vereins*, 1878 ff.

ZNW   *Zeitschrift für die Neutestamentliche Wissenschaft*, 1900 ff.

ZSS   *Zeitschrift der Savigny-Stiftung für Rechtsgeschichte, Romanistische Abteilung*, 1880 ff.

Maps

by M. Avi-Yonah

Chapter One
Sources

Jewish literature in the Hebrew and Aramaic languages from the period of the Second Temple until the end of the Talmudic period may be divided into three sectors. The first is the traditional Hebrew (and Aramaic) Scripture, known as the Written Law. This is presupposed rather than discussed in the following pages. The second group of writings —'non-canonical'—generally known as the Apocrypha (e.g. the Apocalypse of Baruch, 1 Maccabees) were not preserved in Hebrew but in a number of translations. They became more or less loosely attached to the scriptural tradition of the Christian Church, and ceased in time to form part of Jewish tradition, though some fragments, in Hebrew or Aramaic (like the Book of Ben Sira) have been discovered in the present century. In recent years books in Hebrew and Aramaic belonging to a Jewish sect or sects whose headquarters were at Qumran on the western shore of the Dead Sea have also been discovered. These, too, did not become part of the Jewish tradition and, like the Apocrypha, will not be discussed directly here.

The third group of writings, which is our direct concern in these pages, consists of the various collections known by the comprehensive designation of Talmudic literature and known traditionally as the Oral Law, in contradistinction to the Written Law of the canonical Scriptures. Though the date of their first compilation as written works can hardly be earlier than the third century c.e., the matter embodied in them had been taking shape in the era of the Second Temple (before c.e. 70), and was transmitted orally from scholar to disciple, with such additions and reformulations and adaptations as each age demanded. Some scholars and disciples kept records; but these were only for private use and not textbooks for study: they had no official standing either in the schools or the law court. As Oral Law, the teaching clearly emphasized the distinction between the Law revealed to Moses and the Prophets, or contained in the 'inspired' books of the early scribes (the Law, the Prophets, the Writings), and the creation of the following generations.

The main collections of Oral Law may be summed up briefly as the Mishnah, the Tosefta, the two Talmuds (Palestinian and Babylonian) and the Midrashim (of various types).

Mishnah

The Mishnah, the first and central collection of Oral Law, is a series of halakot (הלכה means regulation, practical decision on law, ritual and religion), arranged according to subject matter (e.g. blessings, Sabbath, women, torts, sacrifices, impurities). 'Mishnah' (from שנה, to repeat) indicates oral teaching, that which is learned by repetition. The editing of the Mishnah was begun by Rabbi Judah the Patriarch (נשיא) around the end of the second century. In the main, however, the work of compiling and editing the Mishnah was done by the Sanhedrin and the Academy (בית המדרש), of which Rabbi Judah was the head.

The Mishnah incorporates several collections, which had been compiled one or two 'generations' before the destruction of the Second Temple, as well as those made by Rabbi Akiba (105-135) and by his disciples (c. 140-170). These collections can be identified mainly from internal evidence, though some external evidence about their existence and contents can also be gathered from other Talmudic sources and from the Apocrypha, the New Testament and the Church Fathers.[1] Scholars differ, however, concerning the exact dating of some collections and their attribution to a particular sage. Neither is there general agreement among the scholars as to the extent of the redaction made by Rabbi Judah and the changes he made in his sources. No doubt, however, attaches to the existence of ancient halakic collections of which the Mishnah is composed. Examples of ancient collections can be found in the tractate *Shekalim* which deals with the regulations concerning the half-shekel contribution to the Temple. It tells how the money was collected, who were the officers responsible for it in the Temple, and what their administrative duties were. The fifth chapter of the tractate gives a list of officials of the Temple: 'These are the officers which served in the Temple: Johanan ben Phineas was over the seals, Ahijah was over the drink-offerings ... Gabini was the herald ... and Phineas was over the vestments.' The Palestinian Talmud relates that the Tanna mentioned a list of men from his own generation, which is indeed confirmed by Josephus for the reign of Agrippa I and afterwards, since several of

[1] See Epstein, *Mevoot*, pp. 15 ff.

those mentioned in the tractate are ascribed similar tasks by the historian.[1]

Baraita and Tosefta

The Mishnah of Rabbi Judah did not include all the existing halakic materials, as it intended to represent an authoritative selection. Other halakic sayings from the Tannaitic period are traditionally known as Baraita (ברייתא), which means 'external' to the Mishnah. Many baraitot have been preserved as quotations in the Talmuds. There existed, however, also a collection of baraitot, analogous to the Mishnah, which took shape shortly after the completion of the Mishnah. This collection is traditionally known as the Tosefta, which means enlargement (of the Mishnah). Its final form is from the middle of the third century.

Talmud

The largest collections of Oral Law are represented by the two Talmuds. The Babylonian Talmud, constructed as a completion and commentary on the Mishnah, was mainly edited at the beginning of the fifth century by Ravina and Rab Ashi at Sura in Babylonia. It is not to be regarded, however, as the work of these heads of the Babylonian Academies but rather as a community product. The first redactions of the Palestinian Talmud are attributed to the second half of the fourth century.

Midrashim

The last group of writings related to the Oral Law are the Midrashim, which can generally be described as commentaries on the Scriptures. The oldest midrashim mostly deal with halakic matters, studied and linked with the legal sections of the Pentateuch. They are *Mekilta* (on Exodus), *Sifra* (on Leviticus), *Sifre Numeri* and *Sifre Deuteronomium*. They represent, basically, the halakic tradition of the Tannaitic period and are therefore rightly called Tannaitic midrashim.

The other main category of midrashim are homiletic commentaries, of which the earliest surviving collection is the *Midrash Rabba*, consisting of commentaries on the Pentateuch and the five Megillot. Some of these midrashim have been compiled at the same period as the Talmuds, though most of them in the following centuries.

---

[1] *P. T. Shekalim* 48c; Jos. *War* VI, 390.

The problem of dating

The identification of earlier collections in the framework of a later redaction is only one of the criteria to be used for dating the Talmudic traditions. Another criterion may be derived from form criticism. Thus the first three Mishnaic passages in the tractate *Baba Kamma* give their Halakah in the first person: 'If I am answerable for the care of a thing, it is I that render possible the injury that it may do', etc.[1] This seems to be an early type of saying, as the Amora, Rav, one of the great traditional teachers of the Mishnah, said: 'The language is that of a Jerusalem Tanna.'[2] The form in question is biblical rather than 'Talmudic', and can therefore be used as a criterion for the antiquity of a tradition.

Indications of date may also be derived from the frequent custom of listing the scholars, who transmitted Halakah in the name of their teachers: 'So and so transmitted in the name of so and so.' The first of such Torah scholars mentioned is Simeon the Just, high priest in the Hellenistic era; but most of the scholars mentioned in the Tannaitic literature as belonging to the period of the Second Temple are from the first century C.E. and mostly from the last decades of the Temple's existence. From this time onwards, names of scholars multiply for each 'generation' (see below p. 8).

Many controversies have been preserved in the Mishnah and other Talmudic writings between the School of Hillel and the School of Shammai, which have been active before the destruction of the Temple. During the Jamnia period after the destruction Halakah was decided according to the School of Hillel, and the preserved controversies therefore obviously point to earlier conditions.

Sometimes a tradition states explicitly that a Mishnaic Halakah is from 'the Mishnah of Rabbi Akiba, but the First Mishnah was otherwise', i.e. the rule in force before Rabbi Akiba.[3] This effort to preserve the memory of the earliest forms of the Halakah went so far as literal fidelity to the words of the sages: 'Hillel says: One *hin* of drawn water renders the Immersion-pool unfit. ([We speak of *hin*] only because a man must use the manner of speaking of his teacher.)'[4] Thus in transmitting the words of Hillel, the Mishnah uses the term *hin* for the measure in question, instead of the usual term *kab*, for the sake of fidelity. This fidelity is a feature of Talmudic literature, consciously

[1] *M.Baba Kamma* 1:2. [2] *B. T. Baba Kamma* 6b. [3] *M. Sanhedrin* 3:4.
[4] *M. Eduyoth* 1:3.

4

emphasized in the following saying: 'In this language Rabbi Ishmael said to him...'[1]

Finally another criterion can be derived from a comparison with non-Talmudic sources, such as the Apocrypha, the Qumran literature, the Jewish Hellenistic writings, the New Testament, and the Church Fathers: this criterion has already been mentioned above in connection with the identification of the sources of the Mishnah. Two further examples will be given here for illustration. The prohibition against drinking water which has stood uncovered is mentioned in the Mishnah.[2] Josephus transmits this same prohibition on the authority of a Greek writer of the third century B.C.E., who says that Pythagoras adopted this custom from the Jews.[3]

Pirke de Rabbi Eliezer, a late homiletic midrash, mentions the custom of naming a child on the eighth day after his birth, at his circumcision, but the custom is already mentioned in the Gospel of Luke on the occasion of the naming of John the Baptist.[4] However, the inferences at times remain conjectural; and accord is difficult to attain on this procedure alone among modern scholars.

The antiquity of the contents of Talmudic literature, however, is not based solely on the antiquity of certain collections, Mishnaic passages or isolated traditions. Since the Oral Law reflects Jewish life and thought from the beginning of Oral Tradition, from the time when in the Second Temple period the books of the Torah and the Prophets became the main subject of study and meditation and the basis of public and private law, the presumption is that Talmudic literature represents basically a cultural and religious history covering many hundreds of years. Thus for instance the tractate *Berakoth* opens with a discussion of the exact time when the *Shema* may be recited in the evening and the morning. This was a matter which was debated among the Tannaim who lived at the end of the first and the beginning of the second century C.E. But the controversy is reported along with a long development, relating how certain passages of the Torah were to be read twice daily, in the morning and the evening, which passages were to be read and the blessings which traditionally preceded and followed the reading. This compendium of a long historical process can be verified in many details from the admittedly early sources, such as the Apocryphal literature and from archaeological

[1] *T. Shabbath* 13:4.   [2] *M. Terumoth* 8:4 ff.
[3] *Against Apion* I, 22; see S. Lieberman, *Ha-Yerushalmi Kifshuto* (1935),p. 49.
[4] *Pirke de Rabbi Eliezer* 48 (ed. Luria, 114b); Luke 1:49.

evidence like the phylacteries which have been found in various places.

Classification of the Oral Law

In Talmudic tradition and in modern research, the Oral Law is divided according to three main criteria. The first approach is according to its contents. Here it is divided into Halakah (practical teaching) and Haggadah (הגדה - homiletical teaching). The second approach is according to its relationship with the Scriptures. The Oral Law has reached us in the form of Midrash or exegesis, that is, statements inferred from, built up on or in some way connected with the Written Law or Scripture. But there are also statements and traditions which have reached us without having any direct connection with the text of Scripture, and which may indeed have been originally formulated without such connection. The third approach is based on the two main periods in the history of the formation of the Oral Law: Tannaitic literature up to the beginning of the third century C.E., and Amoraic literature from then to the end of the fifth century.

Halakah and Haggadah

Halakah comprises the whole of the legislative and juridical part of the Oral Law, which reached into all parts of the life of the individual and the community. The halakic rulings, however, included also the discussions by which the verdict was reached, and the conflicting opinions which were only decided in the course of time. The Mishnah contains the various topics of the Halakah, and the halakic commentaries on Exodus, Leviticus, Numbers and Deuteronomy mentioned above (p. 3) are also 'practical teaching', as are of course much of the two great collections, the Babylonian and Palestinian Talmuds.

The sphere of Haggadah cannot be defined as accurately as the Halakah. It includes ethical and social thinking, as traditionally pursued, the world view of the sages, explanations of why various precepts were given and their various degrees of importance, scriptural exegesis, beliefs and opinions ranging into folklore, apophthegms, sermons or homilies (mainly in the form of extracts), expansions of the biblical narrative, traditions concerning Jewish life from after the time in which Scripture was given, biographical notes or short biographies of outstanding sages. Sometimes Halakah and Haggadah are given in separate collections, the Mishnah, as has been said, being halakic, while the *Midrash Rabba* is chiefly composed of haggadic sayings.

6

But the boundaries are not always so clear, and the two Talmuds constructed round the Mishnah contain halakic and haggadic material side by side. But even in the Mishnah short haggadic sayings occur, and one tractate of the Mishnah, *Pirke Aboth*, is wholly devoted to the ethical and religious meditative sayings of the greatest of the early sages. On the other hand, all the collections of Haggadah contain some halakic statements.

Both Halakah and Haggadah have come down to us, as they were transmitted orally, in two main forms: one without any direct or formal connection with Scripture, and another specifically connected with Scripture (Midrash). While the main sources of the halakic and haggadic sayings were undoubtedly the precepts of the Torah and the words of the prophets, and the sages regarded themselves as echoing the words of the Torah and as realizing them in spirit and in practice, their utterances could be formulated without any definite reference to texts of Scripture or were extensions of Halakah or Haggadah which had lost their perhaps original link with particular texts. Mishnaic Halakah includes such statements as: 'From what time in the morning may the *Shema* be recited? So soon as one can distinguish between blue and white,' (*Berakoth*, 1:2); 'On the first day of Adar, they give warning of the Shekel dues', (*Shekalim*, 1:1); 'A man may betroth a woman either by his own act or by that of his agent', (*Kiddushim*, 2:1). Most of the sayings of the Mishnah tractate *Pirke Aboth*, referred to above, are given without reference to any scriptural texts, as for instance the haggadic saying 'Not learning but doing is the chief thing', (1:16).

Much Halakah and Haggadah is derived from the study of Scripture. The sage studied a verse, compared it with other verses, interpreted it (דרש) and so arrived at a conclusion or attached his comment to it. Thus we read in the Mishnah: '*And the officers shall speak unto the people, saying, What man is there that hath built a new house and hath not dedicated it, let him go and return to his house,* [Deut. 20:5]. ... It is all one whether he builds a house for straw, a house for cattle, a house for wood, or a house for stores,' (*Sotah*, 8:2); '*As when a man goeth with his neighbour into the forest to hew wood,* [Deut. 19:5]. Just as in a forest both the injurer and the injured have the right of entry, so too is this the case wherever both have the right of entry, but it excludes a person's private property into which the injurer and the injured have not both the right of entry,' (*Sifre Deut.* 182);

7

'This is my God, and I will glorify him [Exod. 15:2]. R. Ishmael says: Can a being of flesh and blood glorify his maker? But [it means] I shall glorify him with precepts, I shall make before him a beautiful lulab [palm branch], a beautiful tabernacle, beautiful fringes, beautiful phylacteries. Abba Saul says: I shall imitate him. Just as he is merciful and compassionate, so be thou merciful and compassionate,' (*Mekilta, Shirah*, chap. 3).

Midrash is not confined to the works described as such but can be found constantly throughout the whole of Talmudic literature.

Tannaim and Amoraim

When the first compilations of Oral Law were edited in the third century (Mishnah, Tosefta), a clear distinction was made between the traditions prior to this work of editing and those which succeeded it. In Talmudic tradition the scholars of the first period are called Tannaim (תנאים - 'teachers', from תני, 'teach'), and hence the literature of this period is generally termed Tannaitic. The Tannaim who were active from *c.* 40 to 220 C.E. are usually divided into five 'generations'.[1] The scholars active after the Tannaitic era are called Amoraim (אמוראים 'speakers, lecturers', from אמר 'speak'). Their sayings, as the completion (Gemara) of Mishnaic or Tannaitic scholarship, were assembled in the two Talmuds, in the Haggadic Midrashim and in other works (Amoraic literature). One external criterion for distinguishing Tannaitic from Amoraic literature is the language. The former is in Hebrew, except for some odd words or phrases from the Aramaic, while the latter is partly in Hebrew and partly in Aramaic. Further, Amoraic literature is generally secondary and diffuse, in contrast to the originality and succinctness of Tannaitic, which is also more precise with regard to traditions from the time of the Temple and the years soon after its destruction.

Historical references

Fairly precise and adequate historical settings are provided by some of the halakic passages; we are sometimes told how a particular regulation was established, how disputes arose about it and how the issue was settled. Haggadah, being often 'narrative', as the word itself indicates, includes many traditions about the lives of the sages: their

[1] For a list of the principal Tannaim and Amoraim according to 'generations' see Mielziner, *Introduction*, pp. 22-55.

work among the people, their conflicts and disputes with non-Jews, their relations with each other and with the outside world as individuals, sages and representatives of the community. Historical information also occurs in the midrashim. Scriptural commentary, exegetical or homiletical, was not merely given in terms transcending time and change, but also as a guide to actual reality. The sage's reflections on Scripture often took the form of a response to the social, political and religious questions of Jewish life, and did so on principle, since Scripture was regarded as the revelation of God's will not only for the generation to whom the scriptural words in question were addressed, but for all time. The sage, whether preaching in the synagogue or addressing a smaller circle of pupils, understood himself to be, not of course a prophet, but the interpreter of God's words, which he 'actualized' for the benefit of the hearers of his time.

What has passed between Jacob and Esau, for instance, was taken to intimate the relations between Israel and the nations, especially the Roman Empire, Esau (or Edom) being often in fact identified with Rome. Canticles was taken to express not only the relationship between God and the people of Israel, but as describing the adventures, travail and suffering of the people during the Great Revolt, the destruction of the Temple and the period of the Bar Cochba revolt. The concluding words of Canticles, 'Make haste, my beloved, and be thou like a gazelle or a young stag upon the mountains of spices' (Cant. 8:14) are taken to mean that 'honour has left Israel.' Some midrashim therefore connect the verse with Israel's instituting sacrifices for the welfare of the Roman Empire. Others recall the period of civil war in Jerusalem leading up to the destruction of the Temple. Submission to Rome and civil war are regarded as reasons for the departure of the divine presence from Israel.[1]

Various commentaries were given on Exodus 20:6, 'but showing steadfast love to thousands of those who love me and keep my commandments'. Some took it to refer to 'our father Abraham and those like him', or 'the prophets and elders', but Rabbi Nathan, some time after the Bar Cochba revolt, interpreted it as follows: 'These are the people of Israel who dwell in the Land of Israel and give their life to observe the commandments. Why are you condemned to death? For circumcising my son. Why are you to be burned at the stake? For reading the

---

[1] At the end of *Canticles Zuta* (ed. Schechter in *JQR*, 1894), p. 673; this midrash is commented upon by G. Allon, *Studies* I, pp. 44 and 266; see also S. Lieberman, *Greek in Jewish Palestine* (1942), pp. 179-84.

Torah. Why are you crucified? For eating of the unleavened bread.'[1]
There are many haggadic sayings which a sage is reported to have
uttered on some particular occasion, which he interpreted in the
light of Scripture. The occasion could be a natural phenomenon,
or some event of individual, social or political significance. It is told
of Rabbi Johanan ben Zakkai (before 70 c.e.) that as he came to
Emmaus, 'he saw a maiden picking barley out of horses' dung, concerning which he interpreted the verse', etc.[2] Although haggadic
stories do not always add to our knowledge of an event known from
other sources, they tell us of the sages' attitudes to it and how the
event was viewed by tradition. They furnish new insights or at least
suggest new viewpoints as provided by sources of a different nature.
Unspecified historical events often underlie Halakah and Haggadah,
or the events are veiled or left purposely unclear. Later tradition
then interprets the Halakah or Haggadah in terms of some definite
occurrence, which may also be favoured by modern scholarship.
Whether such interpretations are valid at all, or to what degree they
are valid, remains inevitably doubtful; and modern views may remain
as little convincing as an Amoraic Haggadah. Thus the Mishnah
Shabbath 6:2, reads: 'A man may not go out with sandals shod with
nails' (on the Sabbath). This Halakah is explained in the two Talmuds
and in a Midrash on the ground that after the Bar Cochba revolt
Jews hiding in caves would see the iron-shod sandals or hear the noise
of them and think the Roman soldiers were approaching, which
would cause panic: women would miscarry, and men be killed.[3]
There is some confirmation for the prohibition of iron-shod sandals
in the archaeological evidence, inasmuch as no sandals with nails
in them have been found in the various sites uncovered in Israel.
But it is quite likely that the prohibition antedates the period in
question. The Halakah simply forbids the wearing of iron-shod
sandals on the Sabbath, just as the wearing of armour, helmet or
other military accoutrements was forbidden on that day. The later,
legendary explanation probably reflects memories of hiding in caves
and the panics which occurred there.
Then again, there are many traditions in the Talmud[4] and later
sources concerning changes made in divine service and prayers be-

---

[1] *Mekilta*, tractate *Behodesh*, end of chap. 6 (ed. Horovitz-Rabin, p. 227).
[2] Ibid., p. 203.
[3] *P. T. Shabbath* VI, 8a; *T. B. Shabbath* 60a; *Deut. Rabba* (ed. Lieberman, p. 81).
[4] *P. T. Berakoth* I, 3c and par.

cause of religious struggles, persecutions or prohibitions; but in fact, they were rarely the cause of such changes. It was the custom, till some time near the destruction of the Temple, to include the ten commandments in the recitation of the *Shema*, morning and evening. In the second half of the first century C.E. the ten commandments were omitted because the 'heretics' claimed that only these were binding and took precedence over the other commandments. Although they are specifically made responsible for this important change in the *Shema*, the 'heretics' are not explicitly identified in the sources. It seems intrinsically likely and is affirmed by various sources. So too, many other changes ascribed by Talmudic[1] or Gaonic sources[2] to religious persecutions, remain quite dubious.

Apart from such historical allusions—correct or otherwise—there are also remnants of historical traditions in the Talmuds and the midrashim, as is only to be expected since the history of Israel was part of the tradition of Oral Law. Sometimes these traditions are linked with Halakah, as in the *Megillath Taanith*, where there is a list of days on which fasts were forbidden because they were days during the period of the Second Temple when Israel had received special favours. The historical reason is assigned in each case.[3] In the Mishnah the regulations for mourning on the ninth day of the month of Ab are followed by a list of 'five things that befell our fathers on the seventeenth of Tammuz and five on the ninth of Ab'.[4]

Some of the events in question are dated to the period of the First Temple or earlier, and probably come under the heading of illustrative exposition (midrash) rather than history. But the events attributed to the period of the Second Temple are probably historical, though not always clearly defined. Historical traditions sometimes appear in Talmudic literature without being connected with Halakah or related customs. The *Seder Olam*, which we have only in a later version, is an example of a group of historical traditions which became part of the Oral Law. In its succinct language it resembles similar brief notices found in various parts of Talmudic literature.[5] Such are, for instance, the statement that six or ten exiles were forced upon the Sanhedrin from some time before the destruction of the Temple until the Sanhedrin was dissolved at Tiberias[6] or the list of notable

[1] *T. B. Rosh ha-Shanah* 32b; *P. T. Rosh ha-Shanah* IV, 59b.
[2] L. Ginzberg, in *Genizah Studies in Memory of S. Schechter* II (1929), pp. 526 ff.
[3] Ed. Lichtenstein, pp. 317 ff. [4] *M. Taanith* 4:6.
[5] See the edition of B. Ratner (1897) repr. 1966.
[6] *Genesis Rabba* 94 (Ed. Theodor-Albeck, pp. 1220-21).

law courts in the Land of Israel and the Diaspora.[1] Other traditions occur with haggadic embellishments, such as the description of the Jewish community in Egypt and its magnificent synagogue in Alexandria before its destruction during the revolt against Trajan,[2] incidents of the Great Revolt and of the Bar Cochba rising and so on.[3]

The strictly historical notices in Talmudic literature concerning the period of the Second Temple are relatively few. One could hardly attempt to give a continuous account of the period based only or even mainly on such sources. Information regarding the period after 70 C.E. is somewhat less sparse, though again there is not enough to provide a systematic history, like the Books of the Maccabees or Josephus. The general picture, as given in Talmudic sources, has to be supplemented by historical data from Roman historians and the Church Fathers, when matters of external politics are to be treated, such as the revolt under Trajan or that of Bar Cochba. The reason for this is that Talmudic literature aimed at transmitting Halakah and Haggadah, not historical tradition.

Nonetheless, this literature touches on many areas of Jewish history. One might almost say that the sources are there for the social history of ancient Judaism, with reservations of course about the precise dating or duration of the various phenomena. The Jewish way of life is described in detail: housing, furnishings and utensils, work in the fields or in the city, commerce, transport and caravans. We know the customs which prevailed for sleeping and rising, for clothing, toilet and jewelry. We can follow the various forms of marriage settlements, the financial arrangements of households, the manner of educating children. Much attention is of course paid to divine service, and there are whole tractates (such as *Tamid*, *Middoth*, *Shekalim* and *Yoma*), special chapters (such as *Sukkah*, chaps. 4 and 5) and various isolated halakot dealing with services in the ancient Temple on weekdays, Sabbaths and feasts. Here, of course, a certain amount of idealization of the past must be allowed for, and its relevance to the socio-religious life of Talmudic times must be carefully analyzed. Such analysis will be fruitful; for though much matter is found throughout our literature on the social order, public leadership and judicial practices (see chapter 10 on Jewish private law), the main light is cast on the spiritual life of the people. Talmudic literature lives in the world of Pharisaic Judaism, without tailoring it to a system, as Josephus tries to do. Negatively, it is remarkable for the absence

[1] *T. B. Sanhedrin* 32b.　[2] *P. T. Sukkah* v, 55a.　[3] *P. T. Taanith* iv 68c-69a.

of all prophetic visions and for the elimination of the 'apocalyptic' which is found in many of the Apocrypha. Positively, we have the Pharisaic world-view, as it was worked out in long internal struggle and much controversy, where the interpretation of Scripture, the definition of the Halakah which was a 'hedge to the Law', and the search for valid methods of their study were the great directives. We can see how within the prevailing Pharisaic mentality, the school of Hillel came to dominate in the fixing of Halakah, but the success of this school did not obliterate the memory of once-powerful rivals. The 'final' Halakah of the Mishnah can often be traced through a pre-history of controversy. Thus in the *Mishnah Pesahim*, chap. 6, an anonymous authority is quoted for the opinion that the killing of the paschal lamb on the eve of the Passover takes precedence of the Sabbath. But the Tosefta and the two Talmuds describe how Hillel the Elder opposed the Bnei Bathyra on this point, and tradition associates the rise of Hillel to the Patriarchate and the decline of the Bnei Bathyra to the fate of this Halakah.[1] There are other traditions about the refusal of sages to accept majority decisions, from the second part of the first century C.E.[2] It is therefore not just the Pharisaic world-view, but the history of its development which can be traced in Talmudic literature. Even in the absence of controversy, the frequent repetitions and parallels in various contexts enable us to trace the meaning of a tradition and the changes it underwent in varying political, social and economic traditions, or in various houses of study.

Generally, haggadic elements are interwoven into the history of controversy, and this adds to the difficulties, as the criteria at our disposal are mainly internal evidence and stylistic features since, as has been said, Talmudic literature treats history by allusion rather than by testimony. We can find, for instance, that accounts of daily life are realistic, and note the absence in Halakah of the supernatural phenomena which recur in Haggadah. Halakic tradition is spare and concise (as in the Mishnah and the Baraita) and the mention of the receivers and transmitters of various traditions gives further support to the historian: 'It once happened that Rabbi Simeon of Mizpah [thus] sowed [his field with two kinds of wheat and came] before Rabban Gamaliel, and they went up to the Chamber of Hewn Stone to inquire' (whether they should grant one *peah* to the poor

[1] *T. Pesahim* 4; *P. T. Pesahim* VI, 33a; *T. B. Pesahim* 66b.
[2] *M. Eduyoth* 5:6; *P. T. Berakoth* IV, 7d; *T. B. Berakoth* 27a-b.

for each separate kind or whether one *peah* would suffice). 'Nahum the Scrivener said: I have received a tradition from Rabbi Measha who received it from his father...,[1] or again, 'Rabbi Akiba said: When I went down to Nehardaea to ordain a leap-year there met me Nehemiah of Beth Deli, and he said to me, "I have heard that in the Land of Israel the Sages, excepting Rabbi Judah ben Baba, do not suffer a woman to marry again on the evidence of one witness," [they require two witnesses instead]' "...I received a tradition from Rabban Gamaliel the Elder that they may suffer a woman to marry again on the evidence of one witness." And when I came and recounted the matter before Rabban Gamaliel he rejoiced at my words and said, "We have now found a fellow [disciple] for Rabbi Judah ben Baba! Whereupon Rabban Gamaliel remembered that certain men were killed at Tel Arza and Rabban Gamaliel the Elder suffered their wives to marry again on the evidence of one witness."'[2]

This style, on which a history of tradition can be based, contrasts with that of Haggadah, where exaggeration and obviously legendary traits recur. Thus the halakic sources (Mishnah, Tosefta etc.) recount journeys made by leading sages of Jamnia to Rome, with fair precision and without miraculous tales. To the same basic names, places and journeys, as also to biographies and controversies of the sages, haggadic tradition adds marvellous embellishments, and historical events are similarly overlaid. The historian cannot entirely neglect such Haggadah. The story of the destruction of Jerusalem being due to a petty quarrel between two Jews, which led the Romans to suspect that revolt was brewing, is haggadic. But it tells us at least that tradition ascribed the destruction of Jerusalem to civil strife, a notion well supported by other sources.

Conclusions

Talmudic literature presents many difficulties to the historian, even to those well-versed in the literature. The relevant material is widely dispersed and occurs in various contexts and genres. Even the Halakah or religious thought is not presented systematically. The student of history has difficulty first in collecting his material, but then more difficulties in dating a particular tradition or collection and separating later accretions from the nucleus. If his solutions are not to be merely academic conjectures, he must bear in mind that his material reflects a reality in a constant state of growth—so that his task is

[1] *M. Peah* 2:6.   [2] *M. Yebamoth* 16:7.

14

not done if he has reconciled contradictions by perhaps imposing later concepts on earlier sources. Tradition in Oral Law was not just verbal repetition, it was the outcome of study—discussions in public academies, houses of study, discourses of preachers, discussions between a rabbi and his disciples. And discussion of the Oral Law was not confined to learned circles. Many members of the public took part in the study and debate. Tradition reflected this lively concern: it absorbed new viewpoints and responded to new realities, it was affected by each new development of method in study. Above all, since Oral Law was not just an academic study but a practical rule of life, for law, religion and ethics, it grew and changed under the impact of reality, while maintaining its central loyalty to the Torah. This mixture of the late and the early, the superimposition of haggadic embellishments, the tendency to idealize the past, the reduction of strictly historical notices in the vast majority of cases to what are outside the main stream of history, render the task even of composing a history of social life or religious thought on the basis of Talmudic literature a difficult one, which has led many historians to dismiss it as unrewarding. But without a proper exploitation of our sources, our knowledge of ancient Judaism would be distorted and truncated, while their correct assessment is indispensable to a full and reliable picture of the ancient world.

BIBLIOGRAPHY

General Introductions

H. L. STRACK, *Introduction to the Talmud and Midrash* (English translation of the fifth German edition, 1931), repr. 1965; M. MIELZINER, *Introduction to the Talmud* (with new bibliography, 1925-67, by A. Guttmann), 4th ed., 1968; G. F. MOORE, Judaism *in the First Centuries of the Christian Era* I, 1927, repr. 1970, pp. 125-216.

Texts and Translations

MISHNAH

Mishnah first edition Naples 1492 (repr. 1970); CH. ALBECK, ed., *Shisha Sidre ha-Mishnah* (Hebrew text vocalized by Ch. Yalon, with short commentary), 6 vols, 1958, 3rd ed., 1968; N. SACKS, ed., *The Mishnah* (with variant readings collected from manuscripts, fragments of the Genizah and early printed editions), so far published: *Order Zeraim* I, 1972; H. DANBY, *The Mishnah* (translated from the Hebrew, with introduction and brief explanatory notes), 1933, repr. 1972; D. HOFFMANN, ed., *Mischnajoth* (Hebrew text vocalized, German translation and commentary), 6 vols, 1887 ff., repr. 1967; K. H. RENGSTORF and L. ROST, eds., *Die Mischna* (Hebrew text, German translation and extensive commentary), 35 tractates so far published, 1912-1972.

TOSEFTA

M. S. ZUCKERMANDEL, ed., *Tosefta* (critical edition), repr. with *Tashlum Tosefta*, by S. Lieberman, 1970; G. KITTEL and K. H. RENGSTORF, eds., *Die Tosefta* (Hebrew text, German translation and commentary), 10 tractates so far published, 1952-72. S. Liebermann, ed., *The Tosefta*, 3 Orders pub. so far, 1955 ff. S. Liebermann, *Tosefta Ki-Fshutah* (comprehensive commentary on his edition) 1955 ff.

TALMUD

Talmud Bavli, first edition, Venice 1520-3, repr. 1970; M. HERSCHLER, ed., *The Babylonian Talmud* (with variant readings collected from manuscripts, fragments of the Genizah and early printed editions), so far published: *Tractate Kethuboth* I, 1972; E. STEINSALZ, ed., *The Babylonian Talmud* (vocalized text with annotations), so far published: *Berakoth, Shabbath, Pesahim, and Eruvin*, 5 vols, 1968-72; I. EPSTEIN ed., *The Babylonian Talmud translated into English*, 18 vols, 1948-52; *Talmud Jerushalmi*, first edition, Venice 1523-24, repr. n.d.; *Talmud Jerushalmi* (Krotoshin edition) n.d.; M. SCHWAB, *Le Talmud de Jerusalem* (French translation), 10 vols., 1871-90, repr. n.d.; A. WÜNSCHE, *Der Jerusalemische Talmud in seinen haggadischen Bestandtheilen* (German translation), 1880, repr. 1967; R. RABBINOVICZ, *Dikduke Soferim. Variae lectiones in Mischnam et in Talmud Babyloniucum*, 15 vols, 1868-88; B. A. RATNER, *Sefer Ahavat Tsion. Variae lectiones of the Talmud Jerushalmi*, 1901-4, repr. 1969.

MIDRASHIM

H. S. HOROVITZ and I. A. RABIN, eds., *Mechilta de R. Ishmael* (critical annotated edition), 1930, repr. 1960; J. N. EPSTEIN and E. Z. MELAMED, eds., *Mekilta de R. Shimon bar Johai* (fragments found in the Cairo Genizah), 1955; J. Z. LAUTERBACH, ed., *Mekilta de R. Ishmael* (Hebrew text and English translation), 3 vols, 1933-52; I. H. WEISS, ed., *Sifra debe Rab*, 1862, repr. 1947; J. WINTER, *Midrasch Sifra* (German translation), 1938; H. S. HOROVITZ, ed., *Siphre debe Rab 1: Siphre ad Numeros* (Corpus Tannaiticum 3), 1917, repr. 1966; K. G. KUHN, *Der tannaitische Midrasch Sifre zu Numeri übersetzt und erklärt*, 1959; L. FINKELSTEIN, ed., *Siphre ad Deuteronomium*, 1969; H. L. JUNGMANN, *Sifre zu Deuteronomium* (German translation and commentary), *fasc.* 1, 1964; J. THEODOR and CH. ALBECK, eds., *Midrash Bereshit Rabba* (critical edition with notes and commentary), 3 vols, 2nd ed., 1965; M. MARGULIES, ed., *Midrash Wayyikra Rabba* (critical edition based on manuscripts and Genizah fragments), 5 vols, 1953-60, repr. 1972; S. LIEBERMAN; ed., *Midrash Debarim Rabba*, 2nd ed., 1964; M. A. MIRKIN, ed., *Midrash Rabba* (vocalized text with commentary; on Pentateuch only), 11 vols, 1956-70; H. FREEDMAN and M. SIMON, eds., *Midrash Rabba* (translated into English with glossary and general, Talmudic, and biblical indexes). 10 vols, 1951; B. MANDELBAUM ed., *Pesikta de Rav Kahana*, 2 vols. 1962; A. WÜNSCHE, *Bibliotheca Rabbinica* (German translation of Midrash Rabba and Pesikta de Rav Kahana), 34 *fasc.*, 1880-85, repr. 1967; H. LICHTENSTEIN, ed., *Die Fastenrolle* (Megillath Taanith, introduction, text and commentary), *HUCA*, 1931-32, repr. 1949.

STUDIES

The early collections in the Mishnah have been discussed by Z. FRANKEL, *Darke ha-Mishnah*, 1859. CH. ALBECK has written on this subject with greater clarity in *Mavo le-Mishnah*, 1957, pp. 3-39, German translation: *Einführung in die Mischna*, 1970; see also *Untersuchungen über die Redaktion der Mischna*, 1923. The most exhaustive treatment of the early collections in the Mishnah, as well as the Mishnaic passages from the Sages during the Second Temple period, is to be found in I. EPSTEIN, *Mevoot le-Sifrut ha-Tannaim*, 1957, pp. 9-269. The Talmudic sources are utilized in a historical survey by J. DERENBOURG, *Essai sur l'histoire et la géographie de la Palestine d'après les Talmuds et les autres sources rabbiniques*, 1867 (repr. 1971). Excessive und uncritical use of Talmudic sources is illustrated by I. HALEVY's books, including *Dorot ha-Rishonim*, 4 vols, 1906 ff. The historical works of A. BÜCHLER exemplify the proper approach to these sources: *Die Priester und der Cultus im letzten Jahrzehnt des jerusalemischen Tempels*, 1895; *The Economic Conditions of Judea after the Destruction of the Second Temple*, 1912. G. ALLON employs these sources well in his historical description of the period after the destruction of the Temple, in *Toledot ha-Yehudim be-Eretz Israel be-Tekufat ha-Mishnah we-ha-Talmud*, 1952-55. Only one collection of historical sources is available: S. KLEIN, ed., *Sefer ha-Yishuv*, 1939; it presents the sources according to the geographical place names in the Land of Israel. This book contains much material but it is in error with regard to some geographical locations.

II THE GREEK AND LATIN LITERARY SOURCES

Jewish historians

PHILO OF ALEXANDRIA (*c.* 20 B.C.E.-45 C.E.?)

While all Philo's works are a most important source for the study of the spiritual development of Hellenistic Jewry, some also contain information on the history of Jewish society and on the political history of the times.

As the son of one of the eminent families of Jewish Alexandria,[1] Philo participated in public life and led the delegation of Alexandrian Jews, under the Emperor Gaius Caligula. He also, as he himself mentions in one of his works, visited Palestine.[2]

Two of his extant works, *In Flaccum* and *Legatio ad Gaium*, deal with contemporary events of which he was an eyewitness and in some of which he was also actively involved. These works, which give an account of the persecutions of the Jews in the time of Gaius Caligula, were both written after the accession of the new emperor, Claudius (41 C.E.). It is evident that the beginning of *In Flaccum*, which recounted Sejanus' actions against the Jews, has been lost, as has also the end of *Legatio ad Gaium*, which related the emperor's downfall.[3]

In addition to describing the prefecture of Avillius Flaccus in Egypt prior to the days of Gaius and the change in the prefect's conduct when Gaius became emperor, the *In Flaccum* also portrays the dramatic events in Alexandria in 38 C.E. when the Jews were driven into a ghetto and deprived of their rights and their economic status. The work concludes with an account of Flaccus' downfall as brought about by Gaius himself.

---

[1] On Philo's family cf. J. Schwartz, in *Annuaire de l'institut de philologie et d'histoire Orientales et Slaves* (1953), pp. 591-602.
[2] *De providentia* 64.
[3] The last paragraph of the work, 373: 'I must now proceed to the palinode'.

Legatio ad Gaium describes the accession of Gaius Caligula, the joy which that event engendered in the hearts of his subjects, the change which afterwards took place in the emperor's mentality and the consequence this had for the Jewish nation. Philo, who led the Jewish delegation dispatched to the emperor by the Alexandrian Jews to defend their rights, describes his meeting with Gaius, the events in Alexandria, and—with severe strictures—Gaius' attempt to set up his statue in the Temple in Jerusalem. Of great interest is Agrippa I's letter in defence of the rights of the Jews.[1] Dealing with their position in the Roman Empire, it emphasizes the extent of the Jewish dispersion and refers to episodes in the history of the relations between Gaius' predecessors and the Jews.

Both works deal with the events of the same period. Both tell of the persecutions which befell the Jews and the punishment which ultimately came upon their enemies (Flaccus, in the first work; Gaius, in the final, lost part of the second). Both commence with an idealization of the position which existed at the outset, and extol the first stages of Flaccus' prefecture and Gaius' rule, thereby emphasizing all the more the subsequent turn for the worse. Nevertheless there appear to be insufficient grounds for the contention that the two books are parts of one extensive work.[2] Philo's 'historical' writing is permeated in general with faith in divine providence, and in particular with the divine concern for the fate of the Jews, as well as with the ultimate victory of justice, the enemies of the Jews coming to learn that in the end God saves the Jews.[3]

Philo wrote his two works at a time when the persecution of the Jews had ceased, and he was thus able to portray with satisfaction the course of events and the just retribution which had come upon the enemies of the Jews. He undoubtedly intended both to encourage the Jews and to instill into the heart of the non-Jewish reader the feeling that it is neither fitting nor expedient to attack the Jews and assail their rights.

---

[1] *Legatio* 276-329.
[2] So e.g. Schürer III, p. 494, pp. 677-683; against this view cf. L. Cohn, 'Einteilung und Chronologie der Schriften Philos', *Philologus*, Supplement VII, (1899), pp. 421-424; J. Juster, *Les Juifs dans l'empire romain, leur condition juridique, économique et sociale*, 2 vols, (1914), p. 6; E. R. Goodenough, *The Politics of Philo Judaeus* (1938), pp. 9-12.
[3] *Legatio* 3; *In Flaccum* 102, 170.

JOSEPHUS (37/38 C.E.-C. 100 C.E.?)

The works of Josephus undoubtedly constitute the chief source for the history of the Jews at the end of the Second Temple era. Born in Jerusalem to a priestly family of the division of Jehoiarib, Josephus (Joseph ben Matthias) was related to the Hasmonaean dynasty, one of his ancestors having married the daughter of Jonathan the Hasmonaean.[1] Nevertheless the house of Josephus was not included in the limited group of the high priestly oligarchy who were the principal spokesmen of Sadducean views in Jewish life. Josephus even joined the party of the Pharisees. In 64 C.E. he was sent to Rome to secure the release of several priests whom the procurator Felix had arrested and sent to Rome. As a result of contacts which he was able to establish through the Jewish actor Aliturus with the Empress Poppaea, he succeeded in carrying out the task entrusted to him. During the Great Revolt he served as the commander of Galilee. Captured by Vespasian, he prophesied to him that he would yet be elected emperor. When the prophecy was fulfilled, Josephus was freed, granted Roman citizenship, and remained in Titus' camp during the siege of Jerusalem. After the destruction of the Temple he took up residence in Rome, where he wrote his great works.

His first work was *The Jewish War*, which appeared originally in an Aramaic version. Its Greek form, written between 75 and 79 C.E.,[2] contains an account of the war between the Jews and the Romans until after the destruction of the Temple, preceded by a survey of the history of the Jews from the days of Antiochus Epiphanes until the eve of the Revolt.

This work of Josephus conformed to the great tradition of Greek historiography (Thucydides, Polybius), which attached particular importance to a description of contemporary history. On the face of it Josephus had all the necessary credentials for writing the history of the war. He was well acquainted with what happened in both camps. He had a great talent for description and narrative. However, his sympathies lay with the Flavian dynasty, as he himself affirms, and this limited his freedom of expression.[3] It made his work and his evaluation of events tendentious throughout. He was also handi-

---

[1] On Josephus' ancestry, cf. *Life* 1-6; see also M. Radin in *Classical Philology* (1929), pp. 193-196.

[2] H. Vincent, in *RB* (1911), pp. 369-371; see also St. John Thackeray, pp. 34-35.

[3] *Life* 361-363; cf. also 364-367 about Agrippa II who testified to the veracity of the work.

capped by his past as the commander of the Jews in Galilee against the Romans and his deep personal involvement in the internal struggles of the Jewish parties, displaying in his work a deep hatred towards John of Gischala and the Zealots in general. He also strove to prove that only the extremists among the Jews and not the Jewish people were to blame for the rebellion.

Josephus' other great work *Jewish Antiquities* (in twenty books) was completed, according to the author's evidence, in 93-94 C.E. (in the thirteenth year of Domitian's reign).[1] This work constitutes a continuous history of the Jewish nation from its beginnings until the Great Revolt. In it Josephus' pro-Roman sentiments are less pronounced, and there is a conspicuous tendency to glorify the Jewish people. Josephus' autobiography, written in reply to the criticism levelled against him by Justus of Tiberias is to be regarded as an appendix to the *Antiquities*.[2] Some time later Josephus wrote his apologetic work *Against Apion*.

For the history of Herod's accession and reign, Josephus' writings (*Antiquities* XIV-XVII; *War* I) undoubtedly constitute a principal source. However, the question of Josephus' own sources for the subject is inseparably bound up with Nicholas of Damascus (see below pp. 29-30). The detailed account which Nicholas gave of Herod's kingdom in his *Universal History*, might well have become the prevailing version in Graeco-Roman historiographic tradition, especially as Herod was associated with recollections of the principate of Augustus whom the popular version of history, as it crystallized in the

---

[1] *Ant.* xx, 267.
[2] It follows from *Life* 359 that the autobiography was published after the death of Agrippa II. Since the autobiography is attached to the *Antiquities*, it may be concluded that the *Antiquities* too was published after the death of the king. Moreover some passages in the *Antiquities* seem to imply that Agrippa II was already dead at the time of its publication; cf. e.g. *Ant.* xx, 212, 145; see also XVII, 28. However, we read in Photius, *Bibliotheca*, cod. 33, p. 6b that Agrippa died in the third year of Trajan (100 C.E.), a statement which clearly contradicts that of Josephus concerning the publication of the *Antiquities* in the reign of Domitian. Schürer I (3rd Ger. edition), pp. 80, 88 held the view that only the autobiography was published in the time of Trajan; on the other hand, other scholars suggest two editions of the *Antiquities*, the first to be dated to the time of Domitian and the second to the time of Trajan. Cf. Laqueur, pp. 1-6; M. Gelzer, in *Hermes* (1952), p. 67. B. Motzo, *Saggi di Storia e Letteratura Giudeo - Ellenistica* (1924), pp. 214-226 differs from the latter scholars in that he maintains that only the *Life* appeared in two editions. Still, there is much to be said for the view which supposes Photius to be mistaken in his statement relating to the death of Agrippa II. Cf. Luther, pp. 54-65; Th. Frankfort in *Revue belge de philologie et d'histoire* (1961), pp. 52-58; see also p. 304, note 4.

course of the century, showed in a most favourable light. Nicholas was not, however, the only author to devote special attention to Herod. We learn of at least one other author, Ptolemy, who also wrote a history of him. This work, which was doubtless quite detailed and consisted of more than one book, has survived in a single fragment dealing with the forced proselytization of the Idumaeans and taken apparently from the discussion of Herod's origin (see below pp. 31-32).

Since Herod was also involved in the policy of the Roman principate and the affairs of the eastern Mediterranean under Augustus, certain events of his reign were likewise dealt with in general historical writings. So, for example, Strabo includes in his historical work a description of Herod's capture of Jerusalem and of his victory over Antigonus (see below p. 30). Judging by extracts from Latin poets, Herod as ruler was well known in Roman society.[1] An anecdote in Macrobius shows that Herod's domestic tragedy and especially the execution of his sons created a deplorable impression on his contemporaries.[2] Yet this viewpoint did not, in effect, conflict with the account of Nicholas, who devoted a great deal of space to his hero's domestic tragedy. And Nicholas also pointed out the political damage which this tragedy caused Herod.

There is yet another element which influences historical writing on Herod in the first century C.E. to which inadequate attention has hitherto been paid. Not all Herod's influential descendants could agree that the king's actions were always to be judged in an entirely favourable light. Prominent figures of the house of Herod in the first century C.E., among them influential rulers such as Agrippa I, Herod of Chalcis, and Agrippa II, were descended from Aristobulus, the son of Herod and Mariamme the Hasmonaean and the great grandson of Hyrcanus II. Hyrcanus, Mariamme, and Aristobulus were executed by Herod on various charges. The denigration of Hyrcanus' actions shortly before his death and of the conduct of Mariamme the Hasmonaean and her sons could obviously not meet with the approval of these descendants of Herod. In their circle the Greek language was well known and there was also a tradition of history writing, as may be inferred from the detailed accounts of the life of Agrippa I used by Josephus in the subsequent part of the *Antiquities*. In this circle Josephus could therefore find some corrections of Nicholas'

[1] Horatius, *Epistulae* II, 2, 184; Persius, *Saturae* v, 179-180.
[2] *Saturnalia* II, 4, 11.

version which he had to take into account even in his earlier *War*. But these corrections certainly did not apply to the relations between Herod and the Jewish nation, nor did they present Antigonus in a different way from that of Nicholas.

In general we may conclude that the prevailing version in Greek history writing was fundamentally friendly towards Herod. He was mainly esteemed as a statesman and ruler, although some reservations at Herod's behaviour towards members of his family were expressed, as was also an appreciation of the tragic position in which the king found himself. By contrast the prevailing view in the Jewish nation was hostile to Herod's memory; and although there is no hint that this view found expression in any historical writings in Hebrew, Aramaic, or Greek, it is nevertheless fully reflected in Jewish literature as a whole.[1]

We have to take this state of affairs into account if we are to evaluate correctly the debt which Josephus owed to Nicholas of Damascus in those parts of his two historical works which describe the events from the rise of Antipater, Herod's father, until after Herod's death. Although Nicholas is not mentioned as a source in the entire account of Herod's reign in the *War*, scholars are agreed that here Josephus relied very much on Nicholas, having in fact used him as his principal source.[2] The reasons for this hypothesis are undoubtedly convincing. There is first the laudatory attitude manifested towards Antipater and Herod himself.[3] Then there is the relatively lengthy account, as compared to the preceding and succeeding chapters, of the events of Herod's life until after the riots that broke out on his death, which likewise points to dependence on Nicholas. Even leaving aside the attachment to Herod and to his house, the viewpoint expressed in the narrative is at times more compatible with the Greek Nicholas than with the Jew Josephus. Thus, for example, the gifts of money which Herod made to the people of Elis for the Olympic games are described as a favour not only to the people of Greece but to the entire civilized world, wherever the fame of these games had reached.[4] Moreover the hostile attitude which Josephus' narrative adopts towards Antipater, Herod's son, accords with the enmity

---

[1] *The Assumption of Moses* 6:2-6; *T. B. Baba Bathra* 3b; Matt. 2:16.
[2] Cf. E. Schürer in *Theologische Literaturzeitung* (1879), p. 570; Hölscher, *Die Quellen* p. 17; W. Otto, *Herodes* (1913), p. 9; St. John Thackeray, p. 40.
[3] *War* I, 331, 386, 400.
[4] *War* I, 426.

towards him shown by Nicholas and reflected in Nicholas' autobiography. Then there is the dramatic tone used in the account of Herod's domestic tragedy which is characteristic of Nicholas' literary technique.

Generally it may be said that in many respects Josephus found in Nicholas a source in accordance with his own line of thought and tendencies. Just as Nicholas was a loyal spokesman of the principate of Augustus, so too Josephus in the *War* was an official historian, as it were, of the Flavian dynasty. In him, too, Josephus could discern an artist who was also a practitioner of the literary technique known to us from the later books of the *War*. Josephus did not consider this work an appropriate place for expressing his disagreement where Nicholas' remarks were in conflict with Jewish national tradition or gave questionable assessments of various figures in Jewish history.

Greatly abridging in accordance with his needs the relevant material contained in the *Universal History*, Josephus presented it according to subject-matter rather than chronologically, as was apparently the order followed in Nicholas' history. On rare occasions Josephus adopted a critical attitude towards Nicholas' statements but abstained from entering into open controversy with him, as he later did in his *Antiquities*. At all events he completely disregarded Nicholas' view about Antipater's ancient Hebrew origin. A problem is presented by some statements which, relating mainly to the deaths at Herod's instigation of his brother-in-law Aristobulus and Hyrcanus II, are made in a spirit hostile to him. Then again the account of the atmosphere at Herod's court, engendered by the suspicions entertained against his sons Alexander and Aristobulus, also gives rise to misgivings.[1] Here Josephus may have used literary traditions which had crystallized in the circles of the descendants of Herod by his wife Mariamme the Hasmonaean.

For the *Antiquities* Josephus utilized other sources besides those which he had used for the *War*. No less significant is the fact that whereas in his first work Josephus was a spokesman for the Roman Empire and the Flavian dynasty, in the *Antiquities* he is first and foremost the apologist of Judaism. At times this circumstance led him to adopt a position opposed to his sources, although he was not always consistent in this. His use of Nicholas for the entire period from the civil war in Palestine until after the death of Herod was even more extensive. He re-employed the material from Nicholas which

[1] *War* I, 493.

he had previously used in the *War*, and then drew further on him, mainly for the period following the conquest of Jerusalem in 37 B.C.E. described in books XV-XVII. Equally conspicuous is the use in book XIV of Strabo and numerous documents.[1] In two places, one in XIV, the other in XV, Josephus found it necessary to criticize Nicholas. Generally, however, in XIV of the *Antiquities*, Josephus only slightly modified the laudatory tone which characterizes Nicholas and which is reflected in the *War*.[2] In the *Antiquities*, too, the narrative adopts a sympathetic attitude towards Antipater while showing hostility to Antigonus the Hasmonaean in his struggle against Herod. Only the quotations from Strabo's historical work alter the picture somewhat. However, the personality of Antigonus, the most energetic fighter against the Romans, was not such as to induce Josephus to involve himself in a controversy with Nicholas since Antigonus might appear rather too much as the prototype of the Zealots.

Scholars are divided on the extent and manner in which Nicholas' *Universal History* is reflected in the books of the *Antiquities* which describe Herod's reign from the conquest of Jerusalem in 37 B.C.E. until 4 B.C.E. (XV-XVII). In these books Josephus openly criticizes Herod's policy several times, and in one passage even contrasts himself explicitly with Nicholas of Damascus. While describing himself as descended from a family related to the Hasmonaean dynasty and as a priest, he regards Nicholas as a courtier writing to glorify his king's name.[3]

Josephus' criticism of Herod occurs in various contexts. Of particular interest is the general comment analysing Herod's character.[4] When Josephus deals with Herod's last illness he interprets it as a divine punishment for his evil deeds.[5] In XV-XVII of the *Antiquities* Josephus undoubtedly adopts an unfavourable attitude towards Herod, much more unfavourable than that shown not only in the *War* but also in *Antiquities* XIV.

But to what extent was this unfavourable attitude based on sources independent of Nicholas? One gains the impression that while for

---

[1] B. Niese in *Hermes* (1876), pp. 478-480, was of the opinion that Josephus got his documents from Nicholas himself, but this cannot be substantiated. Cf. also Laqueur, pp. 221-230.

[2] *Pace* Laqueur, pp. 128-221.

[3] *Ant.* XVI, 179-187; the view that the *Antiquities* here echo not Josephus but a 'Jewish Anonymous' (so Otto, *op. cit.*, pp. 11-12; G. Hölscher, *Die Hohenpriesterliste bei Josephus und die evangelische Chronologie* (1940), pp. 3-4) is hardly plausible.

[4] *Ant.* XVI, 150-159.   [5] *Ant.* XVII, 168.

most of the topics on which Josephus criticizes Herod he could have obtained the factual material for his criticism from Nicholas himself, his evaluation of the king's actions was his own. Josephus' unfavourable attitude towards Herod in these books of the *Antiquities* is to be ascribed chiefly to his being more dominated by religious and national sentiments, as the apologist of Judaism. There is no need to assume that Josephus adopted this attitude under the influence of some anonymous Jewish writer with anti-Herodian tendencies, and there are certainly no grounds for assuming that his hostility, which in most of its expressions in the *Antiquities* bears a Jewish national-religious character, derives from a Greek source independent of Nicholas. For the description of the events following Herod's death, the riots in Judaea and the pleas put before Augustus in Rome, Josephus likewise used Nicholas. Here a comparison between Josephus and excerpts from Nicholas' autobiography is instructive.[1] But from now on the dependence on Nicholas and in general on one consecutive identifiable source ceases. In the *Antiquities* XVIII-XX Josephus employed various sources as required by the different subjects dealt with. Much of his narrative is naturally devoted to a portrayal of the events in Judaea from the establishment of the province until the Great Revolt and to the history of the members of the Herodian dynasty who ruled over various parts of Palestine. Among the topics in the history of Judaea with which he deals are: Quirinius' census and the Jewish reaction to it; the desecration of the Temple by the Samaritans; the procuratorship of Pilate, which is described in relatively great detail; Vitellius' activities in Judaea; Gaius Caligula's edict and Petronius' action; Agrippa I's reign in Judaea; the restoration, after Agrippa's death, of direct Roman rule in Judaea; the procuratorship of Tiberius Alexander; Cumanus' procuratorship so filled with dramatic episodes, the most important of which was the quarrel between Jews and Samaritans which ultimately led to his removal from office. He describes in some detail also the procuratorship of Felix, with emphasis on the rebellious agitation of this period and on the struggle between the Jews and the non-Jews in Caesarea. A brief survey of the rule of the last procurators (Festus, Albinus, Florus) concludes the part dealing with the history of the province of Judaea prior to the Revolt.

These chapters embody material relating to the history of the house of Herod. While special attention is here paid to the rule of the

[1] E. Täubler in *Byzantinische Zeitschrift* (1925), pp. 36-40.

26

tetrarch Herod Antipas[1], Josephus' narrative gives particular prominence to the personality of Agrippa I, whose history is described in greater detail than that of any other figure with the exception of Herod. This detailed account, it should be stressed, refers largely to the period preceding Agrippa's accession, the hardships suffered by him then as a private person being portrayed in a manner unparalleled in Josephus' historical writings as a whole.[2] The *Antiquities* then gives information on Herod of Chalcis and Agrippa II.

The biography of Agrippa I includes a lengthy chapter of Roman history, which recounts the plot to assassinate Gaius Caligula and its execution,[3] and then gives an account of Agrippa's accession.[4] In the earlier parts of Agrippa's biography there are similarly various details which clearly belong to the history of Rome rather than to that of the Jews. Josephus likewise reports at some length on the relations between the Parthians and the Romans.[5]

There are several episodes associated with the history of the Jews in the Diaspora which are obviously detached items, as for instance the discussion of the Jews of Babylonia and in particular the brothers Asinaeus and Anilaeus, or the conversion to Judaism of the royal house of Adiabene.[6] Touching briefly on the riots in Alexandria in the days of Gaius Caligula and of Claudius, Josephus quotes official documents relating to them.[7] He tells of the expulsion of the Jews from Rome in the days of Tiberius, and includes an erotic story explaining the reason which prompted that Roman emperor to act against the priests of the cult of Isis.[8]

The variety of topics dealt with is also reflected in the changing sources, which Josephus did not always succeed in integrating chronologically, the chronological sequence being at times somewhat confused. A relatively large amount of information, included by Josephus in the final books of the *Antiquitites*, has no direct bearing on the history of the Jews.

The parallel account in the *Jewish War* gives in the main the history of Judaea. Yet here too some events, later recounted in the *Antiquities*, have been omitted. Thus, for example, there is no reference to the early procurators or anything relating to them, the first one mentioned being Pilate, and not all the episodes about him reported in the *Antiquities* are included here. Still more conspicuous is the

[1] *Ant.* XVIII, 36-38; 102-105; 109-119. [2] *Ant.* XVIII, 143-236.
[3] *Ant.* XIX, 1-235. [4] *Ant.* XIX, 236. [5] *Ant.* XVIII, 39-52.
[6] *Ant.* XVIII, 310-379; XX, 17-96. [7] *Ant.* XIX, 278-285. [8] *Ant.* XVIII, 65-84.

absence of important events in the history of Herod Antipas, as also the omission of the detailed biography of Agrippa I before his accession to the throne. The *War* also omits the sections dealing with the history of Babylonian Jewry and with the development of relations between the Parthians and the Romans, as well as the story of the plot against Gaius Caligula.

The question of Josephus' sources for the period from Augustus' arrangements for Judaea until the eve of the Revolt is a complex one. Born in 37/38 c.e., Josephus was an eyewitness of some of the later events described by him. Yet it is clear that for his principal account he used literary sources. Josephus has given us no hint of the authors of his sources, and only for few of them (e.g. for the account of the plot against Caligula) have names been suggested by scholars. But although unable to establish the authors of the sources, we can to some extent at least form an opinion of their nature.

For the principal events in the history of the province of Judaea, described by Josephus in his two works, he had, it seems, written sources. Naturally the closer the events came to the final years of the Second Temple, the more he was able at times to use his direct, personal knowledge. That he had at his disposal one continuous source describing the history of Judaea from the beginning of the establishment of the province until the outbreak of the Revolt in the days of Florus cannot under any circumstances be maintained. It is more probable that, in addition to his oral sources and direct knowledge, he derived his information from several written sources, as required by the different periods and events.[1]

It would also appear that the unusually detailed history of Agrippa I's life was taken from a particular work sympathetically disposed towards him and undoubtedly written by a close friend. The account of the plot against Gaius Caligula was doubtless drawn from a Roman senatorial source, identifiable perhaps with the Latin historian Cluvius Rufus.[2] Whether Josephus incorporated this Latin source in Agrippa's biography or whether this was done by the latter's

---

[1] E. Norden in *Neue Jahrbücher für das klassische Altertum* (1913), pp. 640-642, who made an attempt to characterize the source underlying the narrative of Josephus relating to Pilate.

[2] Cf. Mommsen, *Hermes* (1870), p. 322; F. Schemann, *Die Quellen des Flavius Josephus in der jüdischen Archäologie* (1887), p. 52; G. Hölscher, *PW*, IX, p. 1985; V. M. Scramuzza, *The Emperor Claudius* (1940), pp. 14-15; G. B. Townend, *Hermes* (1960), p. 102. Doubts have been raised by e.g. D. Timpe, *Historia* IX (1960), p. 474 n. 4, and pp. 500-501; L. H. Feldman in *Latomus* (1962), pp. 320-333; R. Syme, *Hermes* (1964), p. 420 (he suggests Servilius Nonianus).

biographer is difficult to determine. The former alternative is decidedly more probable seeing that Josephus wrote his work in Rome where he lived for a long time and had ample access to Latin sources. It should also be borne in mind that for other passages in his work he also used Roman historical sources.[1] Account should likewise be taken of his general statement on the need for historical truth, in which he in effect alludes to various Latin historians.[2] The two stories of the Jewish-Babylonian brothers and of the conversion to Judaism of the royal house of Adiabene reached Josephus as well-formed literary units, but it should not be assumed that both of them had previously been combined within the framework of a single literary work.[3]

Greek and Roman authors

NICHOLAS OF DAMASCUS
(c. 64 B.C.E. - beginning of the first century C.E.)

Historian, rhetorician and many-sided author, Nicholas was born in Damascus, of which city he was proud. His father occupied various positions in the public life of Damascus and went on missions on its behalf. Nicholas, who belonged to the Peripatetic school, was known for the broad interests which characterized the members of that school. Distinguished as an orator and a diplomat, he maintained contact with several leading contemporary figures. He acted as tutor to the children of Antony and Cleopatra. Shortly after their downfall he joined the court of Herod, in whose diplomatic service he was active at least in 14 B.C.E. In that year he accompanied Herod on his journeys to Asia Minor, where before Marcus Agrippa he defended the rights of the Jewish inhabitants of the Greek cities. In 12 B.C.E. he accompanied Herod on his journey to Italy. When relations between Herod and Augustus became strained in consequence of the Jewish king's reprisals against the Nabataeans, Nicholas succeeded in appeasing Augustus. Towards the end of Herod's reign he played an important role in the legal proceedings against Herod's eldest son Antipater. After Herod's death he defended the interests of Archelaus

---

[1] *Ant.* XVIII, 39-54.   [2] *Ant.* XX, 154.

[3] E. Täubler, *Die Parthernachrichten bei Josephus* (1904), p. 62, thinks that the narrative dealing with the pair of Jewish-Babylonian brothers derives from oral accounts of Parthian Jews. The story of the Judaization of Adiabene comes, according to the same scholar, from a written source ('eine erbauliche Missionsschrift'; pp. 62-65). Schalit maintains that the two narratives reached Josephus in Greek, but that their original language was Aramaic.

against the latter's opponents, and once again succeeded in persuading Augustus to grant his principal request and to confirm most of Herod's will.

Nicholas' most important literary achievement was his *Universal History*. Comprising 144 books and commencing with the ancient history of the eastern kingdoms, the work became more detailed as it came closer to the author's own times. Herod had urged him to write the great work, parts of which at least presumably circulated during the king's lifetime. Since Nicholas was a member of Herod's court and played a not insignificant role in the events in Herod's reign, it is not surprising that the *Universal History* should have described in great detail the history of that reign and the personality of the king. Of this work only a few excerpts referring to the Jews have survived. Yet we are deeply indebted to Nicholas for our knowledge of the Jewish history in the period of the Second Temple. This is because Josephus mainly depended on Nicholas in his Jewish *Antiquities* and *War* not only for everything relating to the history of Herod's kingdom and the events following Herod's death, but also for the history of the Hasmonaean dynasty. See also on Josephus, pp. 21-26 above. Very interesting, too, are the surviving extracts of Nicholas' autobiography relating to the history of Herod and to the events that took place after his death.

STRABO (*c.* 64 B.C.E. - the twenties of the first century C.E.)

Born in Pontus of a distinguished family, Strabo travelled extensively and according to his own testimony visited numerous countries. He clearly had a personal knowledge of various parts of Asia Minor and stayed for some time in Rome but apparently visited neither Syria nor Palestine. Strabo was equally celebrated as a historian and a geographer. His historical work, which began where Polybius had left off, comprised forty-three books besides four introductory ones. The main extant fragments of this historical work, which have survived through Josephus' *Antiquities*, relate to Jewish subjects, the earliest event referred to in them being the pillaging of the Temple in Jerusalem by Antiochus Epiphanes,[1] while the latest is the execution by the Romans of Antigonus the Hasmonaean. From the excerpts cited by Josephus it can be seen that Strabo employed various literary sources. Strabo's fragments have a special value in that they enable us to obtain a picture, independently of Nicholas who was

[1] Jos. *Against Apion* ii, 83-84.

Josephus' main source for this period, of certain events associated with the history of the Hasmonaean dynasty and Herod's accession. The sixteenth book of Strabo's *Geography*, which has survived in its entirety, contains a description of Palestine and a historical sketch of the emergence of the Jewish nation and religion. The first Jewish historical figure after Moses mentioned here is Alexander Janneus, regarded by Strabo as the first Jewish king. It is impossible to establish with any certainty who served as Strabo's source for his description of Pompey's conquest of Jerusalem in 63 B.C.E. or for his brief account of Herod's kingdom and of his sons' fate after his death. For the events of 63 B.C.E., Theophanes, the historian of Pompey, may have been the source.[1] As Strabo was a contemporary of Herod, and of his sons there is no need to assume dependence on Nicholas here although this is possible.

For Strabo's views on Judaism, see the final chapter of vol. II.

PTOLEMY (end of the first century B.C.E.?)

In a grammatical work dating from the end of the first or the beginning of the second century C.E. and ascribed to Ammonius, mention is made of a history of King Herod written by someone named Ptolemy.[2] This history undoubtedly comprised more than one book; for the quotations from this work, referring to the origin of the Idumaeans, is said to be taken from the first book.

As Ptolemy is one of the most common names in the Greek onomasticon in general, it is difficult to identify this writer with one of the authors known by that name. Nevertheless it has been suggested (by Schürer, Otto, Hölscher) that he is to be identified with the *grammaticus* Ptolemy of Ascalon who lived, it is conjectured, at the end of the first century B.C.E.[3] This would make Ptolemy's work on Herod in effect a contemporary production, but this identification is far from being conclusive.[4]

Although Josephus nowhere mentions Ptolemy as the author of a work on Herod, it has been suggested (by Hölscher) that this Ptolemy was one of the principal sources for Josephus' account of Herod's

---

[1] F. P. Rizzo, *Le fonti per la storia della conquista pompeiana della Siria* (1963), pp. 35-37.
[2] Ammonius, *De adfinium vocabulorum differentia*, ed. K. Nickau, (1966), no. 243.
[3] M. Baege, *De Ptolemaeo Ascalonita* (1882), p. 6.
[4] The reservations of Jacoby who points out that the list of the works of Ptolemy of Ascalon does not include works of non-grammatical character.

kingdom. However, no real proof has been advanced to substantiate this view.

PLINY THE ELDER (23/24-79 C.E.)

Born at Novum Comum in Gallia Cisalpina, Pliny passed through a rich military and administrative career in the western provinces of the Roman Empire, and was much attached to the Flavian dynasty. He was an industrious scholar whose main works were a history which continued the history of Aufidius Bassus and was known as *a fine Aufidii Bassi* (now lost) and his vast encyclopaedic work, the *Natural History*. The latter contains also a considerable amount of information on the Jews and Palestine, most of which refers to the country's physical characteristics and its products, above all to the Dead Sea and its bitumen. From a historical point of view, special importance attaches to the chapters in the geographical section of the work.[1] After a description of Egypt and at the beginning of an account of the various parts of Syria comes a description of Palestine which assumes the distribution of the Jewish population within Judaea, Galilee, and Peraea. It also gives an account of the division of Judaea into toparchies. A comparison between the list in Pliny and that in Josephus' *War* reveals several stages in the administrative history of Judaea. Pliny's statements about the Essenes are also important, for unlike Philo and Josephus he emphasizes their association with the Dead Sea. In his geographical description Pliny is not entirely free of mistakes. Thus, for example, he locates the city of Tarichaeae to the south of the Sea of Gennesaret instead of to the north of Tiberias. In the whole work there is, in fact, no evidence that Pliny was personally acquainted with Judaea; the assumption that he visited and stayed in Judaea is based only on an uncertain reconstruction of an inscription from Arados, according to which Pliny served as an officer in the siege of Jerusalem in 70 C.E.[2] Pliny does not indicate his sources for his description of Judaea. One gains the impression that while for the account of the administrative division he made use of a source contemporaneous with Herod,

---

[1] *Natural History* v, 66-73.
[2] The inscription is *OGIS* no. 586 (= IGLS VIII, no. 4011); the restoration was suggested by T. Mommsen in *Hermes* (1884), pp. 644-648; cf. also E. Groag in *Jahrbücher für Classische Philologie*, Supplement XXIII (1897), p. 783. Against Mommsen's restoration cf. H. G. Pflaum, *Les carrières procuratoriennes équestres sous le Haut-Empire romain* I (1960), pp. 106-111 (following Münzer); R. Syme in *Harvard Studies in Classical Philology* (1969), pp. 204-208.

he adapted his list to the conditions prevailing in his own times, the seventies of the first century C.E., under the rule of the Flavian dynasty.

TACITUS (c. 55-120 C.E.)

Among the Roman historians who wrote about the Jews, Cornelius Tacitus ranks first by virtue of his two large works, the *Histories* and the *Annals*, which have survived only in part. The former, which deals with the history of the Roman civil war following Nero's death and the history of the Flavian dynasty, was written in the time of Trajan, in the first decade of the second century C.E. Only the first four books of the *Histories* and the beginning of the fifth have been preserved. Here Tacitus deals with the commencement of the siege of Jerusalem. His account of the end has not survived. In this context Tacitus gives his famous excursus on the Jewish nation and its origin, the nature of its religion and also a description of its land and its history until the outbreak of the Great Revolt. Several chapters deal with the siege and the position in Jerusalem during it.[1]

It is quite impossible to equate Tacitus' sources for his account of the ancient Jewish history with those for his description of the siege itself. There is no reason to assume that he derived the various versions quoted by him on the origin of the Jews from a single source. It should not, on the other hand, be imagined that every version he mentions was taken by him from a specific source. It should also be added that although here and there statements of Tacitus on the ancient history of the Jews may be paralleled from Greek sources, he could have found the material in earlier Latin sources.

The chapters that treat of the siege of Jerusalem raise the question of the relation between Tacitus and the *War* of Josephus. Although certain details are common to both authors, there are also differences between them. That Tacitus relied directly on Josephus is unlikely, and while an indirect use is possible, it is not very probable. Other sources suggested are Pliny the Elder and Antonius Julianus.[2]

Interesting points bearing on the history of the Jews are scattered in other books of the *Histories*, such as the reference to the efforts of

[1] *Historiae* v, 2-13.
[2] One Antonius Julianus was procurator of Judaea (cf. Jos. *War*. VI, 238). He seems to be identical with a writer on Jewish life whose work is implied by Minucius Felix, *Octavius* 33,4. Schürer I, pp. 33-34; E. Norden in *Neue Jahrbücher für das Klassische Altertum* (1913), pp. 664-666; A. Rosenberg, *Einleitung und Quellenkunde zur römischen Geschichte* (1921), p. 256; A. M. A. Hospers-Jansen, *Tacitus over de Joden* (1949), pp. 113, 172-177; Paratore, pp. 664-668.

Agrippa II and Berenice on behalf of the Flavians in the struggle for mastery in the empire.[1]

Tacitus' other work, the *Annals*, which deals with the Julio-Claudian period, was written later, and at least some of its books appear to have been published after the Jewish revolts in the days of Trajan.[2] In the *Annals* there is no consecutive discussion on the Jews, but merely descriptions of events associated with the history of the Jews or of Judaea.[3] On Tacitus' attitude towards the Jews, see the final chapter of vol. II.

SUETONIUS (69 C.E.-*c*. 140 C.E.)

A contemporary of Tacitus and the biographer of the emperors, Suetonius refers to the Jews in various passages in his biographies of the twelve emperors. In this way he gives us here and there valuable information on the Jews in the Roman imperial period. Some of the information in Suetonius is also found in the other sources, but some has no parallel elsewhere, such as the mourning of the Jews of Rome at the death of Julius Caesar, the unsympathetic attitude of Augustus to Judaism, or Suetonius' own recollections of the examination of an old man aged ninety, so as to oblige him to pay the 'Jewish Tax.'[4] The biographies of Vespasian and Titus are of special interest, containing as they do details of the war in Galilee and Judaea.

DIO CASSIUS (latter half of the second century-beginning of the third century C.E.)

Born in Bithynia and a prominent figure in the Roman imperial administration, Dio Cassius in his extensive work on Roman history deals in various contexts with the Jews and with different events in their history. For several subjects of prime importance Dio Cassius is the principal source in the later historiographical tradition, as for instance with regard to the Jewish revolts in the reigns of Trajan and Hadrian (the Bar Cochba revolt).[5]

Dio Cassius first deals with the Jews in connection with Pompey's capture of Jerusalem.[6] Here he mentions the characteristic features

---

[1] *Historiae* II, 81.
[2] On the date of the composition of the *Annals*, see Syme, II, pp. 465-480; J. Beaujeu in *Revue des Études Latines* (1960), pp. 200-235 (before 121 C.E.).
[3] Cf. esp. *Annals* II, 42, 85; XII, 54.
[4] *Life of Julius* 84,5; *Life of Augustus* 93; 76,2; *Life of Domitian* 12,2.
[5] Dio Cassius LXVIII, 32, 1-3; LXIX, 12, 1-14,3.
[6] Dio Cassius XXXVII, 15, 2-17, 4.

of the Jewish religion, whose followers succeeded in obtaining for themselves freedom of worship in the Roman Empire. Acquainted with the monotheistic principle of Judaism and with the fact that the Jews did not erect images to their God, Dio Cassius lays particular stress on two features of Jewish religion, the Temple and the day of Saturn (the Sabbath). He is aware especially of the probem of proselytism and observes that the name of Jew applies also to non-Jews who have adopted Jewish customs. It was, he states, the success of the religious propaganda of the Jews which was used as a pretext for their expulsion by Tiberius. He is moreover our only source for the information that among the Roman soldiers besieging Jerusalem under the command of Titus there were some who deserted to the Jews in the belief that Jerusalem was impregnable.

BIBLIOGRAPHY

PHILO

Opera quae supersunt. Editio maior, ed. by L. COHN and P. WENDLAND, 7 vols, 1896-1930, reprinted 1962; Die Werke in deutscher Übersetzung, ed. by L. COHN, I. HEINEMANN et al., 7 vols, reprinted 1962; Greek Text with English Translation, ed. by F. H. COLSON, G. H. WHITAKER and R. MARCUS (The Loeb Classical Library), 12 vols, 1929-70; Les oeuvres, (Greek text and French translation), ed. by R. ARNALDEZ, J. POUILLOUX, C. MONDÉSERT, et al. 25 vols so far published, 1961-72; F. DELAUNAY, Philon d'Alexandrie, Écrits historiques, 1870; H. LEISEGANG in JBL, 1938, pp. 377-405; H. BOX, Philonis Alexandrini 'In Flaccum', 1939; E. M. SMALLWOOD, Philonis Alexandrini 'Legatio ad Gaium', 1961.

JOSEPHUS

Opera, ed. by B. NIESE, 7 vols, 1887-95, reprinted 1955; Greek Text with English Translation, ed. by H. ST. JOHN THACKERAY, R. MARCUS and L. H. FELDMAN (The Loeb Classical Library), 9 vols, 1926-65; Opera, ed. by S. A. NABER, 6 vols, 1888-96; H. BLOCH, Die Quellen des Flavius Josephus in seiner Archäologie, 1879; J. VON DESTINON, Die Quellen des Flavius Josephus in der jüdischen Archäologie, XII-XVII, 1882; F. A. CHR. SCHEMANN, Die Quellen des Flavius Josephus in der jüdischen Archäologie, XVIII-XX, 1887; A. V. GUTSCHMID, Kleine Schriften IV, 1893, pp. 336-375; C. WACHSMUTH, Einleitung in das Studium der alten Geschichte, 1895, pp. 438-449; B. NIESE, in Historische Zeitschrift,

1896, pp. 193-237; H. PETER, *Die geschichtliche Literatur über die römische Kaiserzeit bis Theodosius I und ihre Quellen* I, 1897, pp. 394-401; E. SCHÜRER, *Geschichte des jüdischen Volkes im Zeitalter Jesu Christi*, 3 vols, 1901-11, esp. vol. I, pp. 74-106; G. HÖLSCHER, *Die Quellen des Josephus für die Zeit von Exil bis zum jüdischen Kriege*, 1904; E. TÄUBLER, *Die Parthernachrichten bei Josephus*, 1904; H. LUTHER, *Josephus und Justus von Tiberias*, 1910; H. VINCENT, in *RB*, 1911, pp. 366-383; N. BENTWICH, *Josephus*, 1914; G. HÖLSCHER in *PW* IX, 1916, cols 1934-2000; R. LAQUEUR, *Der jüdische Historiker Flavius Josephus*, 1920; W. WEBER, *Josephus und Vespasian*, 1921; H. ST. JOHN THACKERAY, *Josephus the Man and the Historian*, 1929; A. SCHLATTER, *Die Theologie des Judentums nach dem Bericht des Josefus*, 1932; A. SCHALIT, in *Klio* 1933, pp. 67-95; A. MOMIGLIANO, in *CAH* X, 1934, pp. 884-7; G. C. RICHARDS in *CQ*, 1939, pp. 36-40; D. TIMPE in *Historia*, 1960, pp. 474-502; R. J. H. SHUTT, *Studies in Josephus*, 1961; L. H. FELDMAN, in *Latomus*, 1962, pp. 320-333, and *Scholarship on Philo and Josephus*, 1937-62, 1963; A. SCHALIT, in *ASTI*, 1965, pp. 163-188; H. SCHRECKENBERG, *Bibliographie zu Flavius Josephus*, 1968.

NICHOLAS OF DAMASCUS

The extant fragments have been collected by JACOBY, *FGH* II A, pp. 324-430; A. V. GUTSCHMID, *Kleine Schriften*, 1894, pp. 536-542; SCHÜRER, op. cit., I, pp. 50-7; P. JAKOB, *De Nicolai Damasceni sermone et arte historica quaestiones selectae*, 1911; E. TÄUBLER, in *Byzantinische Zeitschrift* 1925, pp. 33-40; JACOBY, *FHG* II C, pp. 229-291; R. LAQUEUR, in *PW* XVII, pp. 362-424; B. WACHOLDER, *Nicolaus of Damascus*, 1962; G. W. BOWERSOCK, *Augustus and the Greek World*, 1965, pp. 134-8; D. A. W. BILTCLIFFE, *Rhenisches Museum für Philologie* CXII, 1969, pp. 85-93; M. STERN, *Studies in Bible and Jewish History dedicated to the Memory of Jacob Liver*, 1971, pp. 375-394 (in Hebrew).

STRABO

The fragments from his historical work have been collected by JACOBY, *FGH* II A, pp. 430-6; see also II C, pp. 196-9; M. DUBOIS, *Examen de la géographie de Strabon*, 1891; R. KUNZE, *Symbolae Strabonianae*, 1892; K. ALBERT, *Strabo als Quelle des Flavius Josephus*, 1902; E. HONIGMANN, in *PW*, 2nd series IV, cols 76-151; W. ALY, *Strabon von Amaseia*, 1957.

PTOLEMY

Schürer, op. cit., I, pp. 48-50; HÖLSCHER, *Die Quellen des Josephus*, 1904, pp. 57, 80; W. OTTO, *Herodes*, 1913, pp. 5-6; JACOBY, *FGH*, II D, pp. 625-6; A. DIHLE, in *PW* XXIII, p. 1861.

PLINY

Text editions by C. MAYHOFF, 1892-1909, and J. BEAUJEU, A. ERNOUT *et al.*, 1947 ff. On Pliny and Judaea see M. STERN, in *Tarbiz*, 1968, pp. 215-229. On the *Natural History* in general, see F. MÜNZER, *Beiträge zur Quellenkritik der Naturgeschichte des Plinius*, 1897; D. DETLEFSEN, *Untersuchungen über die Zusammensetzung der Naturgeschichte des Plinius*, 1899; on Pliny's life, see K. ZIEGLER, in *PW* XXI, cols 271-285; R. SYME, *Harvard Studies in Classical Philology* LXXIII (1969), pp. 201-236. On the description of the Essenes by Pliny see C. BURCHARD, *RB*, 1962, pp. 533-569.

TACITUS

Annals, 1960, and *Historiae*, 1961, both ed. by E. KOESTERMANN; Of the vast literature on Tacitus himself, see R. SYME, *Tacitus*, 2 vols, 1958; E. PARATORE, *Tacito*, 2nd ed., 1962; R. HÄUSSLER, *Tacitus und das historische Bewusstsein*, 1965; R. T. SCOTT, *Religion and Philosophy in the Histories of Tacitus*, 1968.

SUETONIUS

Text edition by M. IHM, 1908; F. DELLA CORTE, *Suetonio eques Romanus*, 1958; H. G. PFLAUM, *Les carrières procuratoriennes équestres sous le Haut-Empire romain* I, 1960, pp. 219-224; G. B. TOWNEND, *Historia*, 1961, pp. 99-109.

DIO CASSIUS

Text edition by U. P. BOISSEVAIN, 1895-1931; E. SCHWARTZ, in *PW* III, pp. 1684-1722 and *Griechische Geschichtschreiber*, 1959, pp. 394-450; E. GABBA, in *Rivista Storica Italiana*, 1955, pp. 289-333; F. MILLAR, *A Study of Cassius Dio*, 1964.

III THE NEW TESTAMENT

As is the case with most of the literary sources dealt with in this chapter, a full treatment of the textual and literary problems involved will be given in the Section Two of *Compendia*, which is entitled

Oral and Literary Tradition in Judaism and Early Christianity. At this stage only those aspects will be discussed which have a direct impact on the use of the New Testament as a source for the subject-matter of the present volume and the subsequent one.

The New Testament consists of documents written by Christians for Christians, and they deal with Christian issues. Although they are very often based on Jewish attitudes, Jewish ideas, and indeed on typically Jewish methods of interpreting the Scriptures, they also testify to a widening gulf between Jewish and non-Jewish Christians on the one hand and the Jews on the other. The fact that the Gospels were written after the break between the Synagogue and the Church had become final in or around 70 c.e. certainly influenced the way Judaism is reflected in these writings. Often, too, we cannot be sure whether the author possessed first-hand information concerning, for instance, Judaea or Galilee in the first century or concerning a particular area of the Diaspora and, even if he had such information, whether he was in a position to use it effectively. The oldest New Testament writings are the letters of Paul, written (roughly) during the fifties of the first century. Here the problem arises which of these letters are genuine, and which must be called deutero-Pauline. The latter were not written by Paul himself but by later authors who, in dealing with problems arising after Paul's death, used his name and the literary form of his letters to give expression to their understanding of the apostle's thoughts. Romans, I and II Corinthians, Galatians, Philippians, I Thessalonians and Philemon are held to be genuine; some scholars have their doubts about Colossians and II Thessalonians. Ephesians and especially I and II Timothy and Titus are generally considered to be Deutero-Pauline. This, however, is of relatively little importance for the problem we are dealing with here. The Pauline letters, while of great value as illustrations of the way in which Jewish thinking and exegetical methods shaped Paul's belief in Jesus as the Christ, contain very little direct information about Jewish history in the first century c.e. The same applies to the Letter of the Hebrews, the so-called Catholic Epistles and the Apocalypse of John, which need not detain us here.

There is much more to be said about the Gospels and the Acts of the Apostles. It is not easy to date them; the Gospel according to Mark is usually regarded as the earliest (*c.* 70 c.e.). The Gospels according to Matthew and Luke are supposed to have been written in the eighties or nineties, and the Acts of the Apostles, composed by the

38

same author as the Gospel according to Luke, a little later. The Gospel according to John is usually dated 90-100 c.e. Although the first three Gospels have much in common, the matter of their sources poses a difficult problem. Very probably Matthew and Luke used the Gospel according to Mark in some form, and besides that much material which Matthew and Luke have in common very probably goes back to one source. This so-called Q source must have consisted mainly of Jesus' sayings, although it is not clear what its precise contents, structure and date were. Besides, it is difficult to establish anything definite about the written sources or oral tradition used by Mark, Matthew and Luke where they do not follow Q or Mark. In general we must assume that many stories about events in Jesus' life, sayings, parables etc. circulated independently or combined in small units. They must have received their present form during the process of oral transmission; the diverse forms of stories or sayings in the three first Gospels demonstrate that until the stage of recording in writing certain liberties were taken for granted.

The framework of the gospel story in the main is certainly a secondary development of the gospel tradition, as is evidenced by the differences between Mark, Matthew, Luke and John in this respect. We cannot be sure that Mark, as our earliest source, is the most reliable. Yet again this is of relative importance only for the topics dealt with in these two volumes. Even if the Gospels do not enable us to determine the exact sequence of Jesus' travels in Galilee, Samaria and Judaea, they do supply us with solid evidence for the historical geography of Palestine.

One of the oldest elements to be incorporated in the Gospels must have been the Passion story. Despite the many differences between the four Gospels, there is more agreement here than anywhere else, and a primitive version of the story of the Passion may have existed before Mark. Here, however, the need to explain why Jesus the Christ had been rejected by the Jewish authorities and tried and crucified by the Romans, coupled with the desire to defend the Christian faith against the criticism of outsiders (which must frequently have started from this point) undoubtedly coloured the description of events. It is not only difficult to reconstruct the Passion narrative in its original form, we must also take into account that theological motives played a significant part from the very beginning. Moreover because neither the people who told the story nor those who wrote it down were experts in legal matters or interested in the techni-

39

calities of Jewish and Roman procedure, we cannot expect the Gospels in their present form to shed much light on what we would like to know. Consequently it is much easier to recognize the theological tendencies in the various accounts of the trial of Jesus than to reach definitive conclusions as to the criminal law, the procedure of the Sanhedrin or the Sanhedrin's right to deal with capital cases. Although the Gospels contain what we call biographical material, and certainly purport to deal with the life and death of a historical human being, culminating in his resurrection, their authors are not interested in historical events as such. They wrote in order to describe the life of Jesus as a charismatic personality in his words and deeds, sent by God to Israel and the world, and to strengthen the faith and insight of Christian communities. Each Gospel has its own theology and consequently its own perspective on certain crucial events. This is particularly clear in the Gospel according to John, which contains much original material obviously moulded by his own particular form of Christology. Yet this Gospel, too, offers some interesting historical and geographical details and throws some light on Jewish teachings about the Law and messianic expectation.

The words of Jesus (particularly the parables) and the stories about him offer the possibility of discovering important features. of Jewish life in Galilee and Jerusalem in the first century c.e. The matters which concern us here are not generally mentioned expressly by the authors—they are taken for granted or mentioned in passing. Thus we hear about the social situation (e.g. the status of tax collectors in Mark 2:13-17 and Luke 19:1-10), agricultural conditions (e.g. Mark 12:1-9), relations between masters and servants (Matthew 25:14-30)), worship in the Temple (Luke 1:5-25, 2:22-51) and in the synagogue (Luke 4:16-30), and also about the organization of the synagogue (Mark 5:22, Luke 13:14), the administration of the Jewish and Roman authorities (Mark 11:15-19), the temple tax (Matthew 17:24-27), customs (Mark 2:13-17), tribute money (Mark 12:13-17), and census (Luke 2:1).

Especially important is the fact that legal regulations codified later in the Mishnah can be dated in the first century with the help of references in the New Testament. To mention only a few examples: the ritual washing of hands (Mark 7:3, cf. *M. Yadaim* 1:1ff) and the practice of *qorban* (making a vow, pronouncing the word; Mark 7:11, cf. *M. Nedarim* 1:2; 8:7). This illustrates the importance of the New Testament as an additional source of information. Since rabbinic tradition was not codified until after a long period during which the halakic material was orally transmitted, it is sometimes very difficult to date individual traditions without the help of external evidence. The writings of the New Testament, which can be dated with reasonable certainty, can sometimes provide such evidence. The references to political rulers in Palestine during these years—Herod the Great in Matthew 2, Herod Antipas in Mark 6:14-29, Luke 23:6-12, Archaelaus (Matthew 2:12), Pilate (Mark 15 and parallels, Luke 3:1, 13:1)— add little or nothing to the picture given of them by Flavius Josephus. They are portrayed in their relations to Jesus or John the Baptist, and quite a few details in the stories in which they occur are not of historical value. Yet they emphasize the fact that these rulers were very suspicious of messianic movements (see e.g. Luke 13:1, and cf. Luke 13:31ff. and Josephus *Ant.* XVIII, 116-119).

Some interesting sidelights are thrown on the relations between Samaritans and Jews (Matthew 10:5, Luke 9:52 ff. 10:33, 17:11,16, John 4 *passim*, 8:48). It should also be noted that transcriptions of Hebrew or Aramaic words given in the New Testament (e.g. Mark 5:41, 7:11, 34, 14:36, 15:34, I Corinthians 16:22) raise problems for the language used by Jews and Jewish Christians in the first century.

In the Acts of the Apostles, companion text of the Gospel of Luke, we find reports of the foundation of the Christian community in Jerusalem and its preaching in Judaea and Samaria, and of the mission among Jews and Gentiles in Syria, Asia Minor and Greece until, finally, Rome is reached. The picture given is selective: the theme of the book is clearly given in 1:8 'But you shall receive power when the Holy Spirit has come upon you; and you will be my witnesses in Jerusalem, and in all Judea and Samaria, and to the end of the earth.' In the first half of Acts Peter appears as a central figure; the second half deals with Paul's travels. There are many details we are greatly interested in that are not mentioned—we do not hear anything, for example, about Christianity (and Judaism) in Alexandria or Egypt in general. This is obviously not only due to the author's specific aim—to describe distinctive episodes in the world-wide mission of Jesus Christ's apostles in the power of the Spirit, starting from Jerusalem—but is also due to lacunae in the source-material at his disposal. The problem of sources in Acts is, again, a very difficult one. The speeches in Acts, reported to have been held at crucial points by the apostles, were composed by the author himself; like the speeches in the works of classical authors they give the author's comment on the events for the benefit of his readers, rather than an actual report of what was said on these occasions. This does not, of course, exclude the possibility that earlier reports and special traditions were sometimes used.

Though the Acts of the Apostles, like the Gospels, should be read and used primarily as a theological work, the book does provide us with useful information about Jewish life in Judaea, particularly in Jerusalem, and in the Diaspora (Syria, Asia Minor, Cyprus, Macedonia, Greece and Italy). We hear for instance of pilgrims from all over the world in Jerusalem at Pentecost (2:1-14), or various synagogues in Jerusalem, a synagogue of the freedmen (former Jewish slaves of the Romans), Cyrenians, Alexandrians, and of the Jews from Cilicia and Asia (6:9). We also hear of a Roman officer in Caesarea who is a Godfearer (10:1-2) and of an influential Jewish sorcerer at the court of the Roman governor of Cyprus (13:4-12). Very often we are told that Paul and his companions on their travels first preached to the Jews in the synagogues before turning to the Gentiles (after conflicts with the Jews). Even if these somewhat stereotyped descriptions betray the author's theological point of view, they provide us with evidence of the existence of synagogues in several places in the Hellenistic world.

The Acts also contain remarkable details about Herod Agrippa I (chap. 12) and Herod Agrippa II (24:13-26:32), and about the Roman procurators Felix (23:23-24:27) and Festus (24:27-26:32). The attitude of the Roman commander in Jerusalem in a difficult situation (21:27-23:35), though not historical in the strict sense, gives us an insight in the position of the Roman troops in Jerusalem. Interesting is the case of Paul's appeal as a Roman citizen to the Emperor in Rome (25:10-26:32). Mention is made of the proconsul Gallio of Achaia (18:12-17) whose office is confirmed and dated by an inscription at Delphi. The acts also mention some Jewish revolutionaries described by Josephus, such as Theudas and Judas the Galilean (5:36ff., Josephus *Ant.* XVIII, 4-10, *War* II, 118, *Ant.* XX, 97-102); besides them the Egyptian Jew mentioned in *Ant.* XX, 169-172 is referred to in 21:38. In all these cases the Acts corroborate or supplement the evidence provided by the works of Josephus and other sources.

BIBLIOGRAPHY

Concerning the Gospels as source-material for the historical geography of Palestine, see G. DALMAN, *Orte und Wege Jesu*, 3rd ed. 1924, reprinted 1967. On matters of literary genre, sources, authorship and date of the writings of the New Testament the current introductions to the New Testament should be consulted, particularly W. G. KÜMMEL *Einleitung in das Neue Testament*, 17th ed., 1973. On the question of the relation between theological presentations and the historical background of the story of Jesus' trial, see the contrasting conclusions of J. BLINZLER, *Der Prozess Jesu*, 4th ed., 1969; P. WINTER, *On the Trial of Jesus*, 1961; S. G. F. BRANDON, *The Trial of Jesus of Nazareth*, 1968; H. VAN DER KWAAK, *Het proces van Jezus, een vergelijkend onderzoek van de beschrijving der evangelisten*, 1969; D. R. CATCHPOLE, *The Trial of Jesus*, 1971.
For aspects of Jewish life mentioned or implied in the Gospels see many of the writings of J. JEREMIAS, particularly his *Jerusalem zur Zeit Jesu*, 3rd ed., 1962, and *Die Gleichnisse Jesu*, 7th ed., 1965 (English translation *The Parables of Jesus*, 1963). On historical issues connected with the Acts of the Apostles much material can be found in *The Beginnings of Christianity*, Part I The Acts of the Apostles, ed. by F. J. FOAKES JACKSON and K. LAKE, vols I-V, 1920-33, especially vol V which contains additional notes.

IV PAPYRI

The many finds brought to light in Egypt have greatly aided the study of both Jewish and ancient history as a whole. More than five hundred papyri and ostraca in Greek shed light on the development of Egyptian Jewry in the Hellenistic, Roman, and Byzantine periods, bearing as they do on its history from the beginning of Greek rule until the Arab conquest of Egypt. These discoveries have been of great significance particularly in elucidating certain aspects of the life of the Jews in Egypt inadequately reflected in our literary sources, such as their economic life, their distribution in various parts of the country, and the taxes they had to pay (principally under Roman rule). Our knowledge of Jewish names has also been greatly enriched and through it our information on the Hellenization of the Jews. Among the papyri are documents which throw light on the civil status of the Jews and on events associated with contemporary political his-

43

tory.[1] Especially characteristic of the papyri as a historical source is the spontaneity of the information contained in them, for unlike the literary, epigraphic, and numismatic sources most of the papyri include incidental details, since they were informal and not meant to be read by a wider public with no direct connection with their contents. Among the papyri are private letters, legal contracts, accounts and tax receipts.

It should, however, be borne in mind that the division of papyri according to their place of discovery is based on the fortuitous circumstances of climatic conditions and of the siting of excavations in this or that area. By overlooking these factors we are liable to reach incorrect conclusions about the relative importance of the various communities of Jews in the cities and villages of Egypt. The district of Fayum in Lower Egypt is especially rich in finds. Among the large quantity of papyri from Oxyrhynchus are also a number of Jewish ones. The ostraca from Thebes are particularly important for the Ptolemaic period, as are those from Apollinopolis Magna (Edfu) for the Roman period.[2] No excavations have been conducted in Alexandria itself, nor have any papyri been found there; but among those brought to light elsewhere some originated in Alexandria and contain information on the life of the Jews in that city.[3] After the suppression of the Jewish revolt in the days of Trajan the number of Jewish papyri decreases although from the end of the third century C.E. onwards we again have documents attesting the existence of Jewish settlements in Egypt.

As has been said, papyri have survived mainly in Egypt. Some of these bear directly on the history of the Jews in Palestine, namely the papyri from the archives of Zeno dating from the third century B.C.E., some of which are associated with Palestine. In Palestine itself papyri have been found at Nessana in the Negev (Byzantine period). Recently the papyri discovered in the Judaean desert and dating from and before the days of Bar Cochba have received wide publicity.

A separate unit is formed by a series of quasi-literary papyri called the *Acts of the Pagan Martyrs* or *Acta Alexandrinorum*, in which the recurring theme is the conflict between Greek Alexandria, represented by its gymnasiarchs, and the Roman Empire.[4] Some of these papyri

[1] Cf. above all the 'Letter of Claudius' (*CPJ*, no. 153) and the documents relating to the Jewish Revolt under Trajan - *CPJ*, Section XI.
[2] Cf. *CPJ*, Sections V and IX. [3] Cf. *CPJ*, Section VII.
[4] The texts are to be found in Musurillo and *CPJ*, II nos. 154-159.

are also called *Acta Isidori, Acta Hermaisci, Acta Appiani,* after the names of the Alexandrian representatives who are described as appearing before the Roman emperor and rebuking him severely. Along with the theme of conflict with the Roman Empire appears the anti-Semitic element characteristic of a large proportion of these papyri, whose Alexandrian authors viewed the Jews as their enemies and the Roman emperors as the supporters of the Jews.

The *Acta Alexandrinorum* were not composed as a single work (as maintained, for example, by Premerstein) but were published at various times. They are to be regarded as compilations based on authentic historical events, for which official documents in the form of minutes were extant, as were also reports of the various deputations from Alexandria which went to Rome to address the emperor. These reports in particular could have been a source for the *Acta Alexandrinorum*. The relation of the various *Acta* to the historical facts may have differed from one compilation to another, this being particularly so as regards the tone used by the representatives of Alexandria in expressing themselves.

Not all the *Acta* mention the Jews. The *Acta Appiani,* dating from the days of Commodus and one of the finest examples of the *Acta Alexandrinorum,* makes no mention of the Jews; this silence reflects the decline of the Jewry of Alexandria after the suppression of the Jewish revolt in the time of Trajan. Especially important for the history of the Jews are the *Acta Isidori*[1] which mirrors events in the time of Claudius, and the *Acta Hermaisci*[2] which dates from the time of Trajan. Of great interest is the papyrus which refers to the prefect Flaccus.[3]

BIBLIOGRAPHY

A. BAUER, *Archiv für Papyrusforschung,* 1901, pp. 29-47; U. WILCKEN, 'Zum alexandrinischen Antisemitismus', *Abhand. der königl. sach. Gesellschaft der Wissenschaften, phil. hist. Klasse,* 1909, pp. 783-839; ED. MEYER, *Ursprung und Anfänge des Christentums* III (1923) pp. 539-548; A. V. PREMERSTEIN, 'Zu den sogenannten alexandrinischen Märtyrerakten,' *Philologus,* Supplement XVI, fasc. II, 1923; H. I. BELL, in *JJP,* 1950, pp. 19-42; H. A. MUSURILLO, *The Acts of the Pagan Martyrs,* 1954; J. CROOK, *Consilium Principis,* 1955, pp. 133-134; *CPJ* II, pp. 55-107.

[1] Musurillo, no. IV.   [2] Musurillo, no. VIII.   [3] Musurillo, no. II.

V ARCHAEOLOGICAL SOURCES

Archaeology is, basically, along with many other related disciplines, a handmaiden of history; its aim is to supply the materials for our knowledge of the human past. The other type of source material is of course the written kind: histories, chronicles, documents of all kinds.

In the period under consideration here, which comprises roughly the Hellenistic and early Roman period in the Mediterranean, written sources are relatively plentiful, even if their preservation has been haphazard. Thus the great historians of the Hellenistic period between the historians of Alexander the Great and Polybius in the second century B.C.E. are known only from extracts or fragments. The same is true of the time of Augustus Caesar. Throughout the period the evidence of archaeology, composed of the finds of many small excavations and a few big ones, allow us to estimate the processes of cultural and economic evolution which are only too often grandly passed over in the major historical works.

Archaeological excavations relevant to Jewish history in Hellenistic and Roman times

All excavations of the Hellenistic and early Roman period from Pompey onwards served to furnish the archaeological background of the period. This applies in particular to the campaigns at Corinth and the great cities of Asia Minor: Pergamon, Sardis, Ephesus, Miletus and Tarsus.

In the Holy Land itself the interest of archaeologists was concentrated on the Old Testament period (archaeologically speaking the Bronze and Iron Ages). The earliest campaigns, that of De Saulcy in 1864 at the 'Tombs of the Kings' and that of Warren (1870) along the walls of the Temple enclosure, were based on the mistaken belief that the tombs were those of the Davidic dynasty and the Temple walls the work of Solomon. In view of the later developments of the technique of excavation it was perhaps fortunate that the main sites of Hellenistic and early Roman times were attacked only later on; but it should be noted that Warren in his work at Jerusalem not only overcame immense technical difficulties (he had to excavate by underground tunnels), but achieved a very high degree of exactitude in his recording.

At the beginning of the present century Bliss and Macalister cleared a Hellenistic city at Marissa; the painted tombs at this site were found accidentally in 1902. Macalister excavated at Gezer in 1902-3 and 1907-9, publishing all his results in three volumes.[1] His work is now being re-checked by W. Dever. In 1905 H. Kohl and C. Watzinger investigated the Galilean synagogues;[2] here, too, the recent work of the Franciscans P. P. Corbo and Loffreda have raised many questions anew.[3] Samaria with its rich Hellenistic and Herodian strata was excavated in 1908-11 by Reisner and Fisher, and from 1931 to 1935 by Crowfoot.[4]

After the First World War Palestine passed under a British mandate and an orderly Antiquities Service was established. Excavations multiplied, mainly by British and American archaeologists. Among the main expeditions which uncovered remains of the Hellenistic-Roman periods were: Fisher, Rowe and Fitzgerald at Beth Shean (Beisan), 1922-33; Mader at Ramet el-Khalil ('Mamre'), 1926-8; Crowfoot at Gerasa, 1925-8;[5] Petrie at Tell Gamma (Jemme), 1926-7; Waterman at Sepphoris, 1931; Johns at Athlith, 1930-5;[6] Sellers at Beth Zur, 1931, 1957; Glueck at Et Tannur, 1937.[7] Jewish archaeologists excavated the Third Wall of Jerusalem (Mayer-Sukenik, 1926-7), the synagogues of Beth Alpha (Sukenik, 1928), Hammath Gader (Sukenik, 1931)[8] and Husifa (Isfiye, Avi-Yonah, 1932).[9] From 1936 to 1959 Mazar and then Avigad worked at the Jewish necropolis of Beth Shearim.[10] The necropolis of Jerusalem from the Second Temple period has yielded over a hundred tombs, most of them plundered long ago, but occasionally found untouched. The whole area was surveyed by Macalister in 1900-1,[11] and reconsidered by K. Galling in the *Palaestinajahrbuch*.[12] Systematic searches were instituted by the late E. L. Sukenik, and continued by N. Avigad. Among the

[1] R. A. S. Macalister, *The Excavations of Gezer*, 3 vols (1912).
[2] *Antike Synagogen in Galilea* (1916).
[3] V. Corbo, S. Loffreda, A. Spijkerman, *La sinagoga di Cafarnao dopo gli scavi del 1969* (1970); V. Corbo, *The House of St. Peter at Capernaum* (1969); cf. G. Foerster, *IEJ*, 21 (1971), pp. 207-211; S. Loffreda *IEJ* (1973) pp. 37-42.
[4] C. A. Reisner, C. S. Fisher, D. C. Lyon, *Harvard Excavations at Samaria* (1924); J. W. Crowfoot et al., *Samaria-Sebaste*, 3 vols (1938-57).
[5] C. H. Kraeling, *Gerasa* (1938).
[6] *QDAP* II, pp. 41-104; III, pp. 145-164; IV, pp. 122-3; V, pp. 31-60; VI, pp. 121-152.
[7] N. Glueck, *Deities and Dolphins* (1965).
[8] *JPOS* (1935), pp. 101-180.
[9] *QDAP* III, pp. 118-131.
[10] B. Mazar, *Beth Shearim* I (Hebrew, 1958); M. Avigad, *Beth Shearim* III (Hebrew, 1971).
[11] R. A. S. Macalister, *PEF* (1900-1).
[12] *Palaestinajahrbuch* (1937), pp. 73-101.

discoveries of the former there was a family tomb near Talpioth which was assumed (mistakenly) to contain Judaeo-Christian burials dating from before 70 c.e.[1] The same claim, made by the Franciscan Fathers (Bagatti, Sallers, Testa) as regards the finding of an ossuary tomb at Dominus Flevit on the Mount of Olives, is not better substantiated.[2] On the other hand, the tomb of the family of Nicanor of Alexandria - 'He who made the doors,' as an ossuary inscription has it - refers to a well-known donor of the beautiful bronze gates of the Temple.[3] Near it Avigad cleared, in 1967, another elaborate family tomb, called after its founder the 'Tomb of the Nazirite.'[4] In 1968 another big tomb was cleared at Give'at Mivtar, north of Jerusalem: its ossuaries included one of 'Simeon builder of the Temple' (probably a stonemason) and of one John who was crucified, one nail still piercing his foot bones (excavated by V. Tsaferis).[5] The 'Tomb of Jason' (Alfasi Street) from the Hasmonaean period, contained interesting evidence as regards the transition from the group family burial in Sadducee style to the ossuary burial preferred by the Pharisees, each individual's bones being set apart for the day of resurrection.[6]

After a pause caused first by the Second World War, then by the Israel War of Independence, excavations were resumed in the early fifies on both sides of the armistice line. The accidental discovery of the Dead Sea scrolls led to the excavations of Qumran (De Vaux and Harding, 1951-6) and then to the clearance of the caves of Murabbat (De Vaux, Harding, 1952)[7] and of the caves in the valleys of Arugoth, Hever and Mishmar (Aharoni, Avigad, Baradon and Yadin, 1960-1).[8] Funk and Richardson began to excavate at Pella (1958)[9] and Lapp cleared the Tobiad structure at Araq el Amir (Birtha of the Ammanitis, Tyrus) in 1961-2.[10] Avi-Yonah worked at the site of the Caesarea synagogue in 1956 and 1962; an Italian expedition under Frova worked on another part of the site from 1959 to 1963,[11] and

[1] E. L. Sukenik, *AJA* (1947), pp. 73-101.
[2] B. Bagatti and S. Sallers, *Gli scavi del 'Dominus Flevit'* (1958).
[3] G. Dickson, *PEF* (1903), pp. 326-332; Avigad, *Eretz-Israel* (1967), pp. 117-125.
[4] N. Avigad, *IEJ* (1971), pp. 185-200.
[5] V. Tsaferis et al., *IEJ* (1970), pp. 18-59.
[6] L. Y. Rahmani, *IEJ* (1967), pp. 61-100.
[7] R. de Vaux, *L'archéologie et les manuscrits de la Mer Morte* (1961); P. Benoit et al., *Discoveries in the Judaean Desert*, 1955ff.
[8] *IEJ* (1961), pp. 1 ff., ibid. (1962), pp. 167 ff.; Y. Yadin, *The Finds from the Bar-Kokhba Period in the Cave of Letters* (1963).
[9] *BA* (1958), pp. 82-96.
[10] *BASOR* (1962), pp. 16-34; (1963), pp. 8-45.
[11] *Caesarea Maritima* (1959).

A. Negev on still another in 1960-2. Corbo excavated at Herodium in 1962-3 and Foerster in 1967-8.[1] The study of the Nabataean cities and sites of the Negev and Transjordan was begun by Horsefield at Petra (1929) and er-Ram (1934).[2] The Colt expedition worked at Subeita (1934-8) and Nessana (1935-6).[3] Later work included that of Negev at Avdat (Eboda, 1958-60), and at Kurnub (Mampsis, 1965-71). The latest excavations, which have greatly contributed to our knowledge of the Hasmonaean and Herodian periods, were those of Yadin at Masada (1963-5),[4] of Kenyon at Jerusalem (1961-7) and those, still continuing, of Mazar south and west of the Temple enclosure (1968 ff.) and of Avigad in the Jewish quarter of the old city of Jerusalem (1969 ff.).[5]

The list given above does not include scores of minor excavations which contributed a detail here and there, and the work on major sites such as Dora and Ascalon, which was discontinued.

The main results of archaeological research
with regard to Jewish history
in Hellenistic and early Roman times

The Hellenistic background of Jewish history is illustrated by the Hippodamic town-plan of Marissa, while the tombs of the Hellenized Sidonians found nearby are evidence for the penetration of Greek interest in zoology into Semitic circles. The excavations in the fortress of the Tobiads at Araq el Amir have revealed a building which seems to have been planned as a temple, possibly another attempt at competition with the Jerusalem sanctuary like the one known from Leontopolis. The penetration of Greek culture even before Alexander is amply demonstrated by the finds of Attic pottery at Tell Gemma and many other sites, such as Athlith; the use of the image of Athena's owl on the coins of the province of Judah (יהוד) is another such indication. The find in a cave with prehistoric remains near Athlith of a Praxitelean-type terracotta statuette of Aphrodite, with a Greek dedication, illuminates the hold of Greek art and culture on the coastal area, especially in Phoenicia.

---

[1] *Liber Annuus* XIII (1962-3), pp. 219-277.
[2] M. R. Savignac and G. Horsefield, *RB* (1935), pp. 245-8; *QDAP* VII, VIII, IX.
[3] H. D. Colt et al, *Excavations at Nessana*, 3 vols (1950-62).
[4] *Masada* (1966).
[5] K. Kenyon, *Jerusalem* (1967); B. Mazar, *The Execavations in the Old City of Jerusalem* (1969, 1971); N. Avigad, *IEJ* (1970), pp. 1-8, 129-140, (1972) pp. 193-200.

MAP I. MAIN EXCAVATIONS

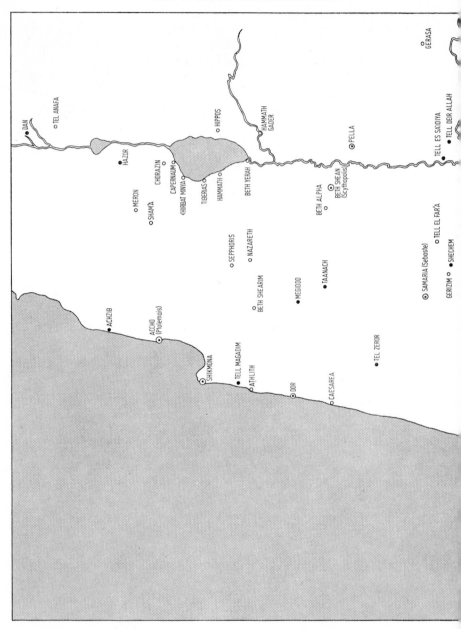

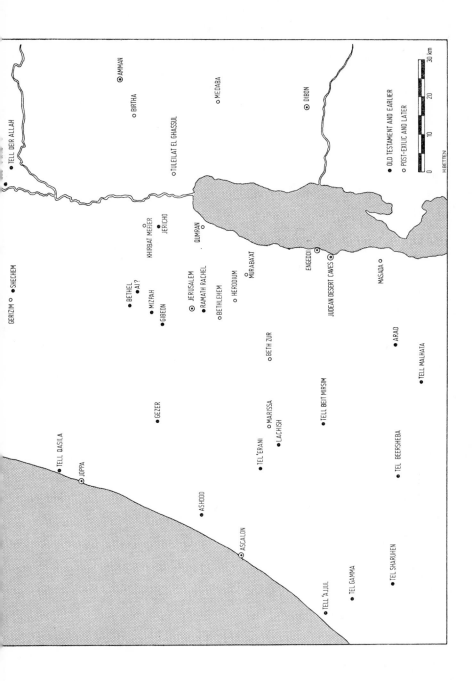

TELL DEIR ALLAH

AMMAN

BIRTHA

MEDABA

TULEILAT EL GHASSUL

DIBON

OLD TESTAMENT AND EARLIER
POST-EXILIC AND LATER

30 km
20
10
0

H.BETTEN

KHIRBAT MEFJER
JERICHO

QUMRAN

MURABA'AT

ENGEDDI

MASADA

JUDEAN DESERT CAVES

GERIZIM SHECHEM

BETHEL
AI ?
MIZPAH
GIBEON

JERUSALEM
RAMATH RACHEL
BETHLEHEM
HERODIUM

BETH ZUR

ARAD

TELL MALHATA

GEZER

MARISSA
LACHISH

TELL BEIT MIRSIM

TEL BEERSHEBA

TEL 'ERANI

TELL QASILA
JOPPA

ASHDOD

ASCALON

TEL SHARUHEN

TELL 'AJJUL
TEL GAMMA

51

The high tide of Hellenism is marked by the discovery of a column base and Ionic capital of huge proportions in the Hellenistic stratum at Jerusalem—probably remnants of a temple (of the Olympian Zeus?) planned by Antiochus IV and never completed. For the rest, the Hasmonaean period can boast only of remains of fortifications: the Hellenistic wall and towers at Samaria breached by John Hyrcanus, Jonathan's wall and tower on the Ophel and the citadel wall, also at Jerusalem, probably the work of John Hyrcanus. The remains of Simeon's fortress and a grafitto 'May the fire from heaven burn the house of Simeon' (probably written by a Greek prisoner of war of the Hasmonaeans) indicate the importance attached to Gezer. At Beth Zur and at Alexandrium (Sartaba) we have remains of Maccabean fortresses of different periods.

The Herodian period is exceptionally well represented by archaeological remains; some of the constructions of Herod are so massive as to be practically indestructible. Among them pride of place belongs to the enclosure wall of the Temple, with successive layers of stones up to ten metres long and one metre high and to the foundations of the Phasael tower in the Jerusalem citadel. Herodian tombs around Jerusalem have provided actual examples of flat circular stones (Matt. 27:60) while among the thousands of ossuaries were examples of all New Testament names.

Outside Jerusalem Herodian remains include the high wall around the traditional Machpelah cave at Hebron, which shows how the Temple enclosure once looked. The Herodian fortresses at Herodium and Masada give us an idea of the palaces of the king; they also supply surprising evidence of his observance of the Jewish commandments—there are no iconic representations at either place, and a synagogue is provided in each. Masada stands also as a monument of the First Revolt; the Roman camps and circumvallation still remain visible below the fortress, while inside it the ritual interests of the Zealots are demonstrated by a series of purification baths (מקוה). The finds from Qumran belong mainly to another chapter, but it will suffice here to note the architecture of this 'monastery' with its communal dining room and its plethora of purification baths. The finds from the time of the Second Revolt (or war of Bar Cochba), show the standard of the markings distinguishing male from female dress, and their aniconic zeal which vented itself on Roman booty.

Archaeology has supplied less certain evidence as to the topography of first century Jerusalem than one might expect: the alleged site the

Lithostratos or the remains of the Bethesda pool are not definitely attributable to this period. Even the line of the Second Wall is still debatable. Outside Jerusalem the theatre of Caesarea (Acts 12:21) still has its Herodian foundations. The fishermen's village of Capernaum has also been uncovered recently.

The oldest synagogues of Galilee are generally attributed to the second and third century C.E., and they still recall in many details their earlier prototypes. Names are written on pillars at Capernaum (Rev. 3:12); a 'seat of Moses' (Matt. 23:2) has been found at Chorazin. The excavations at Beth Shearim have, together with the finds in the synagogues, disclosed a liberal interpretation of the second commandment by the rabbis of the third and fourth centuries. Images of men and beasts were now permitted in paint or in flat relief; only the three dimensional shape was still banned. Beth Shearim has also produced evidence for belief in life after death, which was characteristic of the Pharisees; the earliest traces of this view are to be found in the tombs near Jerusalem where a gradual transition from family tomb to individual burial has been observed. On the other hand the claims made for certain ossuary burials assigning them to the Judaeo-Christian community before the destruction of the Second Temple do not seem to have much substance—they are mainly based on a mark of two intersecting lines, which has been interpreted as a cross.

Outside the Holy Land archaeological excavations have supplied us mainly with the background for the Acts of the Apostles. For instance the theatre at Ephesus and the many statues of the Artemis of Ephesus (Acts 19:28-29), one of which has been found even at Caesarea, serve to give concrete shape to the story of Paul's difficulties with the worshippers of the goddess. In Athens the Areopagus hill is still shown near the Acropolis as it stood in the time of Paul; in Corinth the main street of the Roman period has been laid bare, and an inscription found mentioning the 'synagogue of the Hebrews' (Acts 18:1,4). A spiritual movement like Early Christianity cannot be expected to leave much material evidence; it is only by very great luck that a church in a private house (Epistle to Philemon 2) has been discovered at Dura Europos with Old and New Testament frescoes, the seat of the bishop, the common agape room and a rudimentary baptistery. The archaeological evidence from the Jewish Diaspora is almost entirely dated to the third or fourth centuries, except for a few Hellenistic synagogues and early Roman inscriptions.[1] Nevertheless by making backward deductions, we can understand to a certain extent Jewish community life in the dispersion in earlier ages also. The synagogues of Delos and Miletus are certainly Hellenistic, that of Priene possibly so. All these structures were originally private houses reshaped to accomodate Jewish cult practices, a tradition which persisted also at Dura Europos. It is only with the third century synagogue at Sardis that we have a large Jewish public building erected as such.[2] Both the synagogues (oriented towards Jerusalem) and the Jewish catacombs (Monteverde and Torlonia at Rome) of the second and third centuries illustrate the ambivalent position of the Diaspora Jewry, between the dominant Greek culture—for even in Rome the Jewish ambiance was Greek, not Latin oriented—and attachment to the Holy Land and the ways of the Jewish forefathers. The symbols used in Palestine and in the Diaspora are the same, and lend themselves to the identical varieties of interpretation. In its figurative art the Diaspora followed the rabbinical transition from prohibition to limited permissiveness; the representations of biblical scenes are in both cases formally linked with Greek mythological scenes, suitably modified. In the later synagogues (Sardis, Naro [Hammam-Lif], Aegina) details of the synagogue arrangements, such as benches for the elders of the community (who sat facing Jerusalem), or reading tables, side rooms for the sacred utensils, can be observed. The epigraphic material from the Diaspora contains a wealth of information as regards the organization of the community, its officers, the onomasticon (mostly Greek or transposed into Greek by association either of sound or of meaning), the proselytes, etc.[3] The mere fact of the prevalence of the Greek koine over Hebrew and/or Aramaic is a valuable indication of the receptivity of the Jews of the Diaspora to teaching in this language, a fact that agrees well with their profound respect for the Septuagint and the wide diffusion of the Philonic and New Testament literature, written in Greek.

Only occasionally do we get a glimpse of the underlying feeling for the Jewish sanctuary both before and after its destruction—e.g. a gold-glass painting representing a romanticized version of the Sanctuary[4].

[1] Most of the archaeological material has been collected by E. R. Goodenough in his monumental *Jewish Symbols of the Greco-Roman Period*, vols 2, 3 and 9-11 (1957 ff.).
[2] D. H. Metten, *The Ancient Synagogue at Sardis* (1965).
[3] This material has been collected and published in *CII* and *CPJ*.
[4] Goodenough, op. cit., III, no. 978.

54

The same is true of the frescoes of the Dura-Europos synagogue excavated in 1931, dating from 245 C.E.[1] The themes of these paintings form the most important evidence for the existence of Jewish figurative art and its interpretation of the Bible (for which see Vol. 2 chap. 20). The ideological relationship between the Babylonian community of Dura, the Jewish Hellenism of Alexandria and the rabbinical centre in Palestine is a most complicated problem; but there can be no doubt of the veneration for the Temple, an image of which was placed over the central niche of the West wall.

Epigraphic sources

Epigraphy is the study of inscriptions cut in stone or metal, graffiti scratched on walls and dipinti painted on them. Ostraca either incised or painted on sherds are commonly assigned to papyrology or palaeography. The inscriptions which form the subject-matter of epigraphy can be divided into public and private categories. The public texts are connected with religion or with civil matters: dedications, lists of priestly or civil functionaries, temple or public accounts, honours sacred or civil conferred on individuals. The private inscriptions are mainly funerary but include dedications made by individuals, prayers, curses etc.

The evidential value of inscriptions lies in their authenticity. They do not come to us by way of the distorting mirror of copying. On the other hand they suffer from two kinds of inherent defects: their preservation has been haphazard, the distribution of the extant texts is erratic, plentiful in one place and absent in another; the preservation of the text itself is often defective and it has to be emended with all the uncertainty this implies. Moreover in public texts, and to a certain extent also in private ones, the text reflects the intentions of the writer; if he intended to deceive the reader in some way, there is usually no way of checking this.

In the period under consideration Palestine and the adjacent countries were situated on the borderline of two cultures: the cosmopolitan Graeco-Roman culture which was fostered by the Roman overlords; and the local Oriental cultures, based on the ancient Oriental religions, which helped the conquered inhabitants to resist their conquerors culturally. As a result of this intersection of cultures, the epigraphic texts

---

[1] M. Rostovtzeff et al., *The Excavations at Dura Europos, Preliminary Report* IV (1936); C. Kraeling, *The Excavations at Dura-Europos, Final Report* VIII, I: *The Synagogue* (1956).

relating to this period can be divided into two groups: the Semitic (Hebrew, Aramaic, Safaitic, but also Phoenician, Thamudian, Nabataean, etc.) and the Graeco-Roman. The Hebrew inscriptions of the post-exilic period are relatively few and refer to cultic matters, mostly dedications; some are epitaphs. The ordinary written texts of the Palestinian Jews were in Judaeo-Aramaic. The bulk of the texts are funerary (the Jaffa cemetery, c. 20% of the Beth Shearim inscriptions, about half of the ossuaries) or dedicatory (the synagogue inscriptions). The Latin inscriptions in the Hellenistic East, Palestine included, refer to matters of government (partly) and the army (mainly). They include epithaphs, inscriptions in honour of the emperors and legates, dedications and milestones. The Greek inscriptions are of the most diverse character, ranging from whole poems to barbaric solecisms of illiterate camel drivers.

What we can learn from the epigraphical material is the prevalence of certain cults (Hellenic or Oriental), contemporary ideas on life after death, the names and dates of governors, the composition of military units of the Roman army and its auxiliaries in the east, the functions of civil magistrates, occasionally the boundary line between two cities or villages. We may also learn the names and functions of the officials of the Jewish communities, their synagogues and their educational establishments. The epitaphs (ossuary inscriptions, the epigraphical material from the cemeteries of Beth Shearim and Jaffa) supply rich material for the Jewish onomasticon, the professions exercised by the humble (Jaffa) and the well-to-do (Beth Shearim). The texts from Greece and Asia Minor provide much information as to the civil status of the Jewish communities or individual Jews living in the cities, the degree of their assimilation with their Greek or Oriental surroundings, their material status, etc. The sum of these texts enables us to draw up a map of the Diaspora with fair indications of the density of settlement in the various provinces and cities.

Because of the integration of Jewish (and early Christian) communities with the social and economic (and even political) fabric of the Roman Empire, the epigraphic sources are extraordinarily varied. For instance, a text referring to the career of some rather obscure Roman senator might be of decisive importance in establishing the date of an event in Palestine.[1]

The religious and institutional attitude of the Jewish Diaspora,

[1] W. Eck, *Senatoren von Vespasian bis Hadrian* (1970), pp. 93 ff.

56

which was of such importance for the spread of Christianity, is reflected in the surviving inscriptions. The Hellenistic texts from Rheneia near Delos appeal to the 'Most High God' for vengeance against murderers;[1] the status of the Jews in Greek cities is reflected by the Iasos inscriptions recording the donations of a Jew for the Dionysia;[2] and the text from Miletus indicates the place of the 'Jews and God-fearing' in the theatre.[3] Jewish ephebes seem also to have existed at Hypaepa towards the end of the second century.[4] The inscriptions of Rome are especially rich in information about the organization of the community, which consisted of a number of synagogues, the functionaries and the language of the Jews of Rome (74% Greek, 24% Latin).[5] The authority of the patriarchs, ethnarchs and sages is appealed to in a text from Argos;[6] the patriarch is made the recipient of prospective fines in text from Stobi.[7] There and in other places (Phocaea, Tlos, etc.) property and houses were dedicated as synagogues, and the donors, including women, were suitably rewarded.[8] The historical vicissitudes of the period are reflected in the inscription mentioning a captive from Jerusalem at Naples, the many manumissions of Jews at Delphi[9] and the ominous reference to the 'former Jews' at Smyrna, a result perhaps of the persecution under Hadrian.[10] Among the inscriptions of special interest in this context we may cite the dedications to Egyptian gods (Sarapis and Isis) from Hellenistic Samaria,[11] and to Atargatis and Hadad, the 'gods that listen to prayer', from Hellenistic Accho-Ptolemais.[12] Among the texts of the Roman period the dedication of a Tiberieum at Caesarea by '...Pilatus praefectus Judeae' is the only epigraphic evidence for this governor.[13] The Temple inscription forbidding gentiles to pass the balustrade in the outer court under pain of death was found in two copies (one now at Istanbul, one at Jerusalem) recalling Acts 21:28.[14] The dedication of a synagogue by Theodotus the son of Vettenus found on the Ophel, Jerusalem, brings to mind the Synagogue of Freedmen in Acts 6:9[15]. The Nazareth (?) decree forbidding in the

---

[1] *CII* I (1936), no. 725.   [2] *Ibid.* II (1952), no. 749.   [3] *Ibid.* no. 748.
[4] *Ibid.* no. 755.   [5] *Ibid.* I, pp. LXVIII ff.   [6] *Ibid.* no. 719.   [7] *Ibid.* no. 694.
[8] *Ibid.* I no. 639; II, nos. 738, 757, etc.
[9] *Ibid.* I no. 556, 709-711.
[10] *Ibid.* II, no. 742.
[11] Crowfoot et al., *Samaria-Sebaste* III, p. 37.
[12] M. Avi-Yonah, *IEJ* (1959), pp. 1-12.
[13] A. Frova ed., *Caesarea Maritima*, pp. 217 ff.
[14] *CII* II (1952), no. 1400.
[15] *Ibid.* no. 1404.

name of 'Caesar' to damage tombs, exhume the dead, transport the dead from one tomb to another, recalls Matthew 28:12-13.[1] Of more doubtful relevance is the inscription attributed to Quirinius and referring to a census of Syria (Luke 2:2).[2] The text of Luke 22:25 is anticipated by the dedication of the Jews of Schedia near Alexandria to the 'Beneficient Gods' Ptolemy III and Berenice I.[3] An inscription found at Pergamon dedicated to the 'Unknown God' recalls Acts 17:23.[4] An inscription from Damascus mentioning a freedman of Lysanias the tetrarch[5] and one from Seeia dedicated to Philip tetrarch of Ituraea and Trachonitis illustrate the statement in Luke 3:1.[6]

Numismatic sources

Coins were first struck by the kings of Lydia in the seventh century B.C.E.; they were adopted almost immediately by the Greek city-states, and soon afterward by the kings of Persia and the Phoenician trading centres. At the end of the Persian period various satraps, commanders of mercenaries and autonomous provinces of the empire (including the province of Judah) were all striking coins, often imitating the Athenian silver drachma, the dominant trade coin of the eastern Mediterranean after the middle of the fifth century B.C.E. Only the Phoenician mints refused to follow the Athenian standard; their heavier staters, and in particular that of Tyre, were accepted as 'holy shekels' by the Jews.

Together with inscriptions, coins bear the stamp of authenticity; their symbols and legends (if legible) communicate to us instantly the intentions of those striking them. Moreover, as distinct from inscriptions, coins were issued in quantities and their chances of survival were much greater, in spite of their being made of utilizable material. Coins were often hoarded and hoard-finds properly recorded give a most valuable indication of the coins in circulation about the time of the hoard (as indicated by the latest coin in it), the trade trends of the period etc. In times when the majority of the population could not read, coins formed an important means of propaganda; the Roman emperors in particular used the symbols and even the legends as a means of creating a favourable image among

[1] A. Dain, *Inscriptions grecques du Musée du Louvre; les textes inédits* (1933).
[2] *DAC* VII, fig. 6914.
[3] *CPJ* III, p. 141.
[4] J. Finegan, *Light from the Ancient Past* (1946), fig. 119.
[5] M. R. Savignac, *RB* (1912), p. 534.
[6] *Princeton Expedition to Syria, Semitic Inscriptions*, no. 101.

their subjects. If dated, coins give valuable indications of the length of rule of the kings and princes minting them; a comparison of dies of the obverse and reverse often gives an idea as to the chronological sequence of coins within a series, or of two series following one another. Overstriking of coins (as was systematically done in the Bar Cochba war), and counter-marking of coins in circulation often helps to establish closely the date of a historical event.

The Hellenistic monarchies set up royal mints while allowing their subject cities some latitude of minting. The Ptolemies coined at Ptolemais, Joppa and Gaza; their silver was used exclusively for their overseas dependencies, the copper being used in Egypt to the exclusion of all other metals. Ptolemaic coins bear on the obverse the head of Zeus or Alexander, on the reverse the eagle. The Seleucids coined with the portrait of the king on the obverse, and Apollo on the reverse; their coinage is more varied in its symbols than the Ptolemaic. The symbols of the cornucopias and anchor were taken over by the Hasmonaeans, who replaced however the caduceus of Hermes with the inoffensive pomegranate. All Hasmonaean coinage is aniconic; the usual type of the small bronze coins shows on the obverse an inscription in the old Hebrew script: '...high priest and the κοινόν (חבר) of the Jews' and on the reverse the cornucopia. Alexander Jannaeus varied the type: he dated his coins, used the symbol of the star and anchor, and added to the Hebrew 'Jonathan the king' a Greek version: 'Of Alexander the king'. Hyrcanus II reverted to the earlier type; his vizier Antipater the Idumaean had his initial 'A' added to the coin in Greek.

The Herodian coinage is largely aniconic, although Herod ('the Great') did introduce the caduceus surreptitiously as well as some ritual objects, such as the thymiaterion, which could be interpreted ambiguously. His rival Antigonus Mathatias stamped small bronze coins with the menorah and the table of shewbread, symbols of the Temple he was defending against Herod and the Romans. Herod in his later years introduced an eagle on his small coins, probably to commemorate the eagle over the door of the Temple which he had put up to the disgust of the orthodox Jews. His successor Archelaus stressed on his coins the fact that he alone of the Herodians had harbours on the sea. Herod Antipas coined at Tiberias with strict observance of the rule against images; but his brother Philip, who had many gentiles under his rule, allowed the images of the emperor and statues of Pan on his coins. Agrippa I took many more liberties with his coins than his grandfather Herod. He not only used the portrait of the emperor but also his own image and that of his son. It is true that these coins were made at Caesarea; the mint of Jerusalem struck impeccably orthodox coins with the sun-shade (symbol of royalty) and ears of barley. Agrippa II did not care to use his own image but felt free to coin in the Roman fashion with the imperial bust. The procurators of Judaea avoided images and used mainly accepted symbols, excepting perhaps the pagan *lituus*.

All these local coins were of bronze, gold and silver being reserved for the imperial mint. It was a sign of revolt when the Zealots, and later on Bar Cochba, minted in silver. The shekels of the First Revolt were issued from Year One to Five; their legends read 'Shekel Israel' over a chalice, and 'Jerusalem the Holy' over a myrtle branch (or pomegranates?). Apart from the date the design does not vary. Smaller bronze coins were struck from the Year Four onwards. The coins of Bar Cochba are struck over Roman tetradrachmas or denarii. They are much more imaginative and varied than the earlier coins in their designs, which include the Temple façade, various vessels, musical instruments etc. The inscriptions refer sometimes to 'Simeon Prince of Israel' and sometimes to 'Eleazar the Priest'—the other legends being 'Year ... of the Redemption [or Freedom] of Israel' or just 'Jerusalem'. The bronzes of Bar Cochba are also more numerous and varied. Both the Zealots and Bar Cochba used the old Hebrew script in an archaic shape.

Coins marked 'Judaea capta' were struck by the Flavians in Rome and Caesarea in various metals. Later Roman coinage of local provenance was mainly city coins. They extend from the beginning of Roman rule to the second half of the third century. The city coins, all of bronze, had the image of the emperor on one side, and on the other various symbols of local interest, temples, the city goddess (Tyche), symbols or images of local and other gods. The study of these reverses is important for the diffusion of the foreign cults (Sarapis, Isis, Atargatis etc.) in the Palestinian cities. The fact, of course, of a city striking coins in Greek indicates the status of a polis; if the legend is in Latin, this indicates the rights of a Roman colony.

Tyrian silver coins circulated in the period of the Second Temple; being of Phoenician standard, they were accepted without a discount for the payment of Temple dues.

Of the coins mentioned in the New Testament, the 'piece of money' found in the mouth of a fish (Matt. 17:27) was probably a Tyrian stater, enough to pay Temple dues for two persons; the 'widow's mite' was two leptas (פרוטות) equalling one quadrans ('farthing', Mark 12:41-42); the tribute 'penny' was a Roman denarius with the image of Tiberius Caesar (Matt. 22:19-21).

BIBLIOGRAPHY

General

MILLAR BURROWS, *What Mean these Stones?*, 1957; W. F. ALBRIGHT, *Archaeology of Palestine*, 5th ed., 1960; C. WATZINGER, *Denkmäler Palästinas*, 2 vols, 1933-5; P. BARROIS, *Manuel d'archéologie biblique*, 2 vols, 1939-53; K. KENYON, *Archaeology in the Holy Land*, 2nd ed., 1965; *Encyclopaedia of Excavations in the Holy Land* (in Hebrew, English edition in preparation), 1970.

Excavations

L. A. MAYER and M. AVI-YONAH in *QDAP*, 1932, with annual supplements in every volume until 1950, continued by M. CASSUTO-SALZMANN in *Atiqot* (English series). For excavation sites see also *Atlas of Israel* (English edition), 1970, map IX, 2.

Epigraphy

The Latin inscriptions have been published by T. MOMMSEN and others in the *CIL*, III, (1873). For the inscriptions of Syria see *IGLS, IGRR, MAMA*; LE BAS and WADDINGTON, *Voyage archéologique en Grèce et en Asie Mineure* and the excavation reports for Delphi, Delos, Sardis, Miletus, Priene, Magnesia and Hierapolis. See further W. K. PRENTICE, *Greek and Latin inscriptions, American Archaeological Expedition to Syria, 1899-1900*, 1908; E. LITTMANN et al., *Greek and Latin Inscriptions; Syria* (Publications of the Princeton University Archaeological expedition to Syria, 1921-2). The catalogues of the Cairo and Louvre Museums also contain a wealth of relevant material. Inscriptions concerning Judaism and the Jews have been collected in *CII* and *CPJ*. Those of Beth Shearim in Greek in M. SCHWABE and B. LIFSCHITZ, *Beth Shearim* II, those in Hebrew or Aramaic by MAZAR, ibid. I and AVIGAD, ibid. III.

Numismatics

The best general catalogue of Palestinian coins is still G. W. HILL, *British Museum Catalogue of Greek Coins: Palestine*, 1914; Jewish coins have been recently catalogued by Y. MESHORER, *Jewish Coins*, 1967; L. KADMAN has published four volumes of a planned *Corpus nummorum Palaestinensium* dealing with the coins of Aelia Capitolina, Caesarea Maritima, Ptolemais and the First Revolt.

APPENDIX
CHRONOLOGY

THE REIGN OF HEROD

The chronological limits of Herod's reign, its beginning and end, as well as a number of other dates in its history, are obtained mainly by comparing the data in our literary sources with the assured dates of general Roman history. Yet problems confront anyone seeking to arrive at a precise determination of the basic dates of Herod's reign, such as his nomination in Rome as king, his capture of Jerusalem from Antigonus, and his death. Several principles concerning the chronological calculations of events in Herod's reign may be mentioned here.

1) In the days of the Second Temple the regnal years were counted from spring, as explicitly stated in the Mishnah:[1] 'On the first of Nisan is the New Year for kings.' This we learn, too, from statements in I Maccabees referring to the time of the high priesthood of Jonathan and Simeon.[2] From the history of the last kings of Judah one gains the impression that even before the destruction of the First Temple the regnal years were counted from Nisan.[3]

2) It is very probable that the system which obtained in Judaea was the non-accession one. This means that that part of the year, whatever its length, which preceded the first Nisan of the reign was reckoned as its first year, so that its second year started from the first Nisan. This system also prevailed in this period in Roman Egypt as well as in Roman Syria,[4] which is of special interest for the custom current in Judaea. This was also the system in vogue according to the Talmud:

---

[1] *M. Rosh ha-Shanah* 1:1.
[2] I Mac. 10:21; 16:14.
[3] H. Tadmor, *JNES* xv (1956), p. 227; M. Noth, *ZDPV* (1958) pp. 150-152. Cf. also U. Rapaport, *Revue numismatique* (1969), pp. 67-73. The counting from Nisan was also observed elsewhere in the region adjacent to Judaea, such as in Damascus and in the Nabataean kingdom. Cf. H. Seyrig, *Revue numismatique* (1964), p. 64, n. 6.
[4] For Roman Egypt, cf. U. Wilcken, in L. Mitteis and U. Wilcken, *Grundzüge und Chrestomathie der Papyruskunde* i, i, (1912), p. LVIII; for Roman Syria, cf. C. Cichorius *ZNW* (1923), pp. 18-19.

'If a king ascended the throne on the twenty-ninth of Adar, as soon as the first of Nisan arrives he is reckoned to have reigned a year'.[1]

1. *The date of Herod's nomination as King (40 B.C.E.)*

This date is determined by Josephus' statement that the event took place during the second consulship of Domitius Calvinus and of Asinius Pollio, that is, in 40 B.C.E.[2] One could be even more precise and assign Herod's nomination as king, in which Antony and Octavian cooperated, to the autumn of that year, since such cooperation was feasible only after the two triumviri had made the pact at Brundisium in September 40 B.C.E.[3] Nor is there any reason to assume that Josephus erred in assigning the event to the year of these consuls. In another place in his account of the history of Judaea where he used a date according to consuls, he was accurate. This was when he referred to Pompey's capture of Jerusalem by the year of the consulship of Gaius Antonius and Marcus Tullius Cicero,[4] which was in 63 B.C.E. But on another occasion when Josephus dated an event according to consuls[5] the picture that emerges is not altogether clear, Quintus Hortensius and Quintus Metellus, the consuls of 69 B.C.E., being mentioned in connection with the Hyrcanus II's accession to the throne after his mother's death, which is however more compatible with 67 B.C.E.[6] It should be noted that in this last case the date according to consuls does not refer to an event associated directly with Roman history, as do Herod's nomination as king and Pompey's capture of Jerusalem.

An argument advanced against 40 B.C.E. as the year of Herod's appointment as king of Judaea[7] is that Josephus' statement does not agree with what is reported by Appian.[8] From the latter it appears that Antony, during his stay in the east in 39 B.C.E., appointed Darius king of Pontus, and made Herod king of the Idumaeans and the Samaritans, Amyntas king of the Pisidians, and Polemon of part of Cilicia. There is thus a discrepancy between Josephus, who states that Herod was nominated king in 40 B.C.E., and Appian,

[1] *T. B. Rosh ha-Shanah* 2a.
[2] Jos. *Ant.* XIV, 389; T. R. S. Broughton, *The Magistrates of the Roman Republic* II (1952), p. 378.
[3] R. Syme, *The Roman Revolution* (1939), p. 217.
[4] Jos. *Ant.* XIV, 66.
[5] *Ant.* XIV, 4.
[6] B. Niese, in *Hermes* (1893), pp. 221-226.
[7] W. E. Filmer, in *JTS* (1966), p. 285.
[8] Appian, *The Civil Wars* v, 75, 319.

who assigns that event to 39 B.C.E. It is, however, clear from Appian's statement that he was talking about Antony's activities after he had left Rome and while he was staying in the east. Assigning these activities to 39 B.C.E. is not in conflict with Herod's receiving the kingship in Rome in 40 B.C.E., while Antony was still there. Noteworthy, too, is the fact that Herod is mentioned by Appian only in connection with the Idumaeans and the Samaritans. It may even be contended that in 39 B.C.E., shortly after Herod was made king in Rome in 40 B.C.E., the borders of his kingdom, which at first consisted of the scanty area of Hyrcanus II's ethnarchy, were extended by Antony. In the various arrangements made by him in the Roman East he gave Herod Samaria and parts of Idumaea (Marissa, Adora), which were not included in his kingdom in 40 B.C.E. There is accordingly no real discrepancy between Josephus' chronology and that of Appian, so that the argument, based on the latter against the date given by the former, automatically fails.

2. Herod's capture of Jerusalem

For the capture of Jerusalem by Herod, who was assisted by the Romans under the command of Sosius, Josephus also gives a date according to the Roman consuls. Thus he states that the capture took place during the consulship in Rome of Marcus Agrippa and Caninius Gallus, that is, the consuls of 37 B.C.E.[1] Josephus adds further data, that it was in the hundred and eighty-fifth Olympiad, in the third month (whatever its significance may be) and on the day of the Fast. According to its literal meaning, this last reference is to the Day of Atonement. Not only is this *the* 'day of the Fast' but Josephus also calls it the 'festival of the Fast' (τῇ ἑορτῇ τῆς νηστείας). He adds that Herod's capture of Jerusalem took place on precisely the same day on which the city was captured by Pompey twenty-seven years earlier.[2] The hundred and eighty-fifth Olympiad ended on June 30, 37 B.C.E., a date which rules out any possibility that Jerusalem was captured on the Day of Atonement (in October) in 37 B.C.E. The meaning of 'the third month' is not at all clear, since if it is taken as the third month of the Jewish calendar it cannot be reconciled with the capture of the city on the Day of Atonement, whether we begin reckoning the months from Nisan or from Tishri. There is another discrepancy between the date according to the consuls (37 B.C.E.) and Josephus' assertion that twenty-seven years

[1] *Ant.* xiv, 487. [2] Cf. *Ant.* xiv, 488.

64

had elapsed from the capture of the city under Pompey (63 B.C.E.) to its capture by Herod. For to obtain a difference of twenty-seven years it would be necessary to assign its capture by Herod to a year later, to 36 B.C.E.

Of Josephus' chronological data one statement can easily be refuted—that which identifies the day of the city's capture under Pompey and under Herod as the Day of Atonement. In the non-Jewish literature of antiquity there is, as is well known, the repeated mention of the ordinary Sabbath as a fast day.[1] From the outset we could have surmised that, in the account of the events associated with the two occasions when Jerusalem was captured, the reference is to an ordinary Sabbath. And Dio Cassius asserts that not only the capture under Herod took place on the Sabbath day ('on the day also then called the Day of Saturn') but also that under Pompey.[2] From Josephus it is clear that Pompey's capture of Jerusalem could not have taken place on the Day of Atonement, since he himself states that it occurred in the third month.[3] That this meant the third month of the siege, which began in the spring of 63 B.C.E., can be seen from the parallel passage.[4] To assume that the siege lasted until October is thus quite impossible.[5]

In rejecting the Day of Atonement as the day on which the city was captured on both occasions, we have also to reject Josephus' statement that the two events took place on the same day, for this assertion is in fact based on the assumption that both occurred on the Day of Atonement. A non-Jewish source is undoubtedly responsible for the mistake in Josephus' narrative, which occurs in the *Antiquities* but not in the *Jewish War*. It may be maintained

[1] Cf. the letter of Augustus to Tiberius in Suetonius, *Life of Augustus*, 76; Pompeius Trogus, in Justinus, *Epitome* XXXVI, 2, 14; Petronius, *Fragmenta* no. 37.
[2] Cf. Dio Cassius XLIX, 22, 4; XXXVII, 16, 4.
[3] Cf. *Ant.* XIV, 66.
[4] Cf. *War* I, 149.
[5] The correct interpretation was suggested already by L. Herzfeld, *MGWJ* (1855), pp. 109-115, and his explanation has been adopted by most scholars. See Schürer I, p. 239, n. 23; 284, n. 11; L. Korach, *Über den Wert des Josephus als Quelle für die römische Geschichte* (1895), p. 29; M. B. Dagut, *Biblica* XXXII (1951), pp. 542-548; Magie, *Roman Rule in Asia Minor* II, 1229. Some scholars, however, still maintain the mistaken view. See, for example, V. Gardthausen, *Augustus und seine Zeit* II I (1891), p. 120; J. Morr in *Philologus* LXXXI 266-269; J. van Ooteghem, *Pompée le Grand* (1954), p. 233, n. 6; Filmer, *JTS* 1966, p. 289. W. Otto, *Herodes* (1913), p. 33, n. 2, holds that assigning Herod's capture of Jerusalem to the Day of Atonement was the invention of an anti-Herodian Jewish source interested in maligning Herod. But this is hardly convincing.

that he did not take it from his chief source, Nicholas of Damascus, who was familiar with Jewish matters and would not have confused the Sabbath with the Day of Atonement, but from Strabo, a source of which in the *War* he had as yet no need.

As regards Josephus' further observation in the *Antiquities* that the city was captured in the third month, the view is to be accepted that this is a mechanical transfer of the statement which, in that same work, refers to its capture by Pompey.[1] On the other hand several indisputable facts emerge. The siege began at the end of winter (λήξαντος τοῦ χειμῶνος), and lasted five months.[2] The latter fact cannot readily be reconciled with Josephus' statement that the capture of Jerusalem took place in the hundred and eighty-fifth Olympiad, which ended on June 30. So as to include the taking of the city within the limits of that Olympiad the siege should have begun at the height of winter (January 37 B.C.E.).

There is a contradiction between the date given by Josephus for the capture of Jerusalem by Herod and that given by Dio Cassius.[3] According to the latter it took place in the consulship of Claudius and Norbanus, that is, in 38 B.C.E. Since Dio Cassius assigns the fall of Jerusalem to 38 B.C.E., he could add that in the following year, 37 B.C.E., the Romans in Syria did nothing noteworthy. However the vast majority of scholars are right in here preferring Josephus to Dio Cassius. For the relative chronology of the events which took place from June 38 B.C.E., the date when the Roman commander Ventidius gained his victory over the Parthians, until the fall of Jerusalem does not fit in with the assumption that the city was already captured in 38 B.C.E.[4]

Recently, however, the suggestion has once more been made, this time by Filmer, that 36 B.C.E. is to be preferred to 37 B.C.E. as the date of the capture of Jerusalem.[5] Several of his assumptions are incorrect, such as that Josephus' principal sources for his narrative were Jewish, or that Jerusalem fell on the Day of Atonement. The only serious argument which can be entertained is Josephus' calcula-

---

[1] Cf. J. Kromayer, *Hermes* (1894), pp. 569-570.

[2] Cf. *Ant.* XIV, 465; *War* I, 351. According to *War* V, 398, the siege lasted six months. For a comparison between the chronological data in Josephus' works, see also R. Laqueur, *Der jüdische Historiker Flavius Josephus* (1920), pp. 211-212.

[3] Cf. Dio Cassius XLIX, 23, 1.

[4] For a summary of the problem, see A. Bürcklein, *Quellen und Chronologie der römisch-parthischen Feldzüge* (1879), pp. 61-65; Schürer I, p. 284, n. 11.

[5] Cf. Filmer, pp. 285-9. For a similar view expressed already in the 19th century, see J. v. Gumpach, *Über den altjüdischen Kalender* (1848), pp. 268-277.

tion that twenty-seven years separated the capture of the city by Pompey from that by Herod. But it is doubtful whether this reckoning of Josephus carries sufficient weight to tip the balance against his own explicit date according to the years of the consuls. Moreover if the city's fall is referred to 36 B.C.E., it would become still more difficult to explain Dio Cassius' assigning it to 38 B.C.E. But the main argument against Filmer's view is as follows. According to him the principal stages of the siege lasted through the summer of 36 B.C.E. We know that a very large part of the Roman army took part in this siege.[1] On the other hand, it is also known that Antony set out on his campaign against the Parthians as early as the spring of 36 B.C.E.[2] It is very difficult to assume that at such a time Antony would have split up his army, leaving a large part of it in Judaea. We also know that in Antony's invasion of Parthia his troops numbered about 100,000 soldiers,[3] and it is difficult to imagine where he could have found a second powerful force to assign to the siege of Jerusalem in that same year. These arguments alone suffice to invalidate any attempt to fix 36 B.C.E. as the date of Herod's capture of Jerusalem.

Not much help is afforded us by the information in Josephus that the siege of Jerusalem fell during a sabbatical year and that consequently the Jews besieged by Sosius and Herod suffered from famine in the city.[4] The sabbatical year lasts from Tishri to Tishri. The results of not sowing the fields in a sabbatical year are experienced during the summer of that year itself and then during most of the following year until after its summer harvest. In its simplest terms Josephus' statement can be understood as intended to convey that 38-37 B.C.E. was a sabbatical year and that its consequences were felt already during the early summer months of 37 B.C.E. However, to combine into a clear, consistent system all the scant information which we have on the sabbatical years during the period of the Second Temple[5] is no easy matter, for when in connection with a sabbatical year or in the context of military operations the sources speak of a shortage of food, it may with equal justification be assumed that the reference is to the summer of the sabbatical year itself or to the autumn,

---

[1] Cf. *Ant.* XIV, 469.
[2] Cf. J. Kromayer, *Hermes* (1896), p. 99; T. Rice Holmes, *The Architect of the Roman Empire* I (1928), pp. 225-226.
[3] Cf. N. C. Debevoise, *A Political History of Parthia* (1938), pp. 124-125.
[4] Cf. *Ant.* XIV, 475.
[5] Cf. Schürer I (3rd Ger. edition), pp. 35-36; R. North, *Biblica* XXXIV (1953), pp. 501-515.

winter, and spring of the following year. Nor does this exhaust all the possibilities. Apparently only the context can help to fix precise chronologies, but at times things are not unambiguous.

In summing up it must be emphasized that there is no reason to reject 37 B.C.E. as the year in which Jerusalem was captured, this being the only date compatible with the political and military events of those years.

3. Herod's death

Despite the attempt of Filmer[1] to reject the accepted date of Herod's death (4 B.C.E.)[2] and instead assign it to 1 B.C.E., the former date should, it seems, be retained. The arguments derived from the chronology of the subsequent rule of Herod's sons and from Roman history, as recently advanced by Barnes, are entirely convincing.[3] Barnes himself suggests December 5 B.C.E. as an alternative to the spring of 4 B.C.E., since the only precise evidence in a literary source speaks of Kislev 7 as the day of Herod's death. It should, however, be remembered that this literary source is the late scholion to *Megillath Ta'anith*,[4] whose statements, in contrast to those in the Aramaic text of *Megillath Ta'anith* itself, are in fact without any value at all.

THE END OF PILATE'S TENURE OF OFFICE

The precise date when Pontius Pilate ended his procuratorship is not clear, for the simple reason that it is impossible to fit all Josephus' data on the subject into a uniform theory which would resolve the discrepancies among them. From a comparison with Roman chronology the most important fact to emerge is that Pilate, after staying ten years in Judaea and being dismissed by Vitellius, hastened to Rome, but before he arrived there the Emperor Tiberius died[5] (16 March 37 C.E.). Thus it was shortly before this date that Pilate was removed from office. But here the difficulties begin.

In Josephus it is related, after the paragraph on Pilate's dismissal, that Vitellius came to Judaea and went up to Jerusalem at a time when the Jews were celebrating the festival of Passover. On that

---

[1] Cf. Filmer, op. cit., 283-298.
[2] For a summary of the arguments in favour of 4 B.C.E., see Schürer I, p. 326, n. 165.
[3] Cf. T. D. Barnes, *JTS* (1968), pp. 204-209.
[4] Cf. *HUCA* (1931-1932), p. 339 and the comments of H. Lichtenstein, ibid., pp. 293-294.
[5] Cf. *Ant.* XVIII, 89.

occasion he remitted to the Jews the taxes (or duties) imposed on agricultural produce and gave the high priestly vestments into the keeping of the priests in the Temple.[1] Vitellius also deposed the High Priest Joseph Caiaphas and appointed in his stead Jonathan son of Ananus.[2] After some time we hear of another visit paid to Jerusalem by Vitellius in the company of Herod Antipas, on their way to fight against the Nabataeans. At this time, too, the visit took place during a Jewish festival;[3] and on this occasion he removed from office the High Priest Jonathan son of Ananus, appointing the latter's brother Theophilus in his place.[4] We are not told which festival was being celebrated during Vitellius' second visit, nor how much time elapsed between his two visits to Jerusalem. On the other hand we learn that on his second visit, on the fourth day of his stay in Jerusalem, he was informed of the death of Tiberius and of Gaius Caligula's accession as emperor. He even administered to the Jews an oath of loyalty to the new emperor.[5] Since Tiberius died on 16 March, 37 c.e., the obvious conclusion to be derived from Josephus' account is that the festival on which the news of the emperor's death was received was the Passover of 37 c.e. Hence the Passover previously mentioned in connection with Vitellius' first visit, immediately after Pilate was removed from office, was the Passover of 36 c.e. Accordingly, at least a year elapsed between Pilate's dismissal before the Passover of 36 c.e. and his arrival in Rome shortly after Tiberius' death, as mentioned by Josephus. If we accept all Josephus' data,[6] we are faced with the difficulty of explaining why Pilate took so long over the journey, despite the general instruction that governors had to return to Rome within three months of leaving their posts[7] and despite Josephus' explicit statement that Pilate hurried (ἠπείγετο) to Rome. While Pilate's delay may be ascribed to the winter, when regular sailings were suspended,[8] what explanation is there for his failure to take advantage of the entire period congenial to sea travel, between the Passover of 36 c.e. and the winter of 36-37 c.e.? Another theory has therefore been suggested which utilizes all Josephus' data.[9]

[1] Cf. *Ant.* xviii, 90.   [2] Cf. *Ant.* xviii, 95.   [3] Cf. *Ant.* xviii, 122.
[4] Cf. *Ant.* xviii, 123.
[5] Cf. *Ant.* xviii, 124; Philo, *Legatio*, 231.
[6] So, for example, Schürer i, p. 387, n. 144; p. 388, n. 145.
[7] Cf. Dio Cassius liii, 15, 6.
[8] Cf. Vegetius, *Epitoma rei militaris* iv, 39; J. Rougé, *Revue des Études Anciennes*, liv (1952), pp. 316-325.
[9] Cf. J. Jeremias, *Jerusalem zur Zeit Jesu* (1962), p. 219, n. 8; J. Blinzler, *Der Prozess Jesu* (1960), pp. 194-196.

According to this theory the festival mentioned by Josephus in connection with Pilate's dismissal and Vitellius' first visit was the Passover of 37 c.e., while the other festival on which Vitellius visited Jerusalem was Pentecost. But this theory cannot be sustained critically since it assumes too large a lapse of time between Tiberius' death and Vitellius' receipt of the news in Judaea. As has been said, Tiberius died on 16 March, 37 c.e. In that year Passover occurred on March 24 or April 20, and Pentecost accordingly fell on May 12 or June 8.[1] In the former event it took two months for the news to reach Vitellius, in the latter, close to three months. It should be noted that this was the favourable season of the year, and it is inconceivable that such a decisive item of news should have taken more than a month to reach Vitellius.[2]

There are thus grounds for the suggestion of those scholars who maintain that a mistake has occurred in at least one of Josephus' statements. Thus it has been suggested that Josephus erred in regarding the festival on which Vitellius first visited Jerusalem as Passover, whereas it was in fact Tabernacles.[3] Very convincing, too, is the view which dissociates Pilate's dismissal and Vitellius' first visit from any Jewish festival, and instead refers the former event to December 36 c.e., the latter to the end of December 36 c.e. or the beginning of January 37 c.e., and Vitellius' second visit to Passover 37 c.e.[4]

THE EVENTS IN THE DAYS OF GAIUS CALIGULA

The chronology of the events in Judaea in the days of Gaius Caligula is derived from a comparison between the data in the three detailed

---

[1] Cf. Blinzler, op. cit., p. 196.

[2] The news of the death of Nero on 9 June, 68 and of the accession of Galba reached Tiberius Julius Alexander in Egypt on July 6 of that year, that is, within 27 days. See C. Préaux, *Mélanges Georges Smets* (1952), p. 574. On the speed at which the ancient ships sailed, see also L. Casson, *TAPA* (1951), pp. 136-148. Cf. also Pliny, *Natural History* xix, 3, on the record speed of six and seven days reached by ships sailing from Sicily to Alexandria.

[3] Cf. U. Holzmeister, *Biblica* xiii (1932), pp. 228-232.

[4] Cf. E. M. Smallwood, *JJS* (1954), pp. 12-21. Von Dobschütz, *Realencyklopädie für protestantische Theologie und Kirche*, xv (1904), p. 398, also holds that there is no connection between Vitellius' first visit and Pilate's dismissal; for, according to him, Vitellius used to visit Jerusalem at the Passover. There is no basis for the suggestion of Otto, op. cit., p. 192, that Vitellius visited Jerusalem only once, out of which Josephus made two visits. The information on the two visits is authenticated by the fact that on each of them another high priest was appointed, Jonathan son of Ananus on the first, and his brother Theophilus on the second.

70

accounts which are extent: Philo's *De Legatione ad Gaium*; Josephus' *Antiquities* and *Jewish War*.[1]

The following is an account of the events as described by Philo. While he and the members of the Jewish delegation from Alexandria were staying at Puteoli after their first meeting with Gaius, they were informed of the emperor's command that a statue of himself was to be set up in the Temple in Jerusalem, after the Jews in Jamnia had demolished the altar erected in honour of Gaius by the non-Jewish minority of that city. Petronius, the governor of Syria, was charged with carrying out the command. Because of the dangerous consequences expected to issue from the Jewish reaction to the command, Petronius did not act precipitately. As the statue was not ready, he charged artists in Sidon to attend to its installation. He also summoned the leaders of the Jews to appear before him, in order to influence them to accept without opposition the emperor's command. Their reply was an unequivocal refusal. Crowds of Jews of both sexes and all ages streamed to Petronius, then staying in Phoenicia, and asked that the sacrilegious decree be revoked. Petronius did not give them a clear answer but decided to send a letter to Gaius, in which he explained the reasons for the tardy execution of the command: first the making of the statue was a slow business; and then, since the harvest season had arrived, he feared that the Jews in their desperation would destroy the crop waiting to be harvested. On receiving the letter Gaius was enraged at the postponement, but restraining his anger, wrote a courteous reply, in which he thanked Petronius for his concern for the future, yet at the same time asked him to hurry with the statue, seeing that by then the harvest should already have ended. Meanwhile Agrippa I, ignorant of the emperor's command, arrived in Rome, having left Judaea before news of the decree was known there. Gaius himself informed him of it, and on hearing it, Agrippa fainted. When he recovered, he wrote a letter to the emperor in which he pleaded with him not to abolish the traditional customs of the Jews. Complying with his friend's entreaties, Gaius sent another letter to Petronius revoking the command to have the statue placed in the Temple in Jerusalem, although permitting those who so wished to erect altars and statues outside Jerusalem.

---

[1] Cf. Philo, *Legatio*, 184-348; Jos. *Ant.* XVIII, 261-309; Jos. *War* II, 184-203. Of the discussions on the chronology of the events, see Schürer I, p. 397, n. 180; Graetz III 2⁵, 761-772; H. Willrich, *Klio* (1903), pp. 467-470; J. P. V. D. Balsdon, *JRS* (1934), pp. 19-24; E. M. Smallwood, *Latomus* (1957), pp. 3-17.

Philo adds that Gaius gave instructions that an immense statues be made in Rome itself and shipped to Judaea unknown to the Jews. Later Philo reverts to an account of the delegation of the Jews of Alexandria and to the meeting it had with Gaius near Rome.[1] It is impossible to know what else Philo wrote about the development of relations between Gaius and the Jews and between the former and Petronius, since the last part of *De Legatione ad Gaium* has been lost.

In the *Antiquities* Josephus reports the following stages in the course of events. Petronius, having received a command to introduce Gaius' statue into Jerusalem, went to Ptolemais at the head of a Roman army to winter there and to commence military operations in the spring should the Jews show any opposition. He wrote of his intentions to Gaius who praised him for his energy. In the meantime enormous crowds of Jews demonstrated before Petronius to express their opposition to the command. A second mass demonstration met Petronius on his arrival at Tiberias. These Jews continued their pressure for forty days, in consequence of which they neglected their fields, for the time of sowing had come. They were joined by the leaders of the Jews, among whom was Agrippa I's brother Aristobulus. The Jewish opposition to Gaius' command had its effect on Petronius. He sent a letter to Gaius in which the decisive note was that so many tens of thousands of people should not be brought to despair. Meanwhile Agrippa, who was then in Rome, succeeded during a banquet in influencing the emperor to issue an order revoking the previous command to introduce the statue into the Temple. The emperor sent the countermand to Petronius. This was before he received Petronius' letter informing him of the stubborn Jewish objection to bringing the statue into Jerusalem. Gaius replied in an angry letter, filled with threats against Petronius, which made it clear that the latter was to commit suicide. But the news of Gaius' death (24 January, 41 c.e.) came before his last letter was received by Petronius. His life was thus saved.

The shorter account in *War* is in the main identical with the description in *Antiquities*, although it contains several details not included in the latter work. Especially important chronologically is the information that the bearers of Gaius' last letter were delayed three months at sea.[1]

In general it may be asserted that all the events connected with

[1] Cf. *Legatio*, 349-367. [2] Cf. Jos. *War* II, 203.

72

Gaius' command to set up the statue in the Temple occurred in 40 C.E.,[1] the problem being when precisely during that year they took place. Here there undoubtedly exists a contradiction between Philo and Josephus. According to the former, the Jewish demonstrations in reply to Gaius' command were associated with the harvest season, that is, were in the spring or at the beginning of the summer of 40 C.E., whereas the latter assigns them to the sowing season. On the other hand, it must be admitted that the comparative chronology of the events described by Josephus appears to be reasonable and is compatible with that laid down by himself. It is neverthelesss difficult to dismiss offhand Philo's reference to the harvest season, particularly since he was not only a contemporary of these events but, as a member of the Jewish-Alexandrian delegation, also closely associated with them.[2]

It is not known when precisely Gaius returned from Gaul to Italy (whether in the spring or the beginning of the summer of 40 C.E.) or when the members of the Jewish delegation at Puteoli were able to have the meeting with him, a short time after which they first heard the news of the impending calamity. If we assume that the Jewish demonstrations at Ptolemais and at Tiberias took place in May and that the members of the delegation heard about them in June, this assumption would fit in with Philo's statement connecting the Jewish demonstrations in Phoenicia with the harvest season. His reference to Agrippa's fainting on being informed by Gaius about the statue and to the emperor's sending a letter countermanding his order need not necessarily be interpreted as requiring us to assume that these events took place within the space of several days. For it is likewise possible that Agrippa was told of the matter as early as at the beginning of summer, but his efforts to have the order annulled bore fruit only at the beginning of autumn (September).

The date of the occurrences in Palestine are closely connected with that of the Jewish delegation's first meeting with the Emperor at Puteoli. Scholars differ on whether the delegation left Alexandria for Rome in the winter of 39-40 C.E. or already in that of 38-39 C.E.[3]

---

[1] Contrary to the view of Willrich, op. cit., pp. 468-469.

[2] The best defence of Josephus' chronology is given by Balsdon in the above-mentioned article. The best argument in favour of Philo's chronology is in the article by Smallwood.

[3] The arguments in support of the former date are given by E. M. Smallwood, *Philonis Alexandrini, Legatio ad Gaium* (1961), pp. 47-50. The argument in favour of the earlier date is presented by P. J. Sijpesteijn, *JJS* (1964), pp. 87-96.

If we adopt the latter alternative we would have to assume that the Jewish delegation waited in Italy for more than a year before being received by Gaius at Puteoli.

FELIX AND FESTUS

The period of Felix's tenure of office as procurator of Judaea is a problem which has for long been the subject of divergent opinions. And scholars have not reached any general consensus on the point. (There is still another problem associated with Felix's previous role as the ruler of Samaria alongside Cumanus the governor of Galilee, as stated in Tacitus' *Annals*; see below pp. 374ff.). On the date of Felix's appointment as procurator of the whole of Judaea scholars are generally in agreement. Tacitus, in the context of the occurrences of 52 C.E., speaks of the dismissal of Cumanus, the predecessor of Felix, while the first event whose date is subsequently given by Josephus refers to 53 C.E. (the twelfth year of Claudius' reign).[1] It therefore appears to be entirely reasonable to assign the beginning of Felix's procuratorship to 52 C.E.

On the other hand the date of the end of Felix's procuratorship is far from clear. The most widely held theory maintains that it was in or about 60 C.E. Other scholars hold that Felix was dismissed in 55 or 56 C.E.[2] And the material in our sources is not unambiguous. It is known that Felix was succeeded as procurator by Festus, who died during his term of office. The latter was followed by Albinus, of whom we learn from Josephus[3] that four years before the Great Revolt, on the festival of Tabernacles (that is, in 62 C.E.), he was already occupying the position of procurator. But the questions that arise are how much before that date did Albinus receive the appointment, and how is the time from 52 C.E. to be divided between Felix and Festus.

[1] Cf. Tacitus, *Annals* XII, 54; Jos. *Ant.* XX, 138.
[2] See Schürer I (3rd Ger. edition), p. 577, n. 38. According to Schürer, who repeats the formulation of Wurm, the procuratorship of Felix ended at the earliest in 58 C.E. and at the latest in 61 C.E., so that the most probable date is 60 C.E. This view is followed by J. Felten, *Neutestamentliche Zeitgeschichte* I (1925), p. 224, n. 4. Graetz, op. cit., pp. 731-734, suggests 59 C.E. and Ed. Meyer, *Ursprung und Anfänge des Christentums* III (1923), pp. 53-54, proposes 61 C.E. as the year when Felix's procuratorship ended. Among those who favour the earlier date are Ed. Schwartz, *Gesammelte Schriften* V (1963), p. 154; Lambertz, *PW* XXII, cols 220-226; E. Haenchen, *Die Apostelgeschichte* (1961), pp. 63-64; C. Saumagne, *Mélanges Piganiol* (1966), pp. 1373-1386.
[3] Cf. Jos. *War* VI, 300-305.

The reasons of those who give a later date for the end of Felix's procuratorship, assigning it to 60 C.E. or around that year, are in the main as follows. a) There are the numerous events which, as related in the *Antiquities*,[1] also took place under the procuratorship of Felix after Nero's accession in 54 C.E. b) In his account of the history of Felix's procuratorship after Nero's accession, Josephus tells of the exploits of the false prophet from Egypt, which he does not include among the earliest events.[2] Mentioned also in the Acts of the Apostles, this incident already belonged to the past at the time of Paul's imprisonment. To this must be added, the advocates of this theory maintain, the two years during which Paul was imprisoned in the time of Felix until the latter was succeeded by Festus (Διετίας δὲ πληρω-θείσης).[3] c) From Josephus' autobiography we learn that he set out in 63/64 C.E. for Rome to obtain the release of Jewish priests imprisoned by Felix.[4] This date is more consistent with the assumption that Felix continued to occupy his post until the beginning of the sixties than with the alternative view that he relinquished it in *c.* 55 C.E.

The main argument of those who favour the earlier date is based on the chronology of Eusebius. In the Latin version of St. Jerome, which reflects Eusebius' original version more faithfully than does the Armenian rendering, we read that Festus succeeded Felix as early as 56 C.E. and that he in turn was succeeded by Albinus in 60 C.E.[5] It is, however, doubtful whether any importance is to be ascribed to these dates. From other instances relating to the history of Judaea in this period it can be seen to what extent Eusebius was inaccurate. So, for example, he assigned Archelaus' deposition to 13 C.E. instead of 6 C.E.,[6] the establishment of Tiberias to 28 C.E.[7] instead of between 17 and 23 C.E., and Sejanus' machinations against the Jewish people to 34 C.E.,[8] three years after Sejanus' death.

Another objection against the later date of Felix's dismissal is that in the *Antiquities*[9] it is related that after Felix had concluded his term of office he was accused by the Jews before the emperor, but was acquitted thanks to the entreaties of his brother Pallas, whom Nero at that time held in the highest esteem. It can be argued that this comment is inconsistent with the later date, since Pallas had already been dismissed from his office (that of *a rationibus*) by Nero

[1] Cf. *Ant.* xx, 160-181.   [2] Cf. *Ant.* xx, 167-172.
[3] Cf. Acts 21:38 (the Egyptian prophet); 24:27.
[4] Cf. *Vita*, 13.   [5] Cf. Jerome, *Chron.*, ed. Helm, 182.
[6] Cf. Jerome, op. cit., 171.   [7] Cf. Jerome, op. cit., 173.
[8] Cf. Jerome, op. cit., 176.   [9] Cf. *Ant.* xx, 182.

in 55 C.E.[1] and thus could not be of help to his brother in *c.* 60 C.E. It should, however, be noted that his dismissal did not cancel his influence; and it may be assumed that he retained a certain status so long as Burrus, the commander of the praetorian guard with whom he was on friendly terms, was alive, that is until 62 C.E.[2]
The explanation which refers the two years mentioned in the Acts of the Apostles to the period of Felix's tenure of office[3] and not to Paul's imprisonment is very improbable, being even in conflict with Eusebius' assertion that Felix ended his procuratorship in 56 C.E., for according to this explanation it took place as early as in 54 C.E.[4]
To sum up it may be stated that the hypothesis which upholds the later date of *c.* 60 C.E. as marking the end of Felix's procuratorship is more probable than that which refers it to the earlier date of 55 or 56 C.E. At the same time it is quite possible to agree that the dismissal of Felix could be assigned to the somewhat earlier date of 58-59 C.E., seeing that in this year we find a new minting of coins in the province of Judaea.[5] It seems not unreasonable to assume that Festus, having succeeded Felix as procurator, struck these coins at the beginning of his term of office.

BIBLIOGRAPHY

A new general study of the chronological problems connected with Jewish history from the capture of Jerusalem by Pompey, or even

[1] Cf. Tacitus, *Annals* XIII, 14.
[2] Cf. *Annals* XIV, 51. Pallas, too, died in that year. On Pallas' last years, cf. S. I. Oost, *AJPh* (1958), pp. 133-138.
[3] So, for example, Lambertz, op. cit., 224.
[4] The last authentic chronological fact from Roman history connected with the history of Paul is the governorship of L. Junius Gallio who was proconsul in Achaea when Paul came from Athens to Corinth (Acts 18:12-17). Gallio assumed office in the summer of 51 C.E. and continued in it until the summer of 52 C.E. See the inscription from Delphi (Sylloge³, no. 801D = Gabba, no. XXII), which is a letter of the Emperor Claudius in which mention is made of Gallio. On the inscription, see A. Deissmann, *Paul* (1927) pp. 261-286; E. Groag, *Die römischen Reichsbeamten von Achaia bis auf Diokletian* (1939), pp. 32-35; A. Plassart, *REG* (1967), pp. 372-378.
[5] In 58-59 C.E., the fifth year of Nero's reign, a large quantity of coins was minted. Before that coins had been struck by Felix in 54 C.E. Generally the minting in Nero's fifth year is also ascribed to Felix. See Y. Meshorer, *Jewish Coins of the Second Temple Period* (1967), p. 103. It is quite possible that after an interval Felix started minting coins again. But, as has been said, it may have been done by a new procurator.

from the founding of the Hasmonaean state to the destruction of the Second Temple, remains a desideratum. E. SCHÜRER, is still the best collection of the material and the clearest statement of the problems. Cf. especially vol I, p. 284 n. 11 (the date of the capture of Jerusalem by Herod); pp. 287-294 (chronological survey of Herod's reign); p. 326 n. 165 (the date of Herod's death), p. 392 n. 167, p. 397 n. 180 (the events under Gaius); p. 465 n. 42 (chronology of Felix and Festus).

More controversial are the results of ED. SCHWARTZ' study of the chronology of Paul, which has a bearing on that of the procurators of Judaea, 'Zur Chronologie des Paulus', in *Nachrichten von der Königlichen Gesellschaft der Wissenschaften zu Göttingen, philologisch-historische Klasse* 1907, pp. 262-299 (*Gesammelte Schriften* V, 1963, pp. 124-169); cf. also his 'Die Ären von Gerasa und Eleutheropolis', ibid., 1906, pp. 340-395.

For the chronology of Herod cf. the recent studies of W. E. FILMER, *JTS*, 1966, pp. 283-298 and the convincing reply of T. D. BARNES, *JTS*, 1968, pp. 204-9. On the chronology of the events under Caligula, cf. J. P. V. D. BALSDON, *JRS* 1934, pp. 19-24; E. M. SMALLWOOD, *Latomus*, 1957, pp. 3-17.

On the chronology of Agrippa II, cf. H. SEYRIG, *Revue numismatique*, 1964, pp. 55-65, which constitutes the fundamental study.

Chapter Two
Historical Geography

Throughout its history Palestine has known two basic situations as a result of its geographical position, the more common state of affairs being domination by a great power, which left a certain degree of autonomy to the local inhabitants. In its earlier history the suzerain powers were the states which had risen in the twin cradles of civilization, the Nile Valley and Mesopotamia. Then came the more distant powers: Persia, the Hellenistic monarchies, Rome and Byzantium. In between these periods of submission to the great powers came periods of political vacuum (generally of much shorter duration) during which a local dynasty became independant and extended its rule over the whole country. Such periods were the reigns of David, Solomon and the Hasmonaeans. In retrospect they appeared to the Jews as periods of divine favour and national glory.

The roots of the territorial divisions in the first century go back to the Assyrian period. The powerful military machine of the Assyrians crushed one state of the Near East after another, and left in their place administrative districts rule by Assyrian governors. This basic arrangement was maintained by the Babylonians (who added Judah to the list of their provinces), the Persians and the Hellenistic kings.

THE PERSIAN PERIOD

According to Herodotus the fifth Persian satrapy (עבר נהרא, 'the land beyond the river', i.e. the Euphrates)[1] comprised all the lands from Poseidion to the borders of Egypt, i.e. all of Syria and Palestine.[2] The satrapy, which was administered from Damascus, was divided into provinces (מדינות), each ruled by 'his excellency' (תרשתא)[3] the governor (פחה) and subdivided into districts (פלך).

The province of Judah, known in the official Aramaic as Yehud,[4] was

[1] Neh. 2:7; Ezra 8:36 (Hebrew); Ezra 4:10, 11, 16, 17, 20, etc. (Aramaic).
[2] Herodotus, *History* III, 89-97.
[3] Neh. 10:2.
[4] Ezra 6:7 and coins, see Meshorer, *Jewish Coins*, No. 1.

78

throughout the period of Persian and Hellenistic rule restricted to the narrow boundaries given to it by Nebuchadnezzar. It extended from Bethel in the north[1] to Beth-Zur in the south[2] and from the Jordan in the east to Emmaus in the west.[3] Its extent from north to south was hence about 40 kilometres, from east to west about 50 kilometres; its area was about 1600 square kilometres. The province was divided into six districts, each with a capital and sub-capital, a division made evident by Nehemiah's list of the builders of the Jerusalem wall.[4] These districts were: 1) Jerusalem[5] (with Netophah-Ramat Rahel as secondary capital);[6] 2) Keilah[7] (Adullam?); 3) Mizpah[8] (Gibeon?); 4) Beth Haccerem or 'Ain Karem[9] (Zanoah);[10] 5) Beth Zur[11] (Tekoah?)[12]; 6) Jericho[13] (Senaah)[14]. The area of Judah was entirely inhabited by Jews.

The other provinces were Samaria, which included within its southern border the three districts of Lod (Lydda), Haramatha (Arimathaea, Rentis) and Aphaerema (et Taiyibe), largely inhabited by Jews. Its capital was Samaria, the ancient capital city of the kingdom of Israel. Inhabited by a mixed population from the Assyrian period onwards, Samaria had from the early Persian period certain claims to rule over Judah; the head of the province, a post hereditary in the Sanballat family[15], was also commander of the 'army of Samaria'.[16] North of Samaria lay Galilee, probably a separate province governed from Megiddo or perhaps Hazor. South of Judah was Idumaea, the land occupied by the Edomites after the fall of Jerusalem. Its capital seems to have been Hebron. West of Idumaea was the province of Ashdod[17] which included all inland Philistia.

A curious situation existed during the Persian period along the coast. Because of the importance of the Phoenician fleets for the Persians and also because of the lack of cultivable lands on the Lebanon coast where the Phoenician cities were situated, the kings of Persia assigned the Palestinian coast to the chief cities, Tyre and Sidon, a Sidonian

[1] Ezra 2:29; Neh. 7:32; Zech. 7:2.
[2] Neh. 3:15.   [3] 1 Macc. 3:42.   [4] Neh. 3.
[5] Neh. 3:9,12.
[6] For the identification of this site with Beth Haccerem see Y. Aharoni, *IEJ* (1956), pp. 148 ff.
[7] Neh, 3:17-18.   [8] Neh. 3:15-19.   [9] Neh. 3:14.   [10] Neh. 3:13.
[11] Neh. 3:16.   [12] Neh. 3:5.   [13] Neh. 3:2.
[14] Neh. 3:3; cf. Ezra 2:35; Neh. 7:38.
[15] Neh. 2:19; A. E. Cowley, *Aramaic Papyri of the Fifth Century B.C.* (1923) No. 30; Jos. *Ant.* xi, 302.
[16] Neh. 2:10; 3:34.   [17] Neh. 4:1; 13:23-4.

town alternating with a Tyrian and so on. The two royal fortresses of Accho (later Ptolemais, now Acre) and Gaza were exceptions to this rule. An incomplete list of these settlements has been preserved by a sailing directory attributed to Scylax of Caryanda.[1] The list has several lacunae, which can be filled in with some certainty. It begins with Tyrian Haifa, 'Aradus' (= Adarus or Boucolon polis) probably Athlith, and Dor (Dora), both Sidonian, then a Tyrian city (perhaps Crocodilon polis = Tell Malat); the Tower of Straton (Sharshon, later Caesarea) is not mentioned in the list, but it must have been Sidonian; Rishpuna (later Apollonia-Arsuf), also not mentioned, could have been Tyrian. Joppa (Jaffa) was Sidonian,[2] Ascalon Tyrian.

East of the Jordan the Assyrian provinces of Karnayim and Hauran seem to have continued to serve as administrative units. The status of Ammon was peculiar: although largely inhabited by Ammonites, it had a Jewish governor from the Tobiad family.[3] The western half of the province, bordering on the Jordan, must have been largely Jewish. Moab and Edom seem to have been left to the Nabataean Arabs.

THE HELLENISTIC PERIOD

The Ptolemies

Alexander's passage through the Palestine was too short to make itself felt in the administrative arrangements; he only replaced the Persian satrap at Damascus by a Macedonian. A Samaritan revolt led to the establishment of a Macedonian colony of veterans at Samaria (later Sebaste, now Sebastya), either by Alexander himself or by the regent Perdiccas after Alexander's death.[4] Conditions were stabilized after the definite establishment of the supremacy of the Ptolemaic kings of Egypt in 301 B.C.E.

Ptolemaic rule extended over the whole of Palestine and southern Phoenicia up to the river Eleutherus north of Berytus. The province was administered from Alexandria; the Persian provinces were kept as hyparchies, subdivided into toparchies (the ancient פלכים). Judaea kept its status as a semi-independent province, a kind of enlarged

[1] See the commentary by K. Galling in *ZDPV* (1938), pp. 66-87.
[2] G. A. Cooke, *North Semitic Inscriptions* (1903), pp. 30 ff.
[3] Neh. 2:19; 4:1; 6:1.
[4] Q. Curtius Rufus, *History of Alexander the Great* IV, 8, 9; Hieronymus, *Chronicon* (ed. Helm), pp. 197, 199.

temple estate ruled by a high priest. Its partitions and boundaries remained unchanged. Samaria had been split into two units within the boundary of the same hyparchy: the *ethnos* of Samaritans and the Macedonian colony of Samaria itself; both had the same governor.[1] Galilee (Galila) is now first mentioned as a territorial unit.[2] Its capital may have been at Beth Shean, now named Scythopolis, perhaps because Scythian mercenaries of the Ptolemies were settled there,[3] or at Philoteria (Beth Yerah) on the sea of Galilee, or at the fortress of Itabyrion (Mount Thabor). The Israelite royal estates in the Jezreel and Jordan valleys, were kept in the hands of the Ptolemaic kings. Along the coast the various cities were freed from their Phoenician tutelage; four of them received Greek names, but only one, Ptolemais, so called in honour of Ptolemy II, became a proper city with the usual Greek magistracies.[4] The others, Boucolon polis, Crocodilon polis and Apollonia remained settlements (πολιτεύματα). The old Philistine cities of Ascalon and Gaza were thoroughly Hellenized and assimilated to the Greek colonies in their status. Idumaea had its capital transferred to Marissa (Mareshah) where various Greek officials resided and where a colony of Hellenized Sidonians had settled.[5] The capital of the coastal province was transferred to Jamnia (Jabneh);[6] it had a common border with Samaria, the frontier guards being stationed at Pegae (later Arethusa and Antipatris, now Rosh ha-Ayin).[7] Joppa became an autonomous harbour town, and Dora (Dor) a royal fortress.[8]

East of the Jordan the large uninhabited areas encouraged Greek colonization and administrative innovations. The Ptolemies apparently split up the Persian provinces and added Moab to their dominions. The new hyparchies were distinguished by the Greek locative suffix - ιτις (Gaulanitis, Auranitis, Trachonitis, Moabitis).[9] A series of Greek cities were established in the areas east of the Jordan: Dion (Tell Hamad), Hippos (Susitha), Gadara (Umm Keis), Pella (Fahil), Abila (Abil), Gerasa (Jerash) and Philadelphia (Rabbath

---

[1] I Macc. 3:10; Jos. *Ant.* XII, 261, 264, 287.
[2] *PCZ*, No. 2.
[3] Avi-Yonah, *IEJ* (1962), pp. 123-8.
[4] Diodorus Siculus, XIX, 93, 7.
[5] Thiersch and J. C. Peters, *The Painted Tombs of Marissa* (1905).
[6] *PCZ*, No. 59006; Jos. *Ant.* XII, 308.
[7] *PCZ* No. 59006 and *PSI*, No. 406.
[8] I Macc. 15:11-14; Jos. *Ant.* XIII, 224; *War* I, 50.
[9] Jos. *Ant.* XIII, 396; XV, 343; XVI, 285; XIII, 382, 397; Syncellus I, 558.

MAP II. HELLENISTIC PALESTINE

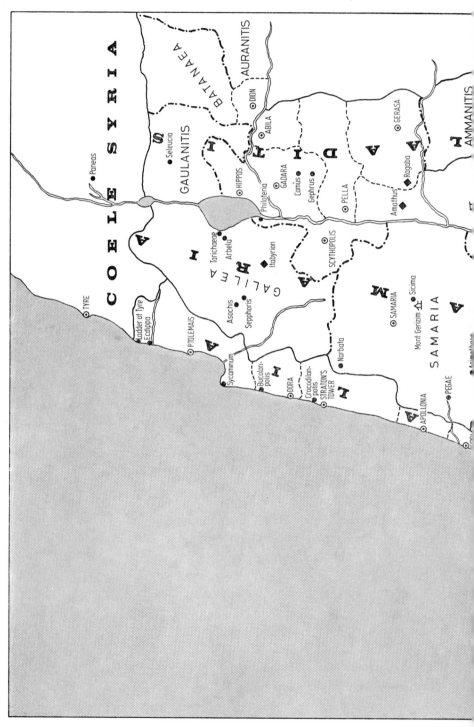

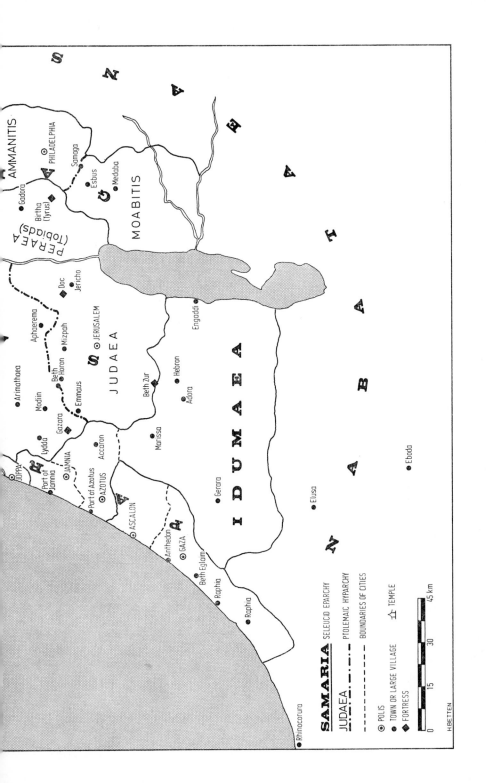

SAMARIA SELEUCID EPARCHY

JUDAEA PTOLEMAIC HYPARCHY
------ BOUNDARIES OF CITIES

⊙ POLIS
● TOWN OR LARGE VILLAGE   ⛰ TEMPLE
◆ FORTRESS

0   15   30   45 km

H.BETTEN

AMMANITIS
● Gadara
Birtha (Tyrus) ◆
PHILADELPHIA ⊙
▲
● Samaga
● Esbus
● Medaba
MOABITIS

PERAEA (Tobiads)
▲

Doc ◆
● Jericho

● Aphaerema
● Arimathaea
● Modiin
Beth ● Horon
● Mizpah
JERUSALEM ⊙
S
JUDAEA

● Engaddi

Gazara ●
● Emmaus
● Lydda
JOPPA ⊙
H
Port of Jamnia ●
⊙ JAMNIA
● Accaron

Beth Zur ◆
● Hebron
● Adora

Port of Azotus ●
⊙ AZOTUS

● Marissa

● Gerara

I D U M A E A

A B A

N

● Eboda

● Elusa

ASCALON ●
▲
● Anthedon
H
⊙ GAZA
● Beth Eglam
● Raphia
● Raphia

● Rhinocorura

Ammon, the modern Amman).[1] The case of the latter was especially significant. By turning the ancient capital of Ammon into a Greek city, its territory was detached from Tobiad supervision; the ancient rulers retained control of the western half of their former domain, which was largely populated by Jews. The capital of the district was Birtha of the Ammonites, also called Tyrus ('Iraq el Emir).[2] The Nabataeans retained their independence, but their port of Aila (Elath) was occupied by the Ptolemies and renamed Berenice.[3]

The Seleucids

In 198 B.C.E. Antiochus III, the Seleucid king of Syria, succeeded in realizing the old claims of his dynasty on Palestine and occupied the Ptolemaic province. The larger scale of the Seleucid empire, which extended from the Persian Gulf to the Aegean, made the small Ptolemaic districts impracticable. Hence their territories were distributed among large districts known as strategies. One such strategy was Coele-Syria, another was Phoenicia, which included the Ptolemaic dominions conquered by Antiochus III.[4] In times of crisis all the western strategies were combined into a province 'from the river Euphrates to the border of Egypt'[5] which was administered by a viceroy. The Seleucid strategy was subdivided into eparchies, of which there were seventy-two in the Seleucid dominions. Several Ptolemaic hyparchies were combined into one Seleucid eparchy. Thus the eparchy of Samaria now included the old hyparchy of the same name in addition to Judaea, Peraea and Galilee.[6] This redistribution of the provinces explains why the Maccabean revolt which broke out at Modin (Modiin) within the toparchy of Lod, i.e. outside Judaea, was met from the direction of Samaria.[7] As the revolt spread, Judaea became an independent eparchy.[8] Idumaea as an eparchy included the former province of Idumaea and that of Jamnia, as well as the royal fortress of Gezer.[9] The coastal plain was formed into an eparchy called Paralia ('sea-coast'). It extended from the Ladder of Tyre (Rosh ha-Niqrah) to the border of Egypt.[10] Beyond the Jordan another eparchy was

---

[1] Stephanus Byzantinus s.v.; Polybius v, 71, 2; Eusebius, *Onomasticon* (ed. Klostermann), 16.
[2] *PCZ*, No. 59003. [3] Jos. *Ant.* VIII, 163.
[4] 2 Macc. 3:5; 4:4; 8:8. [5] 1 Macc. 3:32.
[6] 1 Macc. 3:10; 10:30; Jos. *Ant.* XIII, 50.
[7] 1 Macc. 3:10. [8] 2 Macc. 14:12.
[9] Diodorus, XIX, 95, 2; 1 Macc. 4:15.
[10] 1 Macc. 11:59; Jos. *Ant.* XIII, 146.

created, called Galaaditis;[1] it included Gaulanitis, Batanaea, the cities beyond the Jordan, Trachonitis (Lejja), Auranitis and Moabitis. The Tobiad domain, now called Peraea, 'the land beyond' (the Jordan) was, as we have seen, attached to Samaria. The Tobiad dynasty itself came to an end under the Seleucids, but their former domain remained inhabited by Jews.

The Ptolemies, with their centralistic tendencies, did not favour the establishment of autonomic Greek cities and restricted them whenever possible. The Seleucids, on the other hand, were vitally interested in enlarging the area of Greek municipal life, as they had found their most loyal adherents among the cities. After the conquest of Palestine they - and in particular King Antiochus IV - followed the same policy. In the existing cities special organizations of loyal citizens were set up, the Seleucid demos in Gaza[2] and 'the Antiochenes' at Ptolemais (whose name, however, they did not change).[3] A number of cities east of the Jordan took as their name Antioch (Hippos, Gerasa)[4] or Seleucia (Abila) or both (Gadara).[5] An 'Antioch' was founded side by side with the Old City of Jerusalem.[6] It extended over the western of the two hills which constituted the ancient city and was provided with a market-place (ἀγορά),[7] a fortress called the Acra,[8] and the foundations of a temple planned on a very large scale. Another Antioch was founded at Dan north of Lake Semechonitis (Huleh).[9] Scythopolis now became a polis proper and received the additional name Nysa in honour both of Dionysius' nurse and a princess of the Seleucid family.[10]

THE HASMONAEAN PERIOD

The first fifteen years after the outbreak of the Hasmonaean revolt (167-152 B.C.E.) did not cause any changes in the historical geography of Palestine, the fighting being mainly concentrated in Judaea and the adjoining territories. The only lasting demograpic change was the partial evacuation of the Jews from western Galilee and the district of Narbata by Simeon the Hasmonaean, and of the Jews

[1] I Macc. 5:20, 26, 27, 37, 45.
[2] Hill, British Museum Coins, Palestine (1914), pp. LXIX, 143.
[3] Ibid. Phoenicia, pp. LXXIX, 129.
[4] B. V. Head, Historia numorum (1911), p. 786; C. B. Welles ap. C. Kraeling (ed.), Gerasa (1938), p. 600.
[5] Head, Historia numorum, p. 786.
[6] 2 Macc. 4:9.   [7] I Macc. 12:36.   [8] I Macc. 1:35.
[9] Jos. Ant. XII, 393-4; War I, 105.
[10] M. Avi-Yonah, IEJ (1962), p. 129.

85

in Galaaditis by Judas Maccabaeus.[1] Another interesting event was the bisection of the city of Jerusalem between the Jews established on the Temple Mount ('Mount Zion' as it was then called) and the Syrians and Hellenizers entrenched round the Acra on the hill opposite.[2] During the campaigns of Judas Maccabaeus the Acra was isolated and the four attempts of the Seleucid generals to relieve it were beaten back successively in the north (at the ascent of Lebonah?), the west (Beth Horon and Emmaus) and the south (Beth Zur).[3] After the retreat of Judas Maccabaeus from Jerusalem following the defeat at Beth Zechariah, he won two battles against the Seleucid governor Nicanor, at Caphar Salama and Adasa north of Jerusalem,[4] but in 160 B.C.E. he was defeated and killed at Elasa (Khirbet Ilasa).[5] The rebels, led by Judas' brother Jonathan, withdrew into the desert of Judaea to the well of Asphar and the desert of Tekoah.[6] The counter-measures of the Seleucid general Bacchides, who fortified a chain of fortresses, were of no avail. The 'Bacchides line' included Thamna in Judaea (Khirbet et Tibbaneh), Pharaton (Wadi Farah), Tekoah, Jericho, Emmaus, Beth Horon, Bethel, Gezer and the Acra of Jerusalem.[7]

In 152 B.C.E. the inner divisions of the Seleucid dynasty obliged one of the rivals to appoint Jonathan the Hasmonaean, the brother of Judas, as High Priest and *de facto* ruler of Judaea. From that moment onwards the increasing weakness of the Seleucid kingdom and the continuing contest for the throne between the descendants (real or ostensible) of Antiochus IV and Seleucus IV enabled the Hasmonaean rulers to act as a balance and to enlarge their dominions step by step.

Until then the official boundaries of Judaea had not changed since the time of Nebuchadnezzar. Beth Zur[8] was still the boundary point in the south, Adullam in the south-west[9] and Emmaus in the west.[10] The first addition was that of the territory of Accaron (Ekron), granted to Jonathan by Alexander Balas in 147 B.C.E.[11] Demetrius I ceded to Jonathan the rule of three districts detached from Samaria: Lydda, Haramatha and Aphaerema.[12] These districts were inhabited by Jews, and Jonathan exercised *de facto* control over them. By this grant Modin, the home town of the dynasty, came under their rule. Antiochus VI, when confirming the grant of the districts, speaks

[1] I Macc. 5. [2] I Macc. 4:60. [3] I Macc. 2-4. [4] I Macc. 7; 2 Macc. 8.
[5] I Macc. 9. [6] I Macc. 9:33. [7] I Macc. 9:51-2. [8] I Macc. 14:33.
[9] 2 Macc. 12:38. [10] I Macc. 3:42. [11] I Macc. 10:89.
[12] I Macc. 10:30; 11:28, 34.

of 'four nomes' ceded.[1] The fourth nome was in all probability Peraea, the former Tobiad area, which was later in Hasmonaean possesion since the conquest of Hyrcanus started from its border.

Jonathan's brother Simeon, the last of the Hasmonaean brothers, finally took the Acra in 141 B.C.E. and thus reunited Jerusalem.[2] He also besieged and occupied Gezer, and established his palace and military headquarters there.[3] Finally, he made Joppa definitely a Jewish town and 'made an outlet to the isles of the sea' for Judaea.[4] The Hasmonaean conquests outside ancient Judaea were temporarily nullified by the intervention of Antiochus VII, the last energetic Seleucid. After the death of this ruler in 129 B.C.E. the death throes of the empire set in. In 142 B.C.E. Simeon had been granted the *de facto* status of an independent ruler,[5] including the right to coin money (which, however, he did not do) and an era of his own.[6] The same rights were granted, or arrogated to themselves, by various Greek cities in Palestine and Phoenicia (Tyre in 125 B.C.E., Sidon in 111, B.C.E., Gaza and Ascalon before 103 B.C.E.). Local rulers, such as Zenon Cotylas in Philadelphia[7] and Zoilus in Dora and the Tower of Straton,[8] replaced the Seleucid officials. The Ituraeans occupied the slopes of Mount Hermon and Lebanon, and gained a foothold on the Mediterranean; the Nabataeans extended their dominions as far as Damascus, the capital of Coele-Syria, under their king Aretas IV.[9] In this free-for-all the Hasmonaeans took care to defend what they regarded as their 'patrimony', the ancient kingdom of David. John Hyrcanus, Simeon's successor, gained a foothold on the king's highway east of the Jordan by taking Medaba and Samaga.[10] (The other international highway through Palestine, the *via maris*, came under his dominion after the cession of Lydda). Hyrcanus then turned his attention to the Samaritans and the Idumaeans. The conquest of Samaria was effected in two stages; first the Samaritan *ethnos* was subdued and their sanctuary on Mount Gerizim ceased to function; nevertheless, the Samaritans kept their national and religious consciousness.[11] Next the Idumaeans were conquered and converted to

---

[1] I Macc. 11:57. [2] I Macc. 13:49-52.
[3] I Macc. 12:43, 47-8; 16:19; R. A. Macalister, *Excavations of Gezer* I (1912), p. 217.
[4] I Macc. 14:5. [5] I Macc. 13:41-2. [6] I Macc. 13:41-2.
[7] Jos. *Ant.* XIII, 235; *War* I, 60. [8] Jos. *Ant.* XIII, 324-5.
[9] Jos. *Ant.* XIII, 392, 418; *War* I, 103, 115.
[10] Jos. *Ant.* XIII, 255; *War* I, 63.
[11] Jos. *Ant.* XIII, 256; *War* I, 63.

Judaism.[1] From the beginning it had been the policy of the Hasmonaeans to tolerate no gentiles in their land; the conquered were asked to convert or to leave. Finally Hyrcanus enlarged the Jewish outlet to the sea by taking Jamnia and Azotus in the south and Apollonia in the north, and by besieging and conquering Samaria, the powerful Greek city which barred his way northwards.[2] During the siege of Samaria, Scythopolis fell into Jewish hands, either by bribery or by conquest, as well as the inner slopes of Mount Carmel.[3] By an administrative decision the district of Acraba (Aqraba) in Samaria, largely inhabited by Idumaeans (now presumably Jews), was attached to Judaea, with which it remained united till C.E. 70.[4] Hyrcanus' successor, Judas Aristobulus, reigned only one year (104-103 B.C.E.), but during that short time succeeded in attaching Galilee to the Jewish dominions. Western Galilee had lost its Jewish inhabitants in the time of Simeon (see above p. 85), but its eastern part had remained largely Jewish.[5] The Ituraeans, who had seized Galilee, were forced to evacuate it. Within the year we find that both Asochis (Shihin) and Sepphoris had become Jewish towns.[6]

Alexander Jannaeus, who succeeded Judas I on the throne, enlarged the Hasmonaean dominions to their greatest extent. Although he was on the whole unlucky in the field, he succeeded by dint of perseverance in taking city after city. At the beginning of his reign he expelled Zoilus the 'tyrant' of Dora and annexed his territories including Mount Carmel, which had belonged to Ptolemais.[7] (The city of Ptolemais itself resisted successfully.) East of the Jordan he failed before Philadelphia, but he took in two campaigns the whole area from Gerasa and Ammathus in the south to the 'Valley of Antiochus' (the Huleh) in the north. His dominions included Gadara, Pella, Hippos, Dion and Gaulanitis.[8] He conquered the Nabataean territory around the Dead Sea, turning this into an inland lake within his kingdom and no doubt profiting from its natural treasures. His conquests in this area extended as far as Zoar.[9] In a further effort to cut the Nabataean trade route to the Mediterranean he took Gaza

[1] Jos. *Ant.* XIII, 257-8.
[2] Jos. *Ant.* XIII, 275, 281; *War* I, 65; *Megillath Taanith*, 22.
[3] Jos. *Ant.* XIII, 280; *War* I, 66.
[4] I Macc. 5:3.
[5] I Macc. 9:2; Jos. *Ant.* XIII, 319; *War* I, 76.
[6] Jos. *Ant.* XIII, 337-8.
[7] Jos. *Ant.* XIII, 335.
[8] Jos. *Ant.* XIII, 256, 393-5; *War* I, 86-8, 104-5.
[9] Jos. *Ant.* XIII, 397; XIV, 18.

after a long siege, together with its daughter cities Anthedon and Raphia, and finally his dominions in that area extended as far as Rhinocorura (el-Arish) on the 'Brook of Egypt', the biblical boundary of the Land of Israel.[1] Only Ascalon was, apparently deliberately, left an independent enclave within the Hasmonaean dominions.[2] The administrative divisions of the Hasmonaean kingdom are less well known than its extent. The Hasmonaeans seem to have organized their territories in provinces, each called by the Ptolemaic administrative term μερίς, (part); these were Judaea in the restricted sense, Idumaea,[3] Samaria, Galilee and Peraea. The inhabitants of the villages subject to the Greek cities, whose inhabitants went into exile if unwilling to accept Judaism, were freed from Greek control. The provinces were subdivided into toparchies; at least twenty-four of the latter, inhabited by Jews, formed the foundation of the organization of the *maamadoth* (מעמדות), the territories from which delegations went up in regular rotation to serve in the Temple of Jerusalem throughout the year.[4]

Jannaeus took great care to fortify the strong points of his kingdom. He built the fortresses of Masada, Alexandrium, Hyrcania and Machaerus which remained the main strongholds of Judaea in the following centuries.[5]

After the death of Jannaeus and of his widow Queen Salome Alexandra (67 B.C.E.), a civil war broke out between their two sons John Hyrcanus II and Judas Aristobulus II. In order to obtain the support of Aretas, King of the Nabataeans, Hyrcanus ceded to him the Nabataean lands around the Dead Sea conquered by Jannaeus.[6] The distintegration of the Hasmonaean state, thus begun, was completed after the siege and capture of the Temple at Jerusalem by Pompey in 63 B.C.E. By order of the conqueror all the Greek cities along the coast from Gaza to Dora, as well as the inland cities of Marissa, Arethusa (formerly Pegae), Samaria, Scythopolis and the cities east of the Jordan, were restored to their former inhabitants. Gaulanitis and the Huleh valley went to the Ituraeans. The Jews lost even Joppa and the estates in the Jezreel Valley.[7] In order to strengthen

---

[1] Jos. *Ant.* XIII, 357-364; *War* I, 87.
[2] M. Avi-Yonah, *Holy Land* (1966), pp. 67-8.
[3] Jos. *Ant.* XIV, 10.
[4] M. *Taanith* 4:2.
[5] Jos. *Ant.* XIII, 417-418; *War* VII, 285.
[6] Jos. *Ant.* XIV, 18.
[7] Jos. *Ant.* XIV, 205, 207.

the Greek cities east of the Jordan Pompey created the League of Ten Cities (the 'Decapolis'), which included Scythopolis. The Hasmonaean state was sorely diminished as a result of these decisions. But if we compare what remained with pre-Hasmonaean Judaea, we notice a great expansion of the Jewish element in Palestine. Not only was Judaea increased by eastern Idumaea, parts of Samaria and Peraea east of the Jordan, but Galilee remained as a detached part within its orbit. Besides, Julius Caesar, who was in general friendly to the Jews, repaired some of the worst damage by restoring to Judaea in 47 B.C.E. Joppa and the Jezreel Valley.[1]

Pompey's arrangements were carried out by his successor Gabinius.[2] An attempt was made to split Judaea into five separate areas, on the model of a similar division of Macedonia. Separate authorities (or συνέδρια) were set up at Sepphoris (now Zippori) for Galilee, at Jerusalem for Central Judaea, at Jericho for the Jordan Valley. at Amathus for Peraea and at Adora for eastern Idumaea.[3] The arrangement did not, however, last long.

To conclude the section on the Hasmonaean period we may sum up briefly the demographic changes it brought about. One noticeable change was the inclusion in Judaea of several districts (Lydda, Arimathaea, Aphaerema, Acrabatene, Peraea) inhabited by Jews. Another was the conversion of the Idumaeans to Judaism. Although undertaken by means which cannot be approved of by the modern mind, the fusion of Jews and Idumaeans was successfully carried out and had become an accomplished fact by the time of the first revolt against Rome, when the Idumaeans, although keeping their identity, fought beside the Jews. Shared misery after the loss of the war united them permanently. The settling of Gezer and Joppa (also Azotus and Jamnia) by Jews also created a lasting situation. (Jamnia, which in the time of Judas Maccabaeus threatened its Jews with extermination, became after 70 C.E. the centre of Judaism). Galilee, which must have had a strong Jewish element even before the time of Judas Aristobulus I, was almost completely Judaized in the first years of Jannaeus. The extensive conquests of this king among the Greek cities bordering on his domain had more problematical results. The stories of destruction and exile spread by the Greek historians and accepted by Josephus must be taken *cum grano salis*.

[1] Jos. *Ant.* XIV, 205, 207.
[2] Jos. *Ant.* XIV, 74-6, 88; *War* I, 155-7, 166.
[3] Jos. *Ant.* XIV, 91; *War* I, 170.

These cities consisted of a Greek (or Hellenized) upper class ruling over native villages; the exile of the landlords did not imply a complete desertion of the area, but rather the villagers' exemption from the burden of rent. We know from our sources and from archaeological evidence that Scythopolis continued to be inhabited and this applies also to Samaria. Gaza, Pella and Gadara seem to have suffered most under the Hasmonaeans; Gaza did indeed keep the name 'the deserted' until Roman times, when it again became a prosperous metropolis (Acts 8:26). In any case this state of affairs did not last longer than one generation.

HEROD AND HIS DYNASTY

The rise of Herod the son of Antipater from a private individual to kingship is outside our scope; we should, however, note two territorial changes which were made some time after he received the title of King at Rome in 40 B.C.E. The town of Marissa had been destroyed by the Parthians and was not restored;[1] its territory, which included western Idumaea (part of Herod's patrimony), was added to the kingdom of Herod. Another addition was that of the territory of the Samaritans (as distinguished from that of the city of Samaria); since they had been detached from the Hasmonaean territory, the Samaritans had led an isolated existence, being neither a city nor a state.[2]

During the hegemony of Mark Antony in the Orient Herod led a miserable existence; he lost to Cleopatra the cities in the coastal plain and the profitable domain of Jericho.[3] It was only after the battle of Actium and after the visit of Augustus to Palestine that he began to expand his territory by the grace of the emperor. Even before that he seems to have obtained the territory of Heshbon by a successful war against the Nabataeans.[4] Now Augustus gave him the coastal cities from Gaza to the Tower of Straton (excepting Ascalon), the inland city of Samaria and the cities of Gadara and Hippos east of the Jordan.[5] Herod repaid the imperial generosity by reconstructing two cities, Caesarea and Sebaste and naming them in honour of the emperor (see below p. 93). In 23 B.C.E. the emperor, angered by the

[1] Jos. *Ant.* xiv, 364; *War* i, 269.
[2] Appian, *Bella civilia* v, 75, 319.
[3] Jos. *Ant.* xv, 95-6; *War* i, 361; Plutarch, *Antony* 36,3; Dio Cassius, xlix, 32.
[4] Jos. *Ant.* xv, 294.
[5] Jos. *Ant.* xv, 217; *War* i, 396.

continued depredations of the Ituraeans along the caravan routes leading to Damascus from the south, added to Herod's domain Batanaea, Trachonitis and Auranitis, in the well-founded expectation that the king of Judaea would be able to keep these areas in order.[1] In 20 B.C.E. Herod received the last addition to his kingdom—the area of Paneas, the Huleh valley and Gaulanitis.[2] These additions rounded off Herod's kingdom to about 20,000 square kilometres.

The ambivalence of the Herodian dynasty as between Judaism and the Graeco-Roman world was also manifest in the territorial and ethnic composition of Herod's kingdom. The first additions, in 40 B.C.E., already set up tensions. A Jewish element (Judaea and Galilee) was combined with the Idumaean (presumably loyal to Herod the Idumaean) and the Samaritan, which had a long history of quarrels with the Jews. The addition by Augustus in 30 B.C.E. of a considerable number of Greek towns still further strengthened the non-Jewish element in Herod's possession. Of these some seem to have accepted Herodian rule willingly (especially those cities which he rebuilt and embellished) while others, particularly Gadara and Hippos, opposed the king.[3] The expansions in 23 and 20 B.C.E. did not add many willing subjects (for the Ituraeans must have resented Herod's policing) but they provided the king and his dynasty with rich lands to be colonized. Herod made full use of this opportunity, settling in Batanaea Babylonian Jews, who succeeded in keeping down the highway robberies and also provided the dynasty with a 'house royal' of proven loyalty.[4]

Herod administered his mixed kingdom in two sections. The Greek cities kept their autonomy but were supervised by a royal commissioner or strategos, who occasionally combined his task with the governorship of a neighbouring province.[5] The colonies of veterans settled at Gaba,[6] Heshbon[7] and possibly Azotus[8] made provision for the cleruchs in the style of the Ptolemies and the Seleucids, and also served to secure important road centers. Like other Hellenistic kings Herod was a great founder of cities. In 25 B.C.E. he refounded Sa-

---

[1] Jos. *Ant.* xv, 343-8; *War* i, 398.
[2] Jos. *Ant.* xv, 359-360, 400.
[3] Jos. *Ant.* xv, 351, 354, 356, 358.
[4] Jos. *Ant.* xvi, 285; xvii, 23-5; *War* iii, 57.
[5] Jos. *Ant.* xv, 254.
[6] Jos. *Ant.* xv, 294; *War* iii, 36.
[7] Jos. *Ant.* xv, 294.
[8] Georgius Cyprius, 1021.

maria as Sebaste,[1] providing the city with a new wall, a forum, a theatre and a temple of Augustus.[2] Caesarea (formerly the Tower of Straton) was rebuilt with a deep-water harbour, which provided ships with a secure anchorage, the only one between Joppa and Accho.[3] The city was also given its temple of Augustus and other gods. Other Herodian foundations included Antipatris (formerly Pegae or Arethusa) named in honour of his father, the village of Phasaelis in honour of his brother, and the fort of Cypros in honour of his mother.[4] Anthedon on the coast was renamed Agrippias and rebuilt.[5] One of Herod's perpetual traumas being the fear of an uprising, he multiplied his fortresses, strengthening the old Hasmonaean strongholds of Alexandrium, Hyrcania and Machaerus, refortifying Masada[6] and building a new fortress at Herodium, which was also destined to become the site of the royal tomb.[7]

Herod ruled the other part of his kingdom, that inhabited by Jews, directly through his officials, keeping to the Hasmonaean division of the 'country' (χώρα) into provinces (μερίς) subdivided into toparchies and villages. All these officials, down to the village scribe, were appointed by the king. Jerusalem was regarded as a city, but it is doubtful if it had a council.[8] In any case it was closely supervised by a royal strategos.[9] It seems, however, that the Jewish judicial system functioned along lines parallel to the royal courts and judiciary.

Herod provided Jerusalem with a fortified palace, protected on the north by three huge towers. Another fortress, called Antonia, dominated the Temple area. The Temple itself was equipped with a new esplanade, which doubled the area of its outer court. The inner courts and the sanctuary itself were rebuilt in the most splendid manner. Herod also provided his capital with a theatre and a hippodrome.[10] During the second half of his reign Herod and his family and court were torn by intrigues centring on the problem of succession. After executing three of his sons, Herod divided his kingdom between the

---

[1] Jos. *War* I, 403.
[2] Jos. *Ant.* xv, 296-8. Cf. S. W. Crowfoot *et al.*, *Samaria-Sebaste*, 3 vols, (1942-57).
[3] Jos. *Ant.* xv, 331-341; *War* I, 408-416; A. Frova, *Caesarea maritima* (1965).
[4] Jos. *Ant.* xvi, 142-3; *War* I, 417; *M. Gittin* 7:7 (Antipatris); *Ant.* xvi, 145; *War* I, 418 (Phasaelis); *War* I, 417 (Cypros).
[5] Jos. *Ant.* xiii, 357; *War* I, 87, 416.
[6] Jos. *Ant.* vii, 207-406; Y. Yadin, *Masada* (1966).
[7] Jos. *Ant.* xiv, 360; xv, 323-5; xvii, 199; *War* I, 265, 419-420, 673.
[8] V. Tcherikover, *IEJ* (1964), pp. 62 ff., 75 ff.
[9] Jos. *Ant.* xvii, 156; 209-210; *War* I, 652; II, 8.
[10]Cf. esp. Jos. *Ant.* xv, 380-425; *War* v, 136-254.

three surviving ones, and the Emperor Augustus confirmed the will. The division was carefully planned and well balanced. The elder son, Archelaus, was assigned Judaea with the bulk of the Jewish population; but this was counter-balanced by Idumaea and Samaria (including the cities of Caesarea and Sebaste). He was honoured by the title of ethnarch, whereas the two other heirs received only the title of tetrarch. The second son, Herod Antipas, ruled over purely Jewish Galilee and Peraea; but his two areas were widely separated. The third son, Philip, received the lands east of the Jordan: the district round Paneas (a town which he embellished and which became known as Caesarea Philippi), the Batanaea, Trachonitis, Gaulanitis and Auranitis. His territory was compact, and its population evenly balanced between Jews and gentiles. The economic values of the lands of the three sons can be judged by their tax revenue, as recorded by Josephus: Archelaus had 600 talents a year, Herod 200 and Philip 100. ($ 720,000 monetary value, $ 10 million purchasing value). Certain areas, *viz.* the townlets of Jamnia and Azotus and the domain of Phasaelis in the Jordan valley, were willed by Herod to his sister Salome, who held them under the supervision of Archelaus. Her share yielded 60 talents, a comparatively large sum if we consider the small size of her area.[1]

Archelaus had a short and turbulent reign and was deposed in C.E. 6. The only mark he left on the map of Judaea was a townlet which he founded, called Archelais.[2] His brothers each founded two cities: Herod Antipas one by the Sea of Galilee called Tiberias and another in Peraea called Livias (also called Julias); Philip, along with the Caesarea Philippi mentioned above, built another Julias (Bethsaida), near the entry of the Jordan into Lake Gennesaret (Sea of Galilee).[3] Philip died *c.* 34 C.E. and his lands were taken over provisionally by the imperial administration. In 37 Herod Agrippa (Agrippa I), Herod's grandson by his son Aristobulus, whose mother was Mariamme the Hasmonaean, received from the emperor Caligula the tetrarchy of Philip together with the principality of Chalcis on the slopes of Hermon, and the title of king.[4] In 39 C.E. Herod Antipas was exiled by Caligula, and Agrippa inherited his tetrarchy.[5] After the accession of Claudius he received Judaea and Samaria and thus united under his

[1] Jos. *Ant.* XVII, 317-321; *War* II, 93-8.
[2] Jos. *Ant.* XVII, 340; Pliny *Natural History* XIII, 44.
[3] Jos. *Ant.* XVIII, 18, 27-8, 36-8; *War* II, 168.
[4] Jos. *Ant.* XVIII, 237; *War* II, 181; Dio Cassius, LIX, 8, 2.
[5] Jos. *Ant.* XVIII, 252; *War* II, 183.

sceptre almost the entire kingdom of Herod, except the cities of Gaza, Hippos and Gadara, which had been detached after Herod's death and placed under the Roman legate of Syria. Agrippa ruled his enlarged kingdom for only three years (41-44 C.E.).[1] His son Agrippa II was given Chalcis by Claudius in 53. He received two thirds of Peraea and half of Lower Galilee (Tiberias and Tarichaeae) in 54, from Nero.[2] Agrippa II died c. 95 and from then on the Herodian dynasty ceased to reign over any part of the Jewish nation.

THE TERRITORIAL DIVISIONS IN THE TIME OF JESUS

When Archelaus was deposed, his lands were administered by a Roman official of equestrian rank. It was during the rule of one of these officials, Pontius Pilate, that the ministry of Jesus took place. The teritorial divisions of the country in these years are therefore of special interest and deserve to be discussed in detail.

Jesus grew to manhood in the small town of Nazareth, which formed part of the tetrarchy of Herod Antipas.[3] The next large town, situated to the north-west, would be Sepphoris; we cannot tell, however, whether Sepphoris had already at that date (before its passing under direct Roman rule in 44) acquired the status of a city. It is much more likely that it was merely the headquarters of a toparchy, one of the five constituting Galilee. Nazareth and Sepphoris were both situated in Lower Galilee[4] which was in all probability subdivided into four toparchies: Sepphoris and Araba in the west, Tiberias and Tarichaeae in the east.[5] The boundaries of *Lower Galilee* reached in the west as far as Beth She'arim (Besara) Tib'on and Ardasqus, but not as far as Gaba; further north the boundary ran along Kefar Sasay,[6] Usha and Shefar'am, and still further north Chabulon and Saab. The southern boundary, which separated Lower Galilee from the Herodian estates in the Jezreel Valley, passed along Gabatha and Simonias, Mahalol, Exaloth and Dabaritta, turning southwards to Nain and Salem. Here it reached the border of the Hellenized city of Scythopolis, a member of the Decapolis, whose territory included the entire Harod Valley. The border of Galilee ran as far as Gebul, turning sharply

[1] Jos. *Ant.* XIX, 274-5, 351; *War* II, 215.
[2] Jos. *Ant.*, XX, 104, 138, 159; *War* II, 223, 247, 252.
[3] Matt. 2:23; Luke 23:7.
[4] Jos. *War* III, 35; Matt. 2:22.
[5] Jos. *War* II, 629; *M. Shabbath*, 17:7.
[6] *T. Gittin* 2:3; *P. T. Gittin* 43c; *T. B. Gittin* 6b.

95

northwards so as to leave most of the Jordan Valley between Scythopolis and the Sea of Galilee in the possession of Scythopolis.[1] In its
last stretch near the Sea of Galilee the border ran along the Jordan,
including Sennabris, but excluding Philoteria-Beth Yerah which then
was situated east of the river.[2] The remainder of the eastern border
of Galilee followed the shores of the Sea of Galilee to the entry of
the Jordan and ran along the Jordan to a point slightly north of
Chorazin. The northern boundary of Lower Galilee passed south of
Baca and Beersabe in Upper Galilee, and south of Kefar Hananiya.[3]
The shore of the Sea of Galilee was the site of three localities mentioned
in the New Testament, two of which were closely associated with
Jesus. These were Tiberias, the largest city in this area,[4] Tarichaeae
or, as it was called in Aramaic Migdal Nunaiyya, the home of Mary
Magdalene,[5] and Capernaum, which is called 'his city' with reference
to Jesus (Matt. 9:1.) because of the length and variety of his activities
there.

The highlands of *Upper Galilee* formed a single toparchy extending
from Mafsheta in the west to Thella on Lake Semechonitis in the east,
and from Meroth to Beersabe in the south.[6] Its principal locality
was Gischala.

Herod Antipas had his residence in Galilee, which was the principal
area under his control. There was, however, a second region held by
him: *Peraea* east of the Jordan.[7] This was a long and comparatively
narrow stretch of land, extending from Amathus in the north to
Machaerus and the river Arnon in the south. Narrow at its northern
and southern ends, it widened in the middle where it bordered on
Philadelphia, thus comprising Zia[8] and Jazer. The capital of the whole
province was Gedor, which was also the headquarters of one of the
four toparchies of the province; the others were Amathus in the north,
and Abila and Livias in the south. Although these two localities
were situated close to each other, each belonged to a different toparchy;
the fertility of the Jordan Valley meant that settlements were close
to each other and hence the units of administration were fairly small.
Peraea faced the district of Jericho and parts of Samaria on the west,

---

[1] On the evidence of the milestones which count from Scythopolis to the Jisr
el-Majami' bridge.
[2] On the evidence of an inscription dated by the Pompeian era of the Decapolis,
P. Delougaz and R. C. Haines, *Church at Khirbet el Karak* (1960), pp. 53-4.
[3] Jos. *War* III, 39; *M. Shebiith* 9:2.
[4] John 21:1. [5] Matt. 15:39; Mark 8:10. [6] Jos. *War* III, 40.
[7] Jos. *War* III, 40. [8] Jos. *Ant.* xx, 2.

Pella on the north, Gerasa, Philadelphia, Heshbon, and Medaba on the west, and the Nabataean kingdom across the Arnon on the south. Its importance was that it provided a strip of Jewish territory east of the Jordan which could be regarded as being almost in touch with Jewish Galilee. Consequently Jews who wished to avoid the 'contamination' of passing through the country of the Samaritans were able to approach Jerusalem by way of Peraea, crossing opposite Jericho and then going up to Jerusalem, as Jesus did on his last journey.

The Great Plain, or the Valley of Jezreel, may have been a royal domain from the days of Naboth's vineyard; it must have then passed into the hands of the Assyrians, Babylonians, Persians and the Hellenistic kings, then into the hands of the Hasmonaeans and the Herodians. At the time of the Jewish war it belonged to Berenice, the sister of Agrippa II, forming a region which was administered from Besara.[1] Previously it must have been administered by Herod Antipas, whose tetrarchy it adjoined. Josephus leaves the matter of the attribution of his area in doubt: for him Galilee ends at Exaloth north of the plain,[2] and Samaria begins at Gineae (Jenin),[3] leaving the area in between as a sort of no man's land. There can be little doubt, however, that the Valley of Jezreel formed part of the domain of Antipas at the time of Jesus; the other possible Herodian claimant, Archelaus, whose territory it adjoined, had been banished to Gaul; and the procurators of Judaea were probably instructed to respect the property rights of the Herodians.

After Archelaus' deposition his ethnarchy was administered by a Roman procurator. This area was basically divided into two regions, that of the cities and that of the former χώρα, Herod's 'royal domain'. The latter was again composed of two separate units: Judaea (with Idumaea, inhabited by Jews, with whom the converted Idumaeans began increasingly to identify) and the region of the Samaritans, who constituted a separate ethnic unit.

Judaea proper was divided into eleven toparchies, most of which corresponded to the old districts of the Persian period. Pliny called the district of Jerusalem *Oreine* ('the mountainous one') which in Hebrew probably corresponds to the 'king's mountain' (הר המלך) insofar as this term had a geographical definition.[4] The former toparchy of Beth Zur was now administered from Herodium, Herod's fortress

---

[1] Jos. *Life* 118. [2] Jos. *War* III, 39. [3] Jos. *War* III, 39.
[4] Pliny, *Natural History* v, 70; *M. Shebiith* 9:3; *T. Demai* 1:11 etc.

97

and the site of his tomb.[1] Jericho remained district capital as before; Keilah ceded its rights to Bethleptepha (Beth Nattif), called Pella by Josephus (the name Pella occurs also on an inscription).[2] Emmaus took over from Gezer, Lydda remained the headquarters of its old district, Thamna (Khirbet Tibneh) took over from Arimathaea, and Gophna (Jifna) from Aphaerema. Acraba extended Judaea further north to Coreae at the expense of the Samaritans. Joppa was listed by Pliny[3] as one of the toparchies of Judaea; Josephus also adds Jamnia, which as we shall see later had a special status.[4] The position of Azotus and its subordinate toparchy of Accaron is not clear; the latter was in any case probably one of the twenty-four centres of *maamadoth* (see page 89 above); but Azotus, although within the boundaries of Judaea, was apparently not regarded as a Jewish town.

Both Jamnia and Azotus had a special status as imperial estates. Herod had willed them, together with Phasaelis in the Jordan Valley, to his sister Salome;[5] on the deposition of Archelaus she also received the townlet he had founded, Archelais.[6] Salome died about 10 C.E. and willed her estates to the Empress Livia; on Livia's death in 20 C.E. they became part of the domain of her son, the Emperor Tiberius, and that was their status at the time of Jesus. These estates were administered by a special imperial procurator who resided at Jamnia.[7] The toparchies were as usual divided into villages, each with its scribe originally appointed by the king.[8] At the other end of the scale was the city of Jerusalem, which did not have the rights of a polis, i.e. it had no autonomy but was administered by a commisioner, though the Sanhedrin had jurisdiction in religious and judicial matters.[9]

Idumaea, which Josephus regards as part of Judaea, had two toparchies. One, Idumaea proper, was probably administered from Betogabris (Beth Guvrin), its old capital Marissa having been destroyed and left in ruins in 40 B.C.E.[1] The other part, eastern Idumaea,

[1] Jos. *Ant.* xiv, 360; xv, 323-5; xvii, 199; *War* i, 265, 429, 673; iii, 54-5.
[2] A. Savignac, *RB* (1904), p. 83.
[3] See p. 97, note 4.
[4] See below, p. 107.
[5] Jos. *Ant.* xvii, 321; *War* ii, 98.
[6] Jos. *Ant.* xviii, 31.
[7] Jos. *Ant.* xviii, 158; M. Avi-Yonah, *QDAP* (1946), pp. 84 ff.
[8] Jos. *Ant.* xvi, 203; *War* i, 479.
[9] Tcherikover, *IEJ* (1964), pp. 62 ff.
[10] Jos. *Ant.* xiv, 364; *War.* i, 269.

formerly administered from Adora, now had Engaddi on the shores of the Dead Sea as its capital. Engaddi's economic importance as a centre of groves and a Dead Sea harbour, which continued into the period of Bar-Cochba, probably outweighted the inconvenience caused by its outlying position.[1]

Josephus defines Judaea as reaching from Anuathu Borcaeus in the north to Iardan (?) in the south, and from the Jordan in the east to Joppa in the west.[2] Anuathu Borcaeus is identified with Khirbet Berqit, thirty-five kilometeres north of Jerusalem; but actually, if we include the toparchy of Acraba in Judaea, the border ran much further north. It began on the Jordan slightly north of Coreae[3] (Tell Mazar) and comprised Alexandrium (Sartaba) in Judaea—for the signals for New Years and New Moons passed through this point, which excludes its belonging to Samaria.[4] Acraba, the capital of the toparchy, and Gerasa (Jureish), the birthplace of Simeon bar Gioras[5] were certainly included in Judaea; passing Anuathu Borcaeus, the border continued westwards along the Shiloh Valley (Wadi Deir Ballut) including Bethsarisa (Khirbet Sirisya) within the territory of Judaea (which included the toparchies of Thamna and Lydda, as we have seen above, p. 86); turning southwards the border passed between Rentis and Ono, leaving Giththam (Saqiye) with Antipatris to Samaria and ending at the Mediterranean coast after following the Pega River (Yarqon). After following the coast line to south of Azotus-by-the-Sea, it ran inland, excluding Safir (Sawafir) but including in Judaea the villages of Saalis[6] and Agla, which were later joined together in the lands of Eleutheropolis, and further south Orda (Iardan?)[7] and Birsama; the southern border included in Judaea Beersheba, Malatha and Masada. The Dead Sea and the Jordan formed the eastern border of Judaea.

Samaria, which according to Josephus formed the third part of the 'country' (χώρα), was in Jesus' time much reduced in area; in the south it lacked the toparchy of Acraba, which as we have seen formed part of Judaea, while on the northern side the territory of the *city* of Samaria (now called Sebaste) encroached on the area left to the

---

[1] Y. Yadin. *IEJ* (1962), pp. 249 ff.
[2] Jos. *War* III, 51.
[3] Jos. *War* I, 134.
[4] *M. Rosh ha-Shanah* 2:4.
[5] Jos. *War* IV, 478, 503.
[6] Jos. *War* III, 20; this is Talmudic Kefar Shihlayim, *P. T. Taanith* 69a.
[7] M. Avi-Yonah *The Madaba Mosaic Map* (1954), p. 73.

MAP III. ROMAN ROADS IN PALESTINE

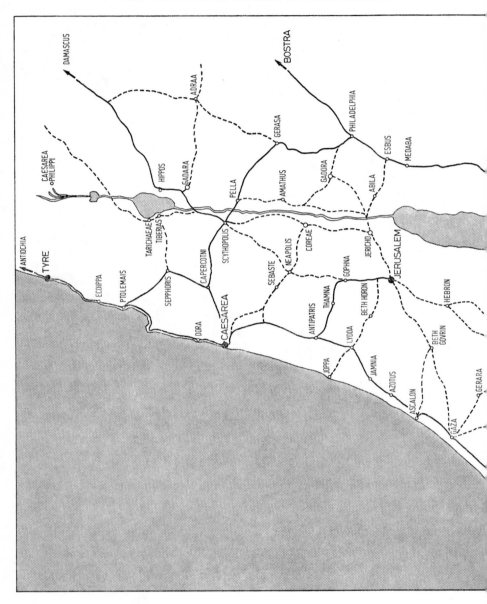

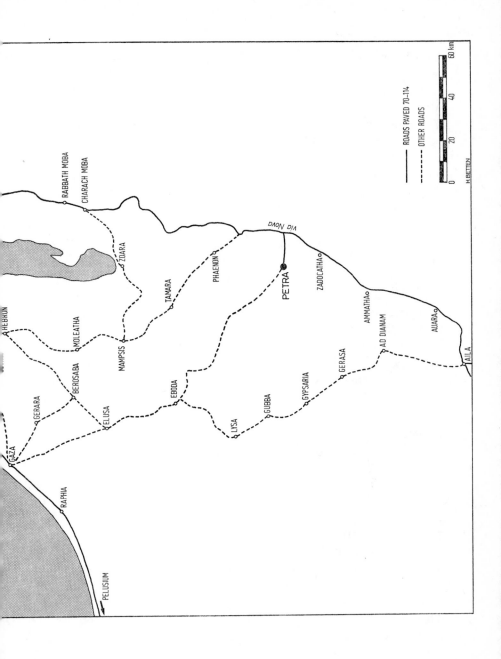

RABBATH MOBA
CHARACH MOBA
ZOARA
TAMARA
PHAENON
VIA NOVA
PETRA
ZADOCATHA
AMMATHA
AUARA
AILA
HEBRUN
MOLEATHA
MAMPSIS
BEROSABA
ELUSA
EBDDA
GERASA
GYPSARIA
GUBBA
LYSA
AD DIANAM
GERARA
GAZA
RAPHIA
PELUSIUM
H.BETTEN

ROADS PAVED 70-114
OTHER ROADS
0   20   40   60 km

IOI

Samaritans. The city of Neapolis (Nablus) was founded only at a later date (71 C.E.) and the Samaritan territory was probably administered from Sichem (Balata) or from the nearby sanctuary of Mount Gerizim.

The remainder of the territory of Palestine was divided into areas of autonomous cities, which in Jesus' time were under the direct supervision of the governor of Syria, who was also the superior of the procurator of Judaea at least in so far as military matters were concerned, for he had at his command the legions of the army of Syria. The most northern city on the coast, Ptolemais, was regarded as part of Phoenicia, although at this period there was no administrative unit of that name. Its territory extended from the Ladder of Tyre to Mount Carmel, including in the interior Caparasima (Kefar Sumaiᶜ). Dora, the next city to the south, had but a small territory; it was also regarded as part of Phoenicia until the time of Diocletian.[1]

After Dora we come along the coast to Caesarea which was in fact at the time of Jesus the seat of the governor (who only came to Jerusalem on special occasions) and hence the capital of the whole province. The territory of Caesarea included the toparchy of Narbata, inhabited by Jews;[2] to the south it reached as far as the Bdellopotamus River. The cities of Apollonia (Arsuf) on the coast and Antipatris (Rosh ha-'Ayin) further inland seem to have enjoyed autonomy, probably in a varying degree, for Apollonia was of old an autonomous city, whereas Antipatris was a foundation of Herod and was probably administered as part of the king's domain.

South of the Judaean city of Azotus lay two old Philistine cities, Ascalon and Gaza, which had become entirely Hellenized in the imperial period. Ascalon, an old 'ally and friend' of the Romans, remained entirely free even in the Hasmonaean period; Gaza, however, had been subjugated by Jannaeus, and later on by Herod; but after the king's death it became an autonomous city once more. Its territory included the satellite cities of Maiumas (the port of Gaza), Anthedon[3] and Raphia.

There were only two inland cities west of the Jordan: Sebaste and Scythopolis. Only the latter was part of the 'League of Ten Cities' (fourteen in fact) which continued into the early imperial era.[4]

[1] 'Itinerarium burdigalense', in P. Geyer ed., *Itinera Hierosolymitama* (1898), 19, 10.
[2] Jos. *War* II, 291, 509; *P. T. Berakoth* 10b.
[3] Jos. *Ant.* XIII, 357.
[4] Pliny, *Natural History* v, 74; Stephanus Byzantinus, s.a. Gerasa.

The division of the country into city areas and other regions which we have observed west of the Jordan also obtained east of it. There, however, the cities occupied a much more prominent place. In the north lay Paneas (Qisaryon, i.e. Caesarea Philippi),[1] which dominated the Ulatha valley; it was at that period regarded as part of Phoenicia and was visited by Jesus together with the territories of the other Phoenician cities, Tyre and Sidon.[2]

Along Lake Gennesaret, on its eastern shore, lay Hippos (Susitha). Its territory included Gergesa (Kursi) on the lake, which is regarded by many authorities as the site of the miracle of the 'Gadarene' swine.[3] (Gadara itself does not seem to have reached the lake, as Kefar Zemach [Samakh] is listed among the villages of Susitha-Hippos.)[4] Gadara (Umm Keis) was situated on a high mountain overlooking the Jordan Valley; its territory was extensive and it was the only one of the cities of Trans-Jordan which could boast of its own poets and philosophers.[5] Further inland we find Abila and Dion (Tell Abil and Tell Hamad). The city of Capitolias was founded in the time of the Emperor Nerva and did not, therefore, exist at the time of Jesus.[6] Going south we find the city of Pella (Fahil) which served as a place of refuge for the Christians of Jerusalem during the siege of Titus, then Gerasa (or as it was known officially: Antioch on the Chrysorrhoas)[7] which reached to the Jabbok river; the chain of autonomous cities ended with Philadelphia. The status of Heshbon and Medaba is not clear at that period; Heshbon was once one of Herod's military colonies but seems to have reverted to the Nabataeans after his death.[8]

The territories without city status east of the Jordan were mostly contained in the tetrarchy of Herod Philip. They included Gaulanitis, which extended east of Lake Gennesaret and comprised Bethsaida; this area was mainly inhabited by Jews who joined the rebels against Rome; in fact Gamala, the capital of Upper Gaulanitis, was one of

[1] Jos. *Ant.* XVIII, 28; *War* II, 168; Matt. 16:13; Mark 8:27; cf. *Ant.* XX, 211; *Life* 74.
[2] Matt. 15:21; Mark 7:31.
[3] Matt. 8:28; cf. 'Gergesa' in Mark 5:1, Luke 8:26; Origenes, *In Joannem* VI, 24. Recent excavations have proved the existence of a large monastery at Kursi.
[4] *T. Shebuoth* 4:10; *P. T. Demai* 22d.
[5] *Anthol. palat.* VII, 417-419 (Meleagros); Diogenes Laertes 6, 99-100 (Menippos); Philodemos (*ibid.*).
[6] B. C. Head, *Historia numorum*, 787; Ptolemaeus V, 14, 18.
[7] C. B. Welles ap. C. Kraeling (ed.), *Gerasa* (1938), p. 600.
[8] Jos. *Ant.* XV, 294.

the strongholds of the revolt and had to be subdued by a long and difficult siege.[1] Further east was Batanaea, also extensively inhabited by Jews, in particular the Babylonians settled there by Herod.[2] The two other areas belonging to Philip were Trachonitis, a wild volcanic region whose inhabitants were notorious robbers, and Hauranitis (Auranitis), which included a fertile plain and the mountainous region of the Hauran mountain. A series of inscriptions dated according to the Seleucid era, when compared with another set dated according to the era of the Province Arabia, enables us to fix with fair certainty the boundaries of Hauranitis and of the Nabataean kingdom.[3]

In addition to the political and city boundaries as described above there was another boundary which may go back to the period of the Second Temple. In a series of later Talmudic texts we find the description of an imaginary line 'held by those returning from Babylonian captivity', and within which the various prescriptions of rabbinical law referring to the 'Land of Israel' were applicable.[4] This line was intended to exclude the non-Jewish areas and is therefore a valuable indication of the extent of Jewish settlement. The line begins with the 'cross-roads of Ascalon' leaving the city itself outside. The 'Tower of Sharshon' (Caesarea) and Dora are also 'beyond the pale'; the line likewise ends with the 'walls of Accho'; and from there it continues along the road from Accho northwards to Kabritha (Kabri), and in a zig-zag line north-eastwards to Ijon (Merj 'Ayyun) in the Lebanon valley. We note that in this area the rabbinical boundary passes further north than the political boundary of Galilee, indicating that there were Jewish villages in the area of Tyre. East of the Jordan the line passes 'Qisaryon', (Caesarea Philippi); it includes Gaulanitis as far as Casphein, and most of Batanaea, but not Trachonitis. Canatha is on the boundary, as is Bezer (Bostra) and the 'great road running through the desert' from Bostra to Philadelphia. Heshbon and Moab are included probably because of biblical reminiscences, and the line follows the 'King's Way' south as far as Gaia near Petra; then it runs north and westwards along the fortified boundary (*limes*) to Raphia and the 'gardens of Ascalon'.

---

[1] Jos. *War.* IV, 4-8, 62-83.
[2] Jos. *Ant.* XVI, 285; XVII, 23-5; *War* III, 57.
[3] Waddington-le Bas, *Inscriptions*, 2242, 2299, 2309. E. Brünnow-A. Domaszewski *Provincia Arabia* III, (1904), pp. 268 ff.
[4] *T. Shebuoth* 4:11; *Sifre Ekeb* (Deut. 11:24) 51; *P. T. Shebuoth* 36c.

DEMOGRAPHY

While the boundary system of the time of Jesus can be reconstructed with fair certainty on the basis of earlier and later sources, we have very little information as to the actual composition of the population and its division into ethnic and religious groups. On the basis of the political division we can roughly separate the Jewish and non-Jewish areas, but without any assurance that these were continuous or that splinters of a different ethnic composition did not exist outside the compact areas of settlement of one group or another. If we take the Hasmonaean period as the basis from which to judge the time of Jesus three generations later, we can allow a compact Jewish population in Judaea proper, including Joppa, Jamnia and Azotus. For the latter two we can, however, assume a certain admixture of gentiles, as their territories were imperial estates, in which the upper administrative ranks were probably filled by non-Jews.[1] Under Herod there seems to have been an infiltration of Greeks into Jerusalem.[2] When Tiberias was founded, Herod Antipas also settled gentiles in the new city,[3] although it was—to judge from the coins struck there—a purely Jewish municipality; until the time of Trajan the coins struck at Tiberias were carefully designed to avoid the human image.[4] The same is true of the other great Galilean city, Sepphoris. It is first mentioned in our sources as a city which could be attacked on the Sabbath on the presumption that its inhabitants would neglect defence on a holy day.[5] Even after it had passed to the Romans in 67, the coins commemorating this change, struck by Vespasian's authority, were entirely aniconic.[6] The existence of royal (later imperial) estates in the Valley of Jezreel and of Asochis (Biqe'at Beth Natofah in the Talmudic sources) brought individual gentiles to reside there, such as possibly the 'king's man' at Cana[7] and certainly a Roman couple in the third century.[8] The population of Capernaum was also to some extent mixed; it was a town on the border of two regions: in the time of Jesus the tetrarchies of Antipas and his brother Philip, and later, Galilee and Gaulanitis; that there were customs collectors there is

---

[1] See p. 98, note 7.
[2] Jos. *Ant.* xvi, 301, for example.
[3] Jos. *Ant.* xviii, 37; *Life*, 67.
[4] A. Kindler, *Coins of Tiberias* (1961).
[5] Jos. *Ant.* xiii, 337.
[6] H. Hamburger *IEJ* (1970), p. 85.
[7] John 4:46.
[8] M. Avi-Yonah *QDAP* (1946), pp. 88 ff.

confirmed by the presence of a Roman centurion, probably a former legionary officer drilling native troops.[1] In his colonizing activity Herod was eclectic; he settled a mixed Judeo-Greek population at Caesarea,[2] Jews at Antipatris and in Batanaea, and gentile cavalry at his colony of veterans at Gaba.[3] We cannot tell how many of his foreign mercenaries, Germans, Gauls and Thracians, settled in the country after their discharge. Under Herod an increasing number of Jews seem to have settled in Ptolemais, Scythopolis, Hippos, Gadara and Gerasa.[4] The existence of Roman garrisons at Jerusalem and Caesarea under the procurators might have led to some gentile settlement even in the former city.[5] Roman veterans of several legions were settled by Claudius at Ptolemais, as is attested by the foundation coins of the colony on which standards of the legions appear along with the image of the founder ploughing.[6] The Jewish element in Jerusalem was continually strengthened by immigrants from other countries. Of the long list of pilgrims from various countries quoted in the New Testament[7]—Parthians, Medes, Elamites, Mesopotamians, Cappadocians, Pontians and Asians (i.e. inhabitants of the Roman province of Asia), Phrygians, Pamphylians, Egyptians, Cyreneans, Romans, Cretans and Arabs—some at least must have settled down permanently in Jerusalem. Babylonian Jews such as Hillel the Elder, and the royal family of Adiabene, came to live in Jerusalem at the same period.[8]

The lurid descriptions of Josephus should not mislead us into believing that Judaea and Galilee were emptied of their Jewish populations in the First Roman War. Even as regards Judaea, which was affected strongly by the Roman operations, the mere fact of the Bar-Cochba revolt sixty-two years after the destruction of the Second Temple is evidence enough that the Judaean peasantry continued to live in their villages. Careful reading of Josephus' story shows clearly that in Galilee, apart from a few specially affected strongholds such as Jotapata, Gamala and Tarichaeae, destruction cannot have been widespread; all these places were resettled and continued as Jewish towns, even if with a somewhat diminished status. Joppa is a special

[1] Matt. 8:5-13; Luke 7:2-10.
[2] Jos. *Ant.* xx, 173; *War* iii, 266.
[3] Jos. *Ant.* xv, 294; *War* iii, 36.
[4] Jos. *War* ii, 466, 477, 478, 480.
[5] Acts 10:1.
[6] Pliny, *Natural History* V, 75; Hill, *British Museum Coins. Phoenicia* (1910), pp. LXXXII ff.; M. Avi-Yonah, *QDAP* (1946), p. 86.
[7] Acts 2:9-11.
[8] Jos. *Ant.* xx, 2; *T. B. Pesahim* 66a.

case in point: it was destroyed in the course of the war not once but twice, but it was resettled each time and continued to be mainly Jewish into the third or fourth century.[1] The vicinity of Jerusalem was indeed strongly affected by the cutting of trees during the war and the expropriation of land after it; but apparently the former owners continued to till their estates as tenants of the imperial treasury. In Jerusalem in any case the Roman garrison, whose barracks included as usual married quarters, lived side by side with a few returned Jews and Judeo-Christians.[2] The gentiles withdrew after the outbreak of the Bar-Cochba revolt. Among the scrolls found in the Judaean desert there are references to the affairs of one Babatha, a Jewish widow, which show that in the south-east corner of Judaea at least relations between Jews and Nabataean Arabs were constant and friendly; in the documents addressed to the Roman authorities and in the sales contracts the names of the witnesses indicate a mixed population.[3] It also seems likely that gentiles took part in the Jewish struggle against the Romans and served in the army of Bar Cochba.

The fatal issue of the Bar-Cochba war brought about a radical change in the demography of Judaea. All the 'circumcised' (including Christians of Jewish origin) were expelled by Hadrian from the region of Jerusalem;[4] only in the extreme south, the so-called 'Daromas' —an area reaching from Engaddi on the Dead Sea to Gerara close to the Mediterranean coast—did Jewish villages survive into the fourth century.[5] The area emptied of Jews was settled by Syrians and Arabs.[6] Other Jewish villages were left in the Jordan valley for fiscal reasons; they were necessary to tend the balsam plantations, which were imperial property and highly valuable.[7]

On the coast, Jewish settlement continued from Jamnia northwards; indeed between the First and the Second War Jamnia became the spiritual centre of Judaism, the seat of the Patriarch and the Sanhedrin. In the plain of Sharon an area of mixed Jewish and Samaritan population ran parallel to the coastline, from Antipatris in the south to Kefar Parshay and Castra in the Carmel range.[8]

[1] Jos. War II, 508; III, 427.
[2] Epiphanius, De mensuris et ponderibus, 14, 15.
[3] Y. Yadin, IEJ 12 (1962), pp. 235 ff.
[4] Eusebius, Historia ecclesiastica IV, 6,3; R. Harris, HTR XIX (1962), pp. 199-206.
[5] Eusebius, Onomasticon 26, 8, 17; 92, 20; 98, 26; 108, 8.
[6] Eusebius, Historia ecclesiastica IV, 6,3.
[7] Eusebius, Onomasticon, 86, 16; 136, 24; Acta Sanctorum, 28.9, VII, 578.
[8] P. T. Hagigah 79b; T. B. Hagigah 25a.

In Samaria proper the Samaritans continued to constitute the majority of the rural population, even after the foundation of the city of Neapolis by Vespasian on the site of the village of Maabartha between the mountains Ebal and Gerizim.[1] The inhabitants of the city continued to worship on Mount Gerizim, either in the Hellenistic-Roman temple of Zeus Xenios on one of its peaks or the Samaritan shrine on the other. The Samaritans seem to have extended their settlement into the toparchy of Acraba which was detached by Vespasian from Judaea and included in the territory of Neapolis; this was presumably easier after the devastation of this region by the Roman troops in the First Revolt.[2] The presence of the Samaritan woman at Sychar (Askar) as evidenced by the New Testament[3] and the fights between Jews and Samaritans at Gineae[4] indicate the extent and density of the Samaritan population, which spilled over into the coastal area.

After the Bar Cochba war Galilee remained the main stronghold of Palestinian Judaism. Isolated Jewish settlements continued to exist on Carmel and in Ptolemais, Achzib and Scythopolis.[5] The migration of twenty-four priestly houses from Judaea to Galilee and their settlement in towns and villages there was an event commemorated in synagogal poetry and inscriptions for a long time.[6] The influx of Jews from Babylonia and Cappadocia into Galilee further served to strengthen the Jewish element there,[7] although some Syrians, Romans and Greeks lived at Tiberias even after this city had become the seat of the central Jewish authorities. The temporary handing over of the municipalities of Sepphoris and Tiberias into gentile hands, as evidenced in part by the coinage of these cities, did not last for long.

A modern description of the demography of a given area would conclude with an estimate of the number of the population and of its component ethnic elements. Unfortunately we do not possess enough reliable statistical material to give precise numbers for the population of Palestine in the period under discussion. The Jewish sources, such as Josephus and the Midrash, give grossly exaggerated figures;

[1] Pliny, *Natural History* V, 69; G. F. Hill, *British Museum Coins, Palestine* (1914), pp. XXVI ff.
[2] Jos. *War* IV, 487, 489.
[3] John 4:5.
[4] Jos. *War* II, 232.
[5] *P. T. Berakoth* 4d; *P. T. Shebuoth* 37a; *T. Terumoth* 2 end; *T. B. Megillah* 24b 24b; *M. Abodah Zarah* 1:4; *Menologium Basilii* (P. G. CXVII, 588).
[6] M. Avi-Yonah, *IEJ* (1962), pp. 137-139.
[7] *P. T. Shebuoth* 36d; *P. T. Yoma* 44b; *P. T. Shabbat* 8a.

thus Josephus implies that the population of Galilee in 67 C.E. amounted to three millions, and the *Midrash Rabba* gives the number of towns
in the coastal plain as 600,000.[1] Apart from these wild exaggerations
there are a number of data in ancient sources which can be utilized
for the purpose of estimating the true size of the population at given
periods; these can be combined with the evidence of archaeological
surveys. One such datum is the number of people returning from
Babylon, as listed by Nehemiah;[2] fifty thousand male adults would
mean a population of a quarter of a million for the whole of Judaea.
In Hasmonaean times Jonathan mobilized forty thousand men, which
suggests that by then the Jewish population had risen to half a million.[3]
In 66 C.E. Josephus raised sixty thousand men in Galilee, hence we
may suppose that the population of this province amounted to
about three quarters of a million.[4] The revenues of Galilee are given
as a fifth of the total revenue of Herod's kingdom;[5] we may therefore
conclude that the Jewish population in Palestine at the period discussed totalled about two and a half million. This assumption may
be further supported by Josephus' statement (in itself absurd) that
the number of pilgrims coming to Jerusalem at Passover was 2,700,000.[6]
If we assume that Josephus thought that every Jew in the country
scrupulously fulfilled his religious obligaton to go up to Jerusalem
every Passover, we can take this number as his estimate of the total
population of Judaea. Another figure that somewhat lightens the
statistical darkness of antiquity can be derived from the Syrian church
historian Bar Hebraeus, who says that the number of Jews in the Roman Empire under Claudius was 6,944,000.[7] As we know that there
were about a million Jews in Egypt, and a total of the rest of the
Diaspora within the boundaries of the empire cannot have exceeded
four million, we are left with roughly the same number for the population of Judaea, namely two and a half million. This maximum seems
to have shrunk to about one and a half million at the time of the
Bar Cochba war, and to about 800,000 after the war, taking into
consideration the number of killed in 132-135, which Dio Cassius
gives as 580,000.[8] The non-Jewish population may be roughly estimat-
ed at a million. It increased considerably to a maximum of about
three million in the Byzantine period. The partial archeological

---

[1] Jos. *Life* 235 and *War* III, 43; *Cant R.* I, 16.
[2] Neh. 7:66; Ezra 2:64.   [3] I Macc. 12:41.
[4] *War* II, 583. (But compare S. Safrai, *Pilgrimage in the Time of the Second Temple*
(1965 in Hebrew), pp. 24-41. Ed.).
[5] Jos. *War* II, 95.   [6] Jos. *War* VI, 425.   [7] Ed. Pocock, p. 73.   [8] LXIX, 14.

surveys carried out in various sections of Palestine both west and east of the Jordan[1] give a proportion of four to one for the Roman Byzantine period, as compared to the number of villages extant in 1900. As the population of the country at that date was about 700,000, living under conditions very similar to those prevailing in antiquity, we may assume that the ancient population of Judaea (and later on Palestina and Arabia) was about four times as numerous as that of the same area in 1900, i.e. that it amounted to about 2,800,000.

COMMUNICATIONS

The earliest roads in Palestine in pre-biblical and biblical times followed the geographical layout of the country and that of its neighbours. The two great international highways, which crossed Canaan and formed links in the land communications between the two great centres of Oriental culture, Egypt and Mesopotamia, were the coastal road (called in Crusader times the *via maris*, a name anachronistically adopted by biblical scholars) and the 'King's Highway' mentioned in connection with the route of the Exodus in its last stages. The coastal road ran from Damascus to one of the Jordan crossings north or south of Lake Gennesaret, and went on by way of the Jezreel Valley (a convenient gap between the mountains of Galilee and Samaria). It cut through the Carmel range at Megiddo, and continued from north to south along the foot of the hills facing the Mediterranean (the plain along the coast proper was impassable because of its swamps and dunes). It passed the famous cities of Philistia, from Azotus to Gaza, and continued to Egypt by way of the Sinai desert. The 'King's Highway' also began at Damascus and continued southwards across Trachonitis, Batanaea to Bostra, then to Rabbath Ammon, and along the cities of Moab and Edom as far as the Red Sea at Elath, from which it went across the Negev and Sinai to Egypt.

Apart from these two main lines of communication there were a number of minor roads of special local importance. The most famous of these was the 'Road of the Patriarchs', the watershed way which connected the Valley of Jezreel by way of Dothan, Shechem, Shiloh, Bethel, Gibeon, Jerusalem and Hebron with Beersheba and the southern wilderness road, also leading to Egypt.

Apart from these great lines of communication there existed of course

[1] A. Saarisalo, *JPOS* (1929), p. 27; *JPOS* (1930), pp. 5 ff. A. Bergman-R. Brandsteter, *BJPES* (1941), pp. 85-90; Tsori, *The Beth-Shean Valley* (1962).

innumerable local roads, linking the various cities of biblical times. Some of these were used as roads of invasion, such as the road leading from the coastal plain of Philistia to Jerusalem, which was used by Pharaoh Shishak, by the Philistines and by Sennecharib,[1] or the roads from the north-east by which the Assyrians invaded Samaria and Judah. These local roads continued to be used throughout the centuries down to the Roman period. Josephus attributes to Solomon the paving of the roads leading to Jerusalem,[2] but there is no actual evidence for such roadmaking before the arrival of the Romans. The various approaches to Jerusalem from the north (by way of Lebonah), from the west (the ascents of Beth Horon, Emmaus and the Elah Valley), and from the south (the watershed by way of Beth Zur) were used in succession by the Seleucid armies in their attempt to relieve Jerusalem, which was blockaded by the forces Judas Maccabaeus. When Judas went to the rescue of the Jews in Gilead, he was guided along the desert roads by the Nabataeans and retreated by way of Ephron and Beth Shean, crossing the Jordan on his way. The later battles of Judas Maccabaeus were all concentrated on the network of communications extending north and west of Jerusalem. When Tryphon invaded Judaea he used the coastal road and the southern approaches; John Hyrcanus advanced in the opposite direction northwards to Samaria and Beth Shean and southwards to Idumaea. The annexation of Lydda to Judaea gave the Hasmonaeans a foothold on the coastal road, which they strengthened considerably later on, while the occupation of Medaba and Samaga by John Hyrcanus gave them a corresponding position on the 'king's highway' which had remained in use throughout the centuries. The conquest of Gaza by Alexander Jannaeus cut the Nabataean highway from Elath and Petra to the Mediterranean shore; ample evidence of this road is to be found in the Nabataean potsherds. The route served in particular for the transport of the products of Arabia Felix to Greece and Italy and was enormously profitable.

Pompey's conquest was effected by an unusual road, running along the west side of the Jordan, from Scythopolis by way of Coreae to Jericho; Herod, in his flight in 40 B.C.E. before the advancing Parthian host, chose a desert road leading by way of Herodium to Oresa (Khirbet Khureisa) and then to Masada.

---

[1] 1 Kings 14:25-8; 2 Chron. 12:2-12; Shishak inscription at Karnak; Isaiah 10:27-32 (Sennacherib).
[2] Jos. *Ant.* VIII, 187.

The roads mentioned in the New Testament are part of the network of routes developed in the preceding centuries. Joseph and Mary would have gone from Nazareth to Bethlehem by way of the watershed road and Jerusalem, just as the flight to Egypt from Bethlehem was effected by way of Ascalon (which was outside Herod's jurisdiction) and the coastal road, rather than via Hebron, Beersheba and the desert—a difficult route for a new-born child and a woman just confined. From Egypt to Nazareth the coastal road and the *via maris* were used, with a side road leading to Sepphoris and Nazareth. In Galilee Jesus used part of the *via maris* to gain Capernaum and another section of the same road to reach Nain. The road from Sepphoris to Jotapata in Upper Galilee passed through Cana. Caesarea Philippi was linked with roads from Tyre and Sidon. In his pilgrimages to Jerusalem Jesus once (according to John 4:4) used the short cut through Samaria; but on the last journey he followed the circuitous route from Galilee into Peraea east of the Jordan, crossing the river at Jericho before going up to Jerusalem.

A radical change in the road system of Palestine came with the First Jewish War. In order to facilitate the movement of Roman troops between the main centres of Roman power in the Orient—Antioch and Alexandria—the Romans began to make a road from Antioch to Ptolemais as early as Nero's time[1] and probably continued it southwards; the march of Titus in 70 from Alexandria to Caesarea[2] served to determine the route of that road.

The fall of Jerusalem led to the establishment of the Tenth Legion (Fretensis) at Jerusalem, while its commander, the legate of the Provincia Judaea, resided at Caesarea. This anomalous arrangement was mitigated to a certain extent by the paving of a new road connecting Caesarea with Jerusalem by way of Antipatris and Gophna. It is possible that this was the road already followed by the apostle Paul when he was conveyed under arrest to Caesarea by way of Antipatris (Acts 23:31). Another road was made about the same time connecting Damascus with Scythopolis, Pella and Gerasa. The last section of this road was completed in 129 when Hadrian was planning his visit to Arabia and Judaea. In the meantime, however, the Romans executed an enormous feat of road-making by paving in 111-114 the *via nova* from Damascus and Bostra to Petra and Elath, which crossed the whole length of the Provincia Arabia (newly won by Trajan).

[1] P. Thomsen. *ZDPV* (1917), p. 18, § 9a[2] and Alt. ibid. (1928), pp. 253 ff.
[2] Jos. *War* IV, 649-663.

The establishment of a second legion, the Sixth (Ferrata – 'Iron-sides'), at Capercotni (later called Legio) under Trajan and Hadrian's visit to Judaea led to further expansion of the network of roads. One road was built from Heshbon by way of Livias to Jericho and Jerusalem, continuing along the way to 'Gaza which is desert' (Acts 8:26 – the now fashionable version 'this is a desert road' makes no sense; it was Gaza which was called 'desert 'in memory of its destruction by Jannaeus and as distinct from the 'New Town' or Neapolis on the shore). The *via nova* was connected with the Galilean network by a link between Gerasa and Philadelphia. The road from Caesarea through the Megiddo pass connected the capital of the province with the camp at Legio, and was continued to Sepphoris into the heart of Galilee.[1] It is quite possible that the existence of this road contributed decisively to the lack of enthusiasm in Galilee for the revolt of Bar Cochba.

Thus with the reign of Hadrian the main elements of the Roman network were completed; what remained was a series of secondary roads which served the cities of Sebaste and Neapolis, a shortcut from Neapolis to Scythopolis, the road from Ptolemais to Tiberias via Sepphoris, which bisected Galilee from west to east, and its continuation from Tiberias towards Damascus.

LATER TERRITORIAL CHANGES

We have seen that at the time of the outbreak of the war with Rome most of Judaea and Samaria, together with Idumaea and one third of Peraea, was administered by the Roman procurator of Judaea. The status of the cities of Ascalon and Gaza is not certain; it is quite likely that they were under the direct control of the legate of Syria. Scythopolis and the cities east of the Jordan which formed the Deca-polis certainly were under the legate at Antioch. Eastern Galilee (the territory of Tiberias and Tarichaeae), as well as Gaulanitis, Batanaea, Auranitis and Trachonitis were administered by King Agrippa II, who also held most of Peraea (the toparchies of Abila and Livias).[2] The coastal cities of Dora and Ptolemais were under the legate of Syria as governor of Phoenicia; the lands south of the line Gerara-Beersheba – Dead Sea – Arnon River – Philadelphia were held by the Nabataean kings, the allies and vassals of Rome.

[1] M. Avi-Yonah, *QDAP* (1946), pp. 96 ff; B. Lifshitz *Latomus* (1960), p. 109ff.
[2] Jos. *Ant.* xx, 159; *War* ii, 252.

The government of Jerusalem during the revolt had no opportunity in its tumultous history to bring about far-reaching administrative reforms. The area under its control included the whole of Judaea and Idumaea including the coastal plain between Azotus and Joppa, and also Peraea east of the Jordan. Samaria and the Decapolis, as well as Gaza and Ascalon, remained loyal to the Romans. The territory of the revolt was thus cut in two: the northern part—Galilee with Gaulanitis including the fortress of Gamala—was separated from the rest although communications passed fairly freely between the two areas. The leaders of the revolt appointed local commanders, thus effecting a rough division of the territory under their control. According to Josephus,[1] Joseph the son of Gorion, the High Priest Ananias, and Eleazar the son of Simeon were in charge of central affairs at Jerusalem; Jesus the son of Sapphas, Eleazar the son of Ananias and Niger the Peraite commanded in Idumaea; John the Essene at Joppa; John the son of Ananias in the Gophna-Acraba district; Joseph the son of Simeon at Jericho; and Manasseh in Peraea, while Galilee was entrusted to the historian himself. Besides these 'legitimate' commanders, Zealot leaders exercised local authority: John of Gischala in the north, Simeon the son of Gioras in his native Acrabatene, and Eleazar the son of Jair at Masada. These arrangements underwent many changes as the territory of the revolt gradually shrunk, until only the garrison of Masada, John of Gischala, and Simeon the son of Gioras at Jerusalem remained in effective control.

With the fall of Jerusalem and the abolition of the central Jewish administration (for the lower grades of local administration remained of necessity in the hands of the remaining native Judaeans) the whole of the area of revolt, together with the cities of Gaza, Ascalon, Scythopolis (as well as some of the cities of the Decapolis east of the Jordan such as Hippos, Gadara, Pella and Abila—possibly even Gerasa and Philadelphia) were placed under the new legate of Judaea, now of praetorian rank and commanding the Tenth Legion, Fretensis. The territory of Judaea was declared imperial property and handed over to the legion, but the lands were no doubt still worked by the Jewish peasants as tenants of the emperor. After the death of Agrippa II his share of Galilee and Peraea, as well as Gaulanitis, was added to Judaea.[2] This arrangement lasted until the revolt of Bar Cochba.

---

[1] Jos. *War.* II, 563-568.
[2] Hierocles, *Synecdemus*, 720, 1-6; his division into Palaestina Prima and Secunda reflects this change.

The Second Revolt seems to have spread to parts of Samaria and the whole of Judaea and Idumaea, but left Galilee only slightly affected. The rebel government soon established an orderly administration; we know from the documents found in the Judaean caves near the Dead Sea that there were local administrators at Herodium and Engaddi (former toparchy headquarters) who conducted business and leased out the former imperial estates in the name of 'Simeon Prince of Israel', dating them in the 'Year...of the Freedom of Israel'.[1] After the disaster of 70 C.E. the process of urbanization, which had begun under Pompey and the Herodians, went on apace. Vespasian declared the cities of Joppa and Neapolis municipalities in their own right; the former had but little territory, but the latter embraced all the Samaritan lands (together with the formerly Jewish toparchy of Acraba) which lay outside the city territory of Sebaste. In Nerva's time the city of Capitolias was founded east of the Jordan.[2] When the Nabataean kingdom was annexed by Trajan, and became the new Provincia Arabia in 106, the cities of Gerasa and Philadelphia were detached from Judaea (or Syria?) and added to the new province, while Petra the metropolis, Heshbon, Medaba and Rabbath Moba became municipal areas.

In Galilee the city of Sepphoris (probably called Diocaesarea after Hadrian ejected the Jewish city council, but certainly from the time of Antoninus Pius on) absorbed the toparchy of Araba. Tiberias, an autonomous city after the death of Agrippa II, received in addition to its own toparchy that of Tarichaeae. The imperial estates in the Valley of Jezreel (inherited from the Herodians) became the territory of the Sixth Legion and ultimately the lands of the city of Legio.

The final steps in the urbanization of Palestine (as the former province of Judaea was called after the revolt of Bar Cochba) were undertaken by Septimus Severus in 200 and Heliogabalus in 221. The former made Lydda into the city of Diospolis (endowing it with the toparchy of Thamna in addition to its own) and Beth Gubrin into Eleutheropolis (with a territory including all Idumaea as well as Bethletepha, detached from Jerusalem); the latter created the city of Nicopolis out of the toparchy of Emmaus. Thus finally only Upper Galilee (also called Tetracomia, the Land of the Four Villages), Gaulanitis, the imperial estates in the Jordan Valley (Peraea, Jericho), and Gerara escaped being turned into cities.

[1] Y. Yadin, *IEJ* (1962), p. 249.
[2] Head, *Historia numorum*, p. 786; Ptolemaeus V, 14, 18.

The whole of Syria Palaestina (or Palestine for short) was after Trajan administered by a legate of consular rank commanding two legions; this doubtful compliment being a result of its reputation as a province prone to revolt. Actually, however, a compromise between the revived Jewish authorities and the Roman government enabled the Jews of Galilee (who had regained control of the cities of Sepphoris and Tiberias) to lead a more or less peaceful life and to devote their energies to the spiritual task of elaborating the codes of Jewish law, the Mishnah and the Palestinian Gemara.

No further changes are known in the historical geography of Palestine until the beginning of the Byzantine period.

BIBLIOGRAPHY

F. M. ABEL: *Géographie de la Palestine*, 2 vols, 1933-8; A. ALT: *Kleine Schriften zur Geschichte des Volkes Israel*, 3 vols, 1953-9; M. AVI-YONAH: *Historical Geography of Palestine* (in Hebrew), 3rd ed., 1962; *The Holy Land from the Persian to the Arab Conquests*, 1966; F. BUHL: *Geographie des alten Palästinas*, 1896; G. DALMAN: *Orte und Wege Jesu*, 3rd ed., 1924; (English translation:) *Sacred Sites and Ways: Studies in the Topography of the Gospels*, 1935: A. SCHLATTER: *Zur Topographie und Geschichte Palästinas*, 1893; E. SCHÜRER: *Geschichte des jüdischen Volkes im Zeitalter Jesu Christi*, 3 vols, 3rd-4th ed., 1901-11; G. A. SMITH: *Historical Geography of the Holy Land*, 26th ed., 1935.

Chapter Three
The Jewish Diaspora

POPULATION FIGURES AND GEOGRAPHIC DISPERSION

One of the most characteristic features of the Second Temple period is that large numbers of Jews were living in the Diaspora. Some of the Diaspora communities were set up during the Babylonian exile and in the period of the Persian Empire. Some were established in the Hellenistic period, either as a result of direct emigration from Palestine or as offshoots of other Diaspora settlements.

Various factors contributed to the geographic dispersion of the Jews and the growth of the Diaspora communities: expulsion, political difficulties and religious persecution in Palestine, internal conflicts in Jewish society, and tempting economic prospects in new countries. The rapid population increase of the various Jewish communities has been remarked upon by Jews and gentiles alike.[1] Another major source of population increase was proselytism, which reached its peak in the first century C.E.

Most of the Diaspora Jews in this period were living within the Hellenistic-Roman sphere of influence. Before Rome had extended its domination to the East, they were the subjects of different states and rulers but from the time of Augustus, at the latest, they came under Roman rule, so that at home as well as in most of these settlements outside Palestine they were dependent on Roman government.

They remained free of Roman control only in Babylonia and in the rest of the Parthian Empire. These eastern Jews thus came to exert a major influence on the entire Jewish nation. It was only towards the end of Trajan's reign that the Jews living in these eastern territories were likewise faced with the threat of annexation to Rome. The danger soon passed, but not without much bloodshed among the large Jewish population living between the Euphrates and the Tigris. Sources from the Hellenistic period already dwell on the extensive dispersion of the Jewish people. According to the Jewish Sybil 'the

---

[1] Already in the Hellenistic age Hecataeus, in *Diodorus Siculus* XL, 3,8; see also Strabo, *Geography* XVI, 2, 28, p. 759; Philo, *Vita Mosis* II, 232; *In Flaccum*, 45; *Legatio*, 214, 245.

whole land shall be filled with you and the entire sea'.[1] Strabo, the historian and geographer of the Augustan period, stated that 'this people has already made its way into every city, and it is not easy to find any place in the habitable world which has not received this nation and in which it has not made its power felt'.[2] Philo gives the following interesting list: 'I must say, it is my home [sc. the Holy City, Jerusalem], and it is the capital not of the single country of Judaea but of most other countries also, because of the colonies which it has sent out from time to time to the neighbouring lands of Egypt, Phoenicia and Syria [the so-called Coele Syria as well as Syria proper], to the distant countries of Pamphylia, Cilicia, most of Asia as far as Bithynia and the remote corners of Pontus, and in the same way to Europe, to Thessaly, Boeotia, Macedonia, Aetolia, Attica, Argos, Corinth, and most of the best part of the Peloponnese. It is not only the continents that are full of Jewish colonies. So are the best known of the islands, Euboea, Cyprus, and Crete. I say nothing about the regions beyond the Euphrates. With the exception of a a small district, all of them, Babylon and those of the other satrapies which have fertile land around them, have Jewish settlers.'[3]

In describing the geographic dispersion of the Jews in his time, Philo thus notes the same Jewish centres that are also known to us from other sources: Egypt, Phoenicia and Syria, various parts of Asia Minor, Babylonia, and the remaining satrapies of the Parthian Empire. The various parts of Greece and the Greek islands are listed in particular detail, not so much because of the prominence of the Jewish settlements there, but rather in order to stress Greece in view of its place in the history of civilisation. It is interesting that no mention is made of the Jewish community of Rome proper, about which Philo speaks in a different context, nor of the Jews in Italy as a whole. Neither the western provinces nor the province of Africa are mentioned. Particularly surprising is the omission of the major Jewish settlement in Cyrenaica about which we have much information from this period.[4]

---

[1] *Oracula Sibyllina* III, 271; on the date of the third book see O. Eissfeldt, *Einleitung in das Alte Testament* (3rd ed. 1964), p. 835; V. Nikiprowetzky, *La troisième Sibylle* (1970), pp. 195-225.
[2] Strabo in Jos. *Ant.* XIV, 115. I have adopted here the translation of R. Marcus. See also M. Stern in *Essays in Jewish History and Philology in Memory of Gedaliahu Allon* (in Hebrew, 1970), p. 172.
[3] Philo, *Legatio*, 281-2.
[4] It is true that in *Legatio*, 283 Philo speaks of the three continents Europe, Asia and Libya (= Africa); however, Egypt too is included in the last-mentioned

In another work, Philo again refers to many countries in Europe and Asia containing Jewish settlements on the islands and on the mainland.[1] In addition to these passages from Philo we must also consider the famous passage from the Acts of the Apostles.[2] Among those who came to Jerusalem for the Feast of Pentecost, mention is made here of pilgrims from Parthia, Media, Elam, Mesopotamia, Cappadocia, Pontus, the province of Asia, Phrygia, and Pamphylia, Egypt, Cyrenaica, Rome, Crete and Arabia.[3]

These sources present a picture of a huge Jewish population in Palestine, in the eastern provinces of the Roman Empire and in the Parthian Empire. There are, however, only a few indications of its actual size. Most of the data relating to Palestine are known to be exaggerated.[4] As one of the reasons why Petronius, the governor of Syria, was reluctant to antagonize the Jews, Philo mentions their numerical strength. 'He had also in mind the vast numbers of the Jewish nation, which is not confined, as every other nation is, within the borders of the one country assigned for its sole occupation, but occupies also almost the whole world. For it has overflowed across every continent and island, so that it scarcely seems to be outnumbered by the native inhabitants.'[5] For the contemporary Jewish community of Egypt Philo cites a figure of one million.[6] We also have some data relating to the Jews of Rome: according to Josephus, eight thousand of them took part in the demonstration designed to dissuade Augustus from bequeathing Judaea to the sons of Herod.[7] In 19 C.E., four thousand Jews of military age were dispatched from Rome to Sardinia as part of the contingent assigned to keep order on that island, the real reason being that the emperor wanted to have them removed from Rome (see below p. 164). After the Great

continent, and thus there is no reason to look here for an allusion to another province situated in Africa.
[1] Philo, *In Flaccum*, 45-6.
[2] Acts 2:9-11.
[3] Cf. also Jos. *War* VII, 43.
[4] Exaggerated numbers concerning the population of Judaea at the end of the period of the Second Temple: Jos. *War* II, 280 (cf. *T. B. Pesahim* 64 b); III, 43; VI, 420; *Life*, 235; Tacitus, *Histories* v, 13, 3. More reality attaches to the number of the defenders of Jerusalem during the siege, as emerges from Jos. *War*; v, 248-250 (23,400).
[5] Philo, *Legatio*, 214; see also *Vita Mosis* II, 27.
[6] Cf. *In Flaccum*, 43. Juster I, p. 209 and A. v. Harnack, *Die Mission und Ausbreitung des Christentums in den ersten drei Jahrhunderten*, (4th ed. 1924), p. 11, accept the evidence. Tcherikover, 'Prolegomena', p. 4 expresses doubts.
[7] Jos. *Ant.* XVII, 300; *War* II, 80.

MAP IV. THE DIASPORA. FIRST CENTURY B.C.E.

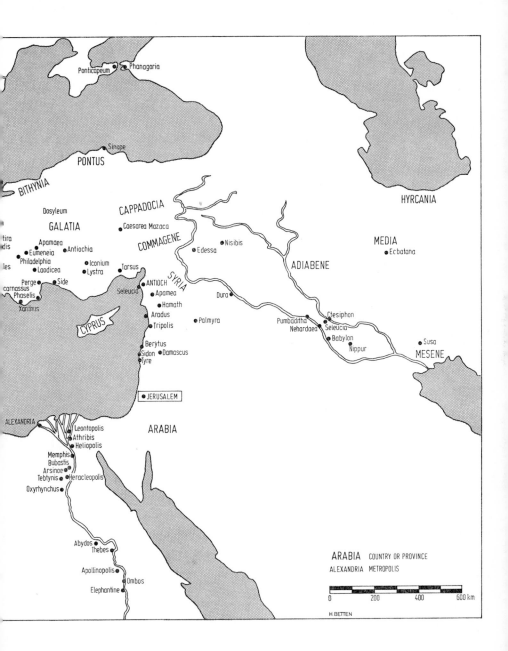

PONTUS

BITHYNIA

Ponticapeum • Phanagoria

Sinope •

HYRCANIA

CAPPADOCIA

Dosyleum

GALATIA   • Caesarea Mazaca

COMMAGENE   • Nisibis   MEDIA

tira   Apamaea   • Edessa   • Ecbatana
idis   • Eumeneia   • Antiochia
     Philadelphia   • Iconium   ADIABENE
les   • Laodicea   • Lystra   Tarsus •
     Perge •   • Side   • ANTIOCH   SYRIA
carnassus   Seleucia   • Apamea   Dura •
    Phaselis •   • Hamath   Ctesiphon
    Xanthus •   Aradus •   Pumbaditha • • Seleucia
                    CYPRUS   • Tripolis   • Palmyra   Nehardaea •   Babylon •
                                                                            Nippur •   • Susa
                                   Berytus •   MESENE
                                 Sidon • • Damascus
                                   Tyre •

                                   • JERUSALEM

ALEXANDRIA •   ARABIA
          • Leontopolis
          • Athribis
          • Heliopolis
    Memphis •
    Bubastis •
    Arsinoe • •
Tebtynis • • Heracleopolis
Oxyrhynchus •

    Abydos •
       Thebes •   ARABIA   COUNTRY OR PROVINCE
                                   ALEXANDRIA   METROPOLIS
 Apollinopolis •
           • Ombos |0   200   400   600 km|
    Elephantine •

                                   H. BETTEN

I2I

Revolt, three thousand wealthy Jews were arrested in Cyrene (see below, p. 135).[1] Of the cities of Syria and Asia, Philo says that they were full of vast numbers of Jews;[2] Josephus had also noted that Syria had more Jews than any other country because of its proximity to Judaea.[3] It is also instructive that in Trajan's reign the Jews of Egypt, Cyrenaica and Cyprus were able to conduct a protracted war against the Roman Empire and the gentile population. Undoubtedly the numerical strength of the Jews in the Roman Empire was considerable, but it is impossible to arrive at an actual estimate nor is there any firm basis for assessing their share in the total population of the Roman Empire.[4] It is also difficult to assess the relative proportions of Jews living in the Diaspora and those in Palestine. We shall, however, not be far out in saying that the total Jewish population of the Roman Empire outside Palestine, and of the Parthian Empire, including the huge Jewish community of Babylonia, considerably exceeded the number of Jews living in their homeland.

EGYPT

The Jewish community of Egypt was the greatest of the major Jewish Disaspora centres in the Roman Empire. Jews had already settled in Hellenistic times throughout Lower and Upper Egypt and filled an important function in the economic and political life of the Ptolemaic kingdom. Thus Philo says: 'They were resident in Alexandria and the country from the slope into Libya to the boundaries of Ethiopia.'[5] The proportion of Jews was particularly high in the city of Alexandria where they were concentrated in two of

---

[1] Jos. *War* VII, 445 (according to the majority of Mss.)
[2] Philo, *Legatio*, 245.
[3] Jos. *War* VII, 43. Harnack, op.cit. p. 11, n. 4 estimates the number of Syrian Jews at a million.
[4] Juster I, 210 estimates the number of the Jews in the Roman Empire, including Palestine, till 70 C.E. at six or seven millions; Harnack, op.cit., p. 13 thinks that the Jews constituted seven per cent of the population of the empire. Against the validity of the number of Jews under Claudius adduced by Bar-Hebraeus, cf. J. Rosenthal, *Jewish Social Studies* (1954), pp. 267-8. S. W. Baron, *A Social and Religious History of the Jews*, I (1952) pp. 170-1 thinks that the Jews reached at that period the number of eight millions and that every tenth person among the population of the Roman Empire was a Jew, while in the Hellenistic East every fifth was a Jew.
[5] *In Flaccum*, 43.

its five sections: in the Delta and in another quarter that is difficult to identify.[1] They also lived in the remaining three quarters, and Jewish synagogues were to be found throughout the city.[2] At least ten papyri relating to the contemporary life of the Jews of Alexandria were discovered in Abusir el-Meleq.[3]

Another major Jewish centre was in the nome of Heliopolis around the Temple of Onias. A long series of inscriptions from Leontopolis (Tel el-Yehudieh) illustrate their life and culture in this area in the time of Augustus.[4] Papyri dating from the first and the early second century C.E. testify to the presence of Jews in some of the provincial towns and villages of Egypt, particularly in Fayum which already had a major Jewish population in the Ptolemaic period, especially in Euhemeria, Philadelphia, Apollonias, Bacchias, and Arsinoe.[5] Mention should also be made of Oxyrhynchus in Middle Egypt,[6] Hermopolis Magna and Ptolemais Hermaeu.[7] Numerous ostraca from Apollinopolis Magna (i.e. Edfu) in Upper Egypt deal with the 'Jewish Tax' imposed by Vespasian after the destruction of the Temple and other taxes payable by the Jews of Edfu.[8] It seems that in this town they chose to live in a special quarter.[9] Neither here nor elsewhere in Egypt, not in the ancient world generally, can the neighbourhoods in which the Jews tended to concentrate be regarded as ghettos. Except during a short interval when they were confined to one of the quarters of Alexandria by the order of the Roman prefect Flaccus, their choice of residence was voluntary (see below, p. 127).

In late Ptolemaic times the Jews of Egypt had already entered into close political contacts with Rome. They also helped the Roman commanders, Gabinius and Julius Caesar, in their Egyptian campaigns. Special importance attached to the fact that the Jews were located at the gateways to Egypt. Hyrcanus II, the high priest and ethnarch of Judaea, who exercised considerable influence over the Jews of

---

[1] On the concentration of the Jews in the Delta see Josephus, *War* II, 495; according to Philo, *In Flaccum* 55, two of the five quarters of Alexandria were labelled Jewish.
[2] Philo, *Legatio*, 132.
[3] *CPJ* nos. 142-9, 151-2.
[4] *C II* nos. 1450-1530; see also D. M. Lewis, *CPJ* III, pp. 144-163.
[5] *CPJ* nos. 409, 411, 413, 416, 420-1, 427, 430, 432-3; cf. also nos. 428, 431, 434.
[6] *CPJ* nos. 410, 414, 422-3, 425.
[7] *CPJ* nos. 412, 424.
[8] *CPJ* nos. 160-229, 236-374.
[9] On the Jews of Edfu see the introduction to *CPJ* II, Section IX, pp. 108-119.

Egypt, sent out letters urging them to help his Roman allies.[1] It is hard to assess to what degree the help extended by the Jews to the Romans during their first attempt to gain a foothold in Egypt affected subsequent relations with the Greeks of Alexandria since Rome's intervention at that time was not designed to annex Egyptian territory but only to further the aims of one of the claimants to the Ptolemaic throne.[2] With the full annexation of Egypt by Octavian in 30 B.C.E. as a result of his victory over Antony and Cleopatra, Jewish affairs in Egypt also came under review. Octavian on the whole reaffirmed their privileges in the matter of religion and self-government, and to lend special emphasis to this measure a stele was erected, enumerating the rights of the Jews in Alexandria. Josephus afterwards erroneously attributed this stele to Julius Caesar, who never had the formal authority to grant such rights since Egypt in the time of Caesar was not yet part of the Roman Empire.[3] Augustus also concerned himself with the internal organization of the Jewish community of Alexandria. While during the early days of his reign the Jews of Alexandria were presided over by an ethnarch,[4] Augustus eventually approved a reform of the community government (πολίτευμα), transferring most of the prerogatives of the late ethnarch—probably the last of the House of Onias—to a Jewish *gerousia*.[5]

The Roman takeover led to some deterioration in Jewish-Greek relations in Egypt as a whole, and in Alexandria in particular. The new regime tried to redefine the various classes if the population and to establish stable social and organizational patterns for the new province. The distinctions between the citizens of the Greek towns, the Hellenes of the provincial towns and villages, and the native population were emphasized. Personal status also impinged on the rights and

---

[1] Jos. *Ant.* XIV, 99, 131.
[2] Tcherikover, 'Prolegomena', pp. 55-6.
[3] Th. Reinach, *REJ* LXXIX (1924), p. 123.
[4] Strabo, in Jos. *Ant.* XIV, 117.
[5] Philo, *In Flaccum*, 74. Contrary to Strabo and Josephus, Philo called the leader of the Jewish community 'head of the nation' (γενάρχης). He also dates the reform of the organization of the Jewish community by Augustus to the time when Magius Maximus was to be appointed prefect of Egypt for the second time (i.e. 11-12 C.E.); cf. A. Stein, *Die Präfekten von Ägypten in der römischen Kaiserzeit* (1950), pp. 22-3. Cf. also P. M. Fraser, *Ptolemaic Alexandria* II (1972), pp. 73-4, 1109. It is true that we learn from the edict of Claudius, Jos. *Ant.* XIX, 283, that when the ethnarch died in 10-11 C.E. Augustus did not prevent the Jews from having another ethnarch. However, in view of Philo's statement, we have to suppose that there were changes which in any case weakened the position of the ethnarch in his relation to the *gerousia*.

duties of the individual vis-à-vis the Roman rulers and determined in particular the rate of poll tax (λαογραφία) levied by the Romans in Egypt. The citizens of the Greek cities were exempt while the Hellenes of the provincial towns paid a lower rate. For the Jews the matter of their personal status was therefore of considerable importance, and they seem to have been resolved to hold out for equal status with the Greeks and for being considered citizens of Alexandria.[1] At the same time the Greeks of Alexandria redoubled their efforts to deprive the Jews even of the privileges they had as compared with the indigenous Egyptian population. The Roman government failed to define the status of the Jews, merely keeping the *status quo* which, under the changed circumstances of Roman rule, may already have assumed a somewhat different significance. Jewish-Greek tension in Alexandria was exacerbated by the resistance of the Alexandrian Greeks put up against the Roman emperors, as reflected in the *Acta Alexandrinorum*. In Greek Alexandria, the gymnasiarchs stood out as the acknowledged spokesmen and leaders of Greek society. They were the chief adversaries of the Roman emperors and of the Jews who were regarded as the emperors' protégés.[2] Little is known about events pertaining to the Jews of Alexandria from the reign of Augustus until the accession of Gaius. Only one episode has been preserved, connected with the visit of Germanicus to Egypt in 19 C.E.[3] When distributing grain to the citizens of Alexandria to tide them over the prevailing famine, he left out the Jews whom he apparently did not consider an integral part of the citizenry.[4] Jewish-Greek tension in Alexandria assumed new dimensions in the times of Gaius Caligula, when the first violent eruption took place, also representing the first major anti-Jewish riots to be recorded in Roman territory. The only possible parallel that can be cited was the slaughter that took place in Seleucia on the Tigris during the disintegration of the Parthian Empire (see below p. 179). The riots in Alexandria marked the first break between the Jews of the Hellenistic Diaspora and the imperial regime. Consequently, the division between

---

[1] Tcherikover, 'Prolegomena' pp. 55-65.
[2] H. A. Musurillo, *The Acts of the Pagan Martyrs*, (1954); *CPJ* nos. 154-9.
[3] Jos. *Against Apion* II, 63. See on the visit of Germanicus to Egypt C. Cichorius, *Römische Studien* (1922), pp. 375-388; E. Koestermann, *Historia* (1958), pp. 348-351; J. van Ooteghem, *Les études classiques* (1959), pp. 241-251.
[4] The explanation put forward by Josephus does not carry conviction; cf. U. Wilcken, *Hermes* (1928), pp. 51-2; D. G. Weingärtner, *Die Ägyptenreise des Germanicus* (1969), pp. 91-9; D. Hennig, *Chiron* (1972), pp. 362-3.

the Greek and Jewish residents of Alexandria became more pronounced and the Jewish community with the assistance of non-Alexandrian and even non-Egyptian Jews organized for its self-defence. The clash itself was initiated by the Greeks who were making use of the special political conjuncture that arose with the accession of Gaius Caligula to the imperial throne in 37 C.E.[1]

Avilius Flaccus was at that time governor of Egypt. One of Tiberius' friends, he had held this office since 32 C.E., and according to Philo had distinguished himself during the first five years by thorough and energetic law enforcement, surpassing his predecessors both in resolution and fairness.[2] As he had had a hand in the intrigues against Agrippina, the mother of Gaius, the death of Tiberius and the accession of Gaius came as a serious personal blow. For some time he still fostered some hopes that his connections with Macro, the commander of the Praetorian guard in Rome who had done much to bring about Gaius' accession, might be of help to him. When Macro lost his position, Flaccus was deprived of his last source of support at the imperial court and had much to fear for his future. This was the occasion used by the leaders of the Greeks in Alexandria, among whom the most notable were Dionysius, Lampon and Isidorus. Lampon had previously been involved in a trial by the Roman authorities but was acquitted and appointed gymnasiarch. Isidorus was the prime mover in the various associations and clubs in the city and after an open conflict with Flaccus had been temporarily forced to leave Alexandria. These Greek leaders now offered the governor an alliance with the Greeks of Alexandria, who would intercede on his behalf at the imperial court, provided he decided in their favour in their conflict with the Jews.[3] Flaccus consequently embarked on an anti-Jewish policy. Discrimination against Jews who were parties to the court cases heard by him was the first step.[4] Some time afterwards Agrippa I, who had been appointed by Gaius as ruler of the former territories of Philip, disembarked in Alexandria on his way from Italy and stayed there as the guest of the Jewish community.

---

[1] See for the narrative of the events A. Bludau, *Juden und Judenverfolgungen im alten Alexandreia* (1906), pp. 66-88; H. I. Bell, *Juden und Griechen im römischen Alexandreia* (1926), pp. 16-24; Tcherikover, 'Prolegomena', pp. 65-6.
[2] *In Flaccum*, 8; cf. Stein, op.cit., pp. 26-7.
[3] See for an interview of Alexandrian leaders with Flaccus P. Oxy. no. 1089 in H. A. Musurillo, *The Acts of the Pagan Martyrs*, 1954, no. II, and *CPJ* no. 154. See also H. I. Bell, *JJP* (1950), pp. 27-9.
[4] Philo, *In Flaccum*, 10-24

The arrival of a Jewish king infuriated the Greeks, and they did all they could to humiliate and embarass him. A known lunatic, one Carabas, was dragged to the gymnasium and given a mock reception as Agrippa, the King of the Jews. Not satisfied with venting their hatred in this symbolic fashion, the crowds stormed the synagogues and with the approval of Flaccus put up pagan idols inside them. By then Flaccus had both feet in the anti-Jewish camp. He expressly declared the Jews to be foreigners in Alexandria and expelled them from four of its five sections, ordering them to concentrate in the fifth, which in fact meant the establishment of the first ghetto; for until then, whenever Jews had to settle in a particular area, they had always done so of their own choice. The Alexandrian mob plundered the houses vacated by the Jews who had been forced to move out and the stores which were closed in mourning for the death of Drusilla, the emperor's sister. It was, however, not only the loss of their property that made the material conditions of the Jews unbearable, but the fact that they could no longer pursue their normal occupations which required their presence in all parts of the city.[1] Expulsion, robbery, and looting were accompanied by widespread murder of Jews. The governor moreover had thirty-eight of the Jewish council members arrested and put in chains.[2] Thus shackled, they were hauled through the market place to the theatre where they were flogged in front of their enemies. Several died under the beating. Flaccus also ordered Jewish homes to be ransacked for arms.[3]

Some relief came in the autumn of 38 C.E., with the arrival of an imperial delegate at the head of a military detachment, who dismissed Flaccus from office and dispatched him to Rome. There his former confederates, Lampon and Isidorus, also turned against him. He was found guilty by an imperial court, his property was confiscated and he was banished to Andros, where he was eventually executed at the emperor's command.[4] Vitrasius Pollio was appointed governor of Egypt in his stead.[5] Though the tension between Greeks and Jews was somewhat allayed, still no clear decision was taken on the legal

[1] *In Flaccum*, 25-57; *Legatio*, 120-135.
[2] Bell, *Juden und Griechen*, p. 21 thinks that the specific accusation raised against the members of the Jewish *gerousia* was connected with the refusal to grant divine honours to the emperor.
[3] Philo, *In Flaccum* 58-94; cf. also a papyrus dated to 34-5 C.E., prohibiting the bearing of arms; cf. L. Mitteis and U. Wilcken, *Grundzüge und Chrestomathie der Papyruskunde* I,2 (1912), no. 13.
[4] Philo, *In Flaccum*, 108-190.
[5] Stein, op.cit., pp. 28-9.

status of the Jews in Alexandria. We also have no information as to what happened about the synagogues which had been profaned and the confinement of the Jews into a single quarter. It seems reasonable to assume that they already returned to the rest of the city during Gaius Caligula's reign and resumed their share in its economic life, but relations remained strained. In the meantime the Jews used the period of respite to consolidate their forces and make ready for the next onslaught.

The decision on the status of the Jews in Alexandria was left to the emperor. Vitrasius Pollio allowed two delegations, one Jewish and one Greek, to be sent from Alexandria, which apparently left for Rome in the winter of 38-39 or 39-40 C.E. Among the most prominent members of the Greek delegation were Isidorus and Apion. The five Jewish delegates included the philosopher Philo, who has also left us a detailed description of the meeting with the emperor. The Greeks of Alexandria had an important ally in Helicon, one of the imperial favourites who was born in Egypt. The emperor was also likely to remember the friendly attitude of Greek Alexandria towards his father Germanicus, who had cold-shouldered the Jews. They could further invoke Jewish opposition to the worship of the emperor which Gaius took in all its seriousness.

The representatives of the Jews intended to submit a memorandum describing their sufferings and setting out their claims. The first meeting with the emperor was very short. He merely answered their greetings and told them he would listen to their arguments as soon as he had time for them . The principal meeting took place only after a considerable delay. The Jews were accorded a cool reception as men who refused to recognize the emperor's divinity. Isidorus, the representative of the Alexandrian Greeks, had managed to stir up the emperor's anger, to the extent that Philo and his colleagues were in fear for their lives, and heaved a deep sigh of relief when they were dismissed with the words: 'I think that these men are not so much criminals as lunatics in not believing that I have been given a divine nature.'[1]

At the death of Gaius on 24 January 41 C.E. the two delegations were still in Rome. The decision now devolved upon the new emperor, Claudius. That King Agrippa had helped Claudius to the throne certainly was a major advantage for the Jews of Alexandria, along with the influence he continued to exert in their favour. Claudius'

[1] Philo, *Legatio*, 166-183, 349-372; Jos. *Ant.* XVIII, 257-260.

decision, which has been substantially preserved in Josephus' *Anti-quities*,[1] and is also alluded to in the emperor's letter to the city of Alexandria,[2] restored to the Jews of Alexandria the privileges accorded to them in the Ptolemaic period and initially upheld by the Romans as well. Claudius also appealed to both parties to abstain from any rioting upon the publication of his edict. It should be noted that the edict contains no provision granting the Jews full citizenship rights in Alexandria. The only possible hint in that direction is the reference in the preamble to the Jews having enjoyed: ἴση πολιτεία at the time of the Ptolemaic kings. This need, however, not be necessarily interpreted to mean personal citizenship status but may relate to the general legal and organizational privileges of the Jewish *politeuma* which were equivalent to the collective rights enjoyed by the Greek polis in Alexandria.[3]

On the same occasion Claudius also issued an edict to all the Jews of the empire by which they were assured the undisturbed right to the full observance of their ancestral customs. At the same time the emperor also exhorted the Jews to practise moderation and confine themselves to keeping their own customs without offending the religious sensibilities of others.[4]

To this series of events also belongs the trial of the gymnasiarchs, Isidorus and Lampon, who had been so active in Caligula's time. Isidorus had also occupied a prominent position in the anti-Jewish Alexandrian delegation to Rome. Information about this trial has come down to us through the *Acta Alexandrinorum (Acta Isidori)*.[5] From these papyri we gather that Isidorus had been instrumental in having some of Claudius' friends, including Macro, the commander of the Praetorian guard, sentenced to death.[6]

---

[1] Jos. *Ant.* XIX, 280-5.
[2] *CPJ* no. 153, ll. 87-8.
[3] On the edict see M. Engers, *Klio* XVIII pp. 88-9; XX, 174-176. In the last article Engers defends the authenticity of the edict and expresses the view that the letter of Claudius to the Alexandrians reflects a change in the policy of Claudius concerning the Jews. On the other hand, Reinach, op.cit., pp. 125-6 maintains that the edict was interpolated. The most sceptical scholar here is Tcherikover, *Hellenistic Civilization*, pp. 409-415.
[4] Jos. *Ant.* XIX, 286-291.
[5] Musurillo, op.cit., no. IV, or *CPJ*, no. 156.
[6] The majority of scholars are of the opinion that the Agrippa concerned is Agrippa II and that consequently the document should be dated to 53 (or 52) C.E.; see L. Fuchs, *Die Juden Aegyptens in ptolemäischer und römischer Zeit* (1924), p. 22; G. de Sanctis *Rivista di Filologia* (1924), pp. 488-9; Reinach, op.cit., p. 141; H. Stuart Jones, *JRS* (1926), pp. 32-4; Bell, op.cit., pp. 28-30

Alexandria in the meantime was in a state of uproar caused by Claudius' accession. This time the Jews were taking the initiative. Claudius ordered the governor of Egypt to suppress the riots. The tense conditions prevailing in Alexandria at that time are reflected in an extant letter on papyrus written in August (41 c.e.).[1] The writer, a resident of the Egyptian countryside, warned his correspondent in Alexandria to beware of the Jews. Apparently the addressee had taken a loan from a Jewish financier, and such contacts with Jews seemed dangerous to the author of the letter.[2]

As in the time of Gaius, two delegations, one of the Greeks and one of the Jews, went to Rome to congratulate the emperor on his accession and put their respective demands and 'complaints before him. Nothing is known about the composition of the Jewish embassy, but of the Greek we possess the full list of the twelve members. It was headed by Tiberius Claudius Barbillus, a friend of Claudius who was at a later date nominated Prefect of Egypt (55-59 c.e.).[3] Claudius' reply to the Alexandrian delegation, which also includes his message to the Jews, has been preserved in a payrus copy of his original letter which was discovered in Philadelphia, in Fayum.[4] The exact date of Claudius' letter has not been preserved. All we have is the date of the edict of the Egyptian governor, Aemilius Rectus, relating to the publication of the emperor's letter, namely, 10 November 41 c.e. A considerable portion of this letter (lines 72-104) deals with the relations between the Greeks and Jews in Alexandria. Claudius refrained from blaming either party for the riots 'or rather, the war conducted against the Jews,' although he had heard the arguments of both parties and Dionysius, the son of Theon, one of the Greek delegates, had pleaded vigorously and responsibly on behalf of the Alexandrians. Noting that he abstained from conducting a thorough enquiry, Claudius warned that whoever dared renew the conflict

and *JJP* (1950), pp. 31-4; A. v. Premerstein, *Hermes* (1932), pp. 174-196; Musurillo, op.cit., pp. 118-124. Bludau, op.cit. pp. 101-4 hesitates, though preferring the connection with the events of 38 c.e. The arguments for the identification with Agrippa I and for 41 c.e. are adduced by Tcherikover, *CPJ* II, pp. 68-9.

[1] *BGU* no. 1079 and *CPJ* no. 152..
[2] See also Dessau, *Kaiserzeit* II, 2, p. 667, n. 3 (against the view that a Jewish usurer is implied).
[3] For the problem of the identification of Barbillus, see H. G. Pflaum, *Les carrières procuratoriennes équestres sous le Haut-Empire romain* I (1960), pp. 34-41.
[4] Cf. P. London no. 1912 in H. I. Bell, *Jews and Christians in Egypt* (1924), p. 23-6 and *CPJ* no. 153.

would feel the impact of his fury. He called upon the Alexandrians to behave gently and humanely towards the Jews, who had been living in that city for a long time, and not to interfere with any matter relating to their religion but to allow them to keep the customs which they had observed in the times of Augustus, as Claudius himself had already stated in his previous edict likewise issued after hearing both parties. He ordered the Jews not to arrogate to themselves any further privileges in Alexandria beyond those they had been enjoying since ancient times, and warned them from sending a separate delegation in the future,[1] and from taking part in the games conducted under the supervision of the gymnasiarchs and cosmetes (κοσμητής),[2] because they should be satisfied with the prosperity they were enjoying in a foreign city.

The fact that Claudius forbade the Jews to participate in the games and called Alexandria a foreign city supports the view that he had not accorded them citizenship rights.[3]

Claudius further warned the Jews of Alexandria against bringing in Jews from Egypt and Syria. They were to obey his instructions under pain of serious measures being taken against them when they would be treated like a pestilence that threatens the world. There is, however, no reason to construe this as a reference to Christianity as some scholars are inclined to do.[4]

The settlement imposed by Claudius remained in force for several decades, and until the Jewish Revolt of 66 c.e. we hear of no upheavals connected with the Jews of Alexandria. In that year, however, the

---

[1] W. Otto, *Berliner Philologische Wochenschrift* (1926), p. 12 holds the view that the two embassies implied there are Jewish, but does not define their nature. On the other hand, H. Willrich, *Hermes* (1925), pp. 482-8 thinks that one of them represented the orthodox and the other the Hellenized part of the community. See also H. Stuart Jones, op.cit. pp. 25-6; Bell, *Juden und Griechen*, pp. 26-7; S. Lösch, *Epistula Claudiana* (1930), p. 11, n. 1; Tcherikover, *CPJ* II, pp. 50-3. Against the theory of two Jewish embassies cf. R. Laqueur *Historische Zeitschrift* CXXXVI (1927), p. 251, n. 1.

[2] This is the common interpretation (Bell, Tcherikover). Cf. also W. Schubart, *Gnomon* (1925), p. 33, n. 2; E. G. Turner, *JRS* (1954), p. 58; a different translation is given by De Sanctis, op.cit., p. 507; M. Radin, *Classical Philology* (1925), p. 370.

[3] See e.g. Tcherikover, *CPJ* II, p. 53.

[4] Some scholars connect this expression of Claudius with the diffusion of Christianity. So e.g. G. de Sanctis, op.cit., pp. 512-513; S. Reinach, *Revue de l'histoire des religions* XC (1924), pp. 108-122. This view has not much to commend it. Cf. Ch. Guignebert, *Revue de l'histoire des religions* XC (1924), pp. 123-132; Lösch, op.cit., pp. 12-24; W. Seston, *Revue de l'histoire et de philosophie religieuses* (1931), pp. 275-304; H. I. Bell, *HTR* (1944), p. 190.

conflict between Jews and Greeks in that city erupted once again. The Greek citizens of Alexandria assembled in the amphitheatre to deliberate upon the dispatch of a delegation to intercede with Nero, who was by then Emperor of Rome. Jews infiltrated into the meeting and when they were discovered they were set upon by the Greeks. All except three managed to escape. The Greeks captured these three and were about to burn them alive. In response, the Jews marched *en masse* to the amphitheatre, brandishing burning torches. Here the Roman governor, Tiberius Alexander, also took sides against them and after an acrimonious exchange of words ordered the legions stationed in Alexandria as well as the forces recently arrived from Libya to march against them. The Roman soldiers launched a con-certed assault upon the Delta quarter, the main residence of the Jews, in order to destroy their homes and loot their property. The strong resistance put up by the Jews was finally beaten down, and a terrible slaughter ensued.[1]

These events should be seen in the light of the tensions generated in the eastern parts of the Roman Empire by the Jewish uprising in Palestine. In these riots more Jewish lives were probably lost than in the previous pogrom in the times of Gaius Caligula, but they were still only the precursor of the far greater calamity which the Jews of Alexandria were to experience towards the end of Trajan's reign. The suppression of the revolt in Palestine and the destruction of Jerusalem naturally also had major repercussions on the Jewish community of Egypt. Some of the most zealous insurgents escaped to Egypt where they continued to spread their views, in order to stir up the local community to a renewed revolt against the Romans. They countered the opposition of the local Jewish leaders by assas-sinating several of them. When the heads of the Jewish council in Alexandria finally concluded that the activities of these extremists could no longer be countenanced, they convened a general meeting at which they spoke out against the danger they represented. Six hundred were seized on the spot, to be delivered to the Romans. Some escaped to the provincial towns and got as far as Thebes in Upper Egypt. When caught and tortured by the Romans the Sicarii again demonstrated the same courage and unswerving loyalty to their principles as they had done in Judaea. No torture could be

---

[1] Jos. *War* II, 487-498; on the events in Alexandria. See also Bell, *Juden und Griechen*, pp. 30-1; Tcherikover, *CPJ* I, pp. 78-9.

devised that would cause them to abandon their views and force them to acknowledge the emperor's supremacy.[1] By the vigorous suppression of Sicarian propaganda and absolute submission to Rome, the Jewish *gerousia* of Alexandria temporarily warded off the annihilation of the local community, which was deferred until the reign of Trajan. Nevertheless the Jews of Egypt were not left unscathed by the Great Revolt and the destruction of the Temple. Not only were they, like all the Jews of the Roman Empire, made liable to the Jewish tax tribute imposed by Vespasian, but 'the House of Onias', the Jewish temple in the nome of Heliopolis, came to be regarded by the Romans with the greatest suspicion. They looked upon it as a potential focus for concerted anti-Roman action, and the Roman governor Lupus was ordered to stop the worship there. He carried out the emperor's orders and closed down the temple. In 73 C.E. his successor, Paulinus, emptied the temple of all its treasures, forbade the Jews to come within its precincts and erased every vestige of its former purpose.[2]

CYRENAICA

The Jewish community of Cyrenaica during the Hellenistic-Roman period may to a large extent be regarded as off-shoot of the Egyptian community. Politically and culturally, it attained considerable standing and its members exerted a major influence on the entire Jewish people. Many Jews of Cyrenaica distinguished themselves by their activities in Palestine. Greek-speaking Jewish writers took a prominent part in the development of Jewish Hellenistic literature and during the great uprising in Trajan's time Cyrenaica was a major centre of Jewish patriotism. We do not know when the first Jews came to settle in this province.[3] Jewish-Hellenistic tradition (Cleidemus-Malchus) has it that the sons of Abraham and Katura took part in Heracles' expedition to Africa.[4] Jews may have already settled there in pre-Hellenistic times. The first clear evidence of Jews living in Cyrenaica dates from the early days of Ptolemaic rule over this country. The Ptolemies who were also the masters of Egypt consistently promoted Jewish colonization in that country. Already

[1] Jos. *War* VII, 409-419.
[2] *War* VII, 420-435; see Bludau, op.cit., p. 91.
[3] Applebaum, *Greeks and Jews in Ancient Cyrene* (in Hebrew, 1969), pp. 110-122.
[4] Jos. *Ant.* I, 240-1.

Ptolemy I, King of Egypt, sent Jewish settlers to Cyrene and to the other towns of Libya in order to consolidate his hold over Cyrenaica.[1] It seems almost certain that they were military settlers, like the Jews whom the Ptolemies settled in Egypt and the Jewish families brought to Phrygia and Lydia at the instigation of Antiochus III. The Jewish population of Cyrenaica continued to grow throughout the Hellenistic period until by the first century B.C.E. they constituted a large proportion of the country's inhabitants. Strabo, in connection with the mission of Lucullus to Cyrene which he undertook on behalf of Sulla in 86 B.C.E., also stresses the role played by the Jews. He notes that the population of the city was composed of citizens, peasants, metics, and Jews.[2]

Under Augustus, the long-standing tension no doubt inherent in the conditions of the Hellenistic period between the Greek municipal authorities and the Jewish *politeuma* of Cyrene came to a head. As a result of the provisions and changes made in connection with the establishment of the principate, the issue once against came to the attention of the Roman government. A letter of Marcus Agrippa to the magistrates, the council and the people of Cyrene has been preserved, in which he states that the Jews had complained to him that although Augustus had instructed the previous governor of Cyrenaica not to interfere with the dispatch of the 'sacred moneys' to Jerusalem (the half-shekel tribute), difficulties were nevertheless put in their way, on the pretext that they owed taxes that were not due from them (see below p. 146). Agrippa therefore ordered that the sacred moneys, insofar as they had been taken away from them, be returned so as to repair the evil caused to them.[3]

The epigraphical material discovered in the Italian archaeological excavations in Cyrene shows to what extent Jews were taking part in the life of that town in the first century C.E. A list of ephebes dating from 3-4 C.E. contains such distinctly Jewish names as Elazar the son of Elazar, or Agathocles the son of Eleazar.[4] Similar names also recur in subsequent years; Chaireas the son of Judah, Simon, Joshua the son of Antiphilus.[5] Of particular interest is an inscription dating

[1] Jos. *Against Apion.* II, 44.
[2] *Ant.* XIV, 115; Plutarch, *Life of Lucullus* 2, 3. See also Gelzer, *PW* XIII, p. 378; P. Romanelli, *La Cirenaica Romana* (1943), pp. 43-4; E. J. Bickerman, *PAAJR* (1951), p. 131; S. I. Oost, *Classical Philology* (1963), pp. 18-19.
[3] Jos. *Ant.* XVI, 169-170.
[4] *Quaderni di archeologia della Libia* (1961), no. 7, p. 21, ll. 48-9.
[5] Ibid. p. 24, ll. 13, 18; J. and L. Robert, *REG* (1962), p. 218.

from Nero's time (60-61 C.E.), listing among the city's magistrates (νομοφύλακες) a Jew by the name of Eleazar the son of Jason.[1] That Cyrene had a prosperous and culturally highly developed Jewish community also results from the fact that several of its members made valuable contributions to Jewish Hellenistic literature. Cyrene was the birthplace of the historian Jason, who wrote the history of the Hasmonaean revolt in five books from a strictly orthodox Jewish point of view but using all the devices of Hellenistic historiography. He certainly lived before Augustus' time.[2] The Second Book of Maccabees is an abbreviated version of his work. It has also been conjectured that Ezekiel, the Jewish dramatist who wrote a play on the Exodus from Egypt, originated from that city.[3]

As for the numerical and financial strength of the community, we are told that after 70 C.E., three thousand wealthy Jews had their property confiscated by the Governor Catullus on behalf of the imperial treasury.[4] Allowing for some exaggeration, we may still assume that Cyrene was one of the major centres of the Jewish Hellenistic Diaspora.

The second most important Jewish centre in Cyrenaica was in Berenice (Benghazi), the westernmost city of Cyrenaica. Three Greek inscriptions may give us an idea of the Jewish *politeuma* of Berenice in the times of Augustus and Tiberius and in the early days of Nero.

The first inscription, dating from the Augustan period, consists of a decree of the *politeuma* and the archons of Berenice honouring a Jew, a Roman citizen named Decimus Valerius Dionysius (apparently 8-6 B.C.E.). for having at his own expense had the amphitheatre plastered and decorated with pictures.[5] The reference seems to be to a Jewish public building rather than to the municipal amphitheatre of Berenice, which was no doubt used in the customary way for gladiatorial displays.[6] The Jewish community exempted the donor from all public charges and decreed that he should be honourably mentioned at every assembly and celebration of the New Month. The archons

---

[1] *Quaderni*, op.cit., p. 16, no. 2.
[2] Some scholars date Jason to the time of the Hasmonaean revolt. See e.g. Tcherikover, *Hellenistic Civilization*, p. 385.
[3] Y. Gutman, *The Beginnings of Jewish Hellenistic Literature* II (in Hebrew, 1963), pp. 66-9.
[4] Jos. *War* VII, 445-6.
[5] The publication of the inscription in *CIG* no. 5362 is faulty. One should use J. and G. Roux, *REG* (1949), p. 286, or *SEG* XVI no. 931.
[6] For a different view see E. Gabba, pp. 64-5.

were instructed to inscribe his name on a stele of Parian marble to be put up in the most prominent place in the amphitheatre.

The second inscription that has come down to us dates from the year 25 C.E.[1] It is again a decree of the Jewish *politeuma*, honouring Marcus Titius, the Roman governor of Cyrenaica and Crete, passed by a meeting held on the Feast of Tabernacles, under the chairmanship of the nine archons of the community (all of them with one exception—Joseph the son of Straton—bearing Greek names and one being a Roman citizen by the name of Marcus Aelius Onasion). The unanimous resolution was a tribute to Titius for the favourable attitude he had shown towards the members of the *politeuma*. As in the case of Decimus Valerius Dionysius, it was decided to have his name inscribed on a stele of Parian marble to be put up in the most prominent place in the amphitheatre.

The third inscription, dating from the second year of Nero's reign (55 C.E.) again represents a resolution of the Jewish community, here called synagogue rather than *politeuma*.[2] Once again a marble stele was put up, this time to commemorate a series of people, most of them archons of the community, who had contributed funds for the repair of the synagogue. Here, too, most of the names are Greek. Some of them are theophoric, such as Dositheus or Theophilus, several being typical of Cyrenaica. There also are several Roman names (such as Cornelius) and a distinctly Jewish name, Jonathan.

Among the other towns of Cyrenaica where Jews are known to have been living at that time mention should be made of Teuchira, on the shores of the Mediterranean, between Ptolemais and Berenice. Excavations have revealed numerous Jewish funerary inscriptions bearing Greek, Hebrew and some Libyan names.[3]

So far there is little evidence of a Jewish settlement in Ptolemais. It consists mainly of a Jewish coin (a quarter of a shekel) and the name Sarah which appears on one of the funerary inscriptions found there. Jewish names also appear on inscriptions found in Apollonia.[4]

---

[1] *CIG* no. 5361; *IGR* I no. 1024; Roux, op.cit. pp. 283-4; Gabba, no. XIX.

[2] G. Caputo, *La Parola del Passato* (1957), p. 134; *SEG* XVII no. 823; B. Lifshitz, *Donateurs et fondateurs dans les synagogues juives* (1967), no. 100; cf. J. and L. Robert, *REG* (1959), pp. 275-6.

[3] J. Gray, 'The Jewish Inscriptions in Greek and Hebrew at Tocra, Cyrene and Barce', in A. Rowe, D. Buttle, and J. Gray, *Cyrenaican Expedition of the University of Manchester*, 1952 (1956), 43-59; *SEG* IX, nos. 559-724; XVI, nos. 876-930; cf. G. R. H. Wright, *PEQ* (1963), pp. 22-64; Applebaum, op.cit., pp. 122-137.

[4] Cf. C. H. Kraeling, *Ptolemais, City of the Libyan Pentapolis* (1962), pp. 17,215,

The destruction of the Temple was a source of major upheavals for the Jews of Cyrenaica no less than for the Jews of Egypt. Nothing has come down to us about any outbreaks of violence either in Cyrene or in the other cities of Cyrenaica at the beginning of the Revolt, as was the case in Alexandria. Upon its suppression, however, many Jewish insurgents managed to escape to Cyrenaica. Among them was a certain Jonathan the Weaver, who set about fomenting revolt among the lower classes of the Jewish population in Cyrene and its environs, asking them to follow him out to the desert where he would show them signs and miracles. Again, as in Alexandria, the local Jewish leadership took action against these extremists and informed Catullus, the Roman governor, of Jonathan's plans. Catullus had Jonathan and his men—who were all unarmed—surrounded by cavalry and infantry. Most of them were slaughtered, and the rest taken prisoner. Jonathan at first managed to escape but was finally caught and brought before the governor where he tried to impugn the position of the higher class Jews by telling Catullus that several of them had been in touch with him and engaged in subversive activities. Consequently one of them called Alexander, to whom the govenor had already been hostile, was executed, together with his wife Berenice. Through Jonathan the Governor also tried to involve Jews of Alexandria and Rome in the affair, including the historian Josephus Flavius, but the emperor refused to indict them. Jonathan was executed in Rome where he had gone to lodge his accusations.[1]

SYRIA AND PHOENICIA

Syria and Phoenicia were major Jewish centres throughout the period reviewed. Since they were so near the homeland, the Jews living there were very much like those living in Palestine, and acted as their close partners and allies.[2] At the same time some of the Jews of Syria also maintained close contacts with the Jews of Babylonia. Palestine and Babylonia were in fact the two sources

---

no. 51 (Tomb of the Kartilioi), p. 268. Kraeling's statement that the coin found there is of the type issued by Simon Maccabaeus is mistaken, since we have till now no coins issued by Simon; for Ptolemais see also F. Preisigke, *Sammelbuch Griechischer Urkunden aus Ägypten* I (1915), no. 5918; on Apollonia see *SEG* XVII nos. 818-819.

[1] Jos. *War* VII, 437-453.

[2] *M. Halah* 4:11: 'He that owns [land] in Syria is as one that owns [land] in the outskirts of Jerusalem'.

from which the Syrian and Phoenician communities recruited their numbers. Their character was largely determined by their intermediate position between these two major foci as well as by the fact that Phoenicia and some part of Syria were among the most Hellenized sections of the entire Orient. The largest Jewish settlement in Syria was undoubtedly in Antioch, the capital of the Roman province of Syria. Jews had settled in this town from its very foundation, and it subsequently became a major Jewish centre in the Graeco-Roman world.

That Antioch was the capital of the Seleucids who for some time also extended their domination over Palestine and later on became the capital of the Roman province of Syria, lent particular importance to the Jewish community of that time, placing it in the same rank as the communities of Alexandria and Rome. The growth of the Jewish population of Antioch was presumably also stimulated by the material advantages of this city and its attractions as a major urban centre. While many no doubt came from Palestine, Jews from Syria itself also tended to concentrate in the capital, and there probably also was some migration from Babylonia and other parts of the Parthian Empire.[1]

Josephus reports that civil rights were granted to the Jews of Antioch by its founder, Seleucus I.[2] Presumably only a minority were granted actual citizenship. During the Seleucid period they did, however, attain extensive *politeuma* or community privileges. These were inscribed on special copper plates of whose existence during Roman times we have definite evidence.[3] There can be little doubt that the annexation of Palestine by the Seleucids about 200 B.C. intensified the contacts between Antioch and Jerusalem. Jewish representatives were frequent visitors in the Seleucid capital; and the Jewish leaders themselves, Onias III, Jason and Menelaus, came to Antioch to present their case and lobby at the court. Onias III sought refuge from his opponents in the famous temple of Apollo at Daphne near Antioch.[4] It is hard to tell to what extent the armed conflict between the Seleucid regime and the Jews of Palestine affected the Jewish colony

---

[1] On the history of the Jewish community of Antioch see C. H. Kraeling, *JBL* (1932), pp. 130-160; G. Downey, *A History of Antioch in Syria* (1961), passim; cf. S. Krauss, *REJ* XLV (1902), pp. 27-49.
[2] *Against Apion* II, 39; *Ant.* XII, 119.
[3] *War* VII, 110.
[4] 2 Macc. 4:33, but we should not infer from this that Jews lived at Daphne at that time.

in Antioch. It is reasonable to assume that many of the Jewish prisoners of war taken in Palestine were brought to Antioch. Later traditions also cite Antioch as the place where Eleazar and Hannah and her seven sons resisted the order of Antiochus IV and preferred martyrdom to the denial of their faith. A particular synagogue is pointed out where these Maccabean martyrs were supposed to have been buried.[1] After the reign of Antiochus IV conditions evidently improved. One of his successors seems to have restored to the synagogue of Antioch the copper vessels taken by Antiochus Epiphanes from the Temple in Jerusalem, and the privileges formerly enjoyed by the Jews were restored.[2]

Under the Romans the Jewish community of Antioch continued to grow and develop. The Jews played a prominent role in the life of the city. They were allowed to retain the privileges accorded by the Seleucids. As in Alexandria and the cities of Asia Minor, there were no doubt some conflicts with the Greek citizen body but we have no record of any eruption before the reign of Caligula. From the course of events at the time of the Great Revolt and the destruction of the Temple it may, however, be conjectured that the problems of Antioch were no less deep-seated than in Alexandria.

Here, too, as in Egypt and Judaea, the reign of Gaius Caligula apparently was a difficult time for the Jews. Our sole informant is Malalas, whose work teems with inaccuracies and can hardly be regarded as a reliable source, although with regard to Antioch he did use some local sources.[3]

Malalas speaks about riots that broke out in Antioch as a result of a conflict between two circus factions, the green and the blue—an event more typical of the Byzantine than of the Julio-Claudian period. They culminated in a major clash between the local Greeks and Jews, as a result of which many Jews were killed and numerous synagogues burned down. In response, Pinehas the High Priest of the Jews, assembled thirty thousand men from Judaea and Galilee and advanced suddenly from Tiberias to Antioch, taking the city by surprise and slaughtering its residents. Gaius was furious with the representative of the Roman regime in Antioch for not having put up an effective resistance to Pinehas, whom he ordered to be seized in Tiberias. His head was cut off, and many other Jews were killed.

[1] J. Obermann, *JBL* (1931), pp. 250-265.
[2] Cf. E. Bickerman, *Byzantion* (1951), p. 82; cf. Jos. *War* VII, 44.
[3] Malalas, *Chronographia*, ed. L. Dindorf (1831), pp. 244-5.

The head of Pinehas the Priest was exhibited on a pole outside the city of Antioch, beyond the river Orontes. The emperor also sent funds for rebuilding those parts of the city that had been burned down. Malalas' report includes so many obvious flights of fancy that it is difficult to determine which, if any, is the grain of truth it contains. Nevertheless it seems we may accept the view that there was severe tension between the Jews and Greeks in Antioch during the times of Gaius Caligula, inspired by his general anti-Jewish policy. It is probable that some bloodshed did occur, but undoubtedly events did not assume the proportions described in Malalas' version. It can also hardly be assumed that the governor, Petronius, would have allowed the situation in Antioch to deteriorate to the extent it did in Alexandria, owing to the unusually precarious position of its governor, Flaccus.[1]

Whatever may have been the course of events, they were only a passing episode in the history of the Antiochene Jewish community, which continued to flourish. Pro-Jewish sentiments and proselytization remained fairly common.[2] The atmosphere was also conducive to the spread of Christianity and Antioch soon became one of its major missionary bases; the name 'Christians' actually originated in this city.[3] Antioch is mentioned together with Apamea and Sidon as one of the three Syrian towns where the gentile majority did no violence to the Jewish minority upon the outbreak of the Great Revolt in 66 c.e.[4] Soon, however, friction arose between the Greek and Jewish inhabitants of Antioch. Under the governorship of Mucianus in 67-69 c.e., the Greeks attempted to deprive the Jews of their former right to receive money in exchange for the oil supplied by the gymnasiarchs, but Mucianus refused to accede to the demands of the anti-Jewish faction.[5] At the same time a Jew by the name of Antiochus, the son of the archon of the Jews of Antioch, for some unknown reason became a traitor to his people and made common cause with their worst enemies. He appeared at a rally in the theatre where he accused his own father as well as other Jews of having hatched a plot for burning down the whole city on a given night. Several foreign Jews who according to him were partners to the plot were seized by the Greeks and burned

---

[1] On the events at Antioch in the time of Gaius see G. de Sanctis, *Rivista di Filologia* (1925), pp. 245-6; Kraeling, op.cit. p. 148; J. Dobiáš, *Dějiny římské provincie Syrské* (1924), pp. 409-410; Downey, op.cit., pp. 192-4; V. Tcherikover, *The Jews in Egypt*, p. 154.
[2] Jos. *War* VII, 45; Acts 6:5, 'Nicolaus, a proselyte of Antioch.'
[3] Acts 11:19-30.   [4] Jos. *War* II, 479.   [5] *Ant.* XII, 120.

alive in the theatre. At his instigation the Antiochians began to practise religious persecution and coercion: Jews—apparently those who claimed citizenship rights —were forced to bring sacrifices after the Greek custom, and whoever refused was executed. Antiochus also, with the aid of the Roman military, kept harassing the Jews on their Sabbath rest. Other Syrian towns were naturally influenced by what was going on in the capital and followed suit.[1]

The persecutions which Mucianus managed to restrain were resumed shortly afterwards when he left his post as governor of Syria. During the interregnum, before the arrival of successor, Caesennius Paetus, in November 70 C.E., a serious fire broke out in the city in which the market and municipal archives burned down. Antiochus reverted to his former accusation. The local populace was in such a state of panic and confusion that it was ready to believe anything, but Naevius Collega, the legate left in charge until the arrival of the new governor, managed to calm the crowds. A careful enquiry showed that the Jews had nothing to do with the matter, the fire having been laid by recalcitrant debtors who wanted to get rid of the records proving their indebtedness.[2]

The former status of the Jews was restored only with the arrival of Titus. On passing through Antioch on his way to Zeugma on the Euphrates, where the ambassadors of the Parthian king were about to offer him a golden wreath as a tribute to his victory over the Jews, the inhabitants of Antioch implored him to expel the Jews from their city. Titus gave a bland reply without stating his intentions. On his return to Antioch he was again given a lavish reception and the request was repeated. This time Titus explicitly, though politely, refused, on the grounds that now that their city had been destroyed the Jews had nowhere to go to. He also refused to rescind their former privileges, and fully confirmed their legal status.[3]

Another Syrian town known to have had a Jewish community is Apamea, which is mentioned together with Antioch and Sidon as being untouched by the major anti-Jewish riots that broke out in the cities of Syria and Phoenicia at the beginning of the Great Revolt.[4]

---

[1] *War* VII, 46-53.
[2] *War* VII, 54-61: cf. Downey, op.cit., pp. 199-200, pp. 204-6, 586-7; Dobiáš, op.cit. 473-4, 509-510. The view of Kraeling (op.cit. pp. 151-2) who combines the two episodes connected with the renegade Antiochus into one does not seem cogent.
[3] *War* VII, 100-111.
[4] *War* II, 479. See also *M. Halah* 4:11 on Ariston from Apamea.

It should also be noted as the birthplace of two famous philosophers, Posidonius in the Hellenistic period and Numenius in the second century C.E., who both referred to Judaism in their works, the latter regarding it in a favourable light. We have no means of ascertaining to what extent they were affected by their immediate contacts with the Jews of their own city.[1]

Among the other towns of Syria special mention should be made of Damascus which undoubtedly had a very ancient Jewish settlement, as is amply shown by the extant literary sources. Thus Paul asked the high priest of Jerusalem for letters of introduction to the synagogues of Damascus so that he might proceed against the Christians there;[2] ultimately he preached Christianity in these very same synagogoues, whereupon his opponents tried to kill him.[3] According to Josephus practically all the women of Damascus were attracted to Judaism and in 66 C.E., when the men were plotting to slaughter the Jews, they had to hide the matter from their wives. According to the same source they rounded up the Jews in the gymnasium and killed as many as 10,500 of them.[4] This, like most figures of the kind cited by Josephus, cannot be taken at its face value but the story may nevertheless serve as an indication that the Jewish population of Damascus was considerable and that Judaism was popular mainly among the women. We also find evidence of a Jewish sect known as the Covenanters of Damascus which emigrated to 'the land of Damascus'.[5]

Since Phoenicia and Palestine were contiguous, the Jews and Phoenicians had maintained close contacts with each other since ancient times. That we have so little concrete information about the Jews living in the Phoenician towns during the period under review can probably be attributed to accidental causes. Hecataeus, at the beginning of the Hellenistic period, already speaks of a major Jewish emigration to Phoenicia;[6] and in the early Roman period we have definite evidence of Jewish communities in Ptolemais,[7] Tyre[8] and Sidon.[9]

---

[1] For the later Jewish incriptions from Apamea see *IGLS* IV, nos. 1319-37.
[2] Acts 9:1.
[3] Acts 9:20-23.
[4] Jos. *War.* II, 559-561; VII, 368 (here the number given is 18,000).
[5] *The Zadokite Documents* (1954), ed. C. Rabin ,VI, 5.19; VII, 19.
[6] Jos. *Against Apion* I, 194.
[7] Jos. *War* II, 477.
[8] *War* II, 478.
[9] *Ant.* XVII, 324; *War* II, 479.

ASIA MINOR

Asia Minor had a big Jewish population throughout the Hellenistic and Roman periods. They seem to have settled there long before and in Sardis at least there was presumably a Jewish community as early as the Persian period.[1] Clearchus, one of the disciples of Aristotle, in his *Dialogue on Sleep* attributes to his teacher a meeting with a Hellenized Jew on the coast of Asia Minor. Clear-cut evidence, however, is available only from the Seleucid period. Antiochus III transferred two thousand Jewish families from Mesopotamia and Babylonia to Lydia and Phrygia in order to secure his hold over these territories. The Jewish settlers were promised religious freedom and allocated lands to build houses and plant vineyards. Their harvest was exempted from taxes for a period of ten years.[2]

During the early period of Roman rule we find large numbers of Jews in the various towns of Asia Minor. In 88 B.C.E., according to Strabo, the Jews of Asia Minor deposited their money in the island of Cos because of the threatened invasion of Mithridates.[3] In 59 B.C.E., the Jews in the Roman province of Asia were instrumental in the indictment of the Roman governor Flaccus, for having confiscated money destined for the Temple in Jerusalem which had been collected in four cities of Asia Minor. Two of the collection centres were in Phrygia (Apamea and Laodicea) and two in north-western Asia Minor —Adramyttium and Pergamon.[4]

Several documents from the period of the Roman Civil Wars also indicate the presence of Jews in the various cities of Asia Minor. Thus we possess a document containing a resolution of Lentulus, the consul of 49 B.C.E. exempting Jews who were Roman citizens from military service.[5] This matter is also dealt with in a letter of Titus Ampius Balbus[6] by which he apparently transmitted the resolution of Lentulus to the authorities of Ephesus.[7] Hence the exemption also seems to have applied to Jews who were Roman citizens living in other towns of Asia Minor.[8] Lucius Antonius' letter

---

[1] Cf. W. Kornfeld, *Mélanges bibliques rédigés en l'honneur de André Robert* (1957), pp. 180-6.
[2] Jos. *Against Apion* I, 176-182; *Ant* XII, 147-153.
[3] Jos. *Ant.* XIV, 113.
[4] Cicero, *Pro Flacco* 28, 67-8.
[5] Jos. *Ant.* XIV, 228-9, 234, 236-240. On Lentulus' consilium see J. Suolahti, *Arctos* II (1958), pp. 152-163.
[6] On those documents see also Juster I, p. 142-6; according to Jos. *Ant.* XIV, 229 Ampius Balbus is mentioned first among the members of Lentulus' consilium.
[7] Jos. *Ant.* XIV, 230.   [8] On Delos, *Ant.* XIV, 231-2.

143

of 49 B.C.E. to the city of Sardis, by which the Jews are ensured religious rights, autonomous jurisdiction and the right to a synagogue[1] belongs to the same time, Less clear is the date of another document relating to Sardis—a decision of the boule and demos of Sardis adopted at the proposal of the magistrates (στρατηγοί) at the request of the Jews residing in that town.[2] In content it largely coincides with Lucius Antonius' letter; it deals likewise with the right of the Jews to form associations and have a synagogue where they may congregate for their prayers; in addition a special area is assigned to them for their living quarters. In the last passage of the resolution the inspectors in charge of the market places are required to see to it that food fit to be eaten by Jews could be brought to the city.

After the assassination of Caesar Roman policy remained unchanged. Dolabella, who for a short period served as governor of Asia Minor after having liquidated Trebonius, one of Caesar's assassins, and before being himself put out of the way by Cassius,[3] again circulated a letter containing a pro-Jewish edict passed at the instigation of Alexander the son of Theodorus, the envoy of Hyrcanus II.[4] According to the letter addressed to Ephesus, the capital of the province of Asia Jews are exempted from military labour, and their right to live according to the customs of their forefathers and congregate for their divine worship is reaffirmed.

Marcus Brutus may also have thrown in his influence in favour of the Jews during his stay in Asia Minor in 42 B.C.E. A resolution of the popular assembly of Ephesus adopted during this period states that the local Jews had requested permission to keep the Sabbath and generally observe the customs of their ancestors, and the assembly granted them these privileges, declaring that no one should interfere with their Sabbath rest.[5]

Another document may possibly relate to the lifetime of Julius

---

[1] *Ant.* XIV, 235. Lucius Antonius acted as quaestor and pro-praetor after Minucius Thermus had left Asia. See *IGR* IV, nos. 400-1. After Fannius had become governor of Asia (50 B.C.E.) he remained proquaestor. See on L. Antonius L. Robert, *Hellenica* I (1940), pp. 54-5; T. R. S. Broughton, *The Magistrates of the Roman Republic* II (1952), p. 260. He is mentioned also in Jos. *Ant.* XIV, 230.

[2] *Ant.* XIV, 259-261.

[3] On Dolabella see Broughton, op.cit. II, p. 344.

[4] Jos. *Ant.* XIV, 225-7.

[5] *Ant.* XIV, 262-4. Brutus was active in Asia Minor early in 42 B.C.E., when he was preparing for war against Antony and Octavian. However, we have to remember that we get the name Brutus in par. 263 only by emendation. Cf. the doubts of Juster I, p. 148, n. 12.

Caesar though it cannot be clearly established. This is the letter addressed by the town authorities of Laodicea in Phrygia to Gaius Rabirius, the governor of Asia.[1] From it we gather that Sopater, an envoy of Hyrcanus II, had delivered to them a letter from the governor stating that Hyrcanus' delegates had requested him to allow the Jews to keep the Sabbath and live according to their laws and that they should not be required to do anything that was contrary to their rights. We further gather from this letter that the governor had overridden the objections of the citizens of the Greek town of Tralles and ordered these provisions to be duly implemented. In the same spirit he also wrote to Laodicea, and the letter in our possession signifies the consent of that city.

A further document—of doubtful date—relates to the city of Miletus. This is a letter of Publius Servilius (Galba?), which again deals with the rights of the local Jews to keep the Sabbath and live according to their religion, a privilege that had been disputed by the local authority, but was upheld by the proconsul.[2]

Still less clear is the date of another document, though it may probably also be attributed to the same decade. This is a resolution of the city of Halicarnassus, which in reliance upon the general Roman custom vouchsafes the Jews the right to celebrate their holidays and conduct their prayers, to keep the Sabbath and construct synagogues close to the seashore.[3] Anybody interfering with the execution of these rights was made liable to a fine payable to the city coffers.[4] We thus see that in the pre-Augustan period the Jews were already pressing for religious rights in several cities of Asia Minor (Ephesus, Sardis, Laodicea, Tralles, Miletus and Halicarnassus) and were supported by the Roman authorities in their endeavour. Apparently however, the problem was not finally resolved and it remained for the principate of Augustus to regulate the situation and lay down fixed rules governing the status of the Jews in the various cities of Asia Minor.

A major stage in this development was the decision of Agrippa in

---

[1] Jos. *Ant.* xiv, 241-243. The emendation Rabirius to the corrupted name in the manuscripts of Josephus was suggested by Th. Homolle, *BCH* (1882), pp. 608-612. He acted as proconsul of Asia in 49-46 B.C.E. *CIL* I, 2(2nd ed.) no. 773; *Inscriptions de Délos* no. 1859.

[2] Jos. *Ant.* xiv, 244-6.

[3] *Ant.* xiv, 256-8.

[4] A. Wilhelm, *Jahreshefte des österreichischen archäologischen Institutes* (1905), pp. 238-241; Juster I, p. 148.

14 B.C.E., who was required to settle the contradictory claims of the representatives of the cities of Ionia and of the Jews, the latter being supported by Herod through his friend Nicholas of Damascus.[1] Again the Jews' contentions were that they were forced to appear in the courts on days sacred to them and that the money destined for the Temple in Jerusalem was seized and they were forced to donate part of it to other purposes although having received official exemption from the Roman authorities.

Agrippa's decision was only one of several adopted by the Roman authorities during the principate of Augustus with respect to the Jews of Asia Minor. There seems to have been a whole series of documents on the same issues. Still extant is a letter of fairly general contents addressed by Augustus to the governor of Asia, Gaius Flaccus Norbanus, who was consul in 24 B.C.E.[2] This letter again deals with the right of the Jews to send the half-shekel donation to the Temple in Jerusalem, without any outside interference. Norbanus Flaccus consequently also issued corresponding instructions to the main cities of Asia Minor, of which his letters to Sardis and Ephesus have been preserved.[3]

We also have the letter of Marcus Agrippa to Ephesus, sent during his stay in the Orient from 23 to 21 or from 16 to 13 B.C.E. likewise dealing with the half-shekel funds.[4] It goes so far as to say that whoever steals the sacred moneys of the Jews shall be deemed to have despoiled a sanctuary and shall be handed over to the Jews even if he has taken refuge in a place of asylum. Another passage, as usual, deals with the keeping of the Sabbath.

A general edict of Augustus dating from 12 B.C.E. reaffirms the rights of the Jews to live according to their ancestral customs, to send money to Jerusalem and to keep the Sabbath.[5] Persons stealing Jewish holy books or sacred funds from synagogues are defined as sacrilegious.

The last document dating from the Augustan period and relating to the Jews of Asia Minor is a letter of procunsul Jullus Antonius

[1] Jos. *Ant.* XVI, 27-61; XII, 125-6.
[2] *Ant.* XVI, 166; on this document and its dating cf. Juster I, pp. 149-150; M. Reinhold, *Marcus Agrippa* (1933), p. 120, n. 84; D. Magie, *Roman Rule in Asia Minor* II (1950), p. 1580; K. M. T. Atkinson, *Historia* (1958), p. 322. E. M. Smallwood, *Philonis Alexandrini 'Legatio ad Gaium'* (1961), pp. 309-310.
[3] Jos. *Ant.* XVI, 171; Philo, *Legatio* 315.
[4] *Ant.* XVI, 167-8.
[5] *Ant.* XVI, 162-165; cf. Atkinson, op.cit., p. 320; G. W. Bowersock, *Harvard Studies in Classical Philology* (1964), pp. 207-210.

to Ephesus.[1] Jullus Antonius served as consul in 10 B.C.E. and died in 2 B.C.E. Some time between these two dates he also served as proconsul in Asia.[2] In this letter, written at the request of the Jews, he reaffirmed the provisions made by Augustus and Agrippa and particularly stressed the right to send money to Jerusalem.

We list below in geographical sequence from south to north the territories and main towns where we have evidence of Jewish settlements in the early imperial period.

I. *Cilicia.* It is only to be expected that from the earliest times there should have been Jews living in Cilicia, the next-door neighbour of Syria. Philo in fact lists it among the countries inhabited by Jews.[3] In the last few generations before the destruction of the Temple, the Jews of Cilicia had a synagogue of their own in Jerusalem or at any rate used to pray in a synagogue shared by Hellenistic Jews. A Christian source furnishes evidence of the presence of Jews in the various towns of Cilicia at a later period.[4] Towards the end of the Second Temple period the king of Cilicia, Polemon, adopted Judaism in order to marry Berenice, the daughter of Agrippa I.[5] We also know that Jews were living in Tarsus, the capital of Cilicia, at the end of the Second Temple period, from the statement that Paul was born in that city.[6]

Two inscriptions discovered in Western Cilicia, near the town of Elaeusa, represent resolutions of the Sabbatistae, a sect worshipping the god of the Sabbath.[7] Dating from the period of Augustus, they testify to the influence of the Jews in Western Cilicia, and to the role of Judaism in the syncretist developments of the period.

Among the other cities of Cilicia, mention should be made of Selinus on the coast, where the existence of a Jewish settlement is corroborated by epigraphic evidence from the second century C.E.—a funerary inscription bearing the name Joseph the son of Theudion.[8] There were Jews in another coastal town, Anemurium, as we learn from an

---

[1] *Ant.* XVI, 172-173.
[2] Cf. Atkinson, op.cit., p. 327; J. and L. Robert, *REG* (1959), p. 177.
[3] *Legatio* 281.
[4] Epiphanius, *Panarion Haer.* XXX, 11, 2.
[5] Jos. *Ant.* XX, 145.
[6] Acts 9:11; 21:39; 22:3; a Jew from Tarsus was buried at Joppa, *CII* no. 925.
[7] *OGIS* no. 573; F. Sokolowski, *Lois sacrées d'Asie mineure* (1957), no. 80; R. Heberdey and A. Wilhelm, *Denkschriften Akad. Wien* XLIV, 6 (1896), p. 67.
[8] G. E. Bean and T. B. Mitford, *Anatolian Studies* (1962), pp. 206-207; *SEG*, XX no. 87.

inscription discovered in Corycus, another Cilician town. About the Jews of Corycus itself nothing is known from literary sources but only from a long series of inscriptions which, however, do not belong to the first century.[1] Similarly the Jewish inscription from Olba dates from the third century,[2] and the inscriptions from Seleucia on the Calcyadnus also are of a fairly late date.[3]

2. *Pamphylia*. Pamphylia was one of the countries notified by the Roman consul in 142 B.C.E. of the renewed alliance with Hasmonaean Judaea in the time of Simeon.[4] Philo also included it among the countries having a Jewish population.[5] Among the cities of Pamphylia, Side was specifically mentioned in the circular of 142 B.C.E. but inscriptions relating ot its Jews date from a later period.[6] The evidence relating to Perge might point to the presence of Jews in that city in Paul's time.[7]

3. *Lycia*. In Lycia, mention should be made of Phaselis[8] and Tlos. In the latter an inscription, apparently dating from the first century C.E. has been found, commemorating a Jew by the name of Ptolemy who had built a cemetery for the local congregation in gratitude for his son's appointment to the post of archon.[9] The evidence relating to Limyra[10] dates from a later period as does that relating to Patara.[11]

4. *Caria*.[12] Here direct information is available about Jewish settlements in several cities. From Halicarnassus we have a popular resolution adopted under the influence of the Romans in which Jews are vouchsafed the right to keep their religious customs and erect a synogogue near the shore (see above p. 145). From Myndus[13] we

[1] On Anamorium see *MAMA* iii, no. 222; *CII* no. 786; on Corycus cf. *MAMA* iii, nos. 205, 237, 262, 295, 344, 440, 448, 607, 679; *CII* nos. 785, 787-794.
[2] *CII* no. 795.
[3] *CII* no. 783-4.
[4] i Macc. 15: 23.
[5] *Legatio*, 281; Acts 2:10.
[6] *CII* no. 781; L, Robert, *Revue de philologie* (1958), pp. 36-47; Lifshitz, op.cit. nos. 36-7.
[7] On Paul's missionary attempt at Perge see Acts 13:13; 14:25.
[8] i Macc. 15:23.
[9] *CII* no. 757; E. Hula, *Eranos Vindobonensis* (1893), pp. 99-102.
[10] On Limyra see *CII* no. 758.
[11] A late Byzantine source Symeon Metaphrastes, refers to Jewish-Christian tension during the old pagan empire; *PG* cxiv, col. 1457.
[12] i Macc. 15:23. [13] Ibid.

have an inscription about a woman having served as 'head of the Synagogue.[1] An inscription from Iasus indicates that a Jew from Jerusalem by the name of Nicetas the son of Jason had arrived there in the second century B.C.E.[2] There also are later inscriptions from this town, and in particular a list of ephebes mentioning the name Judah.[3] About the Jewish community in Tralles we learn from the fact that the Romans intervened in their favour in the forties of the first century B.C.E. (see above p. 145). An inscription dating from the third century relates to a Jewish synagogue there.[4] About Nysa there is no direct evidence before the third or fourth century C.E. when we have an inscription relating to the construction of a synagogue.[5] Again for Hyllarima we have an inscription relating to a synagogue in the third century C.E.[6]

5. *Pisidia.* Here we have epigraphic material dating from the third century relating to the town of Termessus.[7] We also know that Paul came to the synagogue in Pisidian Antioch.[8]

6. *Lycaonia.* We again know that Paul preached in the synagogue of Iconium and that the Jews' violent reaction to this sermon caused him and Barnabas to flee from the city.[9] About Lystra we know that it was the birthplace of Timothy the son of Greek father and a Jewish mother.[10]

7. *Phrygia.* Phrygia had a Jewish settlement as far back as the Hellenistic period. One of the two countries—the other being Lydia—where Jews from Babylonia were settled by Antiochus (see above p. 143), it subsequently occupied a prominent position among the Jewish communities of Asia Minor. The main cities of Phrygia which were

[1] *CII* no. 756; Lifshitz op.cit. no. 29.
[2] *CII* no. 749.
[3] L. Robert, *REJ* CI (1937), pp. 85-6; *Hellenica* I (1940), pp. 28-9.
[4] L. Robert, *Études Anatoliennes* (1937), pp. 409-412; Lifshitz, op.cit. no. 30.
[5] *Athenische Mittheilungen* (1897), p. 484, n. 2; L. Robert, *Hellenica* XI-XII (1960). p. 261; Lifshitz, op.cit. no. 31.
[6] A. Laumonier, *BCH* (1934), pp. 379-380, no. 44; Lifshitz, op.cit. no. 32.
[7] L. Robert, *Hellenica* XI-XII (1960), p. 386.
[8] Acts 13:14. The Antiochene Deborah who occurs on an inscription from Apollonia (*CII* no. 772) hailed probably from Pisidian Antioch. Still Antioch on the Maeander should not be excluded. See B. Levick, *Roman Colonies in Southern Asia Minor* (1967), p. 128, n. 1.
[9] Acts 14:1. [10] Acts 16:1-3.

inhabited by Jews in Roman times include Laodicea where the Temple funds confiscated under Flaccus were collected (see above p. 143). The Roman governor Rabirius is known to have intervened 'on behalf of the Jews (see above p. 145). About the Jewish settlement in Hierapolis we know mainly from later inscriptions which tell of special Jewish archives in that city as well as of Jewish craftsmen there.[1] Apamea was another one of the four cities where Jewish Temple funds were confiscated in Flaccus' time. Interestingly enough, the amount confiscated in Apamea was higher than that taken in Laodicea or Pergamon, although less than in Adramyttium.[2] The inscriptions relating to the Jews in Apamea date from the third century C.E.[3] Jewish influence may also be discerned in coins of the third century reflecting the biblical story of Noah.[4] A substantial number of inscriptions from Acmonia testify to the existence of a Jewish settlement there.[5] One of them[6] tells of one Julia Severa, the wife of Lucius Servenius Capito, the high priestess of one of the pagan cults in Nero's time who at the same time gave proof of her pro-Jewish sentiments—probably quite common among the upper classes in Phrygia—by building a synagogue. This synagogue was at a later date repaired by three leaders of the local community.[7] A first or second century inscription from Synnada speaks about the local synagogue leaders (ἀρχισυνάγωγοι).[8] No information is available about the Jews of Eumeneia before the third century C.E.;[9] an inscription from Dorylaeum hints at the existence of a community there.[10]

8. *Lydia*. Jews had undoubtedly been living in Lydia since very ancient times (see above p. 143). Sardis was the most important Jewish centre in this country about whose importance we learn

[1] CII nos. 775-780.   [2] Cicero, *Pro Flacco* 28, 68.   [3] CII nos. 773-4.
[4] B. V. Head, *Catalogue of the Greek Coins of Phrygia* (1906), p. 101, no. 181.
[5] CII nos. 762-771. No. 760 should also be connected with Acmonia and not with Blaundos; see L. Robert, *Hellenica* x (1955), pp. 250-1; on the Jews of Acmonia also *Hellenica* xi-xii (1960), pp. 409-412.
[6] CII no. 766; *MAMA* vi no. 264; Lifshitz no. 33.
[7] On Julia Severa cf. also *MAMA* vi nos. 263, 265. We should not think of her as of a full proselyte (so e.g. W. M. Ramsay, *The Cities and Bishoprics of Phrygia* I 2 (1897), 673), but rather as of one who displayed in some way sympathy for Judaism. Cf. Groag, *PW* x, pp. 947-8. One of her husband's relatives entered the Roman Senate in the reign of Nero. Cf. C. S. Walton, *JRS* (1929), pp. 44-5
[8] CII no. 759.
[9] CII no. 761; see also L. Robert, *Hellenica* xi-xii (1960), pp. 414-439.
[10] For Jews of Dorylaeum see also J. and L. Robert, *REG* (1941), p. 260.

from documents dating from the Roman Civil Wars.[1] Excavations conducted in that city by an American archaeological expedition have brought to light several third-century inscriptions[2] shedding further light on the life of the local Jews who, from a previous inscription giving a list of springs,[3] had already been known to have a synagogue of their own. The presence of Jews in Philadelphia, southeast of Sardis, may be inferred from the Apocalypse.[4] This is further corroborated by an inscription from the third century C.E. relating to a synagogue of the Hebrews.[5] From Magnesia on the Sipylus we have the inscription of a Jew who in his lifetime had built a tomb for himself and his family.[6] That there was a synagogue in Thyatira in the time of Hadrian is evidenced by an inscription mentioning a σαββατεῖον which is apparently equivalent to a synagogue. A woman from Magnesia who was close to Judaism is reported to have been living in Macedonian Philippi in Pauline times.[7] From Hypaepa we have an interesting inscription from the end of the second or third century C.E.[8]

9. *Ionia*. The efforts of the Jews to secure and maintain their privileges in Ionia have already been described on pp. 145-6. The Ionian cities known to have had a Jewish settlement in Roman times were: Phocaea, from where we have the dedication of a synagogue from the third century C.E.;[9] Smyrna, for which, in addition to several later inscriptions,[10] we have the Christian tradition about the martyrdom of Polycarp;[11] Teos, where a Jew, a Roman citizen, built a synagogue, apparently in the third century C.E.;[12] Priene, where so far the only evidence consists of the vestiges of a synagogue dug up there, including marble plaques with the relief of a menorah and a

---

[1] Jos. *Ant.* XIV, 235, 259-261.
[2] L. Robert, *Nouvelles inscriptions de Sardes* (1964), pp. 37-57.
[3] W. H. Buckler and D. M. Robinson, *Publications of the American Society for the Excavations of Sardis, Sardis VII*, I (1932), no. 17,1.7; *CII*, no. 751.
[4] Apoc. 3:9.
[5] *CII* no. 754; Lifshitz, op.cit. no. 28.
[6] *CII* no. 753.
[7] *CIG* II no. 3509; Acts 16:14.
[8] *CII* no. 755. There is no ground whatever to take ἡ ᾿Ιουδδηνῶν κατοικία as a Jewish settlement; see L. Robert, *Villes d'Asie Mineure* (1962), p. 282, n.1.
[9] *CII* no. 738; Lifshitz, op.cit. no. 13.
[10] *CII* nos. 739-743. The first two also in Lifshitz, op.cit. nos. 14-15.
[11] *Martyrium Polycarpi*, 12-13; 17-18.
[12] *CII* no. 744; L. Robert, *Hellenica* I (1940), pp. 27-8.

menorah carved on one of the pillars;[1] Colophon, where Jewish influence is manifest in an oracle of the nearby temple of Claros that has come down to us.[2] Ephesus, besides being the provincial capital of Asia, also was one of the major economic centres of Asia Minor. Jews seem to have lived there since the early Hellenistic period.[3] Quite a number of them were Roman citizens, and the Romans upheld the rights of the community both during the civil wars and the principate of Augustus (see above p. 143). A synagogue at Ephesus was used by Paul in his first missionary campaign.[4] The Alexandrian Jew Apollos also gave his sermons there. On his return to Ephesus Paul again used its pulpit for three months running, but aroused so much opposition that he preferred to make his headquarters elsewhere in the city, where he was busy disseminating Christianity for two years.[5] The fact that he stayed there so long is easily explained by the importance of the city for Jews and Greeks alike; for from there he was able to spread his Christian propaganda throughout Asia Minor.

Inscriptions relating to the Jews of Ephesus date from a later period, not before the third century C.E. demonstrating the haphazardness of epigraphic findings.[6] The first evidence of a Jewish settlement in Miletus is furnished by the letter of the Roman governor to the municipal authorities of that city (see above p. 145). It was there that Paul met the elders of the Christian community of Ephesus. An interesting inscription was found in 1906 in the theatre of Miletus, indicating the seating accommodation of the Jews.[7]

10. *Mysia.* In Mysia two principal towns are to be noted, Adramyttium and Pergamon. Adramyttium was already a major Jewish centre in 61 B.C.E., and the half-shekel contributions were collected there.[8] Though we continue to hear about the Jews of this city, no

---

[1] E. R. Goodenough, *Jewish Symbols in the Greco-Roman Period* II (1953), p. 77.
[2] Cornelius Labeo, in Macrobius, *Saturnalia* I, 18, 18-21; K. Buresch, *Klaros Untersuchungen zur Orakelwesen des späteren Altertums* (1889), pp. 48-55; W. Kroll, *Rhein. Museum* (1916), pp. 314-5; A. D. Nock, *Revue des études anciennes* (1928), p. 286; M. P. Nilsson, *Geschichte der griechischen Religion* II 2nd ed. (1961), pp. 477-8.
[3] Jos. *Against Apion* II, 39.
[4] Acts 18:19, 24-6.
[5] Acts 19:8-10.
[6] *CII* nos. 745-7; Goodenough op.cit., II, pp. 102-3.
[7] Acts 20:17; *CII* no. 748; Gabba, no. XXXIII.
[8] Cicero, *Pro Flacco*, 68.

far-reaching conclusions can be drawn from the later evidence available. Pergamon, the former capital of the Attalid Kingdom, was also a collection centre for Jewish Temple funds, and it had already establish-ed contact with the Jewish state in the Hellenistic period. We thus have a popular resolution of Pergamon in favour of the Jews dating from the times of John Hyrcanus,[1] which also mentions still earlier connections between Pergamon and the Jews.[2]

11. *Bithynia.* This is another country included in Philo's list.[3] Later inscriptions relating to Jews in different places were also found.[4] There were also Jews in Pontus,[5] Paphlagonia,[6] Galatia,[7] and Cappadocia.[8] The origins of the Jewish settlement in Armenia are obscure.[9]

12. *The islands.* As for the islands of Asia Minor, there is no doubt that there were Jews living in Rhodes during the Roman period. Considering that this island played a primary role in the political and economic life of the eastern Mediterranean in Hellenistic times, Jewish contacts with it probably long antedate our period. However, although we have evidence of people from the Palestinian cities staying in Rhodes,[10] we still have no epigraphic evidence of any con-nection between the Jews and Rhodes during the main Hellenistic period. The first extant report relating to any connections between Judaea and Rhodes is a letter sent by the Roman consul in 142 B.C.E.[11] which might possibly be interpreted to mean that as in all the other places it cites, there also was a Jewish settlement in Rhodes. We further know that some of the well-known Greek writers and philosophers who lived and taught in Rhodes in the first century B.C.E. (Posidonius of Syrian Apamea, Apollonius Molon of Alabanda

---

[1] Jos. *Ant.* xiv, 247-255.
[2] For the influence of the Jewish religion in Pergamon see also M. P. Nilsson, *Eranos* (1956), pp. 167-173; G. Delling, *Novum Testamentum* (1964-5), pp. 73-80,
[3] *Legatio* 281.
[4] L. Robert, *Hellenica* xi-xii (1960), pp. 386-413.
[5] Philo, *Legatio* 281.
[6] Lifshitz op.cit. no. 35.
[7] For Jews at Germa see W. M. Ramsay, *BCH* (1883), p. 24. The proof for the existence of a Jewish community at Ancyra derives mainly from Scaliger's emendation to Jos. *Ant.* xvi, 165.
[8] 1 Macc. 15:22, here King Ariarathes is mentioned; Acts 2:9.
[9] J. Neusner, *JAOS* (1964), pp. 230-240.
[10] D. Morelli, *Studi classici e orientali* (1956), pp. 148, 167.
[11] Cf. 1 Macc. 15:23.

in southern Asia Minor) wrote about the Jews, though with marked disapproval (see final chapter of vol. 2).

From the beginning of the Roman period we have an interesting report of a Jewish *grammaticus* by the name of Diogenes, who used to preach every Sabbath in Rhodes during the reign of Augustus, while Tiberius was staying on the island (between 6 B.C.E. and 2 C.E.).[1] Several inscriptions from the imperial period bear further testimony to the Jewish community of Rhodes. One inscription which may represent a list of donors mentions a person from Jerusalem by the name of Menippus.[2] Another tells of a woman by the name of Euphrosyne who was either Jewish or sympathetic to Judaism.[3]

The island of Cos first appears in Jewish history in connection with Judah the Maccabee. On their return to Judaea in 161 B.C.E. his emissaries to Rome received a letter of safe-conduct from the Roman consul to the authorities of Cos.[4] The Jews of Asia Minor deposited their money in that island during the war with Mithridates.[5] We also hear about the association of Herod and his son, Herod Antipas, with the island of Cos. (see below pp. 244, 285). One of the Greek inscriptions from that island refers to a Jewess or to a 'God-fearer'.[6]

The island of Samos is also mentioned among the places which the Roman consul in 142 B.C.E. asked to give safe conduct to Judah the Maccabee's emissaries.[7] It apparently already had a Jewish settlement at that time. Reports of a Jewish community on the island of Chios date from a later period.[8]

Cyprus, which lies right opposite the coast of Palestine, probably had a very early Jewish colony. It was in fact the site of the first encounter between Jews and Greeks, and the name Kitiyim (Kittim), from the name of the town of Kition in Cyprus, came to denote in Jewish literature the inhabitants of Greece, Macedonia and the entire West.[9] In Roman times the Herodian dynasty forged close ties with

---

[1] Suetonius, *Life of Tiberius* 32,2; J. Hubaux, *Latomus* (1946), pp. 99-102.

[2] *IG* XII, I, no. II.

[3] *IG* XII, I, no. 593; cf. L. Robert, *Études Anatoliennes* (1937), p. 411, n.5; *Nouvelles inscriptions de Sardes* (1964), p. 44.

[4] Jos. *Ant.* XIV, 233 with the comments of B. Niese, *Orientalische Studien Theodor Nöldeke gewidmet* II (1906), pp. 817-829.

[5] *Ant.* XIV, 111-3; Th. Reinach, *REJ* XVI (1888), pp. 204-210.

[6] W. R. Paton and E. L. Hicks, *The Inscriptions of Cos* (1891), no. 278.

[7] I Macc. 15:23; see also G. Dunst, *Klio* (1970), pp. 73-8.

[8] *CII* no. 954; see also G. Dunst, *Archiv für Papyrusforschung* (1958), p. 172; J. and L. Robert, *REG* (1959), p. 223.

[9] For the name Kittim in Jewish literature see also Y. Yadin, *The Scroll of the War of the Sons of Light against the Sons of Darkness* (1962), pp. 22-5.

Cyprus,[1] and Philo mentions it as one of the islands that was 'full of Jews'.[2] The Jewish settlement of Cyprus is also stressed in the Acts of the Apostles. It was the birthplace of Barnabas, Paul's partner in his missionary campaign, as well as of other Christian missionaries.[3] The numerical and physical force of the Jews of Cyprus also comes to the fore in the revolt that broke out in Trajan's time in which Cyprus was no less involved than Egypt and Cyrenaica.

The presence of Jews is documented in several of the major towns of the island. In Salamis the Jews had several synagogues at the time Paul and Barnabas were active there.[4] During the revolt in the times of Trajan the city was devastated by the Jews,[5] and upon its suppression the Jewish community was destroyed, to be revived only at a much later date.[6] In the New Testament we also hear about Paphos in the south-western part of the island.[7] Paul and Barnabas both came there and met the Roman governor who was under the influence of a Jew by the name of Bar Jesus. That trade relations were maintained with Palestine is proved by the Hasmonaean and Herodian coins and the coins of the Roman governors of Judaea which were found in Paphos.[8]

About the Jewish community of Golgoi, which lies further inland, we hear only later.[9] Reports about the Jews of Lapethos also should not be dated before the third century C.E.[10]

THE KINGDOM OF BOSPORUS

The close economic and political relations between the northern part of Asia Minor (Pontus) and the northern shore of the Black Sea helped to promote Jewish settlement in the Roman vassal kingdom of Bosporus—a military dependency of Rome. At least from the first century we have epigraphic evidence showing that Jews were

---

[1] Jos. *Ant.* XVIII, 131.
[2] *Legatio* 282.
[3] Acts 21:16; 11:20.
[4] Acts 13:5.
[5] Jerome, *Chronicon* ed. R. Helm (2nd ed. 1956), p. 196; Orosius VII, 12, 8; Syncellus I (ed. Dindorf), p. 657.
[6] T. B. Mitford, *Byzantion* (1950), pp. 110-6; Lifshitz, op.cit. no. 85.
[7] Acts 13:6.
[8] D. H. Cox, *NNM* CXLV (1959), pp. 25-26, nos. 191-200.
[9] *CII* no. 735; Lifshitz, op.cit. no. 82.
[10] *CII* no. 736; Lifshitz, op.cit. no. 83; Mitford, op.cit., pp. 141-3, no. 12; Lifshitz, op.cit. no. 84.

living in three of the towns on the northern Black Sea coast: Panticapaeum in the East Crimea (Kertsch) which was flourishing at
that period,[1] Gorgippia (Anapa), and Phanagoria. An inscription
from Gorgippia, dating to 41 c.e., refers to the manumission of a
female slave by the name of Chryse by one Pothos the son of Straton.[2]
That the manumittor was a Jew is indicated by the fact that the
manumission was carried out in a synagogue. Moreover, as was
usual, it was fictitiously dressed up as a dedication to the deity but
in this case the god in question was referred to by three epithets
primarily used for the Jewish godhead—the Highest, the Almighty,
the Blessed (θεῷ ὑψίστῳ παντοκράτορι εὐλογήτῳ). Some doubts as to
the man being a Jew were raised by the use of the pagan formula at
the end of the inscription in which the manumittor calls upon Zeus,
the sun and the earth to witness the transaction. It seems, however
that the usage of this formula was so common[3] as to have become a
dead letter that had lost its pagan character.[4]

The Jewish inscriptions from Panticapaeum (from the first century
c.e.) also relate to the manumission of slaves.[5] The first, dating
from 81 c.e., tells of a Jewish widow who, with the consent of her
two heirs, set free her slave in the synagogue provided he continued
to pray there.[6] The local Jewish community assumed joint responsibility for the transaction (συνεπιτροπευούσης δὲ καὶ τῆς συναγωγῆς τῶν
Ἰουδαίων). The second inscription deals with a manumission likewise
carried out in a synagogue at about the same time as the first, and
again contains a proviso relating to synagogue worship and the
function of the Jewish community. Another fragmentary inscription
has come to us from Phanagoria—again representing the manumission

---

[1] M. Rostowzew, *Skythien und der Bosporus* i (1931), pp. 195-7.
[2] B. Latyschev, *Inscriptiones Regni Bosporani Graecae et Latinae* ii (1890), no.
400; *CII* no. 690.
[3] S. Eitrem - L. Amundsen, *Papyri Osloenses* iii (1936), pp. 192-3; R. Taubenschlag, *The Law of Greco-Roman Egypt in the Light of the Papyri* (1955), p. 97, n.
151.
[4] Doubts that the manumittor was a Jew have been raised. That he was is
maintained with reason by E. R. Goodenough, *JQR* (1956-7), p. 221. For a
a similar inscription from Gorgippia 67 c.e. see B. Lifshitz, *Rivista di Filologia*
(1964), pp. 157-161.
[5] Latyschev, op.cit. nos. 52-53; *CII* nos. 683-4; see also nos. 685-9.
[6] See e.g. E. Schürer, 'Die Juden im bosporanischen Reiche und die Genossen-
schaften der σεβόμενοι θεὸν ὕψιστον eben daselbst', *Sitzungsberichte der königlich
preussischen Akademie der Wissenschaften* (1897), p. 3 (p. 202); F. Sokolowski,
HTR (1954), pp. 178-9. The interpretation of S. Krauss, *Synagogale Altertümer*
(1922), p. 240, n. 1 seems unlikely.

of a slave similar in text to the inscriptions from Panticapaeum, and as appears from the remaining fragments, also of Jewish origin.[1] The existence of a Jewish community in Olbia near the mouth of the river Bug is attested to by an inscription of unknown date dealing with the erection of a Jewish synagogue.[2]

A series of inscriptions from Tanais near the mouth of the Don, north-east of the Sea of Azov are associated with the worhsip of the Supreme God (Θεὸς Ὕψιστος).[3] The spread of this cult in Tanais as in other places—Asia Minor, for instance—is most easily accounted for by attributing it to Jewish influence.[4] The inscriptions date from the second and third century C.E.

GREECE

In the late Hellenistic period Greece began to lose its economic and cultural prominence in the Mediterranean world. This decline was accompanied by a fall in population which continued throughout the period of the Roman Empire.[5] Mourning for the glory that was Greece was a consistently recurring theme. Here and there, however, there still were some enclaves of prosperity as a result of the long peace Greece experienced after Octavian's victory and the establishment of the principate—a peace which remained undisturbed for hundreds of years.

The diminished position of Greece during the imperial period is reflected in the history of the Jews in that country, who do not seem to have had any major impact on the Jewish world of those times. On the whole the country was in a state of economic stagnation with a relatively poor population unlikely to attract great numbers of Jews, but there were still some Jewish communities in the first century C.E., usually founded during the preceding period. According to Philo there were Jews living in his time in Thessaly, Boeotia, Aetolia, Attica, Argos, most of the Peloponnese as well as on the islands

---

[1] Latyschev, op.cit. no. 364; *CII* no. 691.
[2] Cf. Latyschev, op.cit. I (2nd ed. 1916) no. 176; *CII* no. 682; Lifshitz, op.cit. no. 11.
[3] Latyschev, op.cit. II, nos. 437-467.
[4] Schürer, op.cit.; M. P. Nilsson, *Geschichte der griechischen Religion* II, p. 664. Goodenough, op.cit., pp. 221-243 goes further and thinks the worshippers of the 'Most High God' were full proselytes.
[5] M. Rostovtzeff, *Social and Economic History of the Roman Empire*, (2nd ed. 1957), pp. 253-4.

of Euboea and Crete.[1] Philo's statements are partly corroborated by
the story of the Acts of the Apostles about Paul's travels in Greece
and his appearances in the Jewish synagogues of the various cities.
They are also borne out by epigraphic material. As elsewhere at
that time, moreover, a considerable number of gentiles in the Greek
towns were attracted to the Jewish faith.

As might have been expected, there was a Jewish community in
Athens proper, and in the second century B.C.E. we already find a
Jew by the name of Simon the son of Ananias mentioned in an inscription.[2] Like the Roman leaders, and following the practice set
by the Hasmonaean rulers, Herod and his court also maintained
close ties with Athens. When Paul came to that city he found a
synagogue there where he preached the Christian gospel to the Jews
and to 'God-fearers' among the gentiles.[3] On an Athenian funerary
inscription of the first century C.E. we find the name of one Ammia
from Jerusalem.[4] In another inscription dating from the first century
B.C.E. or C.E., the name of a Jewish woman by the name of Sambatis
from Ancyra in Asia Minor is mentioned.[5] Two funerary inscriptions
of the Roman imperial period, though of unspecified date, mention
two Jewish women from Antioch, Mathia and Martha.[6] The name
Mathia (the daughter of Philo) also recurs in another inscription
from the first century B.C.[7] where the reference is to a woman from
Aradus in Phoenicia who was married to a certain Socrates from Sidon.
Two other funerary inscriptions from the first century C.E. relate to
Samaritan women, one of them married to a man from Antioch.[8]
Among the Jewish women buried in Athens in the first century C.E.
there was also one who had come from Miletus—a certain Martha the
daughter of Nicolas.[9] Theodorus the son of Theodorus of Marissa,
mentioned in a first century inscription, may likewise have been
Jewish.[10]

It is also interesting to note that the participant in Plutarch's table

[1] *Legatio* 281-2. [2] *IG* II, 2nd ed., no. 12609. [3] Cf. Acts 17:17.
[4] Cf. *IG* II, 2nd ed., no. 8934. [5] Cf. Ibid. no. 7931.
[6] Cf. Ibid. nos. 8231-8232.
[7] Cf. Ibid. no. 8358. For Athenian Jews see L. B. Urdahl, *Symbolae Osloenses*
(1968), pp. 39-56; J. and L. Robert, *REG.* (1964), p. 157; (1969), pp. 431, 453-4.
[8] *IG* II, 2nd ed., nos. 10219-10220; on Samaritans in the inscriptions see J.
and L. Robert, *REG.* (1969), pp. 476-.8
[9] *IG* II, 2nd ed., no. 9756.
[10]Ibid. no. 9285. Some difficulty attaches to the date suggested by the editor
(first century C.E.), since the city was destroyed by the Parthians in 40 B.C.E.,
and we have no information as to its existence in the first century C.E.

talk who speaks well about the Jewish religion and compares it to the worship of Dionysius is an Athenian, Moiragenes, who may well have been under the influence of Jews living there.[1] During the Roman period two Peloponnesian cities, Patrae and Corinth—the capital of the province of Achaea—enjoyed special prominence. Corinth almost acceded to the same status it had once enjoyed before its destruction by the Romans in 146 B.C.E. In line with its standing it seems highly likely that this city had the most important Jewish community in Greece, south of Macedon. Paul chose one of its synagogues to preach the Christian gospel to Jews and God-fearing Greeks.[2] We also know that there was a head of the synagogue by the name of Crispus and another called Sosthenes, and that there were many pro-Jewish gentiles in the city. As in Rome there was synagogue of the Hebrews (see below, p. 167). Though a Greek inscription to that effect, discovered in the excavations at Corinth,[3] belongs to post-Pauline times, it seems reasonable to assume that the same synagogue had existed in Paul's period or else that a new building had been erected instead of the old one.

From Patrae we have an inscription relating to Jews but its date is not clear.[4] We also have no definite epigraphic evidence about other Jewish settlements in the Peloponnese during the period under review. An inscription from Laconia mentions one, Justus of Tiberias, but its date has not been established.[5] Other Jewish inscriptions from Messenia, Argos and Mantinea are undoubtedly of a later period,[6] as are the inscriptions from non-Peloponnesian Greek cities like those found in Larissa in Thessaly.[7] Particular interest attaches to the inscriptions of the synagogue in the island of Aegina.[8]

All the three major urban settlements of Macedon—Thessalonica Philippi and Beroea—boasted a Jewish population. In Thessalonica Paul found a Jewish synagogue which also attracted 'God-fearing' men from among the Hellenes.[9] He also spread his gospel in the

[1] Plutarch, *Quaestiones convivales* IV, 6, 1, p. 671 C.   [2] Acts 18:4.
[3] *CII* no. 718; Gabba no. XXXIV.
[4] *CII* no. 716.
[5] *IG* v, 1, no. 1256; J. and L. Robert, *REG* (1966), p. 374.
[6] *IG* v, 1, no. 1398, l. 91-92; *CII* nos. 719-721.
[7] *CII* nos. 697-708.
[8] *CII* nos. 722-3; Lifshitz, op.cit. nos. 1-2. For Jews at Delos in the Hellenistic age see *CII* nos. 725-731; see also Jos. *Ant.* xiv, 213, 231 (on Paros, or Parium, 213); for Delphi see *CII* nos. 709-711.
[9] Acts 17:1-9; for Samaritans at Thessalonica at a later period see B. Lifshitz and J. Schiby, *RB* (1968), pp. 368-378.

Jewish synagogue of Beroea where he again found a willing ear among pro-Jewish Greeks and women from the wealthier classes.[1] There also was a Jewish synagogue in Philippi, a Roman colony founded in 42 B.C.[2] It seems that there also was a considerable number of Jews on the island of Crete. A tradition referred to in the histories of Tacitus linked the origin of the Jews with that island.[3] One of the wives of Josephus Flavius came from a prominent Jewish family in Crete.[4] Cretan inscriptions relating to Jews, however, date from a later period.[5] Quite a number of Jews, including men of wealth, also lived in the small island of Melos. Like the Jews of Crete they provided considerable funds to Pseudo-Alexander, the Herodian pretender who set himself up to be the son of Herod and Mariamme the Hasmonean, to finance his trip to Italy, and some of them accompanied him on his journey.[6]

ITALY

As early as the second century B.C.E. the Jewish community of Italy may be considered of special importance, Rome at that time already being the capital of the Mediterranean world. We have no definite information about the beginnings of Jewish settlement in Italy but they may probably be placed in that century. Since there were Jews living at that time in Greece, Asia Minor and the Mediterranean islands which were all in constant political and economic contact with Italy, it is only natural for some of them to have moved to Rome and other Italian cities. The political associations of Hasmonean Judaea with Rome, as reflected in the treaty concluded under Judah Maccabaeus (161 B.C.E.) and renewed in the times of Jonathan, Simeon and John Hyrcanus, involved frequent trips of Jewish notables to Rome and brought Italy very much within the Jewish orbit.

The earliest known event in the history of the Jews in Italy is the intervention of the *praetor peregrinus*, Cn. Cornelius Hispanus, in 139 B.C.E. against the religious propaganda of the Jews in

[1] Acts 17:10-12; for later Jewish inscriptions from Macedon see L. Robert, *REJ* CI (1937), pp. 82-85; *Hellenica* III (1946), pp. 104-107.
[2] Acts 16:11-12.
[3] Tacitus, *Histories* V, 2.
[4] Jos. *Life* 427.
[5] M. Guarducci, *Inscriptiones Creticae* I (1935), p. 12, no. 17.
[6] Jos. *Ant.* XVII, 327; *War* II, 103.

Rome and their attempt to set up places of Jewish worship within the Roman *pomerium* ('sacred precincts').[1] The expulsion of
the Jewish proselytizers fits in with a long series of attempts on
the part of the Roman authorities to prevent the influx and spread
of foreign ideas and religions which were likely to undermine
traditional Roman values. The same praetor who took steps
against Jewish religious propaganda in the same year also drove
the astrologers out of Rome. We further know of repeated attempts
to counteract and abolish the influence of the Greek rhetoricians and
philosophers in 161 and 154 B.C.E. and of a continuous struggle, down
to the imperial period, against invasion by Egyptian cults. The
Jewish missionaries may have come from Palestine or from Asia
Minor or from anywhere else in the Hellenistic world. However that
may be, the expulsion of the Jews from Rome and the destruction
of their places of worship in that city by no means put an end to the
mutual relationship. The Roman Republic gradually drew closer,
politically and economically, to the eastern countries and gradually
came to annex first Asia Minor and then Syria and Palestine as well.
These developments were evidently beneficial to the Jews in Italy.
In the first half of the first century B.C.E. there was already a large
and influential Jewish community in Rome. At any rate it had attained considerable proportions before the conquest of Jerusalem
by Pompey,[2] since as early as 59 B.C.E. only four years afterwards,
we hear about its size and influence, and the gold they had been
sending to Jerusalem in previous years.[3] This can hardly be reconciled
with the view that the captives who came to Rome with Pompey's
booty formed the main nucleus of the city's Jewish community.[4]
The Jews of Rome were by that time already involved in the political
and social dissensions that characterized republican Rome in its final
phase. The Jews largely sided with the *populares* against the supremacy
of the Senate and the Roman aristocracy, whose political traditions
made them less favourably disposed towards the new religious elements
coming into the city. It is also possible that the Jews had their misgivings about the legislation passed in 64 B.C.E. against the formation

[1] Valerius Maximus I, 3, 3.
[2] M. Radin, *The Jews among the Greeks and Romans* (1915), pp. 227-231; H. J.
Leon, *The Jews of Ancient Rome* (1960), pp. 4-5.
[3] Cicero, *Pro Flacco*, 28, 66-7.
[4] Philo, *Legatio* 155. He does not expressly connect the emergence of the Jewish
community at Rome with the capture of Jerusalem by Pompey, but only states
that the majority of Roman Jews stemmed from freedmen.

of colleges or associations,[1] even though they may not have been directly affected by it.[2] The policy of leaders hostile to the Senate, like the tribune Clodius, who intended to restore the various *collegia* and facilitate conditions for the cults imported from the East was undoubtedly more congenial to the Jews who had settled in Rome.

From the outset the Jews of Rome maintained their strong national loyalty to their home country. They not only sent the half-shekel tribute to Jerusalem, like the Jews in the rest of the Diaspora, but being at the centre of contemporary political life they also became the lobbyists of the Jews living in other countries. A case in point was the indictment, in 59 B.C.E., of the former governor of Asia, Flaccus, for his depredations in that province. The charges against him included the confiscation of the gold collected by the Jews in four Asian towns for the support of the Temple in Jerusalem. Flaccus, a member of the *optimates* faction and one of the prime agents in the suppression of Catilina's plot, was defended by the two most outstanding counsellors of Rome in that period: Hortensius and Cicero. The latter in his advocacy missed no opportunity of stressing the influence which the Jews of Rome, with their large numbers and effective agitation,[3] were exerting on the proceedings. Although Flaccus was acquitted,[4] this was but one in a long series of attempts on the part of the Jews of Rome to use their influence in favour of Jewish interests in other countries.

In the internal struggles in Rome culminating in the civil war conducted by Pompey and the Senate against Julius Caesar, local Jewish sympathies undoubtedly lay with the latter. Not only was he the leader of the *populares*, so that they could expect him to show more understanding and consideration for their interests, but he also was the opponent of their own great enemy, Pompey, the conqueror of Jerusalem who had robbed the Jewish state of its former independence. Although the official leaders of the Jews, Hyrcanus II and Antipater, assisted Pompey in his campaign against Caesar,[5] the Jewish masses throughout the world never forgave him, especially since Julius Caesar explicitly supported Aristobulus II, the ousted Hasmonaean, and intended to send him to Palestine at the head of an

[1] Asconius, ed. A. C. Clark, p. 7.
[2] J. Lewy, *Zion* (1941-2), pp. 125-134.
[3] Cicero, *Pro Flacco* 28, 66.
[4] Macrobius, *Saturnalia* II, I, 13.
[5] Lucanus, *Pharsalia* III, 216; Appianus, *Bella Civilia* II, 71, 294.

armed Roman force to regain his throne. Caesar's friendly attitude to the Jews of Palestine and the various Roman provinces after Pompey's victory is well documented. Obviously the Jews of Rome also benefited from this benevolent policy as well as from the fact that although he had outlawed all *collegia* other than those founded in ancient times, he expressly allowed the existence of the Jewish associations.[1] Hence, we are told, the Jews of Rome more than any other national group mourned the death of Caesar upon his assassination in March 44 B.C.E.[2]

The fact that the delegation sent from Judaea after Herod's death in 4 B.C.E. to prevent the succession of his sons was joined by thousands of Jews in Rome indicates the extent to which that community had grown.[3]

Augustus who disapproved in general of the spread of foreign cults in Roman society had little sympathy for the Jewish religion. He actually praised his grandson Gaius for not visiting the Temple in Jerusalem and offering sacrifices there during his passage through Judaea in 1 C.E.[4] Nevertheless he continued on the whole Julius Caesar's policy. The presence of Jews in Rome was very noticeable as may be seen from the literary works of the period.[5] Among the Jewish synagogues in the city one was called after Augustus himself and another after his son-in-law and lieutenant, Agrippa (see below, p. 166). The extent of his consideration for Jewish religious sensibilities may be gauged from the fact that he provided for an alternative date for the distribution of money and grain to the Jews in case the date of the general distribution to the Roman people should fall on a Saturday.[6]

Under his successor, Tiberius, the status of the Jews of Rome deteriorated considerably. For the first time since 139 B.C.E. we hear of an official action against them, in an attempt made by the authorities to curb the influence the Egyptian and the Jewish creeds were gaining among the higher circles of Roman society, and to preserve the purity of the native religion. Tiberius was simply continuing the traditional policy of the Roman government since the battle of Actium, which

---

[1] Suetonius, *Julius* 42, 3; Jos. *Ant.* XIV, 215.
[2] Suetonius, *Julius* 84, 5.
[3] Cf. Jos. *Ant.* XVII, 300; *War* II, 80.
[4] Suetonius, *Life of Augustus* 93.
[5] Horatius, *Sermones* I, 4, 139-143; 5, 96-104; 9, 60-78; Ovid, *Ars amatoria* I, 75-80, 413-416; *Remedia amoris* 217-220.
[6] Philo, *Legatio* 158.

was designed to stem the spread of Oriental cults, especially that of the Egyptian goddess Isis.[1]

The steps taken by Tiberius against the Jews were occasioned—at least ostensibly—by reports of irresponsible behaviour by Egyptian priests and Jewish missionaries. Egyptian priests of the goddess Isis had allegedly, under the disguise of religion, inveigled a lady from the higher ranks of society to take part in an erotic rite. Several Jews had convinced a proselyte, also a lady of senatorial rank, to send gifts of purple and gold to the Temple in Jerusalem but instead of transferring them to Judaea, had diverted them to their own purposes. Consequently in 19 C.E., at the prompting of Tiberius, the Senate adopted a resolution (senatus consultum) against the worship of Isis and the Jewish religion. The offending Egyptian priests were crucified, the image of their goddess was thrown into the Tiber, and her ritual paraphernalia were burned. As for the Jews, four thousand men of the freedmen class who were fit for military service were sent by the consuls to the island of Sardinia to put down local marauders while the rest, Jews and converts alike, were driven out of Rome.[2] Philo points out that these anti-Jewish measures were largely inspired by Sejanus, who became the commander of the praetorian guard in 16-17 C.E.[3] It is doubtful whether all the Jews living in Rome actually left. At any rate, the fall of Sejanus in 31 C.E. no doubt facilitated their speedy return. In the time of Gaius Caligula and particularly during the early days of Claudius we again encounter large numbers of Jews living in the imperial capital.

Claudius' attitude to the Jews in the Roman Empire in general was a reaction against the anti-Jewish policy of his predecessor, Gaius Caligula. All anti-Jewish measures were revoked. The privileges of the Jews of Alexandria were reaffirmed and Agrippa I, who had helped Claudius to establish himself on the throne, was made king of the whole of Palestine. On the other hand, Claudius was unwilling to extend to the Jews any further privileges beyond those they had enjoyed under the emperors preceding Gaius Caligula.

As in all other matters it was Claudius' express intention to continue in the footsteps of Augustus in the sphere of religion, strengthening

---

[1] K. Latte, Römische Religionsgeschichte (1960), p. 283.
[2] Jos. Ant. XVIII, 65-84; Tacitus, Annals II, 85; Suetonius, Life of Tiberius 36; Dio Cassius LVII, 18, 5a; Seneca, Epistulae Morales 108, 22; E. T. Merrill, Classical Philology (1919), pp. 365-372; J. R. Rietra, C. Suetoni Tranquilli vita Tiberi (1928), pp. 39-47; E. M. Smallwood, Latomus (1956), pp. 314-329.
[3] Legatio 159.

the native Roman form of worship and preventing its corruption and domination by foreign cults. Hence his attempt to renew the discipline of the *haruspices* and to swell the numbers of the patrician families so that the ranks of the traditional priesthood of Rome might be replenished.[1] At the same time he took steps against the spread of astrology—an oriental import—and imposed a ban on the worship of the Gallic Druids. It may be conjectured that Jewish religious proselytizing in Rome proper aroused his serious dismay at the best of times, and it is not surprising that he should have been violently provoked by any sign of resulting social unrest, as occurred with the appearance of the first Christian missionaries in the capital. When the Jews became restive, Claudius reacted with a severity reminiscent of Tiberius. It seems that he initially ordered their expulsion from Rome but refrained from the enforcement of the edict, partly perhaps under the influence of Agrippa I. On the whole he confined himself to restricting assemblies for public worship in 41 C.E. although it seems that as regards the ring-leaders responsible for the riots and Christian activists the original edict was enforced.[2]

Such upheavals notwithstanding, the Jewish community of Rome continued to flourish. In Nero's reign the arrival of Paul and the spread of Christianity beyond the borders of Palestine no doubt stirred up the community while non-Jewish society also saw that it had to contend with a new religion that had come out of Judaea, which was trying with a new, dangerous vigour to subvert the foundations of Roman tradition. Accordingly in 64 C.E. the authorities made a clear distinction between Judaism and the new Christian religion: the Christians were seized, tortured and killed as scapegoats for the burning of Rome, but the Jews remained unharmed. However, the suggestion that the Jews had persuaded Nero to persecute the Christians seems quite unwarranted.[3]

Historical sources, archaeological findings and the epigraphic material discovered in the Jewish catacombs of Rome which already began to be studied in the early seventeenth century all go to show that in ancient times there were Jews living all over the city of Rome. Most of the inscriptions, however, date from a later period than the first

[1] A. Momigliano, *Claudius, the Emperor and his Achievement* (1934), pp. 20-38; V. M. Scramuzza, *The Emperor Claudius* (1940), pp. 145-156.
[2] Suetonius, *Life of Claudius* 25, 4; Dio Cassius LX, 6, 6; Acts 18:2; Orosius, *Adversus paganos* VII, 6, 15.
[3] Against this view see already E. Meyer, *Ursprung und Anfänge des Christentums* III (1923), p. 500, n.2; Leon, op.cit. p. 28; F. Millar, *JRS* (1966), p. 233.

century C.E. for which the residential distribution of the community is not adequately documented. The first catacomb to be discovered was that of Monteverde (1602), east of the Tiber. Some two and a half centuries later, in 1859, the catacomb of Vigna Randanini on the Via Appia was discovered. Subsequently another four Jewish catacombs were found, the latest and most significant discovery being the catacomb in the Villa Torlonia on the Via Nomentana (1919).[1] The oldest Jewish catacomb discovered is that in Monteverde, which may already have been in use in the first century B.C.E. during the initial consolidation of the community. It continued in use at least down to the end of the third century. The other two catacombs, on the Via Appia and Via Nomentana, were in use from the first down to the third century C.E.

Undoubtedly the highest concentration of Jews in the first century B.C.E. was on the right bank of the Tiber (Trastevere) as is also specifically indicated by Philo:[2] 'He [scil. Augustus] knew that the large district of Rome beyond the river Tiber was owned and inhabited by Jews.' The same distribution also applied in the subsequent generations. The inscriptions point to a considerable number of synogogues in Trastevere, including some whose names definitely show that they were built in the times of Augustus. The main indication that a given synagogue was located in Trastevere is the presence of inscriptions relating to it in the catacombs of Monteverde which are next to this neighbourhood. Among these synagogues mention should first of all be made of that called after Augustus ('Αυγουστησίων) to which reference is made in six inscriptions, most of them discovered in the Monteverde catacombs.[3] It is almost certain that this synagogue was founded in the time of Augustus. The same may apply to the synagogue named after Agrippa, Augustus' right-hand man ('Αγριπ-πησίων) and a known benefactor of the Jews.[4] Another synagogue in Trastevere was named after Volumnius (Βολυμνησίων), the relevant inscriptions also being from the Monteverde catacombs. The identity of this Volumnius is not clear, although some scholars tend to think that the reference is to one of the procurators of Syria in the times of Herod and Augustus.[5]

[1] Cf. H. J. Leon, HUCA (1928), pp. 299-314; The Jews of Ancient Rome, pp. 46-53.
[2] Legatio 155.
[3] CII nos. 284, 301, 338, 368, 416, 496.
[4] CII nos. 365, 425, 503.
[5] E. Bormann, Wiener Studien (1912), pp. 362-3; G. la Piana, HTR (1927), p. 354, n. 23; for a different view see Leon, op.cit. pp. 158-9.

As for the synagogue of the Hebrews in Trastevere,[1] it is regarded by some as the synagogue of the Hebrew or Aramaic-speaking Jews,[2] while others argue more convincingly that it was the first synagogue established by the Jews in Rome at a time when there were no others and its members as yet saw no reason to make any distinction between themselves and members of other synagogues.[3]

These four synagogues certainly existed in the Julio-Claudian period, but it is not at all clear whether the same applies to the other three synagogues in Trastevere: the synagogue of the Calcaresians,[4] apparently called after its location in the street or neighbourhood of the lime-kiln workers; the Tripolitan synagogue[5] whose founders apparently came from the Phoenician—or perhaps from the African—city of Tripolis; and the synagogue of the Vernaclesians,[6] apparently owing its name to the fact that its founders were locally-born Jews.

Thus of the eleven synagogues known to us from Jewish inscriptions found in Rome,[7] at least seven were in Trastevere.

Another quarter which according to the inscriptions had Jews living in it is the Subura, a neighbourhood of miscellaneous shops between the southern end of the Viminal and the western end of the Esquiline.[8] The inscriptions mention a synagogue of the Siburesians whose members were buried in the catacomb of the Via Nomentana.[9] Another synagogue was on the Campus Martius.[10] The location of two other synagogues known to us from the epigraphic material cannot be determined. These are the synagogue of Elaea,[11] one of the references to which is contained in an inscription in the catacomb of Vigna Cimarra off the Appian way, and the synagogue of the Secenians,

---

[1] *CII* nos. 291, 317, 510, 535.
[2] N. Müller and N. A. Bees, *Die Inschriften der jüdischen Katakombe am Monteverde zu Rom* (1919), pp. 23-4; A. Momigliano, *Rassegna Mensile di Israel* VI, p. 290.
[3] La Piana, op.cit., p. 356, n. 26; Leon, op.cit. p. 149.
[4] *CII* nos. 304, 316, 384, 433, 504, 537.
[5] *CII* nos. 390, 408.
[6] *CII* nos. 318, 383, 494.
[7] I exclude from the list the so-called Synagogue of the Herodians, the existence of which is based on a fallacious restoration of *CII* no. 173. Cf. A. Ferrua, *Epigraphica* III (1941), 34; Leon, op.cit. 159-162.
[8] S. B. Platner and T. Ashby, *A Topographical Dictionary of Ancient Rome* (1929), pp. 500-1.
[9] *CII* nos. 18, 22, 67, 140, 380.
[10] *CII* nos. 88, 319, 523; Leon, op.cit. pp. 144-5.
[11] *CII* nos. 281, 509.

which is mentioned only in a single inscription[1] found in the catacombs of the Via Nomentana.[2]

From Juvenal's satire we learn about the connection of Jews with the Porta Capena, near the beginning of the Via Appia leading to Capua.[3] It is difficult to say whether there were Jews living there permanently, but it is quite conceivable that there were.[4]

It is also difficult to tell when Jews first began to settle in ancient Porto, the port of Rome, and in Ostia. The inscriptions frequently cited in connection with Porto were actually brought there from Rome and cannot serve as evidence of the existence of a local Jewish community.[5] On the other hand the existence of a Jewish settlement in Ostia is definitely proved by the discovery in 1961 of a Jewish synagogue there. The excavations show that part of the building was erected towards the end of the first century C.E., but the original building was changed and expanded during the second and third centuries and received its final form in the fourth century.[6]

We also have clear evidence of the presence of Jews during the Julio-Claudian period in the major towns of Campagna, Puteoli, Naples, Capua and Pompei.

Puteoli was at that time a major port connecting Italy with Alexandria and the East. Its Jewish inhabitants were deceived by Pseudo-Alexander, the false pretender (see above p. 160) who appeared some time after Herod's death. They supplied the pretender with considerable funds.[7]

As in many other places, the Jewish community of Puteoli supplied converts to Christianity; and Paul found co-religionists there. Claudia Aster, a Jewish captive from Jerusalem, is mentioned in an inscription from Naples,[8] while the presence of Jews in Capua during the first century C.E. is attested by a Greek burial inscription found

---

[1] *CII* no. 7.
[2] On various conjectures concerning the names of those synagogues see Leon, op.cit., pp. 145-7, 149-151.
[3] *Saturae* III, 10-16.
[4] See on one hand T. Mommsen, *Gesammelte Schriften* III (1907), p. 419, n. 3; La Piana, *HTR* (1927), p. 346; S. Collon, *Mélanges d'archéologie et d'histoire* (1940), pp. 90-1; and for a different opinion Leon, op.cit. p. 137. In any case I do not think that we should identify Porta Capena with Porta Idymaea of *Saturae* VIII, 160, as suggested by B. L. Ullman in *Classical Tradition, Literary and Historical Studies in Honor of Harry Caplan* (1966), p. 277.
[5] H. J. Leon, *HTR* (1952), pp. 165-175.
[6] M. F. Squarciapino, *La Sinagoga di Ostia* (1964).
[7] Jos. *Ant.* XVII, 328; *War* II, 104.
[8] *CII* no. 556.

in Jerusalem mentioning Maria the wife of Alexander of Capua.[1] The relatively numerous inscriptions relating to Jews found in Pompei all undoubtedly date from before 79 C.E., when the city was destroyed. Reference is made to Jewish women by the name of Maria and Martha and to the slave of a Jewish man as well as to Sodom and Gomorrah.[2] We have no first hand information about the Jews of Sicily in that period but we know that the Greek historian and rhetor, Caecilius of Caleacte was a Jew.[3] A contemporary of Augustus and a slave by origin, he is the first Jew known to have become famous as a Greek author writing on non-Jewish subjects, as distinct from the usual type of Hellenized Jew who was primarily preoccupied with Jewish subjects.[4] As we have seen, four thousand Jews were sent in 19 C.E. to the island of Sardinia on military service, but it is difficult to assess whether they formed the nucleus of a Jewish colony there.[5] Nor have we any concrete evidence of Jewish settlements during the Julio-Claudian period in the Latin provinces of the empire and in the African and Mauretanian provinces, which is particularly surprising in view of the ancient ties between Jews and Phoenicians which favour the assumption that Jews had settled in Carthage even before the Romans took over. For a later period we do in fact have such evidence both for Africa[6] and Mauretania.[7] That neither Philo nor the New Testament should allude to Jews living in these areas is therefore all the more astonishing.

Paul, towards the end of his life, intended to preach the Christian gospel in Spain and Illyricum.[8] Since it was his custom to go to countries where the ground had been prepared by the Jews, it may be assumed that there already was a Jewish settlement in Spain during

---

[1] S. Klein, *Jüdisch-palästinisches Corpus Inscriptionum* (1920), p. 24 no. 48; *CII* no. 1284.
[2] *CII* nos. 562-7; J. B. Frey, *RB* (1933), pp. 365-383; G. Giordano and I. Kahn, *Gli Ebrei in Pompei in Ercolano e nella citta' della Campania Felix* (1966).
[3] *Suda*, s.v. Καικίλιος, ed. A. Adler, III, 83; *FGH* IIB, 183, T 1; see also Th. Reinach, *REJ* XXVI (1893), pp. 36-46; Schürer III, 632.
[4] On inscriptional material bearing upon Sicilian Jewry see J. and L. Robert, *REG* (1952), p. 202; (1960), p. 212; (1961), p. 268; (1962), p. 223.
[5] On Jews in Sardinia see Juster I, p. 183.
[6] P. Monceaux, *REJ* XLIV (1902), pp. 1-28; M. Rachmuth, *MGWJ* (1906), pp. 22-58; J. Ferron, *Cahiers de Byrsa* (1956), pp. 105-117; W. H. C. Frend, *JTS* (1970), pp. 92-6. Especially important is the Jewish necropolis at Gamart near Carthage.
[7] Schürer III, p. 55; Juster II, pp. 208-9; R. Thouvenot, *Revue des études anciennes* (1969), pp. 356-9.
[8] Romans 15:28.

the Julio-Claudian period, especially as later traditions frequently stress the ancient origins of the Jewish community in the Iberian peninsula.[1]

BABYLONIA AND THE PARTHIAN KINGDOM

Throughout the Second Temple period there was a large Jewish community living under direct Parthian rule or within their sphere of influence, beyond the boundaries of the Roman Empire. That large numbers of their compatriots were not dependent on the Romans and not subject to their policy was a source of consolation and inspiration for the Jews of Palestine and the Roman Empire, just as in the countries of Christendom during the Middle Ages Jews were comforted by the knowledge that many of their people were beyond the reach of the Christian rulers, under the wings of Islam. The fact that within the Parthian domain the majority of Jews were living in Babylonia, with a further concentration in northern Mesopotamia on the borders of the Roman Empire, enhanced their military and political significance in view of the tension that prevailed between Rome and Parthia during most of our period. The conversion of the royal house of Adiabene gave added weight to their position. According to Philo, the existence of a Jewish colony under Parthian rule was a consideration borne in mind by Petronius, the governor of Syria, when assigned the task of implementing Gaius Caligula's anti-Jewish measures which were appropriately modified.[2] The Jews of the East were also prominently stressed by Agrippa I in his letter to Gaius Caligula.[3] Similarly Josephus dwells repeatedly on the large number of Jews beyond the Euphrates.[4]

The main Jewish centre in the Parthian Empire was in Babylonia, where there was an uninterrupted settlement since the Babylonian exile. The main seat of the Jews of Babylonia was the town of Nehardaea on the Euphrates, a walled city easily defensible thanks to to its geographic position.[5] Located in an area densely inhabited by Jews, it was one of the collection centres for the half-shekel tribute of the Babylonian community.[6] During the period in question we have

[1] Y. Baer, *A History of the Jews in Christian Spain* I (1961), pp. 15-16.
[2] *Legatio* 216.
[3] *Legatio* 282.
[4] *Ant.* XI, 133; XV, 14.39.
[5] J. Obermeyer, *Die Landschaft Babylonien im Zeitalter des Talmuds und des Gaonats* (1929), pp. 244-265.
[6] Jos. *Ant.* XVIII, 311-2.

no specific information about other major Jewish settlements in Babylonia proper, but evidently the fault lies with the state of our source material. There can be no doubt that there were Jews living throughout the country, in smaller or greater numbers. We hear about the activities of a Jewish merchant by the name of Ananias in the town of Spasinou Charax near the Persian Gulf in connection with the conversion of Izates of Adiabene.[1] There was also a Jewish settlement in Seleucia on the Tigris, the largest Hellenistic city of the Parthian Empire. Its numbers were considerably increased by the influx of refugees after the destruction of the semi-independent Jewish state under the leadership of Anilaeus, when for some time the Jews held the balance between the Greek and the eastern element in the city.[2] When their position subsequently deteriorated, many of them moved to Ctesiphon, the winter capital of the Parthian kings.[3]

The second largest bloc of eastern Jews in that period was in northern Mesopotamia, which included the territories of ancient Assyria. It seems likely that Jews were first settled there during the exile of the Ten Tribes. The most prominent Jewish settlement was Nisibis which played the same role in the north as did Nehardaea in the south and also was a collection centre for the half-shekel funds.[4] Jewish settlements presumably existed also elsewhere, especially in Edessa and in Arbela, the capital of Adiabene, east of the Jewish centre of Nisibis. While the conversion of the royal house of Adiabene to Judaism was largely an outcome of their numerical strength in these territories, this was in turn no doubt enhanced by the conversion.

Of ancient origin also were the Jewish colonies in Iran, especially in Media and Elam.[5] Towards the end of the Persian occupation of Palestine Jews from the neighbourhood of Jericho are known to have been deported to Hyrcania, south of the Caspian Sea.[6]

During the occupation of Palestine by the Seleucids in the second century B.C.E. the Jews of Babylonia and of Palestine temporarily found themselves under the same government. Though after the dissolution of the Seleucid Empire and the conquest of Babylonia by

---

[1] *Ant.* xx, 34.
[2] *Ant.* xviii, 374.
[3] Cf. *Ant.* xviii, 377.
[4] On the hypothesis of a southern Nisibis, apart from the more famous one in the north see Schürer iii, p. 9, n. 18.
[5] Acts 2:9.
[6] On the deportation of Jews to Hyrcania see Syncellus, ed. Dindorf, i, p. 486; Orosius, *Adversus paganos* iii, 7, 6.

the Parthians they were again separated politically, relations continued to remain very close. The invasion of the eastern provinces of Rome by the Parthians, who installed the Hasmonaean king Antigonus on the Judaean throne (see below, p. 220 f.) for a short period created a political climate conducive to close mutual relations. Hyrcanus II, the high priest and ethnarch of Judaea who was captured by the Parthians, was subsequently released and allowed to live among his people in Babylonia, who treated him with the respect due to his former rank, until he went back to Judaea at Herod's request.[1] Babylonian Jewry also maintained close contacts with Herod. The first high priest appointed by Herod was Hananel, a Babylonian Jew. Jewish settlers from Babylonia, led by Zamaris, became the allies of Herod and helped him to establish control over Batanaea, Gaulanitis and Trachonitis. In the person of Hillel, the Babylonian community provided scholarship in the homeland with one of its most prominent figures. Media was the birthplace of another well-known Jewish scholar of the period, Nahum the Mede.[2] Under the active guidance of Judah ben Bathyra the city of Nisibis became a major centre of Jewish learning even before the destruction of the Temple in Jerusalem.[3]

Two extraordinary events marked the history of the Jewish community in the Parthian Empire during the first half of the first century C.E.: the conversion of the royal dynasty of Adiabene and the attempt to establish a semi-independent Jewish state in northern Babylonia.

The conversion of the royal house of Adiabene was the acme of the Jewish proselytizing movement of the ancient period. It was the first time a gentile royal dynasty had gone over to the Jewish faith, an example to be later emulated by Dhu Nuwas, the king of southern Arabia, at the beginning of the sixth century C.E. and by Bulan, the king of the Khazars in the eighth century C.E. The conversion filled the Jews with great pride, for along with their missionary success came the sense of real power gained by their nation and the enhancement of its status both in the Roman and in the Parthian empire.

The kingdom of Adiabene with its capital Arbela originally extended over the territories of ancient Assyria, north-east of the Tigris, near its tributaries known as the Upper and Lower Zab. In course of time it annexed further territories, west of the Tigris. Situated near

[1] Jos. *Ant.* xv, 14-19.
[2] On Nahum the Mede, see *M. Nazir* 5:4; *Shabbath* 2:1.
[3] On Judah b. Bathyra I see Neusner I, pp. 43-9.

Armenia in the north, which was the main bone of contention between Rome and Parthia close to the fords of the Tigris in the west,
and at the gateway to Atropatene in the east, it occupied an important
strategic position and therefore played a not inconsiderable military
and political role in the Julio-Claudian era.

The person directly responsible for the conversion of the royal family
was King Izates II, the son of Monobazus I and his wife-sister, Queen
Helena. In his youth he was sent away to Spasinu Charax, the capital
of the Mesenian kingdom, where the Tigris and the Euphrates flow into
the Persian Gulf.[1] He was probably removed from the court to ease the
tension due to the competition between him and Monobazus' sons
by his other wives. A further motive might have been to forge
closer political and economic ties with Mesene. In fact the king of
Mesene cultivated the boy, gave him his daughter in marriage and
granted him extensive estates from which he derived a considerable
income.[2]

Izates had probably met Jews and heard something about their
religion while he was still at his father's court, where the ground was
already prepared for the acceptance of Jewish ideas. The turning
point in his life, however, came during his stay in Spasinu Charax,
where a Jewish merchant by the name of Ananias was making active
Jewish propaganda among the king's harem. Izates was deeply
influenced by his teachings and thoroughly imbued with Jewish
ideas, though he did not have himself circumcised.

Towards the end of his father's reign, Izates was called back to
Adiabene and Ananias went along with him. Monobazus gave Izates
one of the provinces of his empire to administer. After his father's
death Izates became, thanks to the influence of his mother Helena,
king of the whole of Adiabene. The brothers and other relatives of
Monobazus except Izates' brother Monobazus (the Second), the son
of Helena and Monobazus I, were arrested. After some time they were
sent as hostages to Rome to the imperial court in line with the system
commonly used by the Parthian kings for getting rid of dangerous
rivals without executing them or holding them in prison for any
length of time.[3]

---

[1] H. Graetz, *Das Königreich Mesene und seine jüdische Bevölkerung* (1879),
pp. 13-14; Obermeyer, op.cit., pp. 90-1; S. A. Nodelman, *Berytus* (1960), pp.
98-100.
[2] Jos. *Ant.* xx, 17-23.
[3] *Ant.* xx, 24-37.

On his return to Adiabene, Izates found that his mother, Helena, was also showing pro-Jewish proclivities. However, both she and Ananias prevented him from being circumcised and becoming a complete Jew, because such a step might, to their minds, arouse the opposition of his subjects and cost him his throne. The decision came only with the arrival of a Jew from Galilee by the name of of Eleazar who regarded circumcision as an essential prerequisite for the acceptance of Judaism. The king was thus converted to Judaism and other members of the royal house followed suit.[1]

Part of the aristocracy used the king's conversion as a pretext for instigating riots, which were soon quelled. Considering the general climate of the period, when other rulers in Syria and Asia Minor were also converted to Judaism and were circumcised, if only in order to marry princesses of the Herodian dynasty, it can hardly be assumed that the conversion aroused deep and widespread opposition. It obviously won for the house of Adiabene the enthusiastic support of its Jewish subjects as well as of the numerous influential Jews living in Babylonia and in the Roman Empire. Although we hear nothing about the spread of Judaism among wider circles of the local population, it stands to reason that others, too, followed the example of the royal family so that the number of Jews in Adiabene increased considerably and by the end of the Second Temple period it may be regarded as a Jewish state.[2]

Izates also played a not inconsiderable role in the internal politics of the Parthian Empire and its relations with the Roman Empire. During the early days of his reign he was already mixed up in an internal Parthian dispute when King Artabanus was deposed after much struggle and travail and asked for his help. Izates successfully mediated between him and his rebellious subjects who consented to restore him to the throne.[3] In gratitude Artabanus showered much honour upon Izates and ceded to him extensive territories beyond the Tigris and south of Armenia, centering upon Nisibis, with its large Jewish population.

After the death of Artabanus in 38 C.E., the Parthian kingdom went through a difficult time. Vardanes, his successor, was in a state of constant rivalry with his brother, Gotarzes. In Armenia the Romans managed to impose an Iberian ruler who was hostile to the Parthians

---

[1] *Gen. Rabba* par. 46 (ed. Theodor-Albeck I p. 467-8).
[2] G. Widengren, *Supplements to Vetus Testamentum* IV (1957), p. 200, n. 5.
[3] A. v. Gutschmid, *Kleine Schriften* III (1892), p. 45.

and provoked Vardanes into military action. The fall of the mutinous city of Seleucia on the Tigris after a long siege in 42 C.E. made it possible for him to divert his forces against Armenia.[1] For this campaign the Parthians needed the help of Izates, Armenia's next-door neighbour, but Izates remained reluctant, fearing direct Roman intervention after their governor in Syria had forcefully anticipated the Parthian move, or indirect pressure being brought to bear upon his family in Jerusalem. Agrippa I, the king of Judaea, might also have had a hand in his decision. A plot in which Vardanes was killed and his brother Gotarzes installed on the Parthian throne[2] prevented punitive action being taken against Adiabene.

The Roman-Parthian conflict overshadowed the rest of Izates' reign. In 47 C.E. Emperor Claudius, giving in to the anti-Gotarzes faction, agreed to send back one of the Parthian hostages, Meherdates, in order to depose the reigning monarch. With the aid of Cassius Longinus, the Syrian governor at that time, Meherdates set up camp in Zeugma on the Euphrates, where his Parthian supporters gathered around him. From there he turned east to Edessa and pursued his campaign through the kingdom of Adiabene. It seems that Izates, at least ostensibly, joined Meherdates' camp but when the two armies had taken up positions on the river Corma, he was one of the first to defect to Gotarzes and help him to win a decisive victory over his enemies.[3]

Izates continued to hold on to his throne after the accession of Vologases to the Parthian throne in 51 C.E.[4] but in the last few years of his life had to face severe internal dissension. Some of the nobility entered into an alliance with Abias, one of the Arab kings. The forces of Izates, however, defeated the Arabs in battle, and their king escaped to one of his forts where he committed suicide after finding himself surrounded by Izates' troops.[5]

---

[1] Tacitus, *Annals* XI, 8-9.
[2] Jos. *Ant.* XX, 69-73.
[3] Tacitus, *Annals* XI, 10; XII, 12-14.
[4] The chronology of the Jewish rulers of Adiabene is not quite clear. We can only state that Izates' rule commenced before the death of Artabanus III (38 C.E.). See N. C. Debevoise, *A Political History of Parthia* (1938), p. 166; U. Kahrstedt, *Artabanus III und seine Erben* (1950), p. 81. It is certain that Izates survived the accession of Vologases I in 51 C.E. However, in 61 C.E. at the time of the invasion of Adiabene by Tigranes the king of Armenia he was already dead, and his brother Monobazus ruled instead. Thus, the death of Izates occurred between 51 and 61 C.E.
[5] Jos. *Ant.* XX, 75-80.

Still undismayed Izates' enemies once again tried their luck, this time with the aid of Vologases, who massed a large army on the borders of Adiabene. But no armed conflict ensued because at the last moment Vologases was forced to depart hurriedly in order to stem a large invasion of the Dahae and the Sacae into his territories.[1]

After his death, Izates was succeeded by his brother, Monobazus II. It appears that he managed to re-establish good relations with the Parthian king Vologases, who did not repeat his attempts to oust the Jewish kings of Adiabene, but on the contrary made Monobazus one of his major allies in his conflict with the Romans. The outbreak of open hostilities between Rome and Parthia in the fifties of the first century C.E. seems to have been at least partly responsible for Vologases' changed attitude to Monobazus, for he now needed the support of Adiabene and was eager to enlist the sympathies of the Jews in the territories held by the Romans beyond the Parthian border. It should also be borne in mind that during the first few years of Monobazus' reign Vologases still had his hands tied by rebellions in Hyrcania in the northern parts of his empire, and therefore could hardly afford to intervene in the affairs of Adiabene.

The course of events in Armenia, where a Parthian royal candidate, Tiridates, was temporarily deposed through Roman intervention in favour of Tigranes V, one of the descendants of Herod, also had its impact on Adiabene. In 61 C.E. the border skirmishes against Adiabene assumed a scale where they could no longer be dismissed as minor marauding expeditions,[2] and Monobazus asked for Parthian military aid against their instigator, Tigranes. In view of the recent ejection of the Parthians from Armenia and their humiliation at the hands of Rome, Vologases saw fit to open war against the Romans. The Parthian expeditionary forces in Armenia, whose purpose was to restore Tiridates to the throne and drive out Tigranes, also included troops from Adiabene.[3] The city of Nisibis in Adiabene became the main headquarters of Vologases. That Monobazus played a prominent role in this war is also demonstrated by the fact that he acted as a witness to the treaty signed by the Parthians with the Roman commander Paetus in 62 C.E., whose army they had defeated. The importance the Romans attached to Monobazus in that period is also reflected in the fact that in 66 C.E. his sons were delivered as hostages

[1] *Ant.* xx, 81-91.
[2] Tacitus, *Annals* xv, 1, 2.
[3] *Annals* xv, 2, 4; see also Dio Cassius LXII, 20, 2.

to Rome together with the sons of Tiridates, the Parthian king of Armenia, and of Vologases himself. He had previously been mentioned along with Vologases as giving hostages to the Roman commander, Corbulo.[1]

Throughout these years the royal house of Adiabene maintained close ties with Jerusalem. Izates sent his sons to Jerusalem to study, and his mother Helena also went there, Izates escorting her a considerable part of the way and furnishing her with a large sum of money.[2] It is easy to imagine the tremendous impression that the arrival of the convert queen must have made in Jerusalem. She behaved like an orthodox Jewess, took nazaritic vows, cultivated close relations with the Jewish sages and donated funds for the Temple 'making a lamp of gold for the opening of the temple precincts and a plaque of gold with the biblical story of the wayward woman inscribed upon it'.[3] During the famine that broke out in Palestine during the governorship of Tiberius Alexander, she assisted the poor by buying grain in Egypt and dried figs in Cyprus. Izates also sent much money at that time to the Jewish leadership in Jerusalem to help relieve the famine. Helena built her royal palace in Jerusalem and stayed there until after the death of her son Izates.[4] She then returned to Adiabene, undoubtedly in order to help her second son, Monobazus, to consolidate his rule. She died there shortly after her arrival. Monobazus had her and Izates, his borther, buried in a splendid mausoleum near Jerusalem, which aroused general admiration and was cited in the second century c.e. by the Greek writer Pausanias together with the famous mausoleum of Halicarnassus as one of the most glorious monuments of its kind in the world.[5] Several other princes of the Adiabene dynasty also stayed in Jerusalem, including Grapte, after whom one of the palaces in Jerusalem was called.[6]

The existence of a Jewish state in Adiabene of necessity also affected Rome's eastern policy. It helped to bolster the self-confidence of the Jews of Palestine who, at the beginning of the Great Revolt, expected to receive tangible support from this source. Members of

---

[1] *Annals* xv, 14; Dio Cassius LXIII, 1, 2; LXII, 23, 4.
[2] Jos. *Ant.* xx, 71; 49-50.
[3] *M. Yoma* 3:10; *Nazir* 3:6; *P. T. Sukkah* I 51d; *T. B. Sukkah*, 2b.
[4] Jos. *War.* v, 253; VI, 355.
[5] *The Description of Greece* VIII, 16, 4-5; see also Jos. *Ant.* xx, 95; *War* v, 55. 119. 147; Eusebius, *Church History* II, 12, 3; Jerome, *Epist.* 108 *ad Eustochium*, PL XXII, col. 883.
[6] *War* IV, 567.

the royal family of Adiabene in fact took part in the revolt, from the struggle with Cestius Gallus right to the very end,[1] but officially Adiabene abstained from open military intervention. As the Parthians were afraid of any further clash with the Romans, the kingdom of Adiabene did not dare to engage in open warfare on its own.

Apart from the Adiabene interlude the second great event in the history of eastern Jewry was the attempt made by Anilaeus and Asinaeus of Nehardaea to set up a semi-independent Jewish state in Babylonia. The two men, weavers by trade, gathered people from the lower classes around them, equipped them with arms and imposed taxes on the shepherds in the vicinity to support themselves and their men. The Parthian governor of Babylonia, to nip their enterprise in the bud, attempted a surprise attack on a Sabbath. Not only was he defeated but the position of the two brothers was so much strengthened that reports about them reached the ears of Artabanus III.[2] The ramshackle state of his empire and various internal considerations caused Artabanus to come to an agreement with them and a meeting was arranged. We do not know what official status was granted to them, but it is clear that they attained virtual autonomy and controlled extensive areas in Babylonia. Their downfall was brought about only by internal dissension. Anilaeus married a Parthian captive who had previously been the wife of one of the Parthian commanders and continued to worship the idols she had brought with her. This obviously infuriated the Jews, who urged Asinaeus to have his brother send the woman away. Anilaeus refused his brother's pleas and when Asinaeus died shortly afterwards, rumour had it that he had been poisoned by his brother's wife. Anilaeus remained the sole leader. In the meantime he had also incurred the enmity of Mithridates, the son-in-law of King Artabanus, by raiding one of his villages and taking men, livestock and captives. Mithridates marched to protect his property and men, but was captured and humiliated by Anilaeus. After his release he decided to have his revenge and overran Anilaeus with a large army, catching him at a disadvantage when his men were tired and thirsty. Anilaeus was defeated and many of his men were killed. With the remnants of his army he fled into the forests, recruited new forces and resumed

---

[1] *War* II, 520; VI, 356; see also V, 474.
[2] It is commonly assumed that the rise of the brothers is to be dated c. 21 C.E. See Debevoise, op.cit., p. 156, n.54; on the other hand, Kahrstedt, op.cit. p. 52 argues for a later date (37 C.E.).

the looting of Babylonian villages, but he had lost his former status and no longer controlled any definite territory. Consequently the gentile residents of the area entered into negotiations with the Jews of Nehardaea and demanded that Anilaeus should be handed over to them. This they refused to do, but they agreed to enter into a peace treaty with the Babylonians with whom they sent a joint delegation to conduct negotiations with Anilaeus. However, as soon as they had discovered his hide-out the Babylonians found a convenient opportunity to launch a surprise attack on Anilaeus' men and kill their leader.[1]

The death of Anilaeus resulted in further reprisals on the part of the Babylonians against the Jews. It seems that Jews from various parts of Babylonia were forced to move to Seleucia on the Tigris where they became involved in the dispute between the Greeks and the native population. At first they served as a reinforcement of the native element, but once the two parties had become reconciled to each other they became the victims. Five years after the arrival of the Jewish refugees in Seleucia a major massacre took place there, and some of them were forced to escape to the neighbouring town of Ctesiphon.[2]

Though for a time the position of the Jews in Babylonia was seriously affected by the failure of Anilaeus' venture, the major Jewish bastion of Nehardaea held out, and soon Jewish life was resumed also in those parts of the country where the repercussions had been particularly severe. There is some information about Jewish life also in other of the west of the Parthian Empire, visibly at Edessa and Dura.[3]

BIBLIOGRAPHY

Among the main accounts of the Jewish Diaspora in the Hellenistic and Roman period we have to mention E. SCHÜRER, *Geschichte des jüdischen Volkes im Zeitalter Jesu Christi* III, 1909, pp. 1-188, which discusses the diffusion of Judaism, the organization of the communities and their status, the problems of citizenship, religious life and proselytism. A major work is that by J. JUSTER, *Les Juifs dans l'empire*

---

[1] Jos. *Ant.* XVIII, 310-370.
[2] *Ant.* XVIII, 371-9.
[3] On the Jewish inscriptions from Edessa see *CII* nos. 1415-18. The earliest literary information on Jews at Edessa is connected with the early diffusion of Christianity, see Neusner, pp. 166-9. On the beginnings of the Jewish community of Dura see C. Kraeling, *The Excavations at Dura-Europos, Final Report* VIII,I: *The Synagogue* (1956), pp. 326-9.

romain, 2 vols, 1914, which deals with the legal status of the Jews under the Roman Empire from the first contact of Rome with the Jews till the early Middle Ages. It is a great repertory of erudition and covers in fact most aspects of Jewish life in the Diaspora apart from the discussion of the legal conditions. The legal status of Jews in the Roman Empire is the topic also of M. BRÜCKLMEIER, *Beiträge zur rechtlichen Stellung der Juden im römischen Reich*, 1939. V. TCHERI-KOVER's *Hellenistic Civilization and the Jews*, 1959, esp. pp. 269-377 is also important. For the Egyptian Diaspora we have the masterly 'Prolegomena' of Tcherikover to *CPJ* and his *The Jews in Egypt in Hellenistic-Roman Age in the Light of the Papyri* (in Hebrew), 2nd ed., 1963.

The fullest treatment of the history of the Jews in ancient Cyrenaica is to be found in S. APPLEBAUM, *Greeks and Jews in Ancient Cyrene* (in Hebrew), 1969. On the Jews in ancient Rome the work of H. J. LEON, *The Jews of Ancient Rome*, 1960, is fundamental, and especially valuable for the excellent study of the inscriptions. The history of the Jews in Babylonia under Parthian rule is narrated by J. NEUSNER, *A History of the Jews in Babylonia* I, 1965.

APPENDIX

THE PROBLEM OF THE EXPULSION OF THE JEWS FROM ROME IN THE TIME OF CLAUDIUS

Several sources deal with the expulsion of the Jews from Rome in the times of Claudius. Suetonius states that Claudius expelled the Jews from Rome after they had consistently caused riots at the instigation of a certain Chrestus.[1] Suetonius does not tell us when this expulsion was supposed to have taken place.

It seems that Claudius took this step in response to early attempts at the propagation of Christianity in Rome, only a few years after the death of Jesus. The spread of Christianity was, it appears, accompanied by riots and dissension among the Jewish community of which the Christians still constituted an integral part. The name Chrestus should thus be read for Christus[2] although some scholars think that some other person by the name of Chrestus is meant

---

[1] *Life of Claudius* 25,4: 'Judaeos impulsore Chresto assidue tumultuantes Roma expulit.'
[2] In Tacitus, *Annals* XV, 44, the name *Chrestiani* appears in the Mediceus before the correction; see H. Fuchs, *Vigiliae Christianae*, (1950), pp. 69-74.

rather than Jesus Christ.[1] However the arguments for identifying the name with Jesus seem more cogent.[2] Although Suetonius' wording sounds as if Chrestus were present in Rome, the word 'impulsore' does not refer to any actual presence but merely points the cause of the rioting.[3] At any rate Suetonius was not aware of the chronology of the life and death of Jesus.[4] In contrast to Suetonius, Dio Cassius tells us:[5] 'As for the Jews who had again increased so greatly that by reason of their multitude it would have been hard without raising a tumult to bar them from the city, he did not drive them out but ordered them, while continuing their traditional mode of life, not to hold meetings.'

From this statement it definitely appears that, although he had every intention to do so, Claudius did not actually expel the Jews from Rome but only restricted their right of assembly. Dio Cassius places this event close to the accession of Claudius, that is, in 41 C.E.

A third source, Orosius, claims that Claudius expelled the Jews from Rome in the ninth year of his reign, that is, in 49 C.E.[6] He bases himself on Josephus and then cites the above statement by Suetonius. Regarding the expulsion itself he thus follows Suetonius, while citing a date different from that given by Dio Cassius. However, Orosius' reference to Josephus is not supported by the latter's writings.

On the other hand the date proposed by Orosius finds some corroboration in the Acts of the Apostles which speak of an expulsion of the Jews from Rome using the expression προσφάτως (recently) in connection with the arrival of one of the Jews so expelled—Aquila—from Italy in Corinth.[7] Orosius' date fits in well with the presumed chronology of Paul's travels.

Another source, the *Scholia* to Juvenal, mentions Jews expelled from Rome who have settled in Aricia.[8] At least some scholars tend to attribute the event referred to by the Scholia to the reign of Claudius.[9] Other scholars think that we are dealing with two events, a) the prohibition of assemblies by an edict of 41 C.E., referred to by Dio Cassius

[1] So recently also Benko.
[2] So e.g. Janne.
[3] See also the interpretations of Labriolle and May.
[4] The conjecture of R. Eisler, ᾿Ιησοῦς βασιλεὺς οὐ βασιλεύσας I (1929), p. 133, n. 1 is rather fantastic.
[5] Dio Cassius LX, 6. 6.
[6] *Adversus paganos* VII, 6, 15.
[7] Acts 18:2.
[8] *Scholia in Iuvenalem vetustiora*, ed. Wessner, p. 64.
[9] Cf. Schürer III, 63; Juster I, 180, n. 9.

and b) an expulsion order mentioned by Suetonius, the Acts of the Apostles and Orosius, which the latter places in 49 C.E.[1] Nevertheless it seems that all our sources point to the same event. It is quite conceivable that initially Claudius may have intended to expel all the Jews from Rome and had issued an edict to that effect, but that he shortly afterwards replaced this with an order banning Jewish meetings. Quite a number of Jews undoubtedly left Rome before the original edict was amended including some who moved to Aricia or, for instance, to Corinth, like Aquila. Perhaps also the original edict remained in force to apply to those who had been prominently involved in the agitation and riots.[2] The Acts of the Apostles need not cause any major chronological difficulties since Aquila may well have left Rome in 41 C.E. have stayed for several years in some other Italian towns and come to Corinth only several years afterwards. The authority of Josephus, erroneously invoked by Orosius, can certainly not be taken as a counter-argument against Dio Cassius, since Josephus actually said nothing of the kind. On the other hand, in relating the events of 49 C.E. in the 11th book of his *Annals* Tacitus makes no mention of any edict for the expulsion of the Jews issued in that year. This may also serve as a weighty argument against the view according to which Dio Cassius' version of the edict should be accepted, merely substituting the date of Orosius for the one given by him.[3]

BIBLIOGRAPHY

L. GEIGER, *Quid de Iudaeorum moribus atque institutis scriptoribus Romanis persuasum fuerit*, 1872, p. 11; J. A. HILD, *REJ* XI, 1885, p. 58, n. 3; H. SMILDA, *C. Suetonii Tranquilli Vita Divi Claudii*, 1896, pp. 123-5; H. VOGELSTEIN and P. RIEGER, *Geschichte der Juden in Rom* I, 1896, pp. 19-20; E. SCHÜRER, *Geschichte des jüdischen Volkes im Zeitalter Jesu Christi* III, 1909, p. 61; K. LINCK, *De antiquissimis veterum quae ad Iesum Nazarenum spectant testimoniis*, 1913, pp. 104-7; J. JUSTER, *Les Juifs dans l'empire romain* II, 1914, p. 171; E. PREUSCHEN, *ZNW*, 1914, p. 96; M. RADIN, *The Jews among the Greeks and Romans*, 1915, pp. 313-315; E. MEYER, *Ursprung und Anfänge des Christentums*

[1] So Smilda, Meyer, A. D. Nock, *CAH* x, p. 500, Momigliano, Bammel, Bruce, Frend.
[2] Also Leon, p. 26.
[3] So e.g. Schürer. Orosius' date is accepted also by H. Stuart Jones, *JRS* (1926), p. 31, Scramuzza and Benko.

III, 1923, pp. 37-8; pp. 462-3; A. V. HARNACK, *Die Mission und Aus-breitung des Christentums*, 4th ed., 1924, p. 10; G. LA PIANA, *HTR*, 1927, p. 376, n. 7; W. SESTON, *Revue de l'histoire et philosophie religieuses*, 1931, pp. 299-301; M. GOGUEL, *Vie de Jésus*, 1932, pp. 75-6; K. LAKE, in Foakes Jackson and Kirsopp Lake, *The Beginnings of Christianity* Part I, V, 1933, pp. 459-460; A. MOMIGLIANO, *Claudius, the Emperor and his Achievement*, 1934, pp. 31-2, 98-9; P. LABRIOLLE, *La Réaction paienne*, 1934, pp. 42-3; H. JANNE, *Mélanges Bidez*, 1934, pp. 531-53; G. MAY, *Revue historique de droit français et étranger*, 4th series 1938, pp. 37-45; V. M. SCRAMUZZA, *The Emperor Claudius*, 1940, pp. 151, 286, n. 20; S. L. GUTERMAN, *Religious Toleration and Persecution in Ancient Rome*, 1951, pp. 149-150; E. BAMMEL, *Zeitschrift für Theologie und Kirche*, 1959, pp. 294-7; H. J. LEON, *The Jews of Ancient Rome*, 1960, pp. 23-7; E. HAENCHEN, *Die Apostelgeschichte*, 13th ed., 1961, p. 58; F. F. BRUCE, *Bulletin of the John Rylands Library*, 1961-2, pp. 313-318; W. H. C. FREND, *Martyrdom and Persecution in the Early Church*, 1965, p. 160; T. D. BARNES, *JRS*, 1968, pp. 43-4; ST. BENKO, *Theologische Zeitschrift*, 1969, pp. 406-418.

Chapter Four
Relations between the Diaspora and the Land of Israel

The great Jewish Diaspora, in the Parthian and in the Roman Empires, was linked by many ties, on various levels and over a long period, with the centre of Jewish life in the Land of Israel. These contacts had a great influence on the way of life and the organization of Jews in the Diaspora, and on the development and destiny of Judaism in the lands in question. But these contacts were also of great importance for the Jews of the homeland, and especially for life in the city of Jerusalem.

Relations between the Diaspora and the centre in the homeland depended on a number of basic factors in Judaism, and on the political and military realities of the period. But in the main, the relationship depended on the quality of Judaism in the Diaspora in the time in question. We know little about the character and quality of Judaism in the Parthian Empire in early times. More ample information in this regard becomes available mainly after the destruction of the Second Temple, and for the second century of the Christian era in particular. As regards the first century C.E. and the period immediately preceding it, we can only piece together fragments of information. However, even for this period we can give a general outline which will be clear enough to indicate its distinctive features and so throw light on the relationship between the Diaspora and the centre. We know a great deal more about the Judaism of the Hellenistic Diaspora, and in particular about the great Jewish centre in Egypt.

The Judaism of the Hellenistic Diaspora was undoubtedly closely linked to Hellenistic culture. Not only was Greek the language used by these Jews in ordinary intercourse, but even a Greek literature was produced, especially in Egypt. It was a literature which was closely identified with the rich culture of the Greeks, and with the mentality which dominated there. Various documents discovered in Egypt during the present century show us how closely the Jews were attached to institutions of Hellenistic law and to concepts tributary to this sphere. But the Jews of Egypt and the Hellenistic

184

world, like the Jews of the other Diaspora centres, generally remained loyal to the Torah both in public and in private life. There were indeed individuals who felt drawn to the alien world outside, either because they deliberately rejected Judaism or because they wished to make their way in the surrounding world. There were also individuals whose ties with Judaism were loose and weak, intellectuals who gave the Torah an extreme allegorical interpretation, and held that the commandments need not be observed as a practical way of life, or that only some of them were binding. But we have no reason to suppose that these formed large circles or set up influential trends in Hellenistic Judaism. It is clear from the sources that all the circles which departed from the spirit and practice of Jewish observance remained isolated. Their attitude cannot be extrapolated to the Diaspora of Egypt as a whole or to the Jews in the rest of the Hellenistic Roman world. There was no general tendency to assimilation with the environment and to the adoption of the cultural heritage of the Greeks. All the literary sources, as also the inscriptions, give us to understand that the religious sentiment of Judaism and the practice of the Jewish law dominated the whole world of the Jewish Diaspora. The same applies to national sentiment and attachment to the Land of Israel. The Jews in Alexandria threw themselves vigorously into the hard struggle for their civil rights. But this struggle, at least in the case of the Jewish community as a whole, was not linked with a desire for spiritual and social assimilation with the culture and society of Alexandria.[1] The Jews of the Diaspora regarded themselves as partners of their fellow-Jews in the homeland in their daily struggles and in all that happened in the Land of Israel. They shared their joys and their sorrows, and most certainly, their hope of deliverance.

Though the Jews of the Diaspora were apparently part and parcel of Hellenistic culture and society, they regarded themselves essentially as Hebrews living abroad. Jewish literature written in Egypt breathes this sentiment. It finds expression when the expectation of deliverance is mentioned,[2] and also in Jewish prayers in time of religious persecution, as in the following: 'King of great power ... look upon the seed of Abraham ... who are unjustly perishing, strangers in a strange land ... And if our life has been ensnared in impious deeds during our sojourning, save us from the hands of the enemy ... As Thou

[1] See Allon, *History* I, pp. 207, 215.
[2] See e.g. Philo, *De praemiis et poenis* XIX.

hast said, "Not even when they were in the land of their enemies have I forgotten them", even so bring it to pass, O lord.'[1]

Though Judaism in the time of the Second Temple became a world religion in its horizon and its universalist trends, this did not mean any weakening of its ties with the Land of Israel and with the people living there. Jewish life and experience centred on the territorial reality of the Land of Israel and Jerusalem its capital, on the Temple built in its midst and the people living in the Land and in Jerusalem. The Land of Israel not only served as the focus of the hope of deliverance and as the Holy Land. It was also central to the workaday world of Jewish life. The essential reality of Judaism, with the observance of the commands of the Torah, the maintenance of its institutions and its authority throughout the Diaspora, was sustained, according to the Jewish religion, by the actual Jewish occupation of the Land, and by the existence of divine worship in the one and only Temple of Judaism and the functioning of its allied institutions.[2] In the period which we are discussing there was still much in the Jewish way of life which remained fluid and undefined. A community wishing to fulfil each command of the Torah was dependent on decisions and practices obtaining in the Temple. The Jewish Diaspora relied on Jerusalem for the fixing of the New Moon and the New Year and for translations of the Bible, as will be shown in what follows.

The peace that reigned in the Roman Empire from the time of Augustus onwards, and the tranquillity on the frontier between the Parthian and Roman Empires during the first century of Roman rule in the Land of Israel made it easy to maintain and strengthen the many ties between the Diaspora and the Land of Israel. The large-scale pilgrimages and the other ties between the Diaspora and the homeland did not begin with the Roman conquest of the East, which took in the Land of Israel. And these ties did not cease even in times when disorders and wars troubled the frontier of the Empire or during the many conflicts between the Romans and the Parthians and later the Persians. But from about the middle of the first century before the Christian Era, the bonds were strengthened and pilgrimages to the Temple multiplied, aided, we may suppose, by the political and military conditions then prevailing.

Among the principal factors in building up this relationship, mention

---

[1] 3 Macc. 6.
[2] *Sifre* on Deut., par. 154 (ed. Finkelstein p. 207).

must be made first and foremost of the Temple in Jerusalem. This sacred building was the only sanctuary of Judaism in the homeland and in the Diaspora where the worship of God was performed as laid down in the Torah. There was indeed a Jewish temple at Heliopolis for the Jewish colony there, known as the Temple of Onias, and it remained in existence till the destruction of the Temple in Jerusalem and for some time after. But the Temple of Onias did not play any great role even in the lives of the Jews of Egypt. It was not situated at the centre of Jewish settlement but in a remote village in the district of Heliopolis. The Temple in question was built to serve the needs of the military colony in Leontopolis and it never functioned as anything else. It was never a factor which could have alienated the Jews of Egypt from Jerusalem and its Temple.

There were synagogues at this period in all places where Jews had settled. But divine worship in the form of sacrifice, one of the main religious rites among the nations and in Israel, was impossible in the synagogue. All that could be done was to send a sacrifice to Jerusalem or to bring it there personally. There were several occasions on which a Jew was obliged to offer sacrifice, as for instance the indeliberate commission of certain faults, the deliberate commission of others, the cure of leprosy, child-birth for the woman, the completion of the period of a Nazirite's vow. It is difficult to tell to what extent the Jews of the Diaspora fulfilled in practice these obligations of ritual sacrifice, and what milder interpretations of these laws were in vogue which made the offering of sacrifice less imperative. As regards Jews in the Land of Israel, we know for example that many women did not in fact offer sacrifice after each child-birth. They only did so after a few births, and this practice was allowed by the Halakah.[1] It is possible that the Jews of the Diaspora could also make use of milder interpretations which lightened the obligation of offering sacrifice. However, the sources testify to numerous occasions on which Jews from the Diaspora did offer sacrifice, both as free-will and as obligatory sacrifices, as for instance Nazirites after the completion of their statutory time.[2] There was a growing number of converts to Judaism at this period in the Diaspora. The process of conversion, both for men and women, had to be completed by the offering of sacrifice, which had not to be done immediately after conversion, though conversion was not complete without it.[3] Further, gentile

[1] M. Kerithoth 1:7.   [2] M. Nazir, 5:4.
[3] M. Kerithoth, chap. 2; T. B. Kerithoth, 8b-9a.

worshippers (φοβούμενοι τὸν θεόν), whose numbers were increasing both in the Hellenistic Diaspora and in that of the Parthian realm, sometimes sent sacrifices or brought them themselves to Jerusalem.[1] The offering of sacrifices by Jews and gentiles from the Diaspora was an important element. Still more important however was the organization of divine worship in Jerusalem at the time of the Second Temple. We may speak with certainty here, at least as regards the period preceding Roman rule in the Land of Israel. The Temple had to provide for the public sacrifices prescribed for ordinary days and for feast-days, and for other charges, such as the salaries of the judges who sat regularly in the Temple and of the correctors of the sacred books. These expenses were not met from income from Temple property, since the Temple of Jerusalem had no such funds for current outgoings. And its revenue did not come in the main from offerings and gifts. Its chief source of revenue was the half-shekel which all Israelites had to contribute every year. The Pharisees held that the expenses of the public sacrifices could not be defrayed from the contributions of individual Jews. Since the obligation of sacrifice fell on all Israel, the money of all Israel was to be used for the offering of the public sacrifices.[2] The Great Synagogue under Nehemiah resolved to take upon itself the charge of 'a third part of a shekel yearly for the service of the house of our God'.[3] The resolution only speaks of providing funds for meeting expenses. There is no mention of its being a fundamental principle, just as there is no hint that the precept applied to the Diaspora. The same situation is reflected in such post-biblical works as the Second Book of Maccabees and the Epistle of Aristeas. Though they aimed at enhancing the status and the glory of the Temple, and though they were addressed to Jews living outside Israel, they make no mention of the obligation of the half-shekel for the Jews of the Diaspora. The obligation is first mentioned in the first century B.C.E., and then appears more frequently after the beginning of the Roman period in Israel.

As regards the payment of the half-shekel, it is difficult to say whether all the Jews living in the Diaspora paid their contribution as regularly as did those living in Israel.[4] But undoubtedly the great majority of the Diaspora Jews were accustomed to do so. We know this from

---

[1] Jos. *Ant.* III, 318.
[2] *Megillath Taanith*, beginning; *M. Taanith* 4:2.
[3] Neh. 10:33.
[4] *M. Shekalim* 1:3; Matt. 17:24-7.

the many references to the wide measure of official support for the levying of the half-shekel, and from the large sums of money which were amassed in the various towns. Philo mentions several times the huge number of half-shekels from the Jewish Diaspora and says that there were collecting-places in every city for the money for the sacrifices, which was then brought up to Jerusalem by groups of Jews, for whom the journey was a festive occasion.[1] Josephus speaks of the Jews of Babylonia, who used Nisibis and Nehardaea as centres for collecting the gifts dedicated to the Temple of Jerusalem, and says that multitudes of Jews accompanied the convoys who brought their gifts to their destination.[2] In his *Pro Flacco*, Cicero relates that Flaccus, during his period of office as Roman governor in Asia, in 62-61 B.C.E., attacked the Jews of Asia Minor who used to send the half-shekel to Jerusalem and confiscated the money. The sums involved he describes as follows:[3] 'At Apamaea, a little less than a hundred pounds of gold was openly seized ... at Laodicaea, a little more than twenty pounds ... At Adramyttium[4] ... at Pergamum a small amount.' Further, we know of large sums of money destined for the Temple by the Jews which were confiscated by Mithridates in 88 B.C.E. on the island of Cos.[5] Tannaitic sources, speaking of the expenditure of shekels by the treasury, says that the first drawing was made before the Passover, on the shekels from the Land of Israel. The second, before Pentecost, was on the offerings from the neighbouring countries, and the third, before the Feast of Tabernacles, was on the money from Babylonia, Media and the remoter lands.[6] The third section was the richest, and included gold staters and darics.[7] Even if the money for the Temple, especially the sums said to have been confiscated or under threat of confiscation, included wealthy persons' gifts as well as the half-shekel, there can be no doubt that the large sums mentioned show that large numbers of Jews contributed. From other circumstances to be mentioned later, it may be gathered that the contribution of the half-shekel was general and was the practice of nearly all Jews, except those whose loyalty was weak and who were on the point of abandoning Judaism completely.

---

[1] Philo, *De specialibus legibus* i, 77-8; *Legatio*, 156.
[2] Jos. *Ant.* xviii, 312-3.
[3] Cicero, *Pro Flacco* 28.
[4] The sum is omitted in the Mss.
[5] Jos. *Ant.* xiv, 112.
[6] *M. Shekalim* 3. [7] *T. Shekalim* 2:3.

We have a number of imperial edicts from the time of Julius Caesar and Augustus, determining the privileges enjoyed by Jews living in various cities of Asia and Africa. These privileges mention again and again the right of collecting money to be sent to the Temple of Jerusalem. The edicts name Ephesus, the cities of Cyrenean Libya and of Cyrene, Sardis, Miletus and Ancyra, capital of Galatia.[1] We read for instance: 'Wherever the Jews have been following their ancient custom of collecting money for religious purposes and sending it to Jerusalem, they may do so without let or hindrance'.[2]

The payment of the half-shekel and the fact of its being sent to Jerusalem gave a real sense of participation in the divine worship offered at Jerusalem. In the Land of Israel itself, this participation also found expression in the division of the country into twenty-four districts, corresponding to the twenty-four priestly courses. And with each course, as it served its week, a delegation (מעמד) went up from each of the divisions of the country, for it was held that no one's sacrifice could be offered unless he was present at it. The delegation then represented the people.[3] There is no mention in the sources of the Diaspora's being included in these arrangements, but we read that in the prayers offered by the members of the delegation their brothers in exile were also included.[4] The sense of participation which went with the contribution of the half-shekel was not confined to the offering of sacrifices in the Temple. It also included the other public services connected with the Temple, such as the payment of the correctors of the Books, the judges sitting regularly in the Temple and so on. All their salaries were paid out of the funds provided by the half-shekel,[5] while the municipal expenses of Jerusalem, especially the water supply and the building or repair of the city walls, were also met from the same source. Primarily, the contribution of the half-shekel was for the public sacrifices of the community. But in the century before the fall of the Second Temple, the Jews increased in number and the income from the half-shekel greatly exceeded the needs of the altar.[6] Jerusalem was regarded as an extension of the Temple area, and hence the rest of the income from the half-shekel was applied to municipal needs, to the maintenance of the walls and the water supply. Jerusalem was also regarded as the city of all

---

[1] Jos. *Ant.* XIV, 185-267; XVI 160-178.   [2] Jos. *Ant.* XVI, 166.
[3] *M. Taanith* 4:2.   [4] *T.B. Taanith* 22b.
[5] *T. B. Ketuboth* 105a; 106a.   [6] *M. Shekalim* 4:1,2.

Israel, and conclusions had to be drawn accordingly as regards the various arrangements adopted for the city.[1] The contribution of the half-shekel was not regarded by the Jews, or by their foreign rulers, as a gift or free-will offering, but as a kind of tax which established the bond by which the Jews were linked to the Temple and to Jerusalem. Since this was the view of the matter taken by foreigners, this attitude served as the basis for imposing on all Jews, in the Land of Israel and in the Diaspora, a tax of two denarii for the temple of Jupiter Capitolinus, after the destruction of the Second Temple.[2] The matter of the half-shekel brings up the question of the pilgrimages for the three feasts. It would appear that all Jews were commanded to make the pilgrimage three times a year: 'Three times in the year shall all your males appear before the Lord God.'[3] However, as will be explained later, this was not the actual practice of all males, not even of the pious and observant. And no real obligation was felt, either in Israel or in the Diaspora, to go up for each feast and so three times a year. It was a precept which could be fulfilled on any of the three feasts, and the pilgrim had then to offer the sacrifices and meet the other obligations connected with his visit to the Temple. The obligation was only felt to be binding insofar as it was practical to do so, and the individual fulfilled it more or less frequently according to his closeness to the Land of Israel, his possibilities and his devotion to the commandments.[4] Pilgrimages were made, in larger or smaller groups, from every place where there was a Jewish community. Philo, who must have made the pilgrimage himself at least once, since he recounts his experiences on the way to Jerusalem,[5] says in one place: 'Thousands of men from thousands of cities stream to the Temple for every feast, some from the east and the west, some from the north and the south.'[6] The half-shekel was brought to Jerusalem by groups and convoys, which, as we see, meant in practice pilgrimage in groups and convoys. The sending of the half-shekel from the Diaspora coincided with the pilgrimages to the feasts, and so the money collected in the lands adjoining Israel was there on the eve of Pentecost,

[1] See Vol II, chapter VII.
[2] Dio Cassius 66,7.2; Jos. *War* VII, 216ff.; cf. *CPJ* II, pp. 113-116.
[3] Ex. 23:27; 33:23; Deut. 16:16.
[4] See Safrai, 'Pilgrimage to Jerusalem at the end of the Second Temple Period', pp. 12-21 in *Studies in the Jewish Background of the New Testament* (1969).
[5] Philo, *De providentia* 64.
[6] *De specialibus legibus* I. 69.

while the money collected in more distant countries was ready to serve the needs of the Temple towards the Feast of Tabernacles.

The growing number of pilgrimages from the Diaspora also influenced the regulations for the intercalary month, that is, the insertion of a thirteenth month, Adar II, every few years, to bring the lunar year into line with the solar. During the period under discussion, the adjustment of the year was still under the jurisdiction of the Sanhedrin, which could, as necessary, add intercalary months in successive years or postpone the intercalation to a following year. Among the reasons for intercalating a year the Tannaitic Halakah mentions consideration for the 'exiles' (גליות). Convoys from abroad setting out on pilgrimage might not arrive in time to celebrate the Passover, and so the intercalation could be made to enable them to do so.[1] We see from this halakah that not only were there group pilgrimages, but that in many cases at least the Sanhedrin in Jerusalem knew of convoys due to reach the city. Pilgrimages in convoys did not exclude others made individually or in small groups. There is plenty of evidence for pilgrims going singly or as individual bands.

In keeping with the large number of festal pilgrimages from the Diaspora, it appears that synagogues of various communities from the Diaspora were established in Jerusalem in the century or so preceding the fall of the Temple. Tannaitic sources and the Acts of the Apostles furnish us with a noteworthy list of such foundations for our period. Synagogues of Jews from Alexandria and Tarsus are mentioned in Talmudic literature,[2] and synagogues of the Freedmen, the Cyrenians, the Cilicians and men from Asia are mentioned in Acts 6:9. The excavations conducted by Weill on Mount Ophel disclosed the remains of a large structure dating from Roman times, which included the installations of a bath-house. A Greek inscription showed what the complex of buildings was used for: 'Theodotus the son of Vettenus, priest and *archisynagogos,* son of the *archisynagogos,* grandson of the *archisynagogos,* built this synagogue for the reading of the Torah and the study of the commandments, and the hostel and the rooms and the water installations, for needy travellers from foreign lands. The foundations of the synagogue were laid by his fathers and the elders and Simonides.'[3] We have no proof that this synagogue

---

[1] *Sifra, Amor* IX (99d); *P. T. Shebiith* IX, 39c.

[2] *T. Megillah* 3:6; *T. B. Megillah* 26a.

[3] *CII* II, no. 1404; recently discussed by M. Schwabe, in *Sefer Yerushalayim* I (1956), pp. 362-5.

is to be identified with any of those mentioned in the literary sources, such as the synagogue of the Freedmen, as some scholars have supposed. Their idea was that the name Theodotus son of Vettenus indicated a connection with a Roman family which must have been of Jewish exile origin and which built the synagogue, after it had gained its freedom, to cater for the needs of pilgrims arriving at Jerusalem. The argument is unacceptable, because the Roman origin of the family is doubtful, and the inscription may refer to yet another synagogue of the Diaspora communities or to a synagogue not connected with any particular Diaspora community, even though the buildings connected with it were put up for needy travellers from the Diaspora. These synagogues may have been to some extents or even in the main, the result of immigration from the Diaspora, when the Jews in question settled in Jerusalem. But, as hat been said, it seems clear that these synagogues were connected wirh pil, grimages to the feasts, and this is explicitly stated in the insciption-found on Mount Ophel.

The pilgrims, and more particularly the pilgrims from the Diaspora, did not travel to the feasts every year. Some of them undoubedlye looked forward to the pilgrimage for many years in advance and madt preparations accordingly. Their pilgrimage was not limited to at shor stay at Jerusalem, and they did not stay just for the duration of the feast, as will be explained later in the section on the Temple. The pilgrimages to the feasts served as occasions for the study of the Torah under the Sages, and this of course required a longer stay in the city; some pilgrims, however, came to Jerusalem for the express purpose of studying the Torah. This is what happened in the case of Paul of Tarsus, coming from a town in Cilicia and remaining a long time in Jerusalem to study the Torah under Rabban Gamaliel the Elder. The existence of the synagogues mentioned above and the hostels beside them not merely lightened the expenses of pilgrims to the feasts, but also helped them in arranging to settle down in the country. There they could meet people who spoke the special dialect of the region they came from, they could get good advice and so on. Further, these synagogues certainly served as centres where contacts were made between the Diaspora communities and Jerusalem. Help and advice was given about sending people to the communities abroad and other relationships of this nature were set up, which will be discussed later.

The burial caves in the neighbourhood of Jerusalem have provided a number of Jewish inscriptions which indicate that the persons in question came from the Diaspora. One inscription refers to a Marya, the wife of Alexander of Capua.[1] A burial cave on Mount Scopus provides an inscription referring to a Justus from Chalcis.[2] A number of inscriptions refer to Jews who came from Palmyra, as may be seen from the language and script of the inscriptions.[3] One inscription refers to a proselyte named Miriam, from Delos,[4] and another to one named Judah, from Lacedaemon.[5] Another inscription speaks of the tomb of Alexander Nicanor and his sons, saying that Alexander had made gates of bronze for the Temple and brought them to Jerusalem.[6] A burial cave from the Kidron valley contains Greek, Hebrew and bilingual inscriptions. Only Jews from Cyrene were buried there.[7] There are also inscriptions referring to Jews from Africa.[8] In no case is there reason to think that these were people whose bodies had been brought to Jerusalem for burial. For the period in question we have no evidence of any such custom, or of any value being attached to burial in the Land of Israel. The people in question were Diaspora Jews who had come on pilgrimage and had died during their stay in Jerusalem. Or they were Diaspora Jews who had come to pass their last days at Jerusalem. The notion of going to Israel and settling down there was important and widespread as early as the time of the Second Temple, and there was never a time when Jews did not go up, in larger or smaller numbers, to the Land of Israel and Jerusalem. It may be supposed that the distinction between festal pilgrims who prolonged their stay and Diaspora Jews who settled down definitely was not always clear.

Under these circumstances, one can understand why one frequently comes upon references to Jews or groups of Jews from the various Diaspora centres, who are found at Jerusalem at the time of the feasts and throughout the whole year. The general picture given in the second chapter of the Acts of the Apostles, describing the activities of the Christian community in Jerusalem at Pentecost, begins by saying:

[1] *CII* ii, no. 1284; F.-M. Abel, *RB* (1902), p. 106.
[2] *CII* ii, no. 1233; F.-M. Abel, *RB* (1913), p. 275.
[3] Y. Kutscher, in *Sefer Yerushalayim* i, pp. 352-3.
[4] According to E. L. Sukenik's rendering in *Memorial Volume for S. Klein and A. Gulak* (1942), pp. 133-4.
[5] See Sukenik, op.cit., p. 134, n.4.
[6] Recently discussed by Schwabe, op.cit. pp. 367-8.
[7] N. Avigad, *IEJ* (1962), pp. 1-12.
[8] *CII* ii, nos. 1226-7; F. M. Abel, *RB* (1913), pp. 269, 272.

'Now there were dwelling in Jerusalem Jews, devout men from every nation under heaven' (v. 5). These Jews, as the sequel shows, spoke various languages, since they included 'Parthians and Medes and Elamites and residents of Mesopotamia, Judaea and Cappadocia, Pontus and Asia, Phrygia and Pamphylia, Egypt and the parts of Libya belonging to Cyrene, and visitors from Rome, both Jews and proselytes, Cretans and Arabians.'[1] We sometimes hear of people from Babylonia in Jerusalem, priests and laymen. The story goes that Hillel the Elder, who, as we know, had come to Jerusalem from Babylon, fell in with an ass-driver who said to him, arrogantly, 'Rabbi, I am better off than you immigrants. You are short of everything on your way here from Babylonia, and I have only to step outside my door to find lodging at the gate of Jerusalem.'[2] A text in the Mishnah speaks of how priests from Babylonia were eager to reach Jerusalem in time to eat of the sacrifices offered on the Day of Atonement.[3] Queen Helena of Adiabene and her children came frequently to Jerusalem, not merely for the feasts, but also at other times of the year.[4] In the year 66 c.e. relatives of King Monobazus, the son of Helena, were engaged, on the Feast of Tabernacles, in the Jewish war against Rome. Distinguished service was also performed by one Silas of Babylonia, who had been living in the Land of Israel for at least some years before this.[5] During the siege of Jerusalem, in the last stage of the war which ended at the Passover of 70 c.e., subjects of the same kingdom of Adiabene were to be found in the city.[6] Another text of the Mishnah lists various sacred gifts brought by Diaspora Jews, which were refused on the ground that the gifts in question could not be brought from outside the Land, according to the Halakah: 'Nittai of Tekoah brought Dough-offerings from Be-ittur, and they would not accept them. The men of Alexandria brought their Dough-offerings from Alexandria and they would not accept them ... Ben Antigonus brought up Firstlings from Babylon and they would not accept them.'[7] The Jewish Christians who were compelled to leave Jerusalem after the persecution of Stephen included people

---

[1] Acts 2:9-11. The word 'Judaea' is difficult because the text seems to suggest that the word was heard in various languages. There are variant readings, and emendations have been proposed.
[2] *Avot d'Rabbi Natan*, version II, chap. 27, ed. Schechter, p. 55.
[3] *M. Menahoth* 11:7.
[4] Jos. *Ant.* xx, 49; *M. Nazir* 3:6; *M. Yoma* 3:10.
[5] Jos. *War* II, 520.
[6] Ibid. VI, 356. [7] *M. Hallah* 4:10-11.

MAP V. THE MAIN ROADS TO JERUSALEM FROM THE DIASPORA

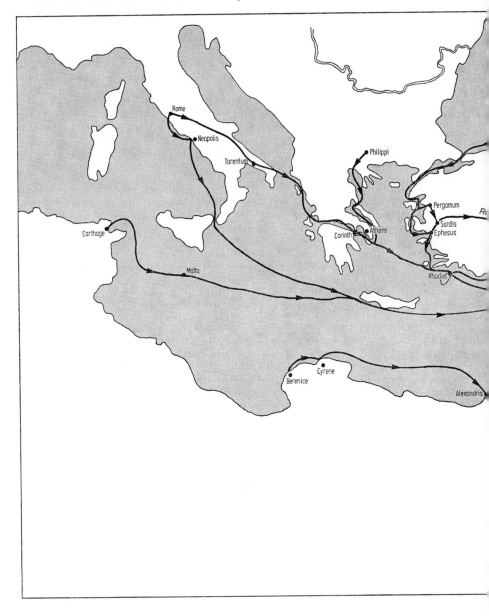

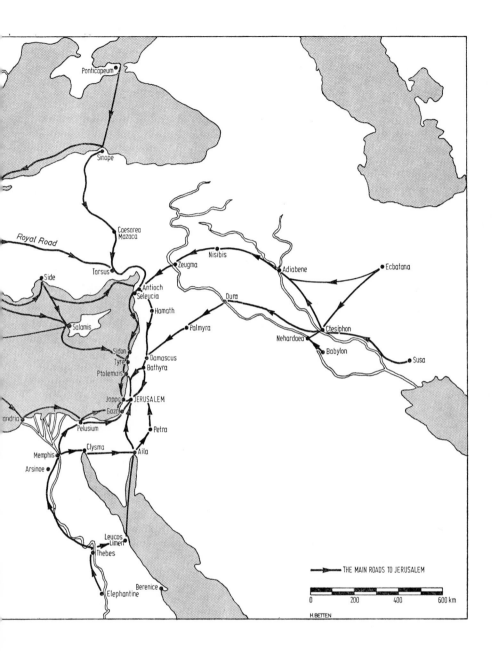

Ponticapeum

Sinope

Royal Road

Caesarea
Mazaca

Side

Tarsus

Zeugma

Nisibis

Adiabene

Ecbatana

Antioch
Seleucia

Salamis

Hamath

Dura

Palmyra

Ctesiphon

Nehardaea

Susa

Sidon
Tyre

Damascus

Babylon

Ptolemais

Bathyra

Jappa

JERUSALEM

Gaza

andria

Pelusium

Petra

Memphis

Clysma

Aila

Arsinoe

Leucos
Limen

Thebes

Berenice

Elephantine

THE MAIN ROADS TO JERUSALEM

0   200   400   600 km

H.BETTEN

197

from Cyprus and Cyrene.[1] And the Simon who was forced to carry the cross of Jesus was a man from Cyrene.[2] Certain Jews and Jewish families from the Diaspora who came to Jerusalem and settled there permanently during the last century of the Second Temple had great influence on life in Jerusalem and on Jewish society in general throughout the country. The families of Hillel and of Bathyra, both from Babylonia, had great influence on the spiritual life, as on the observance of the Torah and on the conduct of public affairs. The first high priest under Herod was Hananel, a Babylonian.[3] Towards the end of the Second Temple period, we know of Nahum the Mede and Hanan the Egyptian among the people who acted as 'judges of civil law', a body which functioned apparently within the framework of the Sanhedrin.[4] The three or four most distinguished priestly families between the time of Herod and the fall of the Temple, who produced many high priests and held other high positions in the Temple, leaving their stamp upon the social life of Jerusalem and on its political struggles, included the houses of Boethus and Phiabi. They had come from Egypt in the time of Herod. A prophet from Egypt whose name is unknown to us stirred up a fever of Messianic expectations during the procuratorship of Felix (52-60 c.e.).[5]

The law on pilgrimages, as in Exodus 23:17 and Deuteronomy 16:16, insists on the command that 'Three times in the year shall all your males appear before the Lord God.' The commandment was interpreted to mean that the Temple sacrifices, the pilgrimage to the feasts and the visit to the Temple were enjoined solely on men. But in fact large numbers of women, including many from the Diaspora, took part in the pilgrimages. Josephus, when describing the Temple, says that the court of the women was occupied during divine service by Jewish women from abroad as well as from the Land of Israel.[6] As regards the actual practice of the Land of Israel, it is clear that women and children took part in public services in the synagogue, in the *hakhel* ceremony (הקהל)—a great assembly of participants which took place every seven years in the courts of the Temple during the Feast of Tabernacles—in the joyous בית השואבה (water-drawing ceremony) and in other such rites.[7] It is not known to what extent

---

[1] Acts 11:19-20.   [2] Matt. 27:32.   [3] Jos. *Ant.* xv, 39.
[4] *M. Ketuboth* 13:1; *T. B. Ketuboth* 105a.
[5] Jos. *Ant.* xx, 167-177.
[6] Jos. *War* v, 199.
[7] *P. T. Hagigah* 1, 75d; *M. Sukkah* 5:2, and elsewhere.

this practice also held good for the Jews of the Diaspora. Women are also mentioned in the inscriptions in Jerusalem referring to Jews from the Diaspora. While they may not have been as closely associated with their husbands as in the Land of Israel, it is quite certain that they participated no less than their husbands when on pilgrimage from the Diaspora.

Proselytes also went up to Jerusalem on the occasion of the festal pilgrimages. Proselytes behaved exactly like Jews in all matters, and there is no reason to suspect that they thought less of the pilgrimages. The inscriptions cited earlier, referring to immigrants or pilgrims from the Diaspora, mention a man and a woman who were proselytes. Various traditional rulings deal with problems connected with the fact that proselytes were to be found in the religious associations in Jerusalem. One halakah for instance says that 'an association for the eating of the Passover sacrifice must not be composed entirely of proselytes, for fear that they may be over-scrupulous about it and so cause it to be annulled.'[1] The Acts of the Apostles, when speaking of the pilgrims who came to Jerusalem for the Feast of Pentecost from various places, mentions proselytes as well as Jews as having come from Rome.[2] It seems that the act of conversion was frequently linked with pilgrimage to a feast. Conversions could undoubtedly take place outside the Land of Israel, but in many cases the proselytes chose to go up to Jerusalem to complete the ceremony, either because they preferred to have it done there, or because there was no Beth Din in the place where they lived. Echoes of conversions taking place during pilgrimages are to be found in the Midrash and in the discussion of rules to be followed in practice. There was the question, for instance, of soldiers who were converted to Judaism on the eve of the Passover. They were permitted to take part in the Passover sacrifice and not obliged to wait seven days for their purification, which was the view held by some.[3]

We have much more evidence about pilgrimages made by gentile worshippers from outside the Land of Israel, as they came to worship God and bring their sacrifices. There are a number of decisions and rulings of the Halakah which reflect this situation. Among them we

---

[1] *T. B. Pesahim* 91b; *P. T. Pesahim* v, 36a. Regarding this text, see Safrai, *Pilgrimage*, p. 102, n. 51.
[2] Acts 2:10.
[3] *T. Pesahim* 7:13; *M. Pesahim* 8:8.

may mention the ruling to the effect that 'if a gentile sent his whole-offering from a region beyond the sea and sent the drink-offerings also, these are offered; but if he did not, they are to be offered at the charges of the congregation',[1]—since the foreigner did not know that a burnt-offering had to be accompanied by libations. There is a text in Josephus which speaks of foreigners from beyond the Euphrates who made a four months' journey in order to offer their sacrifices to God in Jerusalem.[2] In the Gospel according to John, in the account of Jesus' last journey to Jerusalem, we read that 'among those who went up to worship at the feast were some Greeks'.[3] At the feast of Pentecost, a gentile Christian, Trophimus, stayed with Paul in Jerusalem, and Paul was accused by the Jews of Asia of having brought him into the Temple, which was against the law.[4] In another text in the Acts of the Apostles we read of the Ethiopian eunuch, who was in charge of the treasury of Queen Candace, coming to Jerusalem to worship God.[5] Talmudic sources also refer occasionally to foreigners who went up to Jerusalem for a feast and even did so frequently.[6] Festal pilgrims who journeyed in convoys brought the half-shekel contribution with them, and, as we have seen, drawings on this fund were timed to coincide with the arrival of pilgrimages from the Diaspora. But as well as the half-shekel and the other gifts connected with the altar, the pilgrims also brought with them their heave-offerings (תרומה—the dues for the priests) and the tithes accruing from the produce of their fields and from their cattle. The Talmudic Halakah rules that the practice of paying priestly dues and tithes from the soil does not obtain outside the Land of Israel. And the ancient *Mishnah Kiddushin* 1:9, lays down that 'any religious duty that depends on the Land may be observed in the Land (alone)'. This means that priestly dues and tithes, being precepts depending on the soil, were not practised except in the Land of Israel. Jews living outside the country had no obligation in this matter. Statements to this effect are found in many Tannaitic sources.[7] However, whether because of a 'prophetic ruling' or a 'commandment of the Sages' or other reasons of Halakah, or because of a lasting tradition of an ancient halakah preceding or contradicting our Mishnah, it was the practice in many parts of the Diaspora to set aside dues, tithes,

---

[1] *M. Shekalim* 7:6.   [2] Jos. *Ant.* III, 318.   [3] John 12:20.
[4] Acts 20-21.   [5] Acts 8:26ff.   [6] *T. B. Pesahim* 3b.
[7] *M. Hallah* 2:1,2; *Midrash Tannaim Deut.* XIV, 22 (ed. Hoffmann, p. 77), and so forth.

firstlings and other priestly gifts. This was probably not done to the same extent or with the same strictness as in the Land of Israel, but it did take place among the Jews of the Diaspora. Thus we read in a homiletical commentary: "'They made me keeper of the vineyards" (Song of Solomon, 1:6). This means the Jews in exile in Babylonia. Prophets rose up among them and said to them, "Set aside priestly dues and tithes."'[1] There is another text which reads: 'Our teachers in the land of exile set aside priestly dues and tithes.'[2] Many traditions note the fact that priestly gifts were set aside in the neighbouring country of Syria, since it was regarded as being in a certain way within the limits of the Land of Israel.[3]

During the first hundred years of the Second Temple, it was common practice to bring to Jerusalem and the Temple not only gifts connected with the altar, such as first-fruits, but also the priestly dues and tithes which were given to the priests and levites, without passing through the Temple in the Land of Israel. The later Hasmonaean kings and the high priests were engaged in a fierce struggle with the circles who favoured the direct distribution of the dues among the ordinary priests in the towns and villages. The high priestly circles, with the support of the Roman authorities, sought to perpetuate a former custom according to which all dues and tithes were brought to the Temple in Jerusalem, while they themselves retained control of the distribution. Nonetheless, it was the prevailing custom in the Land of Israel, as early as the time of the struggle against the Hellenizers, to give the dues and tithes directly to the priests and levites.[4]

Towards the end of the Second Temple period, the practice of bringing dues and tithes to Jerusalem fell so much into disuse that it is not mentioned in Tannaitic literature and Josephus. It is known only from traditions about early times. But where Diaspora Jews set aside dues and tithes, they tried to bring them, or their redemption-money, to Jerusalem. An edict of the proconsul of Asia addressed to the people of Miletus obliged the city authorities to allow the Jews of the city 'to deal with their produce according to their laws.'[5] This has rightly been explained as meaning that the Jews of Miletus should

---

[1] *Avot d'Rabbi Natan*, version I, chap. 20, ed. Schechter, p. 73.
[2] *P. T. Hallah* IV, 60a.
[3] *M. Hallah* 4:7, 8, 11; *T. Hallah* 1:6; *T. B. Ketuboth* 25a, and elsewhere.
[4] See Allon, *Studies* I, pp. 83-92; S. Belkin, *Philo and the Oral Law* (1940), p. 70; A. Oppenheimer, in *Memorial Volume for B. de Vries* (1969), pp. 70-83.
[5] Jos. *Ant.* XIV, 245.

be allowed to set aside their tithes and bring them to Jerusalem,[1] since the permission of the gentile ruler was not required in order to set aside tithes and distribute them among the priests or the poor of the locality. The edict equates the produce with the payments which fulfilled sacred duties, that is, the half-shekel, with whose transfer to Jerusalem the permission was essentially concerned. In his account of the obligatory gifts to be made to the priests, Philo says: 'But that none of the donors should taunt the recipients, it [the Torah] ordered the first-fruits to be first brought into the Temple and then taken thence by the priests.'[2] His statement is based on the ancient Halakah and the custom of the Jews of Egypt. Even after the destruction of the Second Temple, the Jews of Egypt continued to bring their dues and tithes to the Land of Israel. A passage of the Mishnah describes a discussion between the Sages about the type of tithe to be set aside in Ammon and Moab in the seventh year. Was it to be the Poorman's Tithe or the Second Tithe? Both parties appealed to the custom of the Jews of Babylon and Egypt respectively, the latter tithing by virtue of an 'act of the elders', the former by virtue of an 'act of the prophets'. In the course of the discussion, Rabbi Tarphon said: 'On Egypt, because it is near, have they imposed the Poorman's Tithe, that the poor of Israel might be stayed thereby in the Seventh Year.'[3] Hence Egyptian Jews sent the Poorman's Tithe to the Land of Israel as well as the gifts for the priests and levites. Later, when they had to pay the half-shekel which the Roman authorities demanded of all Diaspora Jews, which had to be sent to Rome for the Temple of Jupiter instead of the half-shekel previously sent to Jerusalem, a small additional tax was also levied on the Jews of Egypt, which is called ἀπαρχή in the ostraca of Edfu and a papyrus from Arsinoë.[4] This ἀπαρχή took the place of the payment of first-fruits, dues or tithes which had been sent by the Jews of Egypt, just as the tax of two denarii took the place of the half-shekel sent to Jerusalem. We have no documentation as regards receipts of payments from Jews of other countries besides Egypt, but it is probable that a similar payment was imposed on them also. So they, like the

[1] A. Büchler, 'Die priesterlichen Zehnten etc.' in *Festschrift for M. Steinschneider* I (1896), pp. 91-109.
[2] *De specialibus legibus* I, 152.
[3] *M. Yadaim* 4:3.
[4] Sherds from Edfu: *CPJ* II, nos. 168-9; and Papyrus from Arsinoe: ibid., no. 421, l. 206. These are discussed on p. 115.

Egyptian Jews, must have originally brought dues and tithes or their redemption-money to Jerusalem.

We have already cited a Mishnah saying that Diaspora Jews brought various gifts for the priests and the altar, which were unacceptable. On most of the points mentioned in the Mishnah, Tannaitic scholars held different views, saying that such gifts could well be sent by the exiles. The very mention of the matter establishes the fact that gifts for priests and levites came to Jerusalem from the Diaspora.

Pilgrims from the Diaspora also brought free-will offerings of gold and silver which went to enrich the Temple. Philo's brother Alexander, the alabarch of Alexandria, had the nine gates of the court of the Temple plated with gold, except the gates of Nicanor—either because a miracle had been performed on them or because of their beauty. Queen Helena of Adiabene and Monobazus presented various articles of gold to the Temple.[1]

In his account of the precept of pilgrimage, Josephus writes that the object was to bring about friendship and affection, since the participants could come together for discussions and festive meals in common.[2] As we shall see later, custom and Halakah in the Temple and in Jerusalem aimed at providing a friendly reception for the visitors to the city and at bringing about a congenial atmosphere for their stay there. These visits did much to bind individual Jews from the Diaspora to the city and the Land, just as they did much for the relationship of the Diaspora as a whole to the homeland. Indeed, they influenced the whole character of Judaism. The central authorities, as will be explained later, sent envoys and letters to the Jews of the Diaspora, to inform them of developments and innovations issuing from the creative hearth of Judaism in the Land of Israel and Jerusalem, and to supervise the life of the communities. But they would not have had the same amount of influence were it not for the fact that so many of the Diaspora Jews went on pilgrimage to Jerusalem and stayed there, got to know personally the teachers of the Torah and became personally and directly linked with what was happening in the city. In Jerusalem and the courts of the Temple could be heard sages, thinkers and visionaries who had come there from the various towns of Israel and from the Diaspora. Every member of the people of Israel who had something to say and wanted a public platform made his way to Jerusalem. Pilgrims from the Dia_

---

[1] *M. Yoma* 3:10; *T. Yoma* 4:4; Jos. *War* v, 201-6.
[2] Jos. *Ant.* iv, 203-4.

spora returning to their homes had therefore a vital link with the actuality and development of Judaism which went beyond the pronouncements of its authorities and sages and matters affecting public life as a whole. While envoys and letters could give information about various rulings, official arrangements and so on, it was only through such personal links as described above that the Diaspora sabbath took on the same character as it had in the Land of Israel. Hence it meant assembling in the synagogue not merely for the readings from the Law and the Prophets, but also to hear a sermon and the discourse of a sage. And there was also the custom of taking meals in common on the Sabbath, a custom which had a great influence on the life of the people.[1] We have mentioned the many bonds on a social and popular level between the Diaspora and Jerusalem. These bonds did not mean that there was any less attachment on the part of the Diaspora to the official institutions of the high priesthood, the Sanhedrin and the envoys sent to the Diaspora. The Sanhedrin in Jerusalem was the supreme institution of Judaism both in the Land of Israel and in the Diaspora. The Jews of the Diaspora naturally had recourse to any Beth Din which existed locally, the court of law of the Jewish community, and to the public courts. But they also depended to a great extent on the Sanhedrin in Jerusalem in all fields of its activities. The rulings and arrangements in religious matters which were adopted in Jerusalem were also communicated to the Jews of the Diaspora. When the feast of Hanukkah was instituted in the Land of Israel the news was given as follows: 'Those in Jerusalem and those in Judaea and the senate and Judas, to Aristobulus ... and to the Jews in Egypt, Greeting, and good health ... Since on the twenty-fifth day of Chislev we shall celebrate the purification of the temple, we thought it necessary to notify you ...'[2] We know that the Jews of Egypt were accustomed to draw up marriage contracts in the terms laid down in the Land of Israel. When the question arose of the legitimacy of the offspring of Alexandrian parents, where the wife had been betrothed to one man but then married another, the matter was referred to the Sages in Jerusalem. Hillel the Elder studied the terms of the contract, and finding that

---

[1] Acts 13:15; 15:21. Regarding Rome, Jos. *Ant.* xiv, 214, and regarding Egypt, *CPJ* i, no. 139 (first century B.C.E.).
[2] 2 Macc. 1:10, 18.

it read that 'the betrothed shall be considered married only when the spouse has brought her to his house', he declared the children legitimate.[1]
At the basis of the legend of the seventy elders sent to King Ptolemy to translate the Bible into Greek—a haggadic tradition found both in the Epistle of Aristeas and in Talmudic literature—there is the fact that the translation of the Bible was made under the supervision and the authority of the Sanhedrin in Jerusalem. So too we find that Rabban Gamaliel the Elder, about a hundred years later, refused to authorize a certain translation of Job,[2] while after the destruction of the Second Temple the Sanhedrin at Jamnia sanctioned a new translation of the Bible into Greek, that of Aquila, which displaced the older Septuagint translation, though this had been regarded as sacred by the Jews of the Diaspora.[3] In the courts of the Temple, people were constantly working at collecting the books belonging to Sacred Scripture, at clarifying the text and at copying the books and checking for scribal errors. These standard and corrected books were also at the disposal of the Jews of the Diaspora. Hence after the dedication of the altar, Judas Maccabeus wrote to the Jews of Egypt to say that all the books that had been scattered on account of the war had been again collected, and that if they had need of any of them, they should send men to fetch them.[4]
We know from many sources, especially the writings of the Church Fathers[5] and the official sources of Roman law contained in the Theodosian Code,[6] of the existence of envoys (שליחים, 'apostoli') as a fixed institution. They were sent constantly, as a matter of course, by the Nasi ('patriarch') in the Land of Israel to the people of the Diaspora. With authority from the centre, the envoys supervised the administration of the communities, inspected the implementation of Law and Halakah, and levied the taxes destined for the office of the Nasi. According to some sources, the envoys were some of the most distinguished sages, who formed a kind of council which was consulted regularly by the Nasi, and conveyed to the Jews of the Diaspora the encyclicals sent out by the Nasi and the Sanhedrin. We have detailed accounts of these matters from the beginning of the third

[1] T. Ketuboth 4:9.
[2] T. Shabbath 13:2.
[3] P. T. Megillah I, 71 c.
[4] 2 Macc. 2:14-5.
[5] Epiphanius, Adversum haereses xxv, 11; Eusebius, On Isaiah 18:1, and others.
[6] xvi, 8, 14.

century C.E. till the abolition of the office of Nasi at the beginning of the fifth century. But in fact we know quite certainly of the existence of these envoys as early as the Synod of Jamnia (70-135 C.E.), and in the early part of the first century, during and before the time of Paul's activities.

Thus Justin Martyr affirms that envoys were sent to the Diaspora from Jerusalem to oppose Christianity.[1] So too Paul, speaking of the charges laid upon him before his conversion to Christianity, tells how he was sent to combat Christianity, bearing letters to the synagogues of Damascus.[2] When he was working as a Christian apostle, we hear that he came to Rome and preached among the Jews there. They told him: 'We have received no letters from Judaea about you, and none of the brethren coming here has reported or spoken any evil about you.'[3] The supervision exercised by the central authorities in Jerusalem over the life of the community in Israel also took in the wide public of the Jews of the Diaspora.

The bond formed between the Diaspora and Jerusalem through the supervision of community life may be further noted in the custom in vogue at the time of the Second Temple, of notifying the Temple in Jerusalem of valid marriages of priests, with the attestation that the wife was a suitable partner according to the laws of the Torah. Thus we read in Josephus: 'And this practice of ours is not confined to the home country of Judaea, but wherever there is a Jewish colony, there too a strict account is kept by the priests of their marriages; I allude to the Jews in Egypt and Babylonia and other parts of the world in which any of the priestly order are living in dispersion. A statement is drawn up by them and sent to Jerusalem, showing the names of the bride and her father and more remote ancestors, together with the names of the witnesses.'[4]

However, the most frequent expression of the dependence of the Diaspora on the authority of Jerusalem is to be found in the proclamation of the New Moon and the intercalation of a month, which took place in the courts of the Temple at Jerusalem. Each New Moon was proclaimed when the evidence had been accepted and the Beth Din had announced that the New Moon had begun. Once every few years the same court determined that a month should be added, to make up

[1] *Dialogus cum Tryphone*, 17, 108.
[2] Acts 9.
[3] Ibid. 28:21.
[4] Jos. *Contra Apionem* I, 32-3.

for the accumulated difference between the twelve months of the lunar year, only 354 days, and the solar year of 365 days. The proclamation of the New Moon month by month, as determined upon and fixed in Jerusalem, was awaited by the Diaspora, so that they could celebrate their feast-days accordingly. The Mishnah relates that the news of the proclamation of the New Moon was transmitted by a series of fire-signals extending from the Mount of Anointing (Mount Olivet) to Pumbeditha.[1] The Mishnah adds that the Samaritans practised a deception and kindled fires on nights when the New Moon had not been proclaimed in order to mislead the Jews. After that, the practice began of sending envoys to announce the New Moon.[2] Even at the time when fire-signals announced the New Moon, envoys used to go to give the news, since the fire-signals were not visible everywhere. This was done at least for the months when feasts were celebrated. The Mishnah gives a list of the months when the envoys went out, even before the signals were dropped. The list is as early as the time of the Second Temple.[3] The intercalation of a month was also announced by the dispatch of envoys and letters. The text of the letters sent to the Diaspora has been preserved in literature.[4] We know from a later period that such letters addressed to the head of the Babylonian Jews were preserved, and used in the solving of halakic problems. The envoys with the news of the proclamation of the New Moon and the intercalation of a month set up close links and enduring contacts, and provided regular checks on Jewish community life. Hence there is a ruling of the Halakah to the effect that evidence that a person used to give priestly blessings and receive priestly gifts in Israel or wherever the envoy announcing the New Moon came in Syria, was valid proof of his priesthood because in these regions covered by the envoys the presumption was that public affairs were properly administered.[5] The same tradition tells us that this rule also applied to Alexandria at first, apparently up to the time of the Jewish revolt under Trajan, before which there was a regular Jewish court of law there.[6] The destructive war lasting for several years, the siege of Jerusalem followed by the destruction of the Temple and the city and the uprooting and dispersal of the institutions connected with them led

[1] M. Rosh ha-Shanah 2:3,4; T. B. Rosh ha-Shanah 23b.
[2] M. Rosh ha-Shanah 2:2.
[3] Ibid. 1:3.
[4] T. Sanhedrin 2:6.
[5] P. T. Megillah 1, 71a.
[6] T. Peah, 4:5.

undoubtedly to a break in the well-established relations. Pilgrimages and the contacts they set up came to an end. We know that the restoration of social life and the rebuilding of a new world are connected with the name and the work of Rabban Johanan ben Zakkai, who was active in Jamnia, though there is no clear tradition as regards the duration of his activity. Some scholars think it lasted only for a few years after the destruction of the Temple, while others hold that he lived till the end of the Flavian dynasty or thereabouts, c. 96 c.e.[1] This was when the succession passed to Rabban Gamaliel II, a member of the dynasty which had presided over the Sanhedrin from the time of Hillel the Elder, and who was the son of Rabban Simeon ben Gamaliel, the head of the Jewish government set up after the outbreak of the revolt in 66. The traditions about the activities of Rabban Johanan ben Zakkai are relatively scarce, and in any case, contain no information about the resumption of ties with the Diaspora in his time, possibly because of the random nature of the sources. However, the activities of Rabban Johanan ben Zakkai were limited territorially and politically, since they were carried on without full permission and recognition on the part of the Roman authorities. In the years immediately after the revolt, he was prevented from developing activities in the Diaspora or renewing the ties with it. In any case, the time of Rabban Gamaliel II, who presided over the Synod of Jamnia from the last years of the first century till 115 c.e. or shortly before that, saw a renewal and even a strengthening, it would seem, of relations with the Diaspora. In spite of the destruction of the Temple, which had been the palpable and traditional framework of these relations, there was no loosening or weakening of the ties, as long as there was a national center in the Land of Israel, first at Jamnia and Lydda in Judaea, and after the revolt of Bar Cochba, in towns of Galilee. No doubt pilgrimages to the Temple, which had had such a popular character, with thousands coming from the Diaspora to each feast, did not begin again, but other bonds took on a much more intensive form.

It seems that the envoys travelled far and wide in the time of the Synod of Jamnia and subsequently. There are many traditions in Tannaitic literature about the travels of the great Sages of Jamnia throughout the Jewish Diaspora. Thus we find that Rabbi Joshua ben Hananiah, one of the leading figures in the time of Rabban Johanan ben Zakkai and active nearly up to the time of the revolt

[1] See Allon, *History* i, pp. 63-64.

of Bar Cochba, visited Alexandria, and was several times in Rome, along with other sages.[1] There are very many traditions about the travels of Rabbi Akiba, whom we find in the 'coastal towns' (possibly Phoenicia), Nabataean Arabia, Zephyrion in Cilicia, Africa, Gaul, Mazaca capital of Cappadocia,Nehardaea, Ginzak (Gazaka) in Media and Antioch, and also a number of times in Rome.[2] There are many traditions which speak of the travels of Rabban Gamaliel, accompanied by some of the great Sages of Jamnia. We hear of 'Rabban Gamaliel and the elders', 'Rabban Gamaliel, Rabbi Eliezer and Rabbi Joshua', 'Rabban Gamaliel, Rabbi Joshua, Rabbi Eleazar ben Azariah and Rabbi Akiba'.[3] The main reason for the journeys to Rome was probably political, but the aim was also to visit the Jews of Rome and set up relationships with them. We find the Sages going into the Halakah and preaching in the synagogues of Rome.[4] The Sages generally travelled in pairs. They preached in public, solved practical problems of the Halakah, inspected communal arrangements, and also collected money from the community for the ordinary expenses of the centre in the Land of Israel, or for other particularly urgent needs. It may be supposed that these contributions, which were officially recognized by the Roman government under the Severan emperors, and so collected on behalf of the Nasi as of legal right, were regarded by the Sanhedrin and the Diaspora Jews as a sort of substitute for the half-shekel formerly sent to the Temple.[5] The contributions were not always collected by the Sages, as the envoys of the Sanhedrin and the Nasi. This was probably done for the most part by the heads of the communities and the local authorities, who sent the money to the authorities in Israel.[6] To some extent, the communities of the Diaspora also sent tithes from the produce of their lands, as is known from occasional references in various Jewish and non-Jewish sources.[7] It is also attested by the dispute, which we have already mentioned, between the Sages of Jamnia after the destruction of the Temple, which clearly shows that the Jews of Egypt sent the Poorman's Tithe to the Land of Israel.

[1] M. Negaim 14:13, and see further on.
[2] T. B. Yebamoth 98a; T. B. Rosh ha-Shanah 26a; T. Baba Kamma 10:17; T. Yebamoth 14:5; M. Yebamoth 16:7; T. B. Abodah Zarah 34a; P. T. Horayoth III, 48a, and elsewhere.
[3] M. Maaser Sheni 4:9; M. Erubin 4:1; T. B. Horayoth 11a; Deut. Rabba 2.
[4] T. Betza 2:12; Ex. Rabba 30.
[5] P. T. Horayoth III, 48a.
[6] P. T. Pesahim VII, 34a; P. T. Gittin I, 44d.
[7] M. Yadaim 4:3; Epiphanies, Haereses XXX, 3, 4 - XXX, 12, 9.

The sole responsibility for the supervision, direction and other relations with the Diaspora did not lie with the envoys who were sent on passing visits. There were also the Sages of Jamnia who were appointed as presidents of the Jewish courts of law in the larger Diaspora communities. We read in one place of the departure for foreign parts of three sages of Jamnia, and of how saddened they were by their departure.[1] The three are mentioned later as presidents of courts of law, Rabbi Judah ben Bathyra in Nisibis, Rabbi Mathia ben Heresh in Rome and Hananiah the nephew of Rabbi Joshua in Pumbeditha.[2] Of these, Rabbi Judah came from Babylonia and was perhaps born there, while the two other sages were from the Land of Israel. The practice obtaining in the Temple period, of sending letters abroad, which was mentioned to Paul by the Jews of Rome, was later resumed. The Roman Jew Todos, one of the leaders of the community there, introduced into Rome the custom of eating kids roasted whole like a Passover sacrifice. He was opposed in this by the Sages of Jamnia, who wrote a letter to him saying: 'If you were not Todos, would we not proclaim the ban against you?'[3]

One of the things which bring out the relationship between the Land of Israel and the Diaspora in the thirty years or so after the destruction of the Temple is the translation of the Bible into Greek, done by Aquila, the proselyte from Pontus. The translation was made under the guidance of Rabbi Joshua ben Hananiah, Rabbi Eliezer ben Hyrcanos and Rabbi Akiba.[4] The work was undertaken for the sake of the Hellenistic Diaspora in the Roman Empire, to provide them with a translation faithful to the 'Masoretic' Hebrew Bible, as understood by the Sages of Jamnia, and to the method of 'Halakic Midrash', which interprets every word, including the particles. This version of the Greek Bible was probably made in such a way as to depart deliberately at times from the Christian interpretation, which was based on the Septuagint version.

All fragments of the Greek translation from the Cairo Genizah are from Aquila's translation. The same applies to the quotations from the Greek Bible in midrashic literature. This shows that the Sages of Jamnia succeeded in introducing Aquila's translation throughout the whole Diaspora, where it took the place of the Septuagint version

[1] *Sifre* on Deut., par. 80 (ed. Finkelstein p. 146).
[2] *T. B. Sanhedrin* 32b. The text reads: גולה (in exile). In the *Babylonian Talmud* גולה by itself refers to Pumbeditha.
[3] *P. T. Pesahim* VII, 34a.
[4] *P. T. Megillah* I, 71c; *P. T. Kiddushin* I, 59a.

held sacred by Hellenistic Judaism, though without displacing entirely the older version. Other works also, composed in the Land of Israel in the thirty years or so after the devastation of the land, such as the Apocalypse of Ezra (4 Esdras) and the (Syriac) Apocalypse of Baruch, were soon accepted and translated in the Hellenistic Diaspora. One proof of this is the fact that they were accepted as part of biblical tradition by Christians.

The text of the Midrash which reads: 'Although the Temple was destroyed, the three pilgrimages each year were not abolished,'[1] contains a large amount of exaggeration. Pilgrimages and visits to the city continued when it was in a state of ruin, and afterwards when it was in the hands of strangers. Throughout the whole of antiquity, after the destruction, there is evidence of pilgrimages which came also from the Diaspora, but merely as a sort of commemoration of the fall of the Temple.[2] There were minor pilgrimages of a sort at feastdays, and the pilgrims paid visits to the doctors of the law and put questions before them at the centre of Torah study.[3] In contrast to these few passing visits, it seems that those who came to settle in the Land of Israel and the young men who made an extended stay to study the Torah increased in number after the destruction of the Temple. Throughout the whole of the Tannaitic and Amoraic periods, there were always a considerable number of sages who came to settle down in the Land of Israel or at least stayed for a number of years. In the main centres of Jewish settlement in the Land of Israel, we even find synagogues or communities of Jews from the centres in the Diaspora.[4] Halakic literature also contains references to immigrants' problems, such as arose when the husband wished to settle but the wife did not, or when there were financial problems connected with immigration.[5]

The usage of proclaiming the New Moon and the intercalated month, which was the enduring bond with the Diaspora, was renewed apparently soon after the destruction of the Temple, since they were

---

[1] *Cant. Rabba* 4.
[2] For the problem arising from Hadrian's decree forbidding the Jews to enter Jerusalem, see S. Safrai, 'The Holy Congregation of Jerusalem', in *Scripta Hierosolymitana* XXIII (1972), pp. 62-78.
[3] Regarding the generation of Jamnia, from Tripoli: *T. Erubin* 9:22; from Asia *T. Hullin* 3:10.
[4] The synagogue of the Babylonians in Sepphoris: *Gen. Rabba* 33 (ed. Theodor-Albeck I, p. 305); in Tiberius: *P. T. Yoma* VII, 44 b; of the Cappadocians: *P. T. Shebiith* IX, 39a, and elsewhere.
[5] *M. Ketuboth* 13:11, and elsewhere.

matters of urgent necessity. There are many references over the years to the sending of envoys and communications regarding these things. The custom of holding from time to time a sort of Sanhedrin session in the chief centres of the Diaspora was introduced at the time of the Synod of Jamnia and continued in force later. The object was to decide upon the intercalation of the year, and so some distinguished sage was sent from the Sanhedrin, accompanied apparently by several others. These, in conjunction with the local sages, made the required ruling. So too we find Rabbi Akiba going to Nehardaea and his disciple Rabbi Meir going to Asia for this same reason.[1]

During the Jamnia period, Judaism recovered from the destruction of Jerusalem and the Temple and built up the spiritual and social life of the people in the new situation where it was without political independence or a material Temple. Community life, prayer and feast-days were organized without reference to the factor of the Temple, which had been the focus of social and religious life. Religious thought, the interpretation given to the practical observance of the commandments and the hope of redemption could not be reconciled to the destruction of the Temple, and the Jewish people looked forward to the time when the Temple would be speedily rebuilt and the order of divine service and the integrity of religious practice would be restored. But at the same time, the fact of the destruction of the Temple was reckoned with, and the continued existence of the Jewish people and its Torah encouraged, even in the new circumstances. The primacy of the Land of Israel and its many ties with the Diaspora disseminated these principles, which crystallized in the Land of Israel and became the heritage of the whole Jewish people.

With the revolt of Bar Cochba, the destruction of the settlements, the dispersal of the institutions and the harsh persecution which followed, relations were broken off for a while between the homeland and the Diaspora. During the revolt, one of the sages of the Land of Israel, Hananiah the nephew of Rabbi Joshua, who had been sent at the time to Babylonia, began to proclaim the New Moon and to intercalate the months for the Jews of Babylonia, acting independently and without regard for what was being done in the Land of Israel. Hananiah sought to persist in this course, even after the institutions in the homeland had begun to function once more, and he was supported by circles close to the head of the Babylonian exiles who sought to establish their independence with regard to the insti-

[1] M. Yebamoth 16:7; T. Megillah 2:5.

tutions in the Land of Israel. Under the combined pressure of envoys from the homeland and of influential sages in Babylonia, Hananiah desisted, and Babylonia like the rest of the Diaspora submitted to the Land of Israel and its restored leadership.[1] Towards the end of the second century, the bonds between Babylonia and the Land of Israel were strengthened with the increasing number of sages from Babylonia who went to the Land of Israel to settle down or stayed there for a number of years before returning to Babylonia. In the middle of the second century, we find that the presidents of the courts of rabbinical law, next to the Nasi in authority, were mostly from the Babylonian Diaspora. The next in command to Rabban Simeon ben Gamaliel, the Nasi at Usha in Galilee, was Rabbi Nathan, the son of the Exilarch, who held that position, as the sources note, because he was the son of the man in question.[2] Rabbi Nathan was dismissed, or resigned from his charge, after he and his deputy had tried unsuccessfully to depose Rabban Simeon ben Gamaliel. But when the latter's son, Rabbi Judah, was Nasi, his second in commmand was Rabbi Hiyya, a member of a distinguished Babylonian family who had come to live in the Land of Israel. This practice continued till the end of the period of the Amoraim.

At the time when Rabbi Judah the Nasi was in office (c. 170-220 C.E.) it became a widespread custom in the Diaspora to bring the dead to the Land of Israel for burial. The most notable example of this is the necropolis at Beth Shearim, which had apparently been the property of Rabbi Judah, having been given him by the Severan emperors. From the few burial-caves uncovered up to the present, it appears that many were buried there from all over the Diaspora in the Hellenistic world and beyond the Euphrates. It seems likely that Beth Shearim was designated as such a burial-place by Rabbi Judah the Nasi. Beth Shearim was a notable example, but not the only one. From this time on, graves of Diaspora Jews have been found in Jaffa and other places.[3] Needless to say, the custom of bringing the dead for burial in Israel was an important element in the links between the Diaspora and the homeland, since it also meant that the relatives came to visit the graves of their kinsfolk.

The various ties described above created in the people the sense of

---

[1] P. T. Sanhedrin I, 19b; T. B. Berakoth 63 a-b.
[2] T. B. Horayoth 13b-14a.
[3] B. Mazar, Beth Shearim I (1967), M. Schwabe and B. Lifshitz, Beth Shearim II, (1967) and N. Avigad, Beth Shearim III, (1971).

being one nation, in spite of being uprooted and dispersed. They felt themselves one nation, not merely through the sharing of historical memories and hopes for the future, but even in the realities of daily life and politics, when relations between Israel and the Roman Empire were well-ordered and correct, or when they were strained and revolt broke out. This state of affairs is aptly described by Philo when speaking of Jerusalem. 'While she', he writes, 'is my native city, she is not only the mother city of the land of Judaea, but also of many other countries.'[1] When relations between the Jewish people and the Roman Empire were good, this affected favourably the position of Judaism in the Diaspora, as stands out clearly from the Roman edicts. It was not officially changed after the fall of the Temple, though Jews were in fact in a worse position. The Jews of the homeland relied on the help of their fellows in the Diaspora in times of revolt, but it is not always clear to what extent help was forthcoming and how relations were maintained. The Roman authorities too, in their dealings with Judaism and with the Jews of the Land of Israel, had to take into account to some extent the existence of the Jewish Diaspora throughout the length and breadth of the Empire and in the Parthian Empire in the East, which was the rival and the enemy of Rome.

BIBLIOGRAPHY

On the letters of the Jews of Egypt in the second book of the Maccabees see E. BICKERMANN, 'Ein jüdischer Festbrief vom Jahre 124 v.Chr.' in *ZNW*, 1933, pp. 233-254.
The relations between the Jews of Egypt and the Land of Israel are discussed in the introduction of V. A. TCHERIKOVER in *CPJ* I, pp. I-III. For a different view see G. ALLON, *History of the Jews in the Land of Israel in the Period of the Mishnah and the Talmud* I, 1958, pp. 202-233 (in Hebrew).
The Jews of Cyrenaica and their relations with the Land of Israel are dealt with by S. APPLEBAUM, *Greeks and Jews in Ancient Cyrene*, 1969, esp. pp. 210-223 (in Hebrew)
On the tombs of the Cyrenaic Jews in Jerusalem see N. AVIGAD, 'A Depository of Inscribed Ossuaries in the Kidron Valley' in *IEJ*, 1962. Some information on the problem of the relations between the Jews of Rome and the Land of Israel can be found in H. J. LEON,

---

[1] Philo, *Legatio*, 281.

The Jews of Ancient Rome, 1960; on the period after the destruction of the Temple see M. VOGELMANN, 'Todos Ish Romi' in *Festschrift S. Mayer*, Hebrew part, 1956, pp. 196-200.
The Jews of Asia Minor are discussed by L. ROTH-GERSON, *The Civil and the Religious Status of the Jews in Asia Minor from Alexander the Great to Constantine* (mimeographed dissertation at the Hebrew University), 1972, pp. 197-209. No special research has been undertaken on the relations between the Babylonian Jews and the Land of Israel in the period we are concerned with. For the principal matters see J. NEUSNER, *A History of the Jews in Babylonia* I, 1965, pp. 1-73, and A. SCHALIT, 'Evidence of an Aramaic Source in Josephus' Antiquities' in *ASTI*, 1965, pp. 163-188.
On the renewal of the relations between the Diaspora and Jerusalem before the destruction of the Temple see J. JEREMIAS, *Jerusalem zur Zeit Jesu* I, 1923, pp. 66-97; S. SAFRAI, *Pilgrimage of the Time of the Second Temple*, 1965, pp. 54-71 (in Hebrew).
Tomb inscriptions from the Jerusalem area in Hebrew, Aramaic and Greek, some of which are of Diaspora Jews, are discussed in *Sefer Yerushalayim* I, ed. by M. Avi-Yonah, 1956, pp. 349-368.
The problem of the 'messengers' in the period of the Second Temple is treated by A. HARNACK, *Die Mission und Ausbreitung der Christentums* I (4th rev. ed.) 1924, pp. 340-4; H. VOGELSTEIN, 'The Development of the Apostolate in Judaism and its Transposition in Christianity', in *HUCA* II, 1925, pp. 99-123.
The dough-offerings and tithes brought by Jews from the Diaspora to Jerusalem are discussed by A. BÜCHLER, 'Die priesterlichen Zehnten und die römischen Stenern in den Erlässen Caesars', in *Festschrift Steinschneider*, part I, 1896, pp. 91-109; SAFRAI, op.cit. pp. 125-132.
On the letters which were sent to inform about the intercalation of years see A. BÜCHLER, 'The Letter of Rabban Shimon ben Gamaliel the Elder and Rabban Jochanan ben Zakkai on the removal of the tithe' in *Festschrift Jehuda to the memory of Jehuda Arie Blau*, 1938, pp. 157-169.

Chapter Five
The Reign of Herod and the Herodian Dynasty

The persecution by Antiochus and the Maccabean revolt led to the spiritual and material independence of the Jewish nation both in Judaea and outside. The Jewish monotheistic faith was saved, with momentous results for the world. In the second century before the current era, after centuries of subjection to imperial powers, an independent Jewish state had arisen under the leadership of the Hasmonaeans, and gradually expanding over the whole of Palestine, had achieved international recognition and status. Palestine became religiously and nationally 'Greater Judaea', and this fact set its stamp on the religious, cultural and ethnic character of the country for a long period. The existence of the Hasmonaean state was further accompanied by a vigorous religious development and by a strengthening of Judaism in the countries of the Diaspora. When Rome gained control of the whole of Syria, Judaea entered the sphere of Roman influence and rule. Pompey's capture of Jerusalem in 63 B.C.E. ended the episode of Jewish independence. The settlement concluded by the Roman commander separated various areas from the state of Judaea and abolished the Hasmonaean monarchy. But neither Pompey nor his immediate successors reversed the wheel of history completely. The large Hellenistic cities, it is true, were freed from Jewish rule; but the greater part of Idumaea, Galilee and important sections of the maritime strip (Sharon) remained Jewish. Hyrcanus II, the chief representative of the Hasmonaean house and the lawful inheritor and ruler of Judaea, was appointed ethnarch of the country, simultaneously holding the high priesthood in accordance with the Jewish tradition still in vigour in the Second Temple period, whereby the high priest was also the political head of the state of Judaea. One of Pompey's successors, Gabinius, governor of Syria in the years 57-55 B.C.E., attempted to break up the unity of the Jewish population by partitioning it into five sanhedrins; but the serious rebellions which broke out in Judaea in the fifties proved to the Roman authorities that it was better to give more power to the native rulers, subject to Rome. These were the conclusions drawn, in the main, by Julius

Caesar, who reunited the Jewish population, restored the port of Joppa to Judaea, granted permission to rebuild the walls of Jerusalem, and increased the prestige of the high priest and ethnarch, Hyrcanus II. The death of Julius Caesar (44 B.C.E.) again threw Judaea into the vortex of the Roman civil wars. The Jewish population suffered fiscal oppression and the enslavement of many of its members. Hyrcanus still retained his position as high priest and ethnarch, and was favoured by successive Roman governments, but in the entourage of Hyrcanus and of the branch of the Hasmonaean family dependent upon him, another family began to come to the fore, one which had been in partnership with Hyrcanus from the beginning —the house of Antipater the Idumaean. Antipater and his sons skilfully enhanced their power and influence throughout the changes and vicissitudes of Roman rule. Under Julius Caesar, Antipater's son Phasael had served as governor of Jerusalem, and another son, Herod, had simultaneously ruled Galilee. After the deaths of Caesar and Antipater, while Rome's eastern provinces were in the sphere of influence of Cassius and Brutus, the killers of Caesar, Antipater's sons maintained their dominant position, even overshadowing in great measure Hyrcanus II, the official ruler of Judaea. Hyrcanus' granddaugther Mariamme also became betrothed to Herod. These developments aroused the hostility of the majority of the Jewish people, who saw that the Hasmonaean dynasty was being supplanted by a foreign house, only half-Jewish, while they themselves were becoming completely subject to Roman power.

The struggle between Herod and Antigonus

A new situation arose for the opponents of the Antipatrids and for the Jews in general after the defeat of Cassius and Brutus by Antony and Octavian at the battle of Philippi (42 B.C.E.). Since both the Antipatrids and, officially, Hyrcanus had been among the supporters of Cassius, their opponents expected to gain a sympathetic hearing from the triumvir Mark Antony, who had been made responsible for the affairs of the East. The group opposing the Antipatrids was divided. Some wished to have them deposed in order to strengthen Hyrcanus' government. Others aimed at replacing Hyrcanus by Antigonus, the younger son of Aristobulus II, the Hasmonaean king who had been deposed by Pompey. Among the various delegations which surrounded Antony when he reached Bithynia, there was a Jewish deputation which accused Phasael and Herod of being in fact usurpers, who had left Hyrcanus ruler in name only. But the personal influence of Herod, who had also hastened to meet Antony, did its work, and Antony turned a deaf ear to his accusers,[1] having a good idea of the general loyalty of the Antipatrids to Rome, and remembering the rebellions of Aristobulus and his sons when he was in Judaea in Gabinius' time. A delegation dispatched by Hyrcanus, ruler of Judaea, composed of three members (Lysimachus son of Pausanias, Joseph son of Mennaeus and Alexander son of Theodorus) appeared only subsequently, when Antony reached Ephesus. Its more essential demands turned on the liberation of the Jews enslaved by Cassius and the restoration of areas overrun by the Tyrians. Antony granted Hyrcanus' requests in these matters, and also confirmed the privileges granted to the Jews by his predecessor Dolabella relating chiefly to their exemption from military service.[2] Antony sent letters to Tyre, Antioch and Arados, to make his decisions more widely known.[3] Antony's appearance in Syria and Judaea and the consolidation of his power in those countries, did little to relieve the inhabitants of the fiscal burden which weighed so heavily upon them. He needed a great deal of money to maintain his army, and the eastern provinces were squeezed to the limits of their financial capacity although they had already suffered severely.[4] Antony's decisions in Bithynia and at Ephesus did not mean that the opponents of the Antipatrids relaxed their efforts. A delegation of a hundred Jewish notables again appeared before Antony with the purpose of persuading him to change the regime in Judaea. In a debate that took place at Daphne near Antioch, M. Valerius Messalla spoke in defence of the Antipatrids, and Hyrcanus again threw his weight into the scales in their favour. Antony not only rejected the demands of their opponents, and refrained from impairing the position of Herod and Phasael, but accorded it official recognition by appointing the two brothers tetrarchs.[5] This appointment did nothing to alter the power relation between them; just as previously they had been more or less equal in status as στρατηγοί (prefects) under the authority of Hyrcanus, so now both were tetrarchs beside Hyrcanus the ethnarch.

[1] Jos. *Ant.* XIV, 301-303; *War* I, 242.
[2] *Ant.* XIV, 304-313.
[3] *Ant.* XIV, 314-323.
[4] M. Rostovtzeff, *Social and Economic History of the Hellenistic World* II (1953), p. 1006; D. Magie, *Roman Rule in Asia Minor* I (1950), pp. 427-8. On Judaea see Appian, *Civil Wars* V, 7, 31.
[5] On the title of tetrarch see W. Schwahn, *PW*, 2nd series V, cols 1089-97.

Herod nevertheless had already acquired a certain superiority by his betrothal to Hyrcanus' granddaugther, Mariamme. Jewish Jerusalem was not lightly reconciled to Antony's decision, nor did Antony's arrest of fifteen of the delegates who had gone to Daphne allay the ferment. A great multitude set out for Tyre, where Antony was holding court, to demonstrate their indignation. Antony treated the demonstrators harshly, ordering them to be dispersed by force, killing and wounding some.[1] It was now absolutely clear that Antony would not hesitate to render full military assistance to the existing Judaean regime.

Real changes could only be effected in Judaea as a result of general changes in the Roman East. Such hopes arose following the invasion of the Parthian forces into the eastern Roman provinces. Labienus the Younger, one of the great figures of the Roman republican party, had been sent before the battle of Philippi to the royal court of Parthia to mobilize military assistance against Antony and Octavian, and was now able to induce the Parthian king to invade Asia Minor and Syria.[2] The Parthian invasion of the Roman territories in the East encountered but feeble military resistance, for part of the inhabitants of the areas against which the Parthian campaign was directed was weary of Roman rule and ready to welcome the Parthian armies with open arms. Thus, for example, the king of Commagene became an ally of the invaders, and Cappadocia, as well as various parts of the province of Asia, fell to the attack of Labienus; only a few of the Carian towns offered a stout resistance to the invaders. The position in Syria was little different. Local governors and various cities made common cause with the Parthians, the closest and most prominent associate of the Parthians being Lysanias, ruler of Chalcis. A revolt against the Romans had already broken out in the Phoenician city of Arados in protest against heavy taxes, and the Roman garrison of the city was wiped out.[3] But Tyre, protected from the Parthian land forces by its geographical position, did not capitulate. The Parthian invasion of Syria did not, of course, omit Judaea, where the invaders could anticipate an especially favourable welcome, as hatred of the

---

[1] Jos. *Ant.* XIV, 327-329; *War* I, 246-247.
[2] On the Parthian invasion of Syria and Asia Minor see A. Bürcklein, *Quellen und Chronologie der römisch-parthischen Feldzüge in den Jahren 713-718 d.St.* (1879); W. W. Tarn, *CAH* X (1934), pp. 47-51; N. C. Debevoise, *A Political History of Parthia* (1938), pp. 108-120; H. Buchheim, *Die Orientpolitik des Triumvirn M. Antonius* (1960), pp. 74-81.
[3] Jerome, *Chronicon*, ed. Helm (1956), p. 158.

Roman authorities had accumulated among the Jewish population. Pacorus, son of the king of Parthia, began an advance along the coast of Palestine, while another Parthian column commanded by Barzapharnes operated in the interior.

Prior to the invasion, the Parthians had reached an agreement with Antigonus through the good offices of Lysanias of Chalcis. Antigonus himself entered his ancestral kingdom with the help of a Parthian cavalry force. As soon as he appeared in the Jewish-populated areas of the Carmel region, he was joined by multitudes of Jews, and swiftly overran Sharon, easily overcoming enemy opposition. From Sharon the way was open to Jerusalem; here, too, he was enthusiastically received and gained control of most of the city, the Temple serving as the principal base for his troops, though Herod and Phasael continued to hold out in the royal palace. Pentecost had brought the Jewish masses to Jerusalem, so Phasael agreed to go to negotiate with the Parthians,[1] accompanied by Hyrcanus. They reached the coast at Achzib, north of Ptolemais. Whatever Phasael's hopes had been in setting out to treat with the Parthians, he soon discovered that he and Hyrcanus were in effect prisoners without prospect of any concessions. One of the Romans present sought to persuade Phasael to escape by sea, but in vain: Hyrcanus and Phasael were placed under undisguised arrest.[2] Herod had remained in Jerusalem, under siege from superior forces. When he heard the news, he determined to escape without delay from the city while it was still possible, and taking with him his troops and his family, made for Masada, where he left his family, with a force sufficient to defend the fortress. He himself prepared to leave for Petra, the Nabataean capital.[3] Meanwhile the Parthians had gained complete control of Jerusalem and continued their advance southward, destroying Marissa on the way. Antigonus became king of Judaea. Phasael took his own life, and Hyrcanus' ears were cropped in order to prevent him from resuming the high priesthood.[4] Herod's hope of freeing his brother by paying ransom to his captors was thus bitterly disappointed, while his appeal to the king of the Nabataeans, to whom he was

[1] Jos. *Ant.* XIV, 330-341; *War* I, 248-255.
[2] *Ant.* XIV, 342-348; *War* I, 256-260. The above-mentioned Roman belonged to a well-known family of merchants, the Ofelli. See J. Dobiáš, *Archiv Orientalni* (1931), p. 253, n. 3.
[3] Jos. *Ant.* XIV, 348-362; *War* I, 261-267.
[4] *Ant.* XIV, 363-369; *War* I, 268-273; Dio Cassius XLVIII, 26,2; Syncellus I, p. 581 (ed. Dindorf).

bound by close ties of friendship, also ended in failure. His sole remaining hope lay with Rome. He reached Egypt, and without lingering at Cleopatra's court, made a winter voyage via Pamphylia and Rhodes to the Italian port of Brundisium.[1]

At Rome he was favourably received by Antony, as he had anticipated, for he arrived at a time when Antony and Octavian had once more drawn closer together, their relationships having deteriorated during the Perusine war. Antony was also actively planning the liberation of the eastern Roman provinces from the Parthians. An energetic man like Herod could be of great assistance in the execution of this task. On his arrival at Rome Herod had intended to beg the throne of Judaea not for himself but for the Hasmonaean Aristobulus III, the brother of Mariamme his betrothed, and a grandson of Hyrcanus II, Judaea's last lawful ruler, since he had counted on the Roman practice of granting power to representatives of the legitimate royal dynasties. But apparently Antony did not feel bound by such considerations; for he chose men loyal to Rome, even if unconnected with previous dynasties, as in Cappadocia, Pontus and Galatia. Antony was well acquainted with Herod's abilities and his loyalty to Rome, whereas Aristobulus, the Hasmonaean candidate, was still a child and incapable of acting independently; hence, Antony decided to transfer power in Judaea directly to Herod. It may be assumed that Herod too, sensing the opportunity, exerted himself in the same direction, and promised Antony ample supplies of money when he had got control of Judaea. Some of the influential men at Rome, such as Valerius Messalla, already friendly with Herod, may well have assisted him also. Once Antony had decided to make Herod ruler of Judaea and had obtained Octavian's complete accord, there remained no alternative but to grant him the title of King, a desideratum in any case, in view of the fact that Herod's rival under Parthian auspices, Antigonus, could claim the title. Further, Herod was not of a priestly family and could not be high priest. As the high priesthood was the loftiest dignity in Judaea, and Herod, like Hyrcanus, received the title of ethnarch only, the recipients of the high priesthood would have vastly overshadowed him. The grant of the royal title to Herod, at all events, was such as to adjust the balance of prestige in his favour. The conferring upon Herod of the kingship of Judaea was decided in a session of the Senate.[2] Herod walked in an impressive procession

[1] *Ant.* XIV, 370-378; *War* I, 277-281.
[2] It seems that in 40 B.C. Herod's kingdom included only the territories which

between Antony and Octavian while the consuls and other dignitaries of the Roman government preceded him to the Temple of Jupiter on the Capitol.[1]

Herod permitted himself no more than a week's stay in Rome; the position in Judaea demanded his presence as soon as possible, since there was no one there to oppose Antigonus, who had gained control of the entire country and was striking coins with Hebrew legends affirming his status as Mattathiah the High Priest, just as their Greek superscription proclaimed him King Antigonus. Only the fortress of Masada, where Herod had entrusted his kindred to his brother Joseph, held out against Antigonus, and it too was in danger due to shortage of water.[2] On the other hand Antigonus' position had begun to weaken; the military supremacy of the Parthians in the East vanished in 39 B.C.E. as Ventidius, the Roman commander appointed by Antony as governor of Syria, had defeated them on the Cilician frontier and exercised virtual control over all Syria; only the inhabitants of Arados, fearing Roman reprisals, refused to submit and were sustaining a prolonged siege.[3] Antigonus' position once again depended on Rome; he attempted to act as other oriental kings had acted before him who had previously inclined to Parthia: he surrendered to Ventidius and paid him a large sum of money.[4] It is to be supposed that although Ventidius refrained from driving Antigonus from Jerusalem, his military superiority nevertheless prevented the Hasmonaean king from operating energetically against the rest of Herod's family. It should indeed be added that Ventidius could not yet afford to mount a regular siege of Jerusalem, for despite the blow suffered by the Parthians, they had not yet despaired and a resumption of the war was to be expected. Ventidius quitted the country, leaving in Judaea only part of his army under the command of Silo, who likewise observed the truce with Antigonus.[5]

At this juncture Herod returned; landing on the coast at Ptolemais, he began the reduction of Galilee. The Roman commanders felt bound to aid him as the official sovereign of Judaea under Roman auspices;

constituted the ethnarchy of Hyrcanus II. New territories were attached to it only in 39 B.C.E. See Buchheim, op.cit., pp. 66-7.
[1] Jos. *Ant.* XIV, 379-389; *War* I, 281-285; cf. also Strabo, *Geography* XVI, 2, 46, p. 765; Tacitus, *Historiae* V, 9.
[2] *Ant.* XIV, 390-391; *War* I, 286-287.
[3] Dio Cassius XLVIII, 41, 4-5.
[4] Jos. *Ant.* XIV, 392; *War* I, 288.
[5] *Ant.* XIV, 393; *War* I, 289.

he was able to overrun considerable areas of Galilee, his immediate aim being to relieve his family, beleaguered in Masada. His main achievement was the capture of Joppa. After Joppa was taken, Antigonus could no longer prevent his advance southward, and Herod was joined by numbers of the Idumaean population. Herod now raised the siege of Masada, effected a junction with Silo's force and invested Jerusalem, even urging its inhabitants to come over to him by promising them a general amnesty. Antigonus, for his part, scornfully denounced Herod to the Romans as devoid of all right to the throne of the Jewish kingdom; if they were really determined to take the kingship from Antigonus because he had gained it by Parthian favour, they should bestow it, he affirmed, upon another member of the Hasmonaean house.[1] The forces of Silo and Herod were, however, inadequate to overcome the spirited resistance of Jerusalem's defenders; the besieging army suffered severely from a shortage of supplies, for the entire environs of the city had been deliberately laid waste by Antigonus' men. Herod ordered his supporters in Samaria to bring supplies to Jericho, but Antigonus' troops, operating behind the enemy lines with the support of the Jewish population of Jericho, interfered with their transport to the army investing Jerusalem. Herod set out for Jericho at the head of a strong force, took the town and garrisoned it, but despite these efforts could not maintain the siege as winter came on (39/38 B.C.E.). The Roman army was sent to winter in the areas he had occupied, but the immediate neighbourhood of Jerusalem was in effect evacuated by the Romans. Antigonus once again endeavoured to reach agreement with them, even quartering part of their forces at Lydda.[2] Herod could not in any case capture Jerusalem with the forces at his disposal. He therefore restricted military operations to other areas, using as his principal base the city of Samaria, where he had placed his family is safe-keeping. He dispatched his brother Joseph to Idumaea, himself determining to conquer Galilee. He took its capital, Sepphoris, without serious resistance and began to wipe out the centres of resistance in the caves of Arbel. Yet despite his not inconsiderable achievements it was doubtful if he had been able utterly to eradicate Galilean resistance. At this point, a deterioration occurred in the relations of Silo and Antigonus, and Silo now had no alternative but to fall in again with Herod's strategy. One of Herod's brothers,

[1] *Ant.* xiv, 394-405, *War* i, 290-6.
[2] *Ant.* xiv, 406-412; *War* i, 297-302.

Pheroras, now received the task of refortifying the stronghold of Alexandrium, which had become the supply base of the Roman army in Judaea.[1]

In reality the decision was to be fought out not between Herod and Antigonus but on the Euphrates, where the Romans and Parthians were preparing for a major engagement. At the battle of Gindarus (38 B.C.E.) the Parthian host was crushed by Ventidius, and the Parthian crown-prince Pacorus died on the battle-field. His death was a heavy blow to the Parthian Empire, since Pacorus was the pivot of the entire Parthian struggle against Rome and enjoyed much sympathy in Syria.[2] His death put an end to the Parthian threat to that province. Ventidius restored Roman sovereignty over the various parts of the country which were still in revolt, and then turned upon the kingdom of Commagene in order to punish its king, Antiochus, for his alliance with the Parthians. The Roman victory over Parthia and the conquest of the whole of Syria left Antigonus as the only serious enemy of Rome in the area, apart from the king of Commagene. Large Roman forces were now free to render substantial aid to Herod. The latter had endeavoured to improve his military situation even before the final victory over Parthia, his chief operation being concentrated in the region of Galilee. Meantime Ventidius had dispatched, on Antony's orders, a Roman army to assist him, yet even this failed to bring about the hoped-for decision in the struggle against Antigonus; the only apparent Roman achievement was a massacre of Jews on the road from Jerusalem to Emmaus.[3]

Herod saw that he could end the war only if larger Roman forces were committed. He determined on a personal meeting with Antony, who was then besieging Samosata, the capital of Commagene, to persuade him to dispatch a considerable Roman force to Judaea. After an adventurous journey Herod reached Samosata. When Antony had successfully concluded the siege, he was easily able to detach some of his best forces for the war in Judaea. The task of eliminating Antigonus and installing Herod in Jerusalem was entrusted to Gaius Sosius, governor of Syria, who promptly sent forces to Judaea and prepared to follow with the rest of his army.[4] But while Herod was still abroad, events occurred in Judaea to undermine his position.

---

[1] *Ant.* XIV, 413-419; *War* I, 303-8.
[2] Dio Cassius XLIX, 20,4.
[3] Jos. *Ant.* XIV, 434-6; *War* I, 317-9.
[4] *Ant.* XIV, 437-447; *War* I, 320-2; 327.

Antigonus braced himself for a last desperate effort against his foes, with the support of the majority of the Jewish nation. Galilee rose in rebellion against Herod for a third time, and his supporters were put to the sword. Joseph, his brother, who had set out for the region of Jericho at the head of some Roman cohorts, fell in battle, and the cohorts, composed chiefly of raw recruits from Syria, were annihilated. Resistance against Herod was also mounted in Idumaea.[1]

Herod received the news while at Daphne. Taking one of the Roman legions and gathering eight hundred men in Lebanon, he reached Ptolemais and began to advance into the interior of Galilee. Without becoming deeply involved there, he moved rapidly towards Jericho in order to cover Samaria.[2] The decisive battle for the area took place near Isana (Burj el-Isaneh),[3] on the road from Jerusalem to Shechem, some twenty miles north of Jerusalem. The action ended in a victory for Herod and his Roman allies, with a mass slaughter of Antigonus' troops, among the dead being Pappus, Antigonus' commander-in-chief.[4] After this battle Herod was able to commence preparations for the siege of Jerusalem in the expectation of being joined by the additional Roman forces under command of Sosius, which were on their way to the country. He further decided to celebrate his marriage with Mariamme the Hasmonaean and so to obtain some sort of legitimacy in the eyes of the Jewish nation. The wedding took place at Samaria, Herod's stronghold.[5] With the arrival of Sosius and his forces a mighty Roman host was concentrated before Jerusalem.[6] As in the Great Revolt of 66 c.e., the main force of the Jewish nation was now gathered in the city. The Jews fought stoutly against the large army of besiegers, inspired with faith in divine aid and ready to endure everything to defend the Temple. But the military superiority of the Romans was immense: three siege-walls were quickly erected around the city. The Romans were able to keep their supply lines open and to prevent surprise sorties on the part of Antigonus' troops. After a five-months' siege, Jerusalem was captured by the Romans (37 b.c.e.).[7]

Antigonus himself was taken prisoner by Sosius, a dreadful massacre

[1] *Ant.* xiv, 448-450; *War* i, 323-6.
[2] *Ant.* xiv, 451-5; *War* i, 327-331.
[3] On the identification of Ješana see W. F. Albright, *BASOR* ix (1923), pp. 7-8.
[4] Jos. *Ant.* xiv, 456-464; *War* i, 332-342.
[5] *Ant.* xiv, 465-7; *War* i, 343-4.
[6] See also A. H. M. Jones, *The Herods of Judaea* (1938), p. 47.
[7] On the chronological problem see pp. 64-8.

ensued, and the city was sacked. Only with difficulty did Herod succeed in restraining his allies by compensating the commanders and Sosius with large gifts of money.[1]

As long as Antigonus was alive Herod could not feel secure on the royal throne, especially as Antigonus had the sympathy of the majority of the nation; he further feared that at some opportune moment Antigonus might claim his rights from Rome and even gain a hearing. Herod therefore brought all his influence to bear upon Antony, who had intended to keep Antigonus for his Roman triumph, to persuade him to put him to death; the Hasmonaean was decapitated at Antioch.[2]

Antigonus, the last ruler of the Hasmonaean line, had begun his military career in a rising against Rome, and spent his entire effective life fighting Rome. Here and there, indeed, he attempted to attain his end by compromising with Rome, even after he had been crowned king of Judaea by the Parthians. His objective was not in fact so unattainable, given the contemporary political reality, but he was continually frustrated by Herod's close connections with the Roman rulers and his tradition of unconditional loyalty to Rome, a loyalty really forced on him since he possessed no roots in Jewish society. Antigonus on the other hand enjoyed the profound sympathy of the Jewish nation, the greater part of which remained faithful to him virtually to the last ounce of its strength. Nor does the fact that Shamaiah and Abtalion, the leaders of the Pharisees, pleaded with the people of Jerusalem to yield to Herod and the Romans,[3] prove the contrary, for they did so out of a desire to prevent futile bloodshed only after the situation had become desparate. Part of the popular sympathy for Antigonus is doubtless to be explained by general loyalty to the Hasmonaean house, by hatred of Roman rule and of its loyal lackeys the Antipatrids. But much of it must be ascribed also to the personality of Antigonus, who exhibited great ability in his warlike operations and his diplomatic negotiations. Though

---

[1] Jos. *Ant.* xiv, 468-486; *War* i, 345-356.
[2] *Ant.* xiv, 489-490; xv, 5-10 (including a quotation from Strabo); *War* i, 357; Dio Cassius xlix, 22,6; Plutarch, *Life of Antony*, 36. On the triumph celebrated by Sosius in September 34 B.C.E. see *CIL* i, i, 2nd ed., p. 76. See also *CIL* ix no. 4855; the coin from Zacynthus in E. A. Sydenham, *The Coinage of the Roman Republic* (2nd ed., 1952), p. 199, no. 1272; Seneca Rhetor, *Suasoriae* ii, 21.
[3] I cannot see much foundation for the remark of Graetz, *Geschichte der Juden* iii, i (5th ed., 1905), pp. 190-1, that the attitude of the Jewish nation and its leaders to Antigonus was marked by antipathy.

Herodian propaganda did much to blacken his repute and diminish his prestige, it would nevertheless appear that his name was revered among the common people. Even in Herod's own family his eldest son Antipater was concerned to profit from the connection and to take Antigonus' daughter as his wife.

Herod as king during Antony's supremacy
in the East (37-31 B.C.E.)

Herod's capture of Jerusalem with the help of the Roman legions put an end to the main Jewish resistance. His monarchy became an established fact. It was basically the creation of the eastern policy of Rome, its form and scope being determined by the calculations and needs of the rulers of the Roman state, first of Antony and subsequently of Augustus.

Herod was only one of Rome's oriental vassal kings, the basis of whose power was laid in these years by Antony. They included various sovereigns in Asia Minor such as Amyntas, King of Galatia, and Archelaus, King of Cappadocia, both of them men who, like Herod, were unrelated to the royal dynasties which had formerly ruled in their countries. Another was Polemo, King of Pontus, a member of a family which had distinguished itself in the war against the Parthian invaders.[1] All these sovereigns were important to Antony as guardians of order in their countries, and as loyal supporters of Roman rule in the East. They also assisted him both materially and financially in his wars against the Parthians, and also against the efforts of Octavian, his great political rival at Rome, to undermine his position.

In the first seven years after the capture of Jerusalem, Herod was confined to the orbit of Antony's political policy. His position was all the more precarious, since he had not yet completely suppressed the remnants of armed resistance offered by the Hasmonaean loyalists in Judaea itself, and a Roman force to the strength of a legion was stationed at Jerusalem in order to protect the King and his regime in case of need.[2] The tension within Judaea further occasioned constant intervention from outside, especially on the part of Queen Cleopatra VII of Egypt, whose influence on Antony grew steadily greater as they became more and more closely associated

---

[1] On Antony's policy in the East in these years and his relations with the vassal rulers in Asia Minor see Magie op.cit. I, pp. 433-6; R. Syme, *The Roman Revolution* (1939), pp. 259-275; Buchheim, op.cit.

[2] Jos. *Ant.* xv, 72.

MAP VI. HEROD'S KINGDOM

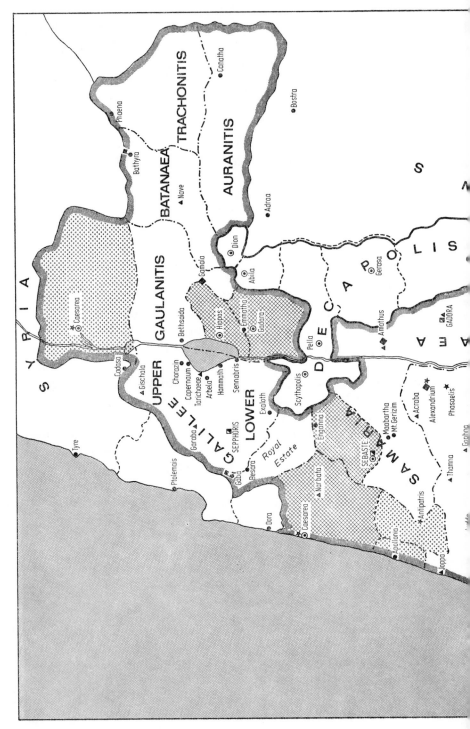

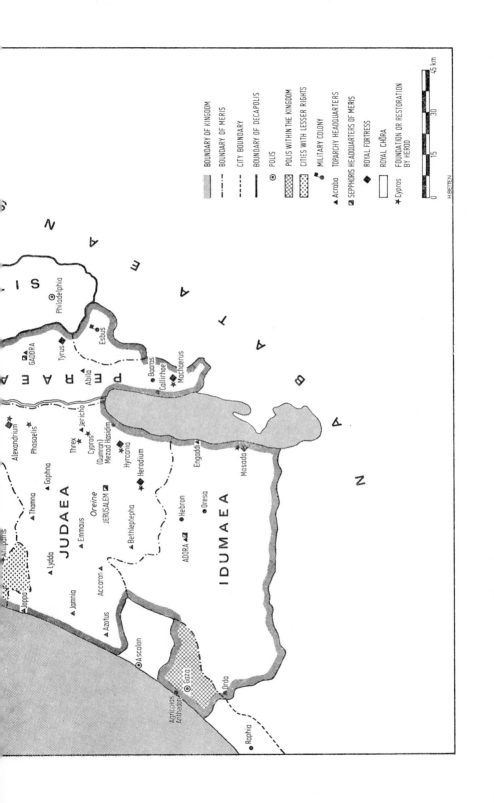

BOUNDARY OF KINGDOM

BOUNDARY OF MERIS

CITY BOUNDARY

BOUNDARY OF DECAPOLIS

⊙ POLIS

POLIS WITHIN THE KINGDOM

CITIES WITH LESSER RIGHTS

MILITARY COLONY

▲ Acraba TOPARCHY HEADQUARTERS

SEPPHORIS HEADQUARTERS OF MERIS

◆ ROYAL FORTRESS

☐ ROYAL CHŌRA

★ Cypros FOUNDATION OR RESTORATION BY HEROD

0   15   30   45 km

H.BETTEN

Philadelphia

GADORA
Tyrus
Esbus
Abila
Baaras
Callirhoe
Machaerus

Alexandrium
Phasaelis
Threx
Jericho
Cypros
(Qumran)
Mezad Hasidim
Hyrcania
Herodium
Engadda
Masada

Gophna
Oreine
JERUSALEM
Bethleptepha

Thamna
Emmaus
Hebron
Oresa

JUDAEA

Lydda
Accaron
ADORA

Jamnia
Azotus
Ascalon

IDUMAEA

Antipatris
Joppa

Agrippias
Anthedon
Gaza
Orda

Raphia

after 37 B.C.E. Her policy was generally hostile to Herod, for she planned to restore the ancient rule of the Ptolemies over Palestine and southern Syria; Antony's hesitations, indeed, prevented Cleopatra from carrying out her policy to the full. Antony did not feel it prudent to liquidate Herod, both because of the possible repercussions in Judaea itself and because of the negative reaction that might ensue in Rome, for officially Herod ruled not under Antony's own auspices, but as a sovereign whose kingship had been acknowledged by the supreme institutions of the Roman state. The material results of Cleopatra's activity were the gradual restriction of the scope of Herod's royal power and a feeling of uncertainty as to the future of his regime in Judaea. This background makes it probable that Herod was unable to initiate an independent foreign policy. Such independent activity was beyond the power of other allied kings, nor did Herod himself exercise it even at the height of his power under Augustus, much less in his difficult days during the reign of Cleopatra. He did indeed open negotiations with King Phraates of Parthia for the return of Hyrcanus II from his place of exile in Babylon.[1] But this step was also in accordance with the political requirements of Antony who may have encouraged him out of a feeling that the presence of Hyrcanus in the Parthian kingdom was a potential danger to Roman interests. Hyrcanus as the eldest representative of the Hasmonaean house and as high priest of the Temple of Jerusalem for many decades was highly honoured by the Jewish multitudes of Babylonia amongst whom he resided with the consent of the Parthian king, and the King himself treated him in the friendliest fashion. In the event of another collision with Rome, the Parthians might well hope that Hyrcanus' name would aid them in gaining Jewish support and serve to counterbalance Herod. To bring Hyrcanus back to Judaea, Herod sent Saramala, a wealthy Syrian, to Parthia. He had long-standing relations with the Parthians, and was also bound by ties of friendship with Herod's family.[2]

In accordance with the settlement of 40/39 B.C.E. Herod's kingdom included Judaea, Galilee, Jewish Transjordan, Samaria, and Idumaea. As Joppa was part of the Jewish state since the time of Julius Caesar,

---

[1] *Ant.* xv, 18-20.

[2] Antony himself before his expedition against the Parthians in 36 B.C.E. started peace negotiations with Phraates, King of the Parthians, with a view to getting back the Roman prisoners and standards held by the Parthians since the death of Crassus. See Plutarch, *Life of Antony* 37; Dio Cassius XLIX, 24, 5; K. H. Ziegler, *Die Beziehungen zwischen Rom und dem Partherreich* (1964), p. 35.

it undoubtedly also came under Herod's rule. Gaza also was among the cities of his realm.[1] In subsequent years the kingdom gradually shrank in extent, as a result of Cleopatra's pressure on Antony, who granted her various areas in Palestine—a procedure which he adopted also in the neighbouring regions.[2]

Cleopatra's demands on Antony were furthered by the internal crisis in Judaea. The expulsion of the Hasmonaean house from the high priesthood and the appointment of Hananel bitterly vexed Alexandra, the King's mother-in-law, who tried to influence Antony to bestow the post on her son, Aristobulus III. Friendly relations were formed between Alexandra and Cleopatra, who interceded with Antony to transfer the high priesthood to Aristobulus. At first Antony displayed no readiness to respond to Cleopatra's petition, but changed his mind under the influence of Dellius, who had discharged various missions on his behalf. Dellius had been personally enchanted, during his visit to Judaea, by the extraordinary beauty of Alexandra's children, and Antony even wrote to Herod to send the youthful Aristobulus to him. Herod naturally was much afraid that the step might lead to Aristobulus' promotion and that the latter would ultimately supplant him, with Antony's encouragement. Aristobulus' journey to Antony was also apt to cause an immediate weakening of Herod's already unstable position in Judaea, and to deliver a considerable blow to his prestige. The move might further inspire Hasmonaean sympathizers, not all of whom had laid down their arms, with new hopes of the restoration of the Hasmonaean family to power. Herod therefore steadily refused Aristobulus permission to leave Judaea, justifying his reluctance to Antony by explaining that he wished to avoid an outbreak of disorder in the country.[3]

Calculating that he could not withstand the pressure exercised upon him at home and from abroad, and perhaps in order to prevent Aristobulus' departure from the country, Herod determined to appoint the seventeen-year old youth High Priest in place of Hananel.[4] Herod soon realized that the new situation was fraught with many dangers. He became more and more suspicious of Alexandra, while she persisted in maintaining close relations with Cleopatra. Aristobulus' appearance

---

[1] Jos. *Ant.* xv, 254. Costobar, Herod's brother-in-law, was appointed governor of Idumaea and Gaza a short time after Herod's accession.
[2] On Antony's donations to Cleopatra see Appendix, pp. 305-7.
[3] Jos. *Ant.* xv, 23-30.
[4] *Ant.* xv, 31-41.

in the Temple in the full splendour of the high priest's raiment on the Festival of Tabernacles (35 B.C.E.), proved to Herod how great was the popularity enjoyed by the young man among the people. Herod seems now to have decided that it was worth risking grave consequences to rid himself of Aristobulus, fearing that otherwise he would be forced to yield place to him. Shortly after the Festival of the Tabernacles, while enjoying the hospitality of Alexandra, the King had his young rival drowned as he sported in the bathing-pool.[1] Outwardly Herod displayed signs of grief over Aristobulus' death, and buried him with much pomp. But his behaviour could not erase his guilt in the eyes of either Alexandra or others. Alexandra again besought the intervention of Cleopatra, who induced Antony to summon Herod to Laodicaea in Syria to render an account of his action. With heavy heart Herod set out, and rumours spread of his execution by Antony.[2] But they swiftly proved to be false. The meeting between Antony and Herod at Laodicaea (34 B.C.E.), led neither to the deposition nor to the execution of the King of Judaea. Herod appears not even to have denied his part in the murder of Aristobulus, but to have justified the deed by the need of safeguarding Roman power from a mass outbreak inspired by the hope of a Hasmonaean revival. Antony was convinced by his argument and even ostentatiously displayed to the world his friendship for Herod.[3] Herod's position nevertheless remained insecure, for Antony now assigned (34 B.C.E.) important areas of the Judaean kingdom to Cleopatra, in addition to the portions he had granted to her in 37 B.C.E. Herod now no longer controlled the fertile Plain of Jericho, with its world-famed opsobalsam plantations and date groves, nor part of the coastal plain. Yet in practice he retained control of part of the areas taken from his kingdom; so much is clear with regard to the Plain of Jericho, which was leased to him by Cleopatra in exchange for an annual payment of two hundred talents.[4] He also served as guarantor for the annual rent owed to Cleopatra by King Malichus of Nabataea, upon whom Antony had imposed a monetary fine in punishment for aiding the Parthians.[5] Areas were now taken from his kingdom as they had been taken from that of Herod, and Malichus leased them from Cleopatra—Herod as has been stated, being his guarantor. This arrangement was to

---

[1] *Ant.* xv, 50-6. See also *War* I, 437. The doubts of H. Willrich, *Das Haus des Herodes* (1929), p. 52 about the murder of Aristobulus by Herod seem out of place.
[2] Jos. *Ant.* xv, 71.   [3] *Ant.* xv, 74-9.
[4] *War* I, 362; *Ant.* xv, 132.   [5] Dio Cassius XLVIII, 41, 5.

prove a source of disaster, since the Nabataean king ceased payment after a time and Herod was charged by Antony and Cleopatra with the task of compelling him to pay. The antagonism between Herod and the Nabataean kingdom runs like a thread throughout the annals of his reign, constituting a continuation of the Jewish-Nabataean struggle which had commenced in the period of Alexander Yannai (Jannaeus). Although friendly relations had formerly prevailed between Antipater and the Nabataeans, they had deteriorated at the time of Herod's flight from Antigonus, and more important still, when Herod became king of Judaea he inherited the political aims and interests of the Judaean sovereigns who had preceded him. As a result the war which Herod waged against the Nabataeans under Cleopatra's instigation accorded also with his own political aims. The campaign, which took place in 31 B.C.E., when the clash between Antony and Octavian was at its height, was a difficult one, and Herod did not overcome the Nabataeans easily. The focus of fighting was in Transjordan: in the first battle, apparently near Dion, he was able to defeat them, but in the second near Canatha, he himself suffered serious defeat. When Herod realized that the fight was lost, he abandoned his defeated army, which retired to its camp. The Nabataeans laid siege to the Jewish encampment and stormed it, which meant that Herod lost a considerable part of his army and was for a time forced to avoid open battle with the Nabataeans, contenting himself with raids upon the areas controlled by them.[1]

A further disaster now befell Herod and his kingdom. An earthquake in Judaea claimed many victims,[2] but Herod was lucky in so far as there were no fatal casualties in the army itself, which, being engaged in warfare, was concentrated in the open field. The defeat near Canatha and the disastrous earthquake left his prospects, nevertheless, very gloomy. The Nabataeans also gave vent to their hostility and contempt for Herod by murdering the envoys whom he sent to open negotiations. But a new victory on the battlefield rescued Herod from the dire straits into which he had fallen, and restored his prestige. The battle took place not far from Philadelphia in Transjordan, many Nabataean troops being killed and many more taken prisoner by the Jewish troops.

[1] Jos. Ant. xv, 108-120; War I, 364-9.
[2] See also R. de Vaux, L'archéologie et les manuscrits de la Mer Morte (1961), pp. 15-16.

In the war against the Nabataeans Herod had proved his ability as a commander, and Judaea its military superiority over the Nabataean kingdom. The impression made by these events in Transjordan was not without effect on Octavian's verdict after the decisive contest between himself and Antony which took place at the same time.

Under the Principate of Augustus

Herod's Nabataean war was advantageous from another point of view. His army, engaged against Malichus, was prevented from taking an active part on Antony's side in the campaign of Actium, although Herod sent Antony money and grain.[1] After Antony's defeat at the battle of Actium (31 B.C.E.), Herod was among those who promptly abandoned the defeated side despite the efforts of Antony to retain his loyalty.[2] Herod also took the first steps to appease the victorious Octavian. Gladiators who had been training at Cyzicus were marching from Asia Minor to assist Antony in Egypt. Herod helped Didius, the governor of Syria, to prevent the link-up. Despite this, Herod's future was far from assured, for he was Antony's man, and had been crowned through his influence. With a heavy heart he set out for Rhodes (30 B.C.E.), where the victor was staying, to hear his decision. The consequences neither justified his fears nor confirmed the hopes of his enemies. Octavian ratified Herod in his kingship of Judaea and bestowed various honours upon him, leaving no doubt that Herod was the man favoured by the Roman ruler. When Octavian appeared in Syria on his way to conquer Egypt, he received an enthusiastic welcome from Herod, who furnished him and his army with the provisions needed for the march from Ptolemais to the Egyptian frontier. Particularly important was his assistance in the crossing of the desert, during which he distributed water and wine in abundance to Octavian's army, doing everything to prove his devotion to his new masters. A gift of eight hundred talents made by Herod to Octavian was an additional manifestation of the material advantage to be derived from Herod's loyalty. Octavian encountered the same readiness on Herod's part to serve and to aid him on his way back from Egypt to Syria.[3]

The fact that Octavian left Herod as King of Judaea is not in fact surprising. The strengthening of the allied vassal kings in the East

[1] Jos. *Ant.* xv, 189; *War* i, 388.
[2] Plutarch, *Life of Antony* 72.
[3] Jos. *Ant.* xv, 187-201; *War* i, 386-395.

still remained one of the corner stones of Roman policy under Octavian. Bosporus, Paphlagonia, Cappadocia and Galatia continued to exist as allied kingdoms after Actium. To a certain extent the victor left in power the men whom Antony had chosen, although the rulers were changed in some states.[1] Octavian did not ignore the simple fact that when the eastern kings took sides with Antony, their action was conditioned by their belonging to Antony's sphere of influence and that they would naturally show the same degree of complete obedience to the new Roman ruler. There was therefore no point in changing rulers of proven ability whose positions in their countries seemed stable. Herod's loyalty to Rome was well known and almost hereditary in his family. He had indeed been loyal to Antony till Actium, but had not persisted in his loyalty after his defeat. Herod had proved his practical ability for over a long period, ultimately also by his war with the Nabataeans and his valiant efforts to win the goodwill of the victor. It is doubtful, at any rate, whether the Romans could have found a more appropriate candidate to rule over Judaea in their name, while the complete annexation of the country to the Empire and the establishment of a Roman provincial regime there did not seem politically worthwhile. Yet it is also to be observed that Octavian's attitude to Herod was strikingly favourable compared with his attitude to the kings of Nabataea and Commagene, who were deposed after a short time.

The general stabilization of political conditions in the central government at Rome, and the institution of the Augustan principate, as well as the removal of the constant threat of Cleopatra and her intrigues against the integrity of Herod's kingdom, formed the background of a period in which Herod began to enjoy immense prestige in the Roman imperial world. Octavian, not content with ratifying his royal power, bestowed honours upon him such as the transfer to the Judaean monarch of Cleopatra's Gallic bodyguard, to perform similar duties at his court.[2] Incomparably more important than honours of this type was the enlargement of Herod's territory, chiefly in the years immediately after the battle of Actium. Octavian not only restored to Herod all the areas that had belonged to him in the year 37 B.C.E., and had been taken from him as a result of Cleopatra's pressure on

---

[1] On the first arrangements of Octavian after the victory see Dio Cassius LI,2. On his relations with the vassal kings see Magie, op.cit. I, pp. 440-5; G. W. Bowersock, *Augustus and the Greek World* (1965), pp. 42-61.

[2] Jos. *Ant.* xv, 217; *War* I, 397.

Antony (e.g. Jericho), but extended the area of his rule in the maritime plain, where additional cities (the Tower of Straton, and Anthedon) were now transferred to him. Some of the Hellenistic towns across the Jordan, such as Hippos and Gadara,[1] previously freed from Jewish suzerainty in Pompey's time, were now annexed to Herod's realm. An additional expansion of Herod's kingdom took place in 23 B.C.E. in northern Transjordan, where Augustus added to it parts of Trachonitis, Batanaea and Hauran.[2] The motive for this annexation was the insecure situation prevailing in the region, which had previously been under the sovereignty of Zenodorus, a local ruler whose principal possessions were situated west and north-west of the area in question.[3] The inhabitants of these areas were practically professional bandits, to the detriment of the neighbouring population and especially of the inhabitants of Damascus.[4] Zenodorus did not do enough to end this situation and appears to have profited from it personally; the complaints of victims were heard before the governor of Syria and reached the ears of Augustus. Augustus perceived that the best way of restoring order would be to hand over these territories to Herod. The latter acted with his customary energy to safeguard the local population; in so doing he encountered numerous difficulties, some caused by Zenodorus, who was envious, and by the Arabs with whom he was connected. Zenodorus also encouraged the people of Hellenistic Gadara to resist Herod. On Zenodorus' death three years later (20 B.C.E.), Augustus granted Herod the original native territory of the deceased prince near the sources of the Jordan.[5] By these various annexations Herod's kingdom was extended to include the entire Land of Israel, including Transjordan, but excluding the enclave of Ascalon and the coastal plain north of Mount Carmel, which had never been part of the Jewish state in the Second Temple period. This meant the end of the settlement made by Pompey and Gabinius, and the State of Judaea regained in general the territories it had held in the time of Alexander Jannaeus and Salome Alexandra.

[1] *Ant.* xv, 217; *War* I, 396.
[2] *Ant.* xv, 343-8; *War* I, 398-9.
[3] On the territory of Zenodorus see Schürer I, pp. 565-567; U. Kahrstedt, *Syrische Territorien in hellenistischer Zeit* (1926), p. 89. On the coins relating to him see *British Museum Catalogue of the Greek Coins of Galatia, Cappadocia and Syria* ed. W. Wroth (1899), p. 281.
[4] See also Strabo, *Geography* XVI, 2,20, p. 756.
[5] Jos. *Ant.* xv, 359-360; *War* I, 400; Dio Cassius LIV, 9,3. The aggrandizement of Herod's kingdom was only one of the many arrangements made by Augustus during his sojourn in the East at that time (20 B.C.E.) cf. Dio Cassius LIV, 9,2.

With the annexation of Zenodorus' territory in 20 B.C.E. the Herodian kingdom reached its maximum expansion, and if Augustus entertained any subsequent intentions of further enlarging its frontiers, they were never implemented. Officially Herod was 'King, friend and ally of the Roman people,' (socius et amicus populi Romani).[1] Initially his royal status had been officially sealed by a resolution of the Roman Senate, perhaps renewed subsequently under Augustus' principate.[2] Herod, in order to emphasize his bond with Rome, also took the title of 'friend of the Romans' (φιλορώμαιος), as other kings had done. This we learn from an Athenian inscription.[3] But it is doubtful whether he really used the title 'friend of Caesar'.[4] It is clear that the significance of Herod's title of 'ally of the Roman people' was not that he was in some degree (however small) free to conduct his own policy and held an independent status vis-à-vis the Roman state. In point of fact he was denied, as were all allied kings, any serious initiative in the sphere of foreign policy, and possessed no licence to wage war on his own accord. His hands were tied to a great extent even in internal policy by the necessity of considering the emperor's intentions and the needs of the Roman state. Nor did it escape his subjects that their supreme sovereign was the Roman princeps, to whom they also owed an oath of allegiance.[5] Nor did Herod ever conceal the fact of his dependence

---

[1] Jos. *Ant.* xvii, 246. cf. also Dio Cassius LIII, 25,1 on Herod's contemporary, Polemo King of Pontus, who was also counted among the friends and allies of the Romans, and also op.cit. LI, 24,7 on Roles the King of the Getae. On the status of the client kings cf. O. Bohn, *Qua condicione iuris reges socii populi Romani fuerint* (1877); P. C. Sands, *The Client Princes of the Roman Empire under the Republic* (1908). On the status of Herod as a client king see Schürer I, pp. 316-7; Sands, op.cit., pp. 226-8; W. Otto, *Herodes* (1913), pp. 57-9; E. Bammel, *ZDPV* (1968), pp. 73-9; A. Schalit, *König Herodes* (1969), pp. 146-167.
[2] Jos. *Ant.* xv, 196.
[3] *OGIS* no. 414; *IG* II, 2nd ed., no. 3440.
[4] Most scholars also connect with Herod the inscription *IG* III, no. 551; *OGIS* no. 427; *IG* II, 2nd ed., no. 3441, where Herod is called φιλοκαῖσαρ. So e.g. Otto, op.cit., pp. 77-8; I. Kirchner in his commentary on *IG* II, 2nd ed., no. 3441; A. Momigliano, *CAH* x, p. 329; B. D. Meritt, *Hesperia* (1952), p. 370 who also restored a new inscription (*SEG* xii no. 150) according to this interpretation. Some scholars still think, however, that φιλοκαῖσαρ refers to Herod, King of Chalcis, the brother of Agrippa I. See Schürer I (3rd Ger. ed.), p. 391, no. 72; Dittenberger in his commentary on *OGIS* no. 427 (and also on *IG* III no. 551); P. Graindor, *Athènes sous Auguste* (1927), p. 82-3. A new discovery of a stone weight seems to prove that Herod the First was called φιλοκαῖσαρ. Cf. Y. Meshorer, IEJ (1970), pp. 97-100.
[5] Jos. *Ant.* xvii, 42. cf. also F. Cumont, *REG* (1901), pp. 26-45; *OGIS*, no. 532. See in general P. Herrmann, *Der römische Kaisereid* (1968).

on the Emperor.[1] Herod was in fact one of the links (with all that this implied) in the political and administrative system of the Roman Empire in the period of the Principate.

Beside his obvious duty of preserving order and security on the frontiers of his kingdom—a duty which constituted the chief justification of his status as King of Judaea—Herod was obliged, like all allied sovereigns, to send military aid to the Roman Empire in its various wars. During Herod's reign, indeed, Rome had no major wars to wage in the East, after 34 B.C.E., least of all after Augustus had reached a general accord with Parthia in 20 B.C.E. and had stabilized the eastern frontier for some time to come.[2] Yet Herod still enjoyed opportunities of proving his loyalty to Rome by the dispatch of forces in time of need. An opportunity of this sort occurred in the years 25-24 B.C.E., when the governor of Egypt, Aelius Gallus, set out on his well-known abortive expedition to southern Arabia. Among the ten thousand troops who took part, there were, beside the Roman force a thousand Nabataeans and five hundred troops from the kingdom of Judaea, sent by Herod.[3]

Another opportunity of affording military assistance to Rome occurred in connection with the military operations of M. Agrippa, Augustus' chief lieutenant, in the Black Sea area in 14 B.C.E.[4] Herod sailed from Judaea to the western coast of Asia Minor and after a voyage by way of Rhodes, Cos and Lesbos, met Agrippa at Sinope on the south of the Black sea and was with him when the Roman statesman settled the affairs of the kingdom of Bosporus and of various regions of Asia Minor.[5] Herod's voyage, which arose from the political requirements of Rome and involved virtually no risk, emphasized his status as royal ally of Rome, enhancing his prestige outside Judaea.

In addition to his military duties, Herod had to pay taxes to Rome,

[1] Suetonius, *The Life of Augustus*, 60 on the personal services rendered by the client kings to the princeps.
[2] Dio Cassius LIV, 8,1-3; *Monumentum Ancyranum*, 29. For the relations between Augustus and the Parthians cf. also Ziegler, op.cit., pp. 45-57.
[3] Strabo, *Geography*, XVI, 4,23, p. 780; Jos. *Ant.* XV, 317. For the expedition of Aelius Gallus see Dio Cassius LIII, 29,3-7; Pliny, *Natural History* VI, 160-1. See also V. Gardthausen, *Augustus und seine Zeit* I,2 (1896), pp. 788-796; A. Kammerer, *Pétra et la Nabatène* (1929), pp. 196-206; T. Rice Holmes, *The Architect of the Roman Empire* II (1931), pp. 19-20; W. Aly, *Strabon von Amaseia* (1957), pp. 165-178. The expedition is now dated 26-25 B.C.E. by Shelagh Jameson, *JRS* (1968), pp. 76-8.
[4] Dio Cassius LIV, 24, 4-7.
[5] Jos. *Ant.* XVI, 16-26.

and here too he was no exception among the allied kings. Antony had made the payment of taxes to Rome a condition of the confirmation of the status of allied kings in the East, and there is no reason to assume that Augustus made any radical change in the arrangements of his predecessors.[1] These taxes were not collected directly from the people by the Roman treasury, but were forwarded by the king himself from his total annual revenues. In this way the people of Judaea were spared the direct activity of Roman representatives. But taxes were not all that Herod had to pay to his Roman overlords. When Antony was at the height of his power, Herod had to pay out most of his income to Antony and his associates.[2] The situation did not change much under Octavian. During his first stay in Syria he received a considerable sum of money from Herod, who also contributed three hundred talents on another occasion, when Augustus was distributing gifts to the Roman people.[3]

Herod's dependence on the Roman Empire was also clearly demonstrated in his general relations with the governor of Syria, and it appears that in various important matters the King of Judaea was bound to defer to the opinion of the governor. Thus, for instance, Herod had to obtain the approval of the governor Saturninus for the steps he wished to take against the Nabataeans.[4] Saturninus in turn took action to protect Herod's interests when Nabataean agents were involved in a conspiracy against him.[5] Saturninus' successor Varus came to Judaea and acted as Herod's advisor during the domestic crisis in the palace after the discovery of the plots of Antipater.[6] It would appear, on the other hand, that Herod, when at the height of his power, was accorded a say in the administration of Syria.[7]

At home, Herod enjoyed all the external trappings of royalty, as the sole sovereign in his realm reigning over Jews and gentiles alike. Augustus further granted him the right to demand the extradition of his subjects who had fled the country, if they were to be accused of crimes. He also ruled that Herod could propose his own successor,

---

[1] Momigliano, *Ricerche*, p. 350.
[2] Jos. *War* I, 358; *Ant.* xv, 5.
[3] *Ant.* xvi, 128.
[4] *Ant.* xvi, 277.
[5] *Ant.* xvii, 57; *War* I, 577.
[6] *Ant.* xvii, 89-132; *War* I, 617-640.
[7] *Ant.* xv, 360; *War* I, 399.

or successors, subject to ratification by the Princeps,[1] just as in general nothing that gravely affected the royal house (such as the execution of princes of the blood) could be done without the sign and seal of the Emperor.[2]

Herod's true position as King of Judaea and as a person of influence in Syria and in the Roman Empire, was in reality determined rather by his actual relations with Augustus and the other great men of the Roman state, than by juridical formulations of his status, senatorial resolutions or public statements. It was a long-standing tradition of the Antipatrids to form close bonds with Roman rulers and with those who could decisively influence Roman policy. After the battle of Actium and the death of Antony, Octavian became an object of Herod's admiration and the winning of the new ruler's favour was the chief real aim of his policy. Undoubtedly these efforts, which were matched by Augustus' conviction that Herod was the right man in the right place, bore fruit. During the greater part of his reign Herod remained a favourite of the Princeps, and only in his last years was his standing somewhat diminished as a result of a series of domestic crises and a new war with the Nabataeans. Herod's attachment to the Princeps was expressed in various ways. For instance, the new cities which he built in his country were called after the Emperor. This was in accordance with a general and widespread trend in the Roman Empire, which led sovereigns to compete with one another in building towns in honour of the Emperor. At this time too they were considering the idea of completing the Temple of Zeus

[1] *Ant.* xv, 343; xvi, 92, 129; *War* i, 454, 458. Those passages imply that Herod's rights in choosing a successor were unlimited. On the other hand, other passages show that Herod's choice had to be confirmed by the princeps, and that the king sent his testament to Rome for that confirmation. See Jos. *Ant.* xvii, 53; *War* i, 573. After Herod's death Augustus only partly fulfilled the wishes of the dead king as expressed in his last testament. However, I do not think that we have to adopt the view of Otto, op.cit., p. 66 according to which Herod's status deteriorated in the last years of his reign. It is better to suppose that from the very beginning his right to appoint his successor, or successors, was limited by the need of confirmation by the princeps.

[2] Aristobulus III, Hyrcanus II and Mariamme were executed without permission being sought from the Roman rulers. The case was different with the execution of Herod's sons: Alexander, Aristobulus and Antipater. Yet we have not to accept the view of E. Taübler, *Klio* (1921), pp. 98-101 that this should be accounted for by the fact that the three princes were Roman citizens. See against Taübler, Dessau, *Kaiserzeit*, ii, 2, 771, n. 2; H. Volkmann, *Zur Recht-sprechung im Principat des Augustus* (1935), pp. 159-161. Herod was actuated in these dealings not by legal limitations, but by political considerations which made it necessary to him to get the approval of the princeps.

Olympius in Athens and of dedicating it to the Genius of Augustus.[1] The two most important cities built by Herod, Sebaste and Caesarea, were called after the Emperor. One of the towers at Caesarea was named after Drusus, the Princeps' stepson. Herod's admiration for Augustus was notably expressed in the imperial cult and the erection of temples in his honour. His great temple at Caesarea itself stood out for all to see, with its twin statues of Rome and the Emperor.[2] Herod further dedicated to Augustus the white marble temple at Paneion near the source of the Jordan,[3] while at Caesarea he established games in his honour. These were first held on the occasion of the festal dedication of the new city of Caesarea, and included contests in music and athletics. There were large numbers of gladiators and wild animals, and also horse-racing. The Emperor himself sent all the necessary equipment for sports of this sort, and the Empress Livia also furnished assistance.[4] Herod's marks of enthusiasm for the Emperor extended beyond the frontiers of his own kingdom, embracing also the provinces of Syria, in whose towns he set up temples to Caesar.[5] In sum, Herod is to be regarded as one of the most enthusiastic propagators of the imperial cult in his time, notwithstanding his care not to practise it in areas with a clear Jewish majority.

Herod also endeavoured to maintain excellent relations with other prominent men of influence. Valerius Messalla had been an old friend and supporter of the Antipatrids ever since Antony's time; under Augustus' rule M. Vipsanius Agrippa, the greatest of the Roman generals of his time and the right-hand man of the Princeps, became Herod's personal friend. Herod may have known Agrippa in previous years, perhaps even at the time of his coronation at Rome in 40 B.C.E., but these relations developed more especially in the years of his first prolonged stay in the East. Between 23 and 21 B.C.E. Agrippa took up residence in the city of Mytilene in Lesbos, and Herod visited him there, apparently in the winter of 23/22.[6] It was at this time that

[1] Suetonius, *The Life of Augustus*, 60.
[2] Jos. *Ant.* xv, 339.
[3] *War* i, 404.
[4] *Ant.* xvi, 136-9.
[5] *War* i, 407. On the diffusion of the cult of Augustus cf. H. Heinen, *Klio* xi, 139-175; G. Herzog-Hauser, *PW*, Supplement iv (1924), cols. 820-833; L. Cerfaux and J. Tondriau, *Le culte des souverains* (1957), pp. 313-339. See also R. K. Sherk, *Roman Documents from the Greek East* (1969), no. 65.
[6] *Ant.* xv, 350. On Agrippa's sojourn at Lesbos cf. Dio Cassius liii, 32,1. On the date cf. Dobiáš, *Dějiny římské provincie syrské* (1924), p. 303; M. Reinhold, *Marcus Agrippa* (1933), p. 84, n. 47.

Agrippa rejected the complaints of the inhabitants of Hellenistic Gadara, Herod's subjects, against their sovereign.

These bonds were strengthened during Agrippa's long stay in the East (16-13 B.C.E.). Agrippa visited Judaea in 15 B.C.E.,[1] receiving an enthusiastic welcome from the King and from the Jewish masses. He visited the new cities built by the King and the three royal strongholds (Alexandrium, Hyrcania and Herodium). His visit to Jerusalem made a particularly strong impression, as also did the numerous sacrifices which he had offered in the Temple as a gesture of goodwill by the Roman power to the national religion of the Jews.

Agrippa's comportment and the respect he accorded to the Temple stood out in contrast with the very different behaviour of his son Gaius who, fourteen years later, in 1 B.C.E. (i.e. after the death of Herod), refrained from visiting the Temple of Jerusalem and so earned the praises of his grandfather Augustus.[2]

As had been noted, Herod joined Agrippa's party on his visit to Asia Minor in 14 B.C.E. when they went through Paphlagonia, Greater Phrygia and Ephesus to Samos. His presence in Agrippa's entourage offered him a suitable opportunity to appear as a public benefactor and mediator between the people and the great Roman, Augustus' son-in-law. Thus, for example, he obtained financial concessions for the people of Chios who owed taxes to the procurators of Caesar. He made a great impression by successfully appeasing Agrippa's wrath against Ilium, on whose inhabitants he had imposed a heavy fine for not helping his wife Julia (Augustus' daughter) when she was in danger of drowning in the River Scamander. Thanks to Herod's intercession Agrippa remitted the fine.[3] The friendship between the two men and Herod's influence on Agrippa had important results for the status of the Jews and the ratification of their privileges in the cities of Ionia, where relations were strained between them and their neighbours, the citizens of the Greek cities. Agrippa decided in favour of the Jews, who were represented by Nicholas of Damascus, a close friend of Herod's. The close relations between Agrippa and Herod are further reflected in the bestowing of the name Agrippias on the city of Anthedon on the coast of Palestine. And the name

---

[1] Jos. *Ant.* XVI, 12-15; Philo, *Legatio* 294-7. cf. also Gardthausen, op.cit., pp. 841-2; Reinhold, op.cit. 112-113; R. Hanslik, *PW*, 2nd series IX, cols. 1262-3.
[2] Suetonius, *The Life of Augustus*, 93.
[3] Jos. *Ant.* XVI, 22-6; Nicholas of Damascus, in Jacoby *FGH* II A, 90 F 134. For the intervention of Herod on behalf of the people of Chios cf. also F. Millar, *JRS* (1963), p. 32.

Agrippa found its way into Herod's family, where it became a normal and accepted surname.[1] Agrippa was merely the most prominent of the leaders of Roman political and social life with whom Herod maintained close relationships. Another was Asinius Pollio, famous as statesman, commander and historian, and consul in 40 B.C.E. when Herod was crowned at Rome. This, and their common friendship with Antony, served as the occasion for a rapprochement between the two. Herod's sons Alexander and Aristobulus resided at Pollio's house during their studies in the imperial capital.[2] Herod's friends included C. Petronius, prefect of Egypt between 24 and 21 B.C.E.,[3] and Titius, who governed Syria in the period between the governorships of Agrippa and Saturninus.[4] Herod was in constant touch with his friends at Rome, and they kept him informed of everything that occurred at the imperial court and in the capital. He also asked them their views on his own domestic policy and was sensitive to their reactions. Among those whose favour Herod attempted to win were also members of the imperial household, both slaves and freedmen. In this he was followed by his own household: his son Antipater had friends at Rome and Herod's sister Salome was regarded as the friend of Livia, wife of Augustus. A friendship also developed between Varus, governor of Syria, and Herod's family.[5]

Following the existing trend among the ruling classes of Rome in the period of the Julio-Claudian principate, and inspired by his own strong desire for publicity and repute, Herod showered benefactions on many Greek cities, aided them financially, erected for them splendid edifices and supported their institutions. Among the cities which enjoyed the generosity of the King of Judaea were such ancient and renowned towns as Athens and Sparta. At Rhodes Herod rebuilt the Temple of the Pythian Apollo, which had been burnt down, and

---

[1] Cf. also R. Daniel, *M. Vipsanius Agrippa* (1933), pp. 31-77.
[2] Jos. *Ant.* xv, 343. Most scholars identify this Pollio with the famous Asinius Pollio, cf. Schürer I, p. 321; Otto, op.cit., p. 71; A. Momigliano, *CAH* x, p. 327; L. H. Feldman, *TAPA* (1953), 79. On the other hand, Willrich, op.cit., pp. 184-5 suggests that the Pollio at whose house Herod's sons stayed was a Jew. A doubt concerning the above-mentioned identification with Asinius Pollio has been expressed also by A. Stein, *PIR* I, (1933), p. 253, no. 1241. R. Syme, *JRS* (1961), p. 30, Addendum, thinks it possible that the Pollio referred to by Josephus is the same as the notorious Vedius Pollio. Still, the arguments for his identification with Asinius Pollio seem stronger.
[3] Jos. *Ant.* xv, 307. See on him A. Stein, *Die Präfekten von Ägypten in der römischen Kaiserzeit* (1950), pp. 17-18.
[4] *Ant.* xvi, 270.
[5] *Ant.* xvii, 303.

made grants of money to the inhabitants for ship-building. He restored the basilica of Chios, which had been devastated in the Mithridatic war, and established a fund at Cos to finance the post of gymnasiarch. His lavish gifts were also bestowed on Pergamum, Samos, and the towns of Lycia, Pamphylia and Cilicia. He aided Nicopolis, the city built by the Emperor in western Greece near the place of his victory of Actium, to erect its public buildings. But Herod gained the greatest publicity from his support of the Olympic games. He presided over one of the Olympiads, either on his way to Rome or on his way back to his country, and actually received the title of permanent Agonothete of the games. He also did much for the Phoenician and Syrian coastal cities near his kingdom. He built baths, fountains and porticoes at Ascalon, which formed a free enclave within his realm, a gymnasium at Ptolemais, temples and markets at Tyre and Berytus; he presented a gymnasium and theatre to Damascus, and built a theatre at Sidon. He built an aqueduct at coastal Laodicea, and walls for Byblos. At Antioch itself he paved in marble the street that ran the length of the city, setting up porticoes on each side of it.[1] He also assisted the inhabitants of Syria in times of famine.[2]

Herod was, as we have said, only one of the royal allies of the Roman people, and the organization of the empire brought him into contact with others. Augustus himself viewed favourably the creation of close bonds between the vassal kings and encouraged marriage-ties among them.[3] While Herod's relations with the Nabataean kings were generally strained, he formed ties of kinship with King Archelaus of Cappadocia, and his son Alexander married Archelaus' daughter Glaphyra. On his way back from Rome in the year 12 B.C.E. Herod and his two sons Alexander and Aristobulus also paid a visit to Elaeousa on the Cilician coast, and were graciously received by Archelaus.[4] Herod further used his great influence with Titius, the legate of

---

[1] *War* I, 422-8; *Ant.* XVI, 18-9; 146-9. On the participation of members of the imperial family in the Olympic games see *SIG* nos. 782, 792. On Herod and Berytus see also *Académie des Inscriptions et Belles Lettres, Comptes rendus* (1927), pp. 243-4; on Herod and Ascalon see J. Garstang, *PEQ* (1922), pp. 114-117; on Herod and Antioch see W. Weber, *Festgabe für Adolf Deissmann* (1927), pp. 26-8; G. Downey, *A History of Antioch in Syria* (1961), pp. 173-4; on Herod and the Greek cities cf. also L. Robert *Etudes epigraphiques et philologiques* (1938), pp. 136-8.
[2] Jos. *Ant.* XV, 311.
[3] Suetonius, *Life of Augustus*, 48.
[4] Jos. *Ant.* XVI, 131.

Syria, to improve relations, which were at a low ebb, between Titius and the king of Cappadocia.[1] As a relative of Herod by marriage, Archelaus was concerned with the struggle at the royal court of Jerusalem in which his son-in-law Alexander and his daughter Glaphyra were involved. He followed all that went on in the Jewish capital with lively attention and also visited Judaea to acquaint himself more closely with the situation and to settle disagreements. His envoy Melas was also active at Herod's court.

Another 'client ruler' with whom Herod maintained relations was Gaius Julius Eurycles, a man of some standing at the time in the empire, who had commanded the Spartan forces in the campaign leading up to Actium and was now the country's *de facto* ruler. Much as Herod and his contemporaries, Eurycles was a feverish builder.[2] Herod seems to have got to know him in the Peloponnesus on one of his journeys to Rome, and Sparta was among the towns which had enjoyed Herod's generosity. Eurycles paid a return visit to Herod in Jerusalem, and there played an important part in the development of the quarrels at the royal court.[3]

On the other hand the Roman government undoubtedly looked askance at any association between an allied king in the East and the Parthian enemy, and no more dangerous suspicion could be cast upon Herod, in Augustus' view, than that of relations with the Parthian kingdom.[4] One of the gravest charges made against his son Alexander was that he wished to flee to the Emperor in order to inform him of Herod's intention to conspire with the Parthian king against Rome.[5] It is also interesting to note that Pheroras, Herod's brother, planned to escape to the Parthians.[6] One affair cast a cloud over the relations between Herod and Augustus in the last years of Herod's reign. Matters between Herod and the Nabataeans had reached a crisis, the root-cause being the situation in Trachonitis. The inhabitants of Trachonitis had not become reconciled to Herod's rule, which involved drastic changes in their whole way of life. In 12 B.C.E., Herod's death was announced while he was in Italy; the rumour brought about open revolt in Trachonitis. which was forcibly put down by

---

[1] *Ant.* XVI, 270.
[2] Pausanias, *The Description of Greece* II, 3,5; III, 14,6.
[3] Cf. G. W. Bowersock, *JRS* (1961), pp. 112-118. On his visit to Jerusalem see also E. Kjellberg, *Klio* XVII, pp. 53-7.
[4] Jos. *Ant.* XVI, 253. See also Kjellberg, op.cit., 54, n. 3.
[5] For similar accusations against Herod Antipas see below p. 287.
[6] Jos. *War* I, 486.

the commanders of Herod's army.[1] The suppression of the rising did not end the episode, since the insurgents continued to enjoy support from the Nabataeans. Syllaeus, the central figure in the Nabataean kingdom in this period and the effective determinant of its policy, was now the greatest enemy with whom Herod had to deal. They had fallen out over Syllaeus' proposed marriage to Herod's sister, which Herod had made conditional on the Arab's embracing Judaism. Syllaeus had refused, on the grounds that the act would endanger his entire standing among his own people. Relations between Herod and Syllaeus therefore went from bad to worse; Syllaeus offered refuge to the leaders of the rebels from Trachonitis, who set up their headquarters in a fortified place in Nabataean territory and thence raided Herod's kingdom, causing casualties and serious damage to property among the frontier population. Herod, seeing that he could not put an end to the trouble so long as the raiders and their chiefs could find shelter across the border in Nabataea, put the problem to the chiefs of the Roman administration of Syria, demanding the extradition of the raiders, and claiming repayment of a loan of sixty talents, which he had made to the Nabataean King Obodas, with Syllaeus acting as intermediary. The negotations, under the auspices of the Romans, concluded with an agreement between Herod and Syllaeus, whereby they were to repatriate the refugees from their respective countries, the Arabs also promising to repay the loan to Herod within thirty days. Syllaeus seems not to have carried out the agreement, and Herod determined to use force to compel fulfilment. He crossed the frontier at the head of an army, and captured the fort of Rhaepta, which was the raiders' base. In the operations which developed following Herod's invasion, many Arabs were killed, including their commander Naqib, a kinsman of Syllaeus. It would seem on the whole that Herod's counter-offensive had assumed wider proportions than the local Roman authorities had envisaged; Herod moreover took additional steps to ensure order in Trachonitis by settling three thousand Idumaeans there. When the news of Herod's action reached Syllaeus, who was then at Rome, he complained to the Emperor. Augustus considered that, by striking into Nabataean territory, Herod had unjustifiably taken the law into his own hands; he further regarded the action as constituting contempt of the supreme powers of the Roman princeps and an infringement of the firmly established principle that allied kings were not permitted to wage war on their own

[1] *Ant.* XVI, 130, 271-3.

initiative, without permission from the supreme ruler at Rome. Augustus addressed a stern letter to the King of Judaea, the burden of which was that 'if till now he had treated him as a friend, he would in the future treat him as a subject'. Nothing, it may be thought, proves more trenchantly than Augustus' angry reaction, the extent to which the status of a friendly allied 'king' was actually a fiction, depending entirely on the will of the Roman ruler. Syllaeus was quick to inform his people of the Emperor's negative attitude to Herod's recent acts; the Nabataeans and the population of Trachonitis were greatly encouraged and could now act without taking account of Herod's possible reactions. The people of Trachonitis again rose in rebellion and began to harry and rob the Idumaean settlement there.[1]

Herod sent Nicholas of Damascus to Rome to explain to the Emperor the entire episode and its motivations, and to effect a reconciliation between Augustus and himself. Nicholas was greatly assisted by a dispute which had broken out among the Nabataeans: King Obodas had died and been succeeded by Aretas IV, who had taken over power without asking the consent of Augustus, as was desirable in cases of this sort. Syllaeus set out to undermine Aretas' power, while Nicholas exploited the hostility of Aretas' representatives at Rome to blacken Syllaeus at the imperial court. He thus prepared the ground for a reconciliation between the Princeps and Herod. In this he was successful. Augustus was appeased. Aretas was confirmed as king of the Nabataeans, while Syllaeus' standing deteriorated and he lost favour with the Emperor. Not long after he was charged by Aretas' representatives with various crimes, among them the assassination of Arab notables. To these charges was added an indictment by Herod's son Antipater, who accused the Nabataean leader of fomenting a conspiracy at Herod's court to murder the King. Syllaeus was found guilty and executed in 4 B.C.E., approximately at the time of Herod's death.[2] Thus ended the grimmest episode in Herod's relations with Augustus, which brought Herod into disrepute in Rome and revealed

---

[1] *Ant.* xvi, 273-292; Nicholas, cf. in Jacoby, *FGH* ii A, 90 F 136 (1).
[2] *Ant.* xvi, 293-9, 335-355; xvii, 54-7; *War* i, 574-7; Nicholas, loc.cit. Strabo, *Geography* xvi, 4,24, p. 782. We have to distinguish between two decisions of Augustus concerning Syllaeus. The first is connected with Nicholas' visit to Rome and the second with Antipater's stay there. The last stage involved the execution of Syllaeus. See also Otto, op.cit., p. 130, note; Stein, *PW*, 2nd series iv, col. 1043; C. Clermont-Ganneau, *Recueil d'archéologie orientale* vii (1906), pp. 305-329; Volkmann, op.cit., pp. 167-9.

to all how frail was the standing of an allied sovereign in the world of the Roman principate. The reconciliation with Augustus officially restored Herod to his former position and gave him reason to hope that the Emperor would ratify his internal arrangements regarding his sons and the bequeathing of power to those of them whom he deemed fit.

The internal administration of the Herodian kingdom

Within his kingdom Herod was an unrestricted despot[1] and his subjects were de facto without rights. The only limitation to his absolute power lay in the apprehension that their patience might be exhausted and that they might rebel against his rule and so destroy one of the chief justifications for his royal power in Roman eyes—namely, his ability to keep order in Judaea. Herod generally succeeded in maintaining peace and security on the frontiers of his kingdom; and as long as he lived, popular bitterness caused no open rebellion on a serious scale, although cases of conspiracy against the royal government, in which individuals or limited groups were implicated, were not lacking. Herod was able to maintain his regime without serious incidents for decades until his death; this he did by iron repression and by timely concessions, by depending on friendly ethnic and social elements, and by elevating new social elements entirely dependent on him for their status and wealth.

The conquest of Jerusalem in 37 B.C.E. put an end to the old Jewish regime in the form it had assumed under the rule of the Hasmonaean house. There was no room in the new Herodian Sanhedrin—which differed in no way from the customary privy councils of Hellenistic kings—for the traditional Jewish elements; its members were the 'king's friends' and entourage. Important affairs of state were brought before the Sanhedrin, and it also tried capital cases whose importance lay in their political consequences; its president was the King and his opinion was decisive. No continuity existed between this Sanhedrin and the previous Jewish body, either in tradition or character, and certainly not in the composition of its membership. Some of the members of the Herodian Sanhedrin were 'Hellenes' and its discussions were doubtless conducted in Greek.

Our literary sources mention several instances in which the royal council acted in situations requiring a decision; thus Herod announced his resolve to appoint Aristobulus III high priest to 'the assembly

[1] On Herod's government see Otto, op.cit., pp. 59-64.

of his friends'[1] and brought before the Sanhedrin the discussion of Hyrcanus' treason and his conspiracy with the king of the Nabataeans.[2] The same Sanhedrin received the announcement of his plan for the marriage of his grandsons,[3] and it was before a Sanhedrin of his friends that the King proclaimed his charges against the wife of his brother Pheroras.[4]

Herod used popular assemblies as a means of communication with the people and as an effective instrument of propaganda for his policy. Assemblies of this sort were held from time to time both in Jerusalem and in other cities of the realm, such as Jericho. The practice of convening such assemblies to explain policy or to direct attention to achievements, had strong roots in the national tradition of previous generations. Yet in Herod's reign, at any rate, not only had such assemblies no right of real decision, but they were meant to play an entirely passive role. Thus, for example, when Herod returned from his journey in Asia Minor in 14 B.C.E., he called a popular assembly in Jerusalem, participated in also by people from outside the city, and described to it all he had achieved on his journey, giving special emphasis to his success in defending Jewish rights in Asia. On this occasion he further announced a twenty-five per cent reduction of taxes.[5] After his return from his trip to Aquileia in Italy (12 B.C.E.), he reported on his experiences to a popular assembly in the Temple and exhibited his heirs to the people.[6] He also announced to a similar assembly his intention of rebuilding the Temple.[7] Somewhat different in character was the gathering which Herod convened in the amphitheatre of Jericho after the plot to tear down the eagle from the gate of the Temple.[8] This was not an indiscriminate mass rally, and only notable holders of responsible posts among the Jews were invited. We may note, too, Herod's use of the popular rally to pronounce sentence of death upon his opponents. The crowd at Jericho was instigated to put to death by stoning the confederates of Herod's sons Alexander and Aristobulus,[9] and the mob behaved similarly at Caesarea towards the officers of his army accused of conspiring on behalf of the two brothers.[10]

Among the Jewish institutions that suffered as a result of the rise of

---

[1] Jos. *Ant.* xv, 31.
[2] *Ant.* xv, 173. See Momigliano, *Ricerche*, 372.
[3] *War* I, 559. [4] *Ant.* XVII, 46-8; *War* I, 571.
[5] *Ant.* XVI, 62-5. [6] *Ant.* XVI, 132-5. [7] *Ant.* xv, 381.
[8] *Ant.* XVII, 161. [9] *Ant.* XVI, 320. [10] *Ant.* XVI, 393.

Herod, besides the Sanhedrin, was the high priesthood. Throughout the Second Temple period the high priesthood had been the most honoured post in Judaea and the high priest who, in the Hasmonaean epoch, had been ethnarch or king of Judaea, was always conceived as the acknowledged leader of the Jewish nation.[1] As Herod was not of Aaronic descent and could not himself assume the high priesthood without causing an unprecedented storm in the nation, he faced a grave problem. To leave the dignity in the hands of the Hasmonaean family or to transfer it permanently to one of the high priestly houses, implied a potential danger to the very existence of Herod's rule, since people would continue to see in the high priestly house the ruling dynasty of Judaea. Herod solved the problem by expelling the Hasmonaeans from the high priesthood and by giving the function to men of different families. He also abolished the practice whereby the high priest continued in office till his death. It is to be remarked, indeed, that he did not introduce the method of frequent changes which became current under the government of the procurators after his death, and for most of his reign his father-in-law Simeon, son of Boethus, was the incumbent. But on the whole he abolished the principle that the high priest should serve for life and transmit his function to his eldest son after him; from Herod's time the relative decline of the high priesthood is perceptible.

In respect of the administrative division of the kingdom, Herod continued along the general lines which had been worked out in the country in the Hellenistic and Hasmonaean periods. The smallest administrative units were the villages; over them were the toparchies, which were again united into larger units known as meridarchies.[2] These seem to have been identical with the historical regions of Idumaea, Judaea, Samaria, Galilee and Peraea. The men placed at the head of these 'meridarchies' were especially loyal to Herod and usually also related to him by blood or marriage. In the first period of his reign his brother-in-law Costobar was governor of Idumaea; at the end of his reign his cousin Achiab seems to have been governor-general of Judaea.[3] The most prominent among these governors was Herod's younger brother Pheroras, who performed the task of governor of

[1] The connection between the priesthood and secular rule in Judaea is emphasized also by non-Jewish sources cf. Pompeius Trogus, in Iustinus XXXVI, 2. 16; Tacitus, *Historiae* v, 8.
[2] Jos. *Ant.* XV, 216. cf. H. Bengtson, *Die Strategie in der hellenistischen Zeit* II, (1944), p. 267.
[3] For a different view see Momigliano, *Ricerche*, p. 371.

Peraea, and combined with this social powers and the title of tetrarch, his son being also designated as successor to his tetrarchy.[1] The entire area of Herod's kingdom was included in the normal administrative division. Neither Jerusalem nor the Greek cities were exceptions to this rule. Gaza was attached to Idumaea,[2] Greek Caesarea and Samaria formed one unit. Sepphoris was the capital of Galilee. Generally the large towns acted as administrative capitals and possessed garrisons. It may be added that they were not exempt from paying taxes to the King. Only one city, Gadara in Transjordan, the ancient centre of Hellenistic culture, attempted vainly to rebel against the royal absolutism. It did so during Agrippa's first stay in the East (22-21 B.C.E.); he arrested the citizens and sent them to Herod. They renewed their complaints under the inspiration of Zenodorus, while Augustus was visiting the East in 20 B.C.E., and asked that their city should be annexed to Syria. But they soon found out that they had no prospect whatsoever of a response from Augustus.[3] Gadara was annexed directly to Syria only after Herod's death, as was also Gaza. It would seem that in general the old Hellenistic cities included in the kingdom's frontiers did not accept their status happily. On the other hand, Herod gained support among the residents of the new towns which he had founded and they became the mainstay of his rule.

Herod disposed of his own military force. No Roman army was stationed in his kingdom after the first years of his reign, and Herod's force was amply sufficient to maintain order. His army was very varied in composition, being partly based on mercenaries from outside the country, amongst whom Galatians and Thracians were prominent. But gradually the men of the new cities Sebaste and Caesarea were utilized for this purpose, and the cities undertook to furnish troops to Herod and subsequently to his Roman successors. At the end of Herod's reign these troops numbered three thousand. This development reinforced the importance of the gentile population in relation to the Jewish, which was of great significance for the subsequent evolution of relations between the Jews and the Roman government. Along with the people of the new Hellenistic towns Herod also recruited soldiers from among the non-Jewish settlers originally settled in military colonies. These, as was the practice in the Hellenistic

[1] Jos. *Ant.* xv, 362; xvi, 228.
[2] *Ant.* xv, 254.
[3] *Ant.* xv, 351; 356-9.

MAP VII. DIVISION OF HEROD'S KINGDOM

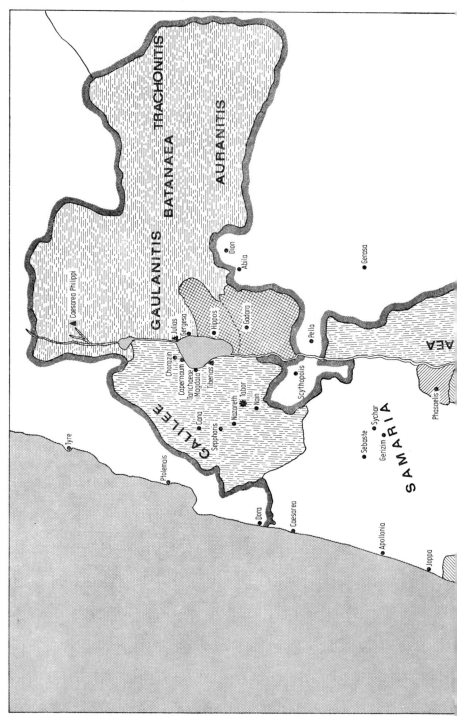

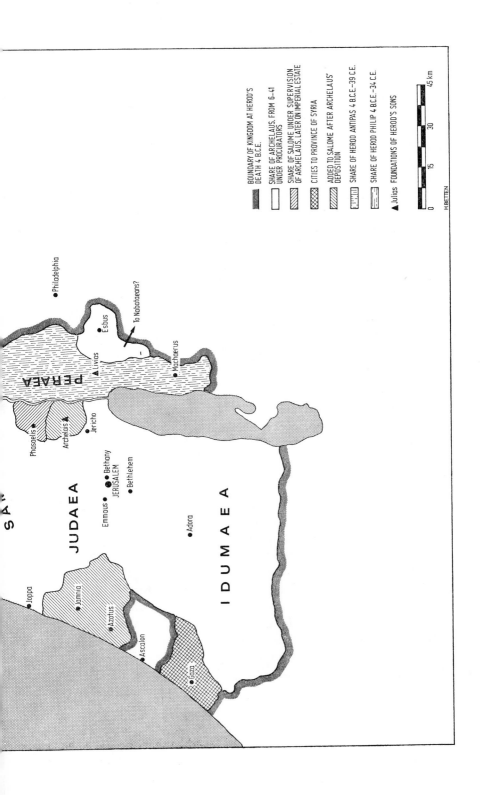

BOUNDARY OF KINGDOM AT HEROD'S DEATH 4 B.C.E.

SHARE OF ARCHELAUS. FROM 6-41 UNDER PROCURATORS

SHARE OF SALOME UNDER SUPERVISION OF ARCHELAUS. LATER ON IMPERIAL ESTATE

CITIES TO PROVINCE OF SYRIA

ADDED TO SALOME AFTER ARCHELAUS' DEPOSITION

SHARE OF HEROD ANTIPAS 4 B.C.E.–39 C.E.

SHARE OF HEROD PHILIP 4 B.C.E.–34 C.E.

▲ Julias FOUNDATIONS OF HEROD'S SONS

0   15   30   45 km

H.BETTEN

Philadelphia

To Nabataeans?

Esbus

Livias ▲

Machaerus

PERAEA

Phasaelis ●

Archelais ▲

Jericho ●

SAM

JUDAEA

Emmaus ●   ● Bethany
● JERUSALEM
● Bethlehem

Joppa ●

Jamnia ●

Azotus ●

Ascalon ●

Gaza ●

Adora ●

I D U M A E A

world, served as a permanent military reserve for the defence of the kingdom. Gaba, the city of cavalry-men in the Plain of Esdraelon,[1] and Heshbon in Transjordan,[2] are known to have been military colonies. Jews, indeed, also served in Herod's army. But as the King's attitude to most classes of the Jewish people was one of suspicion, he could draw on them only selectively for his army, confining his recruitment to those elements which he considered more loyal than the nation in general. Such were, in his view, the Idumaeans, to whom he was related by blood. He used them also for purposes of military settlement, three thousand being settled in Trachonitis to protect the region from raids. After Herod's death, indeed, proof was forthcoming that even the loyalty of Idumaean troops was not overstaunch, for they too felt greater solidarity with the Jewish people as a whole than with the house of Herod. Another Jewish element upon which Herod relied was the Jewish immigrants from Babylonia; these were settled by Herod in northern Transjordan and became the mainstay of security in Batanaea and Gaulanitis. Herod seems also sometimes to have recruited other Jews, as in 31 B.C.E., when he was engaged in the difficult war with the Nabataeans, and there was no reason to fear that they would go over to the enemy. Among the commanders we encounter men with Roman names, such as Rufus and Gratus, and these probably furnished the army with their professional knowledge and skill. Herod was extremely sensitive to events and moods in his army, as may be seen from his reaction to the sympathy evinced by officers and men for Alexander and Aristobulus.[3] The hostile attitude of the armed forces was of major concern to Herod's son, Antipater.[4]

Herod's taste for grandeur was notably expressed in the magnificence of his royal court, which resembled in every respect the courts of the Hellenistic monarchs of the East. Here too 'friends' and 'kinsmen' of the king were to be encountered, who fulfilled central functions of state and were in direct personal contact with the sovereign. The king, of course, was the object of organized adulation not only at court, but throughout the kingdom. The anniversary of his accession was celebrated through the length and breadth of the realm,[5] and he was honoured by statues erected by his subjects in non-Jewish

[1] For the location of Gaba see B. Maisler, *HUCA* (1952-1953), pp. 75-84.
[2] Jos. *Ant.* xv, 294.
[3] *Ant.* xvi, 134; 375-393; *War* i, 491.
[4] *Ant.* xvii, 2.
[5] *Ant.* xv, 423.

areas.[1] Functions were also created with particular reference to the person of the King and of his wives, in accordance with the tradition of eastern sovereigns. We hear, for instance, of the post of chief huntsman[2] and, of course, of eunuchs.[3] Many of Herod's principal assistants were Greeks, the most important being Ptolemy, who appears to have been responsible for the financial administration of the kingdom and perhaps also filled the role of prime minister. He had an estate in Samaria from the King.[4] Some of the great luminaries of contemporary Greek literature were also to be found near Herod; the most important of them undoubtedly being Nicholas of Damascus, a distinguished historian, orator, philosopher, composer of tragedies and of works on natural science. Nicholas was orginally in the service of Antony and Cleopatra, but some time after their fall he moved to the kingdom of Judaea and became Herod's trusted counsellor and special envoy. He accompanied the King on his journey to Asia Minor in 14 B.C.E. and there defended the privileges of the Jews before Agrippa. He also went to Rome with a delegation from Herod and played a central part in appeasing Augustus when angered by the Nabataean affair late in Herod's life. He claimed to have helped to broaden Herod's education, through studies of rhetoric and history. Herod for his part urged Nicholas to write his *Universal History*, a huge work of 144 books, one of the most comprehensive creations of historiography known to us in ancient times. He devoted much space in this composition to the reign of his benefactor Herod. The work stood out among contemporary Greek writings inasmuch as it cited occasionally biblical tradition as its authority and showed respect for this tradition.[5]

Nicholas was not the only Greek writer at Herod's court. Philostratus, the Academic, one of Antony and Cleopatra's intimate circle, also seems to have spent some time there. But unlike Nicholas, Philostratus seems to have been with Herod even in the years before Actium.[6]

---

[1] *OGIS*, no. 415. [2] Jos. *Ant.* XVI, 316. [3] *Ant.* XVI, 230; XVII, 44-5.
[4] *Ant.* XVI, 191; 197; 257; 321; 330; *War* I, 473. On his estate of Arous cf. *Ant.* XVII, 289; *War* II, 69. On its location see F. M. Abel, *Géographie de la Palestine* II, p. 251.
[5] On Nicholas see B. Wacholder, *Nicolaus of Damascus* (1962), and the introduction on the sources.
[6] The connection between Philostratus and the kingdom of Judaea emerges from Crinagoras, in *Anthologia Graeca* VII, 645; A. S. F. Gow and D. L. Page, *The Greek Anthology*, *The Garland of Philip I* (1968), p. 211, no. xx. cf. also C. Cichorius, *Römische Studien* (1922), pp. 314-318 and Page, op.cit. II, p. 228.

Qualified Greeks also performed tasks as tutors and teachers to the princes of the blood. Athletes, musicians and actors were attracted to Jerusalem by the money and prizes offered to them,[1] and a theatre was among the institutions erected by Herod in the city.

Herod's attachment to Greek culture is easily explained by his general ties with the Greek-speaking world and by the atmosphere prevailing in the world of the Roman principate, for Augustus and his entourage were themselves well-known as enthusiastic patrons of literature. Some royal contemporaries of Herod distinguished themselves as authors; it is sufficient to mention his relative by marriage Archelaus of Cappadocia and his younger contemporary Juba, King of Mauretania. Herod himself wrote his memoirs in Greek.

Generally it may be assumed that the official language of the kingdom both for external contacts and within the governmental institutions themselves, at court, in the sessions of the royal Sanhedrin and in the army, was Greek. In addition to Ptolemy and Nicholas, already referred to, Greeks served in important posts in the royal administration. Ptolemy, brother of Nicholas of Damascus (not the Ptolemy referred to above as finance minister) was also working there. The king's secretary was a man called Diophantus;[2] men with Roman names such as Volumnius and Iucundus,[3] were relatively numerous. Here and there we hear of non-Jewish orientals in royal service, such as Soaemus the Ituraean, one of his trusted courtiers, or the Arab Corinthus, one of the royal bodyguard.[4] On the whole, however, the possibility must be taken into account that at this period Jews frequently bore Greek names; hence we are not always permitted to decide that a man with a Greek name mentioned as active in Herod's service was a non-Jew. The number of Greeks at the royal court, in the administration and the army, was nevertheless large.

Nicholas, in his autobiography, while discussing the situation created after the King's death in 4 B.C.E., gives the number of 'Hellenes' who performed various duties as over ten thousand, this being one of the reasons of the Jewish revolt which ensued.[5] The character of Herod's monarchy finds general expression in his coinage. Herod, as is well known, did not coin in silver, but was content to mint bronze, like the Hasmonaean rulers before him. But the important point to

[1] *Ant.* xv, 270.
[2] *Ant.* xvi, 319.
[3] On Volumnius cf. F. Bleckmann, *Klio* xvii, pp. 111-112.
[4] *Ant.* xvii, 55-7.
[5] *FGH* ii A, 90 F 136(8), p. 424.

256

be noted is that the legends on Herod's coins are exclusively Greek and designate, generally in the genitive and sometimes in the nominative, Herod's royalty: 'Of Herod the King' or 'Herod the King'. The symbols on Herod's coins are in part pronouncedly pagan and the absence of Jewish symbolism is noticeable.[1]

Herod excelled, more than the other Jewish rulers of the Second Temple period, in the building of new cities, in the restoration of old ones and in the erection of splendid edifices. With his political activities restricted, it seems as if he found here an outlet for his energy by which he could gain publicity and perpetuate his name. His greatest achievements were the foundation of Caesarea in place of the Tower of Straton, a town originally captured by Alexander Jannaeus; and of Sebaste on the site of Samaria, the Hellenistic city destroyed by John Hyrcanus.

The foundation of Caesarea met a vital need and the city became the principal port of Herod's kingdom, which had lacked a harbour of the first rank, while it is doubtful if Joppa or the southern ports could now cater for the vital economic needs of the kingdom. The new port of Caesarea was directly connected with the rich agricultural hinterland of Samaria, Sharon and the Plain of Esdraelon, and swiftly took its place as the chief port of the kingdom of Judaea and as one of its principal cities. It soon became Jerusalem's main rival for primacy in the kingdom;[2] besides the large harbour, which was said to be larger than Piraeus, Herod erected in the city a series of splendid buildings, including a palace, a large temple of Augustus, visible from afar and containing colossal statues of Augustus himself and of Roma; a series of impressive towers, the finest of which was called after the Emperor's stepson Drusus, and a theatre and amphitheatre. The building of the city continued for thirteen years and seems to have been completed in the year 10-9 B.C.E. The new town was inaugurated with much pomp, with musical and athletic competitions, horse racing, gladiatorial contests and wild beast shows. The games were dedicated to the Emperor and made quinquennial.[3]

The second great city refounded by Herod was Samaria, which had been to a certain extent restored by the Romans, chiefly by Gabinius, but achieved new prosperity thanks mainly to the efforts of Herod,

[1] On Herodian coins see Y. Meshorer, *Jewish Coins of the Second Temple Period* (1967), pp. 64-8.
[2] Jos. *Ant.* xv, 331-341; *War* i, 408-414.
[3] Jos. *Ant.* xvi, 136-8; *War* i, 415.

who bestowed upon it the name of Sebaste (Greek for Augusta) in honour of the Emperor. In rebuilding Sebaste Herod was influenced in great measure by considerations of security. He had long felt himself as much at home at Samaria as at Jerusalem; it had already been a base for his military operations against Antigonus, so he now determined to establish it as a stronghold from which to dominate the Jewish people. The new town had a large periphery (twenty stadia), surrounded by a strong wall, and Herod also exerted himself to make it of outstanding beauty. A temple of Augustus rose on the western part of the city-hill. The settlers of the new town were re-cruited from among his veterans and the population of the nearby districts. We are told that their number amounted to six thousand; they received allotments of land and composed the citizen-body, the King assuring their general prosperity by sharing among them the fertile lands of Samaria near the city. He further provided a con-stitution for the new city, which doubtless exhibited great loyalty to the King and served him as a source of military recruits, a function it continued to perform after his death, in the period of direct Roman rule.[1] Sebaste's loyalty to Herod also explains why Herod executed his sons Alexander and Aristobulus there.[2] Sebaste was further distinguished from both Caesarea and the old Hellenistic towns of the country in that Jews did not (so far as we know) live there. Herod certainly settled no Jews there as citizens, and it would not seem that conditions were subsequently such as to enable them to reside in the town. Apparently the foundation of these large towns, Caesarea and Sebaste, to some degree upset the balance of forces in the country in favour of the pagan element, which constituted a continuation of the policy of Pompey and Gabinius.

Among the small towns built by Herod were the citadel Herodium, south-east of Jerusalem, Phasaelis in the Valley of Jericho,[3] and Antipatris near Rosh ha'Ayyin. He also built the fortress of Machaerus east of the Dead Sea, and strengthened and embellished Masada.[4]

[1] *Ant.* xv, 292; 296-8; *War* i, 403. On Sebaste cf. G. A. Reisner, C. S. Fisher, D. G. Lyon, *Harvard Excavations at Samaria, 1908-1910* I (1924), pp. 170-180; J. W. Crowfoot, K. M. Kenyon, E. L. Sukenik, *The Buildings at Samaria* (1942), pp. 31-5; 39-41; 123-9.
[2] *Ant.* xvi, 394.
[3] On Phasaelis see G. Harder, *ZDPV* (1962), pp. 49-63; on Cypros, ibid. pp. 49-54; on Herodian Jericho see J. B. Pritchard, *The Excavation at Herodian Jericho 1951*, *AASOR* for 1952-1954 (1958).
[4] On the excavations at Masada see Y. Yadin, *IEJ* (1965), pp. 1-120; id., *Masada, Herod's Fortress and the Zealots' Last Stand* (1966).

Jerusalem too now became, thanks to Herod's building projects, one of the finest capitals in the entire East. Among the projects worthy of special note were the royal palace, the new Temple ('Herod's Temple'), the immense towers at the north-west corner of the city (Hippicus, Phasael and Mariamme), the fortifications of the old citadel (named by Herod the Antonia after his benefactor Antony), a theatre and an amphitheatre. He built palaces at Jericho, Sepphoris and Ascalon (which was actually outside his kingdom), at Beth ha-Ramata in Transjordan and elsewhere.[1] The strong fortresses at Alexandrium, Herodium and Hyrcania were regarded as objects worthy of a visit by the Roman Agrippa.

Herod had to budget for heavy expenditure. The cost of the army and the cost of keeping up proper connections with persons of influence, doubtless formed no small or negligible percentage of such expenditure. Expenses were greatly increased by the upkeep of the splendid court, and first and foremost by the erection of new buildings and cities, as well as by the King's well-known prodigality to foreign cities. Part was covered, no doubt, by taxes, after the share owed to the Roman state had been deducted. These taxes were in part direct, devolving upon agricultural produce, but some were of the type imposed on economic activities such as sales and purchases.[2] The tax revenues amounted to the impressive sum of a thousand talents, to judge by the summaries of revenue preserved in connection with the transfer of Herod's kingdom to his successors. The increase of revenue was made possible, no doubt, by the development of new areas of the kingdom and by the conditions of prolonged peace which assisted the economy of the Judaean kingdom within the Mediterranean world. But simultaneously we hear of grave complaints concerning the heavy taxes which weighed upon the people in Herod's reign.[3] They were undoubtedly heavy and it is hard to determine the relationship between the scale of taxes raised by Herod and that which obtained previously. But it is of interest to observe that the total revenue under Herod was less than the total revenue under

---

[1] Jos. *Ant.* xv, 380-425. On Herod as a theatre-builder see Ed. Frézouls, *Syria* (1959), pp. 210-212. In general on Herod's buildings see C. Watzinger, *Denkmäler Palästinas* II (1935), pp. 31-78; S. Perowne, *The Life and Times of Herod the Great* (1956), pp. 115-142; A. B. Byvanck, *Bonner Jahrbücher* (1958), pp, 57-59.

[2] Jos. *Ant.* xvii, 205.

[3] *Ant.* xvii, 308; cf. *War* ii, 85-6.

Agrippa I, although the increase under the latter can be partly explained by the development of additional agricultural areas of the kingdom. It is further to be noted that whatever the tax scale in Herod's kingdom, the burden was not shared equally among all parts of the population, and under Herod the Jewish peasantry bore the main weight of taxation.[1]

It is also clear that the taxes themselves did not suffice to balance the total expenditure, and the King needed additional income. This came, in part, from his private domains. Some of these were an inheritance from his father's family, but in the main they comprised the former estates of the Hasmonaean royal house which passed naturally to the possession of the new king. These embraced fertile agricultural tracts in various parts of the country, in the 'Great Plain' (Esdraelon), in the Shephelah and in the Jordan Valley.[2] They were leased to tenants and were a source of regular income to the royal house. Part of these lands was used by Herod to settle veterans and to grant 'land in gift' to his prominent ministers. It should also be noted that Herod confiscated the property of the numerous opponents whom he put to death, more especially in the first stages of his reign after the capture of Jerusalem in 37 B.C.E.[3] To Herod, in fact, all means of obtaining money were permissible.[4] He also reaped profit from business abroad, a good example being his participation in the exploitation of the copper mines of Cyprus.[5] Herod's own purse and the economic progress of his realm benefited from the flourishing state of the Mediterranean world as a whole which followed the institution of the principate of Augustus and the re-establishment of a stable peace throughout the empire. This peace, which came after a prolonged period of warfare, when heavy taxes were extorted and travel was insecure by land and sea, led to the revival of international commerce and to the firm grounding of agriculture in the various provinces of the empire. The Kingdom of Judaea was also influenced by this development. After the civil war under Hyrcanus and Aristobulus, Pompey's conquest, frequent rebellions, the lootings of Crassus, the oppression of Caesar's killers, and above all the bloody struggle between Antigonus and Herod,

[1] S. Applebaum, *Kiriath Sepher* (1960-61), pp. 13-15.
[2] On royal estates see A. Alt, *Kleine Schriften* II (1959), pp. 389-391.
[3] Jos. *Ant.* xv, 5.
[4] *Ant.* xvi, 179.
[5] *Ant.* xvi, 128. On the mines of Cyprus see T. R. S. Broughton, in T. Frank, *An Economic Survey of Ancient Rome* IV (1938), p. 694.

which inflicted the gravest damage upon the population's material well-being, there came a period of relative tranquility. Between 31 and 4 B.C.E. the state of Judaea was untouched either by external warfare—if we except border raids into Nabataea—or by interior disorders likely to damage the country's economy. Thanks to this, agriculture could recover. Here and there, indeed, we hear of years of drought and famine and the need of royal assistance. The Jewish peasant was certainly burdened by taxation, while many Hasmonaean supporters were driven from high economic positions at the beginning of Herod's reign, and much Jewish capital flowed into the pockets of Antony and his friends. Much of the money extorted from the Jewish peasantry was squandered to enhance Herod's reputation in foreign countries. But after Antony's fall the Roman authorities ceased to extort money without limit from the kingdom of Judaea, and even large-scale confiscations of land ceased to be a common phenomenon. The external links developed by Herod in various ways also influenced the development of trade relations between certain countries and Judaea. The connections between Herod and the Jewish upper classes in the Diaspora countries also assisted the evolution of economic relations between Judaea and abroad, and specific regulations of the Roman authorities permitted the Jews of the Diaspora communities to send money to the Temple at Jerusalem.

Great credit must be accorded to Herod for his work for agriculture by settling peasants on new lands. We know more specifically of his project in northern Transjordan, where Jews from Idumaea and Babylonia were settled. The Babylonian settlers led by Zamaris were exempt from taxes in Herod's reign, and by protecting the area from local brigands and raiders from across the border, they established a firm framework for the progress of agriculture in Trachonitis and Gaulanitis. Another area in which Herod and his successor Archelaus effected numerous changes was the Jordan Valley, chiefly around Jericho.[1] But in what measure these were to the liking of the Jewish peasantry is difficult to say.

The struggle at Herod's court

Herod's rise was marked by his marriage with Mariamme, the daughter

---

[1] On the character of the military colonies in Transjordan see S. Applebaum, *Studies in memory of Zvi Avneri* (1970), pp. 79-88; on Jericho see L. Mowry, *BA* (1952), pp. 33-6.

of Alexander, who was son of Aristobulus II and of Alexandra daughter of Hyrcanus II. By this marriage Herod endeavoured to achieve a certain legitimization of his kingship in the eyes of the Jewish nation, for Mariamme's status and the prospect of bequeathing the kingship to his sons by their marriage created a certain continuity between the Hasmonaean and the Herodian line. But his relations with Mariamme were difficult from the outset and became continually more so. Herod had married her at the height of the struggle with Antigonus, and at that stage of events she and her mother Alexandra supported Herod's war wholeheartedly. Hyrcanus II's return from his Parthian captivity also symbolized and strengthened, to all appearances, the alliance between Herod and that branch of the Hasmonaean house. But the legitimate claims of Aristobulus III to the high priesthood and Alexandra's use of the Egyptian Queen Cleopatra's aid to promote her sons's cause, quickly undermined the relations between Herod and his Hasmonaean kindred by marriage, The murder of Aristobulus permanently impaired good relations between them. Another factor in the breakdown was Herod's behaviour after the fall of Antony, at a time when Herod feared for his position and was quite uncertain whether Octavian would confirm his kingship. The very existence of Hyrcanus II, once ruler of Judaea with Roman approval, appeared to him as a considerable danger. Hyrcanus was accused of treasonable links with the Nabataean king and put to death on that charge.[1] The murder of her brother and grandfather affected decisively Mariamme's attitude to Herod, and could only be worsened by the King's jealous attitude towards his wife, with his suspicions inflamed by his sister Salome. Mariamme was put to death in 29 B.C.E.[2] and her mother Alexandra a short time afterwards.[3]

The execution of Mariamme the Hasmonaean effectively abolished the official rank of 'Queen' at Herod's court. She had been regarded not just as one of Herod's wives, but as an independent factor representing the rights of the Hasmonaean dynasty to the throne. Herod, out of consideration for the trend of popular feeling among the nation, had sent away from the court his first wife Doris, who had borne him his first son Antipater. And he had not taken another wife as long as Mariamme was alive. Thus the children born to him

---

[1] Jos. *Ant.* xv, 161-178; *War* i, 433.
[2] *Ant.* xv, 202-236; *War* i, 438-443.
[3] *Ant.* xv, 247-251.

by Mariamme were regarded as the heirs-apparent of his kingdom. After Mariamme's execution Herod married several times, and he had as many as nine wives in succession or otherwise, during his reign, among the more famous being a second Mariamme, daughter of the High Priest Simeon (son of Boethus of Alexandria) the mother of his son Herod, and the Samaritan Malthace, the mother of Archelaus and Antipas, who succeeded Herod at his death. Herod himself and the nation as a whole at first continued to regard the children of Mariamme the Hasmonaean as the heirs to the throne. Mariamme had borne Herod five children, three of them sons (Alexander, Aristobulus and a third whose name has not reached us, as he died in infancy). Alexander and Aristobulus had been educated at Rome for six years, had absorbed the culture of the capital, and had formed many and various ties there. It is to be assumed that their membership of the Hasmonaean family had gained for them the affection of the Jews of Rome. In 17 B.C.E. Herod himself went to Rome to bring them back to Judaea. Their position now seemed strong; and both were handsome and of regal bearing. The elder, Alexander, was the more outstanding personality of the two and swiftly became popular with Herod's army. Herod married him to Glaphyra, daughter of King Archelaus of Cappadocia, thus enhancing his own prestige and influence, since the marriage meant that Alexander had weighty support even outside Judaea. Herod married Aristobulus to Berenice, daughter of his sister Salome.[1]

Mariamme's sons thus returned to Jerusalem, to enjoy an exalted position and wide popular sympathy. This signalled the renewal of the alliance between Herod and this branch of the Hasmonaean family, but it was a blow to those who had previously worked against the remaining Hasmonaean influence and had pushed the King into sentencing Mariamme to death. Among them was Herod's sister, Salome. They recognized their danger, as the crown-princes made no secret of their anger at the injustice done to their mother, and also made it plain that they would revenge themselves on the guilty parties. They also treated the other royal wives and their sons with contempt. Glaphyra, Alexander's Cappadocian wife, regarded her sister-in-law Berenice as a woman of inferior rank. Besides Salome, Pheroras, the King's brother, and Antipater his eldest son also regarded it as essential to work against Alexander and Aristobulus. It may

---

[1] *Ant.* XVI, 6-11; *War* I, 445-6; on the Macedonian names in Herod's family see F. Pfister, *Historia* (1964), p. 77.

also be conjectured that other interested people such as the family of Boethus, whose representatives had been overshadowed by the sons of Mariamme the Hasmonaean, joined the group which was working against them. In a short time the atmosphere at the court was poisoned, and from then on the hostility between the two sides left its mark on the reign of Herod. Relations quickly deteriorated, especially during Herod's sojourn in Asia Minor (in 14 B.C.E.). Herod was gradually won over by the enemies of Mariamme's sons, since the latter roused in him the old antagonism to the Hasmonaean family. To counterbalance Alexander and Aristobulus he increasingly favoured his first-born son Antipater, according prominence to his status as prince of the blood. For the same reason he recalled Antipater's mother, Doris, to the court and recommended Antipater to Augustus. When Agrippa returned to Rome in 13 B.C.E., Antipater went with him to foster ties with the Emperor.[1]

Things now went from bad to worse. Antipater formed numerous ties at Rome, for Herod had prepared the ground there by letters to his friends. Even from Rome, Antipater managed to manipulate affairs at Jerusalem so effectively that Alexander and Aristobulus were accused of plotting the murder of their father. Herod, unwilling to take decisive action of his own, appeared himself with his two sons before Augustus, at Aquileia in Italy (12 B.C.E.).[2] At the meeting, a reconciliation between the two sides was effected.[3] On his way back to Judaea, Herod met Archelaus of Cappadocia, who was naturally pleased at the improved relations between his son-in-law Alexander and Herod. Herod then declared at a national assembly in the Temple court that he was bequeathing the throne to Antipater, with Alexander and Aristobulus next in line.[4]

The settlement certainly could not satisfy Alexander and Aristobulus, for it meant the effective exclusion of Mariamme's sons and the transfer of the senior position to Antipater. Antipater for his part felt unsure of his future, fearing that Alexander and Aristobulus might successfully recover their former position. Both sides prepared for

---

[1] *Ant.* XVI, 66-86; *War* I, 447-8.
[2] Some scholars maintain that this was the last of Herod's journeys to Rome. See e.g. L. Korach, *MGWJ* (1894), pp. 533-5; Otto, op.cit., p. 125, note; on the other hand, Schürer I, 293, n. 17 supposes an additional journey to be dated to 10 or 9 B.C.E. It seems to me that Korach and Otto are right, and that Josephus in *Ant.* XVI, 271; 273; 276 refers to the journey of 12 B.C.E.
[3] *Ant.* XVI, 87-126; *War* I, 452-4.
[4] *Ant.* XVI, 130-5; *War* I, 455-466.

what was to come. Antipater now enjoyed Herod's confidence and the support of Ptolemy, one of the important ministers of state (see above, p. 255). Alexander and Aristobulus, for their part, endeavoured to build up their connections with the influential elements in the army and at court. Salome, the King's sister, also persisted in her enmity to the sons of Mariamme, and the fact that Aristobulus was her son-in-law did not mellow her in the least; she used her daughter Berenice to find out what he was doing or planning, and took advantage of her relationship to blacken the brothers in the King's eyes.

The tension at court caused primarily by the more or less open struggle for the succession between Antipater and the sons of Mariamme, was compounded by a quarrel between Herod and his brother Pheroras, the tetrarch of Peraea. Pheroras, indeed, may have sensed that both his life and his position were in danger. For there had been another source of strain. Pheroras had refused to marry Herod's daughter and had married instead one of his own slave-women, with whom he had fallen in love. He loyally refused to divorce her, or to marry another of the King's daughters.[1]

A turning-point in the declining relations between Herod and Alexander was the disclosure of close contacts between Alexander and three of the eunuchs who were closest to the King. Under torture, the eunuchs confessed that Alexander hoped to seize the power which he claimed as his birth-right after Herod's death, and that he had made precise preparations to do so, with the support of many of the officers of the army. The confession was the occasion for a reign of terror at the royal court. The King lost his self-confidence and his suspicions knew no bounds. One of the suspects who had been tortured at his orders, affirmed that Alexander and Aristobulus had plotted to murder their father while hunting and to flee to Rome to claim the kingship. But the confession seemed incredible in this form even to Herod, and even less convincing was the affirmation under torture, by a younger man, who claimed that Alexander had written to his friends in Rome to call him thither as he had information of relations between Herod and the Parthians. Alexander, despairing of being acquitted of these charges, wrote to his father that a conspiracy had been formed against him in which both Pheroras and Salome and some of the King's closest friends were involved, all inspired by the one aim, to rid themselves of the constant fear that haunted them. The situation

[1] *Ant.* xvi, 188-219; *War* i, 467-487.

at the royal court now became intolerable. At this point came the intervention of King Archelaus of Cappadocia, who had come to Jerusalem, which brought about a temporary compromise between the sides.[1] But all the factors that had bedevilled the atmosphere at the court continued to operate. Another trouble-maker also appeared at Jerusalem, Eurycles of Sparta who, on ascertaining the conditions prevailing in Jerusalem, exerted his influence in favour of Antipater, against the sons of Mariamme. Another honoured guest, Euaratos of Cos, who supported Alexander, was but a partial counterweight to Eurycles.[2]

A pretext for fresh steps against the brothers was provided by their connection with two dismissed officers, Iucundus and Tyrannus. Having lost Herod's favour, they were now members of Alexander's group, and aroused Herod's suspicions. He ordered them to be arrested and tortured, till they confessed that Alexander had tried to induce them to kill Herod. This disclosure led to the arrest of the commander of the fortress of Alexandrium on the charge of promising the two brothers refuge in the fortress. The commander himself would not admit the charge, but his son became a hostile witness, producing a letter in Alexander's writing alluding to the plan.

Alexander pleaded in self-defence, that the letter was forged. The officers involved with Alexander in the supposed conspiracy were stoned to death by the mob at Jericho. Alexander and Aristobulus denied any plan to kill their father, but confessed to an intention to flee from him on account of the atmosphere of suspicion that surrounded them. Alexander even admitted that they had intended to go to Archelaus, on the assumption that the latter would send them to the Emperor at Rome. This last admission of Alexander was decisive for Herod, for his son's appearance at Rome with connivance of Archelaus would have weakened his position politically. Herod commissioned two of his people to go to Archelaus and to transmit to him his protest against his participation in a plot concerted by his sons; thence they were to continue their journey and deliver to Augustus Herod's letter containing the proofs he had assembled against his sons.[3] Augustus advised Herod not to act in person as judge of his sons, but to remit the matter to a court meeting at Berytus, where representatives of the Roman authorities in Syria would be sitting, and also

[1] *Ant.* xvi, 229-270; *War* i, 488-512.
[2] *Ant.* xvi, 300-312; *War* i, 513-533.
[3] *Ant.* xvi, 313-334; *War* i, 526-9; 535.

Archelaus of Cappadocia. Herod accepted Augustus' proposal, though refusing to agree to the presence of Archelaus. A court of 150 assessors, including Saturninus, governor of Syria, assembled at Berytus. A majority of its members agreed that the two sons should be sentenced to death. News of the verdict spread swiftly. It was received with sorrow not only by the civilian population but also by Herod's army, with whom Alexander had maintained close relations. One of the senior officers, whose sons were among Alexander's friends, was even bold enough to reproach the King for his behaviour to his sons and to inform him of the bitterness prevailing in the forces over the sentence. But the result of the officer's action was contrary to what he had expected: Herod had no sooner extracted from him the names of the officers and men who dissented, than he arrested all of them. Three hundred of the military suspected of connections with Alexander and Aristobulus were put to death by the mob at Caesarea, while Alexander and Aristobulus themselves were brought to Sebaste and there suffered death by strangulation (7 B.C.E.). Their bodies were interred at the fortress of Alexandrium.[1]

With the brothers' death, the prospect of the Hasmonaean dynasty returning to power after Herod's death receded. The way was paved for Antipater. Alexander and Aristobulus, indeed, left children, but the great future which awaited the descendants of Alexander and Glaphyra was to lie outside Judaea and beyond the pale of the Jewish nation and religion. On the other hand a brilliant future was in store for the descendants of Aristobulus and Berenice in Judaea itself. Yet while the brothers were alive Alexander was undoubtedly the more important personality of the two. The Jewish nation mourned their death; and when in course of time after Herod's death a Jewish charlatan appeared claiming to be Alexander, he gained great sympathy among the Jews of the Diaspora (in Crete, Melos, and Italy), till the fraud was exposed by the personal intervention of Augustus.[2] The execution of the brothers was not the end of the struggle within Herod's family. The last three years of his reign were marked by the rise and fall of Antipater. He was to all appearances the heir apparent. But he could not feel that his future was really assured. The arrangements for the succession might yet change and the in-

[1] *Ant.* XVI, 356-394; *War* I, 536-551; Nicholas, in Jacoby, *FGH* II A, 90 F 136(2), p. 423.
[2] *Ant.* XVII, 324-338; *War* II, 101-110; cf. also Volkmann, op.cit. pp. 90-2. The case of the Pseudo-Alexander is not an isolated one in the history of the Roman Empire. See F. Millar, *A Study of Cassius Dio* (1964), pp. 214-218.

heritance might be divided. Antipater therefore attempted to increase his influence at Rome and to strengthen his hold in Judaea. His uncle Pheroras co-operated with him for a time, but Salome held aloof. Antipater does not seem, like Alexander, to have been successful in forming close bonds with the commanders of the army. It was also to be expected that he would be hated by many for his part in the execution of the sons of Mariamme. On the other hand his marriage to the daughter of Antigonus, the last Hasmonaean king,[1] did something to prepare the ground for a reconciliation, since his children by her could claim to be Hasmonaeans no less than those of Herod and Mariamme.

Meanwhile other sons and grandsons of Herod were growing up. The sons of Alexander and Aristobulus became potential rivals of Antipater. The royal court was full of intrigues and harboured all the symptoms characteristic of an oriental court during the old age of the reigning sovereign. Antipater's influence was at first decisive. His maternal uncle also married Berenice, Aristobulus' widow,[2] and he himself tried hard to win over Herod's friends at Rome by sending them gifts. Above all, he tried to strengthen his connections with Saturninus, governor of Syria, and with his brother who also received many valuable gifts from him.[3] Bonds became especially close between Antipater and Pheroras, despite the opposition of Herod, whose relations with his brother had at this time deteriorated, the cause for the quarrel being again Pheroras' wife, whom Herod regarded as an obstacle to proper relations between himself and his brother. Furthermore, Pheroras' home became to some extent the centre of combined opposition to Herod, as is instanced by the fact that Pheroras' wife paid the fine imposed on the Pharisees for their refusal to take the oath of loyalty to the Emperor and to Herod. Salome was well aware of the relationships between Pheroras and Antipater and constantly drew her brother's attention to the danger they involved. Herod's action compelled Antipater to give up all public links with Pheroras. They continued, however, in secret.[4]

Antipater worked things so well that his father agreed that he should go to Rome to visit the Emperor.[5] The mission had a double object: to continue diplomatic activity at the imperial court against Syllaeus,

[1] Jos. *Ant.* XVII, 92.
[2] *Ant.* XVII, 9; *War* I, 553.
[3] *Ant.* XVII, 6-7.
[4] *Ant.* XVII, 32-51; *War* I, 566-572.
[5] *Ant.* XVII, 52-53; *War* I, 573.

and to obtain Augustus' confirmation of Herod's testament, which made Antipater his first and main successor. In the event of Antipater's decease during his father's lifetime, the succession was to go to Herod, son of the King by Mariamme of the house of Boethus. Antipater certainly had an additional purpose for his journey, namely, to strengthen his links with the imperial court at Rome. He hoped even while abroad to keep himself informed of what was going on in Judaea.

But events did not develop as he had hoped. His chief ally in these years, Pheroras, died, and after his death Herod conducted a comprehensive enquiry among the dead man's household. The enquiry, carried out with the customary torture, extracted several confessions which appeared to justify Salome's previous charges regarding the links between Antipater and Pheroras. Herod was now certain that his eldest son and his brother had conspired to kill him; poison moreover had been found in Pheroras' house, brought especially from abroad. As a result of these disclosures Doris, Antipater's mother, lost her high position, and Herod divorced his wife Mariamme, daughter of Boethus, as he believed her also to be implicated in the affair. The King struck her son's name from his will and deposed her father from the high priesthood.[1]

The first news of the changes in Judaea reached Antipater on his way back from Rome. The rumour of the death of his partner and confidant Pheroras reached him at Tarentum; on his arrival at Cilicia he learned of his mother's disgrace. After some hesitation Antipater decided to continue his journey to Judaea in the hope that his presence in Jerusalem would help to dispel the suspicions that had arisen concerning him. But his new situation soon became clear. He was coldly received at Caesarea. When he reached Jerusalem he was brought before a commission of enquiry, one of whose members was Varus, governor of Syria; Nicholas of Damascus acted as chief prosecutor. As a result of the preliminary investigation Antipater was thrown into chains, and Herod informed Augustus of his alleged crimes.[2]

Simultaneously Antipater's intrigues at Rome against the King's sister Salome came to light. He had been in touch with Acme, a Jewish slave-woman of the Empress Livia; Acme had undertaken to arouse Herod's suspicions against Salome by means of forged letters

[1] *Ant.* xvii, 58-78; *War* i, 578-600.
[2] *Ant.* xvii, 83-133; *War* i, 608-640.

which would convince Herod that Salome had worked against his interests at Rome. Herod had originally intended to send Antipater to Rome to answer for his actions to Augustus. He now changed his mind under the influence of his friends, who argued that Antipater might find a way out of the tangle with the help of his connections at Rome; he therefore continued to keep Antipater in custody.[1]

Herod, sick and in his seventieth year, determined to draft a new will in which he bequeathed his kingdom to his son Antipas, since his two sons Archelaus and Philip were in disfavour on account of Antipater's intrigues. He had made their behaviour at Rome seem suspect.[2]

Augustus' reply to Herod's letters empowered the King of Judaea to do as he saw fit with his son Antipater, either by exiling him or by putting him to death.[3] Herod decided to have Antipater executed, and his body buried in the fortress of Hyrcania.[4] Just before his death Herod again altered his will, granting the kingdom to Archelaus, and leaving Antipas only Galilee and Peraea. To Philip he left Gaulanitis, Trachonitis and Batanaea, while Jamnia, Ashdod and Phasaelis went to Salome in reward for her consistent loyalty to her brother throughout his reign.[5] Herod died in 4 B.C.E., and was interred, in accordance with his will, in the fortress of Herodium.[6]

Herod and the Jewish nation

Herod's reign is to be regarded in large measure as a revolution second only in importance to that which had taken place after the persecution by Antiochus and the Hasmonaean revolt. Now, as then, the foundations of the old social order had collapsed. Many of the upper classes of the Hasmonaean epoch had been killed, many had been deprived of their economic power, and most had lost their previous influence. But it must also be remembered that along with this revolutionary

[1] *Ant.* XVIII, 134-145; *War* I, 641-5; Nicholas, in Jacoby *FGH* II A, 90 F 136 (5-7), pp. 423-4. See also E. Täubler, *Byzantinische Zeitschrift* (1925), pp. 33-6.
[2] *Ant.* XVII, 146; *War* I, 646.
[3] *Ant.* XVII, 182; *War* I, 661. Herod's attitude to his sons, three of whom he executed, is reflected in an anecdote where Augustus says that he would rather be Herod's pig than his son. Cf. Macrobius, *Saturnalia* II, 4, 11. It seems that Macrobius goes back to a source contemporary with Augustus. See G. Wissowa, *Hermes* (1881), p. 499. It seems worthwhile referring to Seneca, *De clementia* I, 15, 3-7 according to which Augustus, during a *consilium* convoked by one Tarius, whose life was in danger from his son, spoke against the execution of the would-be parricide and suggested banishment instead.
[4] Jos. *Ant.* XVII, 187; *War* I, 664.
[5] *Ant.* XVII, 188-9; *War* I, 664, 668.
[6] *Ant.* XVII, 199; *War* I, 673.

change, a certain continuity had been maintained between the society of the Hasmonaean monarchy and that which took shape under Herod.

Herod's rise was marked by close links with one branch of the Hasmonaean family, that of Hyrcanus II, whose granddaughter was Herod's wife. This link was strengthened by Hyrcanus' return from exile in the Parthian kingdom. It need not be supposed that this itself converted large numbers of Hasmonaean loyalists into faithful adherents of the Herodian house, but it provided an opening for individuals to change their adherence, all the more so since in the first years of the reign Mariamme was still devoted to her husband's cause. When subsequently relations at court deteriorated, Herod's power had grown so much stronger that even some of the most loyal adherents of the Hasmonaean dynasty were ready to betray their former masters in order to curry favour with the new sovereign.[1] In addition it should be emphasized that the Herodian family itself had belonged to the ruling elite under the Hasmonaeans and that certain influential groups had long been sympathetically inclined towards it. These Herodian groups, along with the Hasmonaean circles hostile to Antigonus, provided a certain continuity, but this was less obvious than the gap. Many members of Antigonus' party had fallen during the war, while another massacre of Hasmonaean supporters had taken place on the capture of Jerusalem in 37 B.C.E., when forty-five of the leaders of Antigonus' faction were executed on Herod's order.[2] Herod faced the task of replacing old elements which had been eliminated from Jewish society, and of elevating new ones on which he could base his power. He attempted to solve the problem in various ways, and we witness the gradual rise in his reign of a new ruling stratum composed of *novi homines* and families who made their way to the upper ranks of Jewish society. This stratum held its ground after Herod's death and even after the deposition of his son Archelaus (6 C.E.). It continued to retain its distinguished position down to the Great Revolt.

What was common to most of these families was that they had no roots in the Hasmonaean past and that their rise was bound up with the victory of Herod, either directly, or as the result of the destruction of the influential families of the previous period. Apart from this, the new families were not all of one type. Some of them came from

[1] See e.g. *Ant.* xv, 47.
[2] *Ant.* xv, 6.

the small minority of the Jewish people, which had taken Herod's side during the war with Antigonus;[1] these were to be found chiefly in Idumaea. But Herod also seems to have had supporters here and there outside Idumaea. We hear explicitly of notables in Galilee who aided Herod and suffered at the hands of his Galilean enemies. It is in fact known that Galilee was on the whole a centre of the most fanatical opposition to Herod, as early as his period as governor of Galilee in the time of Julius Caesar. On the other hand the impression is that he was then able to forge close links with certain groups of the upper classes in Galilee, who remained loyal to Herod in the years to come. In this context it is of interest to note that at the end of Herod's life the high priesthood was bestowed upon the Galileans Matthias son of Theophilus and Joseph son of Ellem.[2]

To some extent Herod's policy followed that of the Tobiads in the Ptolemaic era. Just as the latter had expressed the spirit of certain groups whose outlook was first and foremost cosmopolitan and Hellenistic, so Herod's policy reflected a cosmopolitan concept of Hellenistic tinge, in the setting of the Roman Empire, much more than a Jewish approach. The Idumaean basis of the Antipatrids corresponds to some extent with the Ammonite basis of the Tobiads. The relations with Samaria which characterized the activity of Joseph son of Tobiah, were continued in the close links maintained by Herod with that city. Herod had worked hard in favour of the town of Samaria before seizing control of Jerusalem. He had rendered material assistance and settled disputes that had broken out there.[3] Herod had numerous friends in Samaria to whom he turned in time of emergency, as for instance when the Roman forces were in need of supplies of wine and oil to continue the siege of Jerusalem. It was at Samaria that he solemnized his marriage with Mariamme the Hasmonaean, and when he fell ill, he had felt safer in Samaria than in Jerusalem.

---

[1] *Ant.* xiv, 479; *War* i, 351.

[2] It is true that in *Ant.* xvii, 78 Matthias is described as a native of Jerusalem. However, this statement proves only that he had been active in Jerusalem for some time before his appointment. It clearly emerges from the Talmudic sources that Joseph ben Ellem, who according to *Ant.* xvii, 166, was a relative of Matthias, hailed from Sepphoris in Galilee. Cf. *P. T. Yoma* i, 38 d; *Horayot* iii, 47 d; *Megillah* i, 72 a; *T. Yoma* i:4 (see S. Lieberman, *Tosefta Ki-Fshutah* iv (1962), pp. 723-4); *T. B. Yoma* 12 b; *Megillah* 9 b; *Horayot* 12 b. So we may suggest that Matthias too was a Galilean by origin. On Matthias and Joseph ben Ellem see also H. Graetz, *MGWJ* (1881), pp. 50-3; A. Schwarz, *MGWJ* (1920), pp. 36-9.

[3] *Ant.* xiv, 284; *War* i, 229.

One of his wives (Malthace) was a Samaritan,[1] and bore him two of his heirs. To use Josephus' expression, Herod built Samaria-Sebaste as one of the strongholds against the people.[2]

As has been made clear above, under Herod's reign the Hellenistic elements in society and in governmental institutions were strengthened. But it is important to note that the rise of a stratum of 'Hellenes' in the kingdom brought no profound results in the development of Jewish society itself, and in no sense produced a merger between the Hellenes and the Jewish upper classes. It should also be observed that even in Herod's lifetime there were no signs that the King intended to promote any fusion of Hellenism and Judaism in Jerusalem or in the new cities he had founded in various parts of his kingdom. It is to be noted in this context that he insisted very strictly on the Jewishness of those who desired to enter into family relationships with his dynasty.

The royal house itself was the centre of social life in Judaea. Herod worked from the first not just as an individual, but also as an Antipatrid, and made his brothers and kinsmen partners in his policy. His brother Joseph was his confidant and right-hand man in the different phases of the war with Antigonus, until he was killed in battle. After the victory over Antigonus, his brother Pheroras became prominent and was appointed tetrarch of Peraea. Important tasks were also imposed on Achiab, another relative.[3]

Herod further tried to use his marriage bond to cement relationships with those whom he destined for central functions in the state. Sometimes he utilized his sister in these matters. Her two husbands, Costobar and Alexa, took an active part in public life in Judaea, and the King himself was following the same principle when he married Mariamme of the house of Boethus and appointed her father High Priest. The Alexa referred to above belonged to the new stratum of dignitaries who had risen with the new dynasty; he and his descendants were to perform important functions in the life of Judaea.

Herod's alliance with the house of Boethus brings us to the most interesting feature in the social development of the Herodian period, namely, that individuals and families of the Diaspora communities came to share in the life of Judaea. Viewpoints, tendencies and moods were sometimes prevalent in high Jewish circles of the Hellenistic

[1] *Ant.* XVII, 20; *War* I, 562; see G. Allon, *Studies in Jewish History* I (1957), pp. 73-4.
[2] *Ant.* XV, 292.
[3] *Ant.* XV, 250; XVII, 184; *War* I, 662.

Diaspora—especially in such great centres as Alexandria—that were very like those by which the policy of Herod was directed. Cooperation with the Roman principate was a guiding principle of their public behaviour and a firm foundation of the status of these groups in the various localities of the Hellenistic East. The King was equally eager to strengthen his links with the Jews from Babylonia. Here one can see Herod's general tendency to favour the rise of elements with no ancient loyalties to the Hasmonaean house. The success of immigrants from Egypt and Babylonia produced lasting consequences. Some of them at least retained the status they had achieved in Herod's reign down to the fall of Jerusalem. Some of them set the tone in Jewish society in that period, as may be seen in general from the composition of the high priestly oligarchy as it crystallized at the end of the Second Temple period.

Herod first assigned the high priesthood to the Babylonian Hananel. In course of time Jesus son of Phiabi was appointed. Various conjectures have been voiced on the origin of this family, but it would seem that Phiabi is an Egyptian name which appears on a Jewish inscription at Tell el-Yehudiyeh (Leontopolis).[1] The family therefore was Egyptian-Jewish and Jesus son of Phiabi may serve as our first example of a high priest of Jerusalem from Hellenistic Judaism. More important than these as regards its connections with the Herodian family and the part it played in the history of Judaea, was the house of Boethus, which came from Alexandria. The founder of its greatness was Simon, whose daughter Mariamme married Herod; Simon was appointed High Priest in place of Jesus son of Phiabi.[2]

It was therefore Herod's general policy to encourage immigration from the Diaspora and to promote such new-comers in social status and in the administration. A good example is the Babylonian Zamaris, who laid the foundations of an influential dynasty in northern Transjordan. The family performed a major function in maintaining order and security in that region, and they continued to remain warm supporters of the policy of Herod and his successors. The centre of their activity was at Bathyra in Batanaea, and they were known as 'the men of Bathyra', the name also used for them in Talmudic literature. Branches of the family were to be found also in Gaulanitis (Gamala) and Galilee (Tiberias), and it included various scholars of the Second Temple period. Subsequently they were as prominent at Jamnia

---

[1] CII, no. 1510; Gabba, no. XIV.
[2] Jos. *Ant.* XV, 320-2.

under Johanan ben Zakkai as they had been in the Jerusalem of Hillel. The rise of Hillel and his family also fits in well with the general pattern of Jewish society in Herod's time and subsequently, which was marked by the rise of Jewish elements from outside Judaea. The Herodian period was a watershed in the life of Judaea. On one side there was the rise of the families allied to the Herodian regime and to Rome, and of those who reconciled themselves with the regime in one way or another. But then again, a family such as that of Judas of Galilee, embodying the extreme opposition of men of principle to the existing order also left its mark on the social and political development of' Judaea.[1]

Herod had been made King to start with against the explicit wishes of the vast majority of the Jewish nation, which had fought with desperate valour for Antigonus and the Hasmonaean house. The hostility between Herod and broad strata of the nation persisted unchanged till his death. His rule was regarded as a tyranny. It is true that he did much on behalf of the Jews of the Diaspora, used his influence with Augustus and Agrippa to protect Jewish rights, and erected a splendid Temple in Jerusalem which aroused the enthusiasm of all beholders.[2] He had periodically reduced taxes.[3] In time of famine he even sold the royal insignia to buy grain, and also convened popular assemblies in which to explain his policy and achievements.[4] He also bestowed favours on certain groups in the country and was active in helping settlers from the Hellenistic and Babylonian diasporas. He was respectful towards Shamaiah and Abtalion, the Pharisee leaders who had advised the people to yield to him in 37 B.C.E., after reasonable hope of resisting him was lost; and he did not punish them for their refusal to swear allegiance to him.[5] We also hear of his friendship for Menahem the Essene and of his respect for the Essenes as a whole.[6]

But none of this sufficed to erase the essential antagonism between Herod and the Jewish people. The liquidation of the survivors of the Hasmonaean family and the killing of the sons of Mariamme the Hasmonaean lit up still more clearly the antagonism between Herod

---

[1] On Herod's policy and social changes in Judaea see M. Stern, *Tarbiz* (1966), pp. 235-253.
[2] *T. B. Baba Bathra* 4a; *Sukkah* 51b.
[3] Jos. *Ant.* xv, 365; xvi, 64.
[4] *Ant.* xv, 305-316; xvi, 62; 132.
[5] *Ant.* xv, 370.
[6] *Ant.* xv, 371-9.

and the popular dynasty of the Hasmonaeans; it brought upon him the hatred of the masses. Although Herod remained on the whole loyal to the Jewish religion, making the acceptance of Judaism a condition of the marriage of his sister Salome to one of the chiefs of the Nabataeans, and citing the Torah as an authority even at the court at Berytus before which he brought the case of his sons Alexander and Aristobulus.[1] In actual fact his entire deportment was such as to offend Jewish religious susceptibilities. His instruction to sell bandits into slavery abroad called in question their entire future as Jews.[2] The alien atmosphere prevailing in the royal administration and the establishment of new cities of Hellenized character as citadels against the Jewish nation, made clear to many the real dangers inherent in Herod's policy. This awareness was accompanied by the feeling that Herod was draining away the strength of the Jewish nation to curry favour with the gentiles.[3] Herod's whole-hearted sympathy with the ideological aims of the Roman principate, including the cult of the divinity of Augustus, and the shrines which he erected in his honour, his boundless adulation of physical force and greedy pursuit of ostentatious splendour, his lack of consideration for human life in the achievement of selfish political ends—all this widened the gulf between the monarchy and the mass of the nation. Herod could rule Judaea only by operating a stern regime of suppression based on military force with a series of fortresses that hemmed in the areas of Jewish settlement on all sides, and with all assemblies and associations prohibited. Transgressors of royal instructions were severely punished. The fortress of Hyrcania was the scene of many executions.[4] A rigorous system of police espionage was introduced, and a secret passage prepared from the Temple for the King's safety.[5] Thanks to the efficiency of the organization and to certain concessions and timely acts of appeasement, Herod was able to prevent the outbreak of open rebellion while his reign lasted. Plots were hatched to assassinate him, but the conspirators got no further than planning. We know of a conspiracy of ten men to kill Herod in the theatre,

---

[1] *Ant.* xvi, 365.

[2] *Ant.* xvi, 1-5. This was consonant with the usage prevalent among the Greeks who objected to the enslavement of a citizen in his own city. Cf. e.g. *P. Hal.*, pp. 122-4. See also A. Gulak, *Klausner Festschrift* (in Hebrew, 1937), pp. 132-5; Y. Gutman, *Dinaburg Festschrift* (in Hebrew, 1949), pp. 68-82; Schalit, op.cit., pp. 230-7.

[3] *Ant.* xvi, 154-9.

[4] *Ant.* xv, 366.

[5] *Ant.* xv, 424.

which was discovered by one of the royal spies; the conspirators were taken, bravely admitted their intention of killing the King, and were put to death after brutal torture. But the informer was also punished. He was attacked and killed before a great crowd; this too called forth violent reaction on the part of the King, and redoubled measures for the future repression of the people.[1] In the latter years of his reign, matters came to an open rift between Herod and the mass of the Pharisees, six thousand of whom refused to take the oath of loyalty to him and were fined accordingly. Some of them were in close contact with Herod's brother Pheroras and his wife and had uttered prophecies against Herod's monarchy, under the influence of eschatological expectations.[2] Bitterness reached its peak in Herod's last days, when extremist elements inspired by the scholars Judas son of Sepphoraeus and Matthias son of Margalus tore down the eagle placed by the King over the Temple gate, and were put to death.[3] When Herod died, the entire populace breathed more freely. Archelaus, his son and heir, himself admitted his father's cruelties,[4] and Jewish representatives stressed to Augustus the great wrong done to them by the dead king.[5] The nation's negative attitude to Herod is reflected throughout Jewish literature. The Talmud speaks of him as a brutal sovereign, 'the slave of the Hasmonaean house'.[6] The hostility is unambiguous in the work known as *The Assumption of Moses*, composed not long after Herod's death.[7] He figures in the New Testament as a slayer of infants.[8]

The disturbances after Herod's death

After Herod's death, nothing could restrain the popular bitterness which had reached its peak as a result of the King's policy towards the end of his reign. According to his testament, Archelaus was to have the kingship and direct rule over Judaea, Idumaea and Samaria.

---

[1] *Ant.* xv, 280-291. [2] *Ant.* xvii, 42-5. [3] *Ant.* xvii, 149-163.
[4] *Ant.* xvii, 201. [5] *Ant.* xvii, 304-310. [6] *T. B. Baba Bathra* 3b.
[7] vi, 2-7. Undoubtedly Herod's name was well known to Latin literature (Horatius, *Epistulae* ii, 2, 184; Persius, *Saturae* v, 180), but the relevant passages, apart from the above-mentioned from Macrobius, are of neutral character. The interpretation of the Herodians mentioned by Mark 3:6; 12:13; Matt. 22:16 is still open to dispute. See E. Bickerman, *RB* (1938), pp. 184-197; H.H. Rowley, *JTS* (1940), pp. 14-27; V. Taylor, *The Gospel According to St. Mark* (1957), p. 224. In any case we should not think that this expression implies a religious-messianic movement connected with Herod.
[8] Matt. 2:16.

Herod Antipas was to become tetrarch of Galilee and Peraea. The northern administrative districts of the kingdom—Gaulanitis, Trachonitis, and Batanaea—were assigned to Philip, on the assumption that he too would hold the title of tetrarch. Salome, the king's sister, inherited Jamnia, Ashdod and Phasaelis. Herod left to Augustus a sum of money, as well as valuable vessels and clothing; he also bequeathed money to the Empress Livia. The entire testament required the Emperor's ratification, and despite the fact that his realm had been administratively divided, Herod had intended it to retain a certain unity, on the assumption that the two tetrarchs would be subordinate to King Archelaus.

When Herod's death became known, Salome and her husband Alexas paraded the troops in the amphitheatre of Jericho[1] and read to them the letter written by the King before his death, in which he thanked the troops for their loyalty and asked them to display the same attitude to his son Archelaus. Ptolemy, who had been entrusted with the royal seal, read out the testament.

The troops spontaneously saluted Archelaus as King and marched in companies under their officers to present their respects. Archelaus saw to it that Herod received as magnificent a funeral as possible, his corpse being brought for burial to the fortress of Herodium.[2] After the completion of the seven days' mourning, Archelaus went up the Temple to meet the people. The masses displayed enthusiasm, but also put forward demands, including calls for tax-relief, for the abolition of the sales and purchase tax, and for the release of prisoners. Some of the Jews also gave free rein to their grief at the execution of the scholars and their pupils who had torn down the eagle from the Temple gate, demanding the punishment of Herod's more intimate counsellors, and the removal of the High Priest Joazar son of Boethus. The approach of the Passover Festival and the gathering of multitudes of pilgrims at Jerusalem increased the tension. Archelaus, who had till then refrained from giving a clear reply to the demands of the multitude, now became involved in a direct clash with the Jews in

---

[1] The story that Herod ordered his sister Salome and her husband to murder, after his death, the Jewish notables shut up in the hippodrome of Jericho, and so to cause mourning throughout the entire nation (Jos. *Ant.* XVII, 174-9; *War* I, 659-660) has undoubtedly a legendary ring and derives from a source hostile to Herod. Nor does the view of Otto, *Herodes*, p. 148 that it was Herod's intention to keep the notables as hostages in order to preclude disturbances, seem likely.

[2] *Ant.* XVII, 188-199; *War* I, 666-673.

the Temple. He sent in troops against the crowd, and a dreadful massacre ensued.[1] He was thus guilty of an act of crude butchery, such as not even Herod had perpetrated since his victory over Antigonus. Archelaus then set out by sea for Rome with his mother Malthace, his aunt Salome and some of Herod's veteran ministers, including Ptolemy and Nicholas of Damascus. Herod Antipas also left for the capital with the intention of persuading Augustus to ratify Herod's penulti- mate will which gave him the senior position. In this he had the sup- port of his aunt Salome and the other Ptolemy, brother of Nicholas, and could rely on the persuasive powers of the orator Irenaeus. When he arrived in Rome he was joined by all those of Herod's relatives who were opposed to Archelaus, prominent among them being Antipater the son of Salome.[2] A Jewish delegation independent of the Herods, to the number of fifty, had also obtained the permission of Varus, governor of Syria, to go to Rome.[3]

Augustus accepted the material submitted to him by Archelaus and Antipas, as well as reports from Varus as governor of Syria, and from Sabinus the financial procurator of the province, concerning the prop- erty of the kingdom; he then summoned the two sides before his consilium. He first heard Antipater son of Salome, who represented Herod Antipas, and accused Archelaus of having effectively arrogated to himself royal authority without awaiting Augustus' ratification. He also denounced Archelaus' cruelty and emphasized the validity of Herod's previous will. Nicholas of Damascus pleaded in Archelaus' defence, but Augustus withheld his decision for the time being.[4]

Simultaneously news reached Rome of the outbreak of a serious rebellion in Judaea. This had several phases and it spread to all the Jewish districts of the country. As soon as Archelaus had left, disorder was renewed; it was temporarily suppressed by Varus, legate of Syria, who left one of the legions of the Syrian garrison in Jerusalem to maintain peace and quiet. This step, however, was inadequate, and the new outbreak was in no small degree caused by the activity of the procurator Sabinus, whose intention was to gain

[1] *Ant.* XVII, 200-218; *War* II, 1-13; Nicholas, *De vita sua*, in Jacoby, *FGH* II A, 90 F, 136 (8), p. 424.
[2] *Ant.* XVII, 219-220; 224-230; *War* II, 14-15; 20-6. According to *War* II, 21, the mother, Malthace, passed over to the side of Antipas.
[3] *Ant.* XVII, 300; *War* II, 80. It results from the last-mentioned source that the Jewish delegation had left Judaea before the revolt broke out. Cf. also Otto, op.cit., p. 168. Cf. in general Täubler, op.cit., pp. 36-40; H. W. Hoehner, *Herod Antipas* (1972), pp. 18-39.
[4] *Ant.* XVII, 230-249; *War* II, 26-38; Nicholas loc.cit.

control of the fortresses and to seize the royal treasuries.[1] The Pentecost Festival which concentrated in Jerusalem thousands of pilgrims from Galilee, Idumaea, Jericho and Peraea, in addition to the inhabitants of Judaea, heightened the tension in the city. Many of the Jewish troops in Herod's army went over to the rebels, but three thousand picked troops, predominantly natives of Sebaste, acted with the Romans. The insurgents laid siege to Sabinus and his associates in Jerusalem.[2]

The rising spread over entire Jewish Palestine. One Judas, son of the Ezechias whom Herod had executed, took command in Galilee. Judas's activity was focused on Sepphoris, capital of Galilee, where he attacked the royal palace and armories and equipped his men with the captured weapons. In Peraea the rebellion was headed by a man named Simon, one of Herod's slaves, who burned the royal palace at Jericho and operated elsewhere against royal property, but fell in battle, being met by Gratus (one of Herod's commanders) and the Romans. Other rebels burned down the palace at Amathus. Another leader of the insurgents was a shepherd named Athronges, distinguished by his physical prowess, who, with his four brothers as strong as himself, attacked Roman and Herodian troops indiscriminately, annihilating a Roman company near Emmaus. Many of Herod's veterans joined the insurgents and fought against Herod's army, which was commanded in Judaea by Achiab the King's cousin.[3] Samaria, on the other hand, took no part in the disorders.

The Jewish revolt after Herod's death had no one leader and no united command. It was essentially a series of spontaneous risings which broke out independently of one another in various parts of the country. They drew their main strength from the lower orders and were headed by men of the same class (Simon, Athronges). The leaders of these risings (Judas, Athronges, Simon) adopted royal titles. It may be conjectured that this phenomenon was linked with eschatological expectations, such as brought individual messianic figures to prominence. The phenomenon of an intimate connection between an anti-Roman movement of pronounced popular character and messianic

---

[1] It seems that our sources relating the history of the disturbances, dependent as they are on Nicholas who was on friendly terms with Varus, put perhaps too much blame on Sabinus. However, there is information in other writers, about the character of Varus, including his cruelty and avarice. See P. A. Brunt *Historia* (1961), p. 210.

[2] Jos. *Ant.* XVII, 254-268; *War* II, 39-54.

[3] *Ant.* XVII, 269-285; *War* II, 55-65; Tacitus, *Historiae* v,9.

leadership, is characteristic also of the period of the Great Revolt seventy years later, as may be seen in the adventures of such men as Menahem, leader of the Sicarii, and Simon bar Giora.[1] Varus saw that strong forces from Syria would be needed to suppress the revolt, and in fact the main Roman force stationed in Syria, including legions and auxiliary units, was now committed against the Jewish insurgents. The army was concentrated at Ptolemais and part of it sent against Galilee. The town of Sepphoris was captured and its inhabitants sold into slavery. Varus himself advanced through Samaria, burned Emmaus, gained control of Jerusalem and put an end to the rebellion by brutally repressive measures.[2] He then returned to Antioch, leaving a legion in Judaea to maintain order. The suppression of the Jewish rebellion by Varus constituted one of the gravest catastrophes which befell the Jewish nation in the period of the Second Temple. Many people of all classes fell victim to it and most of the Jewish part of the country suffered heavily. The memory of the disorder was engraved in the national memory as the 'War of Varus' (פולמוס של אסוורוס).[3]

Augustus had taken his decision on the future administration of Judaea before the fighting in that country had ended. He rejected utterly the demand of the fifty-man delegation which had appeared before him in the Temple of Apollo with the support of thousands of Jews in the city of Rome—to abolish completely the rule of the Herodian family and to annex Judaea directly to the Province of Syria. Archelaus' case was then again presented by Nicholas of Damascus, and Augustus confirmed the general lines of Herod's testament. Archelaus received Judaea, Samaria and Idumaea, with an annual revenue of two hundred talents, and Philip the north-easterly portions of the kingdom with an income of one hundred talents. Augustus modified Herod's will in one important particular: by not granting the title of King to Archelaus, who had to be content with the title of ethnarch. Augustus diminished the senior status which Archelaus was to have enjoyed by his father's will. He indeed promised to grant Archelaus the royal title if he proved worthy of it. He further acceded to the urgent appeals of the delegates of the Hellenistic cities of Herod's kingdom (Gaza, Gadara, Hippos) and freed them of all connection

---

[1] W. R. Farmer, *NTS* IV (1957-58), pp. 147-155.
[2] Jos. *Ant.* XVII, 286-298; *War* II, 66-79.
[3] On the so-called פולמוס של אסוורוס See *Seder Olam Rabba*, 30, ed. B. Ratner (1897), p. 145.

with the house of Herod by annexing them directly to the Province of Syria. As a reward to the inhabitants of Samaria for not taking part in the rebellion, he reduced by a quarter the taxes levied from them.[1]

The rule of Archelaus, Herod Antipas and Philip

Archelaus' rule in Judaea (4 B.C.E.-6 C.E.) was marked from the beginning by disappointment and frustration. Although he had successfully obtained most of the inheritance assigned to him by his father in spite of the efforts of his brother and kindred, he had not obtained the royal title held by Herod. His prestige had undoubtedly suffered as a result of the events both in Judaea and at Rome, prior to Augustus' decision. The people of Judaea could not but detest a man who had begun his rule with such frightful bloodshed. On his return from Rome he had to extinguish the last embers of the rising and it was he who ultimately put an end to the activity of Athronges and his brothers in Judaea.[2]

On assuming power, Archelaus also took the name of Herod, which is the name that appears most commonly on his coins.[3] In general he endeavoured to follow his father's policy, but without his father's success in maintaining close relations with the emperor. Among his Jewish subjects he was no more popular than his father had been. Archelaus further angered the Jews by marrying, in contravention of Jewish law, the widow of Alexander, his deceased brother, who had in the meantime married Juba, King of Mauretania. He also perpetuated the alliance with the priestly house of Boethus. Although Joazar son of Boethus had been deposed from the high priesthood, the function was given to his brother Eleazar. After some time Archelaus conferred it on another incumbent, Joshua ben See.[4] The method of frequently changing the high priests was thus introduced. Like his father and brothers, Archelaus was also much occupied in building projects and development. Thus, for example, he brought water from the region of Na'aran to the Plain of Jericho in which he planted date-palms; in the same area he built the town of Archelais,[5] and rebuilt

---

[1] Jos. *Ant.* XVII, 299-323; *War* II, 80-100; Nicholas loc. cit.
[2] *Ant.* XVII, 284; *War* II, 64.
[3] On the name Herod on the coins of Archelaus see Meshorer, op.cit., p. 69; see also Dio Cassius LV, 27, 6.
[4] Jos. *Ant.* XVII, 339; 341.
[5] On Archelais cf. Abel, op.cit. II, p. 249; on its dates see Pliny, *Natural History* XIII, 44.

the palace at Jericho which had been burnt down by the rebels under Simon.[1]

Archelaus' rule was as unpalatable to the Samaritans as it was to the Jews. This was one of the rare occasions on which the Jews and the Samaritans made common cause, and their leaders charged Archelaus with behaving brutally towards them in contravention of Augustus' instructions. Augustus summoned Archelaus to Rome to answer to the charges, accepted the view of the plaintiffs and exiled him to Vienna in Gallia Narbonensis (6 C.E.).[2]

Herod Antipas alone of Herod's sons proved himself a very capable statesman and ruler. He not only ruled his tetrarchy successfully for forty-three years in relative quiet, although his territory included the restless Jewish population of Galilee, but also achieved, like his father, international prestige. From many points of view there is much to be said for those who urged that Herod's penultimate will, allotting the first place to Antipas rather than to Archelaus, should have been ratified. Antipas also inherited from his father his love of pomp, becoming after him the most important city-builder in the history of the Herodian dynasty. He was also the first Jewish ruler to introduce the organization of the Greek polis among the Jewish population of his state. But Herod Antipas was much inferior to his father in one thing at any rate—as a military leader. He maintained a considerable force in his tetrarchy and piled up arms. But when he had to prove his military strength and skill in a conflict with the Nabataeans, he failed the test and his army was defeated. It may be noted, however, that the military potential at his disposal was much smaller than that of his father, and that Antipas did not take part personally in the decisive battle.

After emerging safely from the crisis which had afflicted Herod's heirs in 6 B.C.E.[3] Antipas retained his position throughout the reigns of Augustus and his successor Tiberius, with whom he appears to have entertained friendly relations unimpaired even in the period of Sejanus' supremacy. The reasons for the coolness prevailing between him and Pilate, prefect of the Province of Judaea,[4] are unknown. The joint struggle conducted at Rome by his father, Herod, and Aretas

---

[1] Jos. *Ant.* XVII, 340.
[2] *Ant.* XVII, 342-8; *War* II, 111-116; Strabo XVI, 2,46, p. 765; Dio Cassius LV, 27, 6.
[3] Cf. the comments on Strabo loc. cit. by Otto, op.cit., pp. 178-180, which are accepted also by Dessau, op.cit. II, 2, pp. 776. For another view see Willrich, op.cit., p. 188.
[4] Luke 23:12.

IV against Syllaeus, had drawn the two kings together and created conditions for a change towards friendly relations between Judaea and the Nabataean kingdom. It seems that even before Herod's death the Nabataean king had married his daughter to Antipas, and this marriage secured peace on the border between the Nabataeans and Antipas' tetrarchy for a long period. When the marriage was broken up, peace on the Nabataean border also came to an end, and the old enmity was renewed. The cause was the love affair between Antipas and Herodias, daughter of his brother Aristobulus (she was already married to Herod, another of Antipas' brothers). Herodias agreed to abandon her husband and to marry the tetrarch, but before the agreement was implemented, Antipas' Nabataean wife heard of it. She left him and returned to her father's house;[1] the fragile peace was over, and disputes broke out on the frontier, leading ultimately to a decisive battle between the two sides. Herod Antipas' commanders were heavily defeated by the Nabataeans, to some extent on account of the treachery of refugees from Philip's tetrarchy who had been enrolled in Antipas' forces. Antipas found it necessary to appeal for help to the Emperor Tiberius, who ordered Vitellius, governor of Syria, to make a punitive expedition against Aretas.[2] Vitellius' operations against the Nabataeans seem to have been initially delayed by the situation created on the Parthian frontier by the Parthian king Artabanus. Only after a settlement of this question had been reached and the crisis had passed, was Vitellius able to prepare a campaign against the Arabs.

True to the tradition of the house of Herod, Herod Antipas was alert to all events outside the country and had special connections with Syria. At the end of Tiberius' reign, it fell to his lot to play an important part as mediator between Rome and the Parthians, when relations between them worsened after the death of Zeno-Artaxas, King of Armenia (35 c.e.). King Artabanus of Parthia made energetic efforts to install one of his own sons as ruler of Armenia; his efforts were countered just as energetically by the Romans who caused the King of Iberia to make his own brother King of Armenia, which thus continued to be a protectorate of the Empire. Vitellius as governor of Syria also encouraged pretenders hostile to Artabanus to claim the

---

[1] For the date of the marriage of Herodias and Herod Antipas see Otto, op.cit., pp. 186-191. See also A. v. Gutschmid, *Kleine Schriften* II (1890), p. 319.
[2] Jos. *Ant.* XVIII, 109-115.

Parthian throne. Both sides were nonetheless ready to resume peaceful relations.[1] Artabanus and Vitellius met in the middle of the River Euphrates on a bridge especially built for the occasion. Herod Antipas played host to the two sides, pitching a splendid pavilion on the bridge.[2] Not even Herod his father had attained this degree of international prestige. Artabanus consented to the peace terms and sent his son to Rome as a hostage.[3] Herod Antipas hastened to dispatch news of the agreement to Tiberius, thus anticipating Vitellius, for which the governor of Syria never forgave him.

Herod Antipas followed in his father's footsteps in his dealings with the Greek world. An inscription from Delos shows the links between Herod and Athens, and an inscription from Cos also testifies to his relations with the Greek world.[4]

Herod's most impressive activity within his tetrarchy was displayed in his city-building. He founded three towns, two of which, Sepphoris and Beth ha-Ramtah, had been developed while Augustus was still alive. The third, Tiberias, was founded by him under Tiberius, between 17 and 22 c.e.[5] Sepphoris, the capital of Galilee and centre of the Galilean revolt in the 'War of Varus', having suffered heavily during the suppression of the rising, was fortified by Antipas and re-

---

[1] On these events see Debevoise, op.cit., pp. 158-163; Magie, op.cit. I, pp. 507-9; Ziegler, op.cit., 60-3.

[2] I accept here the chronological sequence of Josephus who dates (*Ant.* XVIII, 96-105) the agreement between Vitellius and the Parthians to the reign of Tiberius. This dating is contradicted by some other sources which connect the event with the reign of Gaius: Suetonius, *Life of Gaius Caligula*, 14,3; Dio Cassius LIX, 27,3 and, as it seems, also Tacitus, who does not relate the event in the surviving part of the *Annals* dealing with the end of Tiberius and presumably described it in one of the last books which told of the reign of Gaius. The case for Josephus' dating has been well stated by E. Täubler, *Die Parthernachrichten bei Josephus* (1904), pp. 39-62. See also Otto, op.cit. p. 194; J. G. C. Anderson, *CAH* X (1934), pp. 749-750; Magie, op.cit. II, 1364, n. 39; F. F. Bruce, *The Annual of Leeds University Oriental Society* (1963-5), p. 19. Against Josephus see A. Garzetti, *Studi in onore di Aristide Calderini et Roberto Paribeni* I (1956), pp. 211-229.

[3] The hostages sent to Rome included a Jewish giant called Eleazar. See Jos. *Ant.* XVIII, 103. See also Columella, *Res rustica* III, 8,2, C. Cichorius, *Römische Studien* (1922), p. 421.

[4] *OGIS*, no. 417; P. Roussel-M. Launey, *Inscriptions de Délos* (1937), no. 1586; Gabba, no. XV; *OGIS* no. 416; A. Maiuri, *Nuova Silloge epigrafica di Rodi e Cos* (1925) no. 456.

[5] On the foundation of Tiberias see M. Avi-Yonah, *IEJ* (1950-1951), pp. 160-9. Avi-Yonah suggests the date 18 c.e.; Hoehner, op.cit., pp. 93-5 prefers 23 c.e.

named Autocratoris (*autokrator*—Greek for the Latin 'imperator').[1] Beth ha-Ramtah was first called Livias after the Empress, and re-named Julias under Tiberius, when Livia took the name Julia on her adoption into the Julian family.

Julias was the stronghold of Antipas in Peraea, but his greatest creation was Tiberias. The town's inhabitants came from various places, some being forced to settle there by royal order in accordance with the practice of Hellenistic sovereigns. Many of the new settlers were without property or social standing, attracted by the economic inducements and social promotion held out to them by the founder. Herod Antipas distributed land among them and built free houses in return for their promise not to leave the place.[2]

Tiberias developed swiftly into a large city. Its foundation saw the inauguration in Judaea of the organizational forms of the Hellenistic polis on the model they had assumed under the Roman Empire. While his father Herod had in fact consistently refrained from founding a polis within Jewish territory itself, Herod Antipas blazed a new trail and established a polis with a preponderantly Jewish population.

As the overwhelming majority of the inhabitants of Galilee and Peraea were Jews, Herod Antipas was compelled to consider their religious feelings. This also appears from his coins, on which he did not have his own image stamped, in contrast to his brother Philip. Although he enjoyed no official status in Jerusalem, his influence was percep-tible there also. He was in the habit of visiting the city, especially at the festivals, when he had the opportunity of coming into touch with the governor. His nickname 'the fox' referred to his cunning, which inclined more and more to diplomatic rather than to violent methods.[3]

Herod Antipas certainly did not imagine that the spiritual ferment among his subjects in Galilee would bring about one of the greatest revolutions in the history of the world. His tetrarchy was the scene of the ministry of John the Baptist, who openly denounced the tetrarch's marriage with Herodias, his brother's wife, and was finally arrested by Antipas and subsequently put to death. Jesus of Nazareth was also active in Antipas' tetrarchy, and Antipas' rule at times cast its shadow upon Jesus' relations with the Galilean Jews of his genera-tion.

---

[1] Jos. *Ant.* xviii, 27.
[2] *Ant.* xviii, 36-8.
[3] Luke 13:32; On relations between Antipas and Pilate, see also H. W. Hoehner in E. Bammel, ed., *The Trial of Jesus* (1970), pp. 84-90.

On the death of Tiberius (37 B.C.E.) Herod Antipas' importance in political life suffered a relative decline. The new Emperor Gaius preferred his nephew Agrippa; and Vitellius, governor of Syria, who held a grudge against him, broke off his campaign against Aretas as soon as he received news of Tiberius' death.[1]

Herod Antipas' efforts to gain the new Emperor's favour were not successful, and he saw his nephew and brother-in-law Agrippa obtain the heritage of Philip and the title of King, while he himself remained with the status of tetrarch. His wife Herodias pressed him to work upon the Emperor to grant him the royal title, and both left for Rome, but their diplomatic lobbying ended in complete failure. Agrippa also exerted his considerable influence upon the Emperor, sending one of his freedmen after them to provoke Gaius against them. Herod Antipas was charged with preparing for war against Rome and with conspiring with the Parthians.[2] He was sentenced to exile (39 C.E.), and his wife went with him.[3] His possessions were annexed to the kingdom of Agrippa.[4]

Philip was the least important of the three sons of Herod who obtained power, both in respect of political influence in general and of connections with the Jewish people in particular. He ruled the north-easterly region of Trachonitis, Gaulanitis and Batanaea, and most of his subjects were non-Jews. This is the explanation of his coinage, which differed from that of his brothers, since he stamped his image upon them. He was known as a man of moderate behaviour who held aloof from large-scale political activity. Josephus tells of his patriarchal style of administering justice, when he travelled from place to place, setting up his court of law in various localities according to need.[5] He too, like the other members of the house of Herod, did much for city-building. He re-built Panion near the sources of the

---

[1] Perhaps the new emperor remembered the respect paid by the Nabataean king to his father Germanicus (Tacitus, *Annals* II, 57, 4).

[2] Some scholars believe that Herod Antipas had some friendly connections with Artabanus, King of Parthia. See e.g. J. P. V. D. Balsdon, *The Emperor Gaius* (1934), p. 197.

[3] According to Jos. *Ant.* XVIII, 252 Antipas was banished to Lyons (Lugdunum) in Gaul, while *War* II, 183 states that his place of exile was in Spain. The correct solution seems to have been suggested by O. Hirschfeld, *Kleine Schriften* (1913), p. 173, n. 2 who thinks of a place situated on the Spanish border, Lugdunum Convenarum. Cf. also F. M. Abel, *RB* (1946), pp. 72-3 and H. Crouzel, *Studia Patristica* x (1970), pp. 275-280.

[4] *Ant.* XVIII, 240-255; *War* II, 181-3.

[5] *Ant.* XVIII, 107.

Jordan, naming it Caesarea; in order to distinguish it from the more renowned Caesarea on the coast, it was customarily called Caesarea Philippi. He also built up Bethsaida on Lake Gennesaret into a city, with a large population, and named it Julias. He was buried there.[1] After Philip's death in the year 34 C.E. the areas he had ruled were annexed directly to Syria and on Gaius Caligula's accession were transferred to Agrippa I (37 C.E.). We have no information as to any intervention by Philip in the affairs of Judaea, but it is very possible that he was one of the four sons of Herod who opposed the introduction of the standards into Jerusalem under Pilate.[2]

The reign of Agrippa I

The reign of Agrippa I coincided with the Jewish nation's last days of glory before the Great Revolt. His reign also constituted the most serious attempt made under the Roman Empire to effect a compromise between Roman rule and the Jewish people, by giving the latter a king it was prepared to regard with favour.

In Gaius Caligula's brief reign Agrippa already stood out as the most prominent personality among the Jews of the Roman Empire. His life is better known to us than that of other distinguished Jews of the time. Born in 10 B.C.E., Agrippa was the son of Aristobulus and Berenice (Herod's niece), grandson of Herod and the Hasmonaean Mariamme. He was educated at Rome, where he could mix with the great. Among his friends there was Drusus son of the Emperor Tiberius; he also enjoyed the ample support of Antonia, Tiberius' sister-in-law, who remained loyal to her friend Berenice, Agrippa's mother.[3] Another friend was Antonia's son Claudius, who was to be Emperor some years later. Agrippa led a spendthrift life at Rome, mainly after his mother's death, the imperial freedmen being a special object of his prodigality. In a short time he was penniless and in extreme distress, but could not approach the Emperor, because after Drusus' death in 23 C.E., Tiberius excluded all Drusus' friends, for fear of awakening too painful memories. Agrippa, plunged in debt, left Rome where he had lived for many years, and set out for his native Judaea.[4]

In Judaea Agrippa enjoyed no official standing, and his want of

---

[1] *Ant.* XVIII, 28; *War* II, 168; *Ant.* XVIII, 108.
[2] Philo, *Legatio*, 300.
[3] *Ant.* XVIII, 143; 165. Cf. also Balsdon, op.cit., pp. 13-14.
[4] *Ant.* XVIII, 143-7.

money did not help his prestige. He first took up residence at Malatha in the south, where he appears to have inherited a country estate,[1] and remained in a state of despair and even on the brink of suicide. Only the encouragement of his wife Cyprus, also a granddaughter of Herod,[2] supported him in his distress and to some extent restored his will to live. His wife further appealed for aid to his sister Herodias, who was married to Herod Antipas. Herod appointed Agrippa *agoranomos* (inspector of markets) of Tiberias, but at a banquet held at Tyre a quarrel broke out between the brothers-in-law. Antipas insulted Agrippa by alluding to his inferior position, and Agrippa, offended, left Galilee for Syria, where an old friend, Pomponius Flaccus, was governor. Flaccus' company already included Agrippa's brother Aristobulus, who was hostile to him and blocked him in every way. The tension between the two brothers finally led to a breach between Flaccus and Agrippa, the immediate cause being Agrippa's plea to Flaccus in the frontier dispute which broke out between Damascus and Sidon. As the Damascenes were aware of Agrippa's influence with Flaccus, they bribed him to act on their behalf. Aristobulus informed Flaccus of the bribe, and Agrippa was compelled to leave Syria and resume his wanderings.

His plight was again desperate. He decided to return to Italy, and having obtained with the aid of his freedmen and his mother the necessary money, was about to sail from the port of Anthedon in the south of Palestine, when he was stopped by Herennius Capito, procurator of Jamnia, who wished to arrest him for a debt owing to the imperial treasury.[3] Agrippa however, succeeded in escaping and reached Alexandria, where he obtained a loan from Alexander the Alabarch, part of which was paid to him in cash and part promised to him when he reached the Italian port of Puteoli. On arriving there he wrote to Tiberius Caesar, who offered him hospitality on the Isle of Capri where he was living at the time. Although a letter from Capito to Tiberius caused a brief deterioration of relations with the Emperor, Agrippa was helped by Antonia, the Emperor's sister-in-

---

[1] On Malatha see A. Alt, *Kleine Schriften* III (1959), pp. 395-6.
[2] Cyprus was the daughter of Phasael, the son of Phasael (the brother of Herod), by his marriage to Salampsio the daughter of Herod himself and Mariamme the Hasmonaean. Cf. Jos. *Ant.* XVIII, 130-1.
[3] *Ant.* XVIII, 147-158. A. H. M. Jones, *The Herods of Judaea* (1938), p. 187 thinks that the debt of Agrippa to the imperial treasury originated in his borrowing from people whose property was later confiscated.

law, to pay the debt owing to the treasury (300,000 drachmae) and relations with the Emperor were restored.[1]

Agrippa's dealings with Antonia were accompanied by a *rapprochement* with her grandson Caligula, the future Emperor. But these connections and some imprudent utterances by Agrippa, in which he expressed a wish for the death of Tiberius and the accession of Gaius, almost caused his undoing, and he was thrown into prison.[2] With Tiberius' death (16 March 37 C.E.), his lot vastly improved. The new Emperor, his friend Gaius, raised him to the rank of king, as successor to Philip.[3] In place of his iron fetters he received a gold chain of the same weight, and was honoured by the Senate with the grant of *ornamenta praetoria*.[4] The grant of kingship to Agrippa was itself nothing exceptional in Gaius' policy at the beginning of his reign: we know, for example, that he cancelled Tiberius' Commagene settlement, abolished the country's provincial regime, and reinstated a monarchy by making Antiochus sovereign, enlarging his realm with territory in southern Asia Minor and compensating him for the financial loss incurred during the period when he was out of office.[5] He also crowned two Thracian princes, Polemo and Cotys, who had been educated with him, as rulers of kingdoms in Asia Minor, Polemo over Pontus and Cotys over Lesser Armenia.[6] Their brother Rhoemetalces III was crowned King of Thrace itself. Sohaemus further became ruler of the Ituraeans by Gaius' favour.[7]

Agrippa now became one of the most important figures in Roman society and gained more influence than was exercised there by any Jew before or after.[8] While his grandfather Herod had been a mere outsider in high Roman society, though his services and talents were appreciated, Agrippa associated with the great men of Rome as one of them in every respect, for better or for worse. But the very fact that he knew Roman society and politics, and the tyranny and caprice of the Caesars and their families intimately and from within, may explain better than anything why he ultimately avoided full

---

[1] *Ant.* XVIII, 159-165.
[2] *Ant.* XVIII, 167-194.
[3] *Ant.* XVIII, 237; *War* II, 181; Dio Cassius LIX, 8,2.
[4] Philo, *Against Flaccus*, 40.
[5] Dio Cassius LIX, 8,2; Suetonius, *Life of Gaius Caligula*, 16,3.
[6] Dio Cassius LIX, 12,2; cf. also *SIG* no. 798.
[7] Dio Cassius, loc. cit.
[8] Dio Cassius LIX, 24, 1 mentions the bad influence exerted by Agrippa and Antiochus of Commagene on Gaius. 'King Agrippa and King Antiochus were with him, like two tyrant-trainers.'

self-identification with Rome. Agrippa was in fact the most pronouncedly Jewish statesman of all the prominent members of Herod's dynasty, and the one who, in his last years, made the good of the Jewish nation his chief concern. Agrippa I's seven years of greatness, which were also his last, expressed his self-identification with the Jewish people and with its needs as he understood them. These years were crowded with activity conducted with understanding and in co-ordination with the majority of his people and its recognized leaders.

In 38 C.E. Agrippa obtained the Emperor's permission to depart for his kingdom. On his way he was received with enthusiasm by the Jews of Alexandria, but his visit there was made the occasion for the outbreak of anti-Jewish riots in the city. Agrippa's appearance in Palestine undoubtedly made a great impression on the Jews of the time, for he was the first Jewish king after a long interval of over forty years. Herod Antipas' exile in 39 C.E. made possible the extension of Agrippa's territory and in 40 Galilee and Peraea were added to his kingdom.[1] Thus Agrippa became king of a large part of the Jewish population of the country. We have no information of what Agrippa did in the north of the country. In the same year he was preoccupied by his attempt to secure the annulment of Caligula's oppressive order—a matter in which he risked his entire political future, his kingdom and his life, until he succeeded, albeit only temporarily and partially, in having the decree annulled. As is well known (see below p. 358), Gaius responded to his friend by consenting not to erect his statue in the Temple at Jerusalem. Agrippa's courage should not be underestimated; it deserves our special esteem when we consider how Gaius behaved towards other kings, among them his friend Antiochus of Commagene, whom he expelled from his kingdom, or King Ptolemy of Mauretania whom he put to death. King Mithridates of Armenia was also deposed by Gaius and flung into prison.[2] At the time of Gaius' assassination (on 24 January 41 C.E.), Agrippa was still in Rome; here prospects of wide political activity of imperial

---

[1] Jos. *Ant.* XVIII, 252. It seems that we should connect with these events the epigram of Philip of Thessalonica which refers to a presentation of some piece of artistic tapestry to a reigning Roman emperor by Cyprus the wife of Agrippa. Cf. *Anthologia Graeca* IX, 778; A. S. F. Gow and D. L. Page, *The Greek Anthology, The Garland of Philip* (1968), no. VI, p. 300; cf. C. Cichorius, *Römische Studien* (1922), pp. 351-5.

[2] Dio Cassius LIX, 25,1; LX, 8,1; Suetonius, *Life of Gaius Caligula*, 26, 1; 35,1; Tacitus, *Annals* XI, 8; Seneca, *De tranquillitate animi*, 11,12.

significance were opened to him. The military had elevated Claudius, Gaius' uncle, to the imperial throne. Important groups in the Roman Senate were toying with the hope and possibility of restoring the Republic. It looked as if matters would reach the point of armed conflict. At this stage of events Agrippa played an important part in mediating between the sides, for he had long been on terms of friendship with Claudius and the hour was now opportune to win his favour in this important activity.[1] Agrippa's efforts were duly rewarded by Claudius after he became emperor. In the course of his general imperial settlement Claudius determined the status of the various client kingdoms. Thus, for example, he restored Antiochus to power in Commagene and Mithridates in Armenia.[2] As part of the general settlement Claudius enlarged the frontiers of Agrippa's kingdom by adding Judaea, including Idumaea and Samaria. Agrippa thus became king of all Palestine, and the provincial regime of Judaea was abolished completely after an existence of thirty-five years. The Jewish state was in effect restored to the territorial extent it had possessed in the time of Herod. Some of the Greek cities such as Gadara and Gaza were not, it is true, reannexed to the kingdom of Judaea and remained under the direct rule of the governor of Syria, but on the other hand the frontiers were extended on the north. The relations between Claudius and Agrippa were accorded solemn and official recognition. A treaty was signed in the Forum, and an edict of Claudius announced to the Roman people the territorial grants made to Agrippa, the formulae being incised on bronze tablets and placed for safekeeping in the Capitol. Agrippa also received the *ornamenta consularia,* and his brother Herod was made king of the state of Chalcis and honoured with the *ornamenta praetoria.* The two brothers obtained from Claudius permission to appear before the Senate to thank him in the Greek language.[3] The attachment of Judaea to the Province of Syria did not cease when Agrippa became king of the whole country and the province of Judaea was abolished. It was very convenient for Agrippa that

---

[1] Jos. *Ant.* XIX, 236-245; 265; *War* II, 206-213; Dio Cassius LX, 8, 2. V. M. Scramuzza, *The Emperor Claudius* (1940), pp. 58-9 points out the difference between *Ant.* and *War* as to the part played by Agrippa in the course of events. However, it is also clear from the narrative of the *War* that Agrippa's activities were of prime importance, which is also confirmed by Dio.

[2] Cf. Magie I, pp. 549, 551.

[3] Jos. *Ant.* XIX, 274-5; *War* II, 215-217; Dio Cassius LX, 8,2-3. Possibly *OGIS* no. 418 also refers to the return of Agrippa I to his kingdom.

P.Petronius, who had done so much for the Jews at the time of Caligula's decrees, was still ruling Syria in 41, for shortly after Agrippa's return to Judaea urgent need of action by the governor of Syria arose. This was in connection with occurrences at the city of Dora, south of Mount Carmel. The town, in fact was not in Agrippa's kingdom, but close to it. Despite Gaius' death, the gentile inhabitants of the town, who had shown little concern for Jewish religious feeling, resumed their provocation by bringing a statue of the Emperor into the Jewish synagogue. Agrippa at once realized the danger thus conjured up, since the act recalled the worst events of Caligula's reign which was offensive to Jewish religion and insulting towards its adherents. He requested Petronius to take drastic steps against the rioters. The governor of Syria acted energetically, charging one of his centurions to arrest the offenders and warning the chief men of Dora to take strict care that in the future no one in their town should be molested for, or prevented from, living according to his ancestral customs.[1] It is to be noted that Agrippa figures prominently in Petronius' official letter to Dora. In course of time, with the appointment of new governor of Syria, Vibius Marsus, relations with the king of Judaea ceased to be cordial, and this had repercussions upon political developments in the years immediately following.

The Jewish nation was proud of its King Agrippa, not only because a Jewish ruler had reached the loftiest dignity, and tried to rule in accordance with the people's will, but also because all knew that he was not just the grandson of Herod, but also a descendant of the Hasmonaeans, thus a Jewish king in every sense.[2] The comparison made by Josephus between Herod and Agrippa,[3] in which he emphasizes how much better Agrippa respected Jewish feelings, appears to reflect the estimate then prevailing among wide circles of the nation. The relatively prolonged period of direct Roman rule, with the oppressive acts of Pilate, and the threat from Caligula, opened the eyes of many to the advantage inherent in the existence of a Jewish king, even if he was only half-independent. Agrippa, for his part, did all he could to be a Jew in every respect in the Jewish-populated areas of his kingdom, and to gain Jewish favour. He gave the Temple the golden chain which had been a gift from the Emperor, offered

---

[1] *Ant.* XIX, 300-312.
[2] For an emphasis on the high-priestly, i.e. Hasmonaean, antecedents of Agrippa cf. Philo, *Legatio*, 278.
[3] Jos. *Ant.* XIX, 328-331.

numerous thank-offerings, defrayed out of his own pocket the expenses of men and women who had bound themselves by vows of abstinence, and so won the hearts of the people.[1] He persisted in this policy till his death, and his popularity finds an echo in the Talmudic sources, where King Agrippa is the Jewish ruler most acceptable to the nation since the reign of Queen Salome Alexandra; The famous Mishnaic words in *Sotah* appear to refer to Agrippa I.[2]

There were, of course, also Jews who were dissatisfied with Agrippa. One of these was a man called Simon who gathered a large crowd in Jerusalem when Agrippa was at Caesarea, and made various charges against him, claiming that he should be prohibited entrance to the Temple as he was impure. The charge was apparently connected with Agrippa's presence at theatrical performances. Agrippa left him unharmed, and endeavoured to appease him.[3]

While Agrippa tried to remain in accord with the masses of the people and to satisfy the demands of the Pharisees, his reign was also marked by the effort to co-operate with the restricted and well-defined oligarchy of the high priesthood. In this there was no great change from the period of Herod and the first procurators. It is only possible to speak of the renewed influence of the family of Boethus, which was certainly the most illustrious of the priestly families in Herod's reign and whose standing had been somewhat weakened under the first procurators in comparison with that of the family of Ananus. Agrippa deposed Theophilus, son of Ananus, who had been appointed high priest in 37 C.E. by Vitellius, legate of Syria, and had served for four years while Agrippa was ruler only in the North. Theophilus had not perhaps shown great readiness to co-operate in the years before Agrippa took over in Jerusalem. In Theophilus' place Agrippa appointed Simon Cantheras of the Boethuseans,[4] this renewal of their glory being in line with the traditional friendship

[1] *Ant.* XIX, 293-4.
[2] *M. Sotah* 7:8; other relevant passages in Talmudic literature are: *M. Bikkurim* 3:4; *T. B. Ketuboth* 17a; *Leviticus Rabba* 3, ed. M. Margulies (1953), pp.66-7, though many scholars have doubts concerning the relation of even *M. Sotah* 7:8 to Agrippa I and prefer to identify the Agrippa mentioned there with Agrippa II. See e.g. M. Brann, *MGWJ* (1870), pp. 541-7; S. Safrai, *Pilgrimage at the Time of the Second Temple* (in Hebrew, 1965), pp. 196-8.
[3] Jos. *Ant.* XIX, 332-4. Cf. G. Allon, *Studies* I, pp. 116-117.
[4] *Ant.* XIX, 297. For an attempt to identify the high priest Simon Cantheras with Simon the Righteous of *T. B. Sotah* 31a, and to date his appointment by Agrippa I as early as the reign of Gaius Caligula, cf. P. Winter, *Zeitschrift für Religions- und Geistesgeschichte* (1954), pp. 72-4. However, it seems doubtful whether Agrippa already had at that time the right to appoint high priests.

between them and the Herodian house. But the house of Boethus had not exclusive enjoyment of the honours thus regained. It seems that Agrippa, bent always on compromise, did not regard it is feasible to forego connections with the house of Ananus, the most important priestly family of the recent years, and later found it desirable to bestow the high priesthood on members of that family. After the removal of Simon Cantheras he proposed to give the post to Jonathan the son of Ananus, who had already served and was one of the most prominent personalities in the history of his house. He refused the function, suggesting his brother Matthias for the appointment.[1]

All these changes in the high priesthood were effected chiefly at the beginning of Agrippa I's reign (not later than the year 42 c.e.). And Matthias son of Ananus did not continue in office till Agrippa's death, but was replaced by Elionaeus.[2] Despite this fact, then, that Agrippa is often regarded as a sovereign who favoured the Pharisees, we cannot discover any indication that he endeavoured to introduce Pharisee element into the high priesthood. Both the families of Ananus and Boethus were definitely Sadducee. Elionaeus, too, who according to the Mishnah was of the house of Caiaphas, must be denied all links with the Pharisees.[3] We may deduce that Agrippa's policy, though intended to win over the Pharisees, was not directed against the existing social order in the form in which it had crystallized from Herod's time onwards. In so far as Agrippa introduced changes, they tended to strengthen old bonds and trends prevailing since Herod's day, and had no revolutionary character. The accession of a king of the Herodian line in Judaea clearly strengthened the influence of the families which stood close to the monarchy. It may certainly be supposed that they had already discharged important functions under the first Roman governors. But now wide prospects were opened to them. Primacy of place among them was held by Helcias, known as 'the Great', whose son Julius Archelaus was betrothed to one of the king's daughters, Mariamme.[4] Among the other personalities in Agrippa's entourage, there was Silas, friend of the king in his day of distress and poverty. He was appointed commander of the royal army at the beginning of the reign, but the old friendship quickly broke up; Silas was demoted from his rank and spent the rest of his life in confinement, Helcias being appointed in his place.[5]

As king of Judaea, Agrippa did not relinquish his links with the Jews

[1] *Ant.* xix, 313-6. [2] *Ant.* xix, 342. [3] *M. Parah* 3:5.
[4] *Ant.* xix, 355. [5] *Ant.* xix, 317-325.

of the Diaspora, least of all with its upper classes. His task in this sphere was not difficult, since the readiness to maintain such links was mutual; they were an established fact and transmitted to him as a tradition of the house of Herod; Agrippa had only to continue to foster them. We have clear information of relations between the alabarch Alexander and Agrippa, some time before he became king, since Marcus, the son of the alabarch, married Agrippa's daughter Berenice (although the marriage itself was cut short by Marcus' death).[1]

By virtue of his function Agrippa had to handle the Christian problem. Here he appears to have acted with severity, and not in accordance with the Pharisaic school as it found expression in Gamaliel's famous speech in the Sanhedrin. His behaviour was more in keeping with the attitude of the Sadducee leaders of the type of Ananus. Thus Agrippa put to death James, the son of Zebedee, and imprisoned Peter.[2]

It was only natural that Agrippa, who was used to servants and aides not of the Jewish religion, should have utilized the services of some of them after his accession. But, of course, there is no reason to assume a hegemony of 'Hellenic' elements in the kingdom, such as had been so characteristic of his grandfather's reign. There was no arbitrary rule by thousands of 'Hellenes' in the pronouncedly Jewish areas of the kingdom, and in Agrippa's time we do not hear of men of the type of Nicholas and Ptolemy. But in accordance with the old Herodian tradition, Agrippa also worked to enhance his reputation in the non-Jewish towns. We do indeed hear of a dispute in which Agrippa was involved at the end of his life with the cities of Tyre and Sidon,[3] but his relations with the Roman colony of Berytus were excellent. Here he erected at great expense a theatre, an amphitheatre designed for the holding of gladiatorial games, and baths. He inaugurated the theatre with musical performances, and organized a magnificent opening of the amphitheatre by providing hundreds of pairs of gladiators gathered from among the criminals held in various parts of his kingdom.[4] We see therefore that outside the Jewish en-

[1] *Ant.* XIX, 276-7.
[2] Acts 12:1-19. Here Agrippa is called Herod, Cf. Ed. Schwartz, *Gesammelte Schriften* V (1963), pp. 48-123; E. Meyer, *Ursprung und Anfänge des Christentums* III (1923), pp. 174-7; E. Haenchen, *Die Apostelgeschichte*, 13th ed. (1961), pp. 324-335.
[3] Acts 12:20.
[4] Jos. *Ant.* XIX, 335-7; On Claudius and gladiatorial games see Dio Cassius LX, 13,1.

vironment he behaved with greater freedom and without much consideration for Jewish tradition. He further struck his own image or that of the Emperor on the coins used in the non-Jewish areas of his realm. It is nevertheless clear that he refrained from doing so on coins meant to circulate among his Jewish subjects.[1]

Agrippa was not content with the conventional appearances of power accepted by the Herodians. He began gradually to strengthen his political position in the Orient and to build up the defences of his Jewish subjects. In this he departed somewhat from the traditional policy of the Herods, who were generally the loyal tools of the Roman imperial power. His personal ties with many members of high Roman society and principally with the Emperor Claudius led him to hope that his actions would not be so strictly supervised, and that he might be given the opportunity of doing things which other rulers could not contemplate. Actually the success of Agrippa's plans was very limited. Thanks, indeed, to his being the most honoured of Herod's descendants, and because he enjoyed the Emperor's friendship, he achieved great initial prestige in the East, even exceeding that of Herod Antipas at the height of his influence. Despite his occasional failures in the implementation of his plans, at least he was not punished for making them, and here Claudius' friendship stood him in good stead.

A striking example of this situation is the frustration of his attempt to strengthen the fortifications of Jerusalem by enclosing the 'New City' with a strong wall. Josephus remarks that had this been carried out, the city would have been impregnable. Agrippa utilized Jewish public funds for this purpose, that is, the funds of the Temple. But he was prevented from completing the work; Marsus, governor of Syria, informed the Emperor of the matter, and Claudius, suspicious for once of Agrippa's intentions, ordered him to stop building. Agrippa was of course forced to obey after he had executed only a small part of his plan.[2]

Another event is instructive as to Agrippa's designs and the political difficulties which beset him. The close ties which had been created between Agrippa and the other eastern kings, were signalled by an assembly at Tiberias, capital of Galilee. The participants included

---

[1] Meshorer, op.cit., p. 79.
[2] Jos. *Ant.* xix, 326-7; Tacitus, *Historiae* v, 12,2. On the relatively insignificant part played by Agrippa in the building of the Third Wall, which was mainly built by the rebels in 66 c.e., see W. F. Albright, in E. W. Hamrick, *BASOR* clxxxiii (1966), p. 26, n. 21.

Antiochus of Commagene, who had personally experienced all the changeability of imperial policy, having been made king by Gaius, deposed by the same emperor, and restored to his kingdom by Claudius; Agrippa had intended his daughter Drusilla to marry Antiochus' son Epiphanes. Another participant was Sampsiceramus, ruler of Emesa, whose daughter Iotape was married to Aristobulus, Agrippa's brother, and whose son Azizus was to marry Drusilla after Agrippa's death, when the betrothal to Epiphanes was cancelled.[1] The two Thracian brothers, Polemo of Pontus and Cotys of Lesser Armenia also came;[2] the latter endeavoured from time to time to conduct an independent policy instead of dancing to the Roman tune.[3] Naturally Agrippa's brother, Herod of Chalcis, was also present. The conference at Tiberias, therefore, brought together the principal allied kings of the Roman East, on whom depended in great measure the defence of the area against the Parthians. The conference might from a certain point of view have constituted the apogee of Agrippa's splendour, insofar as he thus became leader of Rome's client kings in the East. The emperors on the whole looked with favour upon social ties between the client kings, but this time they had exceeded what was desirable to Roman statesmanship. Agrippa's outstanding personality, the affection prevailing between him and the Jewish nation—an unusual phenomenon in the history of the Herodian dynasty—the memory of the Jewish ferment under Gaius Caligula, the constant threat of Parthia to the Roman East—all these conspired to make the conference at Tiberias seem dangerous to Vibius Marsus, governor of Syria, who was responsible for the defence of the eastern Roman provinces against the Parthians. Marsus feared a political and military bloc inconvenient to Rome, which might enable the various eastern kings to join the Parthians and the Jews in a common effort directed against the Empire. The suspicions voiced only a few years previously against Herod Antipas were still fresh, and it should further be noted that the tension between Rome and Parthia had not diminished at the beginning of Claudius' reign and the question of who should rule Armenia was again a source of dispute between the two powers. Claudius had restored to the Armenian throne Mithri-

[1] *Ant.* XVIII, 135.
[2] On this Polemo see W. Hoffmann, *P.W.* XXI, cols 1285-7. He identifies him with Polemo, King of Cilicia who later married Berenice the daughter of Agrippa (*Ant.* XX, 145). However, the identification is by no means certain. Cf. Magie II, 1407, n. 26.
[3] Cf. Tacitus, *Annals* XI, 9, 2 for his reaction to the Roman plans in Armenia.

dates, previously deposed by Gaius, but energetic action on the part of the governor of Syria was necessary in order to prevent intervention in Armenian affairs by the Parthian Vardanes.[1] It should also be remembered that the royal dynasty of Adiabene had become converted to Judaism in these years, and its emissaries maintained close contacts with Jerusalem and were even resident there.

With all this no doubt in mind, Marsus took vigorous steps against the conference. Appearing suddenly at Tiberias, he announced to each of the kings that he must quit the place without delay. The kings obeyed the legate and returned to their countries. Agrippa seems to have been gravely offended by Marsus' attitude and their relations from then on were unfriendly.[2]

Agrippa died while he was at Caesarea, celebrating with great splendour a festival in the honour of the Emperor (44 C.E.).[3] He had reigned for seven years, in the last of which he had ruled the whole of the country. The Jewish people were deeply grieved by his passing, but the foreign troops of Sebaste and Caesarea were jubilant and insulted both the dead king and his daughters.[4]

In actual fact the reign of Agrippa I constituted an ephemeral episode in the history of relations between the Roman Empire and the Jewish nation. In the national memory it remained the last brilliant period before the fall of Jerusalem, but it exercised no serious influence on the development of Judaea and did little to change the processes at work in its administration and social life. And the relative strengths of the Jewish and non-Jewish populations of the country and their part in the administration and the Roman army did not change. From this point of view it was Herod who had determined developments. It can only be conjectured that had Agrippa lived longer

---

[1] *Annals* XI, 9-10. It is true that Tacitus relates the events under 47 C.E.; but from the fact that Marsus the governor of Syria took part in them it follows that we have to date them to the life of Agrippa I, since Marsus was dismissed from the governorship of Syria no later than 45 C.E. See also Dobiáš, op.cit., p. 422, n. 49. On Claudius' activities in Armenia see Scramuzza, op.cit., p. 191; Ziegler, op.cit., pp. 64-5.

[2] Jos. *Ant.* XIX, 338-342.

[3] E. Schwartz, op.cit., pp. 127-8 thinks that these games (*Ant.* XIX, 343) should be connected with a festival inaugurated by Herod in connection with the foundation of Caesarea (cf. also Meyer op.cit., III, 167). Yet it seems more plausible to interpret the games as related to the Britannic triumph of Claudius. See Kirsopp Lake in *The Beginnings of Christianity*, Part I, Vol. v (1933), pp. 446-452. There is no reason to suppose that Agrippa was poisoned, as is suggested by J. Meyshan, *IEJ* (1954), p. 187, n. 2.

[4] *Ant.* XIX, 345-359; *War* II, 219; Acts 12:21-3.

he would have made a deeper impression in this sphere. The fact that he was hated by the gentile inhabitants of such new cities as Caesarea, who doubtless had belonged to the local supporters of Herod, shows that they were sensible of the aims of their new ruler. But, as has been stated, his reign leaves no discernible traces on the development of Judaea.

It is further doubtful whether Agrippa followed a long-term policy in his relations with the Roman Empire. It can hardly be assumed that he entertained the hope of rebelling against Rome in concert with the Parthians. He would seem to have been interested in strengthening the Jewish people within the Jewish kingdom as a Roman protectorate, and in enhancing his own prestige in the Roman world by creating close ties with sympathetic elements at the imperial court and in Roman society outside it.

The reign of Agrippa II

Agrippa II survived as his father's only son beside three sisters, his brother Drusus having died in his youth. At his father's death he was still young (he was born in 28 c.e.) and living at Rome. Theoretically he could anticipate succeeding to his father's kingdom, or at least to part of it. But apparently the Roman government's experience with Agrippa I in his last years had seemed to spell danger, and a convenient pretext to deny the transfer of the paternal inheritance to his son was found in the latter's tender age.[1] Agrippa nevertheless already enjoyed a certain prestige and the Emperor Claudius' unconcealed favour. Thanks to this he was able to continue the traditional function of the Herodian princes in the Julio-Claudian period, which was that of representing the Jewish people before the emperor. A suitable opportunity to do so offered itself about the time of the death of Agrippa I, as a result of the restoration of direct provincial rule in Judaea. On the outbreak of a dispute over the vestments of the high priest (see below, p. 360) Agrippa's intervention, with that of his uncle, Herod King of Chalcis, and of his cousin Aristobulus, brought the Jews success in the affair.

On the death of Herod of Chalcis, Agrippa II became the most prominent figure of the Herodian house and, it could in fact be said, the only member of the family who continued to display an active interest in everything which concerned the Jewish policy of the

---

[1] *Ant.* xix, 362; *War* ii, 220.

Roman government. His intervention was particularly necessary after the disturbances under the procuratorship of Cumanus. His efforts again bore fruit and the dispute between Jews and Samaritans was decided in favour of the Jews (see below p. 365). While active in Rome in this affair he was already ruling Chalcis, although it is not clear whether he had already been granted the royal title.[1] Thus commenced Agrippa's career as client ruler in the Roman Empire—a career that lasted over forty years. Changes took place in the territorial extent of his kingdom some time afterwards, when Claudius granted Agrippa Philip's previous tetrarchy, which had constituted the original nucleus of the kingdom of Agrippa I. Chalcis, on the other hand, was now removed from his rule (53/4 C.E.).[2]

Agrippa's kingdom grew considerably at the beginning of Nero's reign (54-5 C.E.). It now included several of the chief Jewish centres in Galilee and Peraea: Tiberias, Tarichaeae, Julias and Abila.[3] In this way Agrippa became king of a large Jewish population which constituted a considerable percentage of the total Jewish population of Palestine. Although Agrippa II never attained the degree of political influence and prestige reached by his father and by Herod Antipas, he was nevertheless henceforward one of the more important of the allied kings under Rome. At the beginning of Nero's reign, when war with Parthia was imminent, Agrippa, like Antiochus of Commagene, was requested to furnish military aid to the Empire.[4] Like his father, Agrippa formed ties with other sovereigns of the Roman east, added by his sisters whom he endeavoured to marry into the families of these rulers. The hoped-for marriage of his sister Drusilla to Epiphanes, son of King Antiochus, did not, indeed, take place, since Antiochus' son refused to adopt Judaism, but Azizus ruler of Emesa consented to conversion. This marriage was ended by the liason between Drusilla and Felix. Berenice, Drusilla's elder sister,

---

[1] *Ant.* xx, 104; *War* ii, 223. The sources differ as to the order of events. On 49 C.E. as the year in which Agrippa II began to rule, see H. Seyrig, *Revue numismatique* (1964), p. 59. The appointment of Agrippa II as ruler of Chalcis underlies the era of 49 C.E.

[2] *Ant.* xx, 138.

[3] *Ant.* xx, 159; *War* ii, 252; these events are mistakenly dated to 61 C.E. by Schürer i (3rd Ger. ed.), p. 588, n. 7; Rosenberg, *PW* x, col. 147. The incorporation of these territories into the kingdom of Agrippa should be related to the era of 56 C.E. known from the coins. See Th. Frankfort, *Hommages à Albert Grenier* (1962), pp. 662-3. Seyrig, op.cit., p. 63 holds the view that Agrippa became king only in 56 C.E., till then bearing only the title of tetrarch.

[4] Tacitus, *Annals* xiii, 7.

married Polemo, King of Cilicia, though this marriage also did not last.[1]

True to the Herodian tradition, Agrippa II was the benefactor of non-Jewish cities outside the country. We know more especially of his contacts with the city of Berytus, where he built a theatre and which he lavishly adorned. To express his loyalty to the Emperor he changed the name of his capital, Caesarea Philippi, to Neronias.[2]

The population of Agrippa's kingdom was mixed and much flexibility was needed to keep the peace. Like Agrippa's army, his administrative staff was composed of Jews as well as gentiles. The Jewish settlers from Babylonia were noted for their loyalty to Agrippa, but during the Great Revolt their loyalty, too, was severely tested and some of them joined the revolt. Agrippa was bound by close ties to Berenice, his eldest sister.[3] She was married three times, first to Marcus, son of the Jewish alabarch of Alexandria, and then two kings, Herod of Chalcis (her uncle), and Polemo of Cilicia. But in the eyes of both the Jewish and the non-Jewish public she was chiefly linked with her bachelor brother and this was even the cause of scandal.[4] Berenice was also the owner of landed estates, but it seems that most of them were the common property of herself and her brother.[5] Although Agrippa was not king of Judaea itself, his status in Jerusalem was important. This was to some extent officially confirmed by Rome, since after the death of Herod of Chalcis Agrippa was entrusted with the appointment of the high priests and the effectual supervision of the Temple and its maintenance. He and Berenice were frequent visitors to Jerusalem, where they resided at the palace of the Hasmonaeans. At times Agrippa II offended public opinion in Jerusalem (see below p. 369) and his intimates, such as Costobar and Saul, took part in the disturbances which broke out in the city in the last years before its fall. Notwithstanding, Agrippa retained his place as the first-ranking Jewish personality from the point of view of the Roman power.

[1] Jos. Ant. xx, 139; 145-6.
[2] Ant. xx, 211; yet it is doubtful whether this change bears any relation to the era of 61 c.e. See Seyrig, op.cit., p. 64.
[3] Berenice is mentioned first among the daughters of Agrippa I; she was sixteen years old at his death (Ant. xix, 354). See G. H. Macurdy, AJPh (1935), pp. 246-253; E. Mireaux, La reine Bérénice (1951); J. A. Crook, AJPh (1951), pp. 162-175; cf. also the Athenian inscription IG ii, 2nd edition, no. 3449.
[4] Jos. Ant. xx, 145; Juvenal vi, 156-8.
[5] On the property of Berenice and Agrippa see Jos. Life, 119; War ii, 595. In general see Alt, Kleine Schriften ii, p. 389.

The Jewish Revolt placed Agrippa in an extremely difficult position. Both he and Berenice made many efforts to calm tempers in Jerusalem, and Agrippa sent a force of cavalry under Philip, son of Iacimus, to aid the opponents of the rising in the capital; its attempt to stop the rebels ended in complete failure. Agrippa was subsequently among the allied kings who placed their military forces at the disposal of Cestius Gallus, the governor of Syria, in his march upon the capital, but the failure of the expedition, which brought with it the complete collapse of Roman authority in Judaea, also led to revolt in the Jewish parts of Agrippa's kingdom.

Tiberias and Tarichaeae rose against Agrippa, and the Jewish inhabitants of Gaulanitis (including Gamala) and of Peraea also broke off connections with Agrippa's government. Furthermore some of Agrippa's own forces deserted to the rebels. One of his most intimate aides, Philip, son of Iacimus, was suspected of temporary collaboration with the insurgents in Jerusalem, and this was later used as a pretext for making charges against Agrippa himself.[1]

The attempt made by Agrippa to suppress the rising in his kingdom before the arrival of Vespasian failed utterly. His forces did indeed lay siege to Gamala, but the fortress was not taken. Further, despite the contacts established by Agrippa with his supporters in Tiberias, he did not succeed in saving the town for his cause. On Vespasian's appearance in the East, Agrippa joined him at Antioch. He was one of the four allied kings to send armies to aid the Romans (two thousand archers and one thousand cavalry); he himself took an active part in the fighting, helped to force the surrender of Tiberias and was wounded in the siege of Gamala.[2]

The changes which took place in the Roman Empire with the death of Nero and the accession of Galba impelled Agrippa to go home, and he was in the capital throughout the struggle between Otho and Vitellius; he returned to the East after secret emissaries had informed him of events there, and the possible rise of Vespasian, for whom his sister Berenice was working very actively.[3]

On his return to Palestine Agrippa continued to aid the Romans in their war in Judaea and when the revolt had been suppressed received a considerable addition to his kingdom, which now extended far

---

[1] Jos. *Life*, 407. A. Baerwald, *Josephus in Galiläa* (1877), p. 38, thinks that Agrippa's loyalty to the Romans was not above suspicion. It seems, however, that there is not much to buttress this supposition.

[2] Jos. *Life*, 352; *War* IV, 14.

[3] Tacitus, *Historiae* II, 81.

northward to include, for example, Arca, north-east of Tripolis, although it is possible that he lost some of the Jewish portions of his kingdom.[1] Agrippa was further honoured with the *ornamenta praetoria*.[2] It is also to be assumed that the liaison which now developed between Titus and Berenice assisted the consolidation of Agrippa's position. Berenice herself took up permanent residence in Rome in 75 C.E., where she remained until 79, exercising great influence at the time. She was compelled to quit the city at the very end of Vespasian's life by pressure of Roman public opinion, returning to Rome after the accession of Titus to the imperial throne, but public opinion was so hostile to a possible marriage between Titus and Berenice that the Emperor found it necessary to send her away.[3] Agrippa II continued in power during most of Domitian's reign; it is clear that he was still ruling in October of 92, but it would seem that he was no longer king when Domitian died, though a newly-found inscription calls for a reappraisal of the problem.[4] His kingdom was annexed directly to the Roman Empire, and the task which the Herodian family had fulfilled in Jewish history thereby came to an end.

BIBLIOGRAPHY

SCHÜRER, VERMES, MILLAR, *The History of the Jewish People in the Age of Jesus Christ* I (1973), pp. 267-357, 442-454, 471-483 is very valuable for its clear statement of the facts; especially important is its chronological framework of the reign of Herod. H. GRAETZ, *Geschichte der Juden* III, 5th ed., 1905, pp. 189-253 and pp. 317-363, contains a vivid narra-

---

[1] Jos. *War* VII, 97.
[2] Dio Cassius LXVI, 15,4.
[3] On Berenice's sojourn at Rome see above all Crook, op.cit. There are two stages of Berenice's activity at Rome, as may be seen from Dio Cassius LXVI, 15,3-4; 18,1. Cf. also Quintilianus, *Institutio oratoria* IV, 1,19; Suetonius, *Titus*, 7,2; *Epitome de Caesaribus*, 10,4,7.
[4] It follows from the inscription of Aere (*OGIS*, no. 426) that Agrippa was still reigning in 92 C.E. From the inscription from Sueida (in M. Dunand, *Musée de Soueida* (1934), p. 49, no. 75), to be dated to the sixteenth year of Domitian, it may be surmised that at the time of Domitian's death the latest Agrippa was no longer reigning. Since we read in Photius, *Biblioth. cod.* 33, p. 6b that Agrippa II died in the third year of Trajan, it is left for us either to reject the information supplied by Photius (so e.g. T. Frankfort, *Revue belge de philologie et d'histoire* (1961), pp. 52-8; H. Petersen, *AJPh* (1958), p. 262, n. 15), or to suppose that he ceased to be king some years before his death. A new inscription dated 108 C.E. and relating to a former officer of Agrippa II who later served under Trajan (see H. Seyrig, *Syria* (1965), pp. 31-4) does not prove that Agrippa continued to reign until the time of Trajan. Cf. also p. 21, n. 2.

tive tinged with a Jewish national point of view. The same may be said of J. KLAUSNER, *History of the Second Temple* (in Hebrew) IV, 1950. W. OTTO, *Herodes, Beiträge zur Geschichte des letzten jüdischen Königshauses*, 1913, is a first-rate scholarly contribution, objective and reflecting the author's wide knowledge of the Hellenistic and Roman world. Its only weakness lies in his views on the sources underlying Josephus (the 'Anonymous Theory'). H. WILLRICH, *Das Haus des Herodes*, 1929, partakes of the nature of a panegyric. As usual, Willrich displays an anti-Jewish bias. A. MOMIGLIANO in *CAH* X, 1934, pp. 316-337 presents an admirably succinct account of Herod's reign. A. H. M. JONES, *The Herods of Judaea*, 1938, is a popular history of the Herodian dynasty, well-written and accurate. Other popular volumes are S. PEROWNE, *The Life and Times of Herod the Great*, 1957, and *The Later Herods*, 1958, and M. GRANT, *Herod the Great*, 1971. F. M. ABEL, *Histoire de la Palestine* I, 1952, pp. 324-406 is interesting above all for the building operations of Herod. A. SCHALIT, *König Herodes, der Mann und sein Werk* (translated from the Hebrew edition of 1960, 1969), constitutes the most circumstantial study of the reign of Herod and places it within the framework of the Mediterranean world under the Principate of Augustus. H. W. HOEHNER, *Herod Antipas*, 1972, is fundamental for all problems connected with Herod Antipas. For the reign of Agrippa I one should add E. CIACERI, in *Processi politici e relazioni internazionali*, 1918, pp. 319-362; and for that of Agrippa II, TH. FRANKFORT, 'Le royaume d'Agrippa II et son annexion par Domitien', *Hommages à Albert Grenier*, 1962, pp. 659-672; H. SEYRIG, 'Les ères d'Agrippa I', *Revue numismatique*, 6th series, 1964.

APPENDIX

ANTONY'S GIFTS TO CLEOPATRA

The exact dating of Antony's territorial grants to Cleopatra, which included areas detached from Herod's kingdom, is a subject of controversy. Plutarch speaks of these transfers after reporting the Tarentum agreement (autumn 37 B.C.E.) and before describing the Parthian campaign of 36, i.e. he dates them in effect to the winter of 37-36 B.C.E.[1] Among the Jewish areas Plutarch mentions the district in which opobalsam trees were grown, i.e. the district of Jericho. Another source relating to Antony's grants is Dio Cassius,[2] who reports the

[1] *Life of Antony*, 36,3.
[2] XLIX, 32,5.

cession of parts of the kingdoms of Malchus, of the Ituraeans and many areas that had belonged to Phoenicia, Palestine and Crete, likewise of Cyrene and Cyprus, to the children of Antony and Cleopatra. Dio Cassius also undoubtedly dates this event to the year 36 B.C.E. but whereas Plutarch speaks of it before the expedition against the Parthians, Dio Cassius mentions it after that event. This may be explained by the fact that Cassius arranges his matter for a given year according to subjects, not in chronological order.[1] Porphyrius also connects Antony's grants to Cleopatra with the year 36 B.C.E., but speaks only of Chalcis.[2]

Josephus in his *War* writes in a general manner of Antony's gifts to Cleopatra, noting explicitly that the opobalsam plantation at Jericho was one of the areas so donated.[3] But he also says that she obtained all the cities south of the River Eleutheros except Tyre and Sidon. This is related in the *War* after the report of the death of Antigonus[4] and before Antony's Armenian campaign (34 B.C.E.).[5]

Josephus discusses this episode in greater detail in the *Antiquities*. He first mentions gifts to Cleopatra in Coele-Syria, but then relates Cleopatra's demand for Judaea and Arabia.[6] Antony refused her request, but nevertheless detached certain areas from the two kingdoms and handed them over to her. He further granted to her, according to the account in the *Antiquities*, the cities between the Eleutheros and Egypt. Josephus does not specify which areas were detached from Judaea, but further on observes[6] that Herod leased from Cleopatra the region of Jericho, which, in other words, then no longer belonged to his kingdom.

The *terminus ante quem* of Antony's grants in the *Antiquities* is again, as in the *War*, his Armenian campaign (34 B.C.E.). The *terminus post quem* is the murder of Aristobulus (end of 35 B.C.E.) and the meeting between Herod and Antony (beginning of 34 B.C.E.). A contradiction is thus created between the chronologies of Plutarch and Dio Cassius, and perhaps also of Porphyrius, on the one hand, and that of the *Antiquities* on the other. Josephus also suggests that Antony's grants of Jewish territory were not limited to the Jericho region, but included other cities, such as Samaria, Joppa, and Gaza, which belonged to

---

[1] W. W. Tarn, *JRS* (1932), p. 145; L. Craven, *Antony's Oriental Policy until the Defeat of the Parthian Expedition* (1920), p. 70 n. 27 prefers the relative chronology of Dio Cassius to that of Plutarch.
[2] Jacoby, *FGH* II B, 260 F 2 (17), p. 1203.
[3] I, 361. [4] I, 357. [5] I, 363. [6] xv, 79. [7] xv, 88-95. [8] xv, 96.

Herod at the beginning of his reign and were restored to him subsequently by Octavian after the battle of Actium,[1] since the only explanation of Octavian's having to restore them to Herod must be that they had been taken away by Antony. It may also be supposed that some of these places were included among the towns between Egypt and the Eleutheros which were granted by Antony to Cleopatra according to the Jewish historian.

As regards Antony's grants, including those affecting the state of Judaea, some scholars prefer the date deducible from Plutarch and Dio Cassius (36 B.C.E.). The principal arguments against Josephus have been set forth by Kromayer.[2] Others however, defend Josephus' chronology.[3] Dobiáš in particular has brought forward strong arguments against Kromayer's view. It is nevertheless difficult to give Josephus decided preference, just as it is difficult to accord it to Plutarch and to Dio Cassius. I do not think that Antony's grant of territory to Cleopatra was done all at once, and steps in this direction may have been taken both in 36 and 34 B.C.E. Jericho may have been taken from Herod as early as 36 B.C.E., whereas the coastal towns, for instance (Gaza, Joppa), may have been taken only in 34 B.C.E.

---

[1] *War* I, 396; *Ant.* XV, 217.
[2] J. Kromayer, *Hermes* (1894), pp. 571-585; Otto, op.cit., 45, n.1.
[3] Schürer I (3rd Ger. ed.), p. 362, n. 5; J. Dobiáš, *Annuaire de l'institut de philologie et d'histoire orientales et slaves* II (1934, Mélanges Bidez), pp. 287-314; Buchheim, op.cit., pp. 68-74; V. Gardthausen, *Neue Jahrbücher für das klassische Altertum* (1917), pp. 164-5; T. Rice-Holmes, *The Architect of the Roman Empire I* (1928), p. 228, n. 11; K. W. Meiklejohn, *JRS* (1934), p. 191, n. 3; H. U. Instinsky, *Studies presented to David M. Robinson* II (1953), pp. 975-9.

Chapter Six
The Province of Judaea

The inauguration and character of the province of Judaea

Judaea passed through various phases before its final annexation to the Roman Empire. The rule of Herod's descendants was the last phase prior to the constitution of Judaea as a Roman province. The removal of Archelaus from his position as ethnarch of Judaea, Samaria and Idumaea (in 6 C.E.) opened a new chapter in the relations between the Jews and the Roman Empire, and administrative structures were then created which determined the political position of the majority of the Jewish people down to the Great Revolt. The population of Judaea was now included within the territory of a new Roman province headed by a Roman governor of equestrian rank. The continuity of this régime was broken only for the few years in which the entire country was united within the realm of Agrippa I.

The large Jewish population in Galilee and Transjordan was assigned to the tetrarchy of Herod Antipas until his deposition in 39 C.E., and from that year on came under the rule of Agrippa I. Under the first Roman governors therefore two of the chief components of the Jewish population (in Galilee and Peraea) were outside the sphere of of direct Roman rule. At this time (till the year 34 C.E.), Philip, Herod's other son, continued to rule the north-eastern areas. After his death Philip's tetrarchy was annexed for several years to the province of Syria, until in 37 it was awarded to the new King Agrippa. It was the first part of Palestine to be assigned to him.

But the administrative unity of Jewish Palestine, restored by Agrippa, also persisted after his death in 44 C.E.; for on the reconstitution of the provincial régime the Jews of Peraea and Galilee, together with the inhabitants of Judaea, passed under the rule of the Roman procurator. In 55 C.E. Tiberias, Tarichaeae and parts of Peraea were attached to the kingdom of Agrippa II; nevertheless it may be stated that from 44 C.E. the greater part of the Jews of the country were under direct Roman rule; thus the administrative unity of Herod's kingdom in the year 4 B.C.E. was in a measure restored.

The deposition and exile of Archelaus occurred in a period in which the system of allied client kings was still being maintained side by side with that of direct annexation and organisation under the régime of a province. The Roman princeps therefore had several choices. He could impose the task of ruling Judaea on one of the members of the Herodian family, which was what Augustus had actually done with Judaea so far; but it would seem to have been impossible to proceed further in this fashion, on account of the unpopularity of the House of Herod in Judaea itself, resulting from the Jews' experience under Herod and his son Archelaus. Augustus found no member of the family capable of maintaining order in Judaea without infuriating its inhabitants. He therefore decided to place Judaea under direct Roman rule for the first time in its history. This seemed to him good policy since as early as the time of Herod's death, Jewish representatives had implored him not to leave power in the hands of Herod's sons.[1] But the inclusion of Judaea under a provincial régime could be implemented in several different ways. The simplest way, on the face of it, was to annex the ethnarchy of Archelaus to the neighbouring province of Syria.

Archelaus' ethnarchy was too small to demand the creation of an independent province, and the Syrian governors had supervised affairs in Judaea even in Herod's time. But weighty considerations prevented such a step throughout the period of Roman rule in Judaea, Roman policy being primarily influenced by the peculiar character of the Jewish population, its religion and its past, which were so different from those of the population of Syria as a whole. This situation demanded a special attitude and the Roman rulers never ignored the problem and never made Judaea an integral part of Syria, though they altered the form of government in Judaea more than once.

Augustus, therefore, saw no alternative to setting up Judaea as an independent province. The general arrangements made by Augustus for the Empire as a whole are known.[2] The Senate sent governors to a portion of the provinces, particularly to those not exposed to serious danger from without. Others in which a considerable legionary force was stationed and whose position obliged a maximum military preparedness, were under the Emperor's direct surveillance. Provinces of this class received *legati pro praetore* representing the princeps,

---

[1] Jos. *Ant.* XVII, 314; *War* II, 90-1; a similar wish of most of the inhabitants of Cilicia and Commagene is related by Tacitus, *Annals* II, 42.
[2] Strabo, *Geography* XVII, 3,25, p. 840; cf. Dio Cassius LIII, 12.

but members of the senatorial order. Such a province was Syria, over which a governor was appointed by the Emperor from among those who had already served as consuls. But a third type of province existed, also under direct imperial responsibility, to which the Emperor sent governors belonging not to the senatorial but to the equestrian order. This accorded with the general process in the Roman Empire whereby a general upgrading of the equestrian order was taking place on the administrative ladder, and its influence was increasing. The most important of the provinces controlled by equestrian governors was undoubtedly Egypt, whose geographical position, convenient for defence against enemies, fertility and time-honoured centralistic organization endowed it with a special status.

Augustus and his successors, apprehensive of dispatching governors of senatorial rank to the Nile Valley, preferred to send governors of equestrian rank (*praefecti*), who also commanded a Roman legionary force.[1] But all the other provinces where equestrian governors ruled were inferior to Egypt in strength, size and wealth; among them was Judaea.[2] Another province belonging to the category was Cappadocia, which was classed as an equestrian province under Tiberius after having been previously maintained as a client kingdom. In the same year (6 C.E.) that Augustus inaugurated the province of Judaea, he introduced changes into the government of Sardinia, which for the next sixty years was under equestrian governors.[3] Other provinces of the same status in the Julio-Claudian period were Thrace, Mauretania and Raetia.

With the exception of Egypt, these provinces had the following common features: they were ruled by knights, no legionary force was stationed in them, and the imperial authorities saw no need to send them a senatorial governor, either because of the special character of these areas, or for reasons of economy.[4] Though the decision taken

---

[1] On the special status of Egypt under the Roman Empire see A. Piganiol, *Museum Helveticum* x, (1953), pp. 193-202.

[2] See the list of equestrian provinces in O. Hirschfeld, *Die kaiserlichen Verwaltungsbeamten bis auf Diocletian* (1905), pp. 371-6. See also Tacitus, *Historiae* I, 11,2: 'Duae Mauretaniae, Raetia, Noricum, Thracia et quae aliae procuratoribus cohibentur.'

[3] On Cappadocia see W. E. Gwatkin, *Cappadocia as a Roman Procuratorial Province*, The University of Missouri Studies v (1930), no. 4, pp. 17-62; on Sardinia see P. Meloni, *L'amministrazione della Sardegna da Augusto all' invasione vandalica* (1958).

[4] The principle suggested for the creation of procuratorial provinces by P. Horovitz, *Revue de Philologie* (1939), pp. 47-65; pp. 218-237, namely that they

at Rome to make Judaea an independent province was due to the peculiar character of the population, it was not thought necessary to dispatch thither a force composed of legionary troops; a force based on auxiliary troops (*auxilia*) seemed quite adequate to safeguard security and order in the new province. As a country surrounded by other Roman provinces and client states of the Empire it was not threatened by danger from external enemies. In view of the fact that the Roman Empire frequently suffered from shortage of manpower for the legions, the detachment of a legion to Judaea would have seemed an unreasonable waste of Roman military power. The removal of Archelaus had been accompanied by no disorders in Judaea, and had even been received with a considerable measure of satisfaction. The tension reigning during the census of Quirinius could be regarded merely as a transitory phenomenon. Augustus could certainly anticipate that quiet would prevail in Judaea in the immediate future, and that the auxiliary force would be sufficient to keep order in the new province. In the event of a serious crisis it was possible to summon aid from Syria.

It would further seem that the rule of equestrian governors involved smaller financial expenditure. Whether Augustus believed that this sort of régime would also prevent friction between the Jews and the authorities and would involve less interference in the internal life of the ruled, is hard to say. At all events, it is doubtful whether the developments of the next few decades justified these hopes. An important problem arises in connection with the relation between the province of Judaea, ruled by an equestrian governor, and the province of Syria ruled by a governor of senatorial rank (*legatus pro praetore*). In the Julio-Claudian period Judaea was undoubtedly already regarded as an independent province. The governors were appointed by the Emperor and enjoyed within their sphere of government all the powers enjoyed by other governors. When Josephus discusses the annexation of Archelaus' inheritance by Rome, he notes explicitly its conversion to a province.[1] Tacitus too enumerates Judaea in the clearest possible manner as a well-defined province like Syria.[2] Josephus, on the other hand, in a passage parallel to the abovementioned, expresses himself quite differently, saying that Archelaus'

all were border provinces, cannot be substantiated. See H. G. Pflaum, *Les procurateurs équestres sous le Haut-Empire romain* (1950), pp. 26-7.

[1] Josephus, *War* II, 117.
[2] *Annals* II, 42,5; cf. *Historiae* V, 9,3; Suetonius, *Life of Claudius*, 28.

territory was annexed to Syria.[1] In effect he means the same when he says that Judaea became an annex of Syria,[2] and Tacitus writes in one place, when treating of the events of 49 C.E.,[3] that the Ituraeans and Jews were transferred to Syria after the death of Kings Sohaemus and Agrippa. We have moreover a series of concrete instances in which the governors of Syria intervened in the internal affairs of Judaea, removed governors from office and were regarded by the people in Judaea as a higher instance to which complaint could be addressed concerning the governors of Judaea.

Immediately upon the inauguration of the province of Judaea the Syrian governor Quirinius was sent to hold a census and 'Coponius was sent with him', i.e. as governor of Judaea.[4] After the brutalities of Pilate, the boule of Samaria directed a complaint to Vitellius, governor of Syria, who sent Marcellus to replace Pilate, ordering the governor to proceed to Rome to render an account of his acts to the Emperor. Pilate obeyed Vitellius' order 'because it was impossible to oppose it'.[5] On the same occasion Vitellius intervened in the internal affairs of Judaea to abolish the market and purchase tax, also permitting himself to make changes in the high priesthood and to administer to the people the oath of allegiance to the new Emperor Gaius Caligula. Again, when Gaius tried to force the people to accept an image in the Temple, the implementation of the task was imposed upon the Syrian governor Petronius. Nor did the Syrian governor's interference in the affairs of Judaea cease in the reign of Agrippa I, and it was Petronius' successor, Vibius Marsus, who dispersed the conference of kings held at Tiberias on Agrippa's initiative. This situation persisted under the last procurators of Judaea. When in the period of Fadus' administration suspicion arose that disorders might break out in Jerusalem, Cassius Longinus, the Syrian governor, also appeared there; and the Jews addressed their petitions to him, as they had previously addressed them to the procurator of Judaea.

As a striking example of the action of the governor of Syria as the higher authority in Judaean affairs, may be cited the action of the

---

[1] Jos. *Ant.* XVII, 355.
[2] *Ant.* XVIII, 2; this is proved by *Ant.* XVIII, 252; XIX, 274.
[3] *Annals* XII, 23. We cannot accept the interpretation put forward by E. Schwartz, *Gesammelte Schriften* v (1963), pp. 152-3, according to which Judaea proper, in contrast to Galilee and Samaria, was directly incorporated into the province of Syria. See also Momigliano, pp. 389-390.
[4] Jos. *Ant.* XVIII, 2; XVII, 355.
[5] *Ant.* XVIII, 89.

Syrian governor Ummidius Quadratus during the riots which took place between Jews and Samaritans when Cumanus was governor of Judaea (48-52 C.E.). The Samaritan leaders appealed to Quadratus, complaining of the Jews. He came to the country, punished the leaders of the Jewish rebels and sent the leading figures in Jewish public life to Rome. He also dispatched thither the Roman officer Celer, who was involved in the affair. According to Tacitus the Emperor granted Quadratus the right to decide matters affecting the procurators, and the court convened by Quadratus also found Cumanus guilty.[1] During the misrule of Florus, the last procurator before the Revolt, although the Jews did not dare to send a delegation to Cestius Gallus, governor of Syria, to complain of his actions, they voiced their complaints to him when he was staying in Jerusalem.

We therefore behold the nearly constant phenomenon of the intervention of Syrian governors in the affairs of Judaea; they intervened, as is well demonstrated, both under the first governors and the last, and the reign of Agrippa I is not exceptional from this point of view. In several cases the intervention may be explained in terms of special authority granted to the governor by the Emperor. Quirinius may be assumed to have received *ad hoc* authority to carry out the census in Judaea before the provincial régime had crystallized, while his appointment of a high priest can also be interpreted as a way of fulfilling his task, which was to make a general settlement of Judaean affairs. It can of course be remarked that Vitellius was not an ordinary governor of Syria but by way of being a supreme inspector general appointed by the Emperor over all the countries of the Roman East;[2] Quadratus, moreover, received special authorization to set up a court to judge Cumanus. Nonetheless, instances of intervention remain which cannot be explained by special authorization.[3]

It is quite clear that from a military point of view the auxiliary forces (*auxilia*) stationed in Judaea were not sufficient to suppress serious revolts and riots in Judaea; their failure in times of crisis might have

---

[1] *Annals* XII, 54,4.
[2] *Annals* VI, 32,3.
[3] The independence of the governors of procuratorial rank is emphasized by P. Horovitz, *Revue belge de Philologie et d'Histoire* XVII (1938), pp. 53-62; pp. 775-792. On the other hand, Hirschfeld, op.cit., pp. 407-8 pointed out the close relationship between the governors of Syria and Judaea. Cf. also Pflaum, op.cit., pp. 146-9, who distinguishes between the independence of the procuratorial governors in matters of law and administration and their dependence in military matters. See also S. Safrai, *Zion* XXVII, pp. 216-222, on the relations between the governors of Judaea and Syria after the destruction of the Temple.

been anticipated. From this point of view at least, the establishment of Judaea as a separate province was not justified by the course of the events. The governor of Judaea in time of serious threat was in effect dependent for military assistance on the governor at Antioch. Since the reactions of the Jewish population to the administrative and financial arrangements and doubtless to acts which affected matters of religion and cult, could sometimes be of great significance from a military angle, the governor of Judaea was in any case obliged, whenever he took decisions, to weigh, at least to a certain degree, what was likely to be the attitude of the Syrian governor. In this context it should also be noticed that the Syrian governor was not just governor of a province and the commander of a large legionary force, but was generally regarded as the most distinguished governor in the Roman Empire, holding the highest charge.[1] From Tiberius' time a powerful army of four legions was at his disposal, in addition to all the auxiliary forces and those of the client kings. He was rightly regarded as the supreme commander of the Roman Orient, responsible for the Euphrates frontier. To this post ex-consuls were appointed from among the most distinguished personalities of the Empire, men of the type of Vitellius, Petronius and Corbulo. It is clear that these men quite overshadowed the equestrian governors ruling Judaea, and in consequence of Judaea's military dependence on Syria, and sometimes also in consequence of the special powers granted to governors of Syria in respect of the neighbouring areas, the province of Judaea could be viewed as a mere annex of the province of Syria.

On the other hand, in view of the independence left to the governor of Judaea in internal affairs (jurisdiction, finance), we cannot hold that in the Julio-Claudian period Judaea was part of Syria administratively, or that the governor of Judaea was continually and effectively subject to the instructions of the Syrian legate.

Only governors of special official standing, such as Vitellius, could remove or elevate governors of Judaea when they thought the situation required it. It should further be noted that the relative strengths of the governors of Syria and Judaea was sometimes influenced by accidental circumstances and personal ties. The standing of procurators such as Felix and Florus was to a large extent assured by the connections they possessed with distinguished elements in Rome itself. It must also be remembered that Pilate was removed by Vitellius a number of years after the fall of his alleged benefactor Sejanus.

[1] R. Syme, *Tacitus* I (1958), p. 442.

The Great Revolt proved that the régime of the procuratorial province was not to be perpetuated on Judaean territory and that the stationing there of auxiliary units was inadequate for the preservation of safety and order. At the siege of Jerusalem four legions were involved (the Fifth, Tenth, Fifteenth and Twelfth), in addition to *vexillationes* and various auxiliary troops. It was therefore decided to keep a legionary force in Judaea after the final suppression of the revolt and to convert Judaea into a regular imperial province, governed by a member of the senatorial order, holding the title of *legatus Augusti pro praetore provinciae Iudaeae*.[1] The Tenth Legion was used to garrison Judaea, and the governor also acted as commander of the legion.[2]

The status of the governors and their relations with the central government and with the ruled

What, initially, was the official title of the governor of Judaea? Opinions were divided on this subject till recently. Most scholars believed that throughout the period from the inauguration of the province down to the Great Revolt, his title was that of procurator. Others, however, distinguished between the period before and after Agrippa I. According to this view the title of the governor in the first period was praefectus, which became procurator only from Claudius' time onward in accordance with the general development of administrative terminology throughout the Empire. The two titles are well known to us already from the republican period.[3] The princeps needed both prefects and procurators from the start. The clear function of the latter included management of the emperor's estates and supervision of the revenues in the various imperial provinces. On the other hand we have reliable testimony, from Augustus' time and down to the first years of Claudius, that the title of praefectus was the accepted title of governors of provinces administered by men of equestrian order.[4] The effective change took place only under

[1] *ILS* nos 1035-6; 1056; *L'année épigraphique* (1934), no. 177; (1957), no. 336; *IEJ* (1969), p. 225. See the list of the governors in Schürer I, pp. 515-9; cf. also E. M. Smallwood, *JRS* (1962), pp. 131-3; H. G. Pflaum, *IEJ* (1969), pp. 230-1. W. Eck, *Senatoren von Vespasian bis Hadrian* (1970), pp. 93-111.
[2] In the inscriptions also the *legatus pro praetore* of Judaea appears as the commander of the Tenth Legion.
[3] C. Nicolet, *Mélanges d'archéologie, d'épigraphie et d'histoire offerts à Jérôme Carcopino* (1966), pp. 691-709.
[4] See Hirschfeld, op.cit., pp. 384-5; A. N. Sherwin White, *Papers of the British*

Claudius, when the title of procurator replaced that of prefect, although we see from the epigraphical material that the latter still remained attached to the governor of Sardinia under Vespasian, as a title secondary to that of procurator, apparently to emphasize the military powers of the procurator.[1] The literary sources which deal with Judaea are not precise in their use of the official terminology and use different titles indiscriminately. The title of procurator appears both in its Greek (ἐπίτροπος) and in its Latin form (procurator), which is also true of the period preceding the reign of Agrippa I,[2] while on the other hand the Greek translation of the term praefectus (ἔπαρχος) appears frequently even after Claudius' time.[3] But the inscription discovered in the theatre of Caesarea, which gives Pontius Pilate the title of praefectus Iudaeae, is decisive in favour of the assumption that praefectus was the official title of the first governors of Judaea. The text of the inscription as restored by Degrassi is as follows:[4]

(Dis Augusti)s Tiberieum
(—Po)ntius Pilatus
(praef)ectus Iuda(ea)e
(fecit, d)e(dicavit)

Since Pilate's title of praefectus fits in well with the general development in the Empire, there is now no longer room for doubt regarding the official title of the governor of Judaea, and it is to be assumed that those literary sources which call the first governors 'procurators' are transferring the later terminology to an earlier period. A general change took place under Claudius and from then on 'procurator' became the term applied to all the governors of provinces ruled by knights, and is mentioned in the official letter sent by Claudius to the city of Jerusalem.[5] The governors of Judaea belonged to the Roman order of equites.

School at Rome 1939, p. 12, n. 7; A. H. M. Jones, Studies in Roman Government and Law (1960), pp. 115-125.
[1] ILS nos 1358-9.
[2] Tacitus, Annals xv, 44; Jos. War II, 117; 169.
[3] Ant. XIX, 363; XX, 193; 197.
[4] A. Degrassi, Atti della Accademia Nazionale dei Lincei, Rendiconti (1964), pp. 59-65; the inscription was first published by A. Frova, Istituto Lombardo, Rendiconti, (1961), pp. 419-34. Cf. B. Lifshitz, Latomus (1963), p. 783; H. Volkmann, Gymnasium (1968), pp. 124-135; L'année épigraphique (1964), p. 18, no. 39; E. Weber, Bonner Jahrbücher (1971), pp. 194-200.
[5] Jos. Ant. xx, 14.

As far as we know, there was only one exception, the freedman Felix who served as governor in the years 52-60 C.E. Felix was appointed to his post under Claudius, whose reign was the golden age of Roman freedmen, when they reached the highest grades of the imperial administration. Felix was also the brother of Pallas, who served the Emperor as supervisor of finances (*a rationibus*). It must also be remembered that Felix was supported initially by influential circles among the Jews themselves (see below pp. 324). There are also some grounds for supposing that he was elevated to the rank of Roman knight before his appointment, although we have a number of cases which prove that freedmen reached high grades in the provincial administration in the Julio-Claudian era.[1]

The position of governor of Judaea did not belong, however, to the first stages in the administrative career of a Roman knight. A person appointed to a post of this type was doubtless a man with previous military and administrative experience.[2] We know something of the administrative record, or of the further progress in the *cursus*, of only a few of the governors of Judaea before their sojourn in the country. One of them is Tiberius Alexander, the son of an illustrious Jewish family of Alexandria, who served as procurator in the years 46-48 C.E. Before coming to Judaea he officiated as governor (ἐπιστράτηγος) of the Thebais in southern Egypt.[3] His procuratorship in Judaea proved to be a springboard to a higher rank, since in 66 C.E. we encounter him as prefect of Egypt. Another procurator of Judaea of whose administrative career we know something is Lucceius Albinus (62-64 C.E.). Like Tiberius Alexander he seems to have performed administrative tasks in Egypt, and we find him in later years as procurator of Mauretania.[4] Felix may have performed administrative

---

[1] The view that Felix got equestrian status is expressed for instance by A. Stein, *Der römische Ritterstand* (1927), p. 114; P. R. C. Weaver, *Historia* (1965), p. 466. It is opposed by F. Millar, *Historia* (1964), p. 182, n. 13. As examples of freedmen fulfilling important tasks in the provincial administration we may cite Hiberus, prefect of Egypt (Dio Cassius LVIII, 19,6) and Licinus, financial procurator of Gaul (Dio Cassius LIV, 21). See also P. A. Brunt, *Latomus* (1966), pp. 461-2; W. Orth, *Die Provinzialpolitik des Tiberius* (1970), p. 55.

[2] On all these problems cf. E. Birley, *Roman Britain and the Roman Army* (1953), pp. 133-153; H. G. Pflaum, *PW* XXIII, cols 1265-6; 1272-8.

[3] V. Burr, *Tiberius Iulius Alexander* (1955); J. Schwartz, *Annuaire de l'institut de Philologie et d'Histoire Orientales et Slaves*, (1953) pp. 591-602; E. G. Turner, *JRS* (1954), pp. 54-64; H. G. Pflaum, *Les carrières équestres sous le Haut-Empire romain* I (1960), pp. 46-9.

[4] Pflaum, op.cit., pp. 75-7; Tacitus, *Historiae* II, 58-9; on his son cf. R. Syme *Harvard Studies in Classical Philology* (1969), p. 235.

duties in Palestine before being appointed governor of Judaea in 52 C.E. (see below, p. 375). It may also be conjectured that the first governor Coponius had previously officiated in some administrative post in Syria.[1]

Distinction in previous tasks or suitable connections furnished the conditions for promotion to the rank of governor. We know that several of the governors of Judaea obtained their posts through their close connections with the ruling circles and with the imperial court in the capital. Pontius Pilate may have been instrumental in furthering the policy of Sejanus, praetorian prefect at Rome and the right-hand man of Emperor Tiberius; Felix was appointed through the influence of his brother Pallas, and with the support of Jonathan, son of Ananus, one of the leaders of the priestly oligarchy of Jerusalem The last governor before the outbreak of the Great Revolt, Gessius Florus, obtained his post thanks to the friendship prevailing between his wife Cleopatra and the Empress Poppaea Sabina.[2]

We cannot establish the origin of all the governors who ruled Judaea until the fall of Jerusalem. Generally speaking, we may note that the governors who ruled in the period preceeding Agrippa I were of Italian origin. The name of the first, Coponius, takes us to the Latin town of Tibur,[3] and the name of Pontius Pilate evokes the conjecture that he was connected with the region of Samnium.[4] The other equestrian officials officiating in Judaea at the same time, such as the procurator of the imperial estate at Jamnia, were also of Italian origin. From an inscription published in 1940, we learn that Herennius Capito, who served for many years in the above post, came from the Italian town of Teate Marrucinorum, and was appointed procurator of Jamnia under the Empress Livia, who died in the year 29 C.E.; he held his place until and after the accession of Gaius Caligula.[5] Many of the officers of the Roman forces active in the country in those years were also Italian. These facts are in keeping with the situation

[1] E. Täubler, *Klio* XVII, p. 101.
[2] Jos. *Ant.* xx, 252.
[3] R. Syme, *The Roman Revolution* (1939), pp. 193, 357.
[4] Cf. H. Peter, *Neue Jahrbücher für das klassische Altertum* XIX (1907), pp. 6-7.
[5] The inscription was first published by P. Fraccaro, *Athenaeum* (1940), pp. 136-144; cf. Pflaum, op.cit. I, pp. 23-6. Another inscription relating to the administration of Jamnia has been published by M. Avi-Yonah, *QDAP* (1946), pp. 84-5. The Mellon mentioned in it was a freedman and subprocurator of Tiberius. See Pflaum, *Les procurateurs équestres*, p. 34, n. 11. Orth, op.cit., pp. 54-5 thinks that Mellon was not a sub-procurator, but one of the successors of Capito; P. R. C. Weaver, *Familia Caesaris* (1972), p. 275.

in the Empire as a whole, for down to Claudius' reign it is hard to find holders of such posts not of Italian or Latin origin. A considerable change took place under Claudius, when the Roman administration was filled by men of Greek or oriental Greek origin. The process is reflected also in Judaea. At least three of the seven procurators who governed Judaea after the death of Agrippa I were of Greek or oriental stock. The first of them was Tiberius Julius Alexander, a Jew by extraction, who gave up his ancestral religion and became in all respects a Hellenized oriental: the Latin writers Tacitus and Juvenal regarded him as an Egyptian (*Aegyptius*)[1]. The procurator Felix was also a Greek by origin, and his brother Pallas tried to trace his genealogy to the kings of Arcadia;[2] Gessius Florus, on the other hand, came from the town of Clazomenae in western Asia Minor.[3] Men of the type of Felix and Florus, officials of inferior rank to them, and officers of the Hellenistic East, like Claudius Lysias who arrested Paul, were generally and naturally sympathetic to the Syro-Greek population and had an initial tendency to take its side in the struggle against the Jewish population. It was not without reason that Felix and Florus were considered to be the worst procurators who ever ruled Judaea, and this has to be taken into account when we describe how sharply relations between the Roman authorities and the Jewish masses deteriorated in the decades preceeding the Great Revolt.

The governor of Judaea was appointed directly by the emperor. The length of the terms of provincial governors was not settled beforehand, but was affected by several factors, such as the general policy of a given emperor with regard to the duration of the office, the governor's connections with influential elements at the imperial court, the desire to promote him in the administrative hierarchy outside Judaea, and the governor's success in maintaining peace and security in his territory, without too much gross tyranny and cruelty. The Emperor Tiberius (14-37 C.E.), for example, was known for his tendency

---

[1] Tacitus, *Historiae* I, 11; Juvenal, *Satires* I, 130.
[2] Tacitus, *Annals* XII, 53,2; see S. I. Oost, *AJPh* (1958), p. 115. The conjecture of R. Besnier, *Revue belge de Philologie et d'Histoire* XXVIII (1950), p. 454 that Pallas and Felix were Syrians is not very attractive. M. Avi-Yonah restored an inscription published by him in IEJ (1966), pp. 258-264 to imply a connection with Felix .This connection seems, however, unwarranted. Cf. *L'année épigraphique* (1967), no. 525.
[3] *Ant.* XX, 252; on the penetration of Graeco-oriental elements into the administration of the Roman Empire see G. Schumann, *Hellenistische und griechische Elemente in der Regierung Neros* (1930); Pflaum, op.cit., pp. 172-4; 206-8.

to leave the same governors in his provinces for a long period.[1] Hence the two longest governorships, those of Valerius Gratus (15-26 C.E.) and of Pontius Pilate (26-36), occurred under this emperor. Pilate might have lasted longer in his task had it not been for his cruelty and the bloodshed which he caused. These acts ultimately caused him to be removed by Vitellius, governor of Syria. The three governors appointed by Augustus ruled on an average three years each (Coponius, 6-9 C.E.; M. Ambibulus, 9-12 C.E.; Annius Rufus, 12-15 C.E.).

Of the governors after Agrippa I, Felix (52-60 C.E.) served the longest, which is to be explained by his family connections. But generally speaking the average term was two years; this was the period served by the governors Fadus (44-46 C.E.), Tiberius Alexander (46-48 C.E.), Festus (60-62 C.E.) and Albinus (62-64 C.E.). Of these five, Festus died while he was still governor. Gessius Florus' term (64-66) ended after two years with the Great Revolt. Ventidius Cumanus' term (48-52 C.E.), which was longer, was brought to an end by the disorders between the Samaritans and Jews, which caused the governor of Syria to intervene.

As regards his salary, the governor of Judaea appears to have belonged to the grade of those receiving 100,000 sestertii. When Tiberius Alexander passed from the grade of epistrategos of Thebais to that of governor of Judaea, his salary rose from 60,000 to 100,000 sestertii. The salary rate of the Judaean governors is computed on the basis of the military forces stationed in the province, as compared with those stationed in other provinces ruled by equestrian governors.[2]

In what measure were the governors of Judaea obliged to submit reports on their conduct to the emperor, and what were the lawful means by which the inhabitants of Judaea could counteract deeds of oppression and financial extortion and bring about the removal and even the punishment of brutal governors?[3]

The late republican period is conventionally regarded as a period of oppression and exploitation of the provinces, and undoubtedly the inauguration of the principate constituted a considerable improvement

---

[1] Jos. *Ant.* XVIII, 172-7; Tacitus, *Annals* I, 80. It is worthwhile comparing the rate of change in the governors of Judaea with that of the prefects of Egypt. See A. Stein, *Die Präfekten von Ägypten in der römischen Kaiserzeit* (1950), pp. 14-37.

[2] B. Dobson, in A. v. Domaszewski, *Die Rangordnung des römischen Heeres* (2nd ed., 1967), XLIV.

[3] On all these problems see P. A. Brunt, *Historia* (1961), pp. 189-227.

for the provinces, since it ended the civil wars and the blatant extortion of money which destroyed their economies.

But not everything was remedied under imperial rule. Even in the Julio-Claudian epoch the power and authority concentrated in the governor's hands were such as to enable them to behave arbitrarily, to inflict sentence of death and to exploit the population for their own material advantage. The reaction to the Roman régime in the West found expression in grave uprising (in Gaul and Britain), and documents from Egypt testify to the grinding tyranny which characterized the Julio-Claudian era. In Judaea itself such governors as Pilate, Felix, Albinus and Florus must be mentioned in this connection.

The acts of the governors could only be supervised with difficulty from the centre at Rome. Agrippa II, when endeavouring to calm the storm which had arisen in Jerusalem at the beginning of the Great Revolt, could affirm in a speech that Florus' actions were not inspired by Rome and that news of events in Judaea reached there only with difficulty.[1] Nor was it possible by Roman law to conduct a lawsuit in Rome against an actual office-holder. It was necessary to wait for the end of his tenure, or to exert influence in order to have him removed from his post. In the same speech Agrippa consoles his audience by saying that the procurator will not retain his place for ever, and hopes that his successors will be more amenable to the wishes of inhabitants of Judaea.

Restrictions were also imposed on the dispatch of deputations to Rome on behalf of the inhabitants of the provinces. We know definitely that the inhabitants of Judaea required special permission from the governor to send a deputation to the Emperor. Thus, for instance, when differences of opinion arose between the Jews and the governor Fadus as to who was to keep the High Priest's vestments, permission was given by Fadus and by Cassius Longinus, governor of Syria, who was then staying in Jerusalem, to send a delegation to the Emperor. On another occasion, when a dispute broke out between the Jews and King Agrippa about the erection of a screen to prevent the latter observing what was going on in the Temple, special permission was again needed from the procurator Festus. In both these cases the governors were not personally interested in the problems which gave rise to the complaint. But what of the oppressive acts of the governors

[1] Jos. *War*, II, 352.

themselves? It is enough to remark that the Jews did not dare to complain of Florus till the governor of Syria himself came to Jerusalem. The Samaritans indeed complained twice to the governor of Syria (of Pilate to Vitellius and of Cumanus to Quadratus). The difference between these two instances and the others may well have lain in the fact that legally Vitellius and Quadratus had received from the Emperor a different status from that held by Cestius Gallus. The normal way of impeaching a governor seems to have been after he had quitted his post, like Cumanus after his removal (52 C.E.), and Felix after he had ceased to function as governor (60 C.E.).[1]
In the case of Cumanus the Jews attained their object, but the Jewish leaders of Caesarea who travelled to Rome to impeach Felix before Emperor Nero failed in their undertaking. The governor might have paid for his conduct but for the intervention of his influential brother Pallas. The uncertainty of success, fear of the connections enjoyed by the governors in Rome, the expense and the risk entailed in failure, were such as to deter the provincials, including those of Judaea, from making too many attempts to influence the government at Rome to depose governors or to bring them to justice after they had left office. Despite all this, the list of legal convictions of governors for malpractices is a long one. It is not indeed divided equally among the various provinces, and the prospects of success on the part of backward provinces lacking ties with the leaders of Roman society were more remote than those of provinces with a known and accepted element of Graeco-Roman civilization. At all events fear of trial deterred many governors; undoubtedly they took into account the possibility of conviction and tried to prevent it in various ways. One was to win the favour of influential groups among the governed so that their support would be forthcoming in times of need.[2] The influence of Jewish elements, especially those associated with the Herodian House, was far from negligible in Rome of the Julio-Claudians. It was the influence of Agrippa II which decided the case brought against Cumanus in favour of the Jews, leading to his exile and the

---

[1] Cf. Dio Cassius LX, 25, 4-6 on Claudius' policy concerning provincial governors. For a list of governors impeached under the early Empire cf. Brunt, op.cit., pp. 224-7. They include procuratorial governors, such as Vipsanius Laenas, governor of Sardinia (Tacitus, *Annals* XIII,30) or Vibius Secundus, procurator of Mauretania (*Annals* XIV, 28). As an example of the failure of provincials to get justice we may cite the case of Eprius Marcellus accused by the people of Lycia in 57 C.E. (*Annals* XIII, 33).
[2] *Annals* XV, 20-21.

execution of one of his military officers who had acted with him in Judaea.

Various governors also took steps to appease the people before quitting Judaea. Albinus released all detainees except those under sentence of death, and Felix even thought of winning over part of the Jews by leaving Paul in prison.[1] The consideration that oppressive acts might try the patience of the provinces too severely and rouse them to rebellion undoubtedly also played its part in the behaviour of governors. Even so forceful a governor as Pontius Pilate recoiled before the resistance of the Jewish masses to his attempt to introduce standards with the imperial image into Jerusalem. Florus too seems to have feared the consequence of his actions when he was governor, and Josephus ascribes to him a plan of deliberately provoking the Jews to revolt in order to save himself from the threat of legal action on their part.[2] Philo tells us much the same regarding Capito, the procurator of Jamnia. According to Philo, he had taken up his post a poor man, had enriched himself by unlawful means, and feared the consequences: hence his attempt to slander the Jews to the Emperor.[3] It may be generally assumed that, as in other provinces, the presence in Judaea of other high Roman officials or the visits of influential Roman personalities were apt to act as deterrents to malpractice on the part of the governor.

In Judaea the procurator of the Jamnia domain, who was in direct correspondence with the Emperor, might for instance serve as an independent source of information to the central authority.[4] But it may be supposed that the influential Roman officials generally made common cause against the provincials and covered up each other's offences. The origin and rank of the governor, his residence at Caesarea, and the background of the military under his command, were all such as to make him feel socially closer to the Hellenized population than to the Jewish. The principal means by which ties could be formed between him and Jewish society was the Herodian family with its international status. And such ties were in fact formed between the governors and representatives of the House of Herod. The relations of Pilate with Herod Antipas were indeed strained for a time, but we

[1] Jos. *Ant.* xx, 215; Acts 24:27; cf. also *Annals* XIII, 31,3.
[2] *War* II, 282-3.
[3] Philo, *Legatio* 199.
[4] Jos. *Ant.* XVIII, 163; cf. Tacitus, *Annals* XIV, 38, on the rivalry between Suetonius Paulinus, the senatorial governor of Britain, and Iulius Classicianus, its financial procurator.

encounter Agrippa II and Berenice in the company of the procurator Festus.[1] Felix succeeded in setting up the closest relationship of all. He married Drusilla, daughter of Agrippa I and sister of Agrippa II and Berenice; she left her husband Azizus, ruler of Emesa, and Felix married her without becoming a Jew. He would seem to have entertained good relations with Jonathan son of Ananus, the most prominent representative of the House of Ananus, which stood at the head of the priestly oligarchy. The latter had also helped to procure the appointment of Felix to the post of procurator of Judaea. But in course of time relations cooled between the two, and according to Josephus, Felix was responsible for the death of Jonathan at the hands of the *sicarii*. There were other leaders of the contemporary oligarchy who formed close ties with procurators of the time. Thus, for example, the ex-High Priest Ananias son of Nedebaeus was an ally of Albinus. It can therefore be said on the whole that despite the preference displayed for the urban population of the Hellenistic cities, chiefly in the time of the last governors before the Revolt, the latter also moved in high circles of Jewish society and close ties were sometimes formed between the two. Only one procurator, Gessius Florus, seems to have been quite exceptional in this respect. The impression is that he behaved in Judaea like a tyrant in every respect, and we do not hear of any connections between him and the upper classes in Judaea. Even relations between him and the Herods were cool, if we may judge from the few allusions we possess.

Military forces, taxation and judicature

The governor was also commander-in-chief of the forces stationed in Judaea. The Roman army was based on two principal elements, the legions and the *auxilia*. The legions were composed of Roman citizens, whereas the men of the *auxilia* were generally, with the exception of the officers, not Roman citizens when they joined, citizenship being granted to them only on discharge. In Judaea, an equestrian province, no legions or parts of legions were stationed permanently, and its governor did not possess the authority to command such units. Only in time of need were the legions stationed in Syria directed to Jerusalem. Syria, as has been stated, was the principal military base of the Roman Empire in the East, and the legions stationed there

---

[1] Luke 23:12; Acts 25:13-27; 26:1-32.

324

were charged with the defence of the Empire against Parthian attacks. Philo also calls the Syrian garrison 'the army of the Euphrates.[1] The entire Julio-Claudian period was marked by tension between the two great powers, Rome and Parthia, the kingdom of Armenia constituting the chief bone of contention between them. Rome's overall strength was superior, but in the areas of direct conflict on the Euphrates frontier and in the nearby areas, the Parthians had no difficulty in holding their own against the Romans or in endangering the Roman power in several areas of the East. Only the transfer of a considerable force from the legions quartered in Europe could ensure the full superiority of the Romans, but this was not always possible in terms of the military situation and the security conditions prevailing on the frontiers of the Empire as a whole. Usually, then, the defence of the Roman East devolved upon the legions of Syria. Hence the Roman authorities were extremely sensitive to events in the neighbouring areas and to any danger threatening the stability of Roman rule from risings in Judaea, the most rebellious province in the entire Roman Orient, which had displayed little insurrectionary ferment since the wars of Mithradates. The central Roman government, indeed, had not at first grasped the significance of the danger. Only gradually did the danger and its implications become clear, and the great risings which broke out subsequently led in course of time to the conclusion that a force composed of legions must be stationed also in Judaea. We hear explicitly that in Tiberius' reign four legions of the Roman Empire's twenty-five were commanded by the governor of Syria, as compared with two composing the garrison of Egypt.[2] We also know which legions were stationed permanently in Syria; they were the III Gallica, the VI Ferrata, the X Fretensis and the XII Fulminata.

It was also the duty of the legions to safeguard the stability of Roman rule in Judaea. At the time of their establishment these legions were enlisted from Italy, but as time went on their character became

---

[1] Philo, *Legatio* 207; 259.
[2] Tacitus, *Annals* IV, 5. On the distribution of the legions and their movements in the Julio-Claudian period see W. Pfitzner, *Geschichte der römischen Kaiserlegionen* (1881); Ritterling, *PW* XII, cols 1211-65; H. M. D. Parker, *The Roman Legions* (1928), pp. 72-140; T. R. S. Broughton, 'The Roman Army', in F. J. Foakes Jackson and Kirsopp Lake, *The Beginnings of Christianity*, Part I vol. V (1933), pp. 427-439; G. H. Stevenson, *CAH* X (1934), pp. 222-4; G. Webster, *The Roman Imperial Army* (1969), pp. 47-65. For the legions of Syria see also R. Knox McElderry, *Classical Quarterly* III (1909), pp. 47-53.

less distinctive and their strength came chiefly from the eastern parts of the Empire. Antony had commenced widescale enlistment in the East, and this process certainly did not cease under the Julio-Claudian dynasty.[1] The legions of Syria intervened in the affairs of Judaea on several occasions. In certain cases the governor of Syria was forced to commit the greater part of the legions at his disposal to the suppression of disorders in Judaea. Quinctilius Varus took with him three legions to put down the revolt there after Herod's death.[2] When Petronius came to the country to carry out Gaius Caligula's order concerning the introduction of the statue into the Temple, he brought with him two legions, that is, half of the legions at the disposal of the Syrian legate.[3] Cestius Gallus set out to suppress the Judaean revolt at the head of a force two legions strong, composed of the entire Twelfth and two thousand men from each of the other three legions.[4] The Roman command also disposed of the forces of the allied client kings. Thus, for example, Vitellius was accompanied on his campaign against the Arabs by light-armed troops and cavalry of the allied sovereigns.[5] Cestius Gallus' campaign was supported by two thousand cavalry and three thousand archers sent by King Antiochus of Commagene. Agrippa II dispatched the same number of infantry and less than two thousand cavalry; Soaemus of Emesa came with four thousand men, a third of them cavalry.[6] During the suppression of the disturbances which broke out in Judaea after Herod's death (4 B.C.E.), Varus' army also contained Arab troops. The allied kings further played an important part in the siege of Jerusalem in the year 70.

But in normal times when no danger of a general revolt threatened, the garrison of the Judaean province sufficed to keep order there. This garrison, entirely composed of auxiliary troops, included units of foot and horse. The Roman auxiliaries were generally organized in cohorts, some of five hundred men (*quingenariae*), some of a thousand

---

[1] Cf. G. Forni, *Il reclutamento delle legioni da Augusto a Diocleziano* (1953), pp. 54, 57; G. E. F. Chilver, *JRS* (1957), p. 31; Parker, op.cit., pp. 169-186. Cf. Tacitus, *Annals* XIII, 35,2.
[2] Jos. *Ant.* XVII, 286 (*War* II, 67).
[3] *Ant.* XVIII, 262; cf. Philo. *Legatio*, 207 (half of the army of the Euphrates). According to *War* II, 186 three legions.
[4] *War* II, 500.
[5] *Ant.* XVIII, 120.
[6] *War* II, 500-501.

(*milliariae*).[1] The cavalry were grouped in squadrons (*alae*). The main strength of the *auxilia* stationed in the country came from the cities of Sebaste and Caesarea. Units composed of men of Sebaste already existed under Herod and in the disorders after his death played an important part in military operations against the Jewish insurgents.[2] After Judaea became a Roman province, the Romans took over this force from the Herods and it was they who composed the main element of the Roman garrison in Judaea.[3] Besides Sebaste, Caesarea constituted the principal source of recruits to the auxiliary forces. Josephus notes in connection with the death of Agrippa I (in 44 C.E.) that the troops who jeered at the dead king were natives of Caesarea and Sebaste,[4] and when discussing the dispute between the gentiles and Jews at Caesarea in Nero's reign, says that the former relied on the fact that most of the Roman military in the city were natives of Caesarea and Sebaste.[5] But elsewhere he speaks only of the Sebastenes,[6] whose cohorts and cavalry *alae* are also mentioned in inscriptions.[7] It would therefore appear that it was the practice to term the auxiliary forces *Sebasteni* for short in the official terminology, on account of the seniority and perhaps the numerical superiority of the latter. The units from Sebaste and Caesarea in the country numbered six, one squadron of cavalry and five cohorts of infantry.[8] These six units numbered not less than three thousand men. Additional auxiliary units may have been stationed in the country on occasion; we hear, for example, of Cornelius who served as a centurion of the Italian cohort (*Cohors Italica*).[9]

In view of the fact that we possess epigraphical evidence for the existence of a *Cohors Italica* of Roman citizens, which operated in the neighbouring areas, there is no adequate reason to dismiss the infor-

---

[1] On the *cohors milliaria* see F. Birley, *Corolla Memoriae Erich Swoboda dedicata* (1966), pp. 54-67.
[2] Jos. *War* II, 52; 58; 63.
[3] On the garrison of Judaea see Schürer I, pp. 362-367; Broughton, op.cit., pp. 439-441; Momigliano, pp. 376-8; 386; C. H. Kraeling, *HTR* (1942), pp. 265-9.
[4] Jos. *Ant.* XIX, 356.
[5] *Ant.* XX, 176.
[6] *Ant.* XX, 122; *War* II, 236.
[7] *CIL* III no. 2916; VIII no. 9359; *ILS* no. 1436; 2738.
[8] Jos. *Ant.* XIX, 365; cf. *War* III, 66. In *Ant.* XX, 122 we read that Cumanus took with him against the Jews one *ala* and four cohorts. It may be that the fifth cohort was then stationed at Jerusalem. Cf. Kraeling, op.cit., p. 268.
[9] Acts 10:1.

mation that men from the cohort also operated in the province of Judaea itself.[1] The main base of the garrison of the province of Judaea was the provincial capital of Caesarea, where most of these units were concentrated.[2] But one cohort was generally stationed in Jerusalem, at least during the major festivals, its duty being to keep order there.[3] Roman garrisons were also stationed at important fortresses throughout the entire country, such as Cypros near Jericho or Machaerus.[4] We also hear of Roman patrols operating in Samaria.[5]

The officers of the garrison of the Judaean province, i.e. the commanders of the infantry cohort and cavalry squadrons, were Roman citizens, though not all of them were so by birth. Claudius Lysias, for instance, the commander of the Jerusalem garrison when Paul was arrested, obtained his Roman citizen rights by paying a large sum of money.[6] We also encounter decidedly Roman names such as Cornelius or Julius among the centurions. But the ranks of the principal units themselves came primarily, as has been stated, from the cities of Sebaste and Caesarea, with all the consequences that this implied for relations between the gentile population, the Jews and the Roman government. While Cornelius was a 'sympathizer' and other soldiers in his unit belonged to the same class of people,[7] generally the gentile opponent of the Jews in the country could rely on the cooperation of the troops of Sebaste and Caesarea, and their leanings were expressed on various occasions. It was they who went beyond Pilate's orders to 'beat up' the Jewish crowds indiscriminately, whether guilty of disorder or not.[8] And it is to be assumed that it was one of these soldiers who, at a time of festival, under the governorship of Cumanus, profaned the Temple by an indecent act.[9] Josephus goes

---

[1] Broughton, op.cit., pp. 441-2. Perhaps this cohort is to be identified with Cohors II Italica civium Romanorum (*ILS* no. 9168; *CIL* xi no. 6117 (Gabba, nos. xxv-xxvi). On the armed police, the δεξιολάβοι (Acts 23:23) see G. D. Kilpatrick, *JTS* (1963), pp. 393-4.
For information on the Roman navy in Syrian and Palestinian waters see P. Thomsen, *ZDPV* (1946-51), pp. 73-89. In fact the *classis Syriaca* was created under the impact of the events of the Great Revolt. See D. Kienast, *Untersuchungen zu den Kriegsflotten der römischen Kaiserzeit* (1966), pp. 88-97.
[2] Jos., *War* iii, 66; *Ant.* xviii, 55.
[3] *War* ii, 224; v, 244.
[4] *War* ii, 484-5.   [5] *War* iii, 309.
[6] Acts 22:28.   [7] Acts 10:7; cf. Matt. 8:5.
[8] Jos. *Ant.* xviii, 62.
[9] *War* ii, 224 (*Ant.* xx, 108).

so far as to conclude that 'it was they who sowed the seed of war in the time of Florus'.[1]
We must not omit to mention in our survey of the auxiliary troops in Judaea in the period of the procurators, the Ascalonite cohort known to us from inscriptions.[2] We have no information of the activity of this cohort in the province of Judaea during the period of the Second Temple, but it may be supposed that Ascalon's stout resistance to the Jewish fighters during the Great Revolt, when one cohort of infantry and one squadron of cavalry helped to defend the towns,[3] reflects the local military potential.

Alongside the regular auxiliary units the governor was permitted to mobilize, in times of emergency, men from various Greek cities and also the inhabitants of the rural areas without urban organization. Cumanus, for example, armed the Samaritans against the Jews,[4] while Cestius Gallus' march upon Jerusalem was joined by a very large number of city-people. After Agrippa I's reign the governors could draw on troops, albeit only through the good offices of the governor of Syria, from the Roman colony of Ptolemais, founded in 45 C.E. for settlers drawn from the veterans of the Syrian legions. A certain importance doubtless attached also to the military settlers planted by Herod at Gaba and Heshbon.

For military aid the governor of Judaea could also call on the rulers of the Herodian family in the north of the country, among whose subjects were the Jewish military veterans from Babylonia settled there by Herod. Agrippa II in fact dispatched cavalry at the beginning of the Great Revolt in order to suppress the rising while it was still in its infancy.[5]

The changes in the provincial régime after the suppression of the Great Revolt also involved changes in the composition of the Roman garrison, since the new administration was set up for reasons of security. The previous garrison, which had consisted chiefly of men from Sebaste and Caesarea, had been removed from Judaea by Vespasian,[6] and the

---

[1] *Ant.* xix, 366. After the suppression of the Revolt these cohorts left Judaea. But in the second century C.E., near Sebaste, there was a *cohors milliaria* of Sebastenes who were Roman citizens. See M. Avi-Yonah, *QDAP* (1946), pp. 94-6; Héron de Villefosse, *RB* (1897), pp. 599-600.
[2] *ILS* nos 2724 and 9057; *CIL* xvi no. 35.
[3] Jos. *War* iii, 12.
[4] *Ant.* xx, 122. Cf. Tacitus, *Annals* xv, 3.
[5] *War* ii, 421.
[6] *Ant.* xix, 366.

Tenth Legion was transferred thither from Syria.[1] It would seem that the Sixth Ferrata joined the garrison of Judaea before the Bar Cochba rebellion.[2]

As a Roman province, Judaea had of course to pay taxes to the Roman state. Actually it was not the first time that the country paid taxes directly to the Empire, for this had been done after Pompey's conquest and under Gabinius' term as governor of Syria and continued until Caesar's settlement with Hyrcanus II. Subsequently, under the monarchy of Herod, a system was set up in which direct contact no longer existed between the Roman authorities and the Jewish taxpayer. With the transformation of Archelaus' ethnarchy into a Roman province, the situation changed and the Romans found it necessary to devise a new method of tax-collection. We may suppose that they left the tax-system established in Judaea in the previous period fundamentally unaltered, introducing changes here and there according to need. But there is no reason to think that they enlarged the general scale of taxes beyond that of Herod's period of rule.[3]

The basis of the new Roman method of taxation was the census, a general numbering of the population which also served as a basis for the imposition of the poll-tax. We know of censuses of this sort, additional to the censuses of Roman citizens, from various provinces. We have much information on the census which was held in Roman Egypt every fourteen years, but information on the census and the situation in other provinces is more fragmentary. It is only natural to assume that the inauguration of a new province, or the institution there of new administrative arrangements, involved a census.[4] We know of a census which was held in Gaul in Augustus' reign under the supervision of Drusus in 12 B.C.E., and was associated with the redivision of the Gallic provinces; the holding of such a census is also proved for Lusitania.[5] In the new Judaean province the census

[1] On the brick stamp impressions of the Tenth Legion see D. Barag, *Bonner Jahrbücher*, (1967), pp. 244-267.
[2] B. Lifshitz, *Latomus* (1960), pp. 109-111. G. W. Bowersock, *Zeitschrift für Papyrologie und Epigraphik* v (1970), p. 43 suggests that the Legio vi Ferrata constituted the garrison of the new province Arabia in 106 c.e.
[3] We know about some diminution of taxes after the annexation of Cappadocia. See Tacitus, *Annals* ii, 56.
[4] Cf. M. Hombert and C. Préaux, *Recherches sur le recensement dans l'Égpyte romaine* (1952); see for the problems of census in the Roman Empire H. Braunert, *Historia* (1957), pp. 192-214.
[5] On Gaul cf. Livy *Periochae* 138; Tacitus, *Annals* ii, 6; on Lusitania see *CIL* x no. 680.

would seem to have been held simultaneously with that held throughout the Syrian province.[1]

We have no further clear information on another overall census in Judaea in the Second Temple period, although traditions of a legendary character exist which allude to a numbering of the population of Judaea at the end of the period.[2] Our sources may not have thought it worthwhile to record the other censuses because they had become a routine matter, hence far-reaching conclusions should not be drawn from their silence. But it may well be that the authorities' experience during the census of Quirinius, which had led to disturbances headed by Judas of Galilee, influenced them not to be overhasty in instituting a new census after a given period, but to use other means of bringing their statistics up to date. It should again be emphasized that outside Egypt we have no certain knowledge of any other province in which censuses were conducted at fixed intervals.

The taxes levied on the products of the soil constituted the basis of the entire fiscal system under the procurators, as had also been the case in the Hellenistic period and under Julius Caesar and Hyrcanus II. Concerning the latter period we learn from the edicts of Julius Caesar that the land-tax amounted to 12.5 per cent of the crop except in the Sabbatical Year.[3] We may assume that the scale of taxation did not alter much in the period of direct Roman rule. It would further appear that Judaea also paid the poll-tax well known to us from Egypt under the name of λαογραφία. In Judaea, as in Egypt, certain elements of the population, such as the inhabitants of the Greek cities, may have enjoyed some rebatements of this tax. We know from a later legal source that the *tributum capitis*, which involved a wider conception than the poll-tax, was imposed throughout Syria on males between the ages of fourteen and sixty-five.[4] A conjecture has been made on the basis of the New Testament that the poll-tax imposed on Judaea at the end of the Second Temple period was at the rate of one denarius.[5] It might also be possible to conclude from the New Testament that the poll-tax in Roman Palestine was called, at least among the populace, and perhaps in the official terminology, by the Latin name of

[1] See Appendix I, pp. 372-4.
[2] On the census in the time of Cestius Gallus see Jos. *War* VI, 422-4; see also *T. B. Pesahim* 64b; Graetz, III, 2, pp. 815-820.
[3] *Ant.* XIV, 203.
[4] Ulpianus, in *Digesta* L, 15,3.
[5] Mark 12:13-17; Matt. 22:15-22; Luke 20:20-26; see also F. M. Heichelheim, in T. Frank, *An Economic Survey of Ancient Rome* IV (1938), p. 237.

331

census, like the population survey which formed the basis of the tax—just as in Egypt the Greek equivalent for *census*, λαογραφία, also meant 'population census'.

But this does not conclude the list of taxes, on a great part of which no information has reached us, but which can in some measure be completed by comparison with the conditions prevailing in other provinces, especially in Egypt. We hear from Josephus himself, for example, of the house-tax paid in Jerusalem under the Roman governors and remitted by Agrippa I.[1]

Where direct taxes were concerned, the Roman authorities did not utilize 'publican' tax-farmers, but collected them through the leaders of the local communities.[2] We have no information on the total sum collected in taxes in Judaea, or whether the Roman government of the province enjoyed a surplus of revenue over expenditure. In the speech put by Josephus into the mouth of Agrippa, the King argues that the Egyptian revenues in the course of one month exceeded the income of Judaea for an entire year, but this furnishes no sure basis for determining the scale of Roman revenue in the latter country.[3]

In Judaea, at any rate, the taxes were felt to be a sore burden. Writing of events in the reign of Emperor Tiberius, who according to our literary sources endeavoured not to press his subjects excessively in matters of taxation,[4] Tacitus remarks that Syria and Judaea became exhausted by the burden (*fessae oneribus*) and begged for a diminution of the scale of taxation.[5] The situation probably became worse under an emperor like Nero, and we know from other provinces what a grave problem was constituted by taxes and financial extortions in the Julio-Claudian period. Thus heavy taxation was one of the causes for the Gallic rebellion in 21 c.e.,[6] and literary, epigraphical and papyrological sources from Egypt testify to the brutality with which the government levied taxes, with consequent impoverishment of the country and depopulation of villages.[7]

The population was affected not only by taxes but also by the numerous

---

[1] Jos. *Ant.* xix, 299; see also Cicero, *Ad familiares* iii, 8,5 ('exactio ostiorum').
[2] *War* ii, 405; 407.
[3] *War* ii, 386.
[4] Dio Cassius lvii, 10,5.
[5] *Annals* ii, 42.
[6] *Annals* iii, 40,3; cf. *Historiae* iv, 17,4. The burden of taxation was a source of dissatisfaction in the time of Nero (*Annals* xv, 45; Rostovtzeff, *Social and Economic History of the Roman Empire* ii, (1957), p. 572, n. 6.
[7] Philo, *De specialibus legibus* iii, 159-163; H. I. Bell, *JRS* (1938), pp. 1-8; G. Chalon, *L'édit de Tiberius Julius Alexander* (1964), pp. 53-68.

customs duties levied at the frontiers, the ports and even inland. Thus customs would seem to have been imposed upon agricultural produce sold in Jerusalem, being levied at the city-gates. These were abolished by Vitellius when governor of Syria.[1] High tariffs were also levied by the Roman authorities on the perfumes and medicaments brought from Arabia, the point of transit of the caravans being Petra. Here the road divided in several directions, one route going to Pelusium and thence to Egypt, another to Gaza, where goods were shipped overseas, another to Philadelphia, Gerasa and Damascus. The tariffs which were levied on these wares at the customs stations attained a very high rate[2] and were paid to publicans. Gaza seems to have been the first station on the route from Petra. At Leuké Komé and at a station east of Palmyra, customs reached a rate of 25 per cent *ad valorem*, and there is no reason to suppose that at Gaza the rate was lower.

There were other important customs stations at the large ports of Judaea, Caesarea and Joppa. The wealth of John the Publican, one of the leaders of the Jews at Caesarea, was also derived from the business of the port.[3] We hear of the high customs-revenues of the port of Joppa under Hyrcanus II, which hardly diminished in the later Second Temple period, although our sources do not mention them for the period of the procurators. Chance information tells us of the presence of various publicans throughout the country. Thus we hear of a chief-publican, Zacchaeus, resident at Jericho, which was a frontier-station between Peraea, subject to Herod Antipas, and the province of Judaea.[4] This Zacchaeus was head of a society of publicans and was known for his wealth. We learn from the gospels of custom officers in Galilee;[5] these may have included in their activities not only customs in the more restricted sense of the term, but also other government revenues. This work permitted them to take strong measure and to avail themselves of the assistance of military forces.

As the expenses of the procurators were high, they attempted to extract money in various ways from the people they ruled. Pilate's move to utilize the Temple treasury to organize the water supply of Jerusalem is well known. It is also known that the leaders of the Jews feared

[1] Jos. *Ant.* xviii,90; but it is quite likely that we have here a reference to some sale tax. See also *Ant.* xvii, 205. On the customs-duties levied in Judaea see S. J. de Laet, *Portorium* (1949), pp. 331-344.
[2] Pliny, *Natural History* xii, 63-5.
[3] Jos. *War* ii, 287; Dessau, p. 802, n.i.
[4] Luke 19:1-10. [5] Matt. 9:10 (Luke 5:29).

that the procurator might lay hands on the monetary surpluses in the Temple treasury. This explains their tendency to spend them on matters which they regarded as more beneficial.[1] And in fact we see that the procurator Florus took from the Temple treasury seventeen talents for no genuine imperial requirement.[2] Others too extracted money from the inhabitants of Judaea on various pretexts. Thus we hear of Capito, Procurator of Jamnia, who came to Judaea poor and grew rich there; Albinus' behaviour is also common knowledge.[3] Much revenue requiring special management accrued to the Roman government from the private estates inherited by the Emperor from the Herods, such as Jamnia. The areas in the vicinity of Jericho were bequeathed by Salome, Herod's sister, to the Empress Livia. After the deposition of the ethnarch Archelaus, much property passed to the Roman authorities.[4] Particularly large revenues flowed into the imperial *fiscus* from the groves of the much-lauded opobalsam trees near Jericho and Engaddi. Thanks to strict management, the Romans were able greatly to increase the revenue from them.[5] In addition to the various taxes there existed also a type of corvée, for it was the practice of the Roman authorities in time of need to seize men and beasts for the *angaria*, i.e. for public works. The *angaria* was a practice that existed continuously in the Hellenistic and Roman East. With regard to Judaea itself, we encounter it in the letter sent by the Seleucid Demetrius I to Jonathan the Hasmonaean.[6] We see further that the *angaria* was one of the nuisances which irked the population of Roman Egypt most sorely. Germanicus attacked the abuse of the *angaria* during his stay in Egypt in 19 C.E., and Cn. Vergilius Capito, prefect of Egypt, dealt with the same phenomenon in his edict of 49 C.E.[7] The New Testament also contains instances of

---

[1] Jos. *Ant.* XVIII, 60; XX, 220. [2] *War* II, 293.
[3] Philo, *Legatio*, 199; *War* II, 273.
[4] *Ant.* XVIII, 2; on imperial estates cf. see O. Hirschfeld, *Kleine Schriften* (1913), pp. 516-575; Rostovtzeff, op.cit. II, p. 669, n. 45; on the fiscus and the confiscations on its behalf cf. F. Millar, *JRS* (1963), pp. 29-42.
[5] On the balsam groves and their exploitation by the *fiscus* see Pliny, *Natural History* XII, 113.
[6] It seems that Josephus in *Ant.* XIII, 52 hit upon the correct meaning of I Macc. 10:33. See also M. Rostowzew *Klio* VI, pp. 249-258.
[7] See the edict of Germanicus in A. S. Hunt and C. C. Edgar, *Select Papyri* II (1934), no. 211; V. Ehrenberg and A. H. M. Jones, *Documents illustrating the reigns of Augustus and Tiberius* (2nd ed., 1955), no. 320. For the edict of Capito see *OGIS* no. 665; on Syria cf. the letter of Domitian to the procurator Claudius Athenodorus found at Epiphania (*IGLS* v no. 1998; *SEG* XVII no. 755); cf. also N. Lewis, *RIDA* (1968), pp. 135-142.

the practice of the *angaria* in Roman Judaea.[1] The seizure of Simon of Cyrene by Roman troops to force him to carry the cross also belongs to this type of practice.[2] The *angaria* imposed by the Roman government is reflected in Talmudic literature: the Mishnah regards it as a Roman practice and as a part of normal life.[3] Talmudic sources also testify to the suffering caused by the *angaria* to pilgrims going up to Jerusalem.[4]

In consequence of the fall of Jerusalem, and of the changes which took place in the administration of Judaea, the plight of the Jewish population became worse in respect of the scale of taxes which they paid. And the Jews of Palestine and the Diaspora were also obliged to pay a special Jewish tax (τὸ Ἰουδαικὸν τέλεσμα) for Jupiter Capitolinus, in place of the half-shekel paid to the Temple of Jerusalem; it was gathered into a special *Fiscus Iudaicus*.[5] It may further probably be deduced from the words of Appian of Alexandria that there was also an increase in the rate of the *tributum capitis* owed by the Jews of the province of Judaea.[6] But the Jewish situation was affected no less by the changes which took place in the ownership of the soil, as much of the land of Judaea was confiscated by the government and many of its inhabitants became tenants, and as such had to pay a high percentage of their produce to the authorities.

The governors of Judaea enjoyed the right of striking coins.[7] Their mint appears to have been at Caesarea, capital of the province. The establishment of the province of Judaea was not made the occasion for a special era, and we see that the governors used the general official calendar of the Empire. Under Augustus they use the era of Actium, afterwards the regnal years of Tiberius, Claudius and Nero. Coins struck in the province of Judaea have been found in other provinces of the Empire, such as Gallia Narbonensis and Epirus.[8]

---

[1] Matt. 5:41.
[2] Matt. 27:32; Mark 15:21; Luke 23:26.
[3] *M. Baba Metzia* 6:3.
[4] *T. B. Menahot* 103b; *P. T. Shekalim* VIII, 51a.
[5] Suetonius, *Life of Domitian*, 12,2; Dio Cassius LXVI, 7,2; *CPJ* nos. 160-229. The Ἰουδαικὸν τέλεσμα was concentrated in a special *Fiscus Iudaicus* (*ILS* no. 1519).
[6] Appian, *Syriaca* 50, 253. For interpretations of the passage see the bibliographical note of E. Gabba in the first volume of the Teubner edition of Appian (1962), pp. 543-4.
[7] Cf. C. F. Hill, *Catalogue of the Greek Coins of Palestine* (1914), pp. 248-268; M. Grant, *From Imperium to Auctoritas* (1946), p. 131; A. Kindler, *IEJ* (1956), pp. 54-7; Y. Meshorer, *Jewish Coins of the Second Temple Period* (1967), pp. 102-6.
[8] Cf. Grant, op.cit., p. 131, n. 12.

We still have coins issued by Coponius, Ambibulus (under Augustus), Valerius Gratus and Pontius Pilate (under Tiberius), and Felix (under Claudius and Nero). All these are bronze. It can generally be stated that all the governors except Pilate displayed much consideration for Jewish religious susceptibilities. We find on the obverse of the coins of Coponius and Ambibulus the barley-ear, and on the reverse the date-palm and bunches of grapes. On the reverse of Valerius Gratus' coins we find the cornucopiae, leaves and fruit, a vine branch and palm leaf. Felix' coins also bear shields and crossed spears, but a tree or palm leaf and bunches of grapes appear over them.

Besides the duties devolving upon the governor of Judaea as commander-in-chief of the auxiliary troops stationed in the province, and as chief inspector of revenues derived from taxes and customs and of expenditure, he was the supreme judicial authority. In principle this also included cognizance of both criminal and civil cases. But in actual fact the practice in the Roman Empire was to leave civil jurisdiction in the hands of the local authorities. In Judaea civil jurisdiction was actually concentrated in the hands of the autonomous Jewish institutions.[1] Nevertheless it is to be assumed that supervision was exercised in principle by the governor and that in principle too he could claim jurisdiction in such matters of civil law as seemed to him of special importance, although this was doubtless rare. On the other hand the intervention of the governor was obviously necessary when one of the parties was not a Jew, although we do not know what sort of practical arrangements were made in such cases towards the end of the Second Temple period.

We know from literary and epigraphical sources outside Judaea, coming from provinces governed by equestrian governors, that the juridical activity for which they were responsible was very considerable.[2] The sphere of criminal law, at any rate, remained in their charge, and they alone possessed the authority to judge capital cases and to inflict the death sentence. There are well-known state-

[1] For the leaving of civil jurisdiction in the hands of the local authorities in the time of Augustus see H. Volkmann, *Zur Rechtsprechung im Principat des Augustus* (1935), pp. 128-9.
[2] In Sardinia we hear about a decision of the procurator concerning a border dispute which is later referred to by the proconsul L. Helvius Agrippa (*ILS* no. 5947; *FIRA* I no. 59). On Thrace see C. Dunant et J. Pouilloux, *Recherches sur l'histoire et les cultes de Thasos* II (1958), p. 82, no. 186 (the procurator hears the case of Thasos and the Roman colony Philippi). On the jurisdictional competence of the procurators in the imperial service in general see F. Millar, *Historia* (1964), pp. 180-7; (1965), pp. 362-7.

ments to this effect in the Gospel according to John and the Palestinian Talmud: in Judaea jurisdiction in capital cases had been removed from the hands of the Jewish authorities.[1] In other provinces also criminal jurisdiction was the exclusive sphere of the governors. Thus the fourth edict of Cyrene, for example, (6-7 c.e.) affirms that it is the duty of the governor to judge capital cases personally or to appoint a jury to do so.[2]

The governors undoubtedly possessed full powers to judge provincials in all capital cases and to pronounce sentences of death without confirmation by a higher instance.[3] The general remarks of Dio Cassius on senatorial governors, who were empowered to pronounce the death sentence, apply also to equestrian governors, whom he mentioned a little beforehand.[4] Josephus may be referring to this in the *War* when he says that Coponius was entrusted by Augustus with full powers including the infliction of capital punishment (μέχρι τοῦ κτείνειν λαβὼν παρὰ καίσαρος ἐξουσίαν).[5] Josephus says much the same in his parallel account.[6] Hence we see that the Roman governors of Judaea made wide use of this right and were not sparing in their use of the capital sentence. Not only Pilate, but also governors who were not among the most oppressive made free use of it. Thus, for example, Cuspius Fadus (44-46 c.e.) sentenced to death a Jewish leader whom he considered to be an arch-rebel and a trouble-maker, and did likewise with Theudas. Tiberius Alexander, who succeeded him, put to death James and Simon, the sons of Judas of Galilee;[7] of governors of the type of Felix and Albinus it is superfluous to speak. The general verdict must be that judicial executions were a common phenomenon in the life of the province of Judaea at the end of the Second Temple period. From this point of view the situation in Judaea did not differ from that prevailing in other provinces of the Roman Empire. It is enough to recall the fact that Volesus Messalla, proconsul of Asia, put to death three hundred people in one day.[8]

We observe that the governors did not decide the fate of certain persons but sent them to be tried at Rome. Thus Felix sent Eleazar son of Dinaeus to Rome, and Quadratus, governor of Syria, did the

---

[1] John 18:31; *P. T. Sanhedrin* I, 18a.
[2] *SEG* IX no. 8, Edict 4, ll. 65-66; *FIRA* I no. 68, p. 409; see F. de Visscher, *Les édits d'Auguste découverts à Cyrène* (1940), p. 128.
[3] T. Mommsen, *Römisches Strafrecht* (1899), pp. 239-241.
[4] LIII, 14,5.   [5] II, 117.   [6] *Ant.* XVIII,2.
[7] *Ant.* XX, 4; 98; 102.   [8] Seneca, *De ira* II, 5,5.

same with several Jewish leaders.[1] In the same context we should mention the priests arrested by Felix for some 'trivial' reason and sent by him to the Emperor at Rome.[2] Why did the governors not decide the cases of these men in the province itself but defer the decision to the Emperor? Clearly, these were not ordinary criminal cases, but possessed an obvious political complexion. However, the governors also judged in political matters and perhaps mainly in such. It could be argued that some of these men were sent to Rome because they were Roman citizens and as such claimed to be tried before Caesar, but this supposition is hardly acceptable. It would rather seem that they were sent to Rome because their cases were connected with exceptional situations and the decisions taken in relation to them were likely to cause grave consequences, hence the reluctance of the local authorities to decide of their own accord. In the case of Eleazar son of Dinaeus, the procurator Felix was also bound by the special terms agreed on between them when Eleazar gave himself up to the Romans. Sentences were carried out by the personnel of the Roman forces in the province, as can be demonstrated by the traditions concerning the crucifixion of Jesus. It would seem that the governor reserved the right to amnesty one of the condemned men in honour of the festival.[3] We do not know of the existence of a similar practice in other provinces,[4] and the conjecture has been voiced that it was the custom of the rulers of Judaea before it became a Roman province, and was retained by the governors, who thus perpetuated a custom of the Herodian rulers.[5]

A peculiar problem existed in relation to those who resided in the province of Judaea and possessed Roman citizenship. Among them were officers of the auxiliary cohorts such as Claudius Lysias, who arrested Paul,[6] and some Jews who had obtained citizenship in various ways; many were probably freed slaves or the descendants of such, as may be learnt from the presence of the 'Synagogue of Freedmen' in Jerusalem.[7] Some of the Jews belonged to the equestrian class.[8] The rights of the Roman citizens are reflected in the account of the arrest of Paul in the Acts of the Apostles.[9] The Roman officer at Jerusalem was about to flog him, but stopped when he learned that

[1] Jos. *Ant.* xx, 161; 131.
[2] *Life*, 13.
[3] Matt. 27:15 and the parallel passages.
[4] E. Bickermann, *RHR* cxii (1935), p. 197.
[5] Momigliano, p. 386.   [6] Acts 22:28.
[7] Acts 6:9.   [8] Jos. *War* ii, 308.   [9] Chaps 21-6.

Paul was a Roman citizen. This is in accordance with the Roman law, which forebade the flogging of Roman citizens.[1] When Paul was brought before the procurator Festus, he could consent to be tried, but could also refuse, and demand as a Roman citizen to be tried before the Emperor in Rome. He chose the second course,[2] and Festus, the procurator, having consulted his *consilium*, granted Paul's request. The imperial court of justice is not here acting as a court of appeal, but as a court of first instance. On the other hand we see that not all the procurators were scrupulous as to the rights of Jews with Roman citizenship.

The procurator Florus ordered the flogging or crucifixion of such Jews of equestrian rank.[3] Florus could here claim that they had become enemies of the Roman people and that as rebels they had lost their citizen rights.[4]

Nevertheless, since we have in fact only a very small amount of comparative material for the Julio-Claudian period, it is at present very hard to define exactly the judicial rights of a Roman citizen in a province when on trial for his life, and the restrictions on the governors in relation to such citizens. Consequently various solutions of the problem have been proposed.

1. One school of historians holds that every Roman citizen in a province in this period was in principle permitted to claim trial before the emperor. But governors who had been granted the *ius gladii* had the power to judge Roman citizens as well. We have no specific evidence of *ius gladii* in the early period, but the powers granted to Coponius can be interpreted as referring to it. However, in the view of certain scholars,[5] this right was granted to Coponius personally, but did not become a tradition with the governors who succeeded him in Judaea. Festus, who sent Paul to Rome, did not therefore possess the authority to judge Roman citizens.

2. According to another view, the *ius gladii* in the Julio-Claudian period did not include the right to try any Roman citizen in the provinces, but only the right to judge Roman citizens serving in the army.[6] Festus, then, had no legal authority to judge Paul without his consent.

---

[1] *Pauli Sententiae* v, 26, 1.   [2] Acts 25:11.   [3] Jos. *War* II, 308.
[4] Cf. Pflaum, *Les procurateurs équestres*, pp. 147-8.
[5] Mommsen, op.cit., p. 244, n. 3. It is also possible that Josephus has in view only persons of provincial status. See Dessau, p. 778, n.1.
[6] Pflaum, op.cit., p. 117; A. H. M. Jones, *Studies in Roman Government and Law* (1960), pp. 51-65.

3. On still another view, the governors had the authority to try Roman citizens in their provinces, but only in matters specified in the Roman *iudicia publica*.[1] Paul's offence was not clearly defined in Roman law. 4. An interpretation recently put forward holds that all the Roman governors as early as the Julio-Claudian period possessed authority to try Roman citizens, and not military personnel alone.[2] But in certain cases in which the accused could not for various reasons obtain justice in the court of the provincial governor, he could claim trial before the emperor. Paul, who was apprehensive of not obtaining fair trial in Judaea, therefore requested to be sent to Rome to Caesar. Festus, having consulted his *consilium*, found reasonable grounds for Paul's request.

The administrative division of the Province of Judaea and the status of Jerusalem

The administrative division of the province of Judaea was a direct continuation of the system prevailing in the reign of Herod. The villages and, over them, the toparchies, remained the smallest administrative units. The cities were also included in the administrative division and acted as capitals of the toparchies or of the larger units, which embraced a number of toparchies. These units remained chiefly in the form they had been given in Herod's time. The city of Caesarea was attached to Samaria and the official name of this division was 'Samaria and Caesarea'.[3] The port of Joppa and the territory of Jamnia were attached to Judaea proper. Notable changes took place only with regard to Idumaea, which in Herod's time was organized in one administrative unit with Gaza. It seems that on Herod's death this link was dissolved, as the city of Gaza was detached from the ethnarchy of Archelaus and attached directly to the province of Syria, remaining so after the inauguration of the new province of Judaea. The area of Idumaea was therefore small and the Idumaean toparchies, excepting Gaza, were attached to Judaea proper. Important urban settlements with an administrative tradition of their own were in any case not to be found there between the destruction of Marissa and the rise of Beth Govrin; as to the composition of the population,

---

[1] A. N. Sherwin White, *Roman Society and Roman Law in the New Testament* (1963), pp. 61-2.
[2] P. Garnsey, *JRS* (1968), pp. 51-9; idem, *Social Status and Legal Privilege in the Roman Empire* (1970), pp. 75-6, 263-4.
[3] *Ant.* xix, 351.

the differences between the inhabitants of Judaea and Idumaea were now effaced. It is of interest to record that even in classical Latin literature no further distinction is discernible between Judaea an Idumaea and both names are used indiscriminately.[1] The areas across Jordan included in the tetrarchy of Herod Antipas formed a definite administrative unit under that ruler, and in course of time, when annexed to the province of Judaea, continued to constitute the same administrative unit, Peraea.

The permanent administrative capital of Judaea proper was Jerusalem. Idumaea, once its peculiar toparchies had been annexed to Judaea, and Gaza had been attached to Syria, no longer possessed a general administrative centre in addition to the capitals of the toparchies. In this period, therefore, Jerusalem also served as the administrative capital of Idumaea. On the other hand it is hard to determine if Sebaste was regarded as the administrative capital of Samaria, or if Caesarea, on account of its inclusion in Samaria, as the capital of the entire province, was also the peculiar administrative capital of Samaria. Permanent rivalry existed between Sepphoris and Tiberias, ever since the foundation of the latter town, as to which was to be the capital of Galilee. Till the establishment of Tiberias, Sepphoris was doubtless the capital of Herod Antipas, but then Tiberias became the principal town. But in the last years before the fall of Jerusalem, when most of Galilee was part of the Roman province and Tiberias had been transferred to the kingdom of Agrippa II, Sepphoris regained its old prominence and was again the capital of Galilee.

We have comparatively detailed information about the toparchies of Judaea proper at the end of the Second Temple period, thanks to two lists preserved in our literary sources, one in Josephus and the other in Pliny.[2] Josephus enumerates the toparchies of Judaea as follows: Jerusalem, Gophna, Acrabatene, Thamna, Lydda, Emmaus, Pella, Idumaea, Engaddi, Herodium and Jericho (eleven in all). He enumerates with them Jamnia and Joppa. Pliny enumerates the toparchies of Judaea in another order and with certain differences: Jericho, Emmaus, Lydda, Joppa, Acrabatene, Gophna, Thamna, Bethleptephene, Oreine (the hill-region in which Jerusalem is situated) and Herodium (ten in all). The most obvious difference between the

---

[1] Virgil Georgics III, 12; Lucanus, Pharsalia III, 216; Martialis II, 2,5; Valerius Flaccus, Argonautica I, 12; Statius, Silvae III, 2,138; Silius Italicus, Punica III, 600; VII, 456. Cf. also Aelianus, De natura animalium VI, 17.
[2] Jos. War III, 54-6; cf. ibid., 567; Pliny, Natural History V, 14,70.

two lists consists in Pliny's omission of the two southern toparchies, Idumaea and Engaddi, and his assigning of the toparchy of Joppa to Judaea, without mentioning Jamnia. Instead of Pella he speaks of Bethleptephene, but it is clear that the two sources are referring to the same toparchy.[1]
It is almost certain that the two lists are not older than Herod's reign, as the fortress of Herodium is mentioned in both.[2] It can only be supposed that Pliny as a stranger to the country used a written list, while Josephus, as a person rooted in the life of Judaea, who knew it from his childhood, could list the toparchies from personal knowledge. It would appear that Pliny's list reflects in the main a written source which treats of the situation in Herod's reign, when Idumaea was still an administrative unit distinct from Judaea, although here and there he adds observations which reflect the situation after the fall of Jerusalem. Josephus, for his part, describes the conditions prevailing in the period after Herod's death and after Gaza had been separated from Judaea and the special toparchies of Idumaea (western Idumaea and its eastern part with its centre at Engaddi) had been transferred to Judaea.
To sum up it may be said that Judaea under the last procurators was composed of eleven toparchies (including the two belonging to Idumaea) and the two additional toparchies of Jamnia and Joppa. This division of Judaea in fact reflects the old division of the Hellenistic and Hasmonaean periods: only the capitals of the toparchies have changed, Aphaerema and Arimathaea having given way to Gophna and Thamna.
However, not only Judaea proper, but the entire province of Judaea and the areas of the client kingdoms of the sons of Herod, in so far as they were maintained, were divided into toparchies. We possess explicit information only of the toparchy of Narbata in north-western

---

[1] In *War* IV, 445 we meet with the same name as in Pliny, and it seems that the name Πέλλη in *War* III, 55 either constitutes a mistake of copyists or that the name Pella, the same as adopted by the well-known town of Peraea, was sometimes used also for the Judaean township. See Abel, *Géographie de la Palestine* II (1938), p. 277.
[2] For the lists of the toparchies and the differences between them cf. Schürer II, pp. 229-234; E. Nestle, *Judaea bei Josephus* (1911), pp. 51-2; U. Kahrstedt, *Syrische Territorien in hellenistischer Zeit* (1926), pp. 114-115; A. H. M. Jones, *JRS* (1931), p. 78; *JRS* (1935), pp. 230-1; *CERP* (2nd ed.), pp. 273, 462, n. 63; Momigliano, pp. 366-8; S. Klein, *The Land of Judaea* (in Hebrew, 1939), pp. 213-218; M. Stern, *Tarbiz* (1968), pp. 215-229; A. Schalit, *König Herodes* (1969), pp. 208-211.

Samaria,[1] and it is only by chance that we do not hear of the names of the other toparchies of Samaria. Tiberias and Tarichaeae were centres of toparchies in Galilee,[2] and Sepphoris was also doubtless a toparchy capital, although this is not mentioned in the sources. It is further to be assumed that there were other centres of this type in Galilee. The toparchy capitals of Peraea included Abila and Julias-Livias (Beth ha Ramtah), both in the south of the area; elsewhere Josephus speaks of Gadara as capital of Peraea.[3] Gadara is identical with Gadora (es-Salt) and should be distinguished from the Hellenistic Gadara; besides being the capital of all Peraea, it was no doubt the capital of one of the toparchies as well. Amathus was also such a capital.[4] We thus get four toparchies in Peraea in the following order from south to north: Julias-Livias, Abila, Gadora and Amathus.

We know nothing of the organization of the toparchies or their heads, but it is clear that the Roman administration was assisted in its operations by the autonomous institutions of the local population. When Judaea became a Roman province, Jerusalem ceased to be the administrative capital of the entire country. Henceforward the Roman authorities transferred the seat of the governor and the military headquarters to Caesarea on the coast.

Tacitus[5] rightly terms Caesarea the capital of Judaea, the governor's normal residence.[6] But it is clear that the latter was in the habit of visiting the various cities of the province, more especially Jerusalem according to need. Jerusalem remained the town with the largest population in the province and the chief focus of its active political, religious and social life. As such it was frequently visited by the governor. Thus, for example, the Procurator Festus went up to Jerusalem three days after he had arrived in the province and assumed office; he stayed there eight to ten days. In Jerusalem the governors generally took up residence in the Palace of Herod.[7]

---

[1] Jos. *War* II, 509.
[2] *War* II, 252.
[3] *War* IV, 413.
[4] A. H. M. Jones, *JRS* (1931), p. 79. At Amathus there was also a royal residence (*Ant.* XVII, 277).
[5] *Historiae* II, 78.
[6] Jos. *War* II, 171 (*Ant.* XVIII, 57); *War* II, 230 (*Ant.* XX, 116); *War* II, 332 and 407; Acts 23:23ff; 25:1ff.
[7] Acts 25:1. On the residence of the governor at Jerusalem cf. E. Lohse, *ZDPV* (1958), pp. 69-76; see also R. Egger, *Das Praetorium als Amtssitz und Quartier römischer Spitzenfunktionäre* (1966), pp. 17-22.

It should also be emphasized that Jerusalem had acquired a great reputation even among non-Jews in the last decades before its destruction and had become famous throughout the entire civilized world. In Pliny's words, Jerusalem was the most renowned among the towns of the East, and not only of Judaea (*longe clarissima urbium Orientis, non Iudaeae modo.*)[1] The days had passed when the name of Jerusalem was vaguely known only to a few representatives of the Graeco-Roman world, or when Polybius could speak of the Jews who dwelt about the Temple known as Jerusalem.[2] A halo of legend surrounded the city not only for the Jews but also for the gentiles, as we can see from the biographer of the Roman emperors Suetonius,[3] who speaks of some who explicitly pledged to Nero the kingdom of Jerusalem after he had lost the rule of Rome (*nonnulli nominatim regnum Hierosolymorum spoponderunt*). Jerusalem's fame is also echoed by an inscription set up to Titus years after its destruction.[4] It describes Jerusalem as a city which had never been captured before (*Hierosolymam omnibus ante se ducibus regibus gentibus aut frustra petitam aut omnino intemptatam delevit*). Externally the city had assumed the aspect of a *polis*, and formally the Roman government treated it as such, as is indicated, for example, by Claudius' rescript in the matter of the high priestly vestments, where its council and people are explicitly referred to.[5] Josephus' account speaks on a number of occasions of the boule of Jerusalem and its members.[6] Dio Cassius, describing the destruction of the Temple, also speaks of the members of the Jerusalem council; the New Testament knows Joseph of Arimathaea as a councillor (βουλευτής), and the Talmud speaks of the existence of a Council Chamber (לשכת בולווטיץ) in the Temple.[7]

It is clear on the other hand that we cannot simply affirm that Jerusalem really became a polis in all respects.[8] Not only were the social and cultural institutions of a Greek polis not maintained there, but regular assemblies of the demos at a fixed time and place were not

[1] *Natural History* v, 14,70.
[2] Quoted by Jos. *Ant.* xii, 136; cf. Livy, *Periochae* 102.
[3] *Life of Nero* 40,2.
[4] *ILS* no. 264; M. McCrum and A. G. Woodhead, *Select Documents of the Principates of the Flavian Emperors* (1961), no. 53.
[5] Jos. *Ant.* xx, 11.
[6] *War* ii, 331; 336; 405; v, 144; 532; vi, 354.
[7] Dio Cassius lxvi, 6,2; Mark 15:43; Luke 23:50; *P. T. Ta'anith* iv, 69a; *Yoma* i, 38c; cf. G. Allon, *Studies in Jewish History* i (in Hebrew, 1957), pp. 48-76.
[8] See also V. A. Tcherikover, *IEJ* (1964), pp. 61-78.

part of the city's constitution. Nor were the members of its boule elected in the Greek fashion. Furthermore, the boule was in effect identical with the traditional Sanhedrin of Jerusalem, which performed *inter alia* the function of city council. It may nevertheless be noted that changes had also taken place in the administration of the Greek cities of the East, departing from the original forms of the Greek polis, whereas the institutions of Jewish Jerusalem had adopted part of the terminology prevalent in the Hellenistic-Roman world. Thus the Sanhedrin began to be known as a boule and to bestow upon Jerusalem the external aspect of a normal polis.

We shall also see that the process of assimilation between Jerusalem and the Greek cities of the East was not limited to terminology. Something of the organizational arrangements and institutions characteristic of Greek towns was gradually introduced into Jerusalem. An instance of this is the appearing of the 'Ten Leading Men' (δέκα πρῶτοι) in the city. We hear specifically that the Procurator Festus sent these 'Ten Leading Men' to Rome together with the High Priest Ishmael and Helcias the Treasurer.[1] We also learn of the existence of 'Ten Leading Men' in other towns of the country—Tiberias and Gerasa. Josephus delivered to the 'Ten Leading Men' of Tiberias the property stolen at the plundering of Agrippa's palace.[2] We also encounter them in inscriptions at Gerasa dated to 66 C.E.; here a δεκάπρωτος appears who holds his function for life.[3]

The primary duty of these men seems to have been to act as the financial committee of the municipal council, but we cannot state whether they served, as at Gerasa, for life, or for a limited period as at other places. Their presence at Jerusalem, at all events, informs us of the gradual penetration of Greek institutions into the life of the Jewish city.

Although the administrative capital was transferred from Jerusalem to Caesarea, and the Roman government based itself more and more on the inhabitants of the Hellenistic cities of the type of Caesarea and Sebaste, the province as a whole, and not merely Judaea in the narrow sense, continued officially to be called Judaea, and this remained its official name till Hadrian's reign.[4]

---

[1] Jos. *Ant.* xx, 194.
[2] On Tiberias see *Life*, 69; 296. See also *War* II, 639 (*Life*, 168).
[3] C. H. Kraeling, *Gerasa* (1938), *Inscriptions* (ed. C. B. Welles), nos. 45-6, pp. 395-6. Cf. O. Seeck, *Klio* I, pp. 147-187; R. Boecklin and J. P. Hyatt, *AJA* (1934), pp. 511-522; E. G. Turner, *JEA* (1936), pp. 7-19; L. Robert, *Documents de l'Asie mineure méridionale* (1966), pp. 74-7.
[4] M. Noth, *ZDPV* (1939), pp. 127-9; R. Syme, *JRS* (1962), p. 90.

The Roman administration therefore continued the late Hellenistic practice established by the Hasmonaeans, who had annexed most of the country to the State of Judaea. This perpetuation of a name current before the direct Roman annexation was justified objectively by the fact that the Jews continued subsequently to comprise the effective majority of the country's population. The name 'Palaestina' does not appear yet in the official administrative and political terminology, but only in literary usage; it is used not only by non-Jewish, but also by Jewish writers such as Philo and Josephus, who found it difficult to apply the name 'Judaea' to the whole of the land of Israel.[1]

Collaboration and Collision under the First Governors

The rule of the first governors, with the exception of one of them, Pilate, was not marked by an exacerbation of relationships between the Roman government and the Jewish people. Hatred of the rule of Herod and Archelaus was so profound among various circles of the Jewish nation that they were ready to welcome direct Roman rule. On the other hand some of the higher classes, the circles about the high priests, and the families formerly close to the Herodian House, also inclined to willing collaboration with the Roman governors, just as formerly with Herod and his son. Beside them rebellious groups began to form which saw any foreign rule as something to be resisted with violence, since the Jews must not be subjected to human rule but to God alone. These ideas were among the factors causing ferment during the initial stages of Roman rule, but after the first stir had subsided, we do not hear of bloodshed before the time of Pilate. From his time onwards there is frequent mention of messianic excitement, of disorder and of the gradual disillusionment of all the hopes placed in Roman rule.

The Roman administration for its part made an effort to discover an appropriate manner of ruling the Jewish people, and showed much consideration for their religious sensibilities. It abstained, for example, from introducing images and pictures into Jerusalem. However, mutual understanding between the two sides was not always achieved. The presence in Jerusalem of a Roman auxiliary cohort far from sympathetic to the Jews was apt to produce frequent conflicts, and the

[1] Ovidius, *Ars amatoria* I, 416; Philo, *De Abrahamo*, 133; *Quod omnis probus liber sit*, 75; *Vita Mosis* I, 163; *De Virtutibus* 221; Jos. *Ant.* I, 145; XX, 259. The Jewish sources preserved in Hebrew or Aramaic do not use Judaea to include the whole of Palestine, and the same is true of the New Testament. See E. Levesque, *Vivre et Penser*, (1943-4), pp. 104-111.

authority given to the governors to appoint high priests and to hold the high priestly vestments, and thus to supervise the Jewish cult, also enraged the Jews. The heavy taxation, the character of a harsh governor such as Pilate, who treated the Jews with less consideration than his predecessors, and the general emotional alienation between the rulers and the subjects, all played their part in deepening the hostility of the Jewish population towards Roman rule.

On the other hand groups which had become conscious of the strength of Rome endeavoured to bridge the antagonisms, fearing that a direct collision might bring disaster upon the entire nation, upon Jerusalem and upon the Temple. These included people with personal interests such as the descendants of Herod, but also many others who were genuinely concerned for the future. But these too displayed a readiness, at a certain moment, to adopt the old Hasmonaean approach and not to accept situations in which the Roman power threatened the very existence of Judaism, as indeed occurred in the reign of Gaius Caligula. The arrival in Judaea of Quirinius governor of Syria in 6 C.E., with the special duty of holding the census in Judaea immediately after the removal of Archelaus, created a general storm (for the census, see Appendix, no. 1). This first census symbolized enslavement and was accompanied by fears of heavy taxes in the future. Censuses elsewhere had been the cause of rebellion and disorders. The movement against the census was headed by Judas of Gaulanitis, a man from Gamala who had already risen against the government on the death of Herod. He was joined by the Pharisee Saddok, and together they enflamed the multitude by pointing out that the census involved complete subjection to Roman power. Thanks to the influence of the High Priest Joazer son of Boethus, calm was in great measure restored and the census was carried through without the outbreak of a general rising.[1] But simultaneously with the Roman government's first great administrative operation an ideology had been openly manifested opposed to the very existence of the Roman government, the ideology of the zealots. Judas the Galilean himself lost his life, apparently at the hands of the Romans, as the result of his actions against Rome,[2] but his sons and disciples persisted in similar activity down to the time of the fall of Masada.

[1] *Ant.* XVIII, 1-3. On the identification of the Judas who was active at the time of the census with the Judas who led of the Galilean rebels in the time of Varus see J. S. Kennard, *JQR* (1945-6), pp. 281-6.

[2] Acts 5:37.

Quirinius removed the High Priest Joazer from his incumbency despite his support of the Roman governor, probably because he was not favoured by most of the nation. The incumbency of the Boethuseans was particularly detested by the populace and associated with the gloomiest memories of the times of Herod and Archelaus, and Quirinius saw his removal as an opportunity of winning their favour. Ananus son of Seth was appointed in his stead, a representative of one of the most prominent families of the priestly oligarchy at the end of the Second Temple period. This Ananus laid the foundation of the greatness of his family, which from that time onward took the place of the Boethuseans at the head of the high priestly oligarchy. As high priest, Ananus maintained his position for a long period, under the three first governors, so that his position was more stable than that of the Boethuseans. The first governors saw no need to introduce personal changes in the priesthood, perhaps because Ananus collaborated with the Roman government, and his influence assisted greatly in the consolidation of its rule in Judaea.

The governorship of Coponius (6-9 C.E.), the first governor of Judaea, passed in relative quiet. The only striking event noted by our sources in connection with his administration was the desecration of the Temple by the Samaritans.[1] They had expressed their enmity to the Jews by scattering bones in the Temple during the Festival of Passover. Coponius left a favourable memory among the Jewish nation and one of the gates of the Temple was named after him.[2]

After Coponius, M. Ambivius or Ambibulus (9-12 C.E.) was appointed governor.[3] Herod's sister Salome died during his term of office, leaving as a legacy to the Empress Livia Jamnia and its toparchy, and also Phasaelis and Archelais in the region of Jericho.[4] These areas became initially the private estate of Livia herself and subsequently that of the imperial family as a whole, being administered by a special procurator. The last governor under Augustus was Annius Rufus, the first under Tiberius was Valerius Gratus. In accordance with the practice of Tiberius' reign, the latter served for the comparatively

---

[1] Jos, *Ant.* xviii, 30. Some scholars connect this event with the famous edict of Nazareth (Gabba, No. xxviii). So e.g. J. Carcopino. *Revue historique* clxvi (1931), pp. 88-91; E. Bickermann, *RHR* cxii (1935), p. 190, n. 1. Yet this is no more than pure conjecture, since even the date of the edict is by no means certain.
[2] The identification of Coponius with Ciphonos of the Gate of Ciphonos referred to in the Mishnah (*Middot* 1:3) is quite likely.
[3] Jos. *Ant.* xviii, 31. Yet his name is uncertain. Cf. the variant readings in Niese.
[4] *Ant.* xviii, 31 (*War* ii, 167).

long term of eleven years (15-26 C.E.). Valerius Gratus deposed Ananus from the high priesthood and appointed Ishmael ben Phiabi, a member of an Egyptian Jewish family which had risen to prominence in Herod's reign; then after a brief period again appointed one of Ananus' family, Eleazar son of Ananus. Eleazar served in the high priesthood no more than a year and was replaced by Simon son of Camith. After a short time Gratus appointed Joseph Caiaphas, who was, with Ananus, the most important high priest in the period of the first governors and served longer than any other incumbent in the procuratorial period. The Gospel of John[1] makes it clear that he was the son-in-law of Ananus and the two collaborated to determine the policy of the high priesthood. Caiaphas continued his incumbency into the days of the Governor Pontius Pilate, who succeeded Valerius Gratus, and it was he who was involved in the trial of Jesus. The long term of his high priesthood requires a special explanation, since he served so many years under Valerius Gratus, who was a pronounced advocate of frequent changes, and also under Pontius Pilate. One explanation is that Caiaphas' incumbency expressed a compromise reached within the priestly oligarchy itself. Another is the personality of Caiaphas, who knew how to act in complete accord with the Roman governors of Tiberius' reign.[2]

In Pontius Pilate's term of office (26-36 C.E.) a considerable deterioration took place in the relations between the Jews and the Roman government. We hear during his term of a series of clashes between the Jews and the Roman administration, and his name survives as that of a harsh and unbending ruler;[3] he was difficult to appease and we are told in connection with his governorship of the practice of bribery, of insults, robberies and frequent executions without trial. His relatively long governorship (only Valerius Gratus surpassed him in this respect among the procurators) is to be explained not by his peculiar efficiency as administrator, but by the practice current under Tiberius of not replacing provincial governors frequently. In the first period of his governorship Pilate fell in with the anti-Jewish policy of Sejanus, the praetorian prefect of Rome (till 31 C.E.). Pilate's relative strength as governor in comparison to that of his predecessors and successors was also due to the fact that down to 32 C.E. there was no governor of Syria, since the official legate Aelius

[1] 18:13.
[2] E. Stauffer, *La nouvelle Clio* (1949-50), p. 506.
[3] Philo, *Legatio*, 301.

Lamia was kept in Rome by Tiberius, and no other governor was appointed in his place.[1] Only in 32 C.E. was a new legate appointed (Lucius Pomponius Flaccus). The previous situation was thus restored and the activity of the governor of Judaea was again overshadowed by the authority of the senatorial legate of Syria. In consequence of this and of the execution of Sejanus in 31 C.E., Pilate's actions were more restricted during the last years of his term than during his first five.

Pilate followed the policy of his predecessors in maintaining good relations with the High Priest Joseph Caiaphas. On the other hand he was not always on good terms with the various representatives of the Herodian House such as Herod Antipas.[2]

Pilate's unbending attitude to the Jewish nation and his contempt for its feelings also found expression in the coins struck by him in Judaea. As is well known (see above, p. 336), the governors of Judaea struck no silver coins and were content, like the Hasmonaean rulers and the Herods, to mint in bronze. We know that the other procurators, careful not to offend Jewish religious feeling, refrained from stamping their coins with the figures of men or animals or of pagan objects whose connection with the pagan cults was obvious. Only Pilate may be regarded as exceptional from this point of view.

During the years 29, 30 and 31 C.E., which were Sejanus' last years and constituted his heyday, the coins struck by Pilate bore pagan symbols in the form of sacred vessels (the *simpulum* and the *lituus*), of the sort encountered in other parts of the Roman Empire. It is true that even now Pilate did not figure the portrait of the Emperor on his issues, but this was in any case not the practice with bronze coins. When the governor of Syria Pomponius Flaccus took up his duties in 32 C.E., a new period of minting began in the province of Syria after a long interval, and with this the special coinage of Judaea ceased. No governor of Judaea after Pilate repeated his attempt to stamp pagan cult-symbols on coins minted in Judaea. Pilate's policy is stranger than ever when compared with that of the procurator Felix who, despite the fact that he was one of the harshest of the governors, did not venture to strike coins with the *lituus* and the *simpulum*.[3]

[1] Tacitus, *Annals* VI, 27,2.
[2] Luke 23:12.
[3] On Pilate's policy as reflected also on his coins see E. Stauffer, op.cit., pp. 495-514; E. M. Smallwood, *Latomus* (1956), pp. 327-8; E. Bammel, *JJS* (1950-1), pp. 108-110. The picture that emerges is consonant with that of Philo and Jo-

The other steps taken by Pilate in Judaea accorded with this new and domineering policy. The first serious clash between Pilate and the masses of the Jewish people came with the introduction into Jerusalem of the standards of a military unit bearing the image of the Emperor.[1] This was a contravention of the practice of previous governors, so Pilate brought the unit to Jerusalem unexpectedly and at night. Even if the step is not regarded as provocative and was not meant as a direct insult to Jewish feelings, it revealed a glaring lack of consideration for them and the end of the policy of tactful handling of the inhabitants of Judaea. Since not all units of the Roman army possessed standards with the imperial portrait, a change may have taken place in the composition of the garrison of Jerusalem which brought a cohort with standards bearing an imperial portrait to the city.[2] Previous governors on such occasions had doubtless found solutions satisfactory to the Jews, but Pilate was determined to follow the usual practice of the Roman army. The act aroused the wrath of the Jews, who streamed in their multitudes to Caesarea to persuade the governor to take the standards out of Jerusalem, and stayed there for several days. Pilate's attempt to frighten them by surrounding them with armed troops proved fruitless; when he discovered their obstinate faith and their readiness to die rather than suffer its profanation, he ordered the standards to be removed from Jerusalem. On this matter, therefore, Pontius Pilate yielded to the Jews' stern resistance and the prospect of open revolt. But he gave full effect to his purpose in another instance in which he felt that he was not clearly deviating from normal practice and that the support of the central government would not be withheld. This was connected with the building of an aqueduct to supply Jerusalem. He took money from the Temple treasury to finance the project, and this step again aroused resentment among the Jews, who demanded that he stop using Temple money. Pilate reacted harshly. He put troops into civilian clothing and ordered them to beat up the Jewish populace

sephus and refutes the attempt of H. Peter, *Neue Jahrbücher für klassische Altertum* XIX (1907), pp. 1-40 to whitewash Pilate. It seems that E. Fascher *PW* XX (1950), cols. 1322-3 is also somewhat influenced by Peter. For a new attempt on the same lines see P. L. Maier, *HTR* (1969), pp. 120-1; see also J. Blinzler, *Der Prozess Jesu* (3rd ed., 1960), pp. 187-193, and for a different view Orth, op. cit., p. 77, n. 6.
[1] Jos. *Ant.* XVIII, 55-59; *War* II, 169-174.
[2] Cf. C. H. Kraeling, *HTR* (1942), pp. 263-289. It is noteworthy, however, that the standards themselves became an object of religious worship for the Roman soldiers. Cf. A. D. Nock, *HTR* (1952), pp. 239-240.

The soldiers, who were drawn from sections of the population markedly hostile to the Jews, displayed an enthusiasm which exceeded even Pilate's. Many Jews were killed and wounded, and Pilate retained the upper hand.[1]

A further conflict broke out between Pilate and the Jews when Pilate brought into Jerusalem shields dedicated to the Emperor Tiberius. This event seems to have occurred after the fall of Sejanus, and Pilate, according to Philo, conceived the deed 'more to grieve the people than to honour Tiberius'. The governor decided to place the golden shields in the Palace of Herod; they bore no image and their display involved the transgression of no specific prohibition in the Jewish religion. Nevertheless the deed infuriated the Jews. It now appeared that they were ready to oppose even the smallest hint of profanation of the sanctity of Jerusalem, all the more because, as seems likely, the shields were inscribed with the names of pagan deities. The people organized themselves for action. Led by four of Herod's sons, they demanded the removal of the shields, as being against Jewish tradition and the policy adopted by all the kings and emperors. When Pilate refused, the Jewish representatives argued that he was using the imperial name merely as a pretext for offending the Jewish law. If he really claimed Caesar's authority, he must show them an explicit order. Meantime the Jews had dispatched a letter to Tiberius voicing their complaints. Tiberius granted their petition and ordered the transfer of the shields to Caesarea where they were to be dedicated in the Temple of Augustus.[2] These clashes were not the only ones that took place during Pilate's term of office. We learn, from the Gospel according to Luke, of the Galileans whose blood Pilate mingled with that of the sacrifices.[3] There is no reason for connecting this massacre with one of the events known to us from the other literary sources at our disposal, for there could undoubtedly have been many other occasions on which pilgrims from Galilee came into conflict with the Romans. Two other men were crucified with Jesus, and when Jesus was condemned to death

[1] Jos. *Ant.* XVIII, 60-2; *War* I, 175-7.
[2] Philo, *Legatio*, 299-305. Josephus does not mention this episode which should not be identified with that of the standards, *pace* Dessau, p. 787, n. 4; cf. E. M. Smallwood, *Philonis Alexandrini 'Legatio ad Gaium'* (1961), p. 302; P. L. Maier op.cit., pp. 109-121. It seems that the episode of the shields took place after the fall of Sejanus, but I doubt whether we can date it with any degree of certainty to 32 C.E., as A. D. Doyle, *JTS* (1941), pp. 190-3 does.
[3] Luke 13:1; see also J. Blinzler, *Novum Testamentum* II, pp. 24-49.

the capital sentence had been pronounced upon Barabbas, no doubt a rebel against Rome. The 'strong-arm' policy now enforced by Pilate created a Jewish zealot reaction, and a tense eschatological anticipation was characteristic of those years. Pilate saw himself bound to suppress these manifestations of revolt without compunction. This, by and large, is the explanation of the trial of Jesus, as also of the decisiveness with which Pilate acted towards the movement in Samaria led by a man whose name has not come down to us. This leader stirred the Samaritans to ascend the Mount of Garizim by promising to show them the sacred vessels hidden by Moses. The Samaritans gathered in a village called Tiratana with the intention of ascending the hill.[1] Pilate prevented it by dispatching troops who wrought much slaughter among the Samaritans and took many prisoners. He further ordered the execution of their men of influence and repute. The boule of the Samaritans complained to Vitellius, governor of Syria, who removed Pilate from his post and ordered him to proceed to Rome to the Emperor to justify himself concerning the complaints brought against him by the Samaritans. Pilate had no alternative but to obey Vitellius and to quit Judaea, where for ten years he had operated to create bad blood. Vitellius took upon himself the direct responsibility for the situation in the province, nominating one of his friends, Marcellus, to take charge of Judaean affairs.[2] Vitellius, feeling the need to ensure peace and order and to calm the inhabitants after the tension which had prevailed under Pilate, appeared at Jerusalem at the Passover Festival and won popular confidence by alleviating and even remitting the tax on agricultural produce, and by handing over the priestly garments to the priests themselves. He thereby abolished an unpopular practice that had been current since the inauguration of the province of Judaea. Among the important steps taken by Vitellius to restore popular confidence in Roman rule was the deposition of Joseph Caiaphas, the loyal ally of Pilate. His brother-in-law, Jonathan son of Ananus, was appointed in his place;[3] he was one of the prominent personalities of Jewish society, and played an important role even after the end of his period as high priest.

Vitellius' attitude to the Jews remained conciliatory. When he set out at the head of his legions and allies on a campaign against Aretas

---

[1] Cf. Abel, op.cit. ii, p. 484.
[2] Jos. Ant. xviii, 85-9.
[3] Ant. xviii, 90-5. Cf. also the section on chronology, p. 69.

king of the Nabataeans, he planned to march from Ptolemais through Judaea. But when the Jewish leaders came to meet him and implored him not to pass through their country, since the introduction of standards was a contravention of the custom of their fathers, Vitellius acceded to their request and diverted his forces by another route through the Plain of Jezreel and Transjordan. He himself returned to Jerusalem accompanied by Herod Antipas and his friends to offer sacrifices during festival time at the Temple; he stayed three days. On that occasion he again changed the High Priest, replacing Jonathan son of Ananus by his brother Theophilus.

These rapid changes, which were contrary even to the practice of previous governors, are not to be interpreted as implying deliberate contempt of the High Priesthood; such an intention is not to be imputed to Vitellius, who had done so much to appease the Jews. The reason may have been Jewish opposition to Jonathan in person. In the meantime, a new emperor had been crowned in Rome, and Vitellius administered the oath of allegiance to the inhabitants of Judaea.[1] The political changes at Rome were shortly to exercise an immense influence on the course of affairs in Judaea, but at first no turn for the worse was felt, Gaius merely dispatching a new governor, Marullus, to the country.[2]

Gaius and the image in the Temple

The accession of Gaius Caligula to the throne (March, 37 c.e.) was received with enthusiasm throughout the Empire. The Jews were no exception, for there seemed no reasonable grounds to be apprehensive of such a change in the central government. Gaius' father Germanicus had, indeed, evinced a certain coldness to the Jews during his stay in Egypt in the year 19 c.e. (see also above, p. 125), but it is very doubtful if this was an expression of a consistent or deliberate anti-Jewish policy; in any case there was no reason to suppose that his son would exhibit anti-Jewish tendencies. The general tradition of the Roman emperors, now reinforced by the close friendship between

---

[1] *Ant.* XVIII, 120-124; cf. *ILS* no. 190 (Aritium, Lusitania); Dittenberger, *Sylloge Inscriptionum Graecarum* (3rd ed.) III, no. 797 (Assos, Asia Minor).
[2] *Ant.* XVIII, 237. The former governor of Judaea was Marcellus, who had been appointed by Vitellius. Because of the similarity of the names (Marullus, Marcellus), it has been suggested by S. J. de Laet, *L'Antiquité classique* (1939), p. 413 that the same person is implied; in this view he was anticipated by F. Westberg, *Die Biblische Chronologie nach Flavius Josephus* (1910), p. 64.

the new emperor and the Jewish Agrippa, was also a surety for the Jewish position. The first two years of Gaius' reign, therefore, constituted for the Jews of Judaea a direct continuation of the previous period. The most striking change was the gradual unification of the two tetrarchies previously under the sovereignty of Philip and Herod Antipas. They were assigned to Agrippa and became a kingdom. Thus about the year 39 C.E. the Jews of the country who had not been within the province of Judaea were united under the rule of a Jewish king. Another change was the appointment of a new legate of Syria. Vitellius was replaced by Petronius, who was related to him by marriage.[1] As was soon to become clear, Petronius displayed an attitude of sympathy to the Jews in no wise inferior to that of his predecessor.

A fundamental change in relations between the Jews and the Roman Empire came about as a result of the policy of Gaius, who upheld the imperial cult more seriously and not, like his predecessors, merely for reasons of policy. In Rome and Italy itself the duty was imposed of worshipping the emperor as a god in his lifetime; this was a practice opposed to that of previous emperors. Philo describes for us in biting phrases Gaius' justification of his claim to a divine cult: 'Like the other owners of animals such as herdsmen, goatherds and shepherds, who are not themselves oxen, goats and sheep but men who enjoy a more honorable lot and a loftier bodily structure, so I also, as master of the noblest of all herds, the human race, must be regarded as different in quality, in other words, I am to be regarded not as a man but as one enjoying a lot more exalted and divine.'[2]

A special temple was built for Gaius at Rome and another in the city of Miletus in Asia Minor. Priests were appointed and sacrifices offered, and the Emperor identified himself with various deities. The seriousness with which he treated his own divine cult provided the enemies of the Jews both in Egypt and Judaea with a pretext for inciting the emperor against them. For the first time in the history of relations between the Jews and the Empire, the question of the imperial cult became a central problem; and for the first time after a long interval

---

[1] Tacitus, *Annals* III, 49. Cf. Suetonius, *Vitellius*, 6; A. Stein, *Der römische Ritterstand* (1927), p 300, n.3.
[2] Philo, *Legatio*, 76; Suetonius, *Life of Gaius Caligula*, 22; Dio Cassius LIX, 26,5; Seneca, *De ira* I, 20,8-9; Jos. *Ant.* XVIII, 256; L. Robert, *Hellenica* VII (1949), pp. 206-238; J. P. V. D. Balsdon, *The Emperor Gaius* (1934), pp. 157-173; L. Cerfaux et J. Tondriau, *Le culte des souverains* (1957), pp. 342-7; F. Taeger, *Charisma* II (1960), pp. 281-295. On Gaius as a psychopath see J. Lucas, *L'Antiquité Classique* (1967), pp. 159-189.

the Jewish nation faced a fateful decision whether or not to revolt against Rome.

The trouble began at Jamnia, a town with a Jewish majority: the gentile minority now found an opportunity to pay back old scores. When rumours spread of the Emperor's enthusiasm for his own cult, the gentiles of Jamnia set up a brick altar in his honour. The Jews saw this as a direct provocation and a desecration of the sanctity of Judaea; the action moreover was nearly unprecedented, for with the exception of the brief period of the persecution of Antiochus Epiphanes, all the gentile rulers of Judaea had recognized the right of its inhabitants to prohibit absolutely all idolatry within their country. Hence the Jews of Jamnia did not hesitate to destroy the altar. The gentile inhabitants complained to Capito, the procurator of Jamnia. Capito's relations with the Jews were already strained, and in Tiberius' reign he had managed to fall out with Agrippa. He sent a report to, the emperor on the developments at Jamnia. Gaius was enraged by the Jews' offence to his divinity, and inspired by several of his intimates (the Egyptian Helicon and Apelles of Ascalon),[1] decided on an extreme step (in the spring or early summer of the year 40 C.E.), namely the introduction of a colossal golden statue into the Temple of Jerusalem.[2] The statue, it seems, was to be of Zeus with the lineaments of Gaius himself.[3]

Knowledge of the Jewish temper gave reason to anticipate that the order would arouse sharp opposition in Judaea, and that it could be carried out only by force. As it was to be expected that resistance would be on a larger scale than could be overcome by the governor of Judaea with the forces at his command, the execution of the order was imposed from the beginning upon Petronius, governor of Syria.

Petronius has become one of the famous personalities in Jewish history, for in the course of these events he imperilled his position and his life to prevent the desecration of the Temple by Gaius. In the year 19 C.E. he had served as *consul suffectus* and had gained a reputation by his legislation in favour of the slave class;[4] in 29-35 C.E. he had been proconsul of the Province of Asia,[5] where he had already

---

[1] On Apelles see also Suetonius, *Life of Gaius Caligula*, 33; Dio Cassius LIX, 5,2.
[2] Philo, *Legatio*, 199-206.
[3] Philo, *Legatio*, 203; cf. Jos. *Ant.* XVIII, 261; *War* II, 185; Tacitus, *Historiae* V, 9,2.
[4] W. W. Buckland, *The Roman Law of Slavery* (1908), p. 664.
[5] Or in 28-34 C.E. Cf. Magie, *Roman Rule in Asia Minor* II, p. 1363, n. 38.

became known to the Jewish nation. In Philo's words:[1] 'he possessed, it would seem, sparks of philosophy and the Jewish reverence for God'; and Josephus too puts into his mouth clear statements of his reverence for the Jewish God and his readiness to endanger himself on behalf of the Jews.

A man of Petronius' stamp could certainly take no pleasure in the Emperor's order. As governor of Syria and responsible for the Parthian frontier he also feared a Jewish rebellion in Judaea. This could spread to the neighbouring lands and produce a general conflagration in the countries of the East, laying the eastern frontier of the Empire open to a Parthian invasion; for despite the death of Artabanus in 38 C.E. and the war which had broken out between Vardanes and Gotarzes, the Parthians were a constant danger to the Roman provinces. Gaius' removal of King Mithradates of Armenia had also increased the gravity of the situation and exposed Armenia to Parthian influence. Even Petronius, however, saw no possibility of resisting the imperial order. He gained a little time from the fact that the Emperor had not sent a statue from Rome to be set up in the Temple of Jerusalem, nor given specific instructions to select for the purpose a statue in one of the shrines of Syria. Petronius therefore gave the task to Phoenician artists, who began to prepare a statue at Sidon.[2] Taking two legions, he encamped at Ptolemais, the permanent base of departure of legions marching from Syria to Judaea.[3] The entire Jewish nation had been thrown into a state of excitement by the threatened calamity; the persecution of Antiochus Epiphanes seemed to have come again; the sanctity of the Temple and the fundamental values of Judaism were again in danger. Crowds of Jews streamed to Ptolemais to deter the governor from carrying out the Emperor's command, and expressed their unqualified preparedness to protect their sacred inheritance. Petronius, realizing, as he had foreseen, that the imperial order could not be implemented without conflict and bloodshed, proceeded to Tiberias with his friends and entourage.[4] Here the scenes of Ptolemais were repeated. Masses of peasants deserted their fields, though it was the season of harvest (early summer, 40 C.E.), and bivouacked

---

[1] Philo, *Legatio*, 245.
[2] *Legatio*, 220-2.
[3] In Jos. *War* II, 186 we hear of three legions.
[4] We should not suppose a long interval between Petronius' visits to Ptolemais and Tiberias. See E. M. Smallwood, *Latomus* (1957), pp. 8-9.

about Petronius for forty days, imploring him not to desecrate the Temple. This time it became clear that here was no movement of hotheads or extreme zealots preaching abstract principles of liberation from imperial rule, but an entire nation, including the upper class and the members of the Herodian family, united in utter opposition to the imperial order. The delegation of the Herodian family, headed by Aristobulus, brother of Agrippa and Helkias the Great, appeared before Petronius and stressed the gravity of the situation, since to persist with the execution of the plan would bring about the economic ruin of the country. Petronius, convinced both by the delegates and by the determination of the masses, resolved to risk postponing the execution of the order.[1] He dispatched a letter to Gaius in which he informed the Emperor of the peril involved in placing the statue in the Temple, emphasizing in particular the consequences of the deed in the light of the Emperor's plans to visit the Orient.[2]

Gaius, it seems, at first refused to cancel his project, but consented to a temporary postponement till the completion of essential agricultural work.[3] In the meantime Agrippa brought his full influence to bear on his friend the Emperor to ward off the adverse decision. The Jewish King, then at the height of his friendship with the Emperor, in effect threw his entire political position and future into the scales to prevent the threat to the welfare of the Jewish people and the outbreak of a general war between Rome and the Jews. By joining political considerations with personal arguments, he was able to induce Gaius to consent to cancel the order in its gravest form, in so far as it involved the setting up of a statue in the Temple itself. A message in this sense was sent to Petronius, but Gaius added the observation that should anyone desire to set up altars and statues or to sacrifice to Caesar outside Jerusalem, he should not prevent it.[4]

The grant of freedom of action to the foes of the Jews outside Jerusalem held the seeds of a new conflict especially in cities of mixed population. There were also rumours that the Emperor intended to surprise the Jews by a lightning operation, bringing a ready-made statue from Rome and setting it up in the Temple of Jerusalem when he came on

---

[1] The remark of H. Willrich, *Klio* III, p. 417 that the attitude of Petronius was due to the fact that he had accepted bribes from the Jews (an explanation put in *Ant.* XVIII, 304 in the mouth of Gaius), reflects the feelings of Willrich himself.

[2] *Ant.* XVIII, 262-288; *War* II, 186-7; 192-202; Philo, *Legatio*, 222-253.

[3] *Legatio*, 254-260.

[4] *Legatio*, 261-334; *Ant.* XVIII, 289-301.

his visit to the East as planned, in the year 41 C.E. Petronius' position naturally suffered, and the Emperor had his death sentence ready.[1] Matters would have reached a crisis sooner or later and the collision between Rome and the Jews, though postponed, would have taken place in the near future; it was only prevented by the sword of Cassius Chaerea, which felled Gaius Caligula on the 24th of January 41 C.E. Tacitus describes events in a lapidary sentence:[2] 'dein iussi a C. Caesare effigiem eius in templo locare arma potius sumpsere, quem motum Caesaris mors diremit'. But the memory of the events of Caligula's reign and fear of their recurrence caused relationships between Rome and the Jews to be strained after the tyrant's death, for it had become clear even to moderate Jews how much the very freedom of the Jewish religion depended on the fickle desires of an absolute, gentile ruler. Again in Tacitus' notable formulation:[3] 'the fear persisted that one of the Caesars might give the same order' (manebat metus, ne quis principum eadem imperitaret).

The decline of procuratorial rule

The last twenty years after the death of Agrippa I down to the outbreak of the Great Revolt were marked by the decline of Roman rule in Judaea and by increasingly difficult relations between the authorities and the various strata of Jewish society. The Roman procurators became more and more oppressive and clashes with the Jews more frequent, while the sympathy shown to the Hellenistic urban element became more and more marked.

The members of the Herodian family who succeeded Agrippa continued to collaborate with the Roman Empire. Although they attempted from time to time to mediate between the local Roman authorities and the Jews, and to alleviate the plight of the latter, it was clear that none of them reverted to the idea of complete self-identification with the Jewish nation which had characterized the last years of the reign of Agrippa I. Thanks to their prestige in the Roman world and to the peculiar status accorded to them in the appointment of high priests, the Herods remained one of the foremost factors in Jeru-

---

[1] Legatio, 337; Ant. XVIII, 302-4; War II, 203. We read in Josephus that the Emperor ordered Petronius to commit suicide, but that the news about the death of Gaius arrived before the order. Cf. Ant. XIX, 9-10: Memmius Regulus who had hesitated to transfer the statue of the Olympian Zeus to Rome was also saved by the death of the Emperor.
[2] Historiae V, 9,2.
[3] Annals XII, 54,1.

salem society. Their connections with aristocratic families in the Hellenistic Diaspora lent weight to their influence, but the fact remained that they no longer reigned as kings in Jerusalem. This also sometimes made it easier to organize united opposition against them, nourished by the awareness that in the last instance it was the Roman ruler first and foremost who decided the affairs of Judaea and not the various representatives of the Herodian family. Sundry groups found the way to uniting for common action even against Agrippa II, principally in matters connected with the honour and prestige of the priestly aristocracy . But it would be wrong to speak of a united front of the priestly oligarchy against the principal representatives of the Herods. Such a front could have been created only on exceptional occasions, for generally the oligarchic front was divided and disintegrated, and in no period since that preceeding the Hasmonaean rising was there such internal disunity. This situation produced sanguinary feuds between the principal claimants to the high priesthood and between the high priests themselves.

Both Herod of Chalcis and Agrippa II utilized to an increasing extent their right to appoint high priests, but their nominees were usually the normal representatives of the high priestly oligarchy, and it should be noted that from this point of view there was a clear continuity between the first period of direct Roman rule and the period of the last procurators. When direct provincial rule was reimposed on Judaea, the office of procurator was bestowed upon Cuspius Fadus (44-46 c.e.), and friction between the Jews and the Romans began again, more intensely than ever. An immediate dispute arose over the high priestly vestments. Fadus summoned the Jewish leaders and proposed that they should deposit the vestments in the citadel of the Antonia, as had been the practice before the legate of Syria had decided the matter. The Jewish leaders were not prepared to renounce previous gains or to renew a situation dishonourable to the Jewish religion. They therefore requested Fadus and the Syrian legate, Cassius Longinus, who had come at the head of a large force to keep order, that they should be permitted to send a deputation on the matter to Rome to the Emperor Claudius, with nothing done in the meantime likely to prejudice the status quo. Fadus and Cassius consented to the request, and the emissaries of Jewish Jerusalem left for Rome to intercede with the emperor. There they received much assistance from Agrippa II, who was then at Rome, and who added his influence to persuade the emperor to grant the request of the Jewish delegates concerning the priestly vestments. The emperor dispatched an official rescript to the Jewish authorities in Jerusalem (in 45 C.E.), informing them of his decision that the sacred vestments should continue in the custody of the Jews themselves, in accordance with Vitellius' arrangements.[1]

Another faculty withheld from Fadus which had been enjoyed by the first Roman governors was the right to appoint high priests. This faculty, with the supervision of the Temple and the Temple money, was accorded Herod of Chalcis.[2] Herod used his powers to remove Elionaeus from his incumbency and appointed in his place Joseph son of Camei, who belonged to a family already prominent in the time of the first procurators.

From the beginning Fadus had faced a growing ferment among the Jews, partly of a religious messianic complexion. At the outset of his governorship Fadus found Peraea plunged in disorder. The Jews of that region and the inhabitants of Philadelphia were in conflict on the question of the borders between Jewish Peraea and the Hellenistic town. Some of the Peraean Jews tried to settle matters without appealing to the Roman government and contrary to the view of their official leaders. Fadus, considering that they were taking the law into their own hands, seized three of the trouble-makers, executed one and sentenced the other two to exile.[3] Another focus of trouble was the frontier of Idumaea and Arabia, where one Ptolemy, the head of a band, was causing damage on both sides; Fadus defeated him and put him to death,[4] but we do not know if he was a Jew or not.

The messianic ferment involved a graver danger of conflagration. A man named Theudas gathered about him a great multitude, whom he persuaded to follow him to the Jordan, promising to dry up the river at a word to enable his followers to cross. Fadus, unwilling to sanction this dangerous concentration of people near the Jordan, sent a squadron of cavalry against them. Many were captured alive but Theudas' head was cut off and brought to Jerusalem.[5]

The successor of Fadus as procurator of Judaea was Tiberius Julius

[1] Jos. Ant. xx, 6-14.   [2] Ant. xx, 15.
[3] Ant. xx, 2-4.   [4] Ant. xx, 5.
[5] Ant. xx, 97-8; Acts 5:36. The execution of Theudas is referred to in Acts as before the activity of Judas the Galilean. That of course contradicts the chronological sequence. See also M. Dibelius, Aufsätze zur Apostelgeschichte (1951), pp. 159-160. It is difficult to suppose that there were two Theudases. So e.g. L. Dupraz, De l'association de Tibère au Principat à la naissance du Christ (1966), p. 147, n. 1. See also J. W. Swain, HTR (1944), pp. 341-9; M. Hengel, Die Zeloten (1961), pp. 235-6.

Alexander (46-48 C.E.), who belonged to one of the most illustrious Jewish families of Alexandria, and nephew of the philosopher Philo. But unlike his father and uncle, Tiberius Alexander had forsaken Judaism for a Roman administrative career. The procuratorship of Judaea was for him merely one of the rungs of the Roman administrative ladder after he had served as *epistrategos* of the Thebais, and a prelude to a much more brilliant future. With such a background and such ambitions, Tiberius Alexander could not be expected to behave towards the Jews with special consideration. It need only be observed that he had certainly had previous contacts with members of the Herodian family; his father had maintained relations with Agrippa I and his brother Marcus was the first husband of the renowned Berenice. Herod of Chalcis, Berenice's second husband, continued to discharge his function as overseer of the high priesthood. During the governorship of Tiberius Alexander he removed Joseph son of Camei from his post and appointed in his stead Ananias son of Nedebaeus, one of the most prominent personalities in Jerusalem society.[1]

There is no reason to think that the Jewish masses welcomed the apostate Tiberius Alexander with enthusiasm, or preferred him in any way to procurators of gentile origin. Tiberius Alexander, like his predecessor Fadus, was faced with rebellious stirrings but was generally able to keep order in Judaea. The anti-Roman movement in Judaea was now inspired by men of the family of Judas of Galilee. Tiberius Alexander, undeterred, ordered the crucifixion of James and Simon, Judas' sons.[2]

The governorship of Tiberius Alexander was also marked by a severe famine in the country. The intervention of Queen Helena of Adiabene, who purchased corn in Egypt and dried figs in Cyprus, alleviated to some extent this catastrophe.[3] Tiberius Alexander left Judaea after two years, no doubt to receive a higher post in the Roman *cursus*, although we hear of him only fifteen years later. He is then found undertaking important duties in the conduct of war against the Parthians under Corbulo (63 C.E.).[4]

The tension between the Roman authorities and the Jews increased under the new procurator Ventidius Cumanus, whose entire period of rule (48-52 C.E.) was marked by grave clashes and disorders.[5]

---

[1] Jos. *Ant.* xx, 103. [2] *Ant.* xx, 102.
[3] *Ant.* xx, 51; 101. [4] Tacitus, *Annals* xv, 28,3.
[5] From Josephus we know only his cognomen (Cumanus); the nomen Ventidius appears in Tacitus, *Annals* xii, 54,2.

As always, the three great festivals of pilgrimage were the seasons marked out for trouble. The first clash known to us took place on a day of the Passover Festival. In accordance with current practice under the procurators, a special auxiliary cohort was keeping order in Jerusalem on the festival day. One of the soldiers committed an act offensive to the Jews. The crowd reacted angrily, the complaint was heard that the insult was directed not against them but against the Almighty, and some hurled accusations against Cumanus himself. The latter answered the charges with acrimony, bidding the crowd keep the peace of the festival and refrain from sedition. The Jews were unimpressed and Cumanus, concentrating a large force in the Antonia, put the mob to flight; many of the Jews were killed as they fled, and the event left the worst possible impression.[1]

A second incident occurred some time afterwards. Seditious Jewish elements, tired of Roman government, set an ambush near Beth Horon for Stephanus, an imperial freedman,[2] and robbed him of his entire property. Cumanus, on hearing of the robbery, gave orders for the nearby villages to be raided and plundered and their notables seized on the pretext that they had made no effort to catch the robbers. During this punitive expedition one of the soldiers took the opportunity to tear up and burn a scroll of the Law in public, cursing and jeering while doing so. As news of the incident spread, a vast crowd of Jews gathered at Caesarea, the seat of the governor, and demanded that the offender should be punished, alleging that an atrocious sacrilege had been committed, and that the Jews could not tolerate so grave an insult to the ancestral religion. The prevailing atmosphere was of impending revolt. Cumanus consulted his council, and to prevent revolt, decided to mete out the maximum punishment to the offender, whose head was cut off.[3]

Disorder reached its peak at the end of Cumanus' term of office. Its cause was a serious clash between the Jews and the Samaritans, which brought about the intervention of the Roman authorities. Pilgrims from Galilee fell foul of the Samaritans near the village of Ginaea in the north of Samaria, and some were killed. Numerous Galileans responded by assembling to attack the Samaritans. The notables of Galilee thereupon appealed to Cumanus to intervene

---

[1] Jos. *Ant.* xx, 105-112; *War* II, 224-7.
[2] See H. Chantraine, *Freigelassene und Sklaven im Dienst der römischen Kaiser* (1967).
[3] Jos. *Ant.* xx, 113-117; *War* II, 228-231.

before something more serious occurred. They demanded that those found guilty of murder should be punished, on the assumption that only then would the crowd of Galileans disperse without violence. Cumanus does not seem to have reacted promptly. In the meantime news of the murder had created a storm in Jerusalem and many Jews banded together to take vengeance on the Samaritans. The organized groups headed by Eleazar son of Deinaeus and Alexander now assumed prominence; attacking the inhabitants of southern Samaria near the toparchy of Acrabatene, they killed some and burned their villages. Cumanus thereupon came out openly in support of the Samaritans. Taking with him a squadron of Sebastene cavalry and four cohorts of infantry from Caesarea, he went to their assistance, also recruiting men among the Samaritan population itself. Many of Eleazar's people were taken prisoner or killed. The Jewish leaders of Jerusalem did all they could to persuade the hotheads not to declare open war upon the Samaritans, which would bring about Roman action against Jerusalem. Most of the common people were convinced by their arguments and only the organized groups of extremist combatants continued active. The men of influence among the Samaritans, for their part, set out for Tyre to see Quadratus, governor of Syria, and to demand the punishment of those who had ravaged their territory. The Jewish leaders also arrived there, led by the former High Priest Jonathan son of Ananus. They claimed that the Samaritans had begun the disorders by attacking the pilgrims, and that Cumanus was to blame for all that had occurred, by refusing to punish the murderers, and by taking bribes from the Samaritans. When Quadratus had listened to the pleas of both sides, he postponed his decision pending a visit to Judaea to investigate what had occurred with greater precision. Reaching Samaria shortly afterwards, he crucified a number of men both Jews and Samaritans. Later, when he reached Lydda, the Samaritans divulged to him that some of the Jews were inciting the people to rise against Rome. The governor of Syria ordered the agitators to be put to death, but also removed Cumanus from his post, bidding him to proceed to Rome to stand trial before the Emperor. One of the Roman officers, Celer, was also ordered to Rome as having been heavily involved in the sanguinary conflicts. The recognized leaders of the Samaritans and the Jews were also sent there, among them the High Priest Ananias and the ex-High Priest Jonathan son of Ananus. Meantime at Rome both sides prepared for a severe struggle before the Emperor. Cumanus and the Samaritans regarded themselves as allies, having worked together during the disorders. They were supported by influential circles among the Emperor's friends and freedmen. They were actively opposed by the young Agrippa, then still resident in Rome, who with the aid of the Empress Agrippina succeeded in persuading the Emperor to decide in favour of the Jews. There are grounds for supposing that the freedman Pallas, then serving Caesar as *a rationibus*, and confidant of Agrippina, also favoured the Jews. Simultaneously one of the chief Jewish spokesmen, Jonathan son of Ananus, was working hard to have Felix, Pallas' brother, appointed procurator of Judaea in place of Cumanus. Felix seems to have been well-known to the Jews previously, for he had evidently been in Judaea on some administrative task or other (see Appendix II pp. 374-6). The alliance between the Jews, Pallas and Agrippina bore fruit. Cumanus was found guilty and sentenced to exile; the officer Celer was sent to Jerusalem to be executed; the Samaritan delegates were put to death in Rome itself, and Felix was dispatched to Judaea (52 C.E.) as procurator.[1]

The governorship of Felix (52-60 C.E.), which began on friendly terms with the Jews, ended with a crisis in their relations with the Roman administration. Both Josephus and Tacitus denounce in the sharpest terms the character of Felix and his administration of the province's affairs.[2] But it should be noted that he was not completely beyond forming certain ties with Jewish society. His government was conducted in association with influential circles among the Jewish upper classes, but sometimes also in opportunistic accord with extremist groups in the other camp. Outwardly at least, his connections with the Herodian family were strengthened by his marriage to Drusilla, daughter of Agrippa I, who abandoned her former husband, Azizus ruler of Emesa, to marry him;[3] the intermediary had been a Jew of Cyprus. It is hard to know if in fact the marriage led to closer bonds with the Herodian family, for unlike various gentile kings who had become Jews on entering into marriage alliances with Herod's family, Felix did not adopt Judaism. Out of consideration for Jewish feelings, this marriage did not obtain the official approval of Agrippa II.

---

[1] *Ant.* xx, 118-137; *War* II, 232-247; Tacitus, *Annals* xII, 54.
[2] The picture drawn of Felix by P. W. Henderson, *The Life and Principate of the Emperor Nero* (1903), pp. 364-6 displays too much unmerited sympathy for the procurator.
[3] Jos. *Ant.* xx, 141-3; cf. Acts 24:24.

But a way to smooth things out was gradually found and Felix even gave prominence to his links with the royal house by bestowing the name Agrippa on the son whom Drusilla bore him.[1]

Felix's relation to the Jewish upper classes was not limited to his marriage with Drusilla. It is important to note that the High Priest Ananias son of Nedebaeus consolidated his position in Judaea and his connections with the Roman administration in the years of Felix' procuratorship; they continued to develop subsequently under the governorship of Albinus. Ananias (high priest in the years 47-59 C.E.) seems to have enjoyed the support of both Agrippa II and of Felix. As a result of this triple alliance he held his position longer than any other high priest in the period of the procurators before the revolt; and only Joseph Caiaphas had held office longer in the period of the first Roman governors.[2] On the other hand the public activity of Jonathan son of Ananus came to an early conclusion, in spite of all that he had done to obtain Felix' appointment. Jonathan's special position as the elder statesman of the Hananids and his great influence both in the country and abroad evoked the dislike of Felix, who began to regard him as an obstacle, for Jonathan felt himself partly responsible for Felix's doings and from time to time found occasion to reprove him. According to Josephus, Felix, determined to be rid of him, bribed one of Jonathan's close friends to contact the extreme elements, the *sicarii*. Some of them came to Jerusalem on the pretext of visiting the Temple and murdered Jonathan with complete impunity.[3]

The murder of Jonathan son of Ananus was a signal for similar actions throughout Judaea. Felix's procuratorship saw the reinforcement of the extreme liberation movement and its development as a permanent factor in the life of Judaea. At the beginning of his term of office Felix took energetic steps against the extremist leaders. He was able to apprehend Eleazar son of Deinaeus, who led the bands of Jewish raiders against the Samaritans under Cumanus. Eleazar was not put to death, but sent to Rome to the Emperor.[4] His subsequent fate is unknown. One of the most impressive messianic ferments of those years was associated with the appearance of a prophet from Egypt, who gathered

[1] *Ant.* xx, 143.
[2] Some scholars suggest shorter term for this high priest. See J. Derenbourg, *Essai sur l'histoire et la géographie de la Palestine* (1867), pp. 231-2; Graetz III 2, pp. 724-7.
[3] *Ant.* xx, 162-165; cf. *War* II, 256.
[4] *Ant.* xx, 161.

about him thousands of believers and persuaded them to ascend the Mount of Olives, promising to show them how the walls of Jerusalem would fall at his command, so that they could enter the city unhindered, while he himself would overcome the garrison and become king over the nation. Felix sallied out with infantry and cavalry against the prophet's followers and killed many of them, thus terminating the activity of the Egyptian seer, who fled for his life and disappeared from the scene.[1] But the suppression of this messianic movement hardly restored peace and quiet throughout Judaea. Felix's massacre merely increased the general bitterness; and the extremists gained in strength everywhere, urging the people to rise against Rome to recover their liberty, and inflicting the death penalty on those who refused to join them. They raided the homes of the wealthy and attacked the villages that resisted them, burning the houses and slaughtering the defenders. The result was that at the end of Felix's term of office Rome had little control of the countryside and the country towns of Judaea.[2]

In Jerusalem itself normal life had almost been brought to a standstill. Agrippa II had bestowed the high priesthood upon Ishmael ben Phiabi the Second, the scion of an illustrious priestly family which had not produced high priests since the time of the early Roman rule forty-five years ago; but Ishmael ben Phiabi was unable to calm the city. The tension between the various classes continued to grow. Armed bands roamed the city streets and fought each other there. There was a very bitter struggle between the high priestly oligarchy and the ordinary priests over the tithes. The high priestly families sought to gain control of the tithes and sent their slaves to the threshing-floors to take them by force, thus depriving the ordinary priests of their due.[3] In other parts of the province, outside Judaea proper, the governorship of Felix was also marked by clashes and disorders. The chief trouble centre was Caesarea, the provincial capital. The starting point of the trouble was the legal struggle between the Syro-Greek majority and the large Jewish minority for civic rights in the city. The Jews supported their claims by the argument that the city had been founded by the Jewish king, Herod. The gentile population did not of course deny this fact, but pointed to the ancient name of the place, Tower of Straton, and emphasized that in the previous period Jews had not lived

[1] *Ant.* xx, 169-171; *War* ii, 261-3.
[2] *Ant.* xx, 172; *War* ii, 264-5.
[3] *Ant.* xx, 179-181.

in the city. They argued, moreover, that had Herod wished to establish a primarily Jewish city, he would not have erected temples and statues there. Little by little the dispute assumed the form of an armed conflict. So long as this was limited to the civilian population of Caesarea, the Jews retained some advantage owing to their wealth and strength. The gentile population depended on the large garrison stationed in the town, composed of men of Sebaste and Caesarea naturally sympathetic to their Syro-Greek brethren. The Roman administration attempted to put down the rioting at its inception, but unsuccessfully. One of the clashes ended with a Jewish victory and Felix sent in the troops against the Jews; they killed many and plundered their property.[1] Felix decided to bring the matter of civic rights in Caesarea before the Emperor, and delegations from both sides were dispatched to Rome.

In the year 60 c.e. Felix's governorship ended and he was replaced by Festus. As Felix was no longer functioning, the Jews of Caesarea seized the opportunity to impeach him before the Emperor, but he won his case thanks to his still influential brother Pallas.[2] At the same time, or perhaps some years later, immediately before the outbreak of the Great Revolt, Nero also came to a decision on the struggle between the gentile population of Caesarea and the Jews; his decision was in favour of the gentiles, who had been assisted by the influence of Beryllus, head of the Emperor's Greek secretariat.[3] Thus the Jews became second-class citizens in the city.[4] The results of the legal and political struggle between the gentile and Jewish populations of the town caused additional tension, since the Jews were not prepared to resign themselves permanently to what they regarded as a disastrous deprivation of rights, while the gentile population saw in the imperial decision an official confirmation of the down-grading of the Jews to second-class citizens.

Festus, succeeding Felix, found Judaea almost in anarchy. The influence of the extremists had grown continuously; armed bands were terrorizing the villages and the *sicarii*, Jerusalem. Messianic

---

[1] *Ant.* xx, 173-8; *War* ii, 266-270.
[2] *Ant.* xx, 182.
[3] Against the identification of Beryllus with the famous Afranius Burrus see E. Katterfeld, *Berliner Philologische Wochenschrift* (1913), p. 59; Dessau, p. 802, n. 4; E. Meyer, p. 52, n. 4.
[4] Jos. *Ant.* xx, 183-4. According to *War* ii, 270 the envoys of the parties were already sent to Rome under Felix; according to *War* ii, 284 the decision was made immediately before the outbreak of the Great Revolt in 66 c.e.

pretenders continued to raise hopes, and one promised salvation to all who accompanied him to the desert. Festus treated him as Felix had treated the Egyptian prophet. He sent out troops and this time both the prophet and his disciples were killed.[1]

Festus also had to grapple with an additional problem, as a result of a dispute which had broken out between Agrippa II and the Jewish leaders in Jerusalem. As has been said, Agrippa II, though not king in Jerusalem, enjoyed wide authority in the appointment of high priests and the supervision of the Temple. He decided that these powers authorized him to heighten parts of his palace—the old palace of the Hasmonaeans—so that he could overlook the Temple courts and see what was going on there. This greatly incensed the Jerusalem leaders, who regarded Agrippa's step as sacrilegious. They countered his action by erecting a wall to block his view of the Temple; this to a certain degree also blocked Roman military supervision during the festivals. The building of the wall therefore called forth a sharp reaction on the part not only of Agrippa, but also of Festus, who saw in it a grave blow to his authority as procurator. Festus ordered the wall to be destroyed, but postponed the execution of the order when the Jews persuaded him that it was a matter of grave significance, equivalent to the destruction of a part of the Temple. Festus therefore consented to their request to send a deputation on the matter to the Emperor. This was led by the High Priest Ishmael ben Phiabi the Second, who, although appointed by Agrippa, considered the dignity of the Temple more important than gratitude to his benefactor. He was accompanied by Helcias the Treasurer and 'the Ten Leading Men of the city' (see above p. 345). The Jews found a willing listener in Poppaea Sabina, the Empress, who is termed by Josephus 'religious' (θεοσεβής).[2]

Nero granted the Jewish petition to leave the wall as it was. The 'Ten Leading Men' returned to Jerusalem, but the High Priest Ishmael and Helcias were detained in Rome as hostages. The real reason seems to have been to avoid excessive offence to Agrippa who, as the loser, was thus not bound to see his antagonists' victorious return to Jerusalem.[3]

Agrippa appointed Joseph son of Simon to the vacant High Priesthood

---

[1] *Ant.* xx, 188.
[2] We may doubt whether this constitutes here a technical term. Cf. E. M. Smallwood, *JTS* (1959), pp. 329-335.
[3] Jos. *Ant.* xx, 189-195.

and after him Ananus, son of Ananus, the son of the High Priest Ananus the first, whose brothers had also been high priests.[1] Ananus' appointment was made just at the time when the procurators were being changed, Festus having died and his successor Albinus not having yet reached the country. Ananus the Second was a high priest of pronouncedly Sadducee views and during his brief incumbency (in 62 C.E.) attempted to put them into practice in the legal sphere. The Sanhedrin which he summoned pronounced a series of death sentences, among those condemned being the leader of the Jerusalem Christians, Jacob (James) brother of Jesus, who was sentenced to be stoned. The Pharisaic circles in the city looked unfavourably upon the actions of Ananus the Second and sent envoys to Agrippa asking him to prevent their repetition. Some also set out to meet Albinus on his way from Alexandria, to inform him that the high priest had no authority to convene a Sanhedrin with competence to judge capital cases without the procurator's permission.

Albinus was convinced and wrote an angry letter to Ananus, even threatening to punish him for his arbitrary acts. Agrippa, persuaded by Albinus, and taking into account the bitterness created in Jerusalem by Ananus' acts, deposed him from the high priesthood after a ministry of only three months. He appointed Jesus son of Damnaeus in his place.[2] At the beginning of his procuratorship Albinus made efforts to restore order in the province by energetic action against the *sicarii*. Although he killed a number of them, he was unable to prevent them growing stronger. Albinus' chief ally in Jewish society was the ex-High Priest Ananias son of Nedebaeus, whose influence attained considerable dimensions in these years. The *Sicarii* recognized this fact and endeavoured to exploit it to their own advantage, wringing concessions from the governor by striking at Ananias and his intimates. Seizing the secretary of Eleazar son of Ananias they took him out of Jerusalem, then informed Ananias that they would release him only on condition that he persuaded Albinus to free ten of their members whom he had captured. Ananias was compelled to induce Albinus to do this.[3] Encouraged by their success, the *sicarii* continued to seize from time to time associates of Ananias, and so liberated many of their imprisoned associates. Their activity in Judaea increased.[4]

[1] *Ant.* xx, 196.
[2] *Ant.* xx, 197-203.
[3] *Ant.* xx, 204-9.
[4] *Ant.* xx, 210; cf. *War* ii, 275-6.

Albinus thus discovered a new source of revenue. In return for ransom paid by relatives he agreed to release numerous prisoners who had been confined by the Roman administration or by previous governors, or had been arrested by the local Jewish authorities. In Josephus' words: 'Only those who did not pay remained in gaol.'[1]
Changes again occurred in the high priesthood under Albinus. Agrippa II removed Jesus son of Damnaeus from his incumbency and appointed Jesus of Gamala in his place.[2] Once again a man had attained the high priesthood who was related by marriage to the Boethusians. Jesus son of Damnaeus did not surrender his position in Jerusalem easily, and fought a series of street battles against Jesus of Gamala in the city after both sides had gathered gangs of roughs. The other leaders of the high priestly oligarchy also took part in the conflict, Ananias son of Nedebaeus, a man of outstanding wealth, being especially prominent. A further factor which intensified the anarchy in Jerusalem was the intervention of several associates of Agrippa II, among them Costobar and Saul, who also gathered strong-arm groups to take their share in the street warfare.[3]
Florus was appointed in Albinus' place in 64 C.E. His procuratorship was marked by the same processes as had gone on under Albinus: the widening of the gap between the Roman administration and the Jewish nation, and the growing struggle between the various elements in Jerusalem itself. Florus, unlike Albinus, had no support from any part of the Jewish nation (see also above, p. 324). A serious public dispute between Agrippa and the priestly groups again broke out under Florus. The Levite Temple singers persuaded Agrippa to convene a Sanhedrin which was to license them to wear sacred vestments like the priests. The Sanhedrin concerned accepted the King's proposal. Agrippa II also introduced further changes in the Temple arrangements, granting all Levites the rank of Temple singers. These changes, which abolished traditions held sacred by the nation for generations, were regarded by the priests and their associates as a grave affront.[4]
The last years of the Temple's existence also saw its completion. Although the main structure had been built by Herod himself, there were portions where construction continued for many years. The number of labourers employed reached thousands, who became

[1] *War* II, 273.
[2] *Ant.* xx, 213.
[3] *Ant.* xx, 213-214.
[4] *Ant.* xx, 216-218.

unemployed when the Temple was completed. Moreover, fearing that if too large a surplus remained in the Temple treasury it would be seized by the Romans, Agrippa II decided to use the money to pave the city with white stone.[1] His last act as overseer of the Temple and the high priesthood was the removal of Joshua ben Gamala from the incumbency and the appointment of Matthias son of Theophilos II, the last high priest before the Revolt.[2]

BIBLIOGRAPHY

The subject is treated in SCHÜRER, VERMES, MILLAR, *The History of the Jewish People in the Age of Jesus Christ* I (1973), pp. 357-427, 455-470, 514-528. H. REGNAULT, *Une province procuratienne au début de l'empire romain*, 1909, mainly discusses the trial of Jesus. E. MEYER, *Ursprung und Anfänge des Christentums* III, 1923, pp. 42-54, gives a good summary of the history of the procurators in the years 44-66 C.E. A richly documented narrative is supplied by J. DOBIÁŠ, *Dějiny římské provincie Syrské* (on the Roman province of Syria, in Czech with a French summary), 1924, pp. 349-462. H. DESSAU, *Geschichte der römischen Kaiserzeit* II, 2, 1930, pp. 776-801 is brief but well balanced. Many problems bearing upon the history of the province are lucidly treated by A. MOMIGLIANO, *Ricerche sull' organizzazione della Giudea sotto il dominio romano* (63 B.C.E.-70 C.E.), 1934. Outlines of the Roman provincial administration in Judaea are given in A. SCHALIT, *Roman Administration in Palestine* (in Hebrew), 1937.

APPENDIX I
THE CENSUS OF QUIRINIUS

The principal problem arising from the sources treating of Quirinius and the census associated with his name, concerns the contradiction between the Gospel according to Luke, which dates the census in the time of Herod, and Josephus, who speaks of it in connection with the conversion of Judaea to a Roman province in 6 C.E. It is clearly only natural that a census should have been held in Judaea when it became a province; on the other hand, a census in the time of Herod himself constitutes a difficult problem. Furthermore both Josephus and the Acts of the Apostles mention Judas of Galilee in connection with the census. The Gospel

[1] *Ant.* xx, 219-222.
[2] *Ant.* xx, 223.

of Luke says that this census was the first to be held in Judaea, which is also implied by Josephus, as only such an assumption can explain the sharp opposition which it aroused among the populace.

To assume that we have here a chronological error on Josephus' part would be decidedly arbitrary, chiefly in the light of the objective need of a census on the inauguration of the province. Hence most scholars believe that the inaccuracy is that of Luke.[1] A number of scholars, however, have supposed that two censuses were really held, both under the supervision of Quirinius, who on this assumption was twice governor of Syria. This supposition is supported by Tacitus and by an inscription from Tibur. According to Tacitus, Quirinius captured the stronghold of the Homonadenses in southern Asia Minor. This event must have taken place, according to Tacitus, after 12 B.C.E. (the year of Quirinius' consulship), but before 1 B.C.E., since Quirinius was then appointed adviser to C. Caesar, Augustus' grandson, in Armenia. It was logical to assume that Quirinius operated against the Homonadenses as legate of Syria, hence that he was governor of the province before 6 C.E. The Tibur inscription, which describes his career, has been interpreted in this sense, i.e. that he served twice as governor (*legatus pro praetore divi Augusti iterum Syriam et Phoenicen obtinuit*). But in the meantime weighty arguments have been found in favour of the supposition that Quirinius actually operated against the Homonadenses as governor of Galatia and Pamphylia, and not as governor of Syria (Syme). The Tibur inscription, moreover, has been interpreted (Groag), to mean that the person referred to in it, although he served twice as *legatus pro praetore*, did not so in the province of Syria, though he would seem to be identical with Quirinius (Roos). It has moreover proved impossible to date Quirinius' earlier term of office in Syria so as to harmonize with the chronology of the Gospel. It results from Josephus that Quirinius was also ordered to hold a census in Syria and this is confirmed by the Apamea inscription. Both the Gospel of Luke and the inscription from Apamea speak explicitly of Quirinius as governor of Syria when the census was carried out. Josephus here uses the expression δικαιοδότης which has been seen as grounds for supposing that he was not referring to the same census as that referred to in the two other sources, and that Quirinius was not governing Syria during Josephus' census, whose execution had been imposed upon him as a special duty. This conclusion, however, seems far-fetched.

[1] For a summary of the reasons see Schürer.

BIBLIOGRAPHY

T. MOMMSEN, *Res gestae divi Augusti*, 2nd ed., 1883, pp. 175-7; E. SCHÜRER I, pp. 322-4, 327, 508-543; W. WEBER, *ZNTW*, 1909, pp. 307-319; M.-J. LAGRANGE, *RB*, 1911, pp. 60-84; W. M. RAMSAY, *JRS*, 1917, pp. 273-5; *The Bearing of Recent Discovery on the Trustworthiness of the New Testament*, 1915, pp. 275-300; H. DESSAU, *Klio*, 1921, pp. 252-8; F. BLECKMANN, *Klio*, 1921, pp. 104-110; E. MEYER I, 1921, p. 51; E. GROAG, *Jahreshefte des österreichischen Institutes*, 1922-4, Supplement, pp. 445-478 and *PW*, 2nd series IV, cols 829-839; W. LODDER, *Die Schätzung des Quirinius bei Flavius Josephus*, 1930; L. R. TAYLOR, *AJPh*, 1933, pp. 120-133 and *JRS*, 1936, pp. 165-8; J. G. C. ANDERSON, *CAH* X, 1934, pp. 877-8; R. SYME, *Klio*, 1934, pp. 131-8; F. CUMONT, *JRS*, 1934, pp. 187-190; T. CORBISHLEY, *Klio*, 1936, pp. 81-93; F. HEICHELHEIM, 'Roman Syria', in T. FRANK, *An Economic Survey of Ancient Rome* IV, 1938, pp. 160-2; A. G. ROOS, *Mnemosyne*, 1941, pp. 306-318; S. ACCAME, *Rivista di Filologia*, 1944-5, pp. 138-170; G. VITUCCI, *Rivista di Filologia*, 1947, p. 255; D. MAGIE, *Roman Rule in Asia Minor* II, 1950, pp. 1322-3; R. K. SHERK, *The Legates of Galatia from Augustus to Diocletian*, 1951, pp. 21-4; H. BRAUNERT, *Historia*, 1957, pp. 192-214; H. U. INSTINSKY, *Das Jahr der Geburt Christi*, 1957, pp. 19-72; GABBA, pp. 52-61; B. LEVICK, *Roman Colonies in Southern Asia Minor* (1967), 203-214 (the inscription of Tibur relates not to Quirinius, but to L. Calpurnius Piso, the consul in 15 B.C.E.; cf. op. cit., p. 209); SCHÜRER, VERMES, MILLAR I (1973), pp. 258-9, 399-427.

The Sources

Luke 2:1-2; Acts 5:37; Jos. *Ant.* XVII, 355 and XVIII, 1-2 (cf. XVIII, 26; XX, 102; *War* II, 433; VII, 253); Tacitus, *Annals* III, 48,1; *ILS* no. 2683; Gabba, no. XVIII (relating to the census of Apamea); *ILS* no. 918; *Inscriptiones Italiae* IV 1, Tibur (1952), no. 130.

APPENDIX II

THE CONFLICT BETWEEN THE SAMARITANS
AND THE JEWS UNDER CUMANUS ACCORDING
TO JOSEPHUS AND TACITUS

The differences between the narrative in the *Jewish War* and that in the *Antiquities*[1] are of little importance. But there is a fundamental difference between Josephus and Tacitus.[2] Josephus conveys without

---

[1] *Wars*, II, 232-247; *Ant.*, XX, 118-137.
[2] Tacitus, *Annals*, XII, 54.

a shadow of doubt that Cumanus had previously served as governor of Judaea and that the conflict between the Jews and the Samaritans occurred during his governorship. From Tacitus, on the other hand, it is to be understood that Felix was already governing part of Palestine when the disorders broke out, the arrangement being that Felix was over Samaria, whereas Ventidius Cumanus was over Galilee (*ut huic Galilaeorum natio, Felici Samaritanae parerent*). Tacitus' conception of Judaea proper is not clear. First, indeed, he remarks that Felix had been in control of Judaea some time previously (*iam pridem Iudaeae impositus*), but as Tacitus generally thinks of Judaea as the whole of Palestine, i.e. Provincia Iudaea, he may here mean only that Felix governed part of the country, omitting further details.

Some scholars accept Josephus' account (thus, for example, Schürer, Eduard Meyer, Dessau and Millar); others (Scramuzza, Hanslik), prefer Tacitus. One of the best solutions, it seems to me, was proposed by Graetz, who believed that both Cumanus and Felix were in the province as governors during the disorders, Cumanus as governor of Samaria and Judaea and Felix as governor of Galilee. According to Graetz, Tacitus was mistaken in saying that Felix was over Samaria, and Cumanus Galilee. The supposition that the whole of the country was not under Cumanus at the time of the disorders between the Jews and the Samaritans, is to some extent borne out by the narrative in the *War*.[1] Here, when Josephus is discussing Felix's appointment as the governor of the Province of Judaea, he specifies that Felix was appointed as procurator of Judaea, Samaria, Galilee and Peraea. No such details appear in connection with any other governor and can be explained by the assumption, that the previous procurator Cumanus was not in charge of all the areas in question.

Other attempts to solve the contradiction between Josephus and Tacitus have been proposed by Momigliano, Smallwood and Brunt. Momigliano thinks that Felix was appointed as governor of Samaria temporarily; this would explain Tacitus' erroneous supposition that Felix and Cumanus had governed simultaneously from the first in different regions of the country. Brunt on the other hand thinks that Felix performed the function of procurator but not of governor, whose presence did not exclude the activities of domanial procurators, such as the procurator of Jamnia.

In my view, at all events, Tacitus' words, in so far as they contradict Josephus', can be interpreted on the assumption that Felix was

[1] II, 247.

performing some duty or other in the Roman administration of Judaea, when the conflict between Jews and Samaritans broke out. It would also seem that on the same occasion Felix formed close ties with several Jewish leaders, which would explain the support subsequently lent by Jonathan son of Ananus in the matter of his appointment as governor of Judaea.

BIBLIOGRAPHY

SCHÜRER I, p. 570, n. 14; GRAETZ, *Geschichte der Juden* III, 5th ed. 1906, pp. 728-730; E. SCHWARTZ, 'Zur Chronologie des Paulus', *Nachrichten v.d. K. Gesellschaft der Wissenschaften zur Göttingen, Phil.-historische Klasse*, 1907, pp. 285-7; (*Gesammelte Schriften* V, 1963, pp. 152-4); E. MEYER, pp. 44-8; DOBIÁŠ, pp. 430-2; DESSAU, pp. 798-9; MOMIGLIANO, pp. 388-391; V. W. SCRAMUZZA, *The Emperor Claudius*, 1940, p. 87; M. ABERBACH, *JQR*, 1949-50, pp. 1-14; R. HANSLIK, *PW*, 2nd series, VIII, cols 817-818; R. SYME, *Tacitus* II, 1958, p. 747; E. M. SMALLWOOD, *Latomus*, 1959, pp. 560-7; P. A. BRUNT, *Historia*, 1961, p. 214, n. 78; E. HAENCHEN, *Die Apostelgeschichte*, 13th ed. 1961, pp. 60-3; F. MILLAR, *JRS*, 1966, p. 159, n. 35; E. KOESTERMANN, *Annalen* III, 1967, pp. 200-3; SCHÜRER, VERMES, MILLAR I, p. 459 n. 15.

Chapter Seven
Jewish Self-government

Gentile rule and Jewish autonomy

During most of the Second Temple period, the Jews of the Land of Israel were under the rule of the empires which held sway in the East. As time passed and empire succeeded empire, the degree and character of Jewish autonomy underwent changes, dictated by the varying political relations between the Jews and the imperial authorities. Yet for most of the period, it is evident that the Jews of the homeland enjoyed a considerable degree of autonomy. In general, they had more autonomy than the Persian satrapies, the Greek hyparchies, or the Roman provinces, although all these were equal in political status within the empire in question. Serious attempts to restrict this autonomy were only made when relations between the imperial administration and the Jews of the Land of Israel reached a crisis, as during the persecutions of Antiochus or the Bar Cochba revolt. However, after a longer or shorter period, the Jews regained their autonomy and could administer their own affairs, as they re-established their own local and national institutions in the Land of Israel. Jewish autonomy generally extended beyond such matters as preserving civil order locally and imposing taxes. Even during periods when the authorities had dispensed with the Jews' assistance (after the destruction of the Temple, for example), the local and national organizations still continued to exist. Administrative tasks, such as preserving civil order and imposing taxes, were limited to the province of Judaea. However, Jews also lived outside Judaea throughout the Second Temple period, and they were linked with the Jewish national institutions—whether these were formally recognized by Rome or not—which as central organs also supervised many areas of Diaspora life. The central Jewish authorities were not, however, restricted to functions prescribed and recognized by the gentile rulers. They performed many tasks in many areas where they had no official power over the Jewish population, and certainly no backing from the gentile rulers. Their real authority was further reduced after the destruction of the Temple, when the Jews were satisfied if the Romans did not actually

377

interfere in their affairs. Only under the Severan emperors, at the end of the second century C.E., were the Jews granted recognition and assistance by the authorities in order to execute various tasks and impose a central authority on their own people. However, the national centre was not re-established after the destruction either through official recognition or by the granting of autonomy to the Jews. The people's determination to preserve Judaism and their inner discipline enabled the sages to rebuild the national leadership, although their activities were at times partially illegal. After a while, the imperial authorities granted *de facto* or *de jure* recognition.

Jewish self-government in both its local and national forms in the cities and towns, was interwoven with the Torah and the observance of the commandments. Not only did it make it possible, or easier, to observe the Law and keep to the Jewish way of life, but it was an essential part of the Jewish ideal, according to the Torah and the Halakah as taught by the sages. At an earlier time, Judah Maccabee had charged his soldiers 'to fight nobly, even to the death for the laws, temple, city, country and commonwealth (πολιτείας)'.[1] Tannaitic Halakah often dealt with the arrangements of the Sanhedrin meetings and its various responsibilities, as well as with Jerusalem and its leadership. The development of the central leadership—i.e. the Sanhedrin—and the public struggles to shape it while the Temple existed, and particularly after its destruction, may be regarded as the bond of Jewish history and culture. After the destruction of the Temple, social and spiritual life was linked with and clarified by developments in the national leadership, which also influenced political events and Jewish settlement.

An important aspect of both the national and civic leadership was the broad basis on which it was founded. During the Second Temple period, the priesthood was definitely the ruling element, but, in the course of time, the sages came to assume an important place in the government. However, authority, it was then held, belonged to the community and the assembly. Fundamentally, the ruling authority was the gatherings of the local citizens to deal with civic matters, and of all the Jews to deal with national matters. This is exemplified by public assemblies in which matters of principle were decided, such as the acceptance of the yoke of the Torah and the sealing of the covenant.[2] When the people decided against mixed marriages and divorced their gentile wives, 'all the men of Judah and Benjamin

[1] 2 Macc. 13:14. [2] Neh. 8-10.

assembled'.[1] At the end of the third century B.C.E., a popular assembly gathered to revoke part of the political authority of the high priest and appointed Joseph son of Tobias as the national representative.[2] When the Maccabean wars were concluded, they gathered 'in a great assembly of the priests and the people and the rulers of the nation and the elders of the country' to determine what kind of government was to be established.[3] On the eve of the destruction of the Temple after the Roman governor had been compelled to flee, the people assembled to establish a government. In certain of these gatherings, only the citizens of Jerusalem were actually present, since they were considered the representatives of all the inhabitants of the Land. When Josephus in Galilee petitioned the Sanhedrin in Jerusalem, he claimed that he had been delegated by the assembly of Jerusalem (κοινὸν τῶν Ἱεροσολυμιτῶν).[4] The national assemblies in which all the people participated dealt, in the main, with matters of principle. Only during the earlier periods, under Ezra and Nehemiah, did such gatherings actually take place. As time passed these lost their practical significance, although the principle of popular government continued to have influence. Against this background, we may understand the various expressions and images identifying the Sanhedrin with the congregation of Israel and the assembly of Israel. Thus, the passage 'if the whole congregation of Israel...' (Lev. 4:13) refers, according to a Tannaitic midrash, to 'the Great Sanhedrin that met in the Chamber of Hewn Stone'.[5] In the midrash on the Song of Solomon the concepts of the people of Israel and the Sanhedrin were interchanged.[6] The Sanhedrin included sages and priests, and the latter were an important element in its composition, but even they were considered in the main, at least in Talmudic tradition, as representatives of the community. The concepts 'elders of the Court' and 'elders of Israel' were identical and were used interchangeably in the Mishnah.[7] Similarly, 'the seven best men of the city' were not the leaders but the representatives, and for certain matters they were regarded as standing for the entire city.[8]

The Sanhedrin, its origin and composition

The Sanhedrin was the principal institution of national self-government

---

[1] Ezra 10:9.   [2] Jos. *Ant.* XII, 164.   [3] I Macc. 14:28.
[4] Jos. *Life* 62,65.   [5] *Sifra Nehardava* 4 (19a).
[6] *T. B. Sanhedrin* 37a; *Cant. Rabba* 1.
[7] *M. Yoma* 1:3; *M. Parah* 3:7.   [8] *P. T. Megillah* III, 74a.

during the period of the Second Temple and after its destruction. The numerous sources describing the Sanhedrin fall mainly into four categories: (1) apocryphal literature, particularly Judith and the first three Books of the Maccabees. (2) Flavius Josephus—*Antiquities*, *Jewish War*, *Life*, and indirectly *Against Apion*; (3) Tannaitic and Amoraic literature; (4) the New Testament, particularly in the Gospels and the Acts of the Apostles. Some information is indirectly available in the writings of Philo.

The importance of the Sanhedrin in Jewish life and particularly the role it played in the trial of Jesus (as well as the trials of James, Stephen and Paul) and in the history of the early Christian Church have led to many studies of the Sanhedrin and its structure, authority, and place in Jewish life. The sources are indeed numerous and have reached us through various traditions and literary forms. The bearers of these traditions had personal knowledge of the Sanhedrin and its activities; hence they interpreted it from their own viewpoint and perspective. Thus Josephus, with his obvious priestly bias, sought to emphasize the pre-eminence of the priesthood, unlike Talmudic tradition which regards the Oral Law as the essence of Jewish life and the sages of the Torah as the people's leaders at all times. As sources, Josephus and Talmudic literature are different from the traditions found in the New Testament, which were influenced by the crises that befell the Christian community and by a long development in its relations with Judaism, within which Christianity originated. In any tradition, particularly in Talmudic literature and the New Testament, one may distinguish between earlier and later sources, their compilation and composition, and their different versions. Hence, a scholar who seeks to present the history of the Sanhedrin or its structure and functions during a particular period, is faced by certain real, or apparent, contradictions within each category of sources, and even more when the categories are compared. Scholars have not always shown balanced judgment in preferring one source to another or one category to another. There are apparent contradictions between the picture presented by Josephus and the New Testament on the one hand, and Talmudic literature on the other, and these seem unresolvable. However, even in such instances, it is not right to simply prefer one category of sources and reject all the others; Talmudic sources, for example, are at times rejected on the assumption that they project a greatly idealized version of life after the destruction of the Temple back into the earlier period. On the other hand, we have no right to reject the various attestations in both Josephus and the New Testament, and categorically to prefer Talmudic sources on the ground that they present the complete and well-structured picture of the national institutions, when compared with the fragmented and adventitious notices in other sources.

An institution which in its essence acted as the people's representative and resembled the Sanhedrin in the scope of its functions surely existed from the end of the Persian and the beginning of the Hellenistic period. Tannaitic tradition links the Great Sanhedrin with the seventy elders who were with Moses in the wilderness. This tradition ought not to be ignored although there are only vague notices of the existence of an institution comparable to the Sanhedrin during the First Temple period. However, during the time of the Second Temple, the image of such an institution becomes increasingly well outlined. It is generally called the Gerousia, and its presence is conspicuous in the sources transmitted from the end of the Persian and the beginning of the Hellenistic period.[1] From the end of the Maccabean period, the name 'Sanhedrin' becomes widespread in sources outside Talmudic literature. In the Talmud, it is given various names: 'The Great Court in the Chamber of Hewn Stone', 'The Court of one and seventy [judges]', or more generally, 'the Elders of the Court', or 'Elders and Sages'. The name 'Great Sanhedrin' or 'Sanhedrin' isǀ not frequent in Talmudic literature. In non-Talmudic sources we have the terms 'Elders' (πρεσβύτεροι) or 'council' (βουλή).[2] Some scholars, on the basis of these various names, have suggested that during the latter period of the Temple's existence, there were two or three separate and parallel institutions: (1) the Court in the Chamber of Hewn Stone, on the whole an institution of Pharisaic sages only, and concerned with religious instruction, supervision of Temple matters and divine service there; (2) the Sanhedrin—for trials and punishment (particularly for offences against the Temple); (3) the boule—the city council of Jerusalem.[3] Although this assumption may resolve many apparent difficulties and contradictions among various sources, it is not borne out by the sources themselves, nor is it in accord with many of them. Neither does such an assumption accord well with the image of Judaism as it emerges in the Torah and the Halakah or Oral Law, which make

---

[1] Judith 4:8; 11:14; 15:8; Jos. *Ant.* XII, 138; 2 Macc. 1:10; 4:44, and elsewhere. See Zucker, pp. 12-49.
[2] See Allon, *History* I, p. 116.
[3] In particular see Büchler, *Das Synedrion.*

no such distinctions among the various public activities, nor with Jewish history. No distinction is made between various religious matters, civil and private justice, and the public leadership in general. We have no choice but to assume the presence of one 'Sanhedrin' that appears under different names, although these might indeed indicate certain changes that took place in the institution in the course of time. The general picture of the central institution of the Sanhedrin is more or less clear throughout this period. It shared the social and political destiny of the people and the changes that took place in their lives. Its status depended on the political status of the people vis-à-vis the gentile rulers, the Ptolemies, Seleucids, and Romans, and also on the attitude of the native political leadership—the early and later Maccabees, and the Herodian dynasty. The status of the Sanhedrin during the reign of the Hellenistic kings differed from what it was during the early period of Roman rule when the Empire's attitude toward the Jewish people was harsh and unyielding. Similarly, its status changed between the time of the first Hasmonaean kings and the reign of Alexander Janneus (who limited civil rights) and again when Herod diminished the Sanhedrin's authority, limiting its areas of activity and eliminating it as a partner in the government.[1] The social structure of the Sanhedrin changed, as Jewish society and culture developed. The struggles between the Hellenizers and the Hasidim, between the Pharisees and Sadducees, and between the sages and the men of rank and wealth, determined in large measure the structure and composition of the Sanhedrin.

Through all these changes and conflicts, the Sanhedrin continued to exist. At times its authority was extensive and it was a genuine partner in the government, as may be seen from Maccabean coins: 'Johanan the High Priest and the Community of the Jews', 'Judah, High Priest and the Community of the Jews', and 'Jonathan, High Priest, etc.'[2] At other times it functioned only as a setting for instruction, with limited juridical power, supervising the Temple services and religious life. The number of the Sanhedrin's members was variously transmitted by Tannaitic tradition: 'The great Sanhedrin was made up of seventy or one and seventy [judges] ... and Rabbi Judah says: seventy [only].'[3] Rather than reflecting different traditions about the actual number of the Sanhedrin's members, this

---

[1] Allon, *Studies* I, pp. 38-41; A. Schalit, *König Herodes* (1969), pp. 301-4.
[2] G. F. Hill, *Greek Coins of Palestine* (1965), pp. 188-212.
[3] *M. Sanhedrin* 1:6.

mishnah points to different opinions about the relationship of the head to the rest of the members; is he counted as one of them or is he above them and therefore not included as a member?[1] This also explains the tradition that on the day when Rabban Gamaliel was removed from the Patriarchate and replaced by Rabbi Eleazar ben Azariah, there were 'seventy-two elders' at the meeting.[2] This does not point to a different number but to a different method of counting which included the two chiefs as members of the full Sanhedrin. The plenum of seventy is not mentioned except in Talmudic tradition as a historical fact, and some scholars regard it as an exegetical matter merely, based on scriptural texts which state that Moses appointed seventy elders.[3] However, the number seventy applied to a large body which led and represented the community or a section of the public is mentioned numerous times in various sources. Thus, when Josephus reached Galilee, he established there a council of seventy elders as the central authority for the whole of Galilee.[4] Seventy men served as representatives of the community of Ecbatana before Varus, Agrippa's legate, in Caesarea Philippi.[5] Elsewhere, we read that the Zealots established a court of seventy men to sentence Zacharias son of Baris to death; they certainly wished to show that he was sentenced before a fully constituted tribunal.[6] Also, we might assume that Jesus' appointment of seventy envoys, mentioned in Luke 10:1, is linked to the conception that an authoritative body must be of seventy members, such a tradition not being based solely on scriptural exegesis. Indeed, the legend concerning the translation of Scriptures into Greek by seventy or seventy-two elders might well be linked to the fact that the Great Sanhedrin numbered either seventy,[7] seventy-one, or seventy-two members.[8]

The Sanhedrin comprised the elements which were of importance in Jewish society during the Second Temple period. First, one must

---

[1] Cf. *T. Sanhedrin* 1:9; *P. T. Sanhedrin* 1, 19c; *T. B. Sanhedrin* 16b.

[2] *M. Zebahim* 1:3; *M. Yadaim* 3:5; 4:2.

[3] A. Kaminka, 'R. Jochanan b. Zakkai and his Disciples', *Zion* (1944), pp. 70-83, and elsewhere.

[4] Jos. *War.* II, 570-1; *Life*, 79.

[5] Jos. *Life*, 56; *War* II, 482.

[6] Jos. *War* II, 334-8.

[7] Seventy, not seventy-two, is the number also found in Josephus (Jos. *Ant.* XII, 86), and in *Masekhet Soferim*, chap. I.

[8] In Tannaitic tradition seventy or seventy-one men formed the leadership in Alexandrian Jewry. See *T. Sukkah* 4:6, and *P. T. Sukkah* v, 52c, and *T. B. Sukkah* 51b.

mention the priesthood or, more precisely, the high priesthood. In its interpretation of the passage in Deuteronomy chap. 17, 'And coming to the Levitical priests, and to the judge who is in office in those days' (v. 9), Tannatic tradition says that it is 'a commandment of the Great Court that priests and levites should be there.'[1] At times the Sanhedrin is designated in tradition as 'the Court of priests, levites and Israelites allowed to marry into the priesthood' (i.e., without any blemish in their origin which would defile their marriages, so that even the priests are permitted to marry among them).[2] It is certain that the priests in the Sanhedrin were an important element throughout the Temple period. However, toward the end of this period, the pre-eminence of the high priesthood declined, but it was quite considerable even during the last days of the Temple. A second important element in the Sanhedrin was the groups of sages, or teachers of the Torah—often called scribes. The sages were the backbone of the Pharisaic movement, or of the Pharisaic circles. We are not certain as to when the sages achieved the high status in the Sanhedrin which enabled them to limit the power and authority of the priesthood and even to impose their opinions in certain areas, and compel the priesthood to follow them. No doubt the process went on for many decades. During the reign of Queen Salome (76-67 B.C.E.), the Pharisees constituted the majority in the Sanhedrin and their influence was overwhelming, as both Josephus and Talmudic tradition attest,[3] but the process began earlier. The changes that occurred later and the death of many sages at the hands of Herod did not entirely eliminate their influence in the Sanhedrin. All the evidence about the activity of the Sanhedrin until the destruction of the Temple emphasizes the presence of the scribes in that body.

The high priests on the whole were Sadducees, and the high priesthood called itself Sadducean, whether it was really and fervently so in its thinking,[4] or whether it was Sadducean merely in social status and by descent.[5] The scribes in the Sanhedrin reflected the Pharisee movement, so that the Sanhedrin contained two principal blocks, the Sadducees and the Pharisees. Alongside them there was a third element, 'the elders,' not the elders who were sages of the Torah but men of worldly rank and importance, nobles, heads of

[1] *Sifre* on Deut. 153.
[2] *T. Sanhedrin* 4:7.
[3] Jos. *Ant.* XIII, 408; in the beginning of *Megillath Taanith*.
[4] Jos. *Ant.* XX, 197-203; *T. Parah* 3:8.
[5] Acts 5:17; 23:6-9.

families, and wealthy personages such as had been a most conspicuous element in the public leadership in the period of the First Temple and at the beginning of the Second Temple. During the period now in question, this element was almost eliminated from the Sanhedrin, but not entirely. Traces of it are found particularly in Josephus and the books of the New Testament, in the expressions: 'the High Priest, the prophet and the council of elders,'[1] 'the chief priests and scribes,'[2] or 'the chief priests, with the elders and scribes and the whole council,'[3] or 'the chief priests and the elders.'[4] Such and similar expressions, probably designated the elements and circles which the Sanhedrin comprised. Not all the members of the Sanhedrin were from Jerusalem. Some lived in other cities. A passage in the Mishnah says: 'The sages once went down from Jerusalem to their own towns', to Ascalon, and beyond the Jordan. In the New Testament we read of 'a man named Joseph', a member of the boule from Arimathaea, and so on.[5] There were also sages who had immigrated from Diaspora lands such as Babylonia, Media, and Egypt.[6]

Membership of the Sanhedrin did not smooth out the differences between the various blocs or circles. Not only did they remain conspicuous as factions or parties under the direction of their leaders and spokesmen, as is particularly evident in the Acts of the Apostles, but they also constituted law-courts of different kinds, at least in so far as we are acquainted with the phenomenon among the priests and sages. It is not certain whether there were formal customs or traditions determining which body dealt with this or that question. However, we know of controversies between 'the Sons of the High Priests' and a certain sage concerning the latter's decision in a maintenance suit[7] and other controversies between 'the priests' and 'the Court' (a term for the sages) concerning regulations that are fairly characteristic of the priests' aristocratic attitude in contrast to the sages' halakic conceptions.[8] From other Tannaitic traditions we learn of the struggle between the high priesthood and the sages concerning halakic instruction and court procedures, in which the priests sought to preserve their own lofty status, which separated them from the rest of the people.[9]

[1] Jos. *Ant.* IV, 218.   [2] Matt. 2:4.   [3] Mark 15:1.
[4] Matt. 27 and elsewhere.
[5] *M. Taanith* 3:6; Luke 23:50.   [6] See above p. 198.
[7] *M. Ketuboth* 13:1.
[8] *M. Rosh ha-Shanah* 1:7.
[9] *M. Ketuboth* 1:5; *M. Shekalim* 1:4.

A Tannaitic tradition, probably a later one, relates that a Sanhedrin is legitimate even without priests and levites.[1] The passage states, however, that it does not possess full authority to constrain 'a dissenting elder' (one who rejects the decision of the court, and teaches practical Halakah contrary to the Sanhedrin's opinion, after he had submitted the question to it), or to deal with capital cases. This authority was in effect only when the plenum sat in the Chamber of Hewn Stone, near the altar, and in periods when divine service was properly instituted.[2] This situation gave the priests a special status in the Sanhedrin. But we learn both from Josephus and Tannaitic literature that in later times the Sadducees were compelled, even when they held executive authority, to reckon with the opinions and teachings of the Pharisees, for the sake of public opinion, in all halakic and religious matters, including all that had to do with Sanctuary regulations.[3] Public opinion certainly forced the high priests to give great weight to the Pharisees' views on the order of business in the Sanhedrin.

This distinction between the principal groups and their place in the Sanhedrin will assist us to understand the problem of the Sanhedrin's leadership. In Tannaitic tradition, the Great Sanhedrin is depicted as a link in the chain of the Torah tradition, with the leading sages of the Torah, the chief Pharisees, at its head. From the Hasmonaean dynasty onwards, its leaders, according to the same tradition, were the 'pairs' of sages, and from Herod's time until the destruction of the Temple, Hillel the Elder and his descendants, Simeon (according to one tradition), Rabban Gamaliel the Elder, and Rabban Simeon ben Gamaliel.[4] Another picture is given by the Gospels and Acts, where the high priest is almost always at the head of the Sanhedrin, as at the trials of Jesus,[5] Stephen,[6] the Apostles,[7] and Paul;[8] similarly, with Jesus' brother in the year 62 C.E.;[9] and prior to this at the trial

---

[1] *Sifre* on Deut. 153.
[2] Ibid. 152-4; *T. B. Sanhedrin* 52 b.
[3] Jos. *Ant.* XVIII, 17; *M. Yoma* 1:5. *M. Sukkah* 4:9; and *T. Sukkah* 3:16. See in particular *T. Yoma* 1:8 and others.
[4] *M. Hagigah* 2:2, and *T. Hagigah* 2:8; *T. B. Shabbath* 15a.
[5] Matt. 26:3, 57.
[6] Acts 7:1.
[7] Acts 5:17-28.
[8] Acts 23:2, 24:1. In one instance, John 11:47-9, there is an apparent change: 'So the chief priests and the Pharisees gathered a council, and said, 'what are we to do?' But one of them, Caiaphas, who was the high priest that year...'
[9] Jos. *Ant.* xx, 200.

of Herod before Hyrcanus II in 47 B.C.E.[1] Moreover, in the trial of the Apostles, we find Rabban Gamaliel, who in Tannaitic tradition was the president of the Sanhedrin, sitting as one of its members: 'But there stood up one in the council, a Pharisee, named Gamaliel, a doctor of the law, held in honour by all the people.'[2] His words are heard and accepted, but he is one of the members, not president of the session.[3] Moreover, in the trial of Herod, Shammai the sage (or Shemaya) who is included among the 'pairs' of sages, reprimands the members of the Sanhedrin who are afraid to judge Herod for his act of murder. This he does as a member of the Sanhedrin but he has no part in the leadership.[4] In almost all the passages in the New Testament where the groups within the Sanhedrin are enumerated, the high priests are at the head of the list;[5] the expressions 'rulers and elders and scribes', are interchangeable with the chief priests and the elders',[6] but there is no equivalence between scribes and elders. In his various accounts of the constitution and government of the Jewish people, Josephus affirms that the high priest is the head of the people and the supreme judge.[7] Nevertheless, one ought not dismiss the Talmudic tradition completely even if one accepts the notion that the tradition in the Mishnah which regards the 'pairs' of sages and their successors as the presidents of the Sanhedrin, is only an ideal, based on the reality after the destruction of the Temple. But such a solution would not do justice to the many traditions about the activity of these personages as chairmen of a body of great importance in the life of the people, with such tasks as the proclamation of the intercalation of the year and the time for setting aside the tithes in various areas.[8] These traditions are linked with many historical and topographical details of Jerusalem. In Tannaitic literature, a number of rulings are attributed to 'Johanan the High Priest', that is, Hyrcanus I or II,[9] and one of the high priests who served in the last days of the Temple, Joshua ben Gamala, is credited in Amoraic tradition with the rulings that determined the establishment of the schools.[10] However, the vast majority of the rulings from the Second Temple period are attributed

---

[1] Ibid. XIV, 163-179.   [2] Acts 5:34.   [3] Ibid. 5:27.
[4] Jos. *Ant.* XIV, 172.   [5] See p. 385, notes 2-4.
[6] Cf. Acts 4:5 and 4:23.
[7] Jos. *Against Apion* II, 193-4; Jos. *Ant.* IV, 30-218, and XX, 251.
[8] *Midrash Tannaim*, Deut. 26:13, pp. 175-6.
[9] *M. Maaser Sheni* 5:15.
[10]*T. B. Baba Bathra* 21a.

to the 'pairs of sages', to Hillel and his descendants. These rulings do not bear the stamp of arrangements for an association (חבורה) or a movement, or even for a broadly based movement like that of the Pharisees. They rather possess a general national significance and are connected with cases concerning property, family matters, and general public arrangements, including those of the Temple. And again, at times these traditions concerning the rulings are linked with precise details from the life of those days and their reality is confirmed by various external sources.

Simeon ben Shetah is credited with the ruling that the husband must give his wife a 'marriage deed', providing for a settlement in the event of death or divorce, and he also determined the obligation to educate the children.[1] Hillel is credited with the ruling on 'Prozbol', which was a declaration made before a court of law by a creditor, listing debts owed him before the end of the Sabbatical Year, so that they would not be cancelled. Among his other rulings was one permitting the seller of a house (who could redeem it within a year according to the laws of the Torah) to deposit his money in the Temple Treasury, in case the buyer refused to accept the money or hid from the seller.[2] Other rulings of great significance for marriage deeds and divorce laws are attributed to Rabban Gamaliel the Elder.[3] And Rabban Simeon ben Gamaliel is said to have propounded and established an important ruling concerning the obligation of women to bring a pair of doves to the Temple. This ruling immediately lowered the inflated price of doves in Jerusalem.[4] The solution, it seems, must be sought in the general opinion of those scholars who assume that the leaders of the Pharisees during the reign of Queen Alexandra (Salome) and then during the period of Hillel and his descendants, were not only at the head of the Pharisees and the sages of the Torah and its transmitters, or at the head of a law court in some section of the Sanhedrin, but also acted as heads of the Sanhedrin from time to time, at least at some of its special meetings. It is evident that the high priest presided over the Sanhedrin when it dealt with problems relating to public and political life. The trials at which the high priest presided, were in fact capital cases, formally concerning individuals, but having general public significance. But for problems in the field of religion, Halakah and jurisprudence, and in matters of domestic policy, the

[1] *P. T. Ketuboth*, end of chap. 8.
[2] *M. Shebiith* 10:3; *M. Arakhin* 9:4.
[3] *M. Gittin* 4:1-3. [4] *M. Kerithoth* 1:7.

leaders of the sages presided over the Sanhedrin. It is never stated that the power of the high priest and his authority flowed from his being elected or from presiding over the Sanhedrin. The high priest was an independent executive authority from the very fact of his being high priest, and the Sanhedrin, the public or the 'community of the Jews' (חבר היהודים) was an executive authority in its own right. 'The Patriarchate,' which was the principal executive authority later, did not exist in the Second Temple period and it seems probable that the fully worked out concept did not exist until the Bar Cochba period. Hence on juridical occasions having public and political significance, such as the trial of Herod, or again of Jesus, Stephen, the Apostles, and Paul, one may find that the high priest presided over or assembled the Sanhedrin (or part of it, as in the case of the trial of Jesus' brother James). The leaders of the sages are mentioned in such trials only as members of the court in session, while in many other matters, the sages presided over the Sanhedrin.

We have mentioned boule (βουλή) among the terms used for the Sanhedrin. It is found in the letter of Claudius in C.E. 45, who writes: 'To the archons, to the boule, to the inhabitants of Jerusalem, and to all the Jewish people,'[1] in other Roman sources,[2] in Josephus,[3] and in the Talmud in various forms. Its members are called בולווטין;[4] one of the chambers in the Temple, in which the high priest sojourned before the Day of Atonement, is called the Chamber of Councillors.[5] Certain people bear this title, such as Joseph of Arimathaea, Ben Gurion, and others.[6] Although the boule is mentioned by Claudius in his letter, which is formulated as though addressed to a Greek polis, and the boule, and 'people,' and even the 'First Ten,' as in the Greek cities, are mentioned with the high priest in connection with a delegation to the Emperor Nero,[7] one ought not conclude from all this that Jerusalem had the civic organization of a polis. First one ought to emphasize that the boule is identified with the Sanhedrin. At its head are mentioned the archons or the high priests, as in the case of the Sanhedrin. The boule also discharged public and national functions, like the Sanhedrin, representing the people and the city,

[1] Jos. *Ant.* xx, 11.
[2] Dio Cassius, LXVI, 6.
[3] Jos. *War* II, 331, 336 and others.
[4] Jos. *Ant.* II, 405; *P. T. Taanith* IV, 69a and others.
[5] *P. T. Yoma* I, 38c; *T. B. Yoma* 8b.
[6] Mark 15:43; Luke 23:50; *Lam. Rabba* I.
[7] Jos. *Ant.* xx, 194.

collecting taxes and so on. The boule not only included such members as Joseph of Arimathaea, but had its scribe, Aristeus of Emmaus.[1] Not all of these facts suit the boule of a polis. The members of this boule, the Sanhedrin, were not chosen in democratic elections or the like, as in a city with an administration like that of a Hellenistic polis. Despite the broad public base of the Sanhedrin, no national assemblies took place in Jerusalem at fixed times and places. In Jerusalem no social-cultural institutions existed such as the gymnasium, which was a fixed part of the structure of the Greek city. The Sanhedrin also served as the city council of Jerusalem, and applied to itself part of the terminology then in use in the Hellenistic-Roman East with regard to civic administration; but there is no justification for regarding the administration of Jerusalem as similar to that of a polis. In the main it was administered in the traditionally Jewish way.[2] The Sanhedrin was the city council of Jerusalem, in other words, was the general council of the nation. In view of the place of Jerusalem in the practical and spiritual life of the people in this period, this phenomenon ought not surprise us. Jerusalem belonged to all the Jewish people and was considered its representative. Even in sectarian literature, Jerusalem is viewed as either the centre of the people or of the sect in question.

The sources contain almost no mention of the manner in which the members of the Sanhedrin were selected. We are not informed who belonged to the circle of the 'Sons of the High Priests', mentioned in Tannaitic sources, or of the 'High Priests' mentioned in the New Testament and Josephus, nor how they were appointed, just as we do not know how the sages, 'the rulers' or the 'elders' who were not sages, were appointed. From the period after the destruction of the Temple, the practice was to 'ordain' the sages who joined the Sanhedrin, as is fairly well known. The sage who was ordained had authority to teach and to deal with judicial matters, and was included in the Sanhedrin. The ordination was regarded as the continuation of the chain of the tradition of the Torah from generation to generation, and the granting of authority to teach the Torah and direct the public. The ordination of Joshua was regarded as the origin of this custom.[3] Although we have no direct evidence for the practice of

---

[1] Jos. *War* v, 532.
[2] See V. Tcherikover, 'Was Jerusalem a Polis?', *IEJ* (1964), pp. 61-78, bibliography on p. 61.
[3] *Sifre* on Num. 140; *T. B. Sanhedrin* 13b.

ordination from the time of the Second Temple, there are good reasons for accepting the opinion of scholars who assume the existence of ordination at that time. The Christian community in Jerusalem which ordained 'a man full of faith'[1] certainly adopted an accepted practice of the Jewish people: the ordination of those who taught the Torah and guided the people in the line of tradition. During the persecutions after the Bar Cochba revolt, Rabbi Judah ben Baba sacrificed his life in order to ordain young disciples,[2] surely not on behalf of a procedure that had been established only a generation or two after the destruction of the Temple. However, even if it was the custom to ordain sages before this time, the ordination was probably not the act of the entire Sanhedrin but a custom in use in Pharisaic circles. The Pharisees sat together with the Sadducees in the Sanhedrin, but it is difficult to assume that they were prepared to ordain, or help to ordain, Sadducean priests who were not sages of the Torah. According to the Pharisees, the Sadducees did not share certain fundamental beliefs of the Pharisees, such as the resurrection of the dead, but above all, did not follow the path of righteousness as the Pharisees saw it. It is much more likely that the ordination of the sages—the recognition that the ordinand maintained the Torah tradition and way of life—and the granting of authority to him was in fact part of the Pharisees' conception of the chain of the Oral Law which is expressed in the beginning of the tractate *Aboth*. The chain began with Moses' receiving the Torah at Sinai and presenting it to his disciple Joshua; from there it passed to the 'pairs' who were at the head of the Pharisaic sages and so to Rabban Johanan ben Zakkai and his pupils at the time of the destruction of the Temple. From the traditions concerning the manner of ordination it would seem that a rabbi ordained his disciple. However, in practice the ordination was an institutional act (being done by a court of law in the presence of at least three men), even though attributed to the sage who presided over the court.[3]

Appointment was for life. This is quite clear for the period after the destruction of the Temple, but it seems that the same is also true of the previous period.

[1] Acts 6:5-6. See also Bacher, pp. 122-7.
[2] *T. B. Sanhedrin* 13b-14a.
[3] See *P. T. Sanhedrin* I, 19a, and *T. B. Sanhedrin* 13b. Tradition mentions that Rabbi Johanan ben Zakkai ordained his own pupils, but in the same context we learn of a court which ordained pupils.

There were only a few cases for which the Halakah required all seventy members to sit in judgment. Most of the Sanhedrin's activities were carried out by a limited group. Discussion of the intercalation of the year, for instance, required only three or seven members.[1]

In the Tosefta,[2] there are detailed accounts of courts with three members, which have twenty-three in another version, one on the Temple Mount, another in the Hel (in front of the Court of the Women), and the third in the Chamber of Hewn Stone. Some scholars accept the tradition of twenty-three members in the courts, and assume that the Great Law Court of seventy-one included all three law-courts with the addition of the Head (or two Heads) of the Sanhedrin, so that the total was seventy-one.[3] In fact, the Sanhedrin's business was probably done, to a large extent, by sections of that body, with separate law courts dealing with different matters. The division, however, may have been based on the tradition of earlier times, reflecting privileges that the priests or sages or some other circle in the Sanhedrin had succeeded in claiming. However, it is doubtful whether we can accept a well-ordered and precise division consisting of three law-courts, each with twenty-three members, adding up to sixty-nine, with two other personages who were the leaders of the Sanhedrin. Further, the number twenty-three is not certain. Sources from the Land of Israel state that the law-courts which met on the Temple Mount and in the Hel contained three members and it is only in the Babylonian tradition that we read that these law-courts had twenty-three members.

The powers and functions of the Sanhedrin

The Sanhedrin had a number of powers and functions in the matter of internal government and spiritual leadership. They included the legislative authority, judicial authority, and executive power. It was also an academic institution, the central institution for the study of the Torah. In this section, we shall discuss some of these powers and functions as they were exercised in practice.

The Books of the Maccabees make it clear on a number of occasions that the Gerousia (Senate) or elders constituted the supreme political authority, and acted as the people's representatives vis-à-vis the

[1] *M. Sanhedrin* 1:2.
[2] *T. Hagigah* 2:9; *P. T. Sanhedrin* 19c; and others. Parts of this tradition are in *Sifre* on Deut. 152, and in *Gen. Rabba* 70, p. 807.
[3] J. Derenbourg, *Essai sur l'histoire et la géographie de la Palestine* (1867), p. 91.

Jewish government, Judah the Maccabee consulted the elders (πρεσ-βύτεροι) as to whether he should attack the enemy before it invaded Judaea and took the city. Similarly, Jonathan the Maccabee convened the elders of the people and planned with them to build the walls of Jerusalem still higher.[1] This conception is reflected in the rulings of the Mishnah (*Sanhedrin* chap. 1) which lists matters for which the authorization of the Sanhedrin is required. 'They may not add to the city [Jerusalem] or the Courts of the Temple save by the decision of the court of one and seventy.'[2] In matters of war: 'they may not send forth [the people] to a battle waged of free choice [to attack] save by the decision of the court of one and seventy'.[3] Josephus uses similar words in his account of the constitution given by Moses: 'And let the king do nothing without the high priest and the council of his senators'.[4] A Tannaitic halakah even determines that the appointment of a king and a high priest cannot be made except by the court of seventy-one.[5] This particular halakah was probably part of political theory (and not real practice); so too the halakah about going forth to battle, which was also more or less theoretical in the political reality of the Land of Israel in the last century of the Temple's existence. Nevertheless, these do testify to the Sanhedrin's importance as conceived by those generations, at least in the tradition of the sages and of those close to them.

As early as the period of the Seleucid rule and particularly in the period of the Maccabees, it was clear that the Gerousia represented the state vis-à-vis the outside world of the gentile authorities and other peoples. Antiochus III relates in his well-known letter that the Jews came to meet him and were led by a council of elders, and the letter goes on to relieve the council of elders from paying taxes.[6] In the Books of the Maccabees, in the contacts between the Jews and the Hellenistic rulers Ptolemy Philopator,[7] Nicanor, and Demetrius, the elders (Gerousia) are mentioned.[8] Similarly, in the exchange of letters between the Jews and the people of Sparta, Jonathan the high priest, Simon the high priest and the elders or Gerousia are mentioned.[9] This picture also emerges during the Roman period, until the time close to the destruction of the Temple.[10]

[1] 2 Macc. 13:13; 1 Macc. 12:35-7.
[2] *M. Sanhedrin* 1:5.   [3] Ibid. 2:4.
[4] Jos. *Ant.* IV, 224.   [5] *T. Sanhedrin* 3:4.
[6] Jos. *Ant.* XII, 138-142.   [7] 3 Macc. 1:8.
[8] 1 Macc. 7:33; 11:23; 13:36; 14:20 and elsewhere.
[9] 1 Macc. 12:7; 14:20.   [10] See p. 389, notes 1 and 7.

Tannaitic tradition particularly emphasizes the function of the Sanhedrin as the supreme authority on halakic problems submitted to it from all parts of the country: 'Rabbi Jose said: at first there were no controversies in the Land of Israel, but the Court of seventy was in the Chamber of Hewn Stone and the rest of the courts of twenty-three were in the cities of the Land of Israel ... If a man were in need of a ruling, he went to the court in his city ... If they had heard it, they told him, and if not, then he and the most eminent among them went to the court in the Temple Mount ... and if here, too, no [answer was provided] then all of them went to the Great Court in the Chamber of Hewn Stone'.[1] The same picture emerges from Josephus, when he describes the constitution given by Moses,[2] but he emphasizes the importance of the high priest in the assemblies of the council of elders.[3] From the Persian period and until the last days of the Temple there are various accounts of halakic questions sent from places in the Land of Israel and from the Diaspora. As early as the Book of Judith, we read that the people of Bethulia sent a delegation to Jerusalem to put questions to the Gerousia relating to the siege.[4] Earlier we mentioned the enquiries made by the Diaspora in the days of Hillel.[5] Near the end of the Temple period, the Mishnah says that Rabbi Simeon of Mizpah had a question to put concerning the laws of Peah (gleanings) and that 'they went up to the Chamber of Hewn Stone to inquire.'[6] In the last days of the Temple, Rabbi Zadok says that there was 'an occurrence in Ahaliyya, and the case came before the Sages in the Chamber of Hewn Stone ...'[7] The development of the Halakah did not take place for the most part in the institutional framework of the Sanhedrin's rulings. Halakah was interpreted and extended in the sages' teaching and in the houses of study; in most instances, such developments did not come before the Sanhedrin. The Pharisaic sages who imposed their interpretation of the Torah and Halakah on the people, succeeded in doing so because they were considered 'well able to construe the meaning of the Scriptures', as Josephus says. Nevertheless, one ought not minimize the importance of the Sanhedrin in deciding Halakah where there

[1] *T. Sanhedrin* 7:1 and parallels.
[2] Jos. *Ant.* IV, 218.
[3] According to Philo, *De spec. leg.* IV, 190.
[4] Judith 11:12-14.
[5] See above p. 204
[6] *M. Peah* 2:6.
[7] *M. Eduyoth* 7:4; the place-name is uncertain.

were differences of opinion as between Sadducees and Pharisees, or within Pharisaic circles or between the different houses of study. At the beginning of *Megillath Taanith*, and in the earlier and later sources that interpret this passage, we learn of a controversy between the Pharisees and the Sadducees which was resolved by the Sanhedrin. It was about the arrangements for the daily whole-burnt offering in the Temple and the date of Pentecost. From the *Mishnah Eduyoth* we learn of accepted halakic decisions to which Akabya ben Mahalaleel refused to submit. He was put under the ban, and died while still under it.[1] Earlier we mentioned rulings that were attributed to the high priests or the heads of the Pharisaic sages. However, in the light of the numerous attestations from the period after the destruction of the Temple concerning various rulings that are also attributed to the *Nesiim* (patriarchs)—many of whom were certainly established by the Sanhedrin and the Patriarchate—one may conclude that these regulations were established by the Sanhedrin in the Temple period and attributed to the presidents of that body.

The Sanhedrin was in charge of and supervised the established national religion. Jewish religion included many areas of daily life and the concern for and supervision of religious matters thus comprised many areas. The Mishnah tractate *Shekalim* begins by saying: 'On the first day of Adar they give warning of the Shekel dues and against [the sowing of] Diverse Kinds [forbidden mixtures]. On the fifteenth thereof they read the *Megillah* in walled cities and repair the paths and roads and pools of water and perform all public needs and mark the graves; and they also go forth [to give warning] against Diverse Kinds.' The Tosefta adds: 'The court in Jerusalem attends to all the public needs that must be done after the rains in order to prepare the paths and the pools for the coming of the pilgrims.'[2] The Mishnah continues: 'Rabbi Judah says: at first they used to root them out and cast them down before the owner, [of fields where Diverse Kinds grew] but when the transgressors grew many, they used to root them out and cast them down by the wayside; [later] they ordained that [where Diverse Kinds grew] the whole field should be accounted ownerless property.' Hence the messengers from the court whose task it was to repair the paths and mark the locations of graves, were even supposed to note where 'Diverse Kinds' were sown, and they were permitted to proclaim the banning of the produce in such a case. In a baraitha to

[1] *M. Eduyoth* 5:6.
[2] At the beginning of *T. Shekalim*.

this passage, we learn that at this period, they opened the locks on all the cisterns along the paths, before the Passover.[1]

Earlier we mentioned the relations between the Sanhedrin and the Diaspora, and the Sanhedrin's concern to prevent any movements or activities that might represent an abandonment of Judaism.[2] Of course, the Sanhedrin itself had to react to any such manifestations in the Land of Israel. Perhaps the most striking instance of this is in the Mishnah tractate *Taanith* (3:8) which describes in detail the deed of Onias the Circle-Maker (first century B.C.E.), when he was asked to pray for rain; he acted with too much 'intimacy' and arrogated to himself, in the opinion of Simeon ben Shetah, too great power as a 'miracle-worker' while making his request for rain. Simeon ben Shetah sent a message to him saying 'Were you not Onias, I would have pronounced a ban against thee'.

We have mentioned several times the influence of the Pharisees on divine service in the Temple. Their power as representatives of the Sanhedrin and the people, enabled them to determine the manner of divine worship in the Temple according to their own tradition and views. This emerges from several instances mentioned by Josephus and from various traditions in the Mishnah. The Pharisees and the Sadducees disagreed, for instance, about the arrangements for the burning of incense in the Holy of Holies on the Day of Atonement. Here the Mishnah says: 'They [Elders of the Court] said to him [the High Priest]: 'My Lord High Priest, we are delegates of the Court and thou art our delegate and the delegate of the Court. We adjure thee by him that made his name to dwell in this house that thou change naught of what we have said unto thee.'[3] Regarding the burning of incense in the Holy of Holies when no one was in the Sanctuary, they adjured the Sadducean high priest not to depart from what they had told him. And in fact throughout the whole year they supervised the activities of the high priest and compelled him to act in accordance with the opinion of the Pharisees and the court.[4] In the latter days of the Temple, Josephus relates that the levites who sang in the Sanctuary requested Agrippa II to convene the Sanhedrin, for a ruling which would allow them to wear fine linen, like the priests, at worship. Agrippa did so and the Sanhedrin decided in their favour, in spite of the priests (whose interests Josephus reflects

---

[1] *P. T. Shekalim* I, 46a. See S. Safrai, *Pilgrimage in the Time of the Second Temple* (in Hebrew, 1965), pp. 111-112.
[2] p. 206.   [3] *M. Yoma* 1:5.   [4] *M. Sukkah* 4:9.

here).[1] The Sanhedrin also supervised the priesthood itself, that is, it determined the purity of the priests' lineage with all the complicated problems set by marriages and proselytes and freed slaves who were attached to the priesthood: 'The Chamber of Hewn Stone—there used the Great Sanhedrin of Israel to sit and judge the priesthood, and if in any priest a blemish was found he clothed himself in black and veiled himself in black and departed and went his way; and he in whom no blemish was found clothed himself in white and veiled himself in white, and then went in and ministered with his brethren the priests.'[2]

We have mentioned, in various contexts, the fixing of the New Moon and the intercalation of the year, as determined by the Sanhedrin in Jerusalem. Here it is well to emphasize that the fixing of the New Moon involved a wide organization for the hearing of witnesses: 'There was a large courtyard in Jerusalem called Beth Yaazek, where all the witnesses assembled, and there the Court examined them. And they prepared large meals for them so that they might make it their habit to come.'[3] The Sanhedrin employed many people in the process of fixing the New Moon, and the whole process gave a great sense of independence to Jewish life.

The Roman authorities did not interfere to any great extent in the judicial procedures pertaining to the law of property. The local institutions in the cities administered these laws, but the jurisdiction of the Sanhedrin was not confined to Jerusalem in such matters. Anyone could bring his case before the Great Court, or one of its authorized branches.[4]

In numerous sources of Tannaitic Halakah, both early and late, it is stated that capital crimes are judged before courts of twenty-three judges, probably the district courts.[5] However, in practice capital crimes were judged only in the Great Sanhedrin in Jerusalem. All the cases of capital crimes known to us which give any indication of where the trials took place, either occurred in Jerusalem or were brought there for judgment.[6] Thus when Josephus established his own Sanhedrin in Galilee, he ordered that 'great matters' and capital crimes

---

[1] Jos. *Ant.* xx, 216-8.
[2] *M. Middoth* 5:4.
[3] *M. Rosh ha-Shanah* 2:5.
[4] See *M. Ketuboth*, beginning of chap. 13, and the baraithas in the two Talmuds.
[5] *M. Sanhedrin* 1:4; 4:1; *T. Horayoth* 1:4; *Sifre* on Deut. 144.
[6] Jos. *Ant.* xiv, 168-9; xx, 200; Acts 22:30, 23:1, 5:17; *M. Sanhedrin* 7:2; *T. Sanhedrin* 6:6, and elsewhere.

were not to be judged in the local law courts that he had established, but should be brought before the Sanhedrin of seventy members. Philo, too, thought that such cases were heard only in Jerusalem.[1] The midrashim which link the Sanhedrin and its meeting place with the altar, also link its right to deal with capital crimes with the proper maintenance of the sacrificial worship.[2] It would seem that they also regard capital trials as taking place only in Jerusalem. Similarly, the halakic and haggadic traditions assume in their accounts that capital cases were heard only in Jerusalem and before the Great Sanhedrin.[3] However, there was no need to bring every case before the plenum of the Sanhedrin, since some matters could be judged by a Sanhedrin court of twenty-three members.

The limitation on capital cases (their restriction to the Great Sanhedrin in Jerusalem) was part of Pharisaic teaching, which took capital cases very seriously and sought to centralize them under the Sanhedrin in Jerusalem.[4] Although they tried to lessen the frequency of capital punishment, they did in fact inflict it throughout the latter period of the Temple.

At the beginning of Roman rule in the Land of Israel, the imperial authorities did not limit the Jews' juridical right, either in property matters or, most probably, in capital cases. While allowing the Jewish courts to function, they themselves exercised a parallel jurisdiction. Nonetheless, it is quite evident that in the event of a conflict between the two authorities, the Roman governor was the final arbiter. In general he left juridical matters to the local Jewish courts, but he could revoke their jurisdiction or determine, as a matter of course, that certain cases should be brought before him. In the course of this period, the Sanhedrin certainly lost to some extent its right to judge capital cases. In the Palestinian tradition we read: 'For forty years, until the Temple was destroyed, the privilege of trying capital cases was withdrawn.'[5] And in the Babylonian tradition, we read: 'For forty years, until the Temple was destroyed, the Sanhedrin went into Exile and dwelt in temporary quarters[6] ... and they did

---

[1] Jos. *War* II, 571; Philo, *De spec. leg.* III 52-63.
[2] *Mekhilta de Rabbi Ishmael, Nezikin,* end ch. 4, p. 264; *Mekhilta de Rabbi Shimon ben Yokhai* on Ex. 21:14 (ed. Epstein-Melamed, p. 171); *T. B. Abodah Zarah,* 8b.
[3] *T. B. Sanhedrin* 42b; *Pesikta Rabbati* 10, (ed. Friedman, 34a).
[4] *M. Sanhedrin* 4; *M. Makkoth* 1:10.
[5] *P. T. Sanhedrin* I, 18a.
[6] Since it no longer dwelt in the Chamber of Hewn Stone, it was not allowed to judge capital cases.

not judge capital cases.'[1] This statement is confirmed by the Gospel of John: 'It is not lawful for us to put any man to death.'[2] On the other hand, sentences of death passed by Jewish courts are mentioned as being carried out, under Roman rule, until the destruction of the Temple. Those who were found guilty were put to death according to Jewish juridical practice and there is no mention in the legal proceedings or in the execution of the sentence that the judgment needed the confirmation of the Roman authorities; and the convicted were not remanded to them for the execution of the sentence. The second trial of Peter involved capital punishment and only the intervention of Rabban Gamaliel prevented its concluding with the death sentence.[3] Rabbi Eliezer ben Zadok, who was a young man at the time of the destruction of the Temple, tells of a death sentence carried out according to Jewish law at which he was present during his childhood.[4] There are other examples of this.

It is not surprising that there are differences of opinion among scholars when they describe the *de jure* and *de facto* status of Jewish self-rule in this field. The problem is important in itself, and acquired even more significance because of its link with the problem of the trial of Jesus; it is almost impossible therefore to sum up the various conflicting opinions. Here, we simply give an account of the matter by adducing the instances known to us, taking into account as far as possible the opinions of the various scholars.

In all instances involving violations of public order or movements of revolt, the Roman authorities intervened, calmed the disturbances, arrested the likely trouble-makers and put them on trial. At most the function of the Jewish institutions was to hand over these people to the authorities, either because they were asked to do so, or because they feared complications and coming under suspicion for not doing enough. Thus the leaders of the community handed over Jesus the son of Ananias, who proclaimed 'Woe, woe, to Jerusalem,' though they considered him as one possessed by the spirit of God. The governor, Albinus (62-64) released him because he found him insane.[5] By contrast, in all offences involving direct desecration of the Temple, the Sanhedrin was allowed to impose the death penalty, although

---

[1] *T. B. Shabbath* 15a; *T. B. Abodah Zarah* 8b. There are essential differences between the Palestinian and the Babylonian traditions, but this is not relevant here.
[2] John 18:31.
[3] Acts 5:27-40.
[4] *M. Sanhedrin* 7:2; *T. Sanhedrin* 9:11.
[5] Jos. *War* VI, 301-5.

under supervision to a certain extent.[1] The supervision was more or less strict, depending on the governor's strength of character and the range of his authority. Under such governors as Pontius Pilate, supervision was stricter than under weaker governors. When conditions suited, under more lenient governors, or during an interregnum, the heads of the Sanhedrin could take a broader view of its jurisdiction in capital cases and took in cases where the Temple was adversely affected only in an indirect way. Thus the high priest Ananus took advantage of the change of governors to bring James the brother of Jesus to trial; on him and others he imposed the death penalty. Some Jews who respected the Law, most probably the Pharisees, complained of Ananus' malfeasance to King Agrippa, who had charge of the Temple, and also to the new governor who was on his way to Judaea. Their gravamen was that Ananus had no right to assemble the Sanhedrin of his own accord.[2] From this instance and others we see that the Roman governor allowed the high priest to assemble the Sanhedrin to judge capital cases even when no offence against the Temple was involved.

The High Priesthood

Another element of the Jewish leadership, along with the Sanhedrin, was the high priest or the high priests in general. The status of the high priest among the leadership of the people was notable as early as the first immigration from Babylonia. From the middle of the Persian period onward, (at the end of the fifth century, after the time of Ezra and Nehemiah), his status in the homeland was clearly defined: he was over the Temple, and responsible for the administration of autonomous Judaea, head of the Sanhedrin or the Gerousia. The high priest, either by himself or together with the Sanhedrin, represented the people when dealing with the empires or Jews of the Diaspora. This situation prevailed throughout the period of the Ptolemies and the Seleucids. The high priesthood reached the zenith of its power in the time of the Maccabees when it was determined that the Maccabees (Hasmonaeans) and their descendants should head the government and the high priesthood. The title of the Hasmonaean rulers as they appeared on their coins were: 'Johanan the High Priest, Judah the High Priest, Jonathan the High Priest,' and so on. Even when the Hasmonaean high priests proclaimed themselves kings, the

[1] Jos. *War* VI, 124-8; Acts 21,22.
[2] Jos. *Ant.* XX, 199-203.

crown of kingship remained combined with the crown of priesthood, and they emphasized and fought for their status as high priests. The status of the high priest was diminished and severely curtailed by King Herod. Until the Maccabean period, except during the rule of Antiochus Epiphanes, the position of the high priest was hereditary, being transmitted in the family of Zadok, from father to son, or to brother. This also was the case in the Hasmonaean dynasty. Herod undermined the stability and authority of the high priesthood by withdrawing it from the Hasmonaeans and revoking their right of succession. Herod appointed the high priests, dismissed them at will and appointed others in their place. As Josephus says: 'In the matter of the appointment of the high priests, Archelaus followed the practice of Herod his father, as did the Romans who succeeded to the rule over the Jews.'[1] Herod had his own reasons for his policy, but in any event, it served to undermine the stability of the high priesthood and diminish its status in the eyes of the people. Besides the external factors, such as the actions of Herod and the Roman rulers, others may be mentioned as contributing to the decline in the high priests' status. The high priests followed the Sadducean trend, while the people tended to follow the Pharisees and became estranged from the high priesthood. The people regarded the Pharisaic doctors of the Law as their teachers, and obeyed them and stood by them in the clashes between the Pharisees and the Sadducean high priesthood. The popular support was shown both by expressions of admiration and by the performance of acts in the Temple which were contrary to the views of the high priests,[2] and which at times even led to violent clashes.[3] Even the high priests' closeness to the monarchy and their national and political position contributed to the dimming of their image and the lessening of their influence among the people. With the identification of the high priesthood with the ruling circles under the Herods and the Romans and its dependence on them, it suffered a moral and social decline. All these factors combined to lessen the standing and power of the high priesthood. Although the people remembered the prestige of the high priest in former times, the Talmud and other writings preserved sayings in which the priesthood of the Temple is spoken of in angry, mocking and defiant terms.[4]

[1] Jos. *Ant.* xx, 249.
[2] *T. B. Yoma* 71b; *T. Sukkah* 3:1, and parallels; also *M. Menahoth* 10:3, and elsewhere.
[3] *M. Sukkah* 3:9; *T. Sukkah* 3:6.
[4] *T. B. Yoma* 8b; *T. Menahoth* 13:19-21; Jos. *Ant.* xx, 207, and other sources.

The high priesthood, nonetheless, until the destruction of the Temple, was the ruling element along with the Sanhedrin in a semi-autonomous Judaea. Not only had it great practical power when dealing with the Roman authorities or administering affairs connected with the Sanhedrin and the Temple; even its spiritual glory and power continued and some high priests were distinguished for their personal behaviour; their deeds are mentioned favourably even in Talmudic literature which generally takes a critical view.[1] The high priesthood was particularly important in the eyes of the Diaspora, where the Jews were not involved to any great extent in the internal struggles and clashes which took place in Jerusalem.

Josephus concludes his *Antiquities* with an account of the high priesthood and states that from the accession of Herod (37 B.C.E.) until the destruction of the Temple (70 C.E.) twenty-eight high priests held office. It seems likely that Josephus did not count a few high priests who served for only a short while, though their memory is preserved in Talmudic sources. Some of them served a considerable period like Joseph (called Caiaphas) who served for eighteen years (18-36 C.E.) or Ananias son of Nedebaeus who served for twelve years (47-59 C.E.), but some served for only a year or even less. In checking what families these high priests belonged to, we note that, except for the last high priest who was appointed by the people at the time of the Great Revolt, the rest of the high priests belonged to a small number of families in which the high priesthood was hereditary. From the House of Phiabi came three high priests: Jesus son of Phiabi, during the reign of Herod, Ishmael ben Phiabi who held the position in the years 15 and 16 C.E., and another of the same name who was chosen in the days of Agrippa II and served in the years 59 to 61 C.E. From the House of Boethus, which came to the fore during the Herodian period (its history is interwoven with the history of the monarchy), came five high priests during this period. More numerous were the high priests from the House of Ananus who held an important place in political life in Judaea in the last years of the Temple. Eight high priests came from this family, among whom the best known was Caiaphas who served in the years 18 to 36 C.E., and Ananus son of Ananus who was a zealous Sadducee; he served only three months in the year 62 C.E. and was then replaced. Later, at the time of the Great Revolt, he held an important position in the Jewish government. In recounting the appointment of Phineas son of Samuel from Kefar

[1] Jos. *Life* 13-16; *M. Sotah* 9:15; *T. B. Pesahim* 57a; *T. B. Baba Bathra* 21a.

Habta, Josephus complains that this high priest who was chosen by the people did not belong to the families from which the high priests were (traditionally) appointed.[1] Such families, along with the high priests who had completed their service, constituted, it would seem, the body or company of 'the high priests' who are frequently mentioned in the New Testament and in Josephus, or the 'Sons of the High Priests', mentioned in Talmudic literature and Josephus.[2] A concise description of the priestly oligarchy in Jerusalem, particularly with regard to its harsh rule over the Temple and the people, is found in Tannaitic tradition; it is transmitted in the name of two sages who lived at the time of the destruction of the Temple: 'And it was of these and such as these that Abba Saul ben Bothnith and Abba Jose ben Johanan used to say, 'Woe is me because of the House of Boethus; woe is me because of their staves! Woe is me because of the House of Kadros; woe is me because of their pens! Woe is me because of the House of (El)Hanan; woe is me because of their whisperings. Woe is me because of the House of Ishmael ben Phiabi; woe is me because of their fists! For they are High Priests and their sons are (Temple) treasurers and their sons-in-law are trustees and their servants beat the people with sticks.'[3]

Tannaitic tradition mentions smaller Sanhedrins with twenty-three members, besides the Great Sanhedrin in Jerusalem. These smaller Sanhedrins were probably identical with the 'Sanhedrins of the tribes' which are mentioned in the sources. The concept 'tribes' represents a use of the Biblical concept, which did not exist in the time of the Mishnah but probably reflects the conception that smaller Sanhedrins should be established in the larger cities and district capitals. According to the Mishnaic Halakah, such Sanhedrins were set up only by the decision of the Great Sanhedrin.[4] We do not have many clear attestations with regard to the existence of smaller Sanhedrins, either in the time of the Second Temple or afterwards. Josephus does not mention them either when he speaks of the constitution or when he describes the establishment of the judicial institutions and administration of Galilee. He refers only to the ordinary courts of law everywhere and one central institution. It seems likely, however, that the mention of the smaller Sanhedrins is not only a matter of

[1] Jos. *War* IV, 148.
[2] *M. Oholoth* 17:5 and elsewhere; Jos. *War* VI, 114.
[3] The quotation here is composed of *T. Menahoth* 13:21 and *T. B. Pesahim* 57a.
[4] *M. Sanhedrin* 1:6; *T. Sanhedrin* 7:1.

theory. According to Matthew and Mark, Jesus warned his disciples that they were liable to be given over to the Sanhedrins for scourging.[1] This accords with the opinion of Rabbi Ishmael that offences punishable by scourging are not decided by courts of three members (which is the opinion of the anonymous Mishnah), but by courts of twenty-three.[2]

Jewish autonomy after the destruction of the Temple

After the fall of Jerusalem and the burning of the Temple, the national leadership was dispersed and the Sanhedrin abolished. It is probable that the Sanhedrin ceased to function even before the last stages of the Temple's destruction and, in any case, the Tannaitic tradition of the mourning practices established in remembrance of the catastrophes that befell Israel includes, along with the practices commemorating the destruction of the Temple, the statement that 'When the Sanhedrin ceased, singing ceased at the wedding feasts.'[3] The dispersion of the national institutions was due not only to the razing of the city and the Temple, and the abrogation of the independence of the Jewish people in Judaea, but also to the mass slaughter in Jerusalem. Other causes of the dispersion were the spiritual collapse and confusion, and the harsh rule of the Romans during the years just after the fall of Jerusalem. These measures included religious persecution and action against certain people who had participated in the revolt or who were regarded by the Roman authorities as leaders of the national aspirations.[4]

The resurgence and reorganization of Judaism after the destruction of the Temple was linked to the work of Rabban Johanan ben Zakkai who started to revive the Sanhedrin in the city of Jamnia. It is not our task here to describe the spiritual resurgence and the political problems connected with the work of Rabban Johanan ben Zakkai. We shall confine ourselves to the problems of the organization and autonomy of Judaism insofar as they come within the scope of his activities.

According to the version in the Babylonian Talmud, Rabban Johanan ben Zakkai succeeded in escaping secretly from Jerusalem while it

[1] Matt. 10:17; Mark 13:9.
[2] *M. Sanhedrin* 1:2. In our versions, the words of Rabbi Ishmael are in the Mishnah itself, but they might be from a baraitha added to the Mishnah. See J. N. Epstein, *Introduction to the Text of the Mishnah* (Hebrew, 1948), p. 963.
[3] *M. Sotah* 9:11.
[4] Jos. *Ant.* VII, 53; *T. B. Taanith* 29a. Eusebius, *Ecclesiastical History* III, 20, 1-2.

was under siege. He presented himself before the Emperor Vespasian, and received from him 'Jamnia and its sages' and 'the dynasty of Rabban Gamaliel',[1] that is, permission for the descendents of Hillel and Gamaliel to return to their former tasks. However, according to the earlier Palestinian traditions he succeeded in receiving permission only for 'observing the commandments and studying the Torah' and, according to another source, he only succeeded in gaining his release from captivity and the freedom of several persons close to him.[2] The differences in the nature of the sources, the political situation and various attestations in Talmudic literature make the Palestinian traditions seem preferable; the Babylonian tradition merely reflects a tradition later than the time of the establishment of Jamnia and the recognition of the dynasty of Rabban Gamaliel. After the revolt, the Jews of the Land of Israel were considered *dediticii* and lost their rights. Rabban Gamaliel was compelled to go into hiding and was not in Jamnia in the years immediately after 70 C.E. The recognition that the authorities extended to the work of Rabban Johanan ben Zakkai was limited or simply meant that they did not intervene in his activities, only some of which they were aware of. His work for the revival of Judaism took in its organizational structure as well as its intellectual and spiritual life. Being leader of the Pharisees, head of the dynasty which claimed leadership there and second-in-line to Rabban Simeon ben Gamaliel among the heads of the Sanhedrin, he succeeded in gathering round him the disciples and survivors of the Pharisaic sages. He took up the matters whose abeyance was felt to be most distressing in the Jewish way of life, such as the proclamation of the New Moon and the fixing of the intercalary years. He also dealt with other problems in Jewish life arising from the destruction of the Temple, such as what to do with the produce of the new harvest from which it was forbidden to eat until the sacrifice of the Omer, or what was to be done with proselytes who, according to the Halakah, had to bring an offering as part of the rite of conversion.[3] The house of study established in Jamnia functioned like the Great Sanhedrin in Jerusalem, but its activity was limited—not only because of the difficult political conditions and the fear of being observed by the authorities but also because many of the sages, including the best of his own disciples, had reservations, it seems, about his activity and

---

[1] *T. B. Gittin* 56b.
[2] *Avot de Rabbi Natan* version A chap. 4, version B chap. 6; *Lam. Rabba*, 1.
[3] *M. Rosh ha-Shanah* 4:1-4; *T. B. Rosh ha-Shanah* 31a.

were not in accord with him after the destruction of the Temple. In any event, in the Jamnia of his time we do not find many of the sages who had previously flourished in Jerusalem and were later active in Jamnia after Rabbi Johanan's time. His Sanhedrin certainly did not deal with capital punishment, and even matters of property were beyond its purview. In contrast to the period after this, we do not learn of any contacts between Rabban Johanan and the Roman authorities, nor did the sages supervise and maintain relations with the leaders in the various cities, nor did they send messengers to the cities in the Land of Israel and certainly not to the Diaspora. The activity of Rabban Johanan was limited in comparison to that of Rabban Gamaliel who followed him; but the work of Rabban Johanan did lay the foundations not only for subsequent Judaism but also for the internal administration of Jewish affairs without the framework of a State, without Jerusalem, and without the Temple that had been the focal point of organized Jewish life. Jewish self-government in this period was established by the sages; the wealthy aristocrats, the remnants of the Sadducean (or non-Sadducean) high priesthood had no part in this. There were many priests among the sages (and it seems that even Rabban Johanan himself was a priest), but all of them were active as sages, although the priesthood perhaps gave some added weight to their leadership and eased their financial burden, so that they could devote themselves to the teaching of the Torah and public administration. It is clear that the priests continued to receive their Heave-offerings and tithes even after the destruction of the Temple, but in the main they were active as sages and not as priests. The high priesthood disappeared as an administrative body, just as the Sadducean movement ceased to aspire to the leadership of the people.

At the end of the Flavian period or during the reign of Nerva (96-98), or Trajan his successor, Rabban Gamaliel succeeded in assuming leadership at Jamnia; it seems that Rabbi Johanan relinquished his position. Either with the accession of Rabban Gamaliel or in the course of time the leadership achieved recognition by the Empire. We find that Rabban Gamaliel and the leading sages of Jamnia travelled to Rome and were received by the authorities.[1] Emissaries of the Empire came to Jamnia to investigate Jewish Law, a matter certainly connected with the recognition of the independent system

---

[1] *M. Maaser Sheni* 4:9; *M. Erubin* 4:9; *Pirke ben Azai* 3:2.

of justice which began to re-emerge at this time.[1] We read in the Mishnah that Rabban Gamaliel went to seek authority from the governor of Syria.[2] During his Patriarchate, the Sanhedrin at Jamnia not only dealt with public religious needs, such as the proclamation of the New Moon, the new translation of Scripture into Greek, the formulation of the Halakah and of prayers, the struggle against the Judaeo-Christians and so forth, but also with the consolidation of the legal system including the laws of property, fines and scourgings, based on the tradition of Scripture and of Oral Law. The position of the sages authorized by the Sanhedrin was strengthened in contrast to that of the local justices who were in charge in the various cities. The Sanhedrin in Jamnia in the time of Rabban Johanan and particularly in the time of Rabban Gamaliel took over most of the tasks that the Sanhedrin performed while the Temple was standing. Of course, there was no Temple to supervise and it had no authority in capital cases. And taxation and the maintenance of order were outside its scope. But in all other matters, such as supervision of public affairs in the Land of Israel and the communities of the Diaspora, the dispatch of messengers to cities at home and abroad, decisions and rulings in Halakah and so on, the Sanhedrin was the supreme court of law to which all questions were brought from all parts. The Sanhedrin and the Patriarchate not only managed to accomplish all these activities but did so with great vitality, enlarging and deepening of their scope.[3] The flowering of Jewish life which characterized the Jamnia period also found expression in the degree of self-government which developed. This autonomy was not conferred by the Roman authorities. The sages built it up and at best the Roman authorities recognized it either *de facto* or *de jure*. Throughout the period after the destruction of the Temple, fundamental limitations were imposed on civic and juridical autonomy. The Roman governor in the Land of Israel, whose position in the Roman administrative system was higher than in the earlier period, was in practice the supreme judicial authority there. As in other provinces, it was his custom to travel through the provincial districts, set up his tribunal and hold assizes. The governor was authorized to delegate his juridical powers to army officers, officials and even citizens

---

[1] *P. T. Baba Kamma* IV, 4b; *Sifre* on Deut. 344.
[2] *M. Eduyoth* 7:7.
[3] *M. Bekhoroth* 4:4; *T. B. Rosh ha-Shanah* 22b; *T. Betzah* 2:15; *T. Hullin* 3:10 and many others.

of his choice. The Roman governor or his delegates were authorized to handle any trial that came their way, or take control on their own initiative. Although these Roman judges generally intended to judge according to Jewish Law, the situation led to a serious curtailment of the legal system of the nation; the Tannaitic sages appealed to the people not to rely on the Roman legal system: 'Any place wherein you find court sessions in the market-place, even though their laws are like the laws of Israel, you are not permitted to rely on them.'[1] Tannaitic Halakah did not recognize the jurisdiction of the Roman legal system, and Tannaitic haggadic tradition sought to emphasize the corruption of the judges and of the legal system of the province.[2] Even though internal discipline assisted the Jews in their reliance on Jewish law-courts, it was the moral stature of the Tannaitic sages which created the situation in which not only Jews but even Christians and other gentiles as well brought matters in dispute between them to the Jewish law-courts. Nonetheless, the mere existence of the Roman legal system, with its power to intervene in any trial it chose, served as a considerable limitation on the process of Jewish law. The sources attest the efforts of the leaders of the community to satisfy the authorities, so that they should not intervene or feel obliged to intervene in various cases, or commit any injustice.[3]

Another limitation that at times created difficulties for Jewish courts was that Jews who regarded themselves as unjustly dealt with by a Jewish judge were able to appeal to the Roman governor and complain about the judge. This was the case particularly in matters which were not regarded as offences in Roman law, such as when a man was sentenced to be scourged for having sexual intercourse with a gentile woman, or when a woman was sentenced for prostitution, or when a judge did not reach his verdict on the basis of Roman legal concepts.[4] Certainly the possibility for complaints was more limited during periods when the political status of the Jewish people was stronger; however, as a matter of principle, the first limitation which we have discussed was always there.

Notwithstanding the above limitations, a Jewish legal system was then established which put its seal on Jewish life for generations; the principal development of the legal system, as it is known to us in

---

[1] *Gittin* 78b; *Mekhilta* at the beginning of *Mishpatim* (ed. Horovitz-Rabin, p. 246).
[2] *M. Gittin* 9:8; *T. B. Shabbath* 116a.
[3] *P. T. Shabbath* 1, 3c; *P. T. Abodah Zarah* 11, 41d.
[4] *P. T. Megillah* 111, 3d; *T. B. Berakoth* 58a.

Talmudic and later literature, came about in the period after the destruction of the Temple.

The Bar Cochba War brought with it the mass slaughter of the sages, the disintegration of the institutions of public leadership, loss of rights on the part of the Jewish people, and a lengthy period of religious persecution including systematic repression of every manifestation of Jewish community life. Various traditions describe the grave risks that the sages took whenever they ordained young scholars to be responsible for the continuity of Jewish life;[1] it was also necessary to destroy all documents such as marriage contracts and certificates of divorce, so that they might not serve as proof in the hands of the authorities for acting against the law courts and the signatories of the documents.[2] It seems likely that the persecutions after the Bar Cochba revolt lasted longer than those after the revolt which led to the destruction of the Temple.

The first stages of reorganization after the Bar Cochba revolt were semi-underground in character; Rabban Simeon, the son of Rabban Gamaliel of Jamnia, remained in hiding and did not participate in any of these gatherings.[3] Only during the reign of Antoninus Pius (138-161) were the persecutions relaxed, including the ban on circumcision.[4] Jewish institutions were revived and Rabban Simeon ben Gamaliel is mentioned as Patriarch,[5] at the head of the Sanhedrin of Usha in Galilee. But we do not hear of any contacts with the Empire in the time of Rabbi Simeon ben Gamaliel. The form of self-government that was established was like that of the Jamnia period. However, throughout the period of the Antonines (138-192), the Jewish people had to build up community life without any star of redemption shining in their midst.

The establishment of self-rule and its extension began with Rabbi Judah the Patriarch who was mainly active from 170-220 approximately. The restoration of the normal political status of Judaism in the Land of Israel and the Diaspora under the Severan emperors was mainly a matter of re-establishing Jewish self-rule and Jewish courts and strengthening the position of the Patriarch.

The Patriarch had police powers that enabled him to impose his decisions. There are numerous testimonies to his general rulings and his verdicts

[1] *T. B. Sanhedrin* 13b.
[2] *T. Ketuboth* 9:5.
[3] *Cant. Rabba* 2; *P. T. Hagigah*, beginning of chap. 3.
[4] *Dig.* 48, 11,1.
[5] *T. B. Horayoth* 13b.

in individual cases and in controversies among the various elements in the leadership of the cities between the members of the boule and the magistrates (στρατηγοί) in connection with tax matters and imperial levies.[1] We have detailed attestation from the period of Rabbi Judah concerning the great power of the Patriarch and the degree of Jewish autonomy in the letter of Origen to Julius Africanus: 'Now, for instance, that the Romans rule, and the Jews pay the two drachmae [half-shekel], how great is the power conceded by Caesar to the Patriarch! [in the text: ethnarch] So that we, who have had experience of it, know that he differs little from a true king. Private trials are held according to the law, and some are condemned to death, And though there is not full licence for this, still it is not done without the knowledge of the ruler, as we learned and were convinced of during the long time we spent in the country of that people.'[2] These words were written c. 240, and the author is referring to an earlier period which fits that of Rabbi Judah the Patriarch.[3]

Several Tannaitic sources from the period in question refer to the fact that the gentile authorities enforced sentences passed by Jewish courts. We ought not assume, however, that the decrees of the Sanhedrin were dependent on the assistance of the authorities for their enforcement, and probably such attestations express the situation in the law-courts in the cities, where the sages of the various cities sat, as we read in a certain baraitha: 'Among the gentiles, they beat him and said to him: 'Do what a certain Rabbi told you.'[4] Certainly this attests the extent of self-rule which the Jews had achieved under the Severan emperors.

Until the time of Rabbi Judah we do not know of many contacts between the central leadership and the circles of wealthy aristocrats. To a large degree, the wealthy class held aloof from the national leadership which developed under the sages, and in many instances even tried to interfere with the sages who had such influence and authority in the great cities under their rule. They refused to help in meeting the general needs, including financial participation in the social welfare institutions which were founded by the sages. Rabbi Judah the Patriarch won them over and succeeded in imposing

---

[1] *Eccles. Rabba* 6; *P. T. Ketuboth*, 34a; *P. T. Yoma* I, 39a; *T. B. Baba Bathra* 132a.
[2] *PG* XI, cols. 41-8.
[3] See O. Bardenhewer, *Geschichte der altkirchlichen Literatur* II (1903), pp. 177-8.
[4] *T. Yebamoth* 12:13.

his influence on them and brought them into the national leadership.[1] Rabbi Judah's procedure aroused the resistance of certain circles among the sages, the more democratic and pious among them were critical of his actions and his regal mode of behaviour and the grandeur that surrounded his court.[2] Earlier, in the days of Rabban Gamaliel, we find that the Patriarch dismissed the head of a city who prevented the witnesses from reaching Jamnia to give testimony in the matter of the proclamation of the New Moon; however, only in the period of Rabbi Judah did the Patriarch appoint a sage to deal with public functions in a given city and also appointed custodians to look after the coffers in which alms were collected and so on.[3] There are numerous traditions about the dispatch of emissaries by Rabbi Judah the Patriarch to supervise civic and community arrangements.[4] Presumably the practice of appointing community heads in the Land of Israel and the Diaspora, which we note in the third and fourth centuries, and until the abolition of the Patriarchate in the fifth century, was established in the days of Rabbi Judah the Patriarch. Thus, power and prestige accrued to the Patriarchate in the Roman Empire. It was permitted to collect contributions from all Jews, including those in the Diaspora. It appointed public leaders, judges, and leaders of the synagogue; and the community heads enjoyed full legal status, as we know mainly from the fourth century. All this began under Rabbi Judah and under the Severan emperors. We can hardly assume that the Jewish community and the Patriarchate received these privileges of self-determination in the time of the Christian emperors or the civil wars of the late third century. We many assume that they were established under the Severan emperors when relations were good with the Jews in general, and with Rabbi Judah the Patriarch in particular.

In Talmudic literature, with echoes in Christian literature from the third century onwards, there is a widespread tradition that the Patriarchal dynasty was descended from the House of David. Thus, the text in Genesis: 'And the staff shall not depart from Judah, nor the ruler's staff from between his feet,' (49:10) was taken to mean the Exilarchs in Babylonia and the Patriarchs in the Land of Israel, who gave a certain continuity to the royal line of David. There may

---

[1] *T. B. Erubin* 86a; *P. T. Moed Katan* iii, 81c.
[2] *P. T. Moed Katan* iii, 81c; *P. T. Demai* i, 22a.
[3] *P. T. Yebamoth* xii, 13a; *T. B. Baba Bathra* 8b.
[4] *T. B. Yebamoth* 105a; *T. B. Pesahim* 3b, and elsewhere.

indeed be no good reason to assert that this tradition first saw the light in the time of Rabbi Judah the Patriarch. However, it is not mentioned before his time, which suggests that it was not in fact known before then. In any case, the tradition was widespread at the time, and created, or at least enhanced, the royal aura that surrounded Rabbi Judah and his court where the honours of royalty were paid.[1] The rights of the Jews, in the Land of Israel and the Diaspora, to hold assemblies, to organize and preserve their way of life, and to establish relations with the centre in the Land of Israel, were recognized in the edicts of Julius Caesar and Augustus. These rights remained fundamentally unimpaired despite the various clashes and strains which accompanied the revolt against Rome. At the end of the second century, under the Severan emperors, these rights were enhanced, and they withstood the period of anarchy and the re-establishment of the empire at the end of the third century, as well as the Christian empire thereafter.

The leadership in the cities

Before we begin our discussion of the problems of city government, we must make some distinctions. In the areas of Jewish settlement no 'cities' possessing the organization of a Greek polis existed except for Tiberias and Sepphoris. We know that Tiberias had the same organizational and administrative arrangements as the Greek cities with a boule and public assemblies. Despite the Greek form of administration, these were Jewish cities, and possessed the characteristic institutions of Jewish cities of this period, not only when Tiberias and Sepphoris became the principal centres of Judaism and the meeting-places of the Patriarchate and the Sanhedrin, but even, to a large extent, during the first century. Jews lived in considerable numbers in the many Greek cities along the coast and in Transjordan and, of course, in the Greek cities in the heart of the country. But there was nothing particularly Jewish about their government. We may assume that the Jews in the mixed Greek cities possessed some form of organization of their own, although we have little information about this.

There were a few large Jewish cities with populations of ten or twenty thousand or more. For the most part, the population was only a few thousand, and in many instances less than that. The Talmudic tradition regarded all these towns or villages as 'cities'; 'villages' were

[1] *Gen. Rabba* 97 (ed. Theodor Albeck p. 1219); cf. L. Ginzburg, *Geniza Studies* I (1928), 220; *P. T. Shabbath* xvi, 15, beginning of c.

places of settlement which were sparsely populated, without public institutions and leadership of their own, and depending for their government on the institutions of the nearby cities. Talmudic tradition determined the institutions that should function in a city. Various attestations combine to support the assumption that generally they did exist and function in the various cities. The great majority of Jews were consequently 'urban', although they supported themselves in the main by agricultural work and the cultivation of agricultural produce, and were not inhabitants of great urban centers. There are numerous traditions about halakic rulings dealing with the status of the citizen in a city, with his rights to benefit from the services of the city, his obligations to pay the municipal taxes incumbent on citizens, the qualities that were demanded of the elected leaders of the city and so on. None of the varying traditions makes any distinction between one inhabitant and another. There is no hint that the status of the citizen was connected with his economic position or the property that he possessed in the city. All the discussions and traditions assume that all inhabitants of the city had the same obligations and privileges, and the only limitation was the length of their residence in the city, which had to exceed twelve months.[1]

Controversies regarding Halakah and practical customs occurred only with regard to the position of those lacking rights, such as bastards or proselytes who had not yet married into the Jewish people; some thought that those of inferior status were not qualified for leadership, while others held the contrary. An ancient mishnah reads: 'They need not trace descent beyond the Altar (a priest) or beyond the Platform (a levite) or beyond the Sanhedrin; and all whose fathers are known to have held public office as public officers or almoners, may marry into the priestly stock and need not trace their descent. Rabbi Jose says: Also any whose name was signed as a witness in the old archives at Sepphoris.'[2] Anyone who had held any function, even if he had only been included as a witness on a document, was considered to be of unblemished origin. We find various forms of Halakah which follow this rule, but on |the other hand, there are various traditions which affirm that 'everyone is qualified to judge property matters, even proselytes and bastards.'[3] It seems likely that after the destruction of the Temple, as time passed, the

---

[1] *M. Baba Bathra* 1:5; *T. Nedarim* 2:5; *P. T. Peah* v, 21a.
[2] *M. Kiddushin* 4:2.
[3] *M. Sanhedrin* 4:2; *P. T. Sanhedrin* IV, 22b; *T. B. Sanhedrin* 36b.

participation of men of questionable origin was permitted in the law-courts and the leadership.

In his *Antiquities* Josephus describes 'the Jewish Constitution' which Moses gave to the Israelites.[1] In this account he includes, in the manner of Jewish tradition generally, the rulings of sages and later practices from his own time. He writes: 'As rulers, let each city have seven men long exercised in virtue and in the pursuit of justice', and he adds: 'to each magistracy (of each city) let there be assigned two subordinate officers of the tribe of Levi.'[2] From this account and from other passages, it appears that a group of seven ruled each city, where they were also judges; thus, in the general view, the judiciary held an honoured place, or even the principal one, in the government as a whole. This rule is attested by Josephus' own conduct when he arrived in Galilee. He appointed seven men in each city to ad-minister its affairs.[3] In this passage, Josephus does not mention the two levitical officials, but these are mentioned in Tannaitic literature.[4] Presumably, it was not a fixed custom, but it was widespread: the levites fulfilled this task just as formerly in the Temple.

The custom of having a group of seven is reflected in the leadership of the Christian community in Jerusalem shortly after the death of Jesus; the community chose 'seven men of wisdom, full of the Holy Spirit' to serve as administrators in the Judaeo-Christian community in Jerusalem.[5] The Judaeo-Christian community undoubtedly adopted Jewish practices in their congregations. The Jewish practice was maintained even after the destruction of the Temple, and one Tannaitic source states that three men form the administrative body of the synagogue, with authority to act on its behalf while a group of seven act on behalf of the city.[6] The group of seven is called 'the seven good men of the city' or more commonly 'administrators' (פרנסים).[7] As well as these, mention is made of a smaller group called archons (ἄρχοντες), particularly in the Book of Judith, which speaks of the authority of the elders and the archons. The number of elders is not stated, but there were three archons.[8] It is probable that the three archons were chosen from the larger administrative body. Talmudic literature also distinguishes between elders and archons

---

[1] IV, 214. [2] Ibid. 287. [3] Jos. *War* II, 568-571.
[4] *Sifre* on Deut. 15. [5] Acts 6:3-5.
[6] *P. T. Megillah* III, 74a.
[7] *T. B. Megillah* 26a; *T. Megillah* 2:12 and elsewhere.
[8] Judith 6:15-16; 8:10; 8:35; 10:6; 13:12.

(ראשים).[1] One of the three archons is head of the city; however, frequently two of the 'administrators' act on behalf of the city since it was generally held that 'nor were less than two persons suffered to hold office over the public in aught concerning property.'[2] Letters from the Bar Cochba revolt were sent from or addressed to two administrators: 'From the administrators of Bet Mashko, from Jesus, and from Eliezer' or 'To the men of Ein Geddi, to Masabala and to Jehonatan bar Beayan'.[3] In the Temple period the leaders and even the archons generally came from the circles of the wealthy and the powerful; Tannaitic literature of the second century emphasizes the contrast between the secular leadership in the cities and the spiritual leadership of the sages.[4] One even hears criticism of the 'Men of violence' who impose their will on the populace and place obstacles before the sages.[5] In the Jamnia period, the status of the sages in the leadership became stronger, the judicial system passed into their hands and became increasingly the preserve of the sages of the Torah, just as the sages become mainly responsible for works of charity and even penetrate to the leadership of the city. Finally, it is told of Rabbi Akiba that he commanded his son not to live in a city whose leaders are sages, since then they fail to devote themselves to the study and teaching of the Torah.[6]

Along with the group of seven, we hear of a larger body which is found principally in the important cities, called the 'association of the city' (חבר עיר). It is mentioned in Halakah, at least from the Jamnia period on, in the context of prayers at festivals and set feasts, of almsgiving and the comforting of mourners, of the distribution of fruits in the seventh year, and similar matters.[7] From various discussions it is evident that not all cities had a *Hever*, but the Talmudic sages certainly knew of its existence in all important cities.[8] We may assume that there was probably a link between the '*Hever* of the city' and the institution or concept 'the congregation of the Jews' (חבר

---

[1] L. Grünhut, ed., *Sefer ha-Liqqutim* IV (1900), p. 19a.
[2] *M. Shekalim* 5:2; *T. B. Baba Bathra* 8b.
[3] P. Benoit and others, *Discoveries in the Judean Desert* II (1961), no. 42, p. 156; Y. Yadin, *The Judean Desert Caves* (1967), no. 12, p. 59.
[4] *Sifre* on Deut. 20.
[5] *M. Sotah*, ad. fin.; *Est. R.* 1; *Avot de Rabbi Natan*, version A chap. 31.
[6] *T. B. Pesahim* 112a.
[7] *M. Berakoth* 4:7; *T. B. Rosh ha-Shanah* 34b; *T. Megillah* 4:29; *T. B. Megillah* 27a; *T. Baba Bathra* 6:13; *T. Shebiith* 7:9.
[8] *P. T. Berakoth* IV, 8c.

היהודים), mentioned on the coins from the Temple period. While the latter designates the whole nation, the former refers to the large-scale urban institution. The attempts to determine more precisely the character and number of its members have not been successful, though its existence seems certain.

Along with the permanent administrative institutions, we find 'the assembly of men of the city', that is, the gathering of citizens (as an institution) which underlies, from a legal and theoretical viewpoint, the administrative institutions of the city. Thus 'the assembly of the men of the city' was responsible for matters in which the other civic institutions were not competent. We have cited the baraitha which states that the seven leaders of the city did not act on their own authority but on behalf of the city. It is also stated that the citizens were permitted to establish a larger or a smaller *Hever* (if they so wished), but, generally, seven was the number chosen to work for the city. According to *Mishnah Megillah*, chap. 3, a halakah limits the possibility of selling the open place of the city and the synagogue. With regard to this halakah, the Talmud states that these limitations applied only when 'the seven good men of the city' sold city property without the consent of 'the assembly of the men of the city'. When they acted with the latter's approval, however, they could sell city property, including the synagogue, as they wished. It was even permitted to divert the money given to charities to other purposes 'if the assembly of men of the city permitted.'[1]

As the Halakah states and the facts of the situation suggest, the appointment of the leadership was debated in public and the leadership was only accepted with the full approval of the public.[2] On the other hand, it should be noted that the central institutions in Jerusalem and afterwards in Jamnia and Usha, had overwhelming influence on the appointment of public leadership in the cities throughout the country. It is possible that the story in Josephus of the appointment of the leadership in Galilee does not reveal the true situation of the time, since he was in charge during a period of emergency. In any case, numerous Talmudic sources reveal the influence of the leadership in Jerusalem on local appointments. One tradition even describes the bitter feelings of the people in the cities towards the councillors of Jerusalem, who took advantage of their privileges to make appoint-

[1] *T. B. Megillah* 26a-b; *T. B. Baba Metzia* 78b; 106b.
[2] *T. B. Berakoth* 55a; *Sifre Zuta* on Num. 27:19, p. 321; *Midr. ha-Gadol* on Lev. 8:3, p. 168; *P. T. Yebamoth* xii, 13a.

ments in order to acquire property throughout the country.[1] But we are unable to give an exact account of these relations and how they ordinarily worked. After the destruction of the Temple, it is clear that the judiciary was transferred from the ordinary elders to the official doctors of the Law. Even if not all three judges who sat in judgment, according to the Halakah, had been ordained as sages, at least one of them had.[2] The ordination of sages was entirely in the hands of the Sanhedrin and the Patriarchate. This gave them great power in the matter of local government.

One baraitha which was already edited before Rabbi Akiba, lists the institutions or services that every city ought to provide: 'A law-court competent to scourge, a prison, a charity fund, a synagogue and a public bath, a public latrine, a doctor and artisan, a scribe, a slaughterer, and a teacher of children.'[3] Not all the items listed were city property or under its control, but the city did ensure that they were there, and to some extent they were under communal supervision and were public matters. The school was not public property, and the children's teacher was not a city employee, but the city ensured that they were there, and from later sources we learn that the city contributed, to a certain extent, to the teachers' wages.[4] Several of the institutions, such as the charity fund and the synagogue, were characteristic of the Jewish city. The synagogue had already existed in the Temple period in all Jewish cities, and the charity fund also was quite common. However, our knowledge of them during this period is limited.

In Talmudic sources there are scattered notices about various officeholders in the Jewish city who fulfilled tasks similar to those discharged in the Greek cities of the East. We mention briefly one of them: the ἀγορανόμος (inspector of markets). The name was taken over from the Greek and the function is known to us from the Greek cities. However, Talmudic tradition emphasizes the importance of the position, and sees it as the fulfilment of the commandment: 'a just ephah and a just hin' (Leviticus 19:36). Traditions differ as to whether the inspector merely supervised weights and the quality of the produce, or whether he could also control prices. Traditionally, the inspector in Jerusalem was not responsible for the prices, but only for the weights.[5]

[1] *T. Sanhedrin* 7:1; *Sifre* on Deut. 17; *P. T. Taanith* IV, 69a.
[2] *T. B. Bekhoroth* 37a.
[3] *T. B. Sanhedrin* 17b; *P. T. Kiddushin* IV, 68b.
[4] *P. T. Peah* VIII, 201a; *Lev. Rabba* 27.
[5] *Sifra Kedoshim* 8 (91b); *T. Baba Metzia* 6:14.

BIBLIOGRAPHY

A general survey of Jewish self-government may be found in H. ZUCKER, *Studien zur Jüdischer Selbstverwaltung im Altertum*, 1936.

Among the books summarizing the history of the Sanhedrin: D. HOFFMANN, *Der oberste Gerichtshof in der Stadt des Heiligtums*, 1878, written in a conspicuously conservative trend. A. BÜCHLER, *Das Synedrion in Jerusalem und das grosse Beth-Din in der Quaderkammer des Jerusalemischen Tempels*, 1902, emphasizes the division into several separate institutions. Recently, S. HOENIG, *The Great Sanhedrin*, 1953, has made a contribution to the history of the Sanhedrin in the Second Temple period, but the central problems are dealt with superficially. H. MANTEL, *Studies in the History of the Sanhedrin*, 1961 deals with a number of problems concerning the Sanhedrin, particularly after the destruction of the Temple. This is an eclectic book, on the whole. On the problem of the composition and the leadership of the Sanhedrin: D. HOFFMANN, 'Die Präsidentur im Sanhedrium', *Magazin*, 1878, pp. 94-9; A. KÜNEN, 'Über die Zusammensetzung des Sanhedrin' in *Gesammelte Abhandlungen zur biblischen Wissenschaft*, ed. R. Budde, 1894; J. JELSKI, *Die innere Einrichtung des grossen Synedrions zu Jerusalem*, 1894; J. TAUBES, *ha-Nasi ba-Sanhedrin ha-Gedola*, 1925.

On the functions of the Sanhedrin, see G. ALLON, *History of the Jews in the Land of Israel in the Period of the Mishnah and the Talmud* I, (in Hebrew), 1957, pp. 114-128. From the literature on the matter of ordination, we may mention the studies of W. Bacher, 'Zur Geschichte der Ordination', in *MGWJ*, XXXVIII, 1893-4, pp. 122-7; H. Y. BORENSTEIN, 'The Laws about Ordination and its History' (in Hebrew), *Ha Tekufa*, 1923, pp. 394-426; also J. NEWMAN, *Semikah*, 1950; E. LOHSE, *Die Ordination im Spätjudentum und im Neuen Testament*, 1951.

On the envoys: H. GRAETZ, *Geschichte der Juden* IV, 4th ed. 1908, pp. 441-4, n. 21; S. KRAUSS, 'Die jüdischen Apostel', in *JQR*, o.s. XVII, 1904-5, pp. 370-383; A. HARNACK, *Die Mission und Ausbreitung des Christentums in den ersten drei Jahrhunderten* I, 1924, pp. 340 ff.; H. VOGELSTEIN, 'The Development of Apostolate in Judaism and its Transformation in Christianity', *HUCA* II, 1925, pp. 100-123; E. LOHSE, op.cit., pp. 60-3.

On the High Priest in the Second Temple period, and particularly in

418

the first century: E. SCHÜRER, 'Die ἀρχιερεῖς im Neuen Testament' in *Stud. und Krit.*, 1872, pp. 593-657; A. BÜCHLER, *Die Priester und der Kultus im letzten Jahrzehnt des jerusalemischen Tempels*, 1895; E. R. BEVAN, *Jerusalem under the High Priests*, 1904; G. HÖLSCHER, 'Die Hohepriesterliste bei Josephus und die evangelische Chronologie', in *Sitzungsberichte der Heidelberger Akademie der Wiss., Phil.-Hist. Klasse*, 1940; G. ALLON, 'On the History of the High Priesthood at the Close of the Second Temple' (in Hebrew), *Tarbiz* XII, 1941-2, pp. 1-24; E. M. SMALLWOOD, 'High Priests and Politics in Roman Palestine', in *JTS*, 1962, pp. 14-34.

On the status of Jamnia and the work of Rabban Johanan ben Zakkai: M. STEIN, 'Give me a Jabneh and its Wisdom' (Hebrew), in *Zion* III, 1938, pp. 118-122. For other views see G. ALLON, 'Rabban Johanan ben Zakkai's Move to Jabneh' (Hebrew), in *Studies on the History of Israel* I, 1957, pp. 219-252, and 'The Leadership of Rabban Johanan ben Zakkai' (in Hebrew), ibid., pp. 253-273; S. SAFRAI, 'Recent Research on the Problem of the Position of Rabban Johanan ben Zakkai after the Destruction' (in Hebrew), in *Memorial Volume of G. Allon*, 1970, pp. 203-226.

On the status of the sages in the leadership: E. E. URBACH, 'Class-Status and Leadership in the World of the Palestinian Sages', in *Proceedings of the Israel Academy of Sciences and Humanities* II, 1968, pp. 38-74.

On the legal status of the Jewish law-courts after 70 C.E., see H. P. CHAJES, 'Les juges juifs en Palestine de l'an 70 à l'an 500', *REJ*, 1899, pp. 39-52. This is an attempt to demonstrate their lack of legal competence. But see the two volumes of G. ALLON, in the series of J. S. Zuri, *History of Hebrew Public Law* (in Hebrew), 1925-34.

On the Davidic lineage of the Patriarchate: I. LEVI, 'De l'origine davidique de Hillel', *REJ* XXXI, 1895, pp. 202-211, and *REJ* XXXIII, 1896, pp. 143-6; on the communal leadership, M. WEINBERG, 'Die Organisation der jüdischen Ortsgemeinden in der talmudischen Zeit', *MGWJ* XLI, 1896-7, pp. 588-604, 639-660, 673-681; S. SAFRAI, 'The Jewish Town in the Land of Israel in the Period of the Mishnah and the Talmud' (in Hebrew), in *Ha-Ir ve-ha-Kehilla*, 1968, pp. 216-227 deals with the leadership in the cities.

Chapter Eight
The Legal Status of
the Jewish Communities in the Diaspora

The legal status of the Jews of the Roman Empire in the first century
C.E., prior to the destruction of the organized Jewish polity of Judaea—and even to some extent after that date—had developed out
of their crystallized status in the Hellenistic kingdoms which ruled
much of the eastern Mediterranean prior to the establishment of
Roman rule. The Roman Republic and the early Principate were,
like their political predecessors, conservative in their approach to
the status of the communities which came under their authority,
and when peoples or cities which had exhibited strong resistance to
the conquest had been dealt with, tended so far as possible to recognize the *status quo ante* and to acknowledge the internal rights
of indigenous communities. Territories might be recast, state properties
appropriated, additional taxes imposed, and new centres of population intruded or established, but generally speaking it was Roman
policy to use existing structures and to respect local rights of property,
cult and law.

In consequence, no accurate or organic evolutionary picture can be
obtained of the legal position of the Jewish communities of the early
empire outside Judaea, without a prior survey of their status in the
Hellenistic kingdoms.

The legal status of the Jewish communities of the Hellenistic kingdoms has not been clarified at every point, and absence of information
on various aspects leaves numerous obscurities. Here again, the
general attitude of Alexander the Great and his immediate successors
to conquered communities furnishes the key to the status of such
groups, and of the Jews among them. This attitude, in common with
that of the Romans, was tolerant of existing rights and made a rule
of confirming them. The normal formula was the confirmation of the
right of each community 'to live according to its ancestral laws'.[1]
Alexander's successors generally followed this precedent, and Antio-

---

[1] Thus in relation to the Greek cities of Asia Minor (Arrian, 1,18,2); the Lydians
(ibid., 1,17,4); the Arabs (Strabo, xvi,741); the Indians (Arrian, vii,20,1) and
others.

chus III, after he had conquered Judaea in 198 B.C.E., used the same formula in the official charter of benefits and rights which he conferred upon the Jewish community of the country.[1] This grant, however, was made to the Jewish people in its own country, represented by the high priest and Gerousia, and focused upon the Temple of Jerusalem. Our problem concerns the Jewish communities of the Diaspora, and while it is legitimate to assume that the general principle of the confirmation of existing rights in relation to Judaea was applied also to the Diaspora communities, further evidence is required to clarify the development of the legal status of Jews in the communities of the Ptolemaic and Seleucid kingdoms.

While Jewish communities already existed in Egypt, and almost certainly in Asia Minor,[2] the reorganization of these countries involved a considerable degree of new migration, of new colonization and the establishment of new cities or the enlargement of existing ones. It is advisable to study in turn the Ptolemaic and Seleucid kingdoms.

Egypt

The Hellenistic Jewish community of Egypt, at the time when knowledge of it becomes available through the medium of historical sources and documents, can be divided into three sections: 1) military settlers and garrison troops; 2) inhabitants of rural areas and villages; 3) inhabitants of urban centres.

We know practically nothing of what happened to the Jews whom the Hellenistic rulers found already settled in Egypt. These included, presumably, members of Persian garrisons such as the 'Jewish force' stationed at Elephantine[3] and probably elsewhere; in the early Roman period Jewish 'Persians' are found in Alexandria,[4] and a 'pseudo-ethnic' Persian military formation existed in Egypt as early as the third century B.C.E. These, however, appear to have had nothing to do with the survival of actual Persian subjects in Egypt.[5] We may indeed conjecture that some at least of the Jews who had served in the Persian army, whether in Jewish units or as individuals, were

---

[1] Jos., *Ant.* XII,142.
[2] Egypt: see note 3; Asia: cf. *Is.* 60:9.
[3] E. Sachau, *Aramäische Papyrus und Ostraka aus der Jüdischen Militärkolonie zu Elephantine* (1911); A. E. Cowley, *Aramaic Papyri of the Fifth Century B.C.* (1923).
[4] *CPJ* II, nos. 146, 149.
[5] *CPJ* I, pp. 13, 51 n. 10.

incorporated into the Ptolemies' forces; but the 'Persians' or 'Persians of the Epigone', who by Roman times ranked among the lower categories of the population, standing not far from the Egyptian element and suffering similar legal disabilities,[1] and who certainly included some Jews, were an independent category whose origin is lost in obscurity.

Numerous other Jews, mostly immigrants, on the other hand, were accepted into the regular Ptolemaic army, serving generally as individuals in 'pseudo-ethnic' units. Like the other members of the forces, they received land-allotments as cleruchs in return for their readiness to serve. This is shown by papyri, at least from the middle of the third century B.C.E.[2] and confirms on the whole the statements of the *Letter of Aristeas*[3] and Josephus[4] that Alexander, Ptolemy Soter and Ptolemy II Philadelphus used Jewish garrison troops, and that Ptolemy II conscripted numbers of released Jewish prisoners of war from Judaea. How far Alexander used Jewish troops may be controversial,[5] but since Jews buried at al-Ibramiyeh on the outskirts of Alexandria in the early third century B.C.E. spoke and wrote Hebrew[6] and were therefore from Judaea, there is no reason to doubt that Ptolemy I enrolled Jewish servicemen. We may have some evidence of the legal basis on which the religious rights of these men and their families were ensured. In 312 B.C.E. as a result of war between Ptolemy and Antigonus, the High Priest Ezechias and a number of other Jews accompanied Ptolemy back to Egypt to settle there, probably fearing reprisals on the part of Antigonus. According to this account, Ezechias had in writing the conditions attaching to their settlement and political status.[7] The word διάφοραν (difference) presents difficulties, and H. Lewy's suggested emendment of διφθέραν (scroll) may well be right,[8] but hardly affects the question whether Ezechias read

[1] For the difficult term Πέρσης τῆς ἐπιγονῆς, see J. F. Oates, *Yale Class. Stud.*, (1963), pp. 51-121, esp. 109ff.
[2] V. Tcherikover, *The Jews of Egypt in the Hellenistic and Roman Period* (in Hebrew, 2nd ed., 1963), pp. 34-6.
[3] 22-4.
[4] *War* II, 487; *Against Apion* II, 35.
[5] Jos. *Ant.* XI, 339; *Against Apion* I, 22, derived from Hecataeus. In the light of the more recent tendency to favour Hecataeus' authenticity, A. Schalit, *JQR* (1960), pp. 297-8, n. 29, accepts completely the service of Jews in Alexander's forces; for a more sceptical view, see V. Tcherikover, *Hellenistic Civilization and the Jews* (1959), p. 272.
[6] *BSAA*, IX (1907), p. 65; (1930), p. 108; *CPJ* III, pp. 138 ff., nos. 1424-31.
[7] Jos., *Against Apion* I, 186 ff., from Hecataeus.
[8] H. Lewy, *ZNW* (1932), pp. 117-132.

to his group a scroll of the Law or the agreement between themselves and Ptolemy governing their settlement in Egypt. The words κατοί-κησιν and πολιτείαν are more appropriate to the second interpretation, and suggest that this was a group settlement, probably in agriculture i.e. under conditions of cleruchy. What the clauses of such a charter were can only be conjectured, but it may reasonably be supposed that they included permission to practise freely the 'ancestral laws' of the Jews, and prescribed the size of the holdings to be allotted to the Jewish settlers. More technical conditions of lease and cultivation may well have appeared. It should be noted that the settlement of a group of military cultivators under the leadership of a Jewish high priest finds a later parallel in Egypt under the Ptolemies (see below), and that some indication exists of the importance of priests and scholars as leaders of similar Jewish colonies in the Seleucid Empire.

The above then, is fair evidence that Jewish agricultural military settlement in Egypt was carried out under royal initiative and super-vision, on a contractual basis. The military settlement of released prisoners of war recorded by Aristeas and Josephus bears a slightly different character, but Aristeas' general account, however embellish-ed, conveys that consideration was elicited for the settlers' religious requirements, implying some form of corporate recognition, if only for cult purposes, by the King.

On the other hand the papyrological evidence indicates that at this period, on the whole, the Jewish troops were scattered individually about various military units,[1] and it is very difficult to know how far their religious needs were either voiced or met. Nevertheless, active service may have been one thing, peaceful residence between training and campaigning another. In the third century B.C.E. we find the village of Psenyris equally divided between Jews and Greeks,[2] but there is no evidence that the former possessed any sort of organization, nor do we know what the status of the Jews was. By the end of the first quarter of the second century (174 B.C.E.) there were already groups of Jewish servicemen living sufficiently close to one another to entertain business relations; a document refers to two Jewish cleruchs of a hipparchy settled by one Dositheos.[3] Tcherikover[4] is cautious as to his Jewish origin, but elsewhere states

[1] V. Tcherikover, *Jews of Egypt*, pp. 32-42; cf. *CPJ* I, p. 9.
[2] *CPJ* I, no. 33.
[3] Ibid. I, no. 24, l. 26.   [4] Ibid., p. 166.

that this name was so frequently used by Jews that it 'became in some sense... Jewish'.[1] Here then, in great probability, we have a unit settled by a Jewish officer and containing a number of Jews. The precise relation between such cleruchies and rural synagogues cannot be stated on evidence. Most of these settlements would seem till at least the mid-second century B.C.E. to have contained mixed Jewish and gentile populations, and the end of the latter period provides several papyri listing such groups.[2] What can be stated is that the middle third of the third century B.C.E. is the date of the first known inscriptions showing the existence of synagogues in Ptolemaic Egypt.[3] These at least must have been the product of the period of settlement during the reign of Ptolemy Philadelphus, which was responsible for the settlement of a large proportion of the Jewish cleruchs. The inscriptions recording the first two of the above mentioned synagogues are dedicated to King Ptolemy III Euergetes I and his family. It is clear enough that these dedications bear an official character and from them it may be inferred that the synagogues, and *ipso facto* the communities that built them, enjoyed the legal recognition of the king and his protection under the law of the realm. This assumption is confirmed by two other synagogue inscriptions, one of which, from Athribis, is dedicated to the royal family jointly by the community and the local superintendent of police (ἐπιστάτης τῶν φυλακιτῶν), himself no doubt a Jew.[4] The other is the inscription from an unknown site and of uncertain date in the Ptolemaic period, recording a grant of *asylia* to a synagogue by one of the Ptolemaic rulers, Euergetes I or II.[5]

We can supplement the slight information on the status of Jewish cleruchs and other villagers in Ptolemaic territory from material relating to Cyrenaica, which was ruled by the Ptolemaic dynasty, though not always politically united with Egypt. Josephus states specifically that Ptolemy I settled Jews in Cyrene and the other cities of the territory in order to strengthen his control of the country.[6] This may be fairly interpreted to mean cleruchic settlement in the

[1] Ibid. pp. 29 and 166.
[2] *CPJ* I, n. 28, (Samareia); 29-31 (Fayum).
[3] *CII* II, no. 1440, (Schedia, 246-222 B.C.E.); 1532 (Arsinoe, 246-222 B.C.E.); *CPJ* I. no. 129 (Alexandrou Nesos, Fayûm, 3rd century B.C.E.); *OGIS* no. 129 (unknown locality, 3rd century B.C.E.).
[4] *OGIS*. no. 96, 2nd or 1st century B.C.E.
[5] *CII* II, no. 1449.
[6] Jos. *Against Apion* II, 44.

vicinity of the cities or round about them.[1] The statement is interesting because it may be indirectly alluded to in the inscription recording the constitution drafted by Ptolemy I for Cyrene;[2] it is there stated in an unfortunately mutilated passage, either that those who go to the οἰκίαι Πτολεμαϊκαί[3] shall not possess citizenship,[4] or that they shall suffer some disability in respect of the same citizenship. The aim of this regulation was probably twofold: on the one hand the city, with its timocratic constitution, which excluded manual workers, traders and poor inhabitants,[5] had small desire to absorb extraneous elements with lesser incomes. Secondly, it was not to Ptolemy's advantage to give his own cleruchs a common interest with the citizens of Cyrene, who had already evinced a propensity to rebellion. This meant that the new settlers would have been settled on royal land (βασιλικὴ γῆ) in the city's vicinity,[6] and would have been without full citizen rights. Their status is confirmed two centuries later by Strabo, who states that the Jews of Cyrene constituted an element distinct from the citizens, metics and peasants.[7] His statement, of course, refers to the Jewish community as a whole, and not only to the Jewish military settlers.

Two other sites in Cyrenaica cast some light on the legal status of Jews in the country in the Hellenistic period. The first is Teucheira, where the tomb inscriptions in the eastern cemetery, chiefly if not entirely Jewish, showed certain common characteristics indicating a connection with Egypt and with the Ptolemaic dynasty.[8] These people were evidently part of the emigration from Egypt which followed the reunion of Egypt and Cyrene under Euergetes II,[9] and the pre-

---

[1] Cf. below, n. 5.
[2] *SEG* IX, no. 1.
[3] Ibid. par. 8, l. 49. P. M. Fraser, *Berytus* (1958), pp. 124 ff. could not find these words, but it is hardly credible that Oliverio should have invented them. The Jewish woman buried in the Kidron Valley in the 1st century C.E. (N. Avigad, *IEJ* (1962), n. 7a) with other Jews from Cyrene, was perhaps an inhabitant of one of these settlements; she calls herself a Πτυλεμαική.
[4] Another much mutilated paragraph of the same law refers to the presence of Ptolemy's mercenaries, presumably in the vicinity of the city (l. 63).
[5] Ibid., par. 7 and 8.
[6] Acts 2:10; Eusebius, *Ecclesiastical History* II, 2; Jos. *Ant.* XVI, 160; cf. e.g. Polybius XV, 25, 12; *Archäologischer Anzeiger* (1962), p. 437, showing that the way texts refer to the Jews of Cyrene indicates that they were distributed about the city (κατὰ Κυρήνην, πρὸς Κυρήνην).
[7] Jos. *Ant.* XIV, 115.
[8] *Scripta Hierosolymitana* VII (1961), pp. 39-40.
[9] Jos. *Ant.* XIV, 116.

ponderantly agricultural character of Teucheira suggests that they were military settlers, (κάτοικοι).[1] This conclusion is strengthened by the peculiar frequency with which the name Arimmas appears both among the Jews and gentiles at Teucheira, where many inscriptions were of immigrants from the less developed Greek countries. Arimmas is a name occurring from the fourth to the first century B.C.E. in Cyrenaica, more especially among a prominent aristocratic family which became closely associated with the first Ptolemies. This suggests that the settlers represented by the Teucheira cemetery, who included a strong Jewish element, were brought in by a member of the above family acting for one of the Ptolemaic sovereigns in the later second century B.C.E.[2]

The location of the second site furnishing information on our subject is unknown; only its name has come down to us, preserved in a letter of Synesius in the early fifth century of the current era, Kappharodis.[3] The name is clearly Semitic, and may be reasonably explained as Kefar Hadash (כפר חדש) or 'new village'. Such a settlement could only have originated with the settlement of Jewish immigrants in the Ptolemaic period, and as its Hebrew name implies the arrival of settlers who spoke Hebrew, a foundation date not later than the end of the third century B.C.E. is probable. The name may also be interpreted as evidence that part at least of the Jewish agricultural settlers were settled in concentrated village-groups,[4] implying some ultimate form of religious or corporate recognition.[5]

In the middle of the second century B.C.E. a modification may have taken place in Ptolemaic policy where the settling of Jewish military cultivators (now known as *katoikoi*) was concerned. Whereas prior to that date no specifically Ptolemaic Jewish units are definitely known to have existed or to have been settled in one area in Egypt, after that date we encounter the establishment of the *katoikia* of the High Priest Onias IV and his forces at Leontopolis, around a fortified temple which endeavoured to reproduce in all essentials the plan and

---

[1] *Script. Hier.*, loc.cit.
[2] Ibid., pp. 36-7. For parallel cases in Egypt (in the time of Euergetes II) of the adoption by cleruchs of the name of the founder of the cleruchy, *P. Tebt.* I, no. 64 (e), 3; no. 61(a), 19 etc.; cf. *P. Tebt.* I, no. 32 for the formation of cleruchies by a πρῶτος φίλος.
[3] *Ep.* 6 (ed. Fitzgerald, p. 93).
[4] Cf. Τόπος Μαγδαλίς, Norsa, Vitelli, *Studi e testi* (1931); *P. Vaticanus* II, I, 35; IV, 12-15.
[5] This form may well have corresponded to Ptolemaic policy in Egypt from the mid-second century B.C.E.; see below.

cult of the Temple of Jerusalem.[1] The episode is too well known to require repetition here, but its implications for Jewish legal status must be considered, the more so since we may perhaps date to the same period the several villages known as Στρατόπεδον 'Ιουδαίων[2] or Castra Iudaeorum,[3] as well as the establishment of a Jewish garrison element at Pelusium.[4] All these names imply the establishment on permanent sites of Jewish fighting units under their own commanders as the product of a peculiar political situation,[5] which made Onias IV useful to the Ptolemies' foreign policy, and Jewish units desirable in respect both of the Ptolemies' internal situation and of their external military needs. The establishment of Jewish military units at given points meant concentrated blocks of land occupied by nucleated villages, which necessitated some form of approved local autonomy of their own. The phenomenon is likely to have given an impulse to the construction of synagogues and the development of organized Jewish community life in some rural areas. This is most strikingly indicated in the territory of Onias, where an epitaph records one Abramos as leader (πολιτάρχης) of two topoi.[6] L. Robert believed that one was the politeuma of Leontopolis, the other of some locality in the vicinity.[7] The main interest of this information lies in the realm of communal organization, but for our present subject it is important to note that it implies the authorization of a limited territorial (as distinct from religious) autonomy in certain defined areas; and since Abramos' epitaph belongs to the early Roman period, it is possible that this form grew out of a purely military authority pari passu with the demilitarization of the katoikia of Leontopolis at the end of Ptolemaic rule.

When we are considering Jewish troops, we may note the Jewish garrison troops of Alexandria. Their existence is inferred by Tcherikover's interpretation of the Phyle of Jewish 'Macedonians' (recorded by Josephus), as a unit of the city's garrison.[8] Josephus states in no fewer than three places that the Jews were granted the title of Macedonians in Alexandria, and in two passages says that this was as mem-

---

[1] Jos. War I, 33; VII, 423; Ant. XIII, 62 ff.; XII, 387.
[2] Jos. Ant. XIV, 133; War I, 191.
[3] Notitia Dignitatum, Oriens, 25.
[4] Jos. War I, 175.
[5] See V. Tcherikover, Hellenistic Civilization and the Jews (1959), pp. 278-282.
[6] CPJ III, Appendix I, no. 1530A.
[7] Hellenica (1940), pp. 18-24.
[8] Jews of Egypt, pp. 41-2.

bers of the garrison;[1] in the third (apparently) they had the title as citizens, whose 'phyle' survived in his own day. On the assumption that Tcherikover was right, the further determination of their standing belongs to the subject of Jewish citizenship in Alexandria rather than to that of their legal category in respect of the Ptolemaic kingdom as a whole.

Apart from military cultivators there were numerous other Jews in the country districts of Ptolemaic Egypt who were of different status.[2] The bulk of these would have ranked as simple *laoi* that is, unprivileged civilians of non-Greek culture, many of whom got their living as small-holders, wage-labourers, tenants, traders and craftsmen, and who were subject to the various taxes and corvées with which the non-privileged were burdened. These certainly included a number of Jews working as *laoi basilikoi*, i.e. peasants cultivating royal land by contracts of varying length[3]. They received seed from the government, worked according to a controlled cropping plan under official supervision, and were confined to the localities of cultivation in the seasons of sowing and harvest. They paid half their crops to the government and were subject to heavy taxes and corvées. On the other hand there were also government officials among the Jews of the *chora*, most of them of the lower grades.[4] The Jewish urban population of Egypt will be considered when we come to discuss the problem of the relation of the Jewish urban communities to the Greek cities in which they lived.

Let us sum up what is to be learnt from the above survey concerning Jewish legal status in Ptolemaic Egypt in the countryside and within the armed forces. The bulk of the Egyptian Jews serving in the armed forces, both in Egypt and Cyrenaica, appear to have been military cultivators holding allotments whose size varied according to their rank. These settlers, as cleruchs, performed all the services and enjoyed all the privileges of members of the armed forces. Their land was the king's, and at least till the second century B.C.E. could revert to him in case of a breach of obligation or after the holder's death.[5] After that date, the tenure of such holdings tended

---

[1] *Against Apion* II, 36; *War* II, 48; *Ant.* XII, 8.
[2] Tcherikover, *Jews of Egypt*, pp. 44-59; *CPJ* I, pp. 15-16.
[3] Ibid. I, 15-16.
[4] M. Rostovtzeff, *Social and Economic History of the Hellenistic World* I, pp. 277-281.
[5] Rostovtzeff, op.cit., pp. 284-9.

to become hereditary. While cleruchs paid taxes, these were less extensive than those paid by the non-military peasant and non-Greek civilian. They further appear to have been subject, at least from the second century B.C.E., to special military courts presided over by a *hipparches*[1]. Thus cleruchs, like all members of the forces, constituted a privileged group, and continued to do so even after native Egyptians began to serve and to receive allotments at the end of the third century B.C.E. The basis of cleruch service was essentially contractual, and there is evidence that at least some Jewish groups served under the terms of a written agreement which may be taken to have safeguarded their freedom of religious practice (Ezechias). There is additional evidence for the existence of Jewish groups of cleruchs resident in one vicinity, but how far these are to be associated with the development of rural synagogues in the late third century B.C.E. is not clear. The latter imply an official recognition of the Jewish cult and a measure of internal communal autonomy. The principle of private corporate bodies, indeed, was not highly developed in Ptolemaic Egypt, and associations of private individuals would appear to have had no rights or duties beyond those of each member. Cases of the ownership of collective property by such associations nevertheless occur, and it is to be assumed, therefore, that this framework, which did not possess a full corporate personality in law, would have sufficed for the erection and maintenance of a synagogue.[2] The establishment of purely Jewish military settlement zones, however, is not proved before the mid-second century, when their existence indicates the development of Jewish internal autonomy over *katoikiai* constituting defined rural areas, probably organized in the early Roman period as *politeumata*. Such existed, in all probability, in Cyrenaica, where groups of Jewish cleruchs were also settled in or near the cities.

The majority of the remaining Jewish population of Egypt belonged to the unprivileged *laoi*. But there were also Jewish members of the civil service functioning in the country areas. Further, there were the Jews who bore the designation of 'Persians of the Epigone'. These suffered from certain legal disabilities, e.g. they could not in the Roman period avail themselves of asylum in the temples—and had become by the late Ptolemaic period members of the lowest class of the part of the population which claimed Greek culture.

[1] R. Taubenschlag, *The Law of Graeco-Roman Egypt* (1955), p. 488.
[2] Op.cit. pp. 47 ff.

By and large the Jewish civilians of the *chora* lacked the privileges of the Greek ruling caste, but they did include one or two high officials.[1] It will therefore be apparent that no one formula can be applied to the legal status of the Jews of Ptolemaic Egypt. The principle determining legal status in the kingdom was that of personality, i.e. the derivation of the person concerned in terms of national group. The three principal groups in the Ptolemaic state were the Greeks, the Egyptians, and subjects derived from other nationalities. The latter could form their own associations (*politeumata*) which exercised a jurisdiction according to their own laws, subject to certain overruling legal principles imposed by the king.[2] But the principle of personality applied, *sensu stricto*, to the juridical sphere, and even then not without exception, since taxability and other obligations to the state were influenced further by the social-economic functions of the subject. Jews serving in the armed forces came under a different jurisdiction from those who were *laoi*, and their economic obligations to the state were different. Jews of Persian status suffered certain disabilities to which neither soldiers, nor *laoi* were subject. Those resident in the Greek *poleis*, on the other hand, might belong to any one of the aforementioned three groups, and others, apparently, held Greek citizenship (see below). In this situation, a legal recognition of Jewish religious requirements would not proceed from the personal status of Jews, but from some general declaration, or from the *ad hoc* recognition of individual associations. Historically, we may surmise such an act of general recognition to be implicit in the tradition transmitted by the *Letter of Aristeas* and connected with the reign of Ptolemy II Philadelphus; *ad hoc* recognition affecting individual groups is reflected in Ezechias' charter, in the official sanction of village synagogues and in the establishment of the religiously autonomous *katoikia* of Onias IV.

It would follow that within the limits of our survey an interesting fact emerges. The Ptolemies would appear to have restricted the recognition of a peculiar Jewish status entirely to the religious sphere; in respect of jurisdiction and obligations the position of the Jew depended on his position in the non-Jewish class-hierarchy, except in so far as the *politeumata* to which he belonged enjoyed rights of internal jurisdiction.

[1] E.g. Helkias, possibly *strategos* of the nome of Heliopolis, and Onias, who may for a period have performed the same function; see *CPJ* i, 17; nos. 127, 132.
[2] Taubenschlag, op.cit., p. 9.

The Seleucid Kingdom

Our information concerning the status of the Jews of the Seleucid kingdom outside Judaea is even more defective than it is concerning that of the Jews of the Ptolemaic dominions. The problem may be divided into the period prior to Antiochus III and the period of his reign and after it. One cause of obscurity in relation to the first period is the almost complete absence of contemporary documentary sources for the Jewish population of Asia Minor, Syria and the remaining Seleucid provinces. Josephus' statements relating to the period concern the status of Jewish city populations in Syria and Asia Minor, and appear to furnish no information relating to the Jewish population in the rural areas. We shall nevertheless see that some fragmentary information may be derived from indirect sources.

Where the second period is concerned, Antiochus III's charter of liberties to the Temple of Jerusalem, its high priest, priesthood and population, is clearly important as an indication of his attitude to the Jewish community throughout his dominions.[1] How far a general principle was derived from these privileges (φιλάνθρωπα) and applied outside Judaea is a matter for conjecture, but we have one document which shows that he favoured the Jewish population as a source of military settlers devoted to his interests. This is the well known letter, reproduced by Josephus, containing Antiochus' instructions to Zeuxis, viceroy of his Asiatic possessions, for the settlement of two thousand Babylonian and Mesopotamian Jewish families in Phrygia and Lydia.[2] The genuineness of the document has been much discussed, but its authenticity has been accepted by recent authorities.[3] The terms of the letter are in accordance with parallel inscriptions since discovered, and make it clear that the settlement as carried out was that of Jewish *katoikoi* planted as farmers in order to secure the Seleucid interest in the areas concerned. Its organizational aspect will be discussed in the following chapter; here it may be noted that eight thousand Jewish fighting men gave a good account of themselves in Babylonia evidently at a date not long before Antiochus' order, in action against an enemy who employed a large force of Gallic mercenaries.[4] The Phrygian-Lydian settlement must have been shortly

---

[1] Jos. *Ant.* XII, 138-144. See Tcherikover, *Hellenistic Civilization*, pp. 82-7; and especially E. Bickerman, *REJ* (1935), pp. 4 ff.
[2] Jos. *Ant.* XII, 148-153.
[3] A. Schalit, *JQR* (1960), pp. 289-91; Tcherikover, op.cit., p. 287.
[4] 2 Mac. 8:20.

after 213 B.C.E. when Antiochus recovered most of Asia; S. Zeitlin[1] has tentatively identified the campaign in which the Babylonian Jews fought the Gauls with Antiochus' war against Molon between 222 and 220.[2] It follows, therefore, that in Babylonia and Mesopotamia there was a Jewish population furnishing good military material, part of which may well have been settled in *katoikiai*. Some evidence in favour of this supposition will be adduced in the course of our enquiry into the organization of the Jewish Diaspora communities. It is also probable that there were *katoikiai* of Jewish troops in Seleucid Syria. The date of the *Book of Obadiah* is unfortunately uncertain, but 'the exiles of Israel who shall possess Phoenicia as far as Zarephath; and the exiles of Jerusalem who are in Sepharad...'[3] can hardly be later than 167 B.C.E., while the association of Sepharad, the Lydian Sardis,[4] with the Zarephat of Phoenicia between Tyre and Sidon, is unlikely to be a coincidence, and favours a date in the late third century for the Jewish military settlements in both places.[5] Obadiah's words further suggest the interesting possibility that some of the *katoikoi* at Sardis came from Jerusalem itself, which would bring down the date of their transfer to shortly after 198, when Antiochus III occupied Judaea.

It is therefore clear that part at least of the Jewish rural population of Asia Minor, Syria and the provinces east of the Euphrates, were military settlers with corresponding status and privileges and their terms of settlement, at least in Lydia and Phrygia, included a specific recognition of their right to observe their ancestral cult,[6] the livelihood of their religious functionaries being made a public charge. This is an *ad hoc* recognition of the right of Jews to practise their religion, but may have arisen out of a general readiness to grant Jews such recognition everywhere, a possibility considerably strengthened by Antiochus' favourable edict on behalf of the Jewish cult in Judaea. It is further likely to have been influenced by an already existing status of Jewish worship in pre-Seleucid Babylonia.[7] Further con-

[1] *The Second Book of the Maccabees* (1954), pp. 174-5.
[2] Polybius V, 51-4.
[3] Obad. 20.
[4] J. Simons, *The Geographical and Topographical Texts of the Old Testament* (1959), par. 1704.
[5] It may be significant that *M. Eduyoth* 6:2 refers to a Kefar ha Bavli ('Babylonian Village' — today Babeliyeh), 3 kilometres east of Zarephat.
[6] Jos. *Ant.* XII, 150.
[7] Cf. the official recognition of the Temple of the Jewish force at Elephantine,

sideration shows that some of the Jewish *katoikoi* of Asia were settled in a distinct district, which may imply a measure of local autonomy, and such autonomy can indeed be deduced from the sources. It seems probable that the Jewish communities of several cities in Asia took their origin in organized bodies of Jewish *katoikoi*. But apart from these groups of Jewish military settlers we have no information at all on the legal status of Jewish rural settlers in the Seleucid and Parthian kingdoms, unless it can be deduced from Talmudic sources, whose study lies beyond the scope of the present enquiry. There is nevertheless one episode which is instructive for our theme, namely, the appearance in Syria of the Babylonian Jewish commander Zamaris, at the head of his five hundred mounted archers and accompanied by his kinsmen.[1] This occurred in the reign of Herod. It is difficult to know whether his group originated in the Parthian or in the Seleucid period; all we can say is that mounted archers were a characteristically Parthian arm, which triumphed, for instance, at the battle of Carrhae. The background of such a group can only be conjectured, but it is surely a manifestation of Parthian feudalism, whose military forces consisted not of a standing army, but of the levy in arms made by each local potentate from among his own kindred and dependents. Such a force, however small, must be seen against a rural background, for horses need pasture and feed, and above all, space. Such a group can only exist in an agricultural area or at least in a desert oasis whose income can be supplemented by taking toll of trade routes, by raiding civilized centres, or by receiving subsidies from a central government. The Ptolemaic cleruchy of Tobiah in the days of Philadelphus can hardly have been greatly different.[2] But the status of Zamaris' group in the Parthian kingdom would have been fundamentally different from that of *katoikoi* serving under the Seleucids: the latter stood in a contractual relationship with the kings, paying them taxes and performing military service as part of a permanent military establishment. Zamaris and his people were related to one another by the mutual bonds of kinship and clientship, and held their land in return for loyalty to their ruler, rendering military service only when a levy was called

where the cult is subject to regulation by the Paha and by the Great King himself; see Cowley, op.cit., no. 21.

[1] Jos. *Ant.* xvii, 23-31. On the troops of Zamaris cf. also S. Applebaum, *Studies in the History of the Jewish People*, (Univ. of Haifa) i (1970), pp. 79-88.

[2] *PCZ*, nos. 59075-6; *CPJ* i, no. 1.

for by him. Herod, when he settled Zamaris in Batanaea, substituted for this feudal relationship[1] the 'katoikic' principle.[2]

The Cities

The problem of Jewish status in the cities of the Hellenistic kingdoms is perhaps one of the most complicated in Jewish history, but it directly affects the status of Jewish city population in the eastern Roman Empire in the first century of the Christian era.

The Jewish attitude to membership of urban communities differed fundamentally from that of the Greeks. The Talmud cites a ruling by Simeon ben Gamaliel (first century C.E.), that a man becomes a citizen of a town after he has resided there a year, or immediately if he buys a house there.[3] This is a thoroughly modern view. For the Greek, membership of a polis depended on the hereditary possession of citizenship, or on a special grant, honorary or otherwise, by the city authority. Such grants grew commoner in the Hellenistic period, when mutual arrangements for common citizenship were made between pairs or leagues of cities, but citizenship still remained an exclusive privilege which could not be obtained automatically or as a matter of course. In this sense the Hellenistic city remained fundamentally tribal.

The issue of Jewish status in the Greek city of the Hellenistic and Roman periods has been bedevilled by too exclusive a preoccupation with the issue in relation to Alexandria, for the simple reason that here alone it is illuminated (or obfuscated) by the existence of papyrological material. The contradiction between the evidence of Claudius' famous edict[4] and the evidence of Josephus[5] has caused the nearly total rejection of Josephus' testimony concerning all the other Greek cities alluded to by him in the context of the present question. It is true that Josephus' statements do not in any case inspire overmuch confidence, but what is true for Alexandria does not *ipso facto* apply to Antioch, Cyrene or Ephesus. Recent evidence from Cyrene,

---

[1] Something of a feudal relationship is nevertheless suggested by Herod's behaviour with his Idumaean fighting men, 3000 of whom he summarily transfers to Trachonitis for settlement in 9 B.C.E. (Jos. *Ant.* XVI, 285). So arbitrary an action is hardly reconcilable with the conditions of stable long-term tenure involved in 'katoikic' practice.

[2] Cf. especially the terms outlined in Jos. *Ant.* XVII, 25.

[3] *T. B. Baba Bathra* 7b and 8a.

[4] *CPJ* II, no. 153; P.Lond. no. 1912.

[5] Jos. *Ant.* XIX, 280-285.

indeed, has shown that however it should be interpreted, the picture was not uniform.
We must begin with the statements of Josephus. Of Alexandria he writes:

1) 'In fact, however the place was presented to them as their residence by Alexander, and they obtained privileges on a par with those of the Macedonians (καὶ ἴσης παρὰ τοῖς Μακεδόσι τιμῆς ἐπέτυχον) ... Down to the present day their local tribe bore the name of 'Macedonians'.' (*Against Apion* II, 35).

2) 'He [scil. Alexander] assigned many of them to his garrisons, and at Alexandria gave them equal civil rights (?) with the Macedonians (καὶ τοῖς Μακεδόσιν ἐν Ἀλεξανδρείᾳ ποιήσας ἰσοπολίτας). (*Antiquities* XII, 8).

3) 'Alexander having received from the Jews very active support against the Egyptians, granted them, as a reward for their assistance, permission to reside in the city on terms of equality with the Greeks (ἐξ ἰσομοιρίας πρὸς τοὺς Ἕλληνας) ... and they were also permitted to take the title of Macedonians.' (*War* II, 487-8).

4) Claudius' rescript: 'Having from the first known that the Jews in Alexandria called Alexandrians were fellow-colonizers from the very earliest times jointly with the Alexandrians and received equal civil rights from the kings' (ἴσης πολιτείας παρὰ τῶν βασιλέων τετευχότας). (*Antiquities* XIX, 281).

5) 'Now the Jews of Asia and those to be found in Cyrenaean Libya were being mistreated by the cities there, although the kings had formerly granted them *isonomia*. And he (scil. Augustus) granted them the same equality of taxation (τὴν αὐτὴν ἰσοτέλειαν) as before.' (*Antiquities* XVI, 160-161).

6) 'Seleucus Nicator granted them citizenship in the cities which he founded in Asia and lower Syria and in his capital, Antioch itself, and declared them to have equal privileges (ἰσοτίμους ἀπέφηνε) with the Macedonians and Greeks who were settled in these cities, so that this citizenship of theirs remains to this very day.' (*Antiquities* XII, 119).

7) 'His (scil. Antiochus Epiphanes') successors on the throne restored to the Jews of Antioch all such votive offerings as were made of brass, and, moreover, granted them citizen rights on equality with the Greeks.' (*War* VII, 44).

435

Josephus also makes great play with the information that the Jews enjoyed the right of calling themselves 'Antiochenes' and 'Alexandrians'.

That Josephus was pleading a controversial case in a polemical atmosphere there is no doubt, und his juridical training was not such as to guarantee accurate use of legal terms. Nevertheless, these terms must be examined.

Isopoliteia is perhaps the easiest term to define. It refers to the privilege of potential citizenship in a given city granted by the same city to a citizen or citizens of another. Normally it was part of a reciprocal agreement of *sympoliteia* between two cities, whereby the citizenship granted to the citizens of the partner became effective in the event of any of them settling in the granting city, and *vice versa*. In the Roman period *isopolites* is used in reference to the reciprocity of rights enjoyed by members of Roman municipalities.[1]

Isotimia in classical literature generally means 'equality of privilege', and is still so used by Strabo.[2] Under the Ptolemies, *isotimos* means 'of equivalent rank' at the Ptolemaic court.[3] *Isomoiria* refers to an equal share in wealth and power.[4] The term occurs in Aristotle and Thucydides.

The meaning of *isonomia* on the other hand, changed in course of time. Originally it appears to have denoted equality among peers, but Cleisthenes applied it to his ultra-democratic order.[5] It was not descriptive of a constitution, but of a state of affairs, 'the ideal of a community in which the citizens had their equal share'.[6] Appian still uses the word *isonomos* in this sense in the second century of the present era.[7]

Isoteleia is, like *isopoliteia*, a precise technical expression. It denotes a privilege bestowed by a Greek city on individuals of metic status, where they were exempted from payment of the *metoikion* and assumed a status intermediate between that of metics and that of citizens.[8]

---

[1] Dionysius of Halicarnassus VIII, 76; Appian *De bello civili* I, 10.
[2] Xenoph., *Hieron*, VIII, 10; Strabo, VIII, 5,4.
[3] P. Rylands, no. 66.
[4] V. Ehrenberg, *The Greek State* (1960), p. 51.
[5] V. Ehrenberg, *Polis and Imperium* (1965), p. 279 ff.
[6] Ehrenberg, op.cit., p. 285.
[7] *De bello civili* I, 15,15.
[8] G. Busolt, *Griechische Staatskunde* (1920), I, p. 299; A. Heuss, *Stadt und Herrscher des Hellenismus in ihren Staats- und Völksrechtlichen Beziehungen*, (1937), p. 64; cf. *BCH* (1924), p. 264; *SEG* III, no. 122 (Rhamnous).

We thus see that only two of the terms used by Josephus in reference to the status of Jews in the Greek cities can be regarded as specific terms susceptible to precise and technical legal definition. The rest are general words describing an ideal or a general state of affairs, and of somewhat elastic meaning. The question of course is to what extent the usage of one or the other had altered in Josephus' day; as far as we have been able to examine the matter, none had changed its fundamental meaning. But it may be noted that *isomoiria* would, in Josephus' time, have sounded archaic, while *isotimia*, *isomoiria* and *isonomia* are abstract political ideals rather than specific political systems or arrangements, and could be very broadly interpreted.

We shall see, discussing the Jewish situation at Cyrene under Augustus, that *isoteleia* was a precise term applied to a real legal status and derived from a contemporary record (see below). There remains *isopoliteia*, a term applied by Josephus to the Jewish status at Alexandria. Of Jewish status in relation to citizen rights in that city during the Ptolemaic period nothing is known beyond Josephus' statements, and such other evidence as we have relates to the Roman period. The existence of some Jews in the earlier Roman period who did possess citizenship, however, suggests that some of their families had received the privilege under the Ptolemies, since the city's attitude to such grants in the Roman period appears to have been predominantly negative. Philo's family appears to have possessed it,[1] likewise the father of the Jew Helenos who submitted a petition to the Prefect in the year 5/4 B.C.E.[2] The terms of Claudius' edict (C.E. 41) make it clear that there were then Jews who were being educated in the city gymnasia.[3] Tcherikover believed that some Jews received citizenship from Ptolemy VIII Euergetes II, who was interested in injecting his own elements into the hostile citizen body.[4] But Josephus' information concerning the 'phyle' of Jewish Macedonians may be more accurate than it appeared to Tcherikover and other scholars.[5] Tcherikover, having interpreted this phyle as a 'pseudo-ethnic' unit of the garrison, concluded that its existence had no bearing on the problem of Jewish

---

[1] By inference from the fact that his brother Alexander was alabarch (*Ant.* XVIII, 159; 259; XIX, 276; XX, 100), and the office was municipal. Cf. also Philo, *Quod omnis probus liber sit*, 6; H. Box, *Phil. Alex. In Flaccum* (1939), p. xxii.
[2] *CPJ* II, no. 151; *BGU*, no. 1140.
[3] *CPJ* II, no. 153, ll. 93-4; cf. 53-5.
[4] *CPJ* I, p. 40; cf. Justin XXXVIII, 8,7.
[5] For a probable Jewish 'Macedonian' at Teucheira, Cyrenaica, *SEG* IX, no. 661.

citizenship.[1] But this conclusion calls for two observations. First, in the cities in which Macedonian settlers composed the first nucleus, the assembly of the garrison constituted, according to Macedonian tradition, the citizen body.[2] Secondly, one of the two 'Macedonians' of Alexandria who register an agreement in the Jewish 'registry' in 14 B.C.E.[3] held land in the city's *chora* and though the prohibition against non-citizens of Greek *poleis* holding city-land may have been relaxed during the later Hellenistic period,[4] the *chora* of Alexandria was so restricted[5] that this 'Macedonian' Jew was almost certainly an Alexandrian citizen.

There remains the question of the *isopoliteia* attributed by Josephus to the Jews of Alexandria. As *isopoliteia* is strictly a reciprocal arrangement between Greek cities, and no such agreements are known between a Greek and a non-Greek body, it is very difficult to acknowledge the possibility of such between the Jewish *politeuma* and the Greek *politeuma* of the city. Tarn, on the other hand, argued that the meaning was that Jews held potential citizenship of the city, which could become valid at such time as any one of them cared to conform with the pagan rites which full membership of the city involved. If 3 Maccabees reflects any sort of historical situation—and it certainly belongs, as has been shown,[6] to the earlier Roman period—acceptance of paganism was a condition of such citizenship.[7] This being the case, it is hardly to be supposed that a formal arrangement existed between the Greek and Jewish organizations of Alexandria providing that any Jew who cared to deny the Second Commandment could become a citizen. There were certainly some Jews who preferred citizenship to their Jewish faith and identity,[8] but they neither needed (nor would have obtained) their community's formal consent, nor asked it. The fact that among the citizens of Alexandria several categories existed, namely *politai*, *astoi*, Alexandrians and those not

---

[1] *CPJ* I, p. 15.
[2] W. Otto, *Zur Geschichte der Zeit des 6 Ptolemäers* (1934), p. 43, n. 1; cf. V. Ehrenberg, *Der griechische und hellenistische Staat* (1932), pp. 72 ff.
[3] *CPJ* II, no. 142.
[4] L. Mitteis, *Reichsrecht und Volksrecht* (1891), 75.
[5] A. H. M. Jones, *CERP* 305-6.
[6] V. Tcherikover, *Scripta Hierosolymitana* VII (1961), pp. 1-26.
[7] 3 Macc. 2:30.
[8] Cf. Antiochus, son of the head of the Jewish community of Antioch (Jos. *War* VII, 47, 50, 55, 60), Elazar son of Jason of Cyrene (see p. 447), is a more doubtful case, although he appears on a pagan dedication. One suspects he might have taken exception to the above Antiochus.

registered in the demes, has very little bearing on this question therefore, the more so because the actual relationship between the categories (not all of which were necessarily distinct from one another)
is not known for certain. If Josephus meant anything specific by
the word *isopoliteia* in relation to Alexandria, it must have been
something different.

After what has been said, it seems superfluous to emphasize that
Josephus' testimony on Jewish *isopoliteia* in Alexandria has been
vitiated by the evidence of the papyrus version of Claudius' letter,[1]
which has no mention of this privilege, but states succinctly that the
Jews of the city were not citizens, thus proving that Josephus' version
has been emended by him or by his source. The same privilege is
nevertheless attributed by him to the Jews of Alexandria in an independent passage.[2] It remains to interpret Philo's evidence on the
status of his fellow-Jews in Alexandria.

Philo does not, so far as I am aware, use the terms, ἰσοπολιτεία, ἴσης
μοιρᾶς, ἴσης τιμῆς or ἰσονομία with reference to Jewish status in his
city. For him the collective rights enjoyed by the Jewish community
constitute a *politeia*, which appears to possess both an abstract and a
concrete significance, i.e. Flaccus' attempt to abolish it (*Against
Flaccus*, 53) means the abolition both of Jewish rights and of the organization which exists to apply them. But in *Legatio*, 156 *politeia*
is used for the Roman citizenship of the Jews of Rome. He also refers
to the established rights of the Alexandrian Jews by the expressions
ἡμετέρων ... δικαίων—our rights (*Legatio*, 366), πολιτικὸν δίκαιον,—
political right (ibid. 371), and τὰ κοινὰ δίκαια—communal rights
(ibid.); the political rights are referred to again in *Against Flaccus*, 53.
On the other hand Philo constantly refers to the Jews of the city as
Ἀλεξανδρεῖς (Alexandrians). In *Legatio*, 183 they are distinguished
from the party of the other Alexandrians. In *Legatio*, 350 they are
the Alexandrian Jews. It is very difficult to know whether he is
using the term Alexandrians in anything more than a broad geographical sense; none of his other expressions are such as to suggest a
more specific status within the framework of the Alexandrian polis
and his use of *politeia* in relation to the Jews of the city may easily
refer to the Jewish communal organization (*politeuma*) only. In his
Against Flaccus, 47, when he refers to the Jews as *politai* he may
equally mean Jews as members of their own Jewish *politeuma*. Tcheri-

[1] Jos. *Ant.* XIX, 281.
[2] Jos. *Ant.* XII, 8.

kover, indeed, has pointed out[1] that elsewhere (ibid. 172) he calls them κάτοικοι, a status not reconcilable with that of *politai* in the sense of members of the Greek polis. He does state that the Alexandrian Jews 'enjoyed' the privilege of being corporally punished by rods instead of by whips (*Against Flaccus*, 79); this information would be consistent with the assumption that they possessed, corporatively, not Alexandrian citizenship, but an intermediate status somewhat above that of the native Egyptians. As in Cyrene, precisely this intermediate status might have been a source of ambiguity and lack of clarity leading to conflict (see below). But Claudius' ultimate verdict was unequivocal; they were not, as a body, citizens of Alexandria.

We must therefore summarize in relation to Jewish status at Alexandria, that a Jewish 'Macedonian' phyle of citizens existed in the Ptolemaic period, probably in an ultimately 'demilitarized' condition. Other Jewish citizens were to be found who had received their privilege by special grant of the king or the city, or by virtue of a gymnasium education. But the explanation of the expressions used by Josephus, including *politeia* for the status of the Jewish community as a whole, must be sought elsewhere, and will be considered when we come to discuss the situation in the Roman period. The terms and expressions used by Philo, relating to the same problem, on the other hand, are ambiguous and their real purport cannot be determined without some third independent confirmatory source.

Outside Alexandria, the situation of the Jews in relation to the Greek cities where they lived during the pre-Roman period[2] was not necessarily the same as that in the Egyptian capital. Here again our information is practically confined to Josephus. How far can we rely on his statements that the Jews of Antioch and the Asiatic cities participated in their city states? Neither of the expressions ἐξ ἴσου μετέχειν or ἰσότιμοι is juridically precise, as we have seen, and neither needs inevitably to be interpreted as implying membership of the Greek citizen body, although Josephus obviously thought this was the case. We shall consider later Josephus' expression 'the rights of the *politeia*', which he applies to the rights of the Antiochene and Alexandrian communities. If, moreover, we except the case of Paul's citizenship of Tarsus, which need not have been awarded in the pre-

---

[1] *Hellenistic Civilization*, p. 315.
[2] For the purposes of this discussion the Roman period is taken to commence in the middle third of the first century B.C.E.

Roman period,[1] our evidence of Jewish citizenship in Syria and Asia prior to the later second century of the current era is scanty. Josephus' statements on Antioch are mutually at variance, for in one place he derives Jewish privileges from Seleucus Nicator,[2] in another from the successors of Antiochus IV Epiphanes.[3] The latter version seems unlikely, in view of Antiochus' attitude to the Jews. C. H. Kraeling suggested that citizenship was given by Nicator to a small group of Jewish ex-soldiers.[4] There seems to be no evidence to confirm or to invalidate this conjecture. The political vicissitudes of the cities of Asia in the time of the earlier Seleucids, on the other hand, were so complex, that it seems impossible to identify with any certainty a situation in which a grant might have been made.[5] There were indeed Jews holding Roman *civitas* in Asia in the last sixty years of the pre-Christian era, but we do not know how they stood in relation to Greek citizenship.[6] What is certain is that the Jews of Asia were claiming or alleging citizenship in their *poleis* in Augustus' time. The report of the formal legal dispute which they conducted with the combined Greek towns of Asia in the presence of M. Agrippa and Herod in 14 B.C.E.,[7] is unfortunately very incomplete, and something has certainly dropped out of the narrative. It begins with a dispute on citizenship—so much is clear, otherwise we would be unable to explain the Greek question. How can Jews claim membership of their community when they do not worship the same gods?[8] But it ends with a confirmation by Agrippa of the *status quo*. Is the *status quo* the possession of citizenship, or does it refer (as Tcherikover thought)[9] to the existing internal rights and privileges (δικαιώματα) of the organized Jewish communities, rights which amounted to religious and judicial autonomy? Josephus ends his account of the case with the words: 'and the Jews won the right to use their own customs...

---

[1] Paul's parents are stated by Jerome (*De viris illustribus* 5; cf. Phil. 3:5) to have migrated from Gush Halav in Galilee to Tarsus as a result of war. One suspects this would have been during the disturbances of 4 B.C.E. Tarsus was under Roman rule from 66 B.C.E.

[2] Jos. *Ant.* XII, 119.

[3] Jos. *War* VII, 44.

[4] *JBL* (1932), pp. 138-9.

[5] Schürer made a gallant attempt (III, pp. 121 ff.), referring the grant to Antiochus II, in accordance with Josephus' information in Jos. *Ant.* XII, 125.

[6] *Ant.* XIV, 223; 225; 231; 234; 236; 280.

[7] Jos. *Ant.* XII, 125-6.

[8] Ibid.

[9] *Hellenistic Civilization*, p. 330.

for Agrippa gave his opinion that it was not lawful for him to make a new rule'. This means that the *status quo* referred to Jewish rights in matters of religious practice and jurisdiction (to use their own customs)—not to citizenship. But if Josephus' phrase συνηγορήσαντος Νικολάου ('their defense-counsel being Nicholas') is accurate, the Greeks were the plaintiffs, hence the assumption is that they were attacking Jewish *politeia* which, by virtue of their argument on difference of religion, must be membership of the polis. Josephus was perhaps confused by the word *politeia* which, as we shall see, may not refer to Jewish citizenship. But on the face of it, there is here an irreconcilable contradiction.

The other evidence bearing on Jewish citizenship in the *poleis* of Asia in this period is scant and ambiguous. Firstly, all the other confirmations of Jewish rights proceeding from the Roman authorities during the sixty or so years of the first century B.C.E. and recorded by Josephus, relate to the internal privileges of the communities, but not to citizen status. There are nevertheless points which might bear on citizenship and require clarification.

1) L. Antonius in his order to Sardis to respect Jewish rights, refers to the Jews of the city as οἱ Ἰουδαῖοι πολῖται ἡμέτεροι (the Jews our citizens) or ὑμέτεροι (your).[1] 'Our citizens' would mean 'Roman citizens', and as there would be little value in demanding the honouring of the rights of Jews with Roman citizenship only, the correct reading is certainly ὑμέτεροι, i.e. (apparently) the Jews who are citizens of Sardis.

2) Later in the same passage, which reproduces the decree passed by the city in confirmation of Antonius' order, the Jews are referred to as οἱ κατοικοῦντες ἡμῶν ἐν τῇ πόλει Ἰουδαῖοι πολῖται (the Jewish citizens living in our city). Tarn thought that this was a contradiction in terms arising from the interpolation of the word *politai* but this would not explain away the ὑμέτεροι.[2] Marcus suggested the reference was to members of the Jewish *politeuma* who might well have been called *politai*.[3] We shall refer again to this interesting suggestion.

3) In their complaint to Agrippa in 14 B.C.E. the Jews of Asia report, *inter alia*, that they have been forced by the Greek cities to participate

[1] Jos. *Ant.* XIV, 235.
[2] W. W. Tarn and G. T. Griffith, *Hellenistic Civilisation* (1952), pp. 222-3.
[3] Jos. *Ant.* XIV (Loeb VII, p. 587, n. f).

in 'liturgies' with their own sacred funds.[1] At first sight the participation in public charges conveys the impression that the Jews
of the cities concerned were citizens. However, generally it would
seem that resident non-citizens, i.e. metics, paid all the taxes and
performed all the services devolving upon citizens, hence the present
text must be dismissed as evidence.

4) Epigraphical evidence from Acmonia in Phrygia may indicate
that some of the Jewish aristocracy were citizens of the town in the
first century C.E. The well-known Iulia Severa founded or built a
synagogue here[2] in the reign of Nero,[3] though high priestess of the city.[4]
Her second husband was Tyronius Rapo;[5] that he was a Jew by origin
(though also a pagan priest) seems to be proved by the inscription of
his relative G. Tyronius Cladus.[6] The Iulii Severi, moreover, appear
to have been distantly related to the Herods.[7] It is clear then, that
some Hellenized Jews of Asia had by this date obtained not only
Roman citizenship (a fact that we have on independent and reliable
evidence), but that they had achieved high office in the city in the
course of a process of assimilation which in some cases, apparently,
involved apostasy. But that such citizenship did not necessarily
involve apostasy at Acmonia is evident from the fact that Julia
Severa built a synagogue. Gentile women sympathetic to Judaism
apparently existed elsewhere in Asia in the 1st century, as witness
the religious and well-to-do ladies at Antioch-in-Pisidia known to
Paul.[8] There is here less a process of one-sided assimilation than of
mutual rapprochement and interpenetration in an atmosphere of
complete tolerance, and although the last sixty years of the last
century B.C.E. were marked by repeated attacks on Jewish communal
rights in the cities of Asia Minor, these seem to have ended completely
after the turn of the century.[9] In any case it is entirely probable that

---

[1] Jos. *Ant.* XVI, 27-30.
[2] It would be important to know which. As the building was called after her,
she may well have been the founder.
[3] *CII* II, no. 766; revised *MAMA* VI, p. 97, no. 264.
[4] *CIG* III, no. 3858.
[5] Ibid.
[6] *CII* II, no. 771. Cf. *PW*, X (1918), col. 946, s.v. Iulia Severa.
[7] Ibid.
[8] Acts 13:50.
[9] Anti-Semitism often develops in direct proportion to Jewish assimilation to
the gentile group. The sudden cessation of its political expression in the early
first century C.E. in Asia constitutes a phenomenon for which we do not yet possess an explanation.

the processes which enabled individual Jewish families to achieve Greek citizenship in such towns as Acmonia had commenced before the period of Augustus.

On the problem of Jewish citizenship in Syria it is possible that archaeology can contribute some information. A bronze plaque found near the Phoenician Ornithopolis bears the words 'Ορνιθοκόμης (sic) and Συναγωγῆς.[1] The contrast of πόλις with κώμη is striking, and indicates that the Jewish community occupied a non-urban settlement in the immediate vicinity of, if not attached to, Ornithopolis. Not far to the north is Sarepta (Zarephath), the site of a settlement of Jewish troops probably in the Hellenistic period (above). This proximity of a 'village' to a Hellenized polis is paralleled in Palestine by Accho (Ptolemais)! and Kefar Accho,[2] also by Lydda and Kefar Lydda.[3] Parallel also is the attachment to Antioch in its early period of a non-Greek settlement with its own wall.[4] Another parallel may be Seleucia-on-Tigris with its attached non-Greek settlement of Opis.[5] From these cases it seems possible to deduce, at least for Ornithopolis and Antioch, that the bulk of the Jews of those cities were not, at least initially, citizens of the poleis concerned.

Claudius' well known rescript to the Alexandrians put an end to the aspiration of the Jews of the city who had hoped to attain Alexandrian citizen status. It is doubtful if this group was large. The problem, if it was existent in the Ptolemaic period, has left no record; when Rome conquered Egypt, and the Jews were relegated en bloc to the same category as the Egyptians, and so compelled to pay the degrading laographia, entry to the privileged Alexandrian citizenship became essential to the Hellenized Jews of Alexandria. To the broader mass of the Jewish community the matter was probably less important, but as the attacks of the Alexandrian demagogues and the city-mob on the Jewish community multiplied, accompanied by an insistence on the homogeneity of the Greek group, stemming from the Greeks' sense of humiliation and inferiority under the new régime, the citizenship issue assumed a broader significance. The Jewish struggle for civic status had a further importance. In Egypt, the

---

[1] CII II, no. 878.
[2] T. Kilaim 4:12; T. B. Yebamoth 45a.
[3] M. Gittin 1:1.
[4] Strabo XVI 2,4, 750c.
[5] Tarn and Griffith, Hellenistic Civilisation, pp. 157-8.

attainment of Roman *civitas* required the prior possession of Alexandrian citizenship.[1] This road was now barred to Egyptian Jews, who could henceforth obtain *civitas* only by manumission from slavery at the hands of a Roman master, by serving in the forces, or by an individual grant from the Emperor. In the light of Pliny's evidence,[2] the last was unlikely to occur.

But the early decades of the empire did not mark regression in Jewish citizen status in every eastern province. There is evidence in Cyrenaica that some progress took place in this sphere round about the end of the first century B.C.E. Strabo, reported by Josephus,[3] groups the population of Cyrene into four classes, namely, citizens, metics, peasants and Jews.[4] This means that the Jews were neither citizens nor metics when Strabo wrote, and the special or ambiguous character of this status in Greek law may have been a cause of trouble between the Jews and the Greeks of the Cyrenean towns and a source of perplexity to Roman administrators. The position does not necessarily contradict Josephus' statement that the Jews of Cyrene (and also apparently of Asia) had been granted *isonomia* by 'the earlier kings'—since the word appears to signify not a legal status but an aspiration or a state of affairs. But the attempt of Cyrene and the Asiatic cities to stop the transmission of the half-shekel to Jerusalem seems to have led to a change in the status of at least part of the Jewish community. This emerges from Josephus' account of the episode at Cyrene, where the city's pretext for impounding the money was a claim on taxes allegedly owed by the Jewish community. The taxes concerned were not Roman *tributa*, as nowhere outside Judaea do we hear of these being collected from the Jews as a separate body. If they were taxes due to the polis only the *metoikion* could have been involved, since otherwise resident non-citizens paid the same imposts and performed the same *munera* as citizens. Precisely this assumption implies that the real issue behind the Jews' non-payment of 'taxes not owed' (τέλη μὴ ὀφειλόμενα) was that of civic status; it also accords with Strabo's statement that the Jews of Cyrene as a whole were neither metics nor citizens, in other words, that their intermediate position was ambiguous and lent itself to attack. That

---

[1] Pliny, *Epistulae ad Traianum* 6, 22.
[2] Loc.cit.
[3] Jos. *Ant.* xiv, 115, 116.
[4] These classes, as Rostovtzeff saw (op.cit. i, p. 33), are not racial but juridical, corresponding to the four chief juridical groups of Ptolemaic Egypt, i.e. members of Greek cities, other Greeks, Egyptians and members of foreign *politeumata*.

this was the issue is further shown by Josephus' information[1] that Augustus, reasserting the Jewish right to transmit the half-shekel to Jerusalem, granted them the privilege of *isoteleia*. If Josephus' words 'the same equality of taxation' are accurate, he thereby confirmed an already existing status. This privilege was granted by Greek cities to certain resident aliens or groups of such residents, and accorded them a status intermediate between that of metic and citizen;[2] it exempted them, as such, from payment of tax as metics.[3] Josephus' information and use of the term, therefore, would appear in this case to be perfectly accurate, since they fit the rest of our information on the episode and also the report of Strabo. It is unfortunately quite unclear from Josephus' text whether the *isoteleia* in question was granted also to the Jews of the Asiatic cities, but this can be understood from his account.[4]

The date of the grant was apparently between 2 B.C.E. and 2 C.E., and it is therefore interesting that precisely in C.E. 2-3 Jewish names begin to appear among the ephebe lists of Cyrene.[5] At Ptolemais a case occurs a little earlier, in 3/2 B.C.E. The Cyrenean evidence led K. M. T. Atkinson, apparently, to the view that all the Jews of Cyrene were from this date citizens of the polis.[6] I do not incline to this view, although I do not see decisive evidence disproving it. But if the timocratic constitution inaugurated by Ptolemy I at Cyrene was still valid there, citizenship would have been restricted to possessors of a minimal census (two minas), and it is more than likely, after the aristocratic revolution of Arataphila in 88 B.C.E. and the inauguration of direct Roman rule in 74 B.C.E., that the ranks of the citizens had been further reduced in line with general policy.[7] If this was so, a very considerable section of the Jewish population would have remained unenfranchised. It is clear from the Berenice Jewish decree of 24/25 C.E. that the members of the Jewish *politeuma* of the city were not then citizens of the Cyrenean Berenice *as a body*.[8] At Teucheira a group of names incised on the city-wall, certainly

---

[1] Jos. *Ant.* XVI, 161.
[2] Busolt, op.cit., p. 299; Heuss, op.cit., p. 64.
[3] Heuss, ibid.; cf. *SEG* III, no. 122.
[4] Jos. *Ant.* XVI, 161.
[5] S. Applebaum, *Jews and Greeks in Ancient Cyrene* (in Hebrew, 1969), p. 144.
[6] *Ancient Society and Institutions; Studies presented to Victor Ehrenberg* (1966), p. 24; *SEG* IX, I.
[7] J. Marquardt, *Römische Staatsverwaltung* I (1881), p. 208.
[8] *REG* (1949), p. 284 ff.; *CIG* III, no. 5361.

including some Jews, are apparently those of ephebes;[1] their date is between the first century B.C.E. and the early second century C.E. It is not easy to know what if any was the connection between the granting of *isoteleia* to the Cyrenean Jews as a corporation and the contemporary appearance of Jewish names in the lists of the ephebes; it is reasonable to suppose that Augustus' decision on the status of Jews as *isoteleis* created an atmosphere in which it became possible for wealthier Jews to enter their sons for the gymnasia of Cyrene with a prospect of citizenship. The known Jewish graduates extend to the year 28 C.E. One ultimate result of the 'reform' was the appearance in the year 60-61 C.E., of Elazar son of Jason among the νομοφύλακες (magistrates) of Cyrene;[2] the office was not unimportant even under Roman rule. If Elazar was fifty when he was elected he would have ended his gymnasium education in the year 28 C.E. It is nearly impossible to estimate how far gymnasium education in these circumstances was tantamount to apostasy. The life of the gymnasia was intimately bound up with pagan rites,[3] and if Jewish participation was subject to certain religious exemptions (as it is, for instance, in an Oxford college), the problem arises, why Jews needed to infiltrate surreptitiously into these institutions. In the Roman period, nevertheless, the phenomenon of Jewish participation in the city gymnasia is not confined to Alexandria down to Claudius' time, or to the cities of Cyrene. Eight names, certainly or probably Jewish, appear on a list at the small Carian city of Iasos;[4] others on a list at Hypaepa in Lydia, call themselves Ἰουδαῖοι νεώτεροι (the young Jews), *neoteroi* being one of three age-groups into which gymnasium pupils were divided.[5] In addition, two Jewish names appear on an ephebe list as late as the third century C.E. at Coronea in Messenia, in the Peloponnese.[6] The last document

[1] *SEG* VII, nos. 424, 439, 440, 441.
[2] *SEG* xx, no. 737; *La Parola del Passato* (1964), pp. 294-6; for the office, Ghislanzoni, *Reale Accad. Lincei* (1925), 408 ff.; A. H. M. Jones, *The Greek City* (1940), p. 239.
[3] For inscriptions demonstrating the intimate connection between the gymnasia and religious rites, cf. Buckler-Robinson, *Sardis*, III (1932), p. 46, no. 21; *SEG* IX, no. 4 (Cyrene); cf. also Tarn, op.cit., p. 97 and the present writer in *Tarbiz* (Hebrew, 1959), pp. 423-4. Nearly all ephebe lists in this period take the form of dedications to Hermes and Heracles.
[4] *REJ* (1937), p. 73 ff.; corrected readings, L. Robert, *Hellenica* (1946), p. 100.
[5] *REJ* (1885), p. 74.
[6] *IG* v (1), no. 1398, ll. 91-2; Robert, op.cit., p. 100. Here also should be mentioned *IGR*, IV, no. 485, a fragmentary ephebe list at Pergamum, in which a Dositheos appears as one of the officers—perhaps a case of apostasy.

is perhaps to be viewed in the light of various changes which took place in relation to citizen status in the period of the Severi, but the other two instances, which belong to the early Empire, cannot today be considered without reference to the recent discoveries at Sardis, where a gymnasium was found in direct association with the synagogue of the city. It is important to know what the relation between the two structures was, and this is an instance where archaeological analysis combined with epigraphy is apt to have important repercussions on the problem before us. Unfortunately the structural problems connected with the relationship between the two buildings are complicated and information leading to final conclusions is lacking at the time of writing.

The facts at the writer's disposal are as follows. The synagogue composes part of the south side of the building complex surrounding the palaestra of the gymnasium. Upon a large part if not the entirety of the south side of the complex abutted a range of shops, some of which, joined on to the synagogue itself, were in the Byzantine period owned or used by Jews.[1] The early phase of the synagogue now visible dates, on present evidence, to the first half of the third century C.E.,[2] overlying an earlier first century building.[3] Finds of inscribed plaster show that the later building, in its westernmost rooms,[4] was interpenetrated organically with the southern gymnasium complex which formed part, at least from the point of view of plan, of the 'Marble Court' and of the two halls to the west of this court, all of which composed the west side of the gymnasium. Between the Marble Court and the northern hall was found, just above the floor, a dedication of the city to Caracalla (211-217).[5] Here, Louis Robert suggested was the *aleipterion* the gilding of whose walls by two women of consular rank, Flavia Politte and Claudia Sabina, is recorded by an inscription found in the Marble Court. The first phase of the palaestra was apparently Severan.[6]

It is therefore to be deduced, on present available evidence, that the gymnasium, or at least its western range and the palaestra, was erected in the Severan epoch, hardly later than 217. C.E. No details are available to the writer on the structural relationship between the

[1] L. Robert, *Nouvelles inscriptions de Sardis* (1964), p. 57.
[2] Ibid., pp. 39,45; cf. *BASOR* (1966), p. 44.
[3] *BASOR* (1966), 34-5.
[4] *BASOR* (1965), 25-6.
[5] Ibid., p. 23.
[6] *BASOR* (1966), p. 38.

walls of the synagogue and those of the west wing of the gymnasium, i.e. the Marble Court and its associated halls. But on present evidence the gap in time between the building of the gymnasium and the erection of the synagogue cannot have been a long one, and both undoubtedly belonged to the same ground-plan, hence the latter cannot have been carried out except in coordination with the former. On the other hand the epigraphical evidence makes it clear that the gymnasium was the work of the pagan community. While therefore it cannot be deduced that there was an organic administrative nexus between the synagogue and the gymnasium, the intimate topographical relationship between the two is such as to argue a symbiosis in which the Jewish community tolerated the gymnasium as an educational institution, found nothing in its activities to offend it, and even participated in its activities. The present evidence, in so far as it is known to the writer, does not on the other hand justify the conclusion that the Jewish community at a given point took over the gymnasium. Nor is the present state of the Sardis evidence such as to prove the establishment of a Jewish gymnasium as part and parcel of the institutions or the Jewish community. But no evidence could demonstrate better the intimate and excellent relations which prevailed between the Jews of Asia and the Greeks in the early third century C.E., and which must have originated in the type of interpenetration between the two communities illustrated in the first century by the Acmonia evidence and the Acts of the Apostles. We have not discovered in the course of our investigation evidence that in any Greek city in the Hellenistic or early Roman period the Jews possessed citizenship as a body. Cyrene admitted what appears to have been a small group of well-to-do Hellenized Jewish families in the early first century of the current era, but despite pressure, Claudius put an end to the Jewish claim to citizenship of Alexandria by his decision of 41 C.E. The evidence in relation to the cities of Asia in the later years of the 1st century B.C.E. is far from clear, but reading between the lines of Josephus' account of the *cause celèbre* in the presence of Agrippa and Herod, the Jews won no marked victory in the matter of citizenship. Yet elsewhere in Asia Minor some well-to-do individuals or families among the Jewish population had achieved this status in the first half of the first century C.E. (Acmonia, Tarsus, Iasos).

These conclusions do not remove all difficulties or obscurities. It is fairly evident that most of the various terms used by Josephus and Philo cannot be explained as referring to citizenship of the polis if interpreted

449

in a strict sense. But whatever the inferences drawn by the users, these terms still possessed a bearing on Jewish status and organization. This is particularly evident when we examine the use, by the above authors and other relevant sources, of the words *polites* and *politeia* and their derivatives.

1) L. Antonius calls the Jews of Sardis 'your citizens' (Jos. *Ant.* XIV, 235). The Sardean decree on the same occasion refers to them as 'the Jewish citizens living in the city' (ibid. 259).

2) Augustus' rescript to the Cyrenean cities (Jos. *Ant.* XVI, 170), orders that matters must be corrected εἴ τινων ἱερὰ χρήματα ἀφῄρηνται τῶν πόλεων ('if sacred moneys have been taken away from any cities'). The Latin version reads *civium* for πόλεων hence the Greek should be emended to πολιτῶν. The reference is to the Jews.

3) The Leontopolis epitaph (*CPJ* III, no. 1530A) of a Jew who has discharged posts in two Jewish communities, refers to him as δισσῶν γάρ τε τόπων πολιταρχῶν (the civil head of two places).

4) Josephus, narrating the demand of the Greeks of Alexandria and Antioch for the abolition of Jewish rights in their cities, says: The Alexandrians and the Antiochenes asked that the Jews should no longer continue to have the rights of *politeia* (*Ant.* XII, 123-4).

5) John Chrysostom refers to the communal organization of the Jews of Antioch-on-Orontes as a *politeia* (*Oratio adversus Iudaios* I).

6) Philo refers to Jewish rights both as πολιτικὸν δίκαιον (political right) *Legatio*, 371 and as τὰ κοινὰ δίκαια (communal rights). In his *Against Flaccus* 47 he speaks of the Jews as *politai*.

7) In the late (probably 4th century C.E.) inscription from the synagogue of Stobi, Macedonia (*CII* I, no. 694), Claudius Tiberius Polycharmos records that he has built the synagogue πολιτευσάμενος πᾶσαν πολιτείαν κατὰ τὸν Ἰουδαϊσμόν, (having fulfilled all the offices according to the requirements of Judaism).

8) We may compare the term used for the Jewish community in a tomb inscription at Venosa, south Italy - *civitas*. (*CII* I, no. 611).

Kraeling, discussing the Jews of Antioch,[1] suggested that the citizen rights of the Antiochene Jews alleged by Josephus (above p. 440), rose out of a misinterpretation of the term *politeia* applied to their communal organization. Marcus in reference to the term *politai* used by L. Antonius (above) for the Jews of Sardis, suggested tentatively that members of the Jewish organized community were so called.[2]

[1] *JBL* (1932), pp. 138-9.   [2] Jos. *Ant.* XIV (Loeb VII, p. 587, n. f).

It is to the credit of Miss M. Smallwood that she has seen the value of this approach and proposed an interpretation of the term which may lead to an ultimate solution of the complex problem as a whole.[1] She points out that the word *polites* may mean the member of a *politeuma*, (in the sense of an association within the framework of a city, whose members were not citizens), as with the *politeuma* of Caunians at Sidon,[2] and draws attention to the fact that the Jews of Alexandria were subject to πολιτικοὶ νόμοι.[3] She goes on to argue, on the strength of Philo's statement[4] to the effect that ξένοι or metics, endeavouring to achieve the prestige of Alexandrian *astoi*, were nearer to *politai*—that Jews in Alexandria held an intermediate status. This at any rate would agree with their possession of certain privileges in the sphere of punishment not enjoyed by Egyptians.[5] From Miss Smallwood's main contention we may proceed to a broader conclusion concerning Jewish civic status in other Greek cities in the earlier Roman Empire.

Philo and Josephus have in common that their accounts reflect a struggle on the part of the Jews of the eastern Mediterranean urban centres to defend a status which they regarded as equal to that of the Greek citizens. So much is borne out by papyri,[6] and by most of Josephus' terms *in pari materia*, in so far as they express the notion of equality (ἴση μοῖρα, ἰσονομία, ἰσοτιμία). A minority of highly Hellenized and presumably wealthy Jews either possessed citizenship or aspired to it in Alexandria and in Asia, and while the aspiration was probably of little practical interest to the mass of the Jews in the same cities, it might become a slogan even for them in given periods of intercommunal friction or anti-Semitic incitement, as in Alexandria in the first forty years of the present era. However small the prospects of success for the average Jew, the claim to civic equality might become significant from a psychological, fiscal and judicial point of view.[7]

---

[1] *Philonis Alexandrini Legatio ad Gaium* (1961), Introduction, pp. 6 ff.
[2] *OGIS* 592.
[3] L. Mitteis and U. Wilcken, *Grundzüge und Chrestomathie der Papyruskunde* II, 2, nos. 21, 47.
[4] *De vita Mosis* I, 35.
[5] Philo, *In Flaccum* 78.
[6] *CPJ* II, nos. 150, 151, 153, 154-9.
[7] In Egypt—to avoid *laographia* and the degradation of being classed with the natives. But generally it must have been advantageous to be judged in Greek courts as opposed to those of the Egyptian *laoi*. In Egypt, we know that many Jews (in so far as records exist) used non-Jewish courts (Tcherikover, *The Jews of Egypt*, pp. 95-115).

But the campaign for its realization ended abruptly with Claudius' judgment in relation to Alexandria and in Judaea with Nero's verdict on Jewish status in Caesarea Maritima (c.e. 60).[1] Prior to that, it seems probable that it was more gently but no less firmly checked by M. Agrippa's judgment in Asia in the last decades of the 1st century B.C.E.

But there was another aspect of the struggle, namely, the Greek offensive against Jewish communal rights, the correct legal term for which is used (perhaps inadvertently) by Josephus in relation to Alexandria and Antioch—the rights of the *politeia, viz.* the rights inherent in and applied by the organized Jewish community in the free practice of its religion and internal jurisdiction. The efforts of the Greek cities of Asia and Cyrene, during the second half of the 1st century B.C.E. of Alexandria under Gaius, and of Alexandria and Antioch immediately after c.e. 70, to restrict or abolish the above communal privileges, developed, I believe, in reaction to the claim made by the Jewish *politeumata* to effective equality with the parallel Greek polity within the same city. As Smallwood puts it, citing Engers in support,[2] 'There were in fact in Alexandria two parallel citizenships, that of the Greeks and that of the Jews,' and this may have been the real meaning behind Josephus' untechnical use of the term ἴση πολιτεία.

If this parallelism of equal (or potentially equal) *politeumata* existed in Alexandria—which Tarn called 'a collection of *politeumata*'[3]—it would have been aided by the fact that in the Roman period, at least, the city lacked the full authority and institutions of a proper polis. As the Ptolemaic capital it had been under the close supervision of the kings, who had to some extent controlled entry to the citizen body, and it lacked a council (βουλή). This last deficiency certainly persisted under Rome, and the emperors controlled most of the city administration, with the exception of cults, the gymnasia and the ephebate,[4] although Claudius intervened on matters of the last two.[5] There were other precedents or analogies which might support the notion of parallel *politeumata* possessing equal rights within one settlement. Such was Delos, which, in the period of its existence

---

[1] Jos. *War* II, 284; Jos. *Ant.* xx, 182-3.
[2] Smallwood, loc.cit.; M. Engers, *Mnemosyne* (1926), p. 159.
[3] *Hellenistic Civilisation*, p. 185.
[4] A. H. M. Jones, *CERP* (1937), pp. 311-12, and 473, n. 16, where the references will be found.
[5] His rescript, *CPJ* II, no. 153, ll. 35-51.

after the slave revolt of 130 B.C.E. was governed by the federated *politeumata* of foreign merchants under an Athenian governor.[1] Seleucia-on-Tigris had a Syrian and a Jewish in addition to a Greek *politeuma*[2]. In the Seleucid empire a number of settlements, most of which became later cities, originated apparently as *katoikiai* with considerable degrees of self-organization but controlled by royal officials (e.g. Seleucia-on-Eulaeos or Susa).[3] This was also the form on which the Cappadocian Anisa was modelled;[4] it possessed a Greek constitution, but was called a *politeuma*, and was supervised by royal officials. This system of partial autonomy and royal supervision would obviously have lent itself to the development of more than one *politeuma*, each of equal status within the settlement, although the Greek association would naturally have regarded itself as superior in privilege and standing. The method as a whole bears a resemblance to what is known of Alexandria in the later Ptolemaic period.

There would also appear to have been examples of 'double' communities existing side by side in the same urban centre under Roman rule. One was Heraclea Pontica, divided between Julius Caesar's Roman colony and the Greek inhabitants, who ultimately, with the Galatians, wiped out the colony.[5] Another may have been Antioch-in-Pisidia, likewise a Roman colony, alongside whose Roman magistrates Greek gymnasiarchs appear.[6] Sinope, another Julian colony, was similarly constituted.[7] In addition we may mention Thugga in Numidia, where a *pagus et c(ives) Thugensium* appear on an inscription in propinquity.[8] We may therefore conclude that while an aspiration to citizenship of the Greek polis might assert itself among highly Hellenized Jews in our period, the basic source of conflict in most of the big Graeco-Jewish urban centres was the potential equality between two parallel organizations, the tension being reinforced both by the cultural abilities and ethnic religious consciousness of the Jewish associations

---

[1] Tarn, op.cit., p. 264; W. S. Ferguson, *Hellenistic Athens* (1911), p. 380.
[2] Jos. *Ant.* XVIII, 372; cf. 378.
[3] Rostovtzeff, op.cit., pp. 489-90.
[4] Ibid. II, p. 840.
[5] Strabo XII, 3, 6 (542-3).
[6] Jones, op.cit., p. 141 and p. 41, n. 31; the gymnasiarchs, *JRS* (1913), p. 267; B. Levick, *Roman Colonies in Southern Asia Minor* (1967), p. 72, doubts the dual character of the town. For such communities generally, F. Hampl, *Rhein. Mus.* (1952), p. 68.
[7] D. Magie, *Roman Rule in Asia Minor* I (1950), n. 33; Strabo XII, 3,11 (338); *Rev.arch.* III, 335, no. 10; 338, no. 5; *IGR* III, no. 94.
[8] Marquardt, op.cit., pp. 124-5.

and by the consequent ambiguity of their civic status. Naturally, the potential equality of parallel *politeumata* did not exist in the same degree in fully institutionalized Greek cities, but the ambiguity of Jewish status and its accompanying tension could still exist, as at Cyrene, and this was the situation which caused Josephus, and perhaps Philo, to employ general terms in a way that might be conceived, by contemporaries and later historians equally, to imply a Jewish claim to membership of the Greek polis, although analysis has shown that nearly all these terms can be reconciled with the potential (or aspired to) equal standing of the Jewish with the Greek *politeuma*.

Rome followed the basic principle of the Hellenistic kings by confirming those privileges, possessed by the Jews in the Diaspora, which enabled them to practise unmolested their ancestral religion. In the Republican period this policy expressed itself in orders issued by Roman governors to Greek cities under their control, compelling them to respect such privileges if they had been infringed. The policy also expressed itself directly in diplomatic pressure in the form of letters to foreign states and cities requesting them to respect the rights of their Jewish communities. This latter action was a by-product of the treaty signed by Judah the Maccabee with the Roman Republic in 161 B.C.E. and renewed by his successors. Whereas the Roman confirmation or support of Jewish privileges took its origin in fundamentally the same principle as the confirmations of the Seleucid and Ptolemaic kings—*viz.* the recognition of the *status quo*, the Roman Republic added an important innovation, namely, the conception of rights which belonged to the Jewish people as a whole throughout the Diaspora. We know of no confirmation issued by a Hellenistic sovereign in favour of all the Jews of his territory; a general act in favour of the Jews of Egypt by Ptolemy II Philadelphus may be surmised but cannot be proved, and Antiochus III's *philanthropa* (privileges) on behalf of Jerusalem concerned Judaea only. It is true that the Greek cities (our information relates to those of Asia and Cyrene, but must have been valid for all Greek towns recognizing Jewish rights) accorded their Jewish residents the freedom to transmit the half-shekel to Jerusalem, and this permission, which must have been subject to royal approval, implies a recognition of the unity of the Jewish people and its national centre. But this was acknowledged, it would seem, by a series of *ad hoc* decisions, and no instance of a royal confirmation has come down to us.

The Roman consul's letter of 142 B.C.E. on the other hand, was directed to all the important centres of the eastern Mediterranean which had sizeable Jewish communities. Julius Caesar's treaty with Hyrcanus II, although it concerned almost exclusively the relations of Rome with Judaea, took some account of the Diaspora communities, in so far as it accorded Hyrcanus the right of settling their disputes on problems of the Jewish 'way of life' (ἀγωγή).[1]

Two questions therefore arise: 1) Did Rome recognize the existence outside Judaea of a Jewish nationality which enjoyed certain privileges connected with the status of its possessors as extra-territorial Jewish citizens? and 2) Were Jewish Diaspora privileges based, in Roman eyes, upon a treaty-relationship such as had existed between Rome and Judaea since 161 B.C.E. and was terminated, if not in C.E. 70, then at any rate with the death of the last reigning member of the House of Herod (Agrippa II) at the end of the 1st century of the present era?

T. Mommsen was convinced that a conception of Jewish nationality was the basis of the Roman juridical attitude to the Jews under Roman rule;[2] the Diaspora Jews of the Empire, he thought, were Jewish nationals living as *incolae* for religious reasons.[3] Juster for his part was convinced that the maintenance of a body of Jewish rights proceeded from the permanent treaty existing between Rome and Judaea, which was placed on a firm basis by Julius Caesar,[4] and re-confirmed not only by Augustus[5] but subsequently by Claudius.[6] The Roman conception of the Jews as a single entity is expressed on two occasions: Augustus confirms the privileges of Jews ὅσοι ποτ' οὖν εἰσί (however numerous they may be);[7] Claudius relates a similar confirmation τοῖς ἐν πάσῃ τῇ ὑπὸ ῾Ρωμαίοις ἡγεμονίᾳ ᾿Ιουδαίοις (throughout the empire under the Romans).[8] It is nevertheless extremely difficult to establish that the Jews of the Empire outside Judaea down to 70 C.E. enjoyed a recognized national status; it is highly doubtful if such a conception existed among the Roman administrators

---

[1] *Ant.* xiv, 195.
[2] *Gesammelte Schriften* iii, pp. 303, 416 ff.
[3] V. Colorni, *Leggi ebraici e legge locali* (1945), pp. 13 ff., also accepts this point of view.
[4] *Les Juifs dans l'empire romain* i (1914), pp. 220 ff.; *Ant.* xiv, 190-216.
[5] Jos. *Ant.* xvi, 162-5.
[6] Jos. *Ant.* xix, 287-91.
[7] Jos. *Ant.* xvi, 166.
[8] Jos. *Ant.* xix, 288.

and jurists. The Jews were *peregrini* with peculiar privileges, unless they happened to possess Roman citizenship, a status which affected the said privileges but did not cancel them. When Julius Caesar accorded to Hyrcanus II as Ethnarch and High Priest the right of judging Jewish religious disputes arising outside Judaea, this might be regarded as constituting an acknowledgement of a national jurisdiction extending throughout the Diaspora, since secular and religious matters could hardly be distinguished in the ancient world. But we have no evidence that this peculiar judicial competence enjoyed by Hyrcanus was inherited by Herod or by any of his sons, and it can hardly have attached to the High Priests who served under the House of Herod or under the procurators. When the word *gens* was applied to the Jewish nation in the inscription at Rome commemorating Titus' victory,[1] it referred to Judaea specifically.

The same difficulties affect the doctrine which sees the source of Jewish privileges in a treaty relationship between Rome and the rulers of Judaea. It has been denied that Herod's relationship with Augustus and the Senate[2] was based on a treaty. But even if we see a treaty behind his title φίλος καὶ σύμμαχος, (friend and ally),[3] and even if we assume that his obligation descended to his sons the tetrarchs, and to his descendants Agrippa I and Agrippa II, the rule of two out of the three tetrarchs was prematurely ended and replaced by direct Roman rule; Agrippa I's reign was brief, and Agrippa II reigned directly only over a fringe-territory whose Jewish population was a minority. These vicissitudes hardly favour the validity of a treaty-relationship as an effective permanent source of Jewish rights; it is much more probable that such privileges as the Jews continued to enjoy in Judaea in the procuratorial interregna (e.g. freedom from the quartering of troops and conscription), were maintained on grounds of general political prudence and policy, while the rights of Diaspora Jewry were maintained as part of a legal continuum constituted by a series of *ad hoc* confirmations proceeding from Rome and embodied in the law of each individual Greek city. It was precisely the national character of the Jewish religious-ethnic consciousness which the Romans failed to understand; careful emperors tolerated it, but emperors with strong Hellenizing propensities who took their own deification seriously, and Roman administrators not over-endowed

---

[1] *CIL* vi, no. 944.
[2] Otto, *Herodes*, p. 57.
[3] Jos. *Ant.* xvii, 246.

with an appreciation of complex phenomena, tended to deal summarily and drastically with the Jews.

This did not mean, of course, that Rome's relation with the rulers of Judaea had no effect on the status of Diaspora Jewry. The consul's letter of 142 B.C.E. included a demand for the extradition by the Greek cities and states of exiles objectionable to Simon the Hasmonaean.[1] The Pergamene resolution in favour of Judaea[2] was adopted under the influence of the Senate. Five of the orders issued by Roman officials to Greek cities instructing them to respect Jewish rights (Paros, Laodicea, Miletus, Halicarnassus and Sardis) cite in authority Caesar's treaty with Hyrcanus II.[3] Herod intervened in favour of Jewish rights in Ionia, enlisting for the purpose the aid of M. Agrippa and the oratory of Nicholas of Damascus.[4] Agrippa I obtained from Claudius the reversal of the discriminatory acts of Flaccus against the Jews of Alexandria and a general confirmation of Jewish privileges throughout the Empire.[5] But this beneficent influence of Jewish rulers proceeded not so much from the letter of a treaty as from a general diplomatic and personal relationship closely bound up with the prestige commanded by these rulers. When Tiberius deported Judaizers of freedman extraction from Rome,[6] and Claudius, having found total expulsion of the Jews from Rome impracticable, nevertheless suppressed their assemblies,[7] their actions were local, but they were sufficient to demonstrate that no one precise and comprehensive law governing Jewish rights existed to be infringed. When in the fifth century Theodosius examined the basis of Jewish privileges, he had to fall back on a negative formula: Iudaeorum sectam nulla lege prohibitam satis constat.[8]

The fact was that virtually all the privileges which Augustus and Claudius officially confirmed to the Jews of the Empire were embodied in a series of city-laws of local application, which, although they possessed common principles, differed in detail from one city to the next. When Julius Caesar excluded the Jewish *politeumata* from his law

---

[1] I Macc. 15:21.
[2] Jos. *Ant.* xiv, 247—dated *c.* 112 B.C.E. by M. Stern, *Zion* (1961), p. 17.
[3] Jos. *Ant.* xiv, 241-258; 213.
[4] Jos. *Ant.* xii, 125 sq.
[5] Jos. *Ant.* xix, 310.
[6] Tacitus, *Annals*, ii, 85: 'quattuor millia libertini generis ea superstitione infecta...'
[7] Dio Cassius lx, 6, 6.
[8] *Cod. Theod.* xvi, 8, 9.

restricting the formation of *collegia* (θίασοι),[1] he got as near as he needed to universal legislation relating to Judaism, but the very nature of the regulation precludes a universal view.

There were, however, two principles, one real and one which various scholars have alleged, which were not of mere local application, and either proceeded from or were confirmed by Rome herself.

One was the exemption of Jews from worshipping the deities of the Roman state, that is, the Capitoline triad and the imperial genius. The second was their supposed exemption from service in the Roman forces.

The Roman rulers were prepared formally to sanction the non-participation of Jews in the pagan cults of their cities of residence; it may be inferred that Agrippa did this in relation to Ionia.[2] The exemption from the Roman state-cult, on the other hand, was tacit, for clearly no formal statute could be promulgated which permitted a given subject community to forego an act whose omission would be an offence on the part of all other subjects of the Empire. P. Petronius as legate of Syria nevertheless virtually ratified in a written order Jewish exemption from the imperial cult in relation to Dora,[3] citing in authority Claudius' edict of C.E. 41.[4]

The problem of the relation of Jews to Roman military service, on the other hand, is much more complex and not a little obscure. There is no doubt that at least five specific exemptions from such service were accorded by Roman officials to the Jews of Asia; the most important of these was issued by Dolabella in 44 B.C.E. in response to the request of Hyrcanus II,[5] as Ethnarch. The order appears to have related to the entire province, as it followed a similar exemption granted by L. Lentulus Crus in 49 B.C.E.[6] M. Agrippa seems to have ratified the exemption for the Jews of Ionia,[7] and while neither his ratification nor Hyrcanus' request refers specifically to the status of the Jews concerned, according to Josephus' text, all the other instructions given by Roman governors and officials of Asia direct the exemption specifically to Jews with Roman citizenship.[8] It could

---

[1] Jos. *Ant.* XIV, 215.
[2] Jos. *Ant.* XVI, 27-30; 59-60; cf. XII, 125-6.
[3] Jos. *Ant.* XIX, 303-311.
[4] Jos. *Ant.* XIX, 310.
[5] Jos. *Ant.* XIV, 230.
[6] Jos. *Ant.* XIV, 240.
[7] Jos. *Ant.* XVI, 27.
[8] Jos. *Ant.* XIV, 225, 230, 231.

be argued that these orders merely confirmed for such citizens what already applied to Jewish *peregrini*, but this seems improbable, because, although Hyrcanus was applying on behalf of all Jews irrespective of *status civitatis*, and on religious grounds,[1] it is known that Lentulus raised two legions of Roman citizens in Asia.[2] It is no less relevant that in his confirmation of Jewish rights between 2 B.C.E.-C.E. 2, a copy of which was set up at Ancyra,[3] Augustus is entirely silent on the exemption of Asiatic Jews from military service. These exemptions, then, seem to have related to Roman citizens only, and were not permanent. But a possible explanation for them can be proposed. Some time between 39 and 34 B.C.E. Augustus is found granting immunity from military service, taxes and other public burdens to the Roman citizens of the village of Rhosos in northern Syria, in reward for their previous service with his forces.[4] As authority for the grant, the Lex Munatia et Aemilia is cited. This law was passed in 42 B.C.E. two years after Dolabella's concession, but some of the Asiatic Jews concerned may well have gained citizenship by previous military service under Pompey in his drive against the pirates, and received exemption for similar reasons. In any case both sides in the civil wars evidently found it politic to conciliate the pro-Roman Jewish element in Asia, and the contemporary concessions are no proof of a permanent or universal exclusion of Jews from the Roman imperial army. The rarity of Jewish service in the Roman forces of the Empire, in the first and second centuries, all the more interesting in view of the active Jewish participation in both the Seleucid and Ptolemaic services, is to be explained rather on religious and political grounds; Roman army life revolved extensively round the ruler-cult, the consecrated standards and the *auguria*; this and the constant tension between the Jews and the Roman power more particularly in Judaea during the first century of the current era, made Jews as reluctant to enlist as it made the authorities reluctant to accept them. Exceptions of course occur,[5] and more may be found in the future. The freedmen whom Tiberius forcibly enlisted to suppress

---

[1] Jos. *Ant.* XIV, 226.
[2] Caesar, *De bello civili* III, 4.
[3] Jos. *Ant.* XVI, 162-165.
[4] *Syria* (1934), pp. 33 ff.; cf. R. K. Sherk, *Roman Documents from the Greek East* (1969), no. 58.
[5] *CPJ* II, no. 229, a centurion, Aninios, serving in the year 116 (!); *CIL* III, 2, p. 914, Dip. V, Mathaios Syros (C.E. 68). At a later date Abinnaios is strongly suspect.

brigands in Sardinia appear to have been Judaizing gentiles rather than born Jews.[1] It is further evident, that the Jews in Egypt serving as *katoikoi* in the Ptolemaic army on the eve of Octavian's annexation of Egypt in 31 B.C.E., ceased to be military personnel under Roman rule unless they enlisted in the Roman army. Our evidence on Jewish service in Egypt is confined to one centurion who was serving in 116 C.E.[2] On the position of parallel elements in Asia in the first century C.E. we have no information, but as here over much of the peninsula Roman rule had begun in the middle of the second century B.C.E. it is a fair assumption that they had lost their military status and connections when Octavian took over the Asiatic provinces. Only in Gaulanitis and Batanaea did Jewish military settlers continue to serve as a distinguishable element at least as late as the beginning of the second century of the current era.[3]

We may therefore conclude that Jewish status outside Judaea was ethnic rather than national, and that the privileges associated with it proceeded not from a treaty relationship or a comprehensive statute, but from *ad hoc* confirmations, individual or *en bloc*, of a series of city-laws, which became part of the Roman *corpus iuris* as an expression of policy. This being the case, the question of whether Judaism was a 'permitted religion' does not seem to arise at all. The source of the question appears to be in Tertullian's famous sentence: 'Quasi sub umbraculo insignissimae religionis certe licitae...'[4] but as Schürer long ago observed,[5] *religio licita* is not a Roman legal expression, while *collegia licita* is. Roman law in relation to Jews, in fact, related to their individual associations (*politeumata*), and the status of these seems to be best expressed by saying that their rights corresponded closely to those of autonomous *poleis* in the Greek sense, because they included autonomy of jurisdiction. The repeated confirmations of Jewish rights under the Empire, beginning with Augustus, and perpetuated by Vespasian and Titus, are sufficient to prove that Judaism was looked upon as 'permitted'; ironically, the imposition of the 'Jewish Tax' after C.E. 70 itself reaffirmed the legality of Jewish worship and institutions.

The question therefore arises, how did the destruction of the Second

---

[1] See p. 457, n. 6.
[2] See p. 459, n. 5.
[3] *Syria* (1965), pp. 31-9 (108 C.E.).
[4] *Apologeticum* 21,1.
[5] Schürer III, p. 111; *Dig.* XLVII, 22.

Temple affect Jewish status? Mommsen,[1] Mitteis,[2] and Juster[3] all held that the rights of Diaspora Jews prior to 70 proceeded from their status as extra-territorial nationals of Judaea, and that after 70 Jewish nationality lapsed, so that such rights were restricted to freedom of religious organization. Schürer[4] was more cautious, holding that Mommsen's juridical formula was too fine, and that even after 70 the basis of the Jewish communities continued to be both national and religious. If we interpret the word 'national' not in the sense of a formal political nationality, but in the sense of 'ethnic', Schürer's view was certainly correct. Titus is known specifically to have resisted demands for the abolition of Jewish communal privileges in Antioch and Alexandria,[5] and generally these remained unmodified outside Judaea, as is indicated not only by the continued ability of the Jews of Alexandria to convene meetings,[6] make arrests[7] and, probably, to dispatch embassies to the Emperor,[8] but also by the persistence of synagogues in Rome and the provinces. For these reasons it cannot be maintained that Jews in the Diaspora became, like those of Judaea, *dediticii*, and the existence of a rabbinical court at Rome under the presidency of R. Mattatiah Harash, is proved for the early years of the second century.[9] Nor would the status of Jews who were citizens appear to have been affected.[10] Jews in Egypt between 70 and 116 are found paying the Ἰουδαϊκὸν τέλεσμα (the Jewish Tax), but they are still, as Roman citizens, immune from the λαογραφία.[11]

[1] Op.cit. III, pp. 416 ff.
[2] *Reichsrecht und Volksrecht* (1891), p. 34.
[3] Op.cit. II, pp. 1-2.
[4] Op.cit. III, pp. 106-7, n. 29.
[5] Jos. *Ant.* XII, 123-4.
[6] Jos. *War.* VII, 412.
[7] Ibid., 416.
[8] *CPJ* II, no. 157 (P. Oxy., no. 1242).
[9] *T. B. Sanhedrin* 32b. The evidence is rejected by Colorni, *Legge Ebrei* (1945), p. 311, but as this court is mentioned in company with the courts of Jamnia, Beror Hayyil, Lydda, Benei Beraq and Sepphoris, it was obviously of outstanding importance.
[10]Mommsen's view (op.cit. p. 404) that Jews of Roman citizenship did not enjoy Jewish privileges cannot, I think, be substantiated. It is directly contradicted by Philo, (*Legatio* 156), when he states that Augustus acknowledged both the *civitas* and communal rights of the Jews of Rome. Cf. also the Berenice inscription (Cyrenaica), *CIG* no. 5361 (*REG* 1949, pp. 281 ff.), where a Roman citizen, M. Laelius Onasion, appears as an archon of the *politeuma*. It seems unacceptable that *civitas* involved loss of conformity with Jewish laws of personal status, although it apparently made the possessor subject to Roman law in all other respects.
[11]*CPJ* II, nos. 162, 174 etc.; I, p. 82, n. 66.

The Jewish Tax, indeed, was the one important administrative in-novation affecting Diaspora Jewry after 70 (τὸ 'Ιουδαϊκὸν τέλεσμα; *capitularia Iudaica*). Materially it may have been more injurious to Rome than to the Jews;[1] its main importance was historical—in that with it was born a new conception, that of the Jews as the special object of fiscal discrimination.[2] Moreover it infringed a legal principle embodied in the δικαιώματα of at least one Diaspora community, viz. that of Asia, where Jews were protected from having to expend their sacred funds on behalf of pagan cults;[3] this exemption must have formed part of Jewish privileges in other cities as well. The Roman legal view, presumably, was that Jewish sacred funds had ceased to exist in so far as they were connected with the Temple. But the Jewish Tax was first and foremost a blow to Jewish moral standing, and as such part and parcel of the atmosphere that produced, for instance, the cynical annihilation of the Jewish aristocracy of Cyrene in 73.[4]

In this connection, we are faced with the problem of what was the reason for Nerva's reform of the Jewish Tax and what was its character? The first observation should be that according to the coins,[5] the re-form concerned the machinery of collection, (Fiscus Iudaicus), since the name of the tax itself was, in Greek, τὸ 'Ιουδαϊκὸν τέλεσμα,[6] in Latin, perhaps, *Iudaica capitularia*,[7] Fiscus Iudaicus being the govern-ment office into which the proceeds of the tax flowed. Secondly, what was *calumnia*? It has two chief significances: the first is infor-mation laid by an informer, *inter alia* concerning illicit religious prac-tices.[8] The second meaning is derived from the *Epitome de Caesaribus*[9] attributed to Aurelius Victor. Whatever the value of this work as a source, the passage which here concerns us seems to reflect genuine history. We are told that Trajan's procurators afflicted the provinces with *calumniae*, and these are described. They are extraction of

---

[1] One of its consequences would have been the cessation of the payment of the half-shekel by Jews outside the Empire, and this may have affected adversely the Empire's trade-balance. This question requires further investgiation.
[2] S. W. Baron, *Social and Religious History of the Jews* II (1952), p. 106.
[3] Jos. *Ant.* XVI, 27-30.
[4] Jos. *War* VII, 437 ff.
[5] F. W. Madden, *History of Jewish Coinage* (1864), p. 199.
[6] Manteuffel, *Tel Edfou*, 1937, I, 146; *CPJ* II, 112 sq.
[7] *CIL* VI, no. 8604.
[8] Seneca, *Epistulae* 108, 22.
[9] 42, 21.

information on income and its sources by threats and bullying.[1] This looks like the real meaning of the word as it appears on the coins of Nerva, nor does it contradict Suetonius' unpleasant account of the examination of a nonagenarian suspected of being circumcised.[2] Bruce may well be right in affirming that this account implies the raising of the age of payment over the sixty-second year.[3] Whether the tax was demanded from 'non-practising' Jews seems to me impossible to ascertain, and probably irrelevant, because 'practising and non-practising' is a modern conception.[4] It is at least clear from Dio[5] that Nerva stopped all charges of Judaization and ἀθεότης (atheism). It may further be observed that the setting of the word 'Iudaicus' on coins of the Empire must have symbolized a considerable revulsion of public feeling in respect of Judaism, since Vespasian had rejected the title of 'Iudaicus'.

BIBLIOGRAPHY

E. SCHÜRER, *Geschichte des jüdischen Volkes im Zeitalter Jesu Christi*, III, 4th ed., 1909, pp. 97-134, and J. JUSTER's great work *Les Juifs dans l'empire romain, leur condition juridique, économique et sociale*, 2 vols, 1914, are of great value. Useful also is the survey of D. ASKOWITH, *The Toleration of the Jews under Julius Caesar and Augustus*, 1915.
On the status of Egyptian Jewry we have the exhaustive studies of V. A. TCHERIKOVER: his 'Prolegomena' to the *CPJ* I, 1957, and the introduction to Section VII in vol II, as well as *The Jews in Egypt in the Hellenistic-Roman Age in the Light of the Papyri*, 2nd ed. (in Hebrew), 1963, pp. 116-159; an English summary, pp. xiv-xxvi; M. BRÜCKLMEIER, *Beiträge zur rechtlichen Stellung der Juden in römischen Reich*, 1939, deals with the legal status of the Jews under the Roman Empire.

---

[1] '... cuius (sc. Traianus) procuratores cum provincias calumniis agitarent, adeo ut unus ex his diceretur locupletium quemque ita convenire; 'Quare habes?' alter: 'Unde habes?' tertius 'Pone, quod habes....'
[2] Suetonius, Domitian, 12,2.
[3] I. A. F. Bruce, *PEQ* (1964), p. 43.
[4] I do not think it is possible to interpret Dio Cassius' words LXVI, 7,2: 'those who continued to observe their ancestral customs' too strictly.
[5] LXVIII, 1,2.

Chapter Nine
The Organization of the Jewish Communities in the Diaspora

The Greek city, which set the norm for much of the life of the Hellenistic world within the broader framework of the Hellenistic monarchies, was itself to such an extent an association of associations—of phyles, phratries, demes and similar bodies—that the recognition and toleration within itself or within its environment of voluntary associations, whether of citizens or non-citizens—was essential to it. Aristotle states that 'all associations are manifestly part of political life'.[1] He distinguishes between groups associated for practical objects (trade, war) or for political ends (the city), and groups associated for pleasure, religion or the like. Athenian law, the only Greek code whose attitude to the establishment of associations has come down to us in defined form, provides that any deme, brotherhood, cult-association, dining-club, social club, or body organized for piracy or commerce, shall be lawful so long as public law does not forbid it.[2] The only known restrictions relating to such bodies appear to have been the prohibition against clubs using temples for their meetings, and that the state's permission was required if such a society wished to set up a statue. Aliens, of course, needed state permission to acquire land for purposes of worship or for the introduction of a new cult.[3]

The heterogeneous composition of the new Greek towns founded in the Middle East and Asia after the conquests of Alexander was such that their life would have been impossible without the perpetuation of the principle of free association. However many non-Greek elements might be formally incorporated into the new citizen body,[4] there normally remained within the settlement non-citizen populations, often of native origin, organized after their own fashion.[5] Freedom of association was therefore deeply inherent in Hellenistic life.

[1] *Eth. Nic.*, 1160a 28: 'All these associations then appear to be parts of the association of the state.'
[2] Cited by Gaius, *Dig.*, 47, 22, 4.
[3] E. Ziebarth, *Das Griechische Vereinwesen* (1896), pp. 166 ff.
[4] Cf. Tarn, Griffith, *Hellenistic Civilisation* (1952), pp. 156-7.
[5] Cf. ibid., p. 157.

It has already been mentioned that the corporate body was never fully developed in Ptolemaic Egypt, and never seems to have achieved the same legal personality as the *collegia* and *sodalitates* of Roman life; associations possessed no rights or duties beyond those of each individual member.[1] *Politeumata* nevertheless could own property[2] and it is evident that cult-associations dedicated temples.[3] Associations are found acquiring property as early as 124 B.C.E.[4] and in the Roman period, when private ownership of land had become recognized in law, they appear as proprietors of plots and buildings.[5]

The four important juridical groups of which the population of Ptolemaic Egypt was composed, were the citizens of Greek *poleis*, other Greeks, aliens and native Egyptians. The third element, in common with the first two, enjoyed the licence to form and maintain its own *politeumata* for cultic purposes, but their regulations were subject to overriding modification by royal directives and orders.[6] To this category belonged the Jewish associations.

We have little information, however, of the existence of details of such associations among the Jews of the rural districts of Egypt in the Ptolemaic period, and little more in the earlier Roman period In our treatment of the status of the Jews we found evidence for aggregations of Jewish settlers dwelling in nucleated rural groups as early as the third century B.C.E. In the latter part of the same century the first synagogues appear in the Egyptian countryside, and these are good evidence of the existence of organized communities; the inscriptions indicate that they existed by royal licence, but we have few details of their officials or the manner of their administration. The existence of the local organized body is indicated by the words οἱ Ἰουδαῖοι (the Jews), for instance at Schedia under Ptolemy Euergetes II,[7] or οἱ ἀπὸ Ξενεφύρεος Ἰουδαῖοι (the Jews from Xenephyris) under the same sovereign at Xenephyris.[8] Both these communities record the erection of synagogues and the second speaks of attached buildings (a pylon, indicating that the synagogue stood within a sacred enclosure), thus showing the capacity for the execution of work and proprietorship. The Xenephyris community is represented by two officials called προστάται. At Alexandrou Nesos in the year 218 B.C.E. we hear

[1] R. Taubenschlag, *The Law of Graeco-Roman Egypt* (1955), pp. 62-3.
[2] Op.cit., p. 268, n. 21.
[3] E.g. *P. Giess.*, no. 99 (80-79 B.C.E.).
[4] P. Tebt., no. 700.
[5] Taubenschlag, op.cit. p. 651.
[6] Op.cit. [7] *CPJ*, III, Appendix I, no. 1440. [8] Ibid., 1441.

of the νακόρος or *hazzan* (sacristan) of a synagogue.[1] A papyrus from Arsinoe, dated to 113 C.E.,[2] provides a list of waterdues owed to the local municipality, and includes payments by two synagogues (called προσευχή and εὐχεῖον respectively), one of the Theban and one of the local Jews, the former being represented by archons.

It has been noted that in the course of the second century B.C.E. a concentrated military settlement (κατοικία) was set up about the Temple of Onias at Leontopolis ('Ονίου γῆ—the land of Onias).[3] This district may be assumed to have possessed a considerable degree of local autonomy by virtue of the temple which formed its centre, and the high priest would have been the senior official of the hierarchy, combining priestly with military and local administrative duties. Unfortunately we have no details of the organization of Leontopolis.[4] In the early Roman period one Abrahamos, who was probably buried in the cemetery of that place, had discharged functions (as πολιτάρχων) in two localities,[5] which L. Robert interpreted to be Leontopolis and some other unknown Jewish community. This would suggest that in the Roman period, with the demilitarization of the *katoikia*, some form of *politeuma* was adopted, even if it had not existed before; the presence of a high priest with military functions might well have precluded even a nominally democratic constitution before that. We may perhaps mention in this connection that another Leontopolis epitaph[6] alludes to the inhabitants of the district as 'citizens' (πολεῖται). Several other concentrated Jewish *katoikiai* probably had their origin in the same period, i.e. in the reigns of Philopator and Euergetes II. They included 'Ιουδαίων στρατόπεδον, Castra Iudaeorum, and Pelusium, but we have no information on how they were administered. Quite possibly affairs were centralized in the hands of the commanding officer, as may have been the case earlier in the cleruchy of the hipparchy of Dositheos, which existed in 174 B.C.E.[7]

It may be added that the town of Oxyrhynchus possessed both a Jewish community and a distinct Jewish quarter (ἄμφοδον), but they are not mentioned before the Roman period.

Cyrenaica has as yet yielded very little clear evidence on the organiza-

[1] *CPJ*, I, no. 129.
[2] Ibid., II, no. 432, lines 57, 60.
[3] Ibid., III, Appendix I, no. 1530, line 4.
[4] Cf. also *CPJ*, I, no. 132.
[5] *Hellenica*, I (1940), 18-24.
[6] *CPJ*, III, Appendix I, no. 1489.
[7] Ibid., I, no. 24.

tion of Jewish rural communities, but the strongly organized character of the Jewish immigrants there, at least from the second century B.C.E., is conveyed by the term συντάγματα (contingents) applied by Josephus to their communities.[1] It has been pointed out that the name Kappharodis (Kephar Haddash) indicates a nucleated village of Jewish settlers who, as Hebrew-speakers, must have come direct from Judaea in the time of Ptolemy I, in accordance with the information furnished by Josephus.[2] We may conjecture a communal organization of the sort accorded to Ptolemaic cleruchs but beyond this we cannot go. The village of N'gharnes, to the east of Cyrene, at the beginning of the first century B.C.E., possessed a council of fifty-three πολυάνομοι, empowered to grant members of the community honorary exemption from 'liturgies' and corvées.[3] As this village paid the ἀγόραστος σῖτος to the government, it seems to have been a katoikic village, and similar institutions may be tentatively ascribed to the Jewish katoikic villages of the country in the late Ptolemaic period; one such may have been Ein Targuna, on or near royal land on the western Jebel.[4]

Evidence of the representation of the tenants of the Ptolemaic lands in Cyrenaica at the beginning of the Roman period may be reflected in a bilingual inscription from Lavinium, belonging, apparently, to the early decades of the first century of the present era.[5] This is dedicated to A. Terentius Varro Murena by the Ptolemaei Cyrenenses represented by Ithalammon son of Apellas and Simon son of Simon. Frank thought that the tenants of the Agri Ptolemaei, i.e. the Roman *ager publicus*, were concerned,[6] and this seems to be right, since the inhabitants of the Cyrenean city of Ptolemais are called Ptolemaenses;[7] those of the Egyptian and Palestinian cities of that name, Ptolemenses;[8] 'Ptolemaeus' means 'of Ptolemy'.[9] On the other hand the name of Ithalammon son of Apellas appears on an ephebe stele at Cyrenean Ptolemais[10] in the year 3-2 B.C.E. But his name seems to be Jewish,

---

[1] Jos. *Ant.*, XIV, 116.
[2] Jos. *Apion*, II, 44.
[3] *SEG*, IX, no. 354; see also Applebaum, *Jews and Greeks in Ancient Cyrene* (1969), pp. 178-9 (Heb.).
[4] For this site, see *BJPES*, XIX, (1955), 188 sqq.; Applebaum, *Jews and Greeks*, pp. 147-151.
[5] *CIL*, XIV, no. 2109; Dessau, *ILS*, no. 897.
[6] *JRS*, XVII (1927), p. 150, n. 2.
[7] P. Romanelli, *Cirenaica romana* (1943), p. 102, n. 3.
[8] *Dig.*, 50, 15,1.
[9] Cic., *de Fin.*, 5, 1, 1.
[10] Unpublished; in Tolmeta Museum.

and occurs as יתשלום on a bronze plate found at Naples.[1] This being the case, both the delegates who dedicated the inscription to Terentius Varro would seem to have been Jews, and it is less probable that they represented the city of Ptolemais than that they spoke for the settlers of the Ptolemaic crown-lands, where Jews were numerous, whether as military settlers or as *laoi*.

Although our information on the organization of rural Jewish communities in Asia Minor and the Seleucid Empire as a whole is much more limited, a careful investigation of sources throws some light on the problem. The order of Antiochus III to his viceroy of Asia, Zeuxis, instructing him to settle two thousand Jewish families from Mesopotamia and Babylonia in Phrygia and Lydia between 212 and 205 approximately,[2] has some details which may be usefully applied in other directions. The text makes it clear that the settlers were military cultivators, since the instruction is to settle them in forts and at the most vital points.[3]

Two important clauses in Antiochus' instructions invite examination. One is the assignment of agricultural land to the settlers, the second the allocation of state-support for the upkeep of the religious functionaries of the newcomers. (τοῖς εἰς τὰς χρείας ὑπηρετοῦσιν). As regards the first item, the land allocated is divided into arable land and vineyards, and the latter item furnishes valuable additional information on the area settled. Examination of the areas of modern Turkey where vines are grown shows that they are today confined to three distinct areas, viz. two areas in the east of the country, on the central Halys and the Upper Euphrates (neither of which need concern us), and a region in central Lydia and western Phrygia extending westward to the coast between Adramyttium and the mouth of the Hermus. It is limited on the south by the Hermus and the Cogamus, on the east by the scarp of the Phrygian highlands between Acmonia and Celaenae-Apamea; on the north by the line from Acmonia through Thyateira to the Caicus and Adramyttium.[4] In ancient times vinegrowing was more widespread, extending farther south to the Maeander, but all the other additional areas of ancient vinegrowing, according to ancient sources, lay near the coast outside Phrygia and Lydia.[5]

---

[1] *CIL*, I, no. 555.   [2] Jos. *Ant.*, XII, 147-153.   [3] Ibid., 149.
[4] Y. Qarmon, M. Braver, *An Atlas of the Middle East*, 2nd ed. (1967) Map 39, ii.
[5] The ancient sources will be found assembled by Broughton in T. Frank, *Economic Survey of Ancient Rome* IV, pp. 609-610 and Magie, *Roman Rule in Asia Minor* I, pp. 84 ff.

It is clear that this vine-growing region, by and large, defines the area of Antiochus III's Jewish settlement, and it contains no fewer than thirteen ancient sites on which the existence of Jewish communities is proved for the Hellenistic or Roman periods by epigraphy or by literary sources.[1] Sardis and Apamea lie immediately outside the area. The above thirteen points included Hierapolis, whose Jewish community is referred to in an inscription as ἡ κατοικία τῶν ἐν Ἱεραπόλει κατοικούντων Ἰουδαίων (the *katoikia* of the Jews living in Hierapolis);[2] on the south edge of the area lies Sardis, whose important community is described by an official document of the city in the last decades of the first century B.C.E. as οἱ κατοικοῦντες ἐν τῇ πόλει Ἰουδαῖοι πολῖται ('the Jewish citizens living in the city').[3] It may be noted that eight of the above places (Pergamum, Thyateira, Magnesia, Acmonia, Eumeneia, Apollonia, Deliler, Hierapolis) lie on the edge of the region, as if forming a defensive ring about it.

It is evident that most of the Jewish settlement-points established by Antiochus III were in or near already existing Greek towns.[4] Some of the Jewish groups were doubtless placed in the towns themselves and allotted lands in the vicinity; others were planned to be independent *katoikiai* in the countryside, for it is known that the Seleucids, unlike the earlier Ptolemies, preferred to settle their non-urban military cultivators in nucleated villages.[5] We may therefore visualize the establishment of two forms of Jewish community in Asia: the rural and the urban, the former an independent entity, the latter forming part of a larger urban community.

Local autonomy is deducible from the second clause of Antiochus III's settlement order, to which attention has been drawn, namely, the provision for the state-support of the settlers' religious functionaries. Schalit has pointed out[6] that the phrase διδόσθω δὲ καὶ τοῖς εἰς τὰς χρείας ὑπηρετοῦσι τὸ αὔταρκες ('and let there be given also to those engaged in public service sufficient for their needs'), refers to those serving religious requirements, and that such are referred

---

[1] Adramyttium, Pergamum, Thyateira, Magnesia ad Sipylum, Blaundos, Sebaste, Sala, Acmonia, Eumeneia, Hierapolis, Apollonia, Deliler near Philadelphia, Phocaea.

[2] *CII*, II, no. 775 (2nd - 3rd century C.E.).

[3] Jos. *Ant.*, XIV, 259.

[4] Cf. A. Schalit, *JQR* (1959-60), pp. 305 ff.

[5] Oertel, *PW*, XI, (1921), sv. Katoikia; 6; Rostovtzeff, *Social and Economic History of the Hellenistic World* I (1953), pp. 472 ff.; E. Bickerman, *Les Institutions des Seleucides* (1938), pp. 80 ff.

[6] *JQR* (1959-60), pp. 311 ff.

to in similar language in relation to the parallel settlement of Onias' *katoikia* at Leontopolis.[1] The word χρεία is also used in reference to religious needs in papyri.[2] Schalit further drew attention to the fact that ὑπηρέτης means *hazzan*,[3] and that Josephus[4] makes it clear that *hazzanim* were of the tribe of Levi.[5]

It is therefore evident that the Jews of the Antiochene *katoikiai* having received specific confirmation of their right to live according to their ancestral laws,[6] were *ipso facto* accorded an organization in which the religious functionaries, apparently the Levites, and possibly the priests, were the responsible officials, since their support was made a charge upon the state. Is it possible to trace this pattern of organization further afield?

Let us consider the Seleucid town of Seleucia-on-Eulaeus, the Persian Susa. An important military centre, part of its population consisted of military settlers; in the Parthian period, when arrangements continued pretty much as they had been under Seleucid rule, we find the ἀκροφυλακῖται (acropolis garrison) of the town thanking the Parthian authorities for restoring the irrigation of their allotments[7]; there can be no doubt that these were descendants of the original Seleucid garrison of *katoikoi* (military settlers) responsible for the city's citadel (ἄκρα). Parallel evidence led Rostovtzeff to conclude that the original constitution of a number of the Seleucid cities which had begun as *katoikiai* had been fundamentally the same as that inferrable at Seleucia-on-Eulaeus, that is, a body of *katoikoi* autonomous in their internal affairs but supervised by royal officials, and not therefore possessing full city-status. In Rostovtzeff's view there are good grounds for assuming the existence of a similar constitution at Dura-Europos, Seleucia-in-Pieria, Seleucia-on-Tigris and—in Asia Minor—at Antiochia-in-Caria, Laodicea-on-Lycus and Antiochia of Pisidia. (We may note that Laodicea-on-Lycus is not far south of Phrygian Hierapolis). We might add as a parallel phenomenon the constitution of the Cappadocian town of Anisa, which ranked as a *politeuma* with regular Greek institutions under the control of a Cappadocian royal official.[1]

---

[1] Jos. *Ant.*, XIII, 67.   [2] Schalit, loc.cit.
[3] Ibid. Cf. Epiphanius, *Haer.*, 30:11.
[4] Jos. *Ant.*, IV, 214.
[5] 'and to each magistracy let there be assigned two ὑπηρέται of the tribe of Levi.'
[6] Jos. *Ant.*, XII, 150.
[7] Rostovtzeff, *Social and Economic History* I, p. 490.
[8] Rostovtzeff, *Social and Economic History* II, p. 840.

Now the royal quarter of Seleucia-on-Eulaeus (Susa) was known in Hebrew as the בירה,[1] and the word is not confined to Persia. It appears also, in its Akkadian form, Birta, for instance, as the centre of Tubias' military cleruchy in Transjordan.[2] At Jerusalem the fortress in the vicinity of the Temple is referred to as the Birah by Nehemiah (2:8), in whose time it was in the charge of a commandant known as שר הבירה (Sar habirah).[3] As early as the time of Persian rule its garrison received both agricultural holdings and pay from the government.[4] The fortress survived till the period of the Maccabees, when it was known as the Baris;[5] this building was presumably dismantled by Antiochus Sidetes,[6] but appears to have been restored, since it served as the object of reconstruction by Herod, who converted it into the Antonia. At least four scholars are known in Talmudic literature who bore the title שר or איש הבירה: 1) Joezer, איש הבירה,[7] a pupil of Shammai and of priestly stock, who held a post in the Temple;[8] 2) R. Aḥa, שר הבירה, who taught at Antioch, and transmitted a halakah to the scholars at Usha;[9] 3) R. Jonathan ben Eleazar, שר הבירה, a contemporary of R. Samuel ben Nahman of Babylon, who addressed to him a halakic enquiry;[10] 4) R. Aḥa, שר הבירה, who lived at the end of the third century C.E., and redeemed captives from Armenia at Antioch.[11] The general assumption is that these men bore the title of שר or איש הבירה hereditarily, and that it originally belonged to the commandant of the fortress attached to the Temple at Jerusalem.[12] But there seems to be no reason why the title should have been confined to the commandant at Jerusalem. We have a suggestive piece of information from Josephus,[13] who tells us that Daniel built a baris at Ecbatana in Media, the man in charge being a Jewish priest, and that this was still so in his own time. There is very little doubt that איש הבירה would have been rendered into Greek as ἀκροφύλαξ or ἀκροφυλακίτης; the titles of ἀκροφύλαξ and φυλακάρχης also appear in reference to officers in Ptolemaic Judaea.[14] Nor

[1] Esther 1:2, 5; 2:3, 5, 8 etc.
[2] *CPJ*, I, no. I, line 13.
[3] Neh. 7:2.
[4] 3 Esdras, 4:56; Jos. *Ant.*, XI, 63.
[5] Jos. *Ant.*, XV, 403.
[6] Cf. *Ant.* XIII, 247 but also Jos. *War*, I, 75; 118.
[7] M. *Orlah*, 2:12.
[8] Cf. T. B. *Baba Metzia*, 90b.
[9] T. B. *Ketuboth*, 88a.
[10] *Gen. Rabba*, 95, 3; *Tanhuma B.*, 12.
[11] *Yuhsin* (Lon.ms.), 109a; T.B. *Yebamoth*, 45a. S. Klein, *Zion* (1939), pp. 39-40.
[12] Cf. Avi-Yonah, *EB* II, (1954), 51 s.v. בירה
[13] Jos. *Ant.*, X, 264-5. [14] *PCZ*, no. 59006; cf. no. 59007.

can there be much doubt that the Jewish inhabitants of Seleucia-on-Eulaeus (Susa) would have referred to the garrison of the Greek citadel as אנשי הבירה, and their commandant as שר הבירה. It is not irrelevant that Josephus' statement[1] can be interpreted to mean that Jews bore personal responsibility for the defence of the towns of Nehardaea and Nisibis, where their communities were very large.[2] It may not be coincidence, therefore, that two of the known שרי הבירה who figure among the Jewish scholars, possessed connections beyond the eastern frontier (Armenia and Babylon), and that another is apparently to be connected with the Antioch area.

It may therefore be possible to offer a tentative reconstruction of the organization of at least some of the Jewish κατοικίαι (military settlements) in Asia, Mesopotamia, Babylonia and Persia. 1) Their organization centred on the priests and Levites, who received their personal stipends from royal funds. 2) The priests sometimes held the command, and as such were responsible for the baris or central strong-point of the settlement area.[3] 3) The position of command was in these cases hereditary in view of the priestly rank of the incumbent. We may note under the Ptolemies the parallel cases of the settlement-group of the High Priest Ezechias and the *katoikiai* established by Onias IV and his sons at Leontopolis; also of Tobiah (Tubias) the Ammonite at the Birta of Ammanitis. His family intermarried with the high priestly family,[4] and had possessed links with the priesthood and the Temple itself in the time of Nehemiah.[5] It is to be added that an organization of this type gives point to the passage in Antiochus III's instruction for the establishment of the Jewish *katoikiai* in Lydia and Phrygia, in which the King emphasizes the importance of the Jewish

---

[1] Jos. *Ant.*, XVIII, 311-2.

[2] It is possible to adduce the presence of Jewish rural *katoikoi* in Mesopotamia, where they no doubt originated with the Seleucids. Whether or not Zamaris' force of mounted archers originated in Seleucid Babylonia we cannot say; it has already been suggested (pp. 433-4) that its feudal character was such that it is more likely to have emerged under Parthian rule. But the settlement of Sina Iudaeorum recorded in *Notitia Dignitatum Orientis* (XXXV,19) in Osrhoene, may well have taken its name from a group of Jewish military cultivators settled by the Hellenistic sovereigns. Interesting in this context is *Not.Dig.Or.*, XXXV, 28, Tovia (? Iovia - Seeck) contra Birtha, in the same region.

[3] It may be recalled that under Herodian rule the centre of Zamaris' *katoikia* was Bathyra, presumably a fortress. (Jos. *Ant.*, XVII, 26).

[4] Birta: *PCZ*, nos. 59075-6; intermarriage with the high priestly family: Jos. *Ant.*, XII, 160.

[5] B. Mazar, *IEJ*, (1957), pp. 143-4.

settlers' religion as a source of loyalty.[1] On the other hand two of the שרי הבירה of the Talmudic sources are not known to have been priests, and some of these commands may have been held by scholars. A number of communities originally founded as *katoikiai* in the Seleucid Empire ultimately became towns, but not all attained full city autonomy. Tarn comments[2] that 'the usual form for the admission of Asiatics into a Greek city was the *politeuma*, in Asia apparently also known as the *katoikia*'. We have already noted, in our study of Jewish Diaspora status, that settlements without full city-autonomy may well have formed the most favourable receptacles for two or more *politeumata*, Greek or non-Greek, dwelling together within one urban or quasi-urban framework. Very suggestive in this respect is the constitution attributed by Tarn[3] to Alexander's 'Alexandrias', each of which, founded on royal land, consisted of a Greek corporation side by side with corporations of Thracians, Persians, etc. The community as a whole enjoyed internal autonomy subject to a standard city-law modified by royal rescripts, but had neither *ecclesia* nor *boule*. These settlements ultimately attained full city-status.

Many of the *katoikiai* also grew into cities, and groups of *katoikoi* were established from the beginning in fully-fledged urban communities. It has been mentioned that the Jews of Phrygian Hierapolis still called themselves a *katoikia* in the third century C.E., while the Jews of Sardis were referred, to officially as Jews living in the city. What we know of their organization may therefore be discussed under the heading of the organization of the Jewish urban communities as a whole (see below, pp. 477ff.).

In Ptolemaic and early Roman Egypt, we are acquainted with the general lines of the Jewish communal organization of Alexandria. Known as a *politeuma*, it is first alluded to in the *Letter of Aristeas*,[4] and in the parallel passage in Josephus' *Antiquities*,[5] which is dependent on it or draws from a common source. Aristeas refers to 'the priests, the elder translators (of the Septuagint), the elders of the *politeuma* and the leaders of the multitude'; Josephus to 'the elder translators and the leaders of the *politeuma*'. Wilamowitz' emendation of Aristeas— 'the elders of the *politeuma* who were the leaders of the multitude', seems unavoidable.[6] This being the case, at the date when Aristeas

---

[1] Jos. *Ant.*, XII, 150.
[2] *Hellenistic Civilisation*, p. 157.
[3] *Alexander the Great* (1951), p. 134.
[4] 310.   [5] XII, 108.   [6] Cf. *CPJ*, I, (1957), 9, n. 24.

wrote, the community was led by the elders, i.e. the *gerousia*, mentioned later by Philo, and to these we may probably add the priests. The exact date of the *Letter of Aristeas* is unfortunately highly controversial, and opinions vary over much of the third and the entire second century B.C.E. Nor do we know when the Jewish ethnarch, who may have replaced the gerousia or presided over it, was first appointed. An ethnarch was ruling in C.E. 11, according to Josephus,[1] but died immediately afterwards (11/12), and a gerousia appears to have been appointed in his place by the new Roman prefect Magius.[2] Strabo, cited by Josephus,[3] describes the powers of the ethnarch as 1) the supervision of contracts; 2) the settlement of internal disputes and 3) the supervision of προστάγματα — as if he were the head of an independent state. It seems to me entirely probable that by προστάγματα royal edicts are meant, and one of two interpretations is possible: either that the ethnarch saw to the implementation of those royal orders (or subsequently of the orders of the Emperor and his deputy, the prefect) which affected the Jewish community, or (and this seems the more attractive alternative) that he applied to the work of the Jewish courts those royal legislative edicts which were such as to modify their practice. These courts are alluded to by Strabo in his reference to the ethnarch's function of judging disputes (καὶ διαιτᾷ κρίσεις). If Strabo is reliable, it would seem that they were presided over by the ethnarch. As to his first function, the supervision of contracts, this is indirectly confirmed by a papyrus recording the registration of a loan-contract between two Jews of Alexandria in 13 B.C.E.[4] at the Jewish records office (διὰ τοῦ τῶν Ἰουδαίων ἀρχείου).

Whether or not the ethnarch was a nominee of the Ptolemaic sovereign or of the emperor, we do not know, but it seems certain, on Philo's evidence, that the Gerousia which replaced him was appointed by the prefect. On the strength of the information of *Tosefta Sukkah* 4:6 and the *Babylonian Talmud Sukka* 51b, that seventy-one thrones adorned the Great Synagogue of Alexandria, it is generally assumed that this was the number of elders constituting that body. We know little of other official functions within the *politeuma*; Talmudic literature describes the regulation of the service of the Great Synagogue by the *hazzan*.[5] An inscription from Jaffa speaks of a φροντιστής (superin-

[1] Jos. *Ant.*, XIX, 283.   [2] Philo, *In Flacc.*, 74.   [3] Jos. *Ant.*, XIV, 117.
[4] *CPJ*, II, no. 143; *BGU*, 1151, lines 7-8.
[5] Krauss, *Synagogale Altertümer*, 1922, p. 124.

tendent) of the Alexandrians[1], but it is uncertain if the reference is to an officer of the Alexandrian community or of a congregation of Alexandrian Jews settled at Joppa. It may however be remarked that if it is the latter, it would have been natural for its members to appoint an officer of the sort they had known in their original home. The superintendents seem to have been in charge of synagogue property (see below).

The Alexandrian *politeuma* headed by its Gerousia was an 'umbrella' organization, which included the entire Jewish population of Alexandria. We know that a number of synagogues existed in the city,[2] and presumably the *politeuma* controlled and represented them in some way. But we have no information on the exact relationship between them and the central body, nor do we know the degree of autonomy enjoyed by the individual congregations or if the Gerousia was elected by them. But we are forced to assume that the body of elders took over the ethnarch's functions, his notarial powers, the presidency of the Jewish court, and the application of government legislation to the judicature.

The Alexandrian *politeuma* did not cease to exist after the destruction of the Second Temple. Titus refused the Greek demand for its dissolution, as he refused the demand for the abolition of the privileges of the Jews of Antioch.[3] The vitality of the Jewish organization of Alexandria is attested by the events of 73, when the Gerousia acted to frustrate the revolutionary incitement of the Zealot refugees, by convening a general Jewish assembly (ἐκκλησία) to expose them, by arresting the revolutionaries and handing them over to the authorities.[4] Here the powers of the Gerousia to convene the *politeuma* and to effect arrests are demonstrated. To these may be added the function of sending delegations to the emperor, as fully demonstrated by Philo,[5] who describes his participation in the Alexandrian community's delegation to Gaius. If the papyri commonly known as the *Acts of the Pagan Martyrs* are to be believed, further Jewish deputations attended upon Trajan[6] and Hadrian.[7]

In addition there is perhaps a trace of the *politeuma*'s activity farther

[1] *CII*, II, no. 918.
[2] Philo, *Legatio ad Gaium*, 132.
[3] Jos. *War*, VII, 110: *Ant.*, XII, 121.
[4] Jos. *War*, VII, 409 ff.
[5] *Legatio ad Gaium*, passim.
[6] Musurillo, *APM*, no. viii; *CPJ*, II, no. 157.
[7] Musurillo, no. ix; *CPJ*, II, no. 158.

afield: we hear of the pleading of Dorotheus the son of Cleopatrides of Alexandria in favour of the exemption from military service of Jews with Roman citizenship, before the proconsul Lentulus.[1] This is probably Cornelius Lentulus Crus, who was recruiting in Asia about 49 B.C.E. It is likely enough that Dorotheus was an envoy of the Alexandrian Gerousia. One further function is almost certainly to be ascribed to the Gerousia, namely, the passing of resolutions in honour of the emperor and his officials. This is not specifically recorded, but it is indirectly demonstrated by Philo's allusion to the presence of steles, inscriptions, gilded spears and crowns dedicated to the emperors in the synagogues of the city.[2] These can hardly have been offered without the sanction of the central Jewish body, and inscriptions imply resolutions.

So far our record distinguishes two elements of the Alexandrian *politeuma*, namely, the Gerousia and the synagogue. There appears to have been a third form of organization, that of the craft guilds. The guilds of the goldsmiths, silversmiths, smiths, wooldressers and textile workers are described by *Tosefta Sukkah* 4:6 as occupying each its own place in the Great Synagogue of the city, hence these bodies must have constituted a permanent and recognized element of Jewish communal life in Alexandria. It is fairly safe to say, on the analogy of town life in the East in this period, that each guild also represented a distinct quarter within the Jewish areas of the city.[3] Parallel evidence comes from Asia Minor and will be discussed in due course. The political importance of these bodies we can only conjecture, but it may well be that they constituted an independent factor which did not always follow the direction of the presumably plutocratic Gerousia, and probably developed a radical line in the first and second centuries of the present era.[4] When Claudius in the year 41 rebuked the Alexandrian Jews for sending two delegations 'as if they lived in two cities', the second,—if we accept the explanation of Tcherikover,[5]—represented the militant elements of the community involved in the disturbances of that time, probably influenced by the Zealot trend. The guilds are as likely as not to have been one of the sources of this trend, and we shall later discuss some evidence that supports this view.

[1] Jos. *Ant.*, XIV, 236.
[2] Philo, *Legatio ad Gaium*, 133.
[3] Cf. e.g. Tiberias: the carpenters' market (*T. B. Erubin*, 29b); the synagogue of the textile-workers (*P. T. Shekalim*, II, 47a).
[4] Tcherikover, *CPJ*, I, 68. [5] Ibid.

We hear very little of the organization of Egyptian Jewry outside Alexandria in the Roman period. But we may note a Jewish quarter (ἄμφοδον) at Oxyrhynchus,[1] and assume that it was under charge of a Jewish warden (ἀμφοδάρχης), since an officer of this title is recorded for the quarter of Arsinoe (the Fayum) where Jews lived, but whose population was mixed.[2] These officers were not appointed by the community, but by the government.

We know something more, thanks to Josephus and to epigraphical material, of the Jewish urban communities of Asia Minor. Josephus' information is almost entirely derived from |the orders of Roman officials issued to various Greek cities in the last sixty years of the first century B.C.E. requiring them to maintain Jewish privileges, and in one or two cases from the resolutions adopted by the councils of those cities in compliance with the same Roman directives. Generally Josephus' reports are based on official documents, and parts of the texts seem to be cited *verbatim* from them. One of them, the letter of the proconsul Gaius Rabirius, was delivered by Sopater the envoy of the High Priest Hyrcanus to Laodicea in Phrygia. It demanded protection for the right of the Jews to observe the Sabbath, their cultic practices and their ancestral laws generally. The same document refers to objections made by the city of Tralles to a similar demand.[3] Broughton believes the proconsul to have been the C. Rabirius recorded at Delos in 49-46 B.C.E.,[4] though he is not known to have governed Asia; but as Hyrcanus appears without the title of ethnarch, the suggestion has been made that this is Hyrcanus I (134-104 B.C.E.). As Hyrcanus maintained friendly diplomatic relations with Pergamum,[5] such intervention is by no means impossible. Whatever the case, there can be no doubt that Jewish privileges of the type alluded to here and in the other documents were all well established in Asia and must have originated in the Hellenistic period.

The most detailed information on the organization of a Jewish urban community of Asia comes from Sardis, in the form of a decree passed by the council and people of the city in 50 B.C.E. to confirm Jewish privileges in compliance with the demand of the Roman *quaestor*

---

[1] *CPJ*, II, no. 423 (c. 85 C.E.).
[2] Ibid., no. 421 (73 C.E.).
[3] Jos. *Ant.*, XIV, 241.
[4] T. R. S. Broughton, *The Magistrates of the Roman Republic*, II (1952), p. 481; *CIL*, I, 2, no. 773.
[5] Jos. *Ant.*, XIV, 247 ff.

propraetore L. Antonius.[1] Since the decree refers to the Jews as 'Jewish citizens living in the city', it may be taken as certain that their community, originally a group of *katoikoi*,[2] was organized in a *politeuma*, which may well have been officially entitled σύνοδος (association), according to L. Antonius' letter.[3] Both he and the Sardean decree acknowledge the right of the community to a distinct quarter of the city for their cultic activities, where they may build and also dwell. The market inspectors (ἀγορανόμοι) of the city are also required to facilitate the import of the necessary food-supplies for the Jewish community. The implication of this last provision is that the community possessed a licensed market where ritually permissible foodstuffs brought in from the countryside could be sold. The decree confirms the right of the Jewish 'synod' to conduct not only its internal affairs, but also its own courts. L. Antonius refers specifically to the place in which the Jews of Sardis decide their affairs and internal controversies. At a later date the proconsul C. Norbanus Flaccus,[4] confirming Jewish privileges in Sardis, adds their right to collect money and to transmit the half-shekel to Jerusalem.[5] The intimate topographical relationship of a city gymnasium to the Sardis synagogue has already been discussed (pp. 448 ff.), and although we cannot deduce from this evidence what part, if any, the Jewish community played in the gymnasium, the existence of 'Ιουδαῖοι νεώτεροι at Hypaepa in Lydia would appear to show that in some Asiatic towns young Jews were organized in their own gymnasia. Such an assumption would encourage us to interpret similarly in relation to Antioch the information that the city's Jews received the cash-equivalent of the oil distributed to citizens by the gymnasiarch.[6]

The following information on the Jewish communal organization of Sardis may therefore be deduced:

They are permitted to worship and practise their ancestral laws; to meet for cultic and communal activities in a defined locality;

---

[1] Jos. *Ant.*, XIV, 259 ff.

[2] Some apparently from Jerusalem; cf. Obad., 20: ‏וגלת ירושלם אשר בספרד‎ ...
It is notable that Sardis became a polis towards the end of the third century B.C.E. (Jones, *CERP*, 46; *SIG*³, 548-9), hence at the date of the Jewish settlement it might have been a mere collection of *politeumata* under royal supervision.

[3] Jos. *Ant.*, XIV, 235.

[4] Men of this name held consulships in 38 and 24 B.C.E. Dahl and Juster identify the man concerned with the second; Smallwood puts his Asiatic governorship in 23 B.C.E.

[5] Jos. *Ant.*, XVI, 171; also Philo, *Legatio ad Gaium*, 315.

[6] Jos. *Ant.*, XII, 120.

to erect communal buildings and dwellings in that locality; to conduct litigation in their own courts; to collect funds and transmit the half-shekel dues to Jerusalem; to conduct their own market in foodstuffs. From the fact that L. Antonius' confirmation was prompted by a Jewish complaint (*Ant.*, XIV, 235), the Jewish synod's activities seem to have included the sending of delegations to the government. The terms πολῖται and πολιτεύωνται applied in the documents to the synod's activities imply, as we should expect, the election or appointment of functionaries and representatives under the auspices of the community. We have no contemporary information as to who these were. But it may be permissible to use the evidence from the Sardis synagogue excavated in recent years.[1] The building as at present known was first erected in the early third century of the present era, but was preceded by an earlier building dating, it would seem, from the first century. Jewish communal institutions from Hellenistic to Byzantine times, moreover, were stable in type and altered little. The association of the Sardis synagogue with Jewish shops, therefore,[2] confirms in a remarkable way the existence of a distinct Jewish quarter, such as is provided for by the Sardis decree of 50 B.C.E. and furnishes a strong presumption that the city's Jewish communal organization perpetuated in the third century C.E. the lines of the Hellenistic and early Roman periods, when the existence of a synagogue is independently attested by an inscription listing the fountains of the city, that of the synagogue among them.[3] This being the case, the evidence provided by the synagogue may not be irrelevant to the organization of 50 B.C.E.

Among the donors of the synagogue's mosaics, we find Aurelius Olympius, Φυλῆς Λεοντίων (of the phyle of the Leontii); a goldsmith whose name has not survived, who is a councillor (βουλευτής); and the goldsmith Aurelius Hermogenes, Σ]αρδιανὸ[ς βουλε]υτής (a member of the council (βουλή) of Sardis).[4] The third was a councillor of the city of Sardis. That the second was, is not quite so evident, though L. Robert accepts him as such. But it is not impossible that his function was councillor of a guild of goldsmiths. Most interesting is Aurelius Olympius. Robert[5] thinks phyle means 'tribe',

---

[1] *BASOR*, 177, (1965), 23, 25-6; 182, (1966), 38, 40, 44.
[2] *BASOR*, 170, (1963), 49-51.
[3] Buckler and Robinson, *Sardis* VII (1932) I, n. 17, line 7; cf. *Revue de Philologie*, (1958), pp. 43-5.
[4] L. Robert, *Nouvelles inscriptions de Sardes* (1964), pp. 44-55, nos. 6, 13, 14.
[5] Loc.cit., 45.

because Leontios is *interpretatio Graeca* of Judah,—and suggests that this is a 'tribe' of the Jewish community. This is an extremely attractive suggestion, especially in view of the probable derivation of part of the original nucleus of Jewish settlers at Sardis from Jerusalem. But it encounters difficulties: Josephus and Eusebius use the word phyle for a family in the high priestly and royal sense,[1] though this is an uncommon usage, and in the Septuagint (e.g. *Num.*, I:4) it always means a tribe or its subdivision (מטה).[2] There is nevertheless another possibility. Aurelius Olympius does not state that he is a craftsman: two of his associates contributing to the pavement of the synagogue, however, are goldsmiths. A Jewish goldsmiths' guild is known at Corycus in Cilicia, on the evidence of one Moses who had been its guildmaster.[3] At Philadelphia (Lydia) the trade-guilds and phyles of the town appear to have coincided;[4] at Apamea an organization by streets replaced the tribal division, and some of the streets were called after trade-guilds.[5] Thyateira (Lydia) was organized by trade guilds (potters, dyers, butchers, tanners, linen workers, bakers, coppersmiths, leatherworkers),[6] and no 'tribes' are mentioned. This being so, the phyle of Leontis might have been a guild of goldsmiths and an integral part of the synod of the Jews of Sardis. In this case we should find a parallel in the organization at Alexandria, where the Jewish guilds constituted an organic part of the Great Synagogue and, one assumes, of the *politeuma*. At Phrygian Hierapolis, where associations (σύνοδοι) of an undefined character are recorded in connection with the council and people,[7] (Jones thought they might have been craft-guilds),[8] two Jewish guilds, those of purple-dyers and carpet-weavers, are known.[9]

The legal position of the Jewish organizations under the Roman Empire will be discussed below, but a comment must be made here concerning the craft-guilds. A profusion of inscriptions from the

---

[1] Jos. *War*, IV, 155: μίαν τῶν ἀρχιερατικῶν φυλήν; Eusebius, *Eccles. History*, III, 12.
[2] The Jewish Macedonian φυλή in Alexandria, even if a military unit, would—if its members were citizens of the Greek *politeuma*—have been a tribe in respect of the city's constitution. Precisely for this reason, it can have no bearing on the constitution of the Jewish *politeuma*.
[3] *CII*, II, no. 793.
[4] *IGR*, IV, no. 1632.
[5] *IGR*, IV, nos. 788, 790, 791; cf. Jones, *CERP*, 70.
[6] *IGR*, IV, no. 1205 etc.; Jones, op.cit., 83-4.
[7] *IGR*, IV, no. 818.
[8] Op.cit., 395.
[9] *CII*, II, no. 777.

Greek cities of Asia Minor in the Roman period makes it plain that professional organizations of craftsmen flourished.[1] This fact has caused some difficulty in view of the existence of the *Lex Iulia de Collegiis*, which dissolved all but the older bodies.[2] Claudius and Nero amended the law to exempt *collegia tenuiorum* (poor men's clubs) from the Lex Iulia, i.e. the special object of the latter was the control of the craftsmen's organizations, whose activities were apt to become politically dangerous in the view of the administration. The situation in the provinces is nevertheless not entirely clear; in the first century professional associations flourished in the West;[3] Trajan suppressed clubs of all types in Bithynia, as the younger Pliny testifies,[4] but till then, they had existed freely. Trajan's restriction was gradually extended to the other provinces on the evidence of Marcian.[5]

There is no doubt that the normal Jewish communal organization was exempt from the Lex Iulia,[6] but this would not necessarily have applied to the Jewish guilds. The Alexandrian Jewish craft-guilds, however, need not have survived Trajan and the virtual annihilation of the Jewish community of Alexandria in 115-117. The evidence for gentile Asiatic guilds, on the other hand, extends through the third and fourth centuries, and the two Jewish guilds recorded at Hierapolis belong to the second or third century. Ziebarth[7] concluded that a liberal policy must have applied in these provinces owing to the political importance of the Greek cities in the eyes of the emperors. We might add that the Asiatic industries—especially the textile and leather trades—were of no less importance to the Roman economy and particularly to the military machine.

The craft organizations were nevertheless a source of ferment in the earlier second century; this is clear from Dio Chrysostom's account of Tarsus, where he says specifically that the λινουργοί (linen-workers, apparently a generic name for the craftsmen of all branches) were an extraordinarily large multitude responsible for turbulence and disorder who regarded themselves as part of the city and were a consider-

---

[1] Cf. Ziebarth's list, *Das Griechische Vereinwesen* (1896), pp. 102 ff. For further literature, Rostovtzeff, *Social and Economic History* I, pp. 178-9; II, pp. 619-20.
[2] Suet., *Aug.*, 32; *ILS* no. 4966; cf. Jos. *Ant.* XIV, 215.
[3] A. N. Sherwin-White, *The Letters of Pliny* (1966), p. 608.
[4] *Epp. Plin. ad Traianum* XXXIII, XXXIV.
[5] *Dig.*, 47, 22, 1.
[6] Jos. *Ant.*, XIV, 215.
[7] Op.cit., 107 ff.

able factor.[1] Such bodies, however, are to be distinguished from the employers' societies which in Rostovtzeff's opinion were the majority.[2] It is at any rate clear, if the phyle of the Leonti was a goldsmiths' guild, that its members were men of wealth and prominence in the community, some of whom held municipal office. But something additional can be learnt of the character of the Jewish textile and leatherworkers' guilds from other sources.

It has already been suggested that the Alexandrian craftsmen's societies were active in the Jewish radical movements of the first and early second centuries (above, p. 476). We may recall the exploits of the weavers Anilaeus and Asinaeus, which began with a dispute between owner and workers in a weaving-mill at Nehardaea,[3] and ended with the founding of an ephemeral 'robber' principality among the swamps of the Euphrates. Significant too is Jonathan the Weaver, the Zealot who stirred up revolt at Cyrene in the year 73; his activities began with a clash with a wealthy Cyrenean Jew, Alexander,[4] and one wonders if this was not in the course of employment; the acute class hatred revealed in the entire episode is striking. We have also evidence of the pronounced freemasonry prevalent among Jewish craftsmen in this period; *Tos. Sukkah* 6:2 speaks explicitly of the ready reception and employment of outside craftsmen by the Alexandrian Jewish societies centred on the Great Synagogue. Something of the same phenomenon is to be perceived in the encounter of Aquila of Pontus and Paul of Tarsus at Corinth; Paul is not only lodged by Aquila, but the two work together 'because they were of the same craft'.[5] Both these men were admittedly of the employer-class, but the principle was the same. Alexandrian Jewish craftsmen travelled to Jerusalem, and tradition traces the first Jewish settlement in Spain to a weaver of the Temple tapestries.[6] Tarsean and Cappadocian artisans are found working in Judaea.[7] Other Asiatic craftsmen from Thyateira[8] and Ephesus[9] are mentioned in the New Testament.

---

[1] Dio Chrysostomus XXXIV, 21.
[2] Loc.cit., 178.
[3] Jos. *Ant.*, XVIII, 314.
[4] Jos. *War.*, VII, 45.
[5] Acts 18:3.
[6] *T. B. Arakhin* 10b; *M. Yoma*, III, 1; *T. B. Yoma*, 38a. Spain: *Encyclopedia Judaica Castellana*, IV, 1949, 139, s.v. España.
[7] S. Klein, *Pal.-Jüd. Corpus Inscr.* (1920), 131, 132; *P. T. Shekalim*, II, 4, 100b; *P. T. Shebiith*, IX, 5, 39a.
[8] Acts, 16:14; Lydia, a seller of purple.
[9] 2 Tim. 4:14, a bronzeworker.

It therefore seems probable that in the first century of the present era, in Asia as in Alexandria, both master-craftsmen and working artisans were an organized factor in the larger Jewish communities—as they were in Asia in the third century—and it seems possible that, on the model both of Alexandria and some Asiatic towns, the craft guilds were part of the Jewish communal organization.

In the course of our survey of the functions of the Jewish *politeuma* of Sardis, we found no mention of a records office, although such may well have existed in connection with the Jewish courts of the city. But such is clearly proved for the community of Phrygian Hierapolis. Here an epitaph commemorates the construction of the tomb by Aurelia Augustas daughter of Zotikos, and threatens illegal reuse of the place with a fine to be paid to the Jewish *katoikia* of Hierapolis, a copy of the inscription having been deposited ἐν τῷ ἀρχίῳ τῶν Ἰουδαίων (in the records office of the Jews).[1] The tomb belongs to the later second or third century of the present era, but may be taken also to reflect conditions of the first. The Hierapolis *katoikia*, therefore, possessed a records office and notary, and in connection with such the function of the synagogue of some communities for the registration of manumissions must be mentioned.[2] The legal aspect of this process is not our subject here, but it gives rise to the possibility that in many communities the synagogue fulfilled the duties of a records office wherever a specific office did not exist separately.

Inscriptions show that two other functions were sometimes discharged by Jewish communal organizations in Asia. The funerary monument of M. Aurelius Moussios at Ephesus was prepared by 'the Jews' at the public expense of the community.[3] At Tlos, Lycia, on the other hand, Ptolemaios son of Leukios hands over his tomb to the community (to belong to all Jews).[4] Thus the maintenance of cemeteries or tombs fell within the competence of the above organizations. The second function was support of the aged: a tomb at Dokimeion in Phrygia directs part of the fine imposed for desecration to the γηρο-κομήσαντες, or 'those that care for the aged'.[5] The Jewish origin of this epitaph, however, is not completely established.

---

[1] *CII*, ii, no. 775.
[2] Panticapaeum, *CII*, i, no. 683 - 80 c.e.; Oxyrhynchus, *CPJ*, ii, no. 473 - 291 c.e.
[3] *CII*, ii, no. 746; revised reading, L. Robert, *Hellenica*, xi-xii, (1960).
[4] *CII*, ii, no. 757.
[5] *MAMA*, iv, no. 31.

The city of Acmonia, Phrygia, furnishes us with another form of organization which may have existed within the framework of the Jewish community, namely, a specific Jewish quarter not necessarily coinciding, as at Sardis, with the homes of the Jewish community as a whole. Two such have been noted in Egypt, but we know no details of their organization, except that they were in charge of wardens (ἀμφόδαρχαι). At Acmonia an epitaph tells us how Aurelius Aristeas in the third century C.E. made various donations to his quarter, which lay near one of the city-gates—on condition that roses were offered annually at his wife's tomb.[1] As he had purchased the plot for his tomb from a Jew, Math(i)os, son of Marcus, and since he ends with a warning against desecration of the tomb with the phrase (directed to desecrators) ἔσται αὐτοῖς πρὸς τὴν δικαιοσύνην τοῦ Θεοῦ, Jewish identity is evident. Robert concludes that the above-mentioned quarter ὁ τῶν Πρωτοπυλειτῶν was a small Jewish quarter near the town-gate, recalling the Jewish quarters near the Porta Capena, the Porta Esquilina and the Porta Collina at Rome. The name of the quarter suggests that it was not new, hence it may well have existed in the early Roman period. Robert observes that the offering of roses on the tomb is a purely gentile custom; on the other hand the fact that no sacrifice is prescribed confirms that the donor was Jewish. Robert's theory of a Jewish quarter perhaps requires more evidence than we have, but if we accept it, we shall note that a testamentary gift with a condition attached can only be made to a body possessed of a juridical personality, and some form of recognized representation. If this was the case, our hypothetical Jewish quarter at Acmonia was supervised by some sort of body elected or self-appointed, but more we cannot affirm.

There may have been a similar Jewish quarter with its own representative body at Arnut-Keni in Bithynia, but here the question is highly problematic. An epitaph here commemorates one Sanbatis who was γραμματεὺς καὶ ἐπιστάτης τῶν παλαίων.[2] It has been usual to explain ἐπιστάτης τῶν παλαίων as 'supervisor of the aged', but the word παλαίος does not seem to be used in reference to human age after the Homeric cycle, and in classical and later Greek means almost exclusively 'old' in the chronological sense (ancient, antique). Οἱ

---

[1] W. Ramsay, REG (1889), p. 23; revised reading and discussion, L. Robert, Hellenica, XI-XII, (1960), pp. 409 ff.
[2] CII, II, no. 800.

παλαίοι therefore would here mean 'old' in relation to some community or quarter.

On the urban organization of Jews in Syria our information is confined to Antioch and Apamea, where it refers almost entirely to the fourth century or later; there can be no doubt, however, that in its general lines this organization was of long standing and can be related to the first century of the present era. Claudius sent a copy of his general confirmation of Jewish rights to the Antioch community in 41;[1] in relation to the year 69, Josephus refers to an archon of the same community,[2] and in 70 Titus refused to abolish its rights.[3] John Chrysostom in the fourth century mentions a Jewish archon and superintendent (προστατής) of Antioch, also patriarchs.[4] He terms the organization of the Jewish community a *politeia*.[5] Talmudic sources prove the existence of a Jewish court of law,[6] which is confirmed by Chrysostom.[7] The latter also speaks of what appears to have been a Jewish hospital.[8] We have seen above that in all probability the Antioch Jews possessed their own gymnasium.

Antioch Jewry was therefore a strongly organized community as befitted the capital of the Seleucid kingdom and the third city of the Roman Empire. The community clearly embraced a number of synagogues; at least three are recorded[9] and there must have been more, thus indicating that the Jewish *politeia* was a 'roof' organization like that of Alexandria. Its executive would appear to have consisted of more than one archon, for the author of the *Pseudo-Chrysostom* was certainly referring to Antioch when he wrote that Jewish archons were elected in September.[10] As two inscriptions refer to gerousiarchs of Antioch,[11] it has been suggested by Schwabe that the community was led by a Gerousia presided over by a gerousiarch, in which case the archons may be presumed to have composed the executive committee. Caracalla was in all probability referring to the Jewish *politeia* when in 213 C.E. he transmitted his judicial decision to the *Universitas Iudaeorum qui in Antiochensium constituti sunt*.[12] This

---

[1] Jos. *Ant.*, XIX, 279.   [2] Jos. *War*, VII, 47.
[3] Jos. *Ant.*, XII, 121.   [4] *Adv. Iud.*, VI, 5.
[5] Ibid., I, 3.   [6] *P. T. Sanhedrin*, III, 21a.
[7] *Adv. Iud.*, I, 3.   [8] Ibid., VIII, 6.
[9] The *Kenesset ha-Shemonit*; the Synagogue of Asabinus and at least one in the south of the city—see C. Kraeling, *JBL*, (1932), p. 140.
[10] *De nativ. S. Ioannis.* See p. 494, n. 3.
[11] M. Schwabe, *Y. Levi Mem. Vol.* (1949), p. 216, no. 7 (Heb.); *IEJ* (1954), p. 252, no. 207.
[12] *Cod. Iust.*, I, 9, I.

verdict, which prohibited the *universitas* from accepting a legacy, indicates that the community was fully empowered to own and administer funds and property.

The possibility of another form of Jewish organization arises in some rural areas of Asia Minor, although it can only be discussed on a hypothetical plane. In Pamphylia epigraphical evidence of Jewish settlement in Roman times is known at the towns of Side[1] and Olba,[2] yet the Roman consul's diplomatic circular in 142 B.C.E.[3] refers separately to Pamphylia and (after Lycia and several other Asiatic cities are mentioned) to Side. On the other hand the husband of Deborah on a Phrygian epitaph[4] is merely called a 'Pamphylos'; and Jacob buried at Beth She'arim in Israel[5] is commemorated as ἀρχισυνάγωγος Πανφυλίας.[6] This suggests that a considerable part of the Jewish population of the region was rural, and unattached to city communities, and that it had a centralized organization which also embraced the countryside. This remains at present no more than a conjecture, but support for it may be seen in the Acts,[7] where Paul preaches at Lystra and Derbe and in the country round about.

Cyrenaica has yielded valuable information on the organization of Jewish communal life in the late first century B.C.E. and the first century C.E., the chief source being three inscriptions of the Roman period from Berenice (Benghazi). The first,[8] dating from 8-6 B.C.E., expresses the thanks of the archons and Jewish *politeuma* of the city to Decimus Valerius Dionysius for plastering and painting the amphitheatre; the decision is registered to exempt Decimus from all 'liturgies'. As Decimus' contribution is termed specifically a contribution to the *politeuma*, there can be no doubt that the amphitheatre was a building belonging to the Jewish *politeuma* itself, where the community assembled.[9] The chief occasions of assembly are referred to in the

---

[1] *CII*, II, no. 781. [2] Ibid., no. 795. [3] I Macc. 15:23.
[4] *CII*, II, no. 772. Apollonia of Phrygia.
[5] M. Schwabe, B. Lifshitz, *Beth She'arim* II (1967), no. 203.
[6] Lifshitz reads Ἰακὼς Καισαρεὺς ἀρχισυνάγωγος, Πανφυλίας inserting a comma after ἀρχισυνάγωγος; this seems to me less acceptable than Schwabe's original interpretation, *BJPES*, IX (1941), 28, where ἀρχισυνάγωγος is taken with Πανφυλίας.
[7] Acts 14:6.
[8] *CIG*, no. 5362; *REG*, (1949), pp. 290 ff.
[9] For a discussion of the form of the building, Applebaum, *Fourth World Congress of Jewish Studies Papers* I (1967), pp. 107-8 (Heb.). It may be observed that the Jews of Tiberias seem to have used their hippodrome as a gathering place (Jos. *Life*, 138).

second inscription,[1] dated 24-25 C.E., which honours the Roman official M. Tittius for his favourable attitude to both the city and the community. This resolution too is to be set up in the amphitheatre, and Tittius is to be publicly eulogized at each assembly (σύνοδος) and new moon (νουμηνία); the dedication itself is made at the Festival of Sukkot (ἐπὶ συλλόγου τῆς σκηνοπηγίας). The third inscription, dated to 56 C.E., is a resolution passed not by the *politeuma* but by the synagogue, which term is here applied both to the community and to its place of worship. The inscription records the members who have contributed to the latter's repair or reconstruction. The list opens, like the two previous inscriptions, with the names of the archons or members of the executive board, but continues with other contributors, commencing with a priest and terminating (so far as can be seen) with several women. In the two earlier documents the archons alone are named.

An interesting fact emerges from a comparison of these three inscriptions: the first records only seven archons, the second nine and the third eleven. The first inscription, it is true, is mutilated, but the chronological order is such that it is probable that in the first there were no more than eight archons at most. What is certain is that the number had risen to eleven in 56 C.E., implying that the community had grown in numbers. It therefore seems likely that the archons were appointed in some sort of proportion to the size of the community, and the probability arises that they were democratically elected by its members.

Another point may be noted in reference to the Berenice *politeuma*. This is, that the city's community in the third inscription is called ἡ συναγωγὴ τῶν ἐν Βερνεικίδι Ἰουδαίων (the synagogue of the Jews in Bernikis). This form of the city's name (Ber(e)nikis), with its peculiar termination, refers not only to the polis but also to its territory and countryside (χώρα) (cf. Thebaid, Megaris etc.), meaning that in the middle of the first century C.E., at least, the synagogue of Berenice included not only the Jews resident in the city but also those who lived in the countryside round about.

Nothing is known of the organization of the important Jewish community of the city of Cyrene; a fragmentary stele of the first century B.C.E. mentioning a synagogue has been found: it records at least five

---

[1] *CIG*, no. 5361; *REG*, (1949), pp. 283 ff.

people.[1] As none has an identifiably Jewish name it is not completely certain that a Jewish synagogue is meant, although the stele fragment, which is adorned with a pediment, is of much the same type as two of those from Berenice.[2] But there is no doubt whatsoever, that the city had a large community, and the episode of the interference of Cyrene with the transmission of the half-shekel to Jerusalem in Augustus' reign, on the pretext of non-payment of taxes by the community, as well as the fact that the action involved not only Cyrene but also the other cities of the province, justifies certain assumptions concerning the activities of all the Jewish community-organizations of the province, the more so as they were able to complain and to obtain redress against the infringement of their rights.

If then we combine what we know of the Berenice *politeuma* with the rest of our information on the Jews in the Cyrenean Pentapolis, we obtain the following picture of the local Jewish organizations and their functions:

1) They held regular general assemblies.

2) Their resolutions were taken by the general meeting on the initiative of boards of officials, at Berenice of a board of elected archons.

3) They took honorary resolutions, honoured members and non-members with steles, and sent delegations and complaints to the authorities.

4) They were responsible for collecting given taxes for the authorities; this may be inferred from the fact that the transmission of the half-shekel was stopped by the city-authorities of Cyrene on the pretext of 'taxes not paid', implying that the community was held responsible for their payment. The practice of collecting the half-shekel from the community must therefore also be added to the activities of the *politeumata*.

5) They were empowered to exempt members from 'liturgies': whether these were 'liturgies' imposed by the communities themselves on their members, or were imposed by the city, is not evident.

6) They possessed and maintained buildings. At Berenice these included an amphitheatre which served as a place of assembly, and also a synagogue.

7) The Berenice organization included the Jews of both the town and the surrounding country.

---

[1] *Annuario della Scuola archeologica di Atene*, XXXIX-XL, 1961-2 (1963), p. 288, no. 116.

[2] See now P. M. Frazer, *Berytus*, (1958), pp. 115-6, no. 8, for an inscription from Cyrene for a Jewish synagogue.

Virtually nothing is known of the organization of the Jewish rural communities of the Cyrenean province in the Roman period. We have noted the evidence that the Jews of the countryside round Berenice (the city's χώρα) were organized with their brethren in the city. The existence of the so-called Jewish 'temple' of Boreion, in the south of the province,[1] indicates the existence of synagogues in non-urban areas.

There is one other detail worthy of consideration. The settlement of Iscina Locus Augusti Iudaeorum is recorded on the shores of the Syrtis by the *Tabula Peutingeriana*, and in the second century sources,[2] but its location is given under another name in earlier records.[3] Its origin as a foundation by the imperial authority is clear from the name, and several sources confirm the settlement of slaves of the imperial household and ex-soldiers on the land by the personal action of the Caesars—e.g. Flaviopolis in Thrace, founded by Claudius and transferred by Vespasian to Asia;[4] a similar settlement in Samos, established by the latter;[5] tracts near Panormus granted by him to veterans and imperial slaves;[6] and lands allotted by the same emperor to tenants and imperial slaves at Abella (Campania).[7] We may therefore follow Monceaux's suggestion[8] that Iscina was a settlement of recalcitrant Jews, whether from Judaea or Cyrenaica or both, carried out by Vespasian or Titus in the seventies or eighties of the first century.[9]

The name is such as to leave no doubt that the settlement occupied imperial domain, and that it possessed no form of municipal status or autonomy. The term *locus* nevertheless tells us something more. Ulpian[10] defines it, outside towns, as part of a *fundus*, and in agrarian legislation it denotes rural property.[11] More especially in southern Gaul it is found denoting villages, and in one case at least, the centre

---

[1] Procopius, *de Aedif.*, vi, 2; now Bu-Grada—see R. G. Goodchild, *JRS*, (1951), pp. 11 ff.; *Antiquity* (1951), 132, 140, 143; *Geographical Journal* (1952), 9.
[2] *Die Peutingersche Tafel*, ed. K. Miller (1962) viii, p. 1; cf. *ib.* p. 15; *Itinerarium Antonini* (ap. O. Cuntz, *Itineraria Romana*, 1929), 65.1; Ptol., *Geog.*, iv, 3,11.
[3] Strabo, xvii, 3,20 (836).
[4] Mommsen, *Provinces of the Roman Empire* i (1909), pp. 306-7, n. 1.
[5] *IGR*, iv, nos. 991, 992.
[6] *Gromatici*, Lachmann, 211.
[7] Ibid., *Lib.Col.*, i, 230.
[8] *REJ* (1902), 7.
[9] Cf. A. Neubauer, *Mediaeval Jewish Chronicles* i (1887), p. 190; S. Applebaum, *Jews and Greeks in Ancient Cyrenaica*, pp. 200-202 (Heb.).
[10] *Dig.*, 50, 16, 27.
[11] Bruns, *Fontes Iuris Romani* (1907), no. 11.

of a large estate.[1] In several places in northern Britain, on the other hand, *loca* were points, often cult-centres, in the border-region, where native fairs were held at fixed intervals under government licence and supervision.[2] It may therefore be suggested with some confidence that Iscina Locus Augusti Iudaeorum was the central point of an imperial estate, which served as a meeting-place of Jews dwelling in dispersed farms or groups of farms about it; and constituting, in all probability, both a fair and a place of worship. We may possibly compare the Topos Magdalis[3] of the Martuba district in eastern Cyrenaica, whose name gives reason to suspect that it was a Jewish settlement.[4]

It is now necessary to discuss the communal organization in the first century of the Jews of the Roman Empire outside Palestine, Syria, Egypt, Cyrenaica and Asia Minor. This is difficult, because the direct contemporary evidence is very small, and a reconstruction can only be made by the use of material of the second to fourth centuries, on the assumption that little changed in this sphere between the first century and the later period. In the treatment of the organization of these groups, it will also be necessary to utilize evidence from the eastern Mediterranean provinces. Under this head, therefore, an attempt will be made to summarize what is known of synagogue organization as a whole.

In all the centres where something is known of Jewish communities in the above-mentioned area —except Rome—the communal organization seems to have been centred on a single synagogue. At Panticapaeum in the Crimea in the first century C.E. the word προσευχή means the prayer-house and the συναγωγή, the assembly of the congregation. But at Berenice of Cyrenaica under Nero συναγωγή denotes both the building and the congregation assembled for business. At Rome the word συναγωγή appears always to apply to the congregation, but the word προσευχή, commonest in Egypt, is found only once at Rome,[5] though it occurs also much later and farther west at Elche (Ilici) in Spain.[6] At Stobi (Macedonia) the prayer-house is 'the holy place' (ὁ ἅγιος τόπος).[7]

The communities refer to themselves, however, as 'the Hebrews'

[1] *CIL*, XII, no. 1524.
[2] Richmond in *Arch.*, (1959), 15; cf. *Chorog. Ravennas*, para. 226-35, (*ib.*, p. 19).
[3] Ptol., IV, 5.
[4] See Tcherikover, *The Jews of Egypt*, pp. 18-19; *CPJ*, I, 4-5 and nn. for Magdola (Migdal) as a name in Egypt indicating Syrian and Jewish settlement.
[5] *CII*, I, no. 531.   [6] *CII*, I, no. 662.   [7] *CII*, I, no. 694.

(οἱ Ἑβραῖοι) at Corinth, Portus near Ostia, and once in Rome; as 'the people' (λαός) at Mantinea, Smyrna, Larissa and Pherae. It is to be noted that at Hierapolis (Phrygia) the community is once called the *katoikia*, once 'the people of the Jews' (ὁ λαὸς τῶν Ἰουδαίων).[1] The term *universitas*, which is used by Caracalla for the 'federation' of the Jewish communities of Syrian Antioch, (above), has been conjecturally used to restore the missing term at the head of the well-known Latin inscription at Castello Porziano near Ostia,[2] and thence has passed into literature as a certainty, although it possesses virtually no authority in this context; in relation to Antioch it is used, in all probability, as an equivalent of the word πολιτεία in the sense of the 'umbrella' organization of a number of synagogues.

The normal Jewish community in Judaea appears to have possessed, in the first century of the present era, a representation of seven men,[3] assisted by two 'ministers' (ὑπηρέται) of the tribe of Levi.[4] The seven functionaries appear also to have acted as judges,[5] and are called by Josephus ἄρχοντες (magistrates). The executive of a synagogue, on the other hand, consisted of three functionaries.[6] The *Book of Judith*, however, describes the communal leadership as consisting of elders (πρεσβύτεροι) and archons.[7] Allon[8] supposed that the former were the ordinary members of the council, while the latter were the executive, corresponding to the three officials of the synagogue. It may be noted that the *Book of Judith* concurs with the information of the *Letter of Aristeas* about elders of the *politeuma* in Alexandria,[9] which relates to a period hardly later than the late second century B.C.E. and may be a good deal earlier. In the first century C.E., the same community has both a gerousia and archons,[10] meaning that the latter were the executive committee. It therefore seems probable that the traditional Jewish communal representation in Judaea formed the chief model for the Diaspora centres, although undoubtedly various modifications took place in them in the course of time. The distinction between executive and council was by no means always maintained; at Berenice, for instance,

---

[1] *CII*, II, nos. 775; 776.   [2] *CII*, I, no. 533.
[3] Jos. *Ant.*, IV, 214.   [4] Ibid.   [5] Ibid.
[6] *P. T. Megillah*, III, 171d.
[7] VI, 15-17; VII, 9-10.
[8] *Hist. of the Jews of Eretz Yisrael in the Period of the Mishnah and the Talmud* I (1954), p. 110 (Heb.).
[9] See pp. 473-4.
[10] Philo, *Against Flaccus*, 74; 117.

there were at first seven, later more archons, who comprised, it would appear, the entire council. In each Roman synagogue it is doubtful whether there was more than one annual archon, but the evidence on the point is indecisive (see below).

Most of the detailed information which we possess on synagogue organization comes from Rome, and it will therefore be convenient to give the particulars, availing ourselves also of evidence from elsewhere within the Empire for comparative or supplementary purposes.

It is clear from Philo that Roman Jewry enjoyed a fully organized life in the time of Augustus,[1] and there is no reason to believe that this state of affairs had not already existed by the fifties of the first century B.C.E., when Cicero faced a Jewish audience while he was conducting the defence of Valerius Flaccus. We know virtually nothing of the history of the development of the various Roman congregations whose names have been preserved; there are eleven of these, not counting some doubtful claimants.[2] It seems natural to suppose that those called the Hebrews, Augustesians and Agrippesians were among the earliest, and the relatively early origin of 'the Hebrews' might seem to be confirmed by the fact that some of its members were buried in the Monteverde catacomb, which is the oldest of the five known Jewish cemeteries. But the Tripolitanian, Vernaclusian and Volumnesian communities also used this burial-place.

The synagogue's chief officer appears to have been the ἀρχισυνάγωγος ('head of the synagogue'). It is to be noted that the Syriac and Aramaic translations of the Gospels render this title by the word רבי, (rabbi), hence it may be supposed that the head of the synagogue was the community's spiritual leader and scholarly authority. But Talmudic sources call holders of the title ראש הכנסת.[3] It is to be assumed that the head of the synagogue was appointed for life; nevertheless at Acmonia for instance, G. Turonius Cladus is (perhaps misleadingly) called ὁ διὰ βίου ἀρχισυνάγωγος, ('life-president'),[4] which could be theoretically interpreted to imply that the post was usually held for a definite period. It would appear—from the same Acmonia dedication—that there might be more than one head acting simultaneously. The account of Paul's reception at the synagogue at Antioch-in-

[1] *Legatio ad Gaium*, 156.
[2] See H. J. Leon, *The Jews of Ancient Rome* (1960), pp. 140-166, for a full list and discussion.
[3] Syriac Gospels - Krauss, *Synagogale Altertümer* (1922), 120; *M. Yoma*, 7:1 etc.
[4] *CII*, II, no. 766.

Pisidia shows that these men performed an introductory function in the life and worship of their congregations; here they invite the visitors to speak if they have 'any word of exhortation for the people'.[1] It is also the head of the synagogue who takes the intellectual initiative in the synagogue at Corinth against Paul's preaching.[2] The heads of the synagogue might, however, sometimes also fill other posts; in Rome one was (or had been) archon,[3] implying that he might also deal with secular practical problems; this is confirmed both at Aegina[4] and Acmonia,[5] where the heads of the synagogue superintend the rebuilding of their respective synagogues. The above-mentioned Roman official specifies, moreover, that he has discharged 'all the posts' in his congregation. The head's primary rôle in the congregation is confirmed by the Latin translation of his title—*princeps synagogae*[6] and by the fact that the Theodosian Code[7] recognized him as an *immunis* and as one of the synagogue's responsible official representatives.

The individual community was represented, for practical purposes, as we have seen, by a committee. At Rome this is never mentioned as a body, but its existence is inferred by the post of Gerousiarch, presumed to be its president. This inference is reasonable so long as we accept the very probable thesis that the officer was not, at Rome, the president of a 'federation' of synagogues and of its central Gerousia, a problem which will be discussed below. The practical importance of the gerousiarchy is perhaps to be perceived in the fact that it is never, in the records which we possess, bestowed upon young men, although it does appear to have been granted, at Bizye (Thrace),[8] to women.[9] Where the Roman congregations are concerned, the precise composition of the committee is problematic. In the capital, archons are mentioned with relative frequency, whereas 'elders' (πρεσβύτεροι) never appear, hence we are left uncertain on the question whether there were any distinctions between executive and ordinary members of the council. Elsewhere, elders appear in Italy,

[1] Acts 13:15.   [2] Acts 18:17.
[3] *CII*, I, no. 265 (Via Appia).
[4] *CII*, I, no. 722.
[5] *CII*, II, no. 766.
[6] Cf. *CII*, I, no. 681, (Sofia), *Joses archisynagogus et principalis*, which, however, is more likely to refer to the archisynagogus' membership of the municipal decurionate (cf. A. H. M. Jones, *The Later Roman Empire* II (1964), p. 731.
[7] 16, 8, 4; 13, 14.
[8] S. Krauss, op.cit., no. 87a.
[9] Cf. women *presbyteroi* at Venosa, Italy (*CII*, I, nos. 581, 590, 597).

Spain, Cyprus, Asia Minor[1] and (early) in Alexandria, where it would seem possible that in the Hellenistic period they were distinct from the archons. At Elche, at a late date, archons and elders are recorded together, showing that in some cases at least they were distinct, and it is to be supposed that the archons were the executive, although at Berenice of Cyrenaica they composed the entirety of the committee.

Among the epitaphs of the Roman communities the title of archon is the most frequent. With Justin Martyr, who wrote in the mid-second century, the word is generic for synagogue officials as a whole (οἱ ἄρχοντες τοῦ λαοῦ),[2] showing the extent to which they figured in the public affairs of the community, and doubtless in its contacts with the gentile world. In the fourth century the *Pseudo-Chrysostom*[3] states that the Jewish communities appoint (*designant*) their archons in the month of September, in other words, in the New Year or at Sukkot. This raises the question as to whether they were elected, and what was their term of office. The statement of the *Pseudo-Chrysostom* would indicate that appointment was annual, and that it was for a definite period would appear to be indicated by the special title ἄρχων διὰ βίου (archon for life) which occurs six times at Rome.[4] A limited term of office is further indicated by the epitaph of Eupsychus, who was twice archon, as well as ἄρχων πάσης τιμῆς (whatever that means) and φροντιστής (superintendent).[5] At Tlos in Asia Minor Ptolemaios commemorates his son who was archon 'among us Jews'[6] a phrase pointing in the same direction. On the other hand the occurrence at Rome of children who were entitled μελλάρχων,[7] i.e. 'archon designate' at the time of their death, shows that in given congregations or at a given period, the post may have become hereditary in certain families. Women, however, never appear in this capacity. On the question of election, on the other hand, we have virtually no information. But the fact that at Berenice the number of archons appears to have grown in the course of sixty years (above) presumably with the growth of the community, suggests that the character of the office was regarded as representative and therefore elective.

Despite the generic use of the term by Justin, the archons are not

[1] *CII* I, no. 663; *CII* II, 735 (Golgoi); 739 (Smyrna); *Ep. Aristeas*, 310 (Alexandria).
[2] *Dial.*, 73:5; 72:4.
[3] *De nativ. S. Ioannis*; the relevant passage may be found in Schürer III, p. 86.
[4] *CII*, I, nos. 266, 398, 416, 417, 480, 503.
[5] *CII*, I, no. 337.   [6] *CII*, II, no. 757.   [7] *CII*, I, no. 85.

mentioned by the later imperial Roman constitutions, which speak only of the elders.[1] As has been made clear in the discussion of the latter, the archons appear to have belonged to the executive committee in Roman synagogues and probably in Alexandria; at Berenice they were board and executive in one. It is nevertheless debated whether in Rome more than one archon functioned for the annual term, since otherwise the appearance of many more archons would be expected.[2] The statistical argument, however, is of doubtful value, since we possess only a fraction of the epitaphs that must have existed. If, however, it is accepted as a hypothesis that only one archon functioned annually (a possibility which leaves us ignorant of what was the position of life-archons in the same congregation)—then we need to know who, besides the Gerousiarch, constituted the rest of the executive. It seems difficult to exclude the 'head of the synagogue' and the 'clerk' (γραμματεύς) from the quorum; further it is unwise to go, but the absence of any generic name for council members would favour the assumption that all of them bore independent titles.

The duties of the archons appear to have been predominantly the secular aspects of synagogue business. They sign a contract at Porto[3] and lease the synagogue's water-supply at Arsinoe in Egypt.[4] An archon is active in the rebuilding of the synagogue of Dura-Europos.[5] These men are among the contributors to communal projects, as at Berenice, where they subscribe to repair the synagogue, as also at Porto. Probably the exarchon, recorded only once, at Rome,[6] was simply one who had discharged the function of archon. Attempts to see in him the head of the 'Federation of Synagogues', at any rate, on the analogy of the Christian term ἔξαρχος which was applied to the head of a group of monasteries, seem ill-supported, since the only known bearer of the Jewish title died at the age of twenty-eight.

The γραμματεύς is the functionary most frequently mentioned in the Roman inscriptions after the archon. He is not a scribe but a clerk, but the position is one of honour and is always filled by mature men. Nevertheless, the fact that he is rarely recorded as filling any other post shows that he was an employee rather than an elected official. But at Arnaut Keni (Bithynia), a γραμματεύς is also found fulfilling

---

[1] C. Theod. 16, 8, 2 etc. [2] Leon, op.cit., pp. 175-6.
[3] CII, I, no. 533, line 2. [4] See p. 466, n. 2.
[5] CII, II, no. 828a. [6] CII, I, pp. 317, 465.

the function of ἐπιστάτης τῶν παλαίων (see p. 484). The title is however in two instances conferred on children, implying that it carried respect and might be transmitted from father to son as a hereditary skill. One assumes that the duties involved records and the correspondence required in dealing with other communities and with the gentile authorities.[1] We have no evidence on the term of office of the γραμματεύς, but it is natural to suppose that it was filled under normal circumstances for life.

The hazzan of the synagogue figures under the name hyperetes once in the Roman epitaphs.[2] In Alexandria he leads the benedictions among a congregation so large that his direction is needed.[3] It is also clear from Josephus[4] and from Epiphanius[5] that he was called ὑπηρέτης in Greek, and was a Levite. Epiphanius,[6] the Gospels[7] and an inscription from Apamea, Syria,[8] show that the hazzan was identical with the deacon prominent in the Christian communities (which took as their organizational model the Jewish synagogue); the latter was responsible for care of the sick and assistance to the poor.[9] The hazzan is probably the equivalent of the νακόρος mentioned as the official of a Jewish prayer-house in Alexandrou-Nesos (p. 465). Besides keeping order during the service, the hazzanim made announcements. Though their functions more nearly approached those of the modern *shamash* (beadle), they were learned men, at least in Judaea and served on the town councils.[10] They also administered corporal punishment when it was inflicted by the community court.[11]

The function of the προστάτης who appears in some communities is controversial.[12] One opinion[13] makes him the equivalent of the

---

[1] As instances in which written documents were required by Jewish communities of the period, may be cited the purchase of burial plots (Porto); the receipt of donations (Aegina); the conduct of litigation (Antioch); the presentation of complaints to the city or to the central authorities (Cyrene); the drafting of honorary inscriptions (Berenice; Alexandria; Acmonia); manumissions (Panticapaeum; Oxyrhynchus).

[2] *CII*, I, no. 172.

[3] *T. Sukkah*, 4:6 etc.

[4] Jos. *Ant.*, IV, 214.

[5] *Haer.*, 30:11.

[6] Ibid.

[7] Luke 4:20; John 7:32. Cf. Krauss, *Synagogale Altertümer* (1922), pp. 126 ff.

[8] *CII*, II, no. 805.

[9] H. Lietzmann, *A History of the Early Church* I, p. 145 (Eng. 1937).

[10] Krauss, op.cit., pp. 123 ff.

[11] M. *Makkot*, 3:12; Krauss, op.cit., p. 125.

[12] Leon, op.cit., pp. 191-2; Juster I, p. 433; Krauss, op.cit., p. 145.

[13] Krauss, loc. cit.

gerousiarch. At Xenephyris in Egypt in the second century B.C.E. two figure as the chief officers of a synagogue,[1] and in a document of 10 B.C.E.[2] a Jew appears as the προστάτης of a loan society. The title was borne by an officer of the Antioch community (p. 485). The term is on one occasion applied to the high priests of Judaea[3] (προστασία τοῦ ἔθνους-leadership of the nation). Its sense here must have been essentially 'representative of the nation to the government' —and vice versa—clearly in no necessarily democratic sense. In common Greek terminology the title was applied to the chairman or president of a considerable variety of committees or councils, political, religious or secular, but it also appears in the sense of a 'champion' or patron, and it is with this meaning that Schürer[4] considered it was used in Jewish institutions, implying the function of legal representation of the community to the outer world.

The φροντιστής is an important and responsible official, to judge by the fact that in one case at Rome, Eupsychus, who had held this post,[5] had also been twice archon, and archon πάσης τιμῆς (of all dignity). The office may have been held also at one of the synagogues of Alexandria or it may have been one of the functions discharged within the central administrative machinery of the Alexandrian community as a whole. At Side in Pamphylia,[6] this officer actually repairs the synagogue building, which means that if his function was technical, he was probably, at least in some places, a wealthy person. The most general use of the term in pagan literature and epigraphy in Roman times[7] is that of a steward, curator or general manager, more especially in the practical sphere, and in at least two cases the men associated with the term were in charge of temples,[8] —in the last case probably concerned with the building of the temple.

The *Patres Synagogae* appear to have borne an entirely honorary rank. They were nevertheless presumably men of importance, probably by virtue of general standing, personality and wealth, since the *Theodosian Code*[9] classes them among the *immunes*. Women also enjoyed this

---

[1] *CPJ*, III, Appendix I, no. 1441.
[2] *CPJ*, II, no. 149.
[3] Jos. *Ant.*, XII, 161.
[4] III, 89.
[5] *CII*, I, no. 337.
[6] *CII*, II, no. 781.
[7] See Liddell and Scott, *Greek-English Lexicon* (1940), ad loc.
[8] *IGR* I, no. 1167, C4: Φροντιστοῦ ἱεροῦ ᾿Αφροδίτης *SEG*, XIX, no. 882: ῾Ιεροσύνη καὶ φροντιστίᾳ Σαβίνου κτλ.
[9] 16, 8, 4.

honour as *matres synagogae*.[1] In Rome each appears attached to his own synagogue, but Mniaseas, a Roman Jew, is πατήρ συναγωγίων (father of synagogues) (*sic*),[2] and Veturia Paulina of Rome, was successively or simultaneously 'Mother' of two congregations, the Campesians and the Volumnesians.[3] Although the position did not, so far as we know, involve specific duties, it is probable enough that it was one of patronage, implying either the rendering of material and monetary aid to the synagogue or to the needy. Moreover, in various cases bearers of the title had discharged responsible functions in their communities before receiving the final honour,[4]

A less frequent post is that of reader, known at Nicomedia in Bithynia as ἀναγνώστης.[5] The post presumably existed in those congregations where knowledge of Hebrew had become restricted, but whether it was a paid or honorary function is unknown.

Some communities—especially the larger—certainly possessed, beside the synagogue itself, various functional institutions which imply the existence of other employees of the organization. Jerome makes it certain[6] that they possessed libraries (from which he appears to have appropriated books in contravention of the fifth commandment), and archives have been referred to in the present chapter. Schools are implied by archaeological considerations as well as by the strong Jewish tradition of child-education; and their existence is supported in Rome by inscriptions recording a διδάσκαλος καὶ νομομαθής (teacher and student of law)[7] and a νομωδ[ιδάσκαλος] (teacher of law).[8] Whether Mniaseas the μαθητὴς σοφῶν (disciple of the sages)[9] was salaried by the community, is unknown. At Antioch we have the record of the existence of a Jewish hospital in the fourth century, (above), although we do not know if it existed before that time. An institution for care of the aged is evidenced at Dokimeion (Phrygia) by an inscription (above); unfortunately the inscription could be either Jewish or Christian. But while its formulation could belong to either community, there is nothing distinctively Christian about it, whereas many Jewish parallels of the formula can be cited in Asia Minor.

One problem exceeds in importance the details of organization in each individual synagogue, and that is the much debated question,

---

[1] E.g. *CII*, I, p. 523. [2] *CII*, I, no. 508. [3] Leon, pp. 157, 166, 188, 254.
[4] E.g. *CII*, I, no. 494. [5] *CII*, II, no. 798.
[6] Jerome, *Ep.* 36,1; *Praef. in Esther*, Migne, *PL*, XXVIII, 1433: Librum Esther... quem ego de archivis Iudaeorum relevans.
[7] *CII*, I, no. 333. [8] Ibid., no. 201. [9] Ibid., no. 508.

whether the Roman community possessed a central federative in-stitution which represented or controlled the various synagogues of the city. Opinions have been divided on the point;[1] the arguments put forward *pro* or *contra* have on the whole been unconvincing on both sides, partly because the evidence is not sufficient to furnish material for a decision.[2] The main evidence in favour of the existence of the 'Federation of Synagogues' is constituted by the inscriptions mentioning respectively an *archon alti ordinis*,[3] archons described as πάσης τιμῆς,[4] and an archon πασης τεσσιμεν (*sic*—the words are clearly corrupt).[5] The expression πάσης τιμῆς (of all dignity) is so vague, in my view, as to offer no evidence on the point at issue, and the last mentioned expression is obscure. The term *alti ordinis*, on the other hand, could refer either to an *ordo* in the sense of a representative body, or to rank in the sense of 'class' or 'degree', in which case it becomes too general to provide any information. We are therefore compelled to fall back on other considerations in order to weigh the possibilities of the existence of a federal body.

Philo has an interesting observation which may have some bearing on the question. He writes in reference to the Jews of Rome: 'But despite this he did not expel them from Rome or deprive them of their citizenship (τὴν αὐτῶν πολιτείαν) because they remembered their Jewish *politeia* too' (ὅτι καὶ τῆς Ἰουδαϊκῆς ἐφρόντιζον).[6] Πολιτεία is here clearly *civitas* (citizen rights), and the noun to be supplied after Ἰουδαϊκῆς, must therefore imply a similar concept. It has been noted elsewhere, (p. 439), that by πολιτεία Philo appears to mean with reference to Alexandria, both the general body of Jewish privi-leges and the organization which put them into action. It would follow that in reference to Rome he was thinking of a similar organi-zation. We may recollect that the term πολιτεία was used in the fourth century by John Chrysostom for the federation of the Jewish com-munities of Antioch, referred to in Latin as a *universitas* (above, p. 485).

Two other considerations might be cited in favour of the view that Roman Jewry possessed a central organization. One is that various members of Roman synagogues were buried in cemeteries alongside

---

[1] Schürer, op.cit., III, p. 81; Juster I, pp. 420 ff.; n. 3; Krauss, op.cit., pp. 137-40.
[2] For a summary of the opposing schools, Leon, pp. 168-70.
[3] *CII*, I, no. 470.
[4] Ibid., nos. 85, 324.
[5] Ibid., no. 216.
[6] *Legatio ad Gaium*, 157.

members of other congregations. Members of no less than eight communities are represented at Monteverde, the Scenian community
buried a member at the Via Nomentana catacomb, and seven Siburen-
sians were laid to rest in the same burial place. There must of course
have been a measure of fluidity between one congregation and another,
but evidently cemeteries were not necessarily connected with individual
synagogues, and the possibility arises that an independent חברה
קדשה existed that was responsible for the allocation of burial-places
and their arrangement on behalf of the entire Roman community.
The second fact of interest is the existence at Rome, in the early
second century of the current era, of the court of R. Mattatiah Harash,[1] which was clearly of more than local importance,[2] and would
certainly have tried cases from all the Roman congregations. Viewed
independently, Paul's reference to the 'heads of the Jews' whom he
invited to visit him in prison[3] would prove little; taken together with
the above facts it may be significant, though none of the three items
of information is decisive.

In this context, moreover, it is desirable to compare the Roman community with the communities of Alexandria, Antioch and Apamea
(Syria). The first two towns certainly possessed 'federations' which
combined all their synagogues; the same was less certainly the case
at Apamea.[4] Both Alexandria and Antioch were royal foundations
whose populations were heterogeneous from the first, hence semi-
autonomous associations of non-Greeks would have been inevitable
and even necessary to them almost from the beginning. Rome on the
other hand was ancient when the first groups of *peregrini* took root in
the city, and the Jews constituted one of the newest groups amongst
them. Moreover a very large number of them were slaves who obtained Roman citizenship on emancipation. It follows that a federative organization of alien groups would have been less necessary or
welcome to a structure which possessed a much greater readiness for
and power of rapid assimilation of new groups than the Greek city.
The latter, tending to safeguard more closely the exclusivity of its

---

[1] *T. B. Sanhedrin*, 32b.
[2] See chap. VIII.
[3] Acts 28:17.
[4] M. Schwabe, *Y. Levi Memorial Vol.* (1949), pp. 216 ff. (Heb.), saw in *CII*,
II, no. 804 from Apamea evidence that the city possessed several synagogues,
and a central council, as three ἀρχισυνάγωγοι and one gerousiarch are mentioned.
But, as we have seen, one synagogue might have several ἀρχισυνάγωγοι, hence
the evidence is not decisive.

citizen body, was ready to view with equanimity the existence of parallel groups. It is therefore *a priori* less likely that Roman Jewry was organized in a federal framework, although there exist some fragments of information which, though not decisive, compel us to leave the question open.

There remains one matter of moment requiring comment, namely, to whom did the Jewish synagogues and associated communal properties belong? It is a fair inference, not specifically stated, to the best of my knowledge, in reference to the Diaspora, that most of the synagogue buildings and their appurtenances were the property of the community that used them. Thus in Ptolemaic Egypt, where the Schedia prayer-house is dedicated to the sovereign by οἱ ᾿Ιουδαῖοι (the Jews),[1] it may safely be assumed that the building was communal property. When a lintel bears the inscription [συν]αγωγὴ ῾Εβρ[αίων] (the synagogue of the Hebrews), at Corinth,[2] this seems equally probable. The same may be inferred at places where the building has been erected or repaired by the joint contributions of a number of members of the congregation and by communal funds, as at Aegina in the fourth century; here the contribution of Theodorus the 'head of the synagogue' is supplemented by revenues and gifts.[3] At Berenice, Cyrenaica, in the reign of Nero, the synagogue is reconditioned with the aid of contributions from members of the congregation.[4] In the case of Acmonia, the redecoration and repairs of the synagogue are carried out by two ἀρχισυνάγωγοι and an archon and obviously at their expense, as they are conspicuously honoured for their work by the community,[5] yet it is unclear whether the building was communal property, since it was built by Iulia Severa, and whether one of the three philanthropists (Turonius Cladus) repairing it was her kinsman or descendant. On the other hand communal proprietorship may be accepted in relation to those buildings to which well-to-do members of the congregation contribute individual parts, as at Carian Hyllarima, in whose synagogue Aurelius Eusambatios and his wife dedicated a door-lintel,[6] or at Mantinea, whose πρόναος (forehall) was donated by the 'father of the community'.[7]

A more complex situation may have existed at Sardis, where the city

---

[1] *CPJ*, III, Appendix I, no. 1440.   [2] *CII*, I, no. 718.   [3] *CII*, I, no. 722.
[4] *SEG*, XVII, no. 823; *La Parola del Passato*, XII (1957), pp. 133 ff.; *BJPES*, (1961), pp. 167 ff.
[5] *CII*, II, 766.
[6] *Hellenica* III, 105, n. 5; XI-XII, 435.
[7] *IG* v, 2, no. 295.

granted the land for Jewish prayer and residence.[1] It is here at least possible that the land was leased by the city rather than sold to the community, all the more so since in the third century, as we have seen, the city's gymnasium was erected in close association with the synagogue. Nor is there any doubt that some synagogues were built by private individuals for the community, and that the former sometimes retained rights in the building. Such was the case at Stobi, Macedonia, in the fourth century,[2] where Claudius Tiberius Polycharmus reserves complete ownership for himself and his descendants, undertaking the perpetual maintenance of the roof of the upper storey. On the other hand there is fair evidence, at least in the Roman period, that synagogues could both acquire and receive property, implying that, even if they were not in communal proprietorship, they were administered by their officers who constituted a legal personality. Thus the Ostia community (which we may assume was identical with its synagogue) acquires a burial place for one of its gerousiarchs at the proposal of one of its officers.[3] A Jew of Tlos (Lycia) at the end of the first century C.E., erects a tomb for his son, archon of the community, and makes it over to the community 'so that it should belong to all the Jews'.[4] It would appear, indeed, that associations were not permitted to receive legacies until the reign of M. Aurelius;[5] but it seems clear, in the light of Julius Caesar's exemption of Jewish communities from his law prohibiting associations,[6] that Jewish *politeumata* were not *collegia*. This should be evident from the fact that their membership was determined by ethnic status and not by election, and that their regulations were to a large extent predetermined by Jewish law instead of being determined *ad hoc* on the creation of each community. Nor does the imperial chancellery's verdict under Caracalla forbidding the Antioch community to accept a legacy,[7] affect the question, since we do not know the circumstances of the case or the reasons for the judgment.

BIBLIOGRAPHY

Here again the basic material is to be found in SCHÜRER III, pp. 71-96 and in the chapter on local organization of the communities in Juster's

[1] Jos. *Ant.* XIV, 260. [2] *CII*, I, no. 694.
[3] *CII*, I, no. 533. [4] *CII*, II, no. 757.
[5] *Dig.*, 34, 5, 20, 12. [6] Jos. *Ant.* XIV, 215-6.
[7] *C. Just.*, I, 9, 1.

first volume, pp. 409-485. A general survey is given also by S. W. BARON, *The Jewish Community* I 1942, pp. 75-117; III, pp. 13-21. H. J. LEON, *The Jews of Ancient Rome*, 1960, pp. 167-194 summarizes the data deriving from inscriptions. Cf. also J. B. FREY, in the introductory chapters of his *Corpus Inscriptionum Iudaicarum* I, 1936. S. KRAUSS, *Synagogale Altertümer*, 1922, is still invaluable.

Chapter Ten
Private Law

I JEWISH PRIVATE LAW

Jewish law did not divide the legal norms into two spheres of private and public law. Even matters which are nowadays of public concern were dealt with in the form of private law. Thus the king's highway is just a form of servitude, to be treated and compared with other private right-of-way.[1] Likewise, much of what would now be criminal law is dealt with as a violation not of public but only of private interest. Causing grievous bodily harm, arson and burglary, for instance, are actionable only upon the claim of the victim, though there was no doubt that the public in general was concerned in these cases. When therefore we speak of Jewish private law, we read back a modern concept into the ancient sources, which should be done only as a kind of shorthand to circumscribe a number of subjects in one word.

Another classification is used by the sages. Among the various subject matters of the Torah they mention דינים i.e. claims *ex delicto* and *ex contractu*.[2] Sometimes the term is דיני ממונות (suits concerning property), as distinguished from the suits concerning fines, flogging or capital punishment. This term seems to exclude delicts, such as thefts and torts, and to be mainly concerned with contracts.[3]

The law of the family, on the other hand, nowadays forming part of private law, does not wholly belong to this sphere. True, a suit concerning a married woman's property certainly could be classified among the דיני ממונות. But impediments of marriage, to take another example, do not fit into this sphere. They are part of the עריות (rules of nakedness), listed together with the rules of the clean and unclean, i.e. with the ritual norms.[4]

Some of these rules derive from biblical law, while the majority have developed within the framework of the Oral Law. Even the latter norms were often ascribed to divine legislation, but those of them which were known to be of late origin were held to be rabbinic ordinances of decisions. Sometimes a rule was simply derived from custom or from a non-Jewish source which can still be traced.

---

[1] *M.Baba Bathra* 6:7.
[3] *M. Sanhedrin* 1:1.
[2] *M. Hagigah* 1:8.
[4] *M.Hagigah* 1:8.

Originally דינים were the actions in court rather than the norms applied
therein. Hence the term came to include the whole process[1] and the
verb דין meant judicial and even academic argument.[2] Finally,
דין became a synonym of logical deduction, especially by way of inference *a minori ad majus*.[3] The reason for this semantic phenomenon
seems to be that part of the Oral Law, particularly the logical inferences, was developed in the law-courts.

Cases of private law could be brought before four different courts.
During the Second Temple period cases would mostly be brought
before the local archons. Even after the destruction of the Temple
many actions were adjudicated by local arbitrators.[4] Sometimes
petition was made to the gentile authorities for their decision according to Roman or even according to Jewish law. However, the sages
insisted on the exclusive jurisdiction of the rabbinical courts. Anyone
who turned to any other court was accused of acting illegally, even
though the judgment in such a court may have been in agreement
with the rabbinical law. The judicial office was taken as part of the
right of teaching the law reserved to ordained rabbis, so that laymen
and gentiles were excluded.[5]

Persons

Talmudic law is based on the principle of personality, i.e. rights and
duties depend upon the traditional law of a man's fathers rather
than upon the norms of the state in which he lives. The law is part of
the divine covenant with the People of Israel and stress is put upon
the distinction between the 'Sons of the Covenant' and gentiles.[6] Therefore, personal law is particularly important in the Jewish legal system.
Rights and duties are generally limited to men. However, by way of
personification certain rules are applied also to non-human beings.
Thus the property dedicated to the Temple is called 'that of the
Exalted', referring to ownership of God himself.[7] The acquisition of
divine property is thus regulated by the ordinary law, though not
equalized exactly to that of ordinary persons. On the other hand, a
beast having unnatural carnal relations with, or killing, a human
being is tried by a court of law just as the person who is a party to

[1] *M. Sanhedrin* 4:1.
[2] *M. Rosh ha-Shanah* 2:9; *Eduyoth* 1:10.
[3] *M. Yadaim* 3:2. [4] *M. Sanhedrin* 3:1.
[5] *Mekhilta, Nezikin* 1. [6] *M. Baba Kamma* 1:3.
[7] *M. Kiddushin* 1:6.

the offence.[1] But these are exceptions based upon biblical provisions and ancient traditions.

In general, the law applied to human beings only, i.e. to persons between birth and death. According to the original view, the embryo is considered as a part of the mother, without rights and duties of its own. The soul is said to have entered into the body at birth,[2] and 'If a woman was condemned to be put to death they may not wait until she has given birth, but if she had already sat on the birth-stool they wait until she has given birth'.[3]

An exceptional position is, however, given to the embryo for the purposes of succession. The unborn son of a priest is already considered owner of his father's slaves, but he is not yet in the position of an ordinary priest who may let his slaves eat from the heave-offerings.[4] The biblical longing of every father to have a son to perpetuate his name made the sages create this exception.

A controversy arose also in the case of the owner of a female slave who had liberated her on condition that the child in her womb should remain a slave. According to one view, the position of the embryo was like hers, i.e. free, while other sages held the embryo to be a slave.[5]

All rights and duties of a person lapse at his death. A creditor, for instance, cannot claim payment from the deceased person's estate if he has not taken care from the beginning to have a real lien. Marriage, likewise, comes to an end at death, except for the dead man's right to the perpetuation of his name, which, however, is rather a right of the family than of the dead individual.

But re-marriage of the wife is permitted only after legal proof of the death had been obtained, and no presumption can fulfil the lack of such proof. Thus 'concerning [them that live in] a town that is besieged, or [that travel in] a ship storm-tossed at sea, or a man that is gone forth to be judged—these must be presumed to be still living; but concerning [them that lived in] a town that was overcome after a siege, or [them that travelled in] a ship that was lost at sea, or a man that has been condemned to death, the more stringent rulings for the dead apply to them.'[6] The more stringent rule for the living, in these cases, prohibits the remarriage of the deserted wife, while

---

[1] *M. Sanhedrin* 1:4.
[2] *Genesis Rabba* 34, 10, ed. Theodor-Albeck, p. 321.
[3] *M. Arakhin* 1:4.   [4] *P. T. Yebamoth* VII, 4, 8b.
[5] *T. B. Kiddushin* 69a.   [6] *M. Gittin* 3:4.

the more stringent rule of the dead prevents the wife, if she is the daughter of an Israelite who married a priest, from eating the heave-offering by virtue of her husband's right. In the middle of the first century C.E., however, the onus of proof was lessened so as to mitigate the fate of soldiers' wives: 'Rabban Gamaliel remembered that certain men were killed at Tel Arza and Rabban Gamaliel the Elder suffered their wives to marry again on the evidence of one witness.'[1] But the court was never granted discretion in the declaration of death or in invoking circumstantial evidence.

While the rabbinical law was the personal law of the Jews, the Babylonian sage Samuel proclaimed at the beginning of the third century that 'the law of the realm is law' at least concerning taxes and other public duties.[2] Where a sage was approached to arbitrate between gentiles, he would certainly apply only the law of the realm. Perhaps he would do so even if the gentile was sued by a Jew. On the other hand norms of Jewish law were often used also with regard to non-Jewish parties, and only exceptional provisions of Jewish law were said to be inapplicable to gentiles.[3] As a reaction to the Roman persecution, the sages did not grant legal remedies to gentile plaintiffs against Jewish defendants, but morally the Jewish defendant was asked to indemnify the wronged person.

Where Jewish women sued under Greek law, they had to be represented by a guardian, but no such disability existed under Jewish law.[4] 'Scripture equalized woman and man for all legal actions mentioned in the law.'[5] Only a minor daughter was under her father's *potestas*, allowing her sale and her marrying off. Even this right was limited by moral considerations, and a father was asked not to give his daughter in marriage until she made her own choice.[6]

After the father's death, the *potestas* of giving the minor daughter in marriage passed to the mother or brother. But when coming of age, the girl could protest against such a marriage and gain her freedom by a unilateral declaration.[7] Another result of parental power was the father's right to his minor daughter's earnings, though not to the usufruct of her property.[8]

The latter right was, however, accorded to the husband with regard to the dowry. If the goods had been listed in the marriage contract,

---

[1] *M. Yebamoth* 16:7.
[2] *T. B. Baba Kamma* 113a.
[3] *T. B. Abodah Zarah* 71b.
[4] *CPJ* nos 19, 149.
[5] *T. B. Kiddushin* 35a.
[6] *T. B. Kiddushin* 41a.
[7] *M. Yebamoth* 13:1-2.
[8] *M. Ketuboth* 4:4.

the husband could even take the capital for himself, the contract guaranteeing the restoration of the given value in case of divorce or widowhood. Only those goods specially given to the woman 'On condition that the husband have no right over them' are fully at the wife's disposal.[1]

Since the majority of wives did not own goods of the latter category, it could be said of them that the injury caused by them was a bad debt, for married women usually had no property to pay for the damage, and the plaintiff would have to wait for their divorce or widowhood in order to collect his due.[2] On the other hand the husband guaranteed his wife's dues to the sanctuary and perhaps other debts as well.[3] True, these disabilities applied only to married women but not to women as such, and were rather the result of the marriage contract. But even unmarried women were subject to restrictions on the assumption that they were not capable of fulfilling certain functions like men. Women, for instance, are not qualified to bear witness,[4] to hold public office, or even to be guardian to minors.[5] According to the rules of succession in Numbers 27, females do not inherit as long as there are males of the same degree. Moreover, the husband was given the right of succession to his wife, but the wife was not given the corresponding rights.[6] It was usual to cite Psalm 45:14, 'the King's daughter is all glorious within' to show that all daughters of Israel should modestly remain at home.[7]

A lack of capacity to perform legal acts existed on the part of minors. Biblical law, obviously, applied to the people who were able to go forth to war and to take part in public affairs. Talmudic law, too, knew the difference between the adult and the minor, but originally no clear-cut age-limit was fixed to distinguish between the two. The general idea regarding minors as well as deaf-mutes and lunatics was to consider them incapable of such acts as were beyond their faculties and capable of those which belonged to their range of experience. Though as a matter of principle all the three categories, the deaf-mute, the insane and the minor, are not qualified, ['the deaf-mute person] may communicate by movements of the mouth and be communicated with by movements of the mouth in matters concerned with movable property. In matters concerned with movable property

[1] *M. Nedarim* 11:8. [2] *M. Baba Kamma* 8:4.
[3] *T. Ketuboth* 4:11. [4] *M. Shebuoth* 4:1.
[5] *T. Terumoth* 1:11. [6] *M. Baba Bathra* 8:2.
[7] *T. B. Shebuoth* 30a.

a purchase or sale effected by children is valid.'[1] Thus the sages accorded them capacity in everyday matters on the assumption that they had the necessary understanding for these matters. No such consideration existed with regard to liability in tort: 'It is an ill thing to knock against a deaf-mute, an imbecile, or a minor: he that wounds them is culpable, but if they wound others they are not culpable.'[2]

For the same reason there was no general age-limit for capacity, but the various commandments and norms had each its special criterion on minors. The guiding principle was always the actual ability to perform the act; he who was able to do so was considered to have reached his majority for the purpose of that particular commandment or norm. A general criterion, viz. physical maturity, was created during the discussion of the levirate marriage. Both that marriage and the alternative ceremony of 'unshoeing' need that maturity, therefore only a maiden who has the prescribed signs of sexual maturity is qualified for them.

This specific age-limit was then extended to apply to commandments in general so that coming of age meant about thirteen years for the male and about twelve-and-a-half for the female.[3]

The position of the slave depended upon his origin. A child of a non-Jewish mother was called a Canaanite slave, to describe his or her destiny to serve as foreseen by Noah in his curse. Such a slave had to be converted to Judaism in the form used for free-born proselytes, and thereby became part of the owner's family.

Within the family the Canaanite slave is, of course, under the *potestas* of the head of the family, and cannot therefore be liable to fulfil certain ritual acts which are dependent on a specific time.[4] The commandment of Exodus 23:14 and Deuteronomy 16:16, on the pilgrimage to the sanctuary for instance, does not include women, slaves that have not been freed and children.[5] Likewise, women and slaves may take a Nazirite vow, but 'greater stringency applies to women than to slaves, since one may compel his slave [to break the vow] but one cannot compel his wife. Greater stringency applies to slaves than to women, since a man may revoke his wife's vows but he cannot revoke those of his slave.[6] The status of slaves is also similar to that of married women with regard to torts. Of both it was said that their injury was 'bad'; if they caused injury to others they were not liable, while

[1] *M. Gittin* 5:7.
[2] *M. Baba Kamma* 8:4.
[3] *M. Niddah* 6:11.
[4] *M. Baba Metzia* 1:5; *T. B. Hagigah* 4a.
[5] *M. Hagigah* 1:1.
[6] *M. Nazir* 9:1.

others who injured them were liable.[1] The Sadducees, therefore, put a vicarious liability for the slave's act upon his owner, but their view was opposed by the Pharisees.[2] Later on both women and slaves were held liable, but payment was deferred till divorce or manumission respectively.[3] According to biblical law, the infliction of grievous bodily harm by the owner disciplining his slave caused the latter's liberation.[4]

Slaves could have no *connubium* with legitimate sons or daughters of Israel. Particularly difficult was the position of a person who was half-slave and half-freedman, for he could marry neither a slave nor an ordinary Jew. Therefore, according to the School of Shammai, the owner was compelled to liberate his part for an undertaking that the slave would pay half of the price at a later date.[5]

As an exception to the patriarchal system of descent, the child of a female slave, like that of a gentile woman, takes the status of his mother. The reason given for this rule is the absence of *connubium* between the child's parents.[6] The child's father was, therefore, not linked to his mother: on the contrary, he was supposed to separate from her immediately. The equalization of the status of mother and child was meant to induce him to do so.

For the transfer of slaves the same form was used as for sale of immovables, namely payment, deed or occupancy.[7] This was probably a result of the fact that human beings were comparable with immovables rather than with chattels. According to later views, however, the legal position of slaves was sometimes assimilated to that of movables.[8] Until the end of the second century C.E., liberation of slaves was not uncommon, but the Babylonian sage Mar Samuel interpreted an opinion of Akiba ben Josef as a prohibition of the liberation of slaves.[9] Besides the manumission *ex lege* in compensation for bodily harm, as already mentioned, the slave would gain his freedom by payment of his value or by deed.[10] It was not clear which of the two forms could be used between the owner and the slave without the assistance of a third person and in which case such an intervention was necessary. This need reflected the assumption that even during his liberation the slave was not a person and could not act on his own behalf.

---

[1] *M. Baba Kamma* 8:4.
[2] *M. Yadaim* 4:7.
[3] *M. Baba Kamma* 8:4.
[4] *T. B. Kiddushin* 24a.
[5] *M. Gittin* 4:5.
[6] *M. Kiddushin* 3:12.
[7] *M. Kiddushin* 1:3.
[8] *P. T. Kiddushin* 1, 3, 59d.
[9] *T. B. Gittin* 38b.
[10] *M. Kiddushin* 1:3.

Other forms of liberation, though mentioned only in the third century C.E., were dedication to the sanctuary, abandonment,[1] *vindicta* (touching with the liberating-rod), wearing the headdress of a freedman, or imperial forms of liberation.[2] The owner's intention of liberating the slave may be inferred from various acts, such as making the slave sole heir,[3] or allowing him to do certain acts which are incompatible with servile status.[4]

Sometimes the slave is not manumitted but the owner is under an obligation of setting him free: 'If a man sold his bondman to a gentile or to anyone outside the Land [of Israel] he goes forth a freedman.'[5] Likewise, a will including an obligation upon the heirs that they liberate a slave will be enforced by the court.[6]

If the slave is of Jewish origin, he has been taken into bondage for his inability to pay a debt or to restore some stolen property. The acquisition may take place through payment or by deed but not by occupancy only.[7] That means that the possessor of a Hebrew slave must always prove his title and cannot, as is the case with the Canaanite slave, rely on his possession. A Jewish female slave, moreover, is sold by her father for eventual marriage either with the purchaser or with one of his sons. Therefore, if this implied condition is not fulfilled at a reasonable time, i.e. at her coming of age, she must be freed *ex lege*.[8]

Hebrew male and female slaves, as far as they still existed in the Second Temple period, are not actually slaves, but rather servants. They must be treated like a free person and their status in law and religion is similar to that of an ordinary Israelite. Where a Hebrew bondman has been sold to repay his theft, his owner may give him a Canaanite slave for a wife. After having worked for six years the Hebrew bondman is entitled to freedom, but he may agree to continue in service until the Jubilee year.[9]

Talmudic law did not recognize the legal personality of corporations, but special norms were applied to the councils of citizens, of a neighbourhood, of the members of the synagogue and trade unions. The market, the baths and the synagogue were considered common property of the local townsfolk, while the Temple area and the inter-

[1] *T. B. Gittin* 38b.
[2] *P. T. Gittin* IV, 4, 45d; *T. B. Gittin* 20a.
[3] *M. Peah* 3:8.
[4] *T. B. Gittin* 40a.
[5] *M. Gittin* 4:6.
[6] *T. B. Gittin* 40a.
[7] *M. Kiddushin* 1:2.
[8] *M. Kiddushin* 1:2.
[9] Ex. 21:2-11 and *Mekhilta de R. Ishmael* ad loc. (ed. Horowitz-Rabin pp. 247 ff.).

urban water cisterns were the property of a larger entity, 'all those who came back from Babylonia.'[1] While the ordinary partnership has no character of a legal person, but represents merely the totality of the partners, an undivided estate is considered, for certain purposes, as the continuation of the deceased person. Thus where in the undivided estate ten heads of cattle were born, one tenth was to be sacrificed,[2] while such an obligation did not fall upon an ordinary herding partnership.[3]

Finally, under the heading of persons, mention must be made of the law of agency. Although rights and duties are usually dependent upon a person's acts, they can also be the result of the acts of another person, if that person is authorized to perform such acts. Women, slaves and minors, for instance, are often included in the act of the paterfamilias who acts on their as well as on his own behalf. Thus a man may offer a half-shekel to the sanctuary on behalf of his wife, slave or minor son without being formally authorized by them to act as their agent.[4] Accordingly a man may act by means of his wife, slave or child, their hand being considered to be a mere extension of his own. Thus, 'What is found by a man's son or daughter that are minors, what is found by his Canaanitish bondman or bondwoman, and what is found by his wife, belong to him.'[5]

In the course of the Temple service there was, moreover, need for an agency between people, each of whom was *sui iuris*. The priests fulfilled their function as agents of the Israelites, dealing with their offerings on their behalf. The local synagogue used to send the annual tax of the half-shekel by way of delegates, who dealt on their behalf with the Temple collectors.[6] At prayers the congregation authorized the reader to be delegate to the public,[7] i.e. 'the agent of the community fulfills the obligation that rests upon the many'.[8]

The rule that 'a person's agent is [qualified] like himself', applying at the celebration of marriage as well as in ordinary contracts, thus seems to derive from the rules of ritual.[9] For that reason, unlike the ordinary contract, there was no need for a deed to make the agreement binding both on the principal and the agent. The authoritization is made by mere parol. Therefore the relation lasts only as long as both

---

[1] *M. Nedarim* 5:5.
[2] Lev. 27:32.
[3] *M. Bekhoroth* 9:3.
[4] *M. Shekalim* 1:6.
[5] *M. Baba Metzia* 1:5.
[6] *M. Shekalim* 2:1.
[7] *M. Berakoth* 5:5.
[8] *M. Rosh ha-Shanah* 4:9.
[9] *M. Kiddushin* 2:1; *T. B. Kiddushin* 41a.

parties are *ad idem*, but the agent may at any time cancel the agency by a unilateral decision and henceforth act on his own behalf only: 'If A said to B, that B should go and betroth on the behalf of A a certain woman, and B went and betrothed her to himself, she is betrothed (by B)...' In this case the agency has come to an end and the act is purely the agent's. Likewise the principal may retreat from his agent's act if the latter had acted against his mandate, against the principal's interest, or if he otherwise had assumed any liability on behalf of the principal.[1] For the same reason Talmudic law usually does not recognize any vicarious liability.[2] Only where the agent had converted goods to his own use on the orders of his principal, where he had stolen property of the sanctuary on the instigation of another, did a liability also fall on the principal. In a number of tort cases vicarious liability was introduced as a norm of 'celestial' as distinct from ordinary justice.

Sometimes a person may act on behalf of another without knowledge of the latter. This action is called 'advantage' (זכיה), and it is based on the assumption that everyone would agree to an advantage accruing purely to his benefit. It seems that this institute was originally used to benefit minors, who could neither act for themselves nor legally appoint an agent (beside the father or guardian, who are agents *ex lege*). In such cases, then, a person was held to be able to act on the minor's behalf, if it was merely an advantage without any liability attached. The self-styled agent could, for instance, receive a gift in favour of the minor but not sell or purchase on his behalf. At a later stage the same institute was used to give effect to a testamentary disposition in favour of an absent person.[3] Finally, the advantage accruing to a third person was permitted in all cases as an extension of the law of agency: 'they may act to another's advantage in his absence, but not to his disadvantage save in his presence.'[4]

The family

Talmudic family structure is based upon the biblical patriarchal system, which for its part is the continuation of the custom of the tribal age. Preference is given to males, within the family as well as in society. A person's status is determined by his descent and for this purpose the paternal rather than the maternal relationship is decisive.

---

[1] *T. B. Kiddushin* 42b.   [2] Ibid.
[3] *M. Baba Bathra* 9:7.   [4] *M. Gittin* 1:6.

This idea is realized both in the duty of family solidarity, redemption,[1] and the right of inheritance.[2] Originally, it seems, the father was entitled to deny his paternity even if the child was born within wedlock and, of course, to admit paternity if the child was born out of wedlock. A later view, however, limited this paternal right to preventing bastardization.[3] Talmudic law, indeed, reflects the transition from a larger to a more limited *patria potestas*. For the purposes of property law, minor sons are still under parental powers. Therefore 'what is found by a man's son or daughter that are minors, what is found by his Canaanitish bondman or bondwoman, and what is found by his wife, belong to him; but what is found by his son or daughter that are of age, what is found by his Hebrew bondman or bondwoman, and what is found by his wife whom he has divorced (even though he has not yet paid her her *Ketubah*), belong to them.'[4] The minor daughter, on the other hand, may be sold by her father as a bondwoman and may be given away in marriage.[5] Similarly the father may revoke the vows of his minor daughter,[6] and after betrothal he may do so together with her bridegroom.[7]

The income of sons as well as daughters from work or finds belongs to the father, but there does not exist a corresponding rule with regard to their income from property.[8] Probably this case was exceptional since few children had property of their own. On the other hand the law did not provide for the minor children's maintenance, the assumption being that this relationship would be settled according to tradition and within the family. Only during the second or third century C.E. a resolution was passed at Usha that everybody was to maintain his minor sons and daughters.[9] A father was, however, responsible for the legal and vocational education of his sons[10] and for the provision of a suitable dowry for his daughters.[11]

As in biblical law, polygamy, though permitted, was in practice an extraordinary exception. Among the great number of Talmudic sages there was none who had contracted a bigamous marriage. In some cases, though, a married man may have taken advantage of a female slave or have lived with a concubine.

The blood relationships mentioned in Leviticus 18 and 20 were a bar to

[1] *T. B. Yebamoth* 54b.
[2] *T. B. Baba Bathra* 109b.
[3] *M. Kiddushin* 4:8.
[4] *M. Baba Metzia* 1:5.
[5] *M. Ketuboth* 4:4.
[6] Num. 30:3-16.
[7] *M. Nedarim* 10:1.
[8] *M. Ketuboth* 4:4.
[9] *T. B. Ketuboth* 49b, 65b.
[10] *M. Kiddushin* 1:7.
[11] *M. Ketuboth* 6:6.

marriage, and any marriage contracted in contravention of these passages was void. Likewise, there could be no Jewish marriage between a Jew and a gentile.[1] Other impediments did not render the marriage void but were considered causes for divorce. A man could not marry his divorcee after her marriage to another person,[2] a woman guilty of adultery could neither stay with her husband nor marry the adulterer after her divorce.[3] A child of an adulterous relationship or a relationship in contravention of Leviticus 18, could not marry among families of legitimate descent.[4] A number of temporary impediments were prescribed to prevent any doubts in parentage and other impediments were added as a 'fence' to the biblical prohibitions. Castration and insanity were bars to marriage; in the former case, however, the father could act on behalf of his daughter (see above). A special enactment recognized marriages of deaf-mutes.[5]

The matrimonial bond is created in two phases, by 'acquisition' of the bride and by taking her into the marital home. Prior to the first ceremony the two families would agree on the material conditions of the young couple,[6] and the bridegroom used to 'appease' the bride to get her consent to the main engagement, the 'acquisition'. This 'acquisition' could take place in one of three forms. The ordinary case was that of payment of the bride-price or at least of a nominal part of it to the bride herself, or, if she were a minor, to her father (or mother or brother, if she had no father). Another form was by deed, made and delivered by the bridegroom. This form seems to have been in use where the bridegroom had no means to pay a bride-price or where he had a right to the bride (as in the marriage of Tobit). The third form, cohabitation, perhaps represents the Judaean custom, according to which the bridegroom lived in his father-in-law's house without any further wedding ceremony.[7]

The engagement could be made subject to a certain condition or with delayed effect, *mutatis mutandis* according to the rules on the disposition of immovables. The material elements of the 'acquisition', indeed, are almost identical with those used at the transfer of property, but the spiritual element put a decisive imprint upon the whole ceremony. This blessing and, consequently, the whole ceremony came to be known as the 'sanctification' of the bride. The engagement

[1] *M. Kiddushin* 3:12.
[2] Deut. 24:4.
[3] *M. Yebamoth* 2:8.
[4] *M. Kiddushin* 4:1.
[5] *M. Yebamoth* 14:1.
[6] *M. Ketuboth* 13:5.
[7] *M. Kiddushin* 1:1.

formula, moreover, used the same word together with the reference to 'the law of Moses and Israel'.

Although the bride lives in her father's house, she is already bound to the bridegroom, with all the duties of a married woman. The engagement can, therefore, only be cancelled with his consent and by an ordinary deed of divorce (גט). The introduction of the bride into the marital home under a special canopy formed the contents of the second ceremony, the nuptials. Again, the act was accompanied by a number of blessings, giving it a religious character.

The law of husband and wife was laid down in the marriage contract (כתובה). Instead of paying the bride-price in cash, the husband assigned the major part in the deed to be paid only at divorce or widowhood. According to an early regulation a minimum sum was required for the undertaking towards a virgin, and half of that amount for a widow or a divorcee. The husband, moreover, would add to this amount a gift on his part and assume the liability for his wife's perishable goods in a total sum payable at divorce or widowhood.

These goods, consequently, became the husband's property and were called goods in the marriage contract, or 'iron sheep'. The rest of the dowry consisted of immovables or other goods not secured in the said form. They were called מלוג the Accadian term for dowry, or 'goods entering and leaving [the marital home] together with her.' During the marriage these goods were under the husband's control including his right of usufruct for the benefit of the household. A third type of goods were those 'over which the husband has no control', either because they were given to the wife on that condition or because they were a gift from the husband.

According to Talmudic law the surviving husband was sole heir to his wife's estate. Therefore a common clause in the marriage contract provided that after the surviving husband's death the property of the wife should revert back to those of the husband's sons who are also sons of the wife. The surviving wife or daughters had a right to support from the estate.[1]

During marriage the husband had to have marital intercourse with his wife, and clothe her according to the most favoured standard of either spouse.[2] The wife, on the other hand, was under a strict obligation of marital fidelity, for any violation of this rule endangered the legitimacy of the man's offspring. She was bound to serve and obey the

[1] M. Ketuboth 4:11-12. [2] T. B. Ketuboth 61a.

husband according to law and custom, to render him her earnings and the fruits of her property.

Where the husband refused to fulfil his conjugal duties he could be fined by a weekly increase of his debt under the marriage contract. A corresponding procedure was used where the fault lay with the wife, in which case a weekly diminution of that amount was prescribed.[1] Originally, divorce was an arbitrary, unilateral act on the part of the husband. One of the reasons given for the cash payment of the bride-price having developed into a promise for the widow or divorcee, was precisely to protect the wife against a rash divorce.[2] While the School of Hillel thought that a husband needed no cause for the divorce, a pietist norm was preserved by the School of Shammai. The husband could not, according to this view, divorce his wife without having found some unchastity on her part.[3] It may be presumed that he was supposed to present this cause to some tribunal prior to the divorce ceremony. Moreover, an insane wife was not to be divorced and left without protection,[4] neither could the husband divorce his wife while she was in captivity before having redeemed her. According to biblical law a man who had raped a virgin and married her, or one who had falsely accused his bride of unchastity, could never divorce her.[5]

A number of causes were recognized to justify an action for divorce on behalf of the wife. If the husband consistently refrained from the fulfilment of his conjugal duties or if owing to his illness or vocation no cohabitation was possible, the court would force him to agree to divorce.[6] Another ground was the fact that the marriage remained childless for ten years,[7] or that the marriage was illegal.

Biblical divorce procedure included the writing of a deed to prevent the husband from raising any further claim over the divorcee.[8] The sages knew various formulae used on this occasion,[9] and an early regulation was to ensure the identification of the spouses by including all secondary names.[10] A number of formalities were specially introduced into the deed of divorce so as to limit the incidence of divorces; thus it must be written specially for the spouses so that no form may be prepared beforehand.[11]

As already mentioned, the husband could perform the divorce by

[1] M. Ketuboth 5:7.
[2] T. B. Ketuboth 82b.
[3] M. Gittin 9:10.
[4] M. Yebamoth 14:1.
[5] Deut. 22:19-29.
[6] M. Ketuboth 7:1-5, 10.
[7] T. Yebamoth 8:4.
[8] Deut. 24:1; Is. 50:1.
[9] M. Gittin 9:3.
[10] M. Gittin 4:2.
[11] M. Gittin 1:1.

himself, if he found a scribe and two witnesses. The wife, on the other hand, had to apply to a court. If judgment was given in her favour, the court would force the husband to agree to the divorce. Although 'the man that divorces is not like to the woman that is divorced; for a woman is put away with her consent or without it, but a husband can put away his wife only with his own consent.'[1] Nevertheless it was held concerning a woman's divorce that the husband is pressed until he expresses his consent.[2]

In general the husband has to pay the amount mentioned in the marriage contract after the divorce. However, in a number of cases, such as where the wife has violated her conjugal duties, she loses all or part of her rights.[3] Divorce, as well as engagement, may be made subject to a condition, whereby its effect is delayed or an interim period of doubtful status created.[4]

The biblical duty of levirate, namely the marriage of the widow of a childless man to his brother in order to perpetuate his name, underwent certain changes. The ceremony of 'unshoeing', originally meant to compel the *levir* to fulfil the duty of marrying the widow, became a legitimate alternative to that act, and according to some sages even preferable to levirate marriage.[5]

After his father's death, a child was in need of protection, especially with regard to his property. The mother was not thought to be sufficiently versed in financial affairs (unless she was appointed by the father). The functions of guardianship, therefore, originally were the responsibility of the paternal next-of-kin. But this remnant of tribal conditions did not last very well in the course of urbanization. Thus a special guardian had to be appointed, at first by the late father, and afterwards by the court. The latter appointment was granted to persons who were not closely related to the ward, for his next-of-kin were suspected of using the office to their own benefit.[6] The first judicial appointments seem, therefore, to have been made in the face of opposition on the part of the child's relatives.

Succession

The transmission of a dead person's property to his heirs is governed by the biblical passage on succession: Numbers 27:6-11. The process

---

[1] *M. Yebamoth* 14:1. [2] *M. Arakhin* 5:6.
[3] *M. Ketuboth* 7:6. [4] *M. Gittin* 7:3-9.
[5] *M. Bekhoroth* 1:7.
[6] *T. B. Baba Metzia* 39a; *P. T. Ketuboth* 1, 8, 25d; *T. B. Ketuboth* 13b.

takes place at the moment of death by operation of law. Originally, it seems, the deceased's firstborn son would be the natural successor to all the property and functions and he, according to his discretion, would decide which part of the property was to be allotted to the other members of the family. The passage of Numbers already expresses the supercession of the system of family property by a form of private ownership. Therefore the firstborn son has only a claim to a double share without excluding the co-heirs from their rights.

Originally, too, the succession applied only to real and personal property but not to things in action. A father wishing to secure the return of a loan to his heirs was to provide so explicitly in the contract, otherwise the debtor had an opportunity to disregard his obligation. Again, Talmudic law already provided for the transmission of credits and other things in action to the heirs, but the additional share of the firstborn was not taken from these parts of the inheritance.[1]

A fortiori the inheritance did not include the debts of the deceased. The creditors had a personal right against him, which came to an end at his death. The son, though perpetuating his father's name and holding his property, was not responsible for his debts.[2] Again, a creditor wishing to collect even after the debtor's death should have provided by deed for a charge on all or part of his immovables. Only by virtue of this charge could he then enforce his claim against the heir as well as against the purchase.

The passage of Numbers precluded the father from disinheriting the firstborn son and appointing a younger son in his stead. On the other hand, the law of succession being part of the law of property, could be considered as *ius dispositivum*, to be changed by the parties concerned. Indeed, opinions differed as to the right of diverting property from the legal heirs and its distribution according to the wishes of the testator: 'If a man apportioned his property to his sons by word of mouth, and gave much to one and little to another, or made them equal with the firstborn, his words remain valid.'[3] A gloss, representing the view that one must not stipulate against the law, adds: 'But if he had said that so it should be by 'inheritance', he has said nothing.'[4] According to another view, a father had the right of changing the shares of legal heirs of an equal parentela but not of favouring an outsider. Finally, one of the sages was of the opinion that,

---

[1] *M. Bekhoroth* 8:9.   [2] *T. B. Ketuboth* 86a.
[3] *M. Baba Bathra* 8:5.   [4] Ibid.

legally speaking, even that practice was possible, |'but the sages have no pleasure in him.'[1]

On intestacy the inheritance descended in the first instance to the children (first parentela), subject to the rules of primogeniture. Upon failure of issue, the inheritance passed to the deceased person's father (second parentela), to the grandfather (third parentela), etc. The descendants of any deceased person who, if he had been living, would have been entitled to the inheritance, represent that person. Males in equal degrees of relationship are always preferred to females. The mother and maternal relatives are excluded from the inheritance.[2]

If a proselyte dies without leaving any child born after his conversion, his inheritance becomes vacant and the first occupier becomes the owner.[3] If a husband survived his wife he became sole heir, except for the rights of others provided in the marriage contract. But even if it was stipulated between the spouses that the dowry should be reserved to the woman's sons, the husband had a life interest in her estate.[4] According to another clause, the husband was to return the woman's property, if she died without issue, to her next-of-kin.[5]

The widow was not entitled to a share in the inheritance but only to her rights under the marriage contract. According to the custom of Jerusalem and Galilee she had an option either to maintenance or to take what was due to her under the marriage contract. Even after having collected maintenance payments, she could still choose to take the capital and stop being supported; after twenty-five years the right of claiming the capital was exhausted. According to the custom of Judaea the option, of either paying maintenance or the capital, belonged to the legal heirs.[6] If the father left a surviving son, the daughters took only payments of maintenance until their marriage.[7] In addition they were also entitled to a suitable dowry.[8]

Although the sages disapproved of the diverting of property from the legal heirs, the law recognized several forms of dispositions in contemplation of death. A testator could make an immediate gift with the reservation of usufruct during his lifetime. In this case he had to use the ordinary form of transfer and he was not able to revoke such a gift.[9]

---

[1] Ibid.
[2] *M. Baba Bathra* 8:2.
[3] *M. Baba Bathra* 3:3.
[4] *M. Ketuboth* 4:10.
[5] *P. T. Ketuboth* IX, 1, 33a.
[6] *M. Ketuboth* 4:12.
[7] *M. Ketuboth* 4:11.
[8] *M. Ketuboth* 6:6.
[9] *M. Baba Bathra* 8:7.

A testator could also by parol make an order to witnesses that they should give a certain amount to a donee,[1] or that they should give certain goods to him.[2] Such a legacy took precedence over the rights of the legal heirs.

A dying man moreover, could dispose of his goods by words only, although in general a gift should be made for fictitious considerations, by way of occupancy on the part of the donee or by deed. A person facing death was exempt from these formalities, so that he should have the last satisfaction of having his wishes fulfilled.[3]

Such a will was implicitly revoked by recovery or by the passing of the danger to life. On the other hand, if the will dealt only with part of the testator's property it was considered as a gift and therefore not revoked by recovery.[4] A gift was also irrevocable where the witnesses had acquired the property in favour of the beneficiary.[5]

Finally, the Greek form of διαθήκη was used for the making of written wills. Of this form it was held that 'a later testament annuls a former one', and 'a testament which is partially invalid is void altogether', and 'he who writes a testament may revoke it.'[6]

Property

The earliest classification of things in Talmudic law was made for the purposes of taking security for debts. Immovables are called 'things which have a security' and movables 'things without security'.[7] The former are so called because the creditor has a security for them and may enforce it in default of payment. Even if the debtor has already sold these goods to a purchaser, the creditor may seize the property until he is paid. This right, then, applies only to immovables which have been charged by a written contract of debt, the assumption being that the purchaser has had notice of the debt and has taken the risk of losing the property. Where, on the other hand, a purchaser acquired movables from the debtor, he did not assume any liability for the repayment of the debt, since he bought 'things without security'. Movables should, thus, be acquired in the market without any liability attached, and the creditor should not trace the debtor's chattels which have passed to a third party.

---

[1] *M. Gittin* 1:6. [2] *M. Baba Bathra* 9:7.
[3] *T. B. Gittin* 13a. [4] *M. Baba Bathra* 9:6.
[5] *M. Gittin* 1:6.
[6] *T. B. Baba Bathra* 152b; *P. T. Sanhedrin* 11, 6, 20c; *T. Baba Bathra* 8:10.
[7] *M. Kiddushin* 1:5.

Deeds of sale usually provide for the transfer of the land, 'including the height and depth'. The meaning of this phrase is to include together with the soil *usque ad coelum et usque ad inferos*. The purchase of a piece of land, therefore, has a right to the air and to any trover underneath his property. 'Whatever is attached to his soil is like the immovable'; according to another view, however, the crop, though not yet detached from the soil, is already movable.[1] Slaves, likewise, were originally treated as immovables, on the ground that they were important enough to justify being used as security. Later views, however, took them for movables.[2]

The problem has been raised whether abstract things should be considered as things and whether they could be the object of contracts. According to one opinion 'usufruct is similar to ownership', and the person who is entitled to the usufruct of a certain property has really a part of the property itself. The opposite view denies this character of usufruct, relying on the difference between concrete and abstract things or perhaps comparing the usufruct with mere rights *in personam*. The sages holding the second view would not, probably, recognize the validity of a sale of future crop, while those who were of the first opinion could perhaps do so.[3]

Other cases of intangible property are those of money and deeds. Money is not in itself considered as a thing but rather as a symbol. Therefore, the tender of money is not a good consideration for the acquisition of movables, though it is for the acquisition of immovables.[4] For the purchase of immovables, indeed, there is only need for a symbolical act, while the purchase of movables requires part-performance.

Originally a debt could not be transferred from the promisee to another person, for such a 'thing in action' was not considered as a thing. However at the beginning of the third century it was held in Babylonia that the promisee could transfer the right in the presence of the promisor,[5] no consent or novation of the debt being required. Thus the debt was on the way to becoming a thing capable of being transferred. On the other hand even at an earlier date it was held that 'letters can be transferred.' There was only controversy as to whether

---

[1] *M. Shebuoth* 6:6.
[2] *P. T. Kiddushin* I, 3 59d; *T. B. Baba Kamma* 12a.
[3] *T. B. Kiddushin* 62b.
[4] *M. Baba Metzia* 4:1; *M. Kiddushin* 1:5.
[5] *T. B. Gittin* 13b.

this came about by mere transfer or by assignment together with transfer.[1] The intention of this rule was to enable the transfer of debts witnessed by deed, and it shows a tendency to identify the deed itself with the debt witnessed thereby.

A person who lost the possession of goods could recover it in two different ways. One view held in the first century B.C.E. said: 'Do not enter into the courtyard of another person to recover your goods without prior permission, for you might be taken as a thief, but knock his teeth and tell him you are going to take your goods.'[2] Another view, however, which probably developed at a later date, prohibited the taking of the law into one's own hands.[3] The plantiff could not easily succeed in action for recovery of possession, since actual possession is in favour of the defendant. Only in exceptional cases was the defendant asked to prove his title.[4] The recovery of immovables was easier. In a number of cases, where the court could not decide, it was held that whoever was stronger and took possession was entitled to keep the property.[5] The defendant, moreover, could not rely on his possession unless it had lasted for three years without protest.[6]

Certain persons cannot rely upon their factual control of the property because theirs is not usually an adverse possession. Examples are spouses, parents and children, tradesmen, partners, tenants, and guardians.[7] Where a person found something on the land of another and the presence of the thing was unknown, the possessor of the land had no claim to what was found. Therefore, 'If he found it in a heap of stones or in an old wall, it belongs to him.'[8]

Distinctions are made in Talmudic property law between private property and property not belonging to an ordinary owner. A special category is formed by goods which are הפקר i.e. not belonging to anybody. We have already mentioned the case of the deceased proselyte leaving no Jewish heirs, when the estate becomes ownerless property. The owner may also declare some of his property to be vacant, thus bringing about the same result.[9] The desert and the sea, moreover, are vacant *ab antiquo*.[10] Certain goods were declared by law to be vacant, e.g. where property was lost and there was no hope of recovery,[11]

---

[1] *T. B. Baba Bathra* 76a. [2] *T. B. Baba Kamma* 27b.
[3] Ibid.
[4] *M. Baba Bathra* 3:3; *T. Baba Bathra* 2:6.
[5] *T. B. Baba Bathra* 34b. [6] *M. Baba Bathra* 3:1.
[7] *M. Baba Bathra* 3:3. [8] *M. Baba Metzia* 2:3.
[9] *M. Nedarim* 4:8. [10] *T. B. Baba Bathra* 54b.
[11] *M. Baba Metzia* 2:1.

or where the owner had committed certain offences by means of the property.[1]

Particular privileges applied to the property of the Sanctuary, though in other respects such property was held and owned in the same way as that of private persons. More like ordinary private property were immovables which belong to all 'Babylonian immigrants', such as the Temple area and the cisterns by the highway. No distinction of principle existed between private and municipal property, such as the street and the synagogue. The latter was considered the common property of all the inhabitants.[2]

For a transfer of property rights something more is needed than a mere declaration of consent. There are normally three modes of acquisition, which seems to be the reason for three forms used for the acquisition of immovables. Payment of the price or of an earnest was obviously appropriate to effect a sale, the execution of a deed to effect a gift, and the taking of possessions to occupy vacant or inherited property. However, the latter forms were equally valid for the conclusion of a sale.[3] The title to movables is acquired by taking possession, or in the case of sale and gift, by delivery.[4]

In the chapter on civil wrongs we shall speak of the lapse of ownership through alternation. Similarly, lost property ceases to belong to its owner, if there is no likelihood of it being restored to him. It then becomes vacant and is occupied by the finder.[5]

Besides full ownership, Talmudic law recognized a number of partial rights in property. A bailee, for instance, is said to have acquired from the bailor the thing deposited with him, if he paid its value to the bailor because it had been lost or stolen. If, later on, the thief was found, he had to pay the capital as well as the fine to the bailee, not to the bailor.[6] While the ownership was still vested in the bailor, the right to bring an action against the thief had thus passed to the bailee.

A co-ownership is created by succession as long as the heirs go on living together in the house. Likewise, other real property may have been acquired by two people in common. According to one view, each of the co-owners of the immovable has an undefined share together with a licence to use also the share of his co-owner. The opposite view accords each of the two the whole of the property,

[1] *M. Shekalim* 1:2.   [2] *M. Nedarim* 5:5.
[3] *M. Kiddushin* 1:5.   [4] *M. Kiddushin* 1:4-6.
[5] *M. Baba Metzia* 2:1.   [6] *M. Baba Metzia* 3:1.

which is possible through splitting the full ownership into two component parts.[1] On the other hand, the upper and lower floors of a building may be owned by different people, the owner of the former having also a servitude over the part of his colleague.[2]

A person may assign his estate to one person for lifetime and to assure a second person to be successor after the death of the first successor, even provide the same thing with regard to a third successor.[3] The estate or possession of the former heir gives him the right of wasting or disposing even of the capital so that the later heir, having merely the estate in expectancy, must be satisfied with whatever remains. According to another view, however, the later heir can recover the property from the purchaser, or the first successor has only the right of usufruct. Moreover, if an heir predeceased his predecessor so that he did not enjoy his right, the whole chain was interrupted and even a later heir did not inherit. In that case the legal heirs of the former heir would take the inheritance.[4]

The rights *in rem* may be split between the owner and the tenant whether by way of a lease or by way of share-cropping. According to a sage of the fourth century C.E., though limited in time, 'a lease during its day is like a sale.[5] A special type of share-cropping is almost like a feudal tenure, giving the tenant, for a rent, most of the rights of ownership.[6]

Although in general the owner may do what he likes with his property, he has to be careful not to damage thereby any other person. A number of nuisances have been defined by Talmudic law[7] and certain restrictions as to the use of land were meant to prevent economic competition.[8] Under the rules of *aequum et bonum* the owner of a parcel of land has a right of pre-emption of the adjoining parcel.[9]

The ordinary lease, as already mentioned, provides for rights *in rem* both to the owner and to the lessee. The rights of the lessor are secured through the idea that the lessee impliedly assumes the obligations of the bailee to protect the property from damage.[10] This does not, however, apply to leases of land, so that the owner has no protection against waste. On the other hand, as lessee, just as everybody else,

---

[1] *M. Nedarim* 5:1.
[2] *M. Baba Metzia* 10:3.
[3] *T. B. Baba Bathra* 137a.
[4] *T. B. Baba Bathra* 129b.
[5] *T. B. Baba Metzia* 56b.
[6] *M. Bikkurim* 1:2.
[7] *M. Baba Bathra* 2:1-12.
[8] *T. B. Baba Bathra* 21a.
[9] *T. B. Baba Metzia* 108a.
[10] *M. Baba Metzia* 6:3-5.

is entitled to compensation for improvements, even though he has made them without authorization.[1]

A real interest is acquired by a secured creditor. An independent craftsman may retain the thing which he worked on until he is paid for his work.[2] Likewise, 'a creditor acquires the pledge,'[3] meaning that he has a right to keep the thing or to sell it, if the debt is not paid in time. According to one sage the creditor may even transfer the pledge for consideration, which should then be deduced from the capital debt.[4] Possessory securities could also be created with regard to immovables. Originally 'If a man lent another money on the security of his field and said to him, 'if thou dost not pay me within three years it shall be mine', then it becomes his.'[5]

At as later stage such land was mortgaged in favour of the creditor and kept in his possession.[6]

But already during the second century B.C.E. a non-possessory security was known in Talmudic law. The normal contract of debt included a clause charging all the debtor's property. This clause did not prevent the debtor from disposing of his goods, but immovables thus disposed of would remain subject to the mortgage, while movables became freed. The former were, consequently, called 'property for which there is security'.[7] At some later date the Greek ὑποθήκη was used to mortgage a particular property.[8]

If a slave had been made subject to a ὑποθήκη and the owner, later on, liberated him, the creditor would have lost his security. But according to a *novella*, the creditor is entitled to payment from the (former) slave and has to write him another deed of liberation on his own part.[9]

Contracts

Talmudic as well as biblical law recognized a number of religious forms to make a promise binding on the person who made it. He could take an oath or make a vow to call upon himself divine punishment, should he go back on his undertaking. In this chapter, however, we will consider the question whether Talmudic law knew also a legal theory of contract, as distinct from the religious and moral concepts of the sanctity of promise.

[1] *T. B. Baba Metzia* 101a. [2] *M. Baba Metzia* 6:6.
[3] *T. B. Baba Metzia* 82a. [4] *M. Baba Metzia* 6:7.
[5] *M. Baba Metzia* 5:3. [6] *M. Shebiith* 10:6.
[7] *M. Kiddushin* 1:5. [8] *T. Shebiith* 8:6.
[9] *M. Gittin* 4:4.

While in modern contracts the emphasis lies upon the promise to do, or refrain from, some specified act, the Talmudic counterpart is based on the idea of restitution. If a person is liable under contract it is mainly to give something, not so much because of the promise, but rather as a result of a kind of quasi-contract. Thus the promisor is under a duty to render consideration for a benefit received or for the forbearance of the other party.

The idea is like that of the obligation arising as the result of an un-solicited gift or service: 'He who went unto his neighbour's field and planted without the owner's authorization' has a right to demand payment for his improvement. Indeed, according to the School of Shammai, the person making the improvement may take away even the fixtures, but the School of Hillel did not permit him to do so.[1] It was therefore, in their opinion, only fair to indemnify that 'volunteer' for his services and expenses. *A fortiori* a promisor, who had benefited from the other party's act of forbearance, should be held liable to fulfil his promise.

The earliest contract was probably the contract of debt, in which the promisor merely undertook to restore a sum of money which he had received in cash. The undertaking may be supported by security and witnessed by witnesses or by a deed. Sometimes another obligation, such as the price of delivered goods or of performed services is, later on, transformed into an ordinary debt.[2] Here, again, it was the idea of a *quid pro quo* upon which the obligation was founded, not the mere promise to pay the given amount.

Labour contracts, likewise, had to be executed by one party, in order to impose the liability upon the other one. If the workmen had performed their task, they certainly had an action for payment of their wages, while the employer, who had paid in advance, could probably raise a corresponding claim for their services. Where, however, no part performance had taken place, both parties were free to go back on their promises, giving only 'cause for complaint'.[3] The next step was that each party became responsible for the damage caused by the breach of promise.[4]

A disposition rather than a contract lies behind the Talmudic sale. One cannot transfer a thing which has not yet come into existence, such as the future crop of a field.[5] Here again a number of forms were

[1] *T. B. Baba Metzia* 101a. [2] *M. Shebiith* 10:1.
[3] *M. Baba Metzia* 6:1. [4] Ibid.
[5] *T. B. Baba Metzia* 33b.

invented to enable a man to sell his future products.[1] Moreover, in order to be able to dispose of a thing, the transferor must be in possession. Therefore, where goods have been stolen, both the thief and the owner are unable to dedicate them to the Sanctuary, the former because they were not his own, the latter because they were not in his possession.[2] On the other hand, there was no need for full performance for the sale to take effect. Even if the purchaser had given a nominal price only, if a deed of transfer had been written in his favour, or if he had taken constructive possession, the disposition was valid. A guaranty, too, was held to be binding because of the consideration received by the surety, namely the satisfaction that the creditor trusts in him.[3] Thus there was no need for valuable consideration in order to create a corresponding duty.

But trust towards the promisor was not the only consideration. At the beginning of the third century the view was expressed that mere 'words as distinct from an act of acquisition, do not cause a 'breach of trust.' Accordingly, if a salesman had received an advance payment for flax and the price of flax rose, the salesman was not bound to deliver at the old price.[4] Since movables were acquired by taking possession, not by payment of the price, there was merely a verbal promise, the breach of which was no 'breach of trust'. The opposite view, however, held by another sage, said that even 'words may bring about a breach of trust', so that the salesman in that case should have delivered the goods at the old price. Thus, according to the latter view, a parol promise to sell was actionable at least under the rules of *aequum et bonum*, which implies the existence of the idea of contract.

A similar development may be traced in the law of partnership. Originally based upon co-ownership, partnership became independent of the latter but still depended upon some property in the beginning. A partnership is formed by two or more persons who 'deposited into a purse' the initial fund.[5] By creating this common fund, the partners put themselves in a position analogous to that of brothers in an undivided inheritance. Therefore, according to one view, the profit should be divided *per capita*, which shows that the personal effort, rather than the investment, was the basis of the partnership. Another view, however, provides for a division of profits in proportion to the capital contributed by each partner.[6] Again, the first opinion seems

---

[1] *M. Baba Metzia* 5:7.
[2] *T. B. Kiddushin* 52a.
[3] *M. Baba Bathra* 10:8.
[4] *T. B. Baba Metzia* 49a.
[5] *M. Ketuboth* 10:4.
[6] *T. B. Ketuboth* 93a; *M. Ketuboth* 10:4.

to accept the partnership as a kind of personal contract, while those who are of the second opinion rely on the real element. The common fund is considered as having grown, and each partner has thus a *ius in rem* to the profit.

The Talmudic institute which is nearest to modern contract is suretyship. Here we have a verbal promise without any act of acquisition, nevertheless putting an obligation upon the promisor. True, the trust put in the promise was thought sufficient consideration, but the same principle could be applied in any other type of promise if the promisee had changed his position for the worse. However, the suretyship must be expressed before the loan or included in the bond before the signature of the witnesses. If a person wanted to become surety afterwards he had to take the debt upon himself, not only to promise repayment of the debt of another. There was also no suretyship for due appearance of the debtor.[1]

Mistake does not constitute a ground for avoiding contracts and the cases where a party claims that 'his purchase was made in error' are actually cases of misrepresentation. Thus, 'if a man sold wine to his fellow and it turned sour, he [the seller] is not answerable, but if it was known [to the seller] that his wine would [soon] turn sour, this is accounted a purchase made in error.'[2] Here the assumption is that the seller, but not the purchaser, knows the hidden defect, so that he is under an obligation of *uberrima fides*.

Likewise, a bridegroom who found his bride not to be a virgin, would claim that 'his bargain was made in error' and hence be absolved from the duty of paying the bride-price.[3] In this case, it was assumed, the bride was under an obligation to disclose the fact, and failing to do so she was guilty of implied misrepresentation. We do not, however, know whether the marriage was also voidable. This would certainly be so if the bridegroom had expressly stipulated that the marriage was contracted on that assumption, and then the bride turned out not to be a virgin.[4]

A sale may also be voided if the price was more than one sixth below or above the market value, or if a hidden defect existed in the goods. The right of retracting from the contract was given only to the aggrieved party.[5]

Duress, too, originally seems to have constituted grounds for setting

[1] Ibid.
[2] *M. Baba Bathra* 6:3.
[3] *M. Ketuboth* 1:6.
[4] *M. Kiddushin* 2:5.
[5] *M. Baba Bathra* 5:6; *M. Baba Metzia* 4:3.

aside the contract. If the authorities, for instance, had requisitioned and sold private property, the purchaser was obliged, under Talmudic law, to return it to the owner. Only during the Great Revolt (66-70 C.E.), or after the second revolt (132-5 C.E.) was such a sale declared valid, so as to protect the possession of Jewish purchasers.[1] But even then the purchaser acquired title only if he had first bought the land from the owner and then from the authorities. On the other hand the court would sometimes be satisfied with a fictitious consent, where an act should have been done out of the free will of the doer. Thus if a husband was bound by law to divorce his wife, 'they may compel him until he said: It is my will.'[2] In such a case, therefore, no claim of duress would be accepted. In the third century C.E. a Babylonian sage went so far as to dismiss any claim of duress to avoid a sale for 'a person never sells entirely out of his free will.'[3] Thus, with regard to contracts of sale, there was no need of consent.

Certain restrictions were imposed by the sages upon the use of conditions in private law. In order to suspend a given transfer or obligation or to discharge it the condition has to be expressed both in the positive and the negative form, the positive must be stated before the negative, the condition before the transfer or the main obligation and, finally, the condition must not be impossible.[4] These formal requirements were, however, waived in certain cases so as to give effect to the condition, but there could be no condition contravening a biblical law. Only in matters of property, according to one sage, a condition should be recognized though contracting out of a legal provision.

A contract may have been frustrated through the act of God or through the act of a party. Again, Talmudic law did not so much deal with the obligation resting on the other party as with the question of who is to bear the loss. 'If a man hired an ass and it went blind or was pressed into the king's service, he may say to the owner, 'Here before thee is what is thine'; but if it died or was lamed, he must provide him with another ass.'[5] Thus in the first case the contract is still enforceable, though the ass may perform only a fraction of the expected work. The lessor, therefore, is not bound to supply another animal and may claim the full amount of rent. The assumption is always that the

[1] *M. Gittin* 5:6.
[2] *M. Arakhin* 5:6.
[3] *T. B. Baba Bathra* 47b.
[4] *M. Kiddushin* 3:4; *M. Baba Metzia* 7:11.
[5] *M. Baba Metzia* 6:3.

loss remains where it fell, i.e. upon the temporary holder of the property. Only when the leased chattel has ceased to be called by its original name, will the owner have to replace it and will then be entitled to payment. On the other hand, 'If a man leased a field from his fellow and the locusts devoured the crop or it was blasted [by tempest], if it was a mishap widespread in that region he may give less than the agreed rental, but if it was not a mishap widespread in that region he may not give less than the agreed rental.'[1] It is, again, a question of allocating the loss between the parties to the contract.

Since personal obligations are not of the essence of the Talmudic contract, it is difficult to obtain a remedy for its breach. Both the employer and the workers are only entitled to entertain a grievance against each other if the other party withdraws from the contract.[2] Likewise, 'he who gave money to his friend so that the latter should buy [and sell] fruits for mutual profit and then his friends said, he had not bought [and sold] any fruits, he can entertain only a grievance [against his friend].'[3]

Although a sale of goods can be annulled by the purchaser for some hidden defect, no corresponding claim for resulting damage will be recognized: 'He who bought jars from his friends and they turned out to be broken vessels, [the seller] must refund the price of the jars but not the price of the [lost] wine.[4]

Private wrongs

The law of torts, more than any other part of Talmudic, law, is based upon the interpretation of scripture. The injury is primarily an offence against divine law and the payment of damages is the result of this offence. Injuries are divided accordingly into a number of torts, called after the various passages, respectively: 'Cases concerning property [are decided] by three [judges]; cases concerning theft or personal injury, by three; claims for full damages or half-damages, twofold restitution, or fourfold or fivefold restitution, and [claims against] the violator, the seducer and him *that hath brought an evil name*.'[5] These actions seem to have occupied most of the time in the local courts, though not as much as the cases of property and contract.

Similar to these injuries and comparable with them are the rules on bailees, which are also based on the biblical law rather than on con-

[1] M. Baba Metzia 9:6.   [2] M. Baba Metzia 6:1.
[3] T. Baba Metzia 4:22.   [4] T. Baba Bathra 6:4.
[5] M. Sanhedrin 1:1.

tract. Even the obligation of false witnesses under the *ius talionis* are listed by one authority among torts.[1] A certain affinity is also felt between the rules of tort and larceny on the one hand and the rules against cheating in commerce and lending on interest.

While most obligations originating from tort depend on the malicious intent of the wrongdoer, no such intent is necessary to make a man liable for damage caused by his personal act: 'Human kind is always an attested danger, whether [the damage is caused] by error or wantonly, whether awake or asleep.'[2] and according to another version 'whether he acted under duress or willingly.'[3]

In general, however, the *mens rea* is a prerequisite of the obligation in tort. The standard of care should be highest with regard to personal acts, while the liability for damage caused by one's property is not as strict. The other element is the act itself, which should be the direct cause of the damage. It is only in such a case that the judge can determine the cause of the damage, otherwise he would have to rely on speculation. According to Rabbi Joshua, 'Four acts do not make the person liable under human but only under celestial law: He who breaks the fence before another person's cattle, he who bends the standing corn of another person towards fire, he who engages false witnesses, and he who knows some evidence in favour of another person but does not appear in court.'[4] However, some of the sages, like Rabbi Meir, tried to provide a remedy for the victim of such an indirect injury, they were 'judging according to the law of indirect action.'[5]

The owner of dangerous cattle is liable to make good any damage caused by it, according to the express provision of the law. However, the sages formulated a logical rule showing the place of this rule in the general system of law: 'Whenever I am under an obligation to guard my property, I have prepared the damage caused by that property.'[6] Thus it is not out of an idea of strict liability that the owner is responsible for the damage, but rather as the result of his negligence.

According to the biblical passages there are four types of injurious property: the goring ox, the pit, the consuming cattle and the fire.[7] Another form of injury is 'man', i.e. injury by direct action.

---

[1] *T. B. Baba Kamma* 4b.
[2] *M. Baba Kamma* 2:6.
[3] *T. B. Baba Kamma* 26b.
[4] *T. B. Baba Kamma* 55b.
[5] *T. B. Baba Kamma* 100a.
[6] *M. Baba Kamma* 1:2.
[7] *M. Baba Kamma* 1:1.

Larceny is treated as a civil wrong only: the thief, therefore, will merely be ordered to restore the stolen property, sometimes together with a penalty of one hundred, three hundred, or even four hundred per cent. If the stolen property has been changed to become something different, or if the owner has expressed his despair of getting it back, the thief thereby acquires legal title and need only restore the initial value.[1] This is an ordinance made in order to assist the repentant thief. Likewise, the purchase of stolen property is protected by an ordinance for the benefit of the market, that the owner of the stolen property shall pay him the purchase price before claiming it back.[2]

BIBLIOGRAPHY

GENERAL

S. EISENSTADT: *Repertorium Bibliographicum literaturae totius iuris prudentiae hebraicae*, 1931; Z. W. FALK: *Introduction to Jewish Law of the Second Commonwealth, Part I*, 1972; B. COHEN: *Jewish and Roman Law*, 1966; A. GULAK: *Yesode ha-Mishpat ha-Ivri*, I-IV, 1923; G. HOROWTIZ: *The Spirit of Jewish Law*, 1953.

PERSONS

B. J. BAMBERGER: *Proselytism in the Talmudic Period*, 1968; J. S. BLOCH: *Israel und die Völker*, 1922, English translation: *Israel and the Nations*, 1927; J. H. LEVINTHAL: *The Jewish Law of Agency*, 1923; S. RUBIN: *Das Talmudische Recht, Sklaverei*, 1920; J. STERN: *Die Frau im Talmud. Eine Skizze*, 1879.

FAMILY

M. BLOCH: 'Die Vormundschaft nach mosaisch-talmudischem Recht', in *Jahresbericht der Landesrabbinerschule*, 1904; D. W. AMRAM: *The Jewish Law of Divorce according to Bible and Talmud*, 1896; L. M. EPSTEIN: *The Jewish Marriage Contract*, 1927; J. NEUBAUER: *Beiträge zur Geschichte des biblisch-talmudischen Eheschliessungsrechts*, 1920 (Mitteilungen der Vorderasiatischen Gesellschaft 24-5).

---

[1] *M. Baba Kamma* 9:1; *M. Gittin* 5:5.
[2] *M. Baba Kamma* 10:3.

SUCCESSION

M. BLOCH: 'Das mosaisch-talmudische Erbrecht' in *Jahresbericht der Landesrabbinerschule*, 1889; R. YARON: *Gifts in Contemplation of Death in Jewish and Roman Law*, 1960; M. MIELZINER: *The Rabbinical Law of Hereditary Succession*, 1900.

PROPERTY

J. HERZOG: *The Main Institutions of Jewish Law*, I, 1936; S. RUBIN: *Das talmudische Recht, Sachenrecht*, 1938.

CONTRACTS

L. AUERBACH: *Das Jüdische Obligationenrecht*, 1870; A. GULAK: *Das Urkundenwesen im Talmud im Lichte der griechisch aegyptischen Papyri und des griechischen und römischen Rechts*, 1935; J. HERZOG: *The Main Institutions of Jewish Law*, II, 1939.

CIVIL WRONGS

S. ALBECK: *Pesher Dine ha-Neziqin ba-Talmud*, 1965; Z. W. FALK, 'Elements of the Jewish Law of Torts', in *Studi G. Grosso*, II, 1968, pp. 159-167.

II HELLENISTIC PRIVATE LAW

What is meant by 'Hellenistic Private Law'? There was, of course, never a concrete system of positive law institutions, deriving from a basically uniform legislation, which could have been the law of each land in the Greek states, or in the countries ruled by men of Greek culture, which had survived Alexander's empire or emerged from it. Nevertheless, we do find in that world of dissimilar state structures more or less stereotyped institutions, forms, and customs of private law which, if not identical, still suggest at least related dogmatic conceptions. This relationship is by no means accidental. Frequently the Hellenistic epoch merely preserved what had already been valid in pre-Hellenistic times. Other phenomena may not be verifiable in the law of the ancient Greek polis, but, while reflecting social, economic, or intellectual conditions typical of Hellenistic civilization, they may be considered as organic developments from or transformations of pre-Hellenistic law. Consequently, one may say that all these phenomena combined to form one 'spiritual whole (which has been aptly

534

termed a 'juridical koine') thus taking their place within the general framework of Greek legal history. To this extent, it seems permissible to speak of 'Hellenistic law' or, rather, an identifiable Hellenistic legal culture.

More than eighty years ago, Ludwig Mitteis already assumed that there existed a common body of dogmatic concepts belonging specifically, though not necessarily exclusively, to Greek juridical thought. It is true that some scholars, especially in the field of the classics, still regard his thesis with scepticism. Nevertheless, for the reasons just pointed out, it is used here as a point of departure for the following survey.

It is, accordingly, our task to present Greek legal phenomena in the particular shape they had received under the political and social conditions of the Hellenistic age. It does not matter that in the work of which this survey is a part, emphasis is laid on the first two centuries of the Christian era. For the integration of the Hellenistic countries into the Roman Empire took place, at least at first, without any notable effect on their tradition of private law, which continued to flourish beyond the fall of the Hellenistic state system as such. Furthermore, the subject of this survey will be Greek law also insofar as only such institutions of private law will be considered as had their origin in a *Greek* milieu. From this point of view, it is immaterial that, under the principle of the *lex fori*, they may have been applicable to Jews and other non-Greeks as well when such persons entered into contracts before Greek notaries or engaged in lawsuits in Greek courts of justice. On the other hand, legal phenomena which by their origin and nature do not belong to the Greek sphere do not qualify as 'Hellenistic' in the sense given here, even though they may have been adopted by Greek populations, or have played a role as part of the total complex of institutions and usages forming the legal reality of the country concerned, as did, for example, biblical law in Seleucid and Roman Palestine, or Egyptian law in Ptolemaic and Roman Egypt. It is even more obvious that no account can be taken of influences from Roman law, which, in some places, made themselves felt at an early time.

Consequently, this study will not deal with any particular system of private law such as actually existed in the Hellenistic world. We shall rather ask—without geographical considerations—how, with respect to private law, the Hellenistic component of their environment appeared to the Jews of that period. For practical purposes our knowledge is, of course, still mainly confined to what has been gathered from the Egyptian papyri and from the comparatively slight material from Palestine and Dura-Europos on the Euphrates. Detailed information concerning local peculiarities of private law in force elsewhere in the Hellenistic world will not be available until the epigraphic sources, existing in sufficient quantities for some regions, have been fully exploited from the point of view of legal history. From the standpoint of the present work, however, the concentration on a few countries which is forced on us at the present stage of research is not disadvantageous, since it was mainly in these very countries that Hellenistic and Jewish civilizations met.

The individual and society

1. We are not well informed concerning the law of persons and family in the city states of Hellenistic and Roman times. Presumably, conditions inherited from the classical epoch were at first maintained in the ancient poleis. We should of course reckon with a gradual adaptation to changed circumstances; thus there may have been some mitigation of restrictions on intermarriage with non-citizens and of discrimination against illegitimate children such as existed, for instance, in Athens during the age of full democracy. But for the moment, this must remain pure conjecture. In any case, this type of exclusive legislation instituted by individual poleis for their citizens, which more or less preserved ancient Greek forms of life, cannot be described as 'Hellenistic' law in the proper sense of the term.

Of greater interest in the present context would be the conditions prevailing in cities founded by Alexander and his *diadochoi*. Unfortunately, we know little more about them than about the ancient poleis. Just as had been the case in these, there existed in the new cities a class of citizens (πολῖται) privileged vis-à-vis those free residents who did not belong to it. We do not know to what extent this privileged status, which should be understood as one primarily pertaining to public law, extended into private law. It should not be forgotten that in the newly-founded cities certain characteristic features of status law, such as in Alexandria and Ptolemais the division of the citizens into phyles, demes, and phratries, were not the product of a lengthy organic development from prehistoric conditions, but artificial, new creations. They lacked the 'tribal' substructure on which they were based in the ancient city-states such as Athens—externally perhaps the model for Alexandria—and which, together with the institutions determining the private law status of persons and family, formed an organic whole consisting of mutually dependent elements. It is true that some of the principles governing the city law of Alexandria recall the classical oikos, i.e. the 'house' based on the common descent of its members, and organized along patriarchal or communal lines. Actually, however, they should be considered as artificial structures conserving isolated elements of ancient institutions, rather than as evidence of real survival of the oikos. This refers to such features as possible privileges resulting from a marital union established before a board of priests (ἱεροθύται),[1] the sacral form, characterized by a sacrifice, of the acceptance of children into the phratry,[2] or the exclusion of illegitimate children from civic rights.[3] Altogether, and notwithstanding peculiarities of positive law doubtless present in many poleis, it would appear to be correct to assume that in Alexandria and other cities founded by Hellenistic rulers, the law of persons and family inclined towards basic principles similar to those applicable to the Greeks of the Egyptian *chora*, i.e. the area directly controlled by the central government. In both cases, widely similar changes in sociological conditions must have been reflected in fundamentally analogous departures from the legal structure of the classical polis.

Fundamental to this change in sociological circumstances was the way in which Greeks, from the end of the fourth century B.C.E. onwards, embraced a new type of community life. Whether or not they joined one of the new city-states constituted along more or less traditional lines, or one of the groups of military colonists (κάτοικοι) in the kingdom of the Ptolemies, or even sought their fortune without associating with any organized group, all these people, converging from all over the Greek world, came as individuals free of ties. The principle which integrated the ancient city state, that is to say, the assumption of a real or fictitious tribal relationship and of a cultic community worshipping certain local gods, was abandoned. In Egypt, and probably elsewhere, Greek and non-Greek immigrants continued for a time to indicate their original citizenship by means of a corresponding addition to their names, but this hardly possessed more than a theoretical significance. Their connection with the religiously-based tribal units of their homeland was, in any case, disrupted from

---

[1] See Wolff, *Marriages*, pp. 34 ff.
[2] *P. Hib.* I, 28 and the comments by J. Seyfarth, *Aegyptus* (1955), pp. 4 ff.
[3] *P. Catt. Recto*, col. IV, 11. 6 ff.; L. Mitteis, *Chrestomathie*, p. 372, col. V.

the start. The formation of new ones, however, was no longer possible in a mobile colonial society which tended towards universal religions (Sarapis), unless they were artificially created by arbitrary legislation, as may have been the case in some of the new city-states.

2. The natural consequence was that the Hellenistic law of persons and family assumed a definitely individualistic shape, though without wholly disowning its origin in the institutions of the city-state.

a. Status differences in the sphere of private law practically disappeared, at least in the chora. There remained only the difference between free persons and slaves. In particular, women were, in principle, capable without limitation of possessing property and acting in their own right. Even the participation of a guardian (κύριος), necessary according to the Greek law of Egypt in the business transactions of women, does not seem to have been everywhere obligatory. There is, for example, no trace of it in the Greek documents of Dura-Europos from the second and third centuries C.E., which probably reflected Hellenistic concepts. In Egypt the guardianship of women, of which, to say the least, there is no mention in the oldest documents,[1] was presumably an arbitrary creation of early Ptolemaic legislation, possibly modelled on the κυριεία of classical Attic law. (This had been done, of course, without much thought, since the Athenian *kyrios* had the power to give the woman in marriage and to manage her property. Therefore his authority was much more comprehensive than that of a mere guardian. It had been suitable only to a concept of the family which, as will be seen presently, was no longer valid in the new colonial society.) The purely formal character of the Ptolemaic institution which, perhaps because it ran parallel to the Roman tutelage of women, was nevertheless maintained until a late age, is apparent from two characteristic features: on the one hand, its operation was restricted to transactions involving disposal of property and creation of liabilities and only insofar as these transactions followed Greek rules and were executed in the Greek language; besides, in early Ptolemaic times, women needed the assistance of a 'guardian' when litigating before Greek tribunals. On the other hand, under the conditions named, even Jewish and Egyptian women, who according to the laws of

---

[1] κύριος does not occur in *P. Eleph*. 1 of 311 B.C.E., and 2 of 285-283 B.C.E.; Mitteis, *Chrestomathie*, nos. 283 and 311. And in *P. Eleph* 4, more or less contemporary with 2, Elaphion, a Syrian camp prostitute, appears with *kyrioi*, but the reason for this may be a slave-like subjection of the girl to each temporary paramour. If this is correct, these *kyrioi* have nothing to do with the official law of later papyri.

their own peoples, were not subject to guardianship, came under this law.[1]

b. Behind the legal, though not necessarily social independence of women, was the fundamental fact that a new type of family, resting entirely on blood relationship, had replaced the classical oikos. The new family was based purely on personal ties graded according to the degree of natural relationship among the family members. Apart from possible special regulations in the legal systems of some cities, there was, consequently, no patriarchal family organization at all. Adoption was now simply a means of forming personal ties; accordingly persons of both sexes might be adopted and perhaps already at an early stage even actively adopt. Sons and daughters could own their own property, which the father controlled in the manner of a guardian during their minority. To be sure, to a large extent parents made use of their personal power over their dependent children. In Egypt, not only the father, but the mother too if she were a widow, could indent the child as an apprentice, hire him out to work, marry off a daughter and even a son, and unless appearances deceive us, even pawn, sell, or expose a child. It is, however, uncertain whether all these actual practices were consonant with prevalent legal persuasion. Some should perhaps be classed as an unscrupulous exploitation of the lack of express legal provisions, or even simply supervision, concerning the exercise of paternal power in the *chora*. Only the Roman authorities seem to have tried to set limits to one or other of these abuses.[2]

c. From the juridical point of view, the changed concept of the family expressed itself most clearly in the rules governing the marital relationship, which, so far as one can see, was still monogamous. Outside the poleis, unrestrained intermarriage was the rule, even with non-Greeks. Sibling marriage, practised also outside Egypt, was of ancient Greek origin, but it has been plausibly suggested that responsibility for this custom must be attributed to the desire to bypass an individualistic law of inheritance favouring the uneconomical division of property. Archaic ideas of a sacred endogamous oikos, which at one time may have lain behind it, had certainly been forgotten long ago.

[1] The fact that an 'Athenian of the *epigone*' could act as the guardian of a Jewish woman engaged in litigation before a Greek *dikasterion* demonstrates the merely formal significance of such assistance (*P. Gur.* 2 of *c.* 226 B.C.E.; A. S. Hunt and C. E. Edgar, *Select Papyri* II, 1934, no. 256.)

[2] Examples in the famous papyrus of Dionysia, *P. Oxy.* II, 237.

But the change showed itself most clearly in the fact that the actual establishment of conjugal union by the spouses themselves now sufficed as the foundation of marriage. The giving in marriage of a girl by her father or guardian, and solemn ceremonies of transfer, as for instance the 'betrothal' (ἐγγύη) of Attic law, were no longer prerequisites for the legitimacy of children. Even less could there be any longer a question of a legal claim of kinsmen to the hand and estate of a brotherless daughter (ἐπίκληρος, i.e. 'heiress to the estate'). It is true that in the eyes of conservative circles marriage remained for some time a transaction to be settled between the father of the bride and the bridegroom, with the bride as its object. Hence in Egypt, for example, the husband's documentary acknowledgement of the marriage and of his receipt of the dowry (συγγραφή ὁμολογίας) was, until the time of the later Ptolemies, often followed by a second instrument documenting the 'handing over' (ἔκδοσις) of the bride to him (συνοικεσίου συγγραφή).[1] This practice, however, only shows how obsolete formal exigencies were allowed to wither away by means of an organic adjustment to altered circumstances, but without any drastic break with the past. They fell victim to a gradual change of custom inherent in the logic of a social development which had done away with the concept of a family in which women were subject to the head of the 'house'. The reason why no record of an 'undocumented marriage' occurs in the papyri from Egypt and Dura-Europos before imperial times is probably simply a gap in the sources. The thing itself is doubtless considerably older than its documentation.

It is, under the circumstances, unnecessary to explain why the juridical effect of marriage on the personal relationship of the spouses was minimal. The husband had no conjugal power over his wife. In Egypt he became her guardian for the purely factual reason that he was her most easily accessible male relative. No legally effective domestic authority derived from this position which was, as we have seen, essentially a formal one. Both spouses could dissolve the marriage at will and without formality, by mutual agreement, or by expelling or deserting the other partner, a record of divorce possessing merely declaratory significance for purposes of evidence. That a husband should provide for the maintenance of his wife, and that the spouses should be faithful to each other, must have been recognized principles

---

[1] *P. Par.* 13, on which see Wolff, *Marriages*, pp. 10 ff. The *self-ekdosis* of a girl, occurring once in *P. Giess.* 2 of 173 B.C.E., was probably another manifestation of such conservative thinking.

even when not explicitly provided for in the marriage contract. However, violation of such duties had no legal consequences except in connection with property settlements following a divorce, and even this only when there were special agreements to this effect.

It is understandable that a legal situation such as this did not contribute to the stability of marriage relations. That the wife (γυνή γαμητή) was theoretically still considered privileged vis-à-vis the concubine is attested by clauses in Ptolemaic marriage contracts, and the explicit confirmation of a woman's freedom to join another man, regularly inserted in the divorce document, proves the existence of the concept of adultery. Nevertheless, the curious fact that not a single concrete case of adultery or concubinage has as yet come to light in the extensive papyrus material of Egypt relating to Hellenistic law can hardly be attributed to an extraordinary stability of the matrimonial bond. On the contrary it is a sign of its weakness, and of the great fluidity of the unions resulting from it.

It is not therefore surprising that the individualistic nature of the marriage law manifested itself also in respect of the married couple's property relations. The principle of keeping estates separate—sometimes with the provision that the power to dispose of the property of either partner was vested only jointly in both of them[1]—was coupled with a dotal system modelled chiefly on the Attic or similar patterns. But whereas the Attic dowry (προίξ) formed a settlement by the wife's family on that of the husband and would ultimately go to the wife's children as a share in the maternal grandfather's estate, the φερνή, as the dowry was called wherever it was not connected with an oikos system, aimed especially at the security of the wife herself. Accordingly, in addition to money, it consisted as a rule of the woman's personal belongings, but as a matter of principle and in contrast to Attic custom, not of real estate and slaves.

While the marriage lasted, title to the dowry was vested in the husband. After divorce, however, or dissolution of the marriage by his death, the wife could file a personal claim against him or his heirs for the cash value of the dowry as laid down when the arrangement was made. If the marriage ended through the death of the wife, her dowry could be held for the children. The dowry of a childless wife had to be refunded to the person who had made the settlement. Another deviation from the Athenian practice which occurred in

[1] E.g. in *P. Giess.* 2 of 173 B.C.E., or *P. Tebt.* I, 104 of 92 B.C.E. (Mitteis, *Chrestomathie*, no. 285).

Ptolemaic Egypt was the insertion in the marriage settlement of a provision that the husband, if he were the guilty party in a divorce, was penalized by having to refund the dowry with an addition, while the wife, if guilty, might lose all or part of her claim for return of the dowry.

d. The law of guardianship mainly followed traditional lines, though once more with a characteristic slackening vis-à-vis the classical situation. As a rule, care for the person of a fatherless child was entrusted to the mother. On the other hand, in matters of property, a minor under fourteen years old (ἀφῆλιξ), and in Egypt all females, needed a guardian who had necessarily to be male, at least if he was to function as *kyrios* (see below).[1] In the absence of direction in the father's will, the office of guardian fell to the nearest of the ward's relatives, including those on the mother's side, starting with the grandfathers, followed by the collaterals. An unmarried woman was under the guardianship of her father as long as she lived in his household. The married woman's guardian was her husband; generally, the head of the house in which a woman lived seems to have had precedence over all others. In Roman Egypt guardians for both women and children might be officially appointed.

The principal task of the guardian was to administer the ward's property and support him from it. To this extent, i.e. as *epitropos*, he had power to dispose of the property, but at the end of his guardianship he was answerable to his ward for any diminution of the possessions in his charge. In Egypt he was also subject to a certain amount of official supervision. In addition, the guardian was charged with the supervision of his ward's own transactions, the validity of which depended on his cooperation. In this capacity he was called *kyrios*. As far as guardianship of women was concerned, this was, as a rule, his sole function, and one no longer taken seriously most of the time.

e. Of the several forms of subjection in private law to another person's overlordship known to pre-Hellenistic legal systems, only full chattel slavery still played a role in the Greek law of Egypt, which was perhaps true of the whole Hellenistic world. Nevertheless, its character, which can be no more than indicated here, again reflects the tendency, inherent in the social structures of the time, to efface differences in the sphere of personal status. Legally, the status of a slave could result only from having been born of a slave woman or from having been

[1] A case in which a mother might have functioned as *epitropos* for her minor (this is not quite certain) son appears in *P. Oxy.* VI, 898, from 123 B.C.E.

captured in war, though this latter cause had become insignificant by the time of the Principate at the latest. Foundlings of unknown parentage, whose freedom no one upheld, might also be kept as slaves, though this was not strictly legal. On the other hand, no change of free status resulted legally from a servitude entered into voluntarily on account of debt, or for any other purpose, even if such voluntary servitude lasted for a lifetime. A true slave was a freely disposable and inheritable possession of his master, and could be pawned or sold. At the same time, however, possibly in imitation of Egyptian traditions, the slave might, when dealing with other persons, act with his master's consent as the free titular of his own property, without the Roman concept of *peculium* being brought into play. Similarly, male and female slaves could enter into legally recognized marriage (in the sense described above) both with other slaves and with free persons.

Manumission was permitted. There were various forms of this, some of them probably imitating those of ancient Greece. The private law status of freedmen did not differ basically from that of the free. However, in virtue of special conditions laid down in the act of manumission—it is not known whether in Egypt this might also be by law—the freedman might have certain obligations, such as that of remaining in the service of the manumittor or his family (παραμονή). This duty had been common in the Greek motherland.

Succession

2. It is clear from the foregoing that in a society not organized as a polis—although the following statements are at least in part applicable to Alexandria and probably to other new poleis also[1]—the function of the law of inheritance could no longer be to preserve existing oikoi, but merely to regulate individual succession to property. Hence—in Egypt at any rate—the validity of a testamentary disposition, whether drafted unilaterally and destined to take effect at the testator's death (διαθήκη), as *donatio* or parental distribution *inter vivos* taking effect immediately, or as a contract between a married couple, depended on certain formal conditions: it had to be drawn up in writing (in Roman times, at the latest, in a notarial instrument), and in the presence of witnesses (six in Egypt). Under the aspect of substantive law, however, the result was the disappearance of typical restrictions to which clan-based laws of inheritance had subjected testators and

---

[1] Exceptions for Alexandria emerge from e.g. sections 6, 14, 15 of the so-called *Gnomon of the Idios Logos*.

heirs. Corresponding to the equality of the sexes, now recognized in the law of persons and family, men and women could bequeath their property in the same manner and according to the same principles, while with respect to the right to inherit, only unimportant traces of an earlier distinction between the sexes survived. In particular, the principle valid for instance in classical Athens, under which only the sons of daughters, but not themselves, were able to succeed, was abandoned.

Every free person, whether man or woman, was at liberty to make a will, if of sound mind. No prerequisites were attached to this liberty (as, for instance, the absence of male progeny in Athens), and the property could be disposed of at will. It seems that in the Egyptian chora even a right of certain close relatives of the decedent to claim a minimum portion of the estate was unknown. Outwardly conforming to ancient Greek rules, but in fact proceeding from opposing dogmatic concepts, a will did no more than make individual bequests in matters of property. From the standpoint of theory, this is true even in the case of a will giving all the testator's property to a single heir (κληρόνομος). The conceptual distinction made by Roman law between *hereditas* and *legatum* had no parallel in Hellenistic law.

According to a statute found in Dura-Europos, the estate of a person dying intestate and without leaving natural issue or adopted children (whose place, if they had died before the decedent, would have been taken by their respective descendants), fell to his father' or', i.e. after him, to his mother, provided that she had not remarried; then successively to his full brothers, full sisters, father's father, father's mother, a 'cousin' (unspecified) on the father's side, and failing all these, to the king. If this list, in which neither the spouse nor any collatoral relations on the side of the mother of the deceased had any place, is complete, it may give some idea of the typical rules governing intestacy in a Hellenistic city state. They do not correspond to those force in regions not governed by polis law. In the chora of Egypt the spouse was certainly mentioned between the categories of the children and of the parents of the deceased, and farther down the list, after brothers and their offspring, came his sisters and their descendents. The position of the grandparents is not known, but they were not likely to have been excluded. The systems of both Dura and the Egyptian chora agree, however, in that they reflect a loosening, and in Egypt the total disappearance, of an order of succession oriented towards the preservation of the existing oikos. Its replacement

544

by a mere succession to property is also shown by the reversion, known to both systems, of an unclaimed estate to the treasury.[1]

The absence of any idea of 'universal succession' corresponded to the Greek legal tradition. Its consequence was that the heir had to meet private obligations on the inheritance only from the inherited property, not from his own. Several heirs inherited an estate jointly. While there is evidence in the papyri of division of estates by mutual consent, it is not known whether or in what form a legally enforceable claim for a splitting of property existed. Further details of the law of inheritance must be omitted here.

Property and obligations

1. The Methods of Private Law. While a departure from tradition, a blurring of contours, and a curtailment of set forms were typical features of the fields of Hellenistic private law dealt with so far, the opposite tendency of clinging in the main to traditional concepts, was the distinguishing mark of the law of property transactions to which we shall now turn. In spite of the fact that the Aristotelian philosophy of justice offered points of possible departure, legal theory was as little grasped as in the preceding era. For reasons which cannot be discussed here, there were still no real legal experts who, in the manner of Roman jurists, might have tried to trace the purpose, justice, and implications of norms and institutions.

Nonetheless, the draftsmen of city-state and royal laws (which are only very incompletely known, unfortunately) often produced satisfactory regulations. Even more important was a class of professionals in Egypt and elesewhere who made a living by drafting deeds and other legal instruments. Improving and adapting patterns that had come down from classical times, sometimes inventing new ones, they succeeded quite well in supplying such standard forms for transactions as were needed by the extensive business of the period.

This was made possible by the custom, going back into the close of classical times, of putting down transactions and agreements in writing and keeping them available to the public. Professional scribes and official 'recorders' (μνήμονες) had probably already existed in pre-Hellenistic poleis. They were the predecessors of the well-organized system of notariats and of public archives, which were established in many Hellenistic states, and especially in Egypt. The basic ideas underlying the system were the same everywhere, though details

[1] For Egypt and Alexandria, see sections 4 and 9 of the *Gnomon*.

varied. It ranked among the most remarkable features of Hellenistic juridical culture.

This is not the place to give a detailed description of the type of deeds developed and perfected by these men. Suffice it to mention the most important of them, the συγγραφή, probably a by-product of the international maritime trade of the fourth century B.C.E. Its particular usefulness lay in the fact that it provided incontestable evidence of the contracts it recorded. But it should be noted that this type of drafting was in general the great medium of progress in the law of property and contracts.

2. Private property—understood as a socio-economic principle—was recognized. It is true that there were significant exceptions to this rule in Egypt, particularly in the Ptolemaic era. Here, in consequence of an economic system rigorously enforced in the sole interest of the royal household and strictly supervised by the authorities, it was for the most part only precarious rights of usufruct that were granted to tenants, often settled by constraint on agricultural land; today these rights would come within the sphere of public law. An intermediate position was occupied by the homesteads (κλῆροι) of military colonists (κάτοικοι). The homestead was originally allotted to the tenant merely as a personal fief for his own benefit, but from late Ptolemaic times onward, it was gradually transformed into genuine property. Since both tendencies were more or less local phenomena, no details need be given here.

From the point of view of juridical construction, Hellenistic law retained the ancient and primitive Greek concept of a sometimes more and sometimes less comprehensive, but not sharply defined, title. It recognized neither the Roman distinction between ownership and possession, nor a limited *ius in re aliena* qualitatively different from the full right of ownership. In practice, the concepts of κυριεία, i.e. the power of disposal, and of κράτησις, i.e. the effective but not necessarily direct physical dominion which nevertheless warranted seizure, were held to be sufficient. The content and relative importance of these concepts were determined by the strength of the position in each case, whether it was ownership in the full sense of the term, a lien, or a right to usufruct, involving to a certain extent *kyrieia* and *kratesis*, including that of a lessee or renter. Joint owners of undivided property possessed *kyrieia* over the right to their portion, i.e. they could freely dispose of it.

The sources do not, however, permit us to assert with certainty that in the administration of justice in Hellenistic law courts the theoretical approach described above was still maintained to its full extent. Still, it is not unlikely that at least some legislations, such as perhaps a great Ptolemaic statute on the forms and matters of litigation, known as the edict (διάγραμμα), preserved traditional Greek principles to a large extent. It may be assumed that the legislators still knew nothing of direct actions for the surrender of property or the restitution of possessions, but only διαδικασίαι, i.e. litigation between contestants for the simple determination of the better title, and tort actions against unjustifiable interference with any legal position, even though the latter might be objectively unjust. In any case, no cogent argument against this follows from the fact that in Egypt, under the Ptolemies and the Romans, petitions were quite commonplace for the exercise of official compulsion in respect of the surrender or vacating of movables and immovables, as were also court rulings to this effect. All this took place in the quasi-juridical domain of administrative officials. These, by virtue of the power of coercion vested in them, were in a position to work directly toward the establishment of the legally-correct and socially desired condition. They had no need to concern themselves with forms of action (δίκαι) based on doctrinaire types of thinking, such as were possibly still determining the justice rendered by the *dikasteria*, i.e. the true courts in the traditional Greek sense. The administrative practice contained no doubt in embryo an independent and dogmatically founded law of property. That it did not develop was probably due to the lack of jurists interested in the systematic approach.

The derivative acquisition of a title protected in this way depended on the disposition of the alienator, who determined (if of course legally competent) at his own discretion the cause and content of the title conceded to the alienee. As we are now aware, no separation comparable to the one made by the Roman law existed between the transaction fixing the cause (e.g. sale or gift) of a transfer and its performance. Consequently, a buyer's title to the object of a purchase came into existence only—and immediately—on payment of the purchase price, regardless of whether the object itself was or was not handed over (principle of 'surrogation'). No formalities were required. The deed, without which in Egypt, and probably elsewhere also, no dealings were ever transacted in land or slaves, and rarely in less important matters, was equipped with a *kyria*-clause (see below), which made its contents incontestable, thus protecting the purchase from avoidance on

547

the part of the seller. An older theory which attributed to it a dispositive effect disregarded the priority in Hellenistic legal thought of the procedural approach and is no longer tenable.

Under Ptolemaic law, acquisition of land and slaves had to be entered (by a καταγραφή) in a register kept by the local notary (ἀγορανόμος). The certificate of the entry issued by the official to the purchaser served notice to the public that he was authorized to further dealings with respect to the object, but did not replace a title actually missing. It offered a third purchaser no absolute protection against eviction. The 'property archive' (βιβλιοθήκη ἐγκτήσεων), more effective yet similar in principle, which the Romans established in place of the *katagraphe*, realized this same legal concept. *Bona fide* acquisition of title by purchase from someone not entitled to alienate the object was not recognized. The existence of prescription is doubtful.

Contracts

a. The Hellenistic art of drafting documents achieved its greatest triumphs in providing standard forms of contract. Here again there was no great progress in the theory. There was, for example, no elaboration of more refined criteria for establishing responsibility for breach of contract, or of a differentiated method of assessing damages. But technical skills were developed which allowed the law to go beyond the more or less fixed types of liability which originally marked its limits. They invented, for instance, the device that a seller might temporarily leave the price with the purchaser, in the manner of a loan thus achieveing the economically desired effect of a purchase on credit without infringing on the traditional juridical tenet that purchase was strictly a cash transaction.[1]

Such results were attained in part thanks to a better view, in the light of experience, of the possibilities of application inherent in the existing types of transactions. Even more important was a breakthrough in the art of draftmanship which took place at the latest in the third century B.C.E. The word ὁμολογεῖν (literally, to speak alike, i.e. to recognize, concede), stemming ultimately from the lawcourts and still used in a rather undetermined sense by the Attic orators, was raised to the level of a technical term for a binding declaration. Combined with the *kyria*-clause, which was a regular part of the deed

---

[1] We 'must, in any case, reckon with eastern or Egyptian prototypes; thus on the example mentioned in the text, see M. San Nicolò, *Beiträge zur Rechtsgeschichte im Bereich der keilschriftlichen Rechtsquellen*, 1931, p. 197.

and guaranteed the facts named as the basis of the transaction, the *homologia* made possible the creation of a liability arising from an event that had occurred prior to the contract or even to one only fictitiously supposed. In practice this meant the overcoming of undesirable consequences of the demand—always retained in principle—for a real substratum for every lien (see below).

The mention of this last demand, however, brings to mind at once limits of the progressiveness of the draftsmen resulting from the fact that they could not rid themselves of certain archaic notions of law. One of these archaisms resulted from the fact that the legal thinking of the time concentrated exclusively on the effects of legal relations in terms of liability (the procedural effects). This lay behind the unswerving adherence of draftsmen, century after century, to a contract schema which did not aim at creating a claim to specific performance, but merely permitted the disappointed creditor to seize, by way of execution (πρᾶξις), the debtor's person and/or property. The debtor could avoid the *praxis* only by payment of a ransom usually exceeding the value of the original debt; in other words, it was only the payment of a penalty agreed on in advance, but not the performance of the undertaking as such, that was enforceable. Certainly, the opportunity, open to contracting parties already in classical times, of determining autonomously the conditions and modalities of such a *praxis* had originally been a prerequisite for the development of the organized contract system that we find in the papyri of Egypt and other countries of Hellenistic law. But the Hellenistic world did not go beyond this point. It never produced contract schemas which, by providing for immediately enforceable claims to performance, secured the satisfaction of the substantial interests of the persons concerned. The almost total absence of a mutually binding *homologia* is one of the consequences typical of this doctrinaire fixation on the aspect of liability alone.

There was, however, still another archaism which obstructed progress toward a contract schema simply conceived from the viewpoint of substantive law. It lay in the clinging to the principle already mentioned, that every contractual relation had to be founded on some real transaction. Hellenistic law did not attach any binding force to the promise as such. As in classical times, the dogmatic justification for granting a *praxis*, as well as the basis for assessing a penalty, was still found exclusively in the concrete damage to property which the creditor would suffer in case of his debtor's default. Historically this may have sprung from an original method of linking default on an undertaking to the tort known to Attic law as βλάβη (damage to property). The practical effect was that each contract had to be founded on an actual act of disposal of property, as a rule moving from the creditor to the debtor (e.g. the handing-over of money lent or the cession of premises given in lease), in consideration of which the debtor assumed his obligation and exposed himself to a possible *praxis*, because the act would have proved to have been in vain in case of default on the obligation (principle of the 'Zweckverfügung,' i.e. act of disposal for a determined purpose). One of the results of this rather backward conception was the impossibility of extending the notion of contractual damages to loss of profit on the part of the creditor due to default on the part of the debtor, since it did not diminish his actual estate.

It is in line with the principles described that in spite of local, temporal, and formal differences, and regardless of variations of content and style, most of the private contracts from Hellenistic times, which have been preserved in immense numbers, present basically a homogeneous schema. This schema contains a statement of the *causa*, necessarily consisting in a 'Zweckverfügung', then the obligation undertaken on these grounds and, finally, as a rule, a clause explicitly providing for a *praxis*. The latter is sometimes absent, but the reason is in most cases that the right of execution follows directly from statutory law. For example, the Ptolemaic *diagramma* seems to have provided for direct action against sureties and those who undertook to guarantee the freedom of an object of purchase from any rights of a third party (cases of ἐγγύη and βεβαίωσις—bail and warranty).

A detailed analysis of common types of transactions, and of the rules governing each case, would exceed the scope of this survey. A few indications must suffice. It is remarkable that the number of these types, which, as we have seen, were turned with great skill to serve many kinds of practical needs, was comparatively small. If the picture presented by the papyrological sources is not deceptive, they were all of Greek origin. It did, of course, happen that parties sought to give effect in a Greek document to a form of transaction embedded in native law (Jewish, Egyptian, etc.). In such a case, the draftsman would try to adjust the substance of the native contract to a type corresponding to Greek legal concepts.

The type most frequently employed seems to have been the loan (δάνειον); basically a cash transaction, it was developed into a general credit contract which could serve a large variety of purposes. Another contract of great practical importance was μίσθωσις. It was used primarily for the leasing of agricultural land, but also for the hiring out of other objects, including the lessor's own person, for labour or services. Further types cannot be listed here, for lack of space. It should be noted, however, that an agreement to buy or sell did *not* belong to the group of transactions creating a liability based on a 'Zweckverfügung', such as is described above. Purchase was strictly a cash transaction. No liability for the buyer arose from it, while the seller might be only indirectly liable by virtue of a warranty (see above).

The necessity of founding every contract on a 'Zweckverfügung' led to the consequence that arrangements which could not be attached to such an act were unattainable. For instance, the handing over of money to a person charged with its delivery resulted in a liability for him,[1] but a counter-claim for a refund of his expenses, which according to Roman law followed from the mandate, would not readily meet with success.

b. If the silence of the sources on this point is to be trusted, it was, in the whole Hellenistic world, almost exclusively the draftsmen of deeds who were professionally concerned with legal problems, as has been said. They were certainly excellent technicians within the limits of their field, but they were not true jurists, interested in the law as such or as a whole. It is not surprising, therefore, that such notions regarding the law of contracts as did not immediately fall into their sphere of activity remained primitive. Two examples are the absence of any trace of a theory concerning the requirements of a valid intention, and the helplessness, already indicated, of the legal experts vis-à-vis the problem of a debtor's responsibility.

All the more characteristic then, is the naïve practical skill with which these draftsmen grasped the advantages offered them by the fact that their notion of the contractual relation did not so much emphasize the personal bond between debtor and creditor, i.e. the *vinculum juris* of the Romans, as the latter's objective right to *praxis*. They discovered that this in itself could be treated as a freely-disposable object. It was possible to authorize a person not party to the contract to carry through the *praxis* provided for by the contract. Likewise, the person authorized by the *praxis* clause might transfer, even without

---

[1] See e.g. *P. Ent.* 89 of 222 B.C.E.

the debtor's consent, this right to a third person (the technical expression was παραχωρεῖν, conveying the idea of stepping aside, or ceding).

With the aid of such simple devices, a number of desirable results were achieved with less effort, and sometimes with better effect, than the Romans attained. There is evidence in the papyri of agency, contracts to the benefit of third persons, and assignment of claims, though these were quite different, from the point of view of legal dogma, from the civil law institutions of the present day to which they outwardly correspond. It was possible, through an addition to the *kyria*-clause of a deed, to authorize every future bearer of the document to carry through a *praxis*; and in one case even the simple leaving of a blank space in the *praxis*-clause for the future insertion of a creditor's name instituted a sort of bearer bond.[1] It should of course be remembered that from a doctrinal point of view all this is very different from outwardly similar phenomena existing in modern legal systems.

c. Additional security to creditors was obtained through sureties and pledges. Both institutions, especially the first-mentioned, rested in the main on principles similar to those of classical times.

(i) The surety was considered to be a second person liable to the creditor. Inasmuch as he was under the same threat of *praxis* as the principal debtor himself, which he could only avert by paying the same ransom, he served to increase the creditor's chances of successfully collecting the penalty: hence the technical expression ἔγγυος εἰς ἔκτισιν (guarantor of the ransom). It was left to the creditor's discretion to seize whom of the two he wished. The surety, who according to modern legal thinking rather resembles a joint debtor, enjoyed no *beneficium excussionis*. His liability depended on no express declaration of his intention; it was sufficient for him to participate in fact in the debtor's transaction and to be named as surety in the latter's deed.

(ii) The various types of real securities to be described on the following pages were, as far as one can see, typically associated with loans. (Security provisos of lessors cannot be dealt with here).

Apart from the simple pledge (ἐνέχυρον), the oldest type of security was the *hypotheke*, extending back into classical times. As then, *hypotheke* still seems to have been a special technical term for the fiduciary sale, repeatedly recurring in the papyri as ὠνὴ ἐν πίστει.

[1] *P. Sammelb.* v, 7532 of 74 B.C.E.

Its object, either land or slaves, remained for the time being in the possession of the pledger. In principle, though this admitted of exceptions, both types of pledge functioned as substitutes for the debt itself. That is to say, on the one hand, that even though the value of the claim secured might exceed that of the object pledged, the debtor was not liable beyond forfeiting the pledge; while, on the other, the unredeemed pledge fell to the creditor without his having to refund a value exceeding the debt (ὑπεροχή). The creditor could proceed to realize his right of seizure in the case of default on the date agreed on. But the security had an actual effect even before this, inasmuch as the creditor was entitled to claim it from the transferee if the pledger had alienated it in the meantime.

At least in Egypt, the *hypotheke* retained its practical importance into a late period, despite its primitive structure. But in Hellenistic times, other and more modern forms of real security gained significance beside the ἐνέχυρον and the ὑποθήκη. In Egypt, and perhaps elsewhere, the *hypallagma* came into use. Like the *hypotheke*, it resulted in the forfeiture of its object (again land or slaves) to the creditor. Its legal structure, however, was not that of a conditional transfer of title, with merely a postponed right of seizure. It consisted only in keeping certain pieces of property available for preferential seizure in the case of a necessary *praxis*. Therefore, its immediate and proper function was limited to simplifying enforcement. However, by submitting to bans on disposal, probably operating *in rem*, pledgers usually bestowed on the *hypallagma* the character of a security.

Vis-à-vis the *hypotheke*, the *hypallagma* was distinguished by its predominant orientation toward the interests of creditors in securing effective satisfaction. Even more was this the purpose of customary agreements, probably also dating back to pre-Hellenistic times, by which creditors were authorized, or even obliged, to sell the pledge after the debt had fallen due. Arrangements of this kind regularly included the right of a creditor to bring a supplementary *praxis* in order to recover a possible deficit (ἐλλείποντα) from the sale. To an ever-increasing extent, this right was coupled with the corresponding obligation to surrender any surplus (ὑπεροχή).

The last of the draftsmen's inventions which we note is ἀντίχρησις. In many cases its purpose and effect were not so much to give the creditor a real security in the proper sense, as to provide him with a means to exert pressure on the debtor. It could also serve as an arrangement for the amortization of the debt. It consisted in the ceding of a farm or urban residence to the creditor for his own use until settlement of the credit granted. Its preferred form was that of a lease for a fictitious rent equated with the interest and/or, if such were the case, the amortization installments.

Torts

A lengthy description of the law of torts, the details of which are in any case only fragmentarily known, is superfluous. It will be sufficient to record a few matters of principle suggested by the Egyptian papyri and to indicate a few of the more important individual torts.

Some textually preserved norms, as well as some references to others, confirm that in the earlier Ptolemaic era no private action on account of an extra-contractual wrong was allowed unless it was based on a tort the character and sanction of which were explicitly defined by statutory law. It may be presumed that this corresponded to a tenet held generally in Hellenistic legal thinking. This statement is, in any case, not contradicted by the fact that the principle may have been exposed to a gradual softening under the bureaucratic administration of justice as handled in the later Ptolemaic and in the Roman epochs by the officials who acted within their far-reaching power of coercion and were no longer strictly bound to observe the statutes. Also typical were probably the sanctions evident from the earlier Ptolemaic papyri. Normally the offender had to pay a monetary penalty to the injured party who might avail himself of the machinery of *praxis* in order to exact it. A slave was subjected to corporal punishment unless his master intervened by paying a cash penalty.[1] Sometimes the wronged party was permitted, in addition to his right to demand compensation, to take independent action on the culprit's own premises in order to eliminate the tortious situation. Such was the case, for example, under an Alexandrian statute regulating the relations of neighbours.[2]

As far as individual regulations are concerned, uniformity of methods can hardly be presumed, except, perhaps, for some imitation of classical models. The systems of Alexandria and of the Ptolemaic kingdom seem to have followed in some respects the example of Athens. In other respects, especially as regards legal terminology, they went their own way. An illustration is offered by their treatment of ὕβρις

---

[1] See e.g. the Alexandrian law of *hybris*, *P. Hal.* 1 col. VIII, 11. 186 ff. (Hunt and Edgar, op.cit., II, no. 202).

[2] *P. Hal.* 1, col. V, 11. 101 ff.

(overbearing behaviour). In a characteristic deviation from Attic polis law, this term no longer denoted insolence considered unbecoming a citizen, which could subject him to criminal prosecution by any citizen who wished to initiate it. It now stood for the strictly private tort of bodily assault. On the whole, the tort law of the Ptolemaic diagramma appears to reflect a realistic account of existing conditions. As characteristic examples may be mentioned regulations combating usury and the infringement by private individuals on the personal freedom of others,[1] or the threat of a threefold penalty to be inflicted on a bailiff who, in carrying through a *praxis*, violated the interests of the creditor.[2]

BIBLIOGRAPHY

The existence and significance, from the point of view of legal history, of a Hellenistic legal culture surviving under Roman rule in the eastern part of the Imperium Romanum, was discovered by L. MITTEIS, whose *Reichsrecht und Volksrecht in den östlichen Provinzen des römischen Kaiserreichs*, published in 1891, still remains a standard work in spite of many modifications to which his findings were naturally subjected in the course of time. A first comprehensive survey of papyrological legal research, necessarily still fragmentary and now outdated in some parts, was presented by L. MITTEIS in the juridical section of *Grundzüge und Chrestomathie der Papyruskunde*, 1912, published by himself and U. WILCKEN. More recent general studies: R. TAUBENSCHLAG, *The Law of Greco-Roman Egypt in the Light of the Papyri*, 2nd ed., 1955; E. SEIDL, *Ptolemäische Rechtsgeschichte*, 2nd ed., 1962. A more precise justification of some viewpoints in the present article, which deviate from those of earlier authors, will be found in the present author's forthcoming treatment of the law of the Greek papyri in the *Handbuch der Altertumswissenschaft*.

On the organization of the Ptolemaic judiciary and other matters forming the background of private law, see H. J. WOLFF, *Das Justizwesen der Ptolemäer*, 1970, and 'Plurality of Laws in Ptolemaic Egypt' in *RIDA*, 1960, pp. 191 ff. (particularly on the principle of *lex fori*).

---

[1] For both, see *P. Col. Zen.* II, 83 from 245-244 B.C.E.
[2] *P. Hib.* I, 34, II. 8 ff., from 243-242 B.C.E. (Mitteis, *Chrestomathie*, no. 34).

Although antiquated as to method, the fullest information concerning the private law of ancient Greece is still to be found in L. BEAUCHET, *Histoire du droit privé de la République Athénienne*, 4 vols, 1897. More modern are A. R. W. HARRISON, *The Law of Athens I: The Family and Property*, 1968, *II: Procedure*, 1971, and the present author's article 'Griechisches Recht' in *Lexikon der Alten Welt*, 1965, cols 2517 ff.

For a definition of the concept of Hellenism, from which the present author differs, however, as regards the chronology, see the foreword to M. ROSTOVTZEFF's *Social and Economic History of the Hellenistic World*, 1941. The artificiality of the pseudo-'tribal' system of Alexandria was already emphasized by J. SEYFARTH, *Aegyptus*, 1955, p. 10. For a description of the Hellenistic immigration into the countries of the East, see ROSTOVTZEFF, op.cit., pp. 1054 ff. On the constitutional status of the Greeks in Egypt, see e.g. TAUBENSCHLAG, op.cit., p. 584, and ROSTOVTZEFF, op.cit., p. 1394, note 121.

On the situation of women in Hellenism, including their status with respect to the laws of marriage and succession, see the recent works of C. PRÉAUX, 'Le statut de la femme à l'époque hellénistique, principalement en Egypte' in *Receuil de la Soc. Jean Bodin XI: La Femme*, 1959, pp. 127 ff. and C. VATIN, *Recherches sur le mariage et la condition de la femme mariée à l'époque hellénistique*, 1970. Unfortunately these writers paid insufficient attention to the interdependence of sociological conditions and private law, and therefore seem to underestimate the extent and significance of changes in the latter as compared to the classical period. P.W. PESTMAN gives a useful survey in *Over vrouwen en voogden in het oude Egypte*, 1969.

The description of the marriage law given in the preceding text is based on the author's *Written and Unwritten Marriages in Hellenistic and Post-classical Roman Law*, 1939, and on his supplementary remarks in *Tijdschrift voor Rechtsgeschiedenis*, 1952, pp. 164 ff. On sibling marriage see J. MODRZEJEWSKI, 'Die Geschwisterehe in der hellenistischen Praxis und nach römischem Recht', *ZSS*, 1964, pp. 52 ff. The authoritative work on marriage property relations is now G. HÄGE, *Ehegüterrechtliche Verhältnisse in den griechischen Papyri bis Diokletian*, 1968.

For details of the law of guardianship, a reference to the hand-books mentioned above is sufficient; on the *kyrieia* over women, in particular, see PESTMAN, op.cit., pp. 241 ff. A survey of facts concerning the law of slavery is given by R. TAUBENSCHLAG, 'Das Sklavenrecht im Rechte der Papyri,' in *ZSS*, 1930, pp. 140 ff. (*Opera Minora* II, 1959, pp. 223 ff.). Juridically inadequate, but instructive from the standpoint of social and economic history is W. L. WESTERMANN, *The Slave Systems of Greek and Roman Antiquity*, 1955, sections 5-8. On conditions in ancient Greece, see M. I. FINLEY, 'The Servile Statuses of Ancient Greece' in *RIDA*, 1960, pp. 165 ff. Some remarks on the παραμονή of freedmen in Egypt appear in A. R. SAMUEL, *Journal of Jur. Papyr.*, 1965, pp. 296 ff. Scholars up to now have shown comparatively little interest in the Hellenistic law of inheritance. Therefore, if we prescind from its too Romanistic approach, H. KRELLER's extremely careful *Erbrechtliche Untersuchungen auf Grund der graeco-aegyptischen Papyrusurkunden*, 1919, is still authoritative, and may remain so in the main. On the Dura-Europos law of intestacy see MODRZEJEWSKI, 'La dévolution à l'état des successions en déshérence dans le droit hellénistique', *RIDA*, 1961, pp. 79 ff.

On the absence of true jurists, see H. J. WOLFF, 'Rechtsexperten in der griechischen Antike', *Festschrift für den 45. Deutschen Juristentag*, 1964, pp. 1 ff.; on the skill of Hellenistic draftsmen see F. PRINGSHEIM, *The Greek Law of Sale*, 1950, pp. 501 ff. J. PARTSCH, 'Die griechische Publizität der Grundstücksverträge im Ptolemäerrechte', in *Festschrift für O. Lenel*, 1921, pp. 77 ff., is authoritative on institutions of pre-Hellenistic times, but outdated on Ptolemaic law. A definitive survey of the types of deeds used in Hellenistic times has not yet been given; meanwhile, see H. STEINACKER, *Die antiken Grundlagen der frühmittelalterlichen Privaturkunde*, 1927, pp. 28 ff., 129 ff.; also SEIDL, op.cit., pp. 59 ff.

Concerning property law, we must be content with referring to the relevant sections of TAUBENSCHLAG's and SEIDL's handbooks, cited above. See besides the collection of source materials in R. TAUBENSCHLAG, 'Der Schutz der Rechtsverhältnisse an Liegenschaften im gräko-ägyptischen Recht' in *ZSS*, 1955 (Opera Minora II, pp. 381 ff.). In view of the adherence in the Hellenistic period to the dogmatic concepts of the previous age, the contributions of M. KASER, 'Der altgriechische Eigentumsschutz' in *ZSS*, 1944, pp. 134 ff., and A. KRÄNZLEIN, *Eigentum und Besitz im griechischen Recht des fünften und vierten Jahrhunderts v. Chr.*, 1963, are important; but on the latter see H. J. WOLFF in *ZSS*, 1964, pp. 333 ff. A study of agricultural property law in the Ptolemaic era is found in PRÉAUX, *L'économie royale des Lagides*, 1939, pp. 459 ff. See further W. KUNKEL, 'Über die Veräusserung von Katökenland', in *ZSS*, 1928, pp. 285 ff. The 'principle of surrogation' was first discovered by F. PRINGSHEIM, see his early work *Der Kauf mit fremden Geld*, 1916, now expanded in his *Greek Law of Sale*.

On the question of the 'dispositive effect' of documents, we must be content with referring to STEINACKER, op.cit., pp. 25 ff., and to the literature cited by him. Compare further M. HÄSSLER, *Die Bedeutung der Kyria-Klausel in den Papyrusurkunden*, 1960. The thesis that καταγραφή signifies the registration of transactions was first established by E. RABEL in *ZSS*, 1934, pp. 189 ff. (*Gesammelte Aufsätze* IV, 1971, pp. 513 ff.), and further developed by the present author in 'Registration of Conveyances in Ptolemaic Egypt' in *Aegyptus*, 1948, pp. 17 ff. (with a complete bibliography and discussion of divergent views of A. B. SCHWARZ and E. SCHÖNBAUER). The reference made above to the function of the βιβλιοθήκη ἐγκτήσεων is an attempt to summarize the theory which F. V. WOESS, *Untersuchungen über das Urkundenwesen und den Publizitätsschutz in römischen Ägypten*, 1924, substituted for that of MITTEIS, according to whom the βιβλιοθήκη was an institution similar to a modern land register (of the German or French type).

Of older literature on the law of contracts in the papyri, see above all V. ARANGIO-RUIZ, *Lineamenti del sistema contrattuale nel diritto dei papiri*, 1927; also F. WEBER, *Untersuchungen zum gräko-ägyptischen Obligationenrecht: Modalitäten der Leistung im Rechte der Papyri*, 1932, who did not, however, realize the archaic character of the Hellenistic 'law of obligations'; the phenomenona from which, in agreement with A. B. SCHWARZ, *Die öffentliche und private Urkunde im römischen Ägypten*, (Studien zum hellenistischen Privatrecht), 1920, pp. 84 ff., he deduced the existence of a debt relationship conceived in terms of substantive law, are fully explicable on the grounds of the theory advanced here. The latter is the result of the present author's study on 'Die Grundlagen des griechischen Vertragsrechts' in *ZSS*, 1957, pp. 26 ff. (republished in E. BERNEKER, *Zur griechischen Rechtsgeschichte*, 1968, pp. 483 ff.). *Zweckverfügung*, or 'act of disposal for a determined purpose', a term proposed in that article, should be understood as relating to procedure, i.e. as forming a basis for the right to *praxis*. It should not be confused with the 'principle of necessary compensation' postulated by SEIDL. The latter is conceived from the viewpoint of the debtor's interests; in other words, it is a concept of substantive law.

For recent discussions of various types of transaction, see H. KÜHNERT, *Zum Kreditgeschäft in den hellenistischen Papyri Ägyptens bis Diokletian*, 1965; H. A. RUPRECHT, *Untersuchungen zum Darlehen im Recht der graeco-aegyptischen Papyri der Ptolemäerzeit*, 1967; D. SIMON,' Quasi-*parakatatheke*; Zugleich ein Beitrag zur Morphologie griechisch-hellenistischer Schuldrechtstatbestände', *ZSS*, 1965, pp. 39 ff.; M. TALAMANCA, *L'arra della compravendita in diritto greco e in diritto romano*, 1958; J. HERRMANN, *Studien zur Bodenpacht im Recht der graeco-aegyptischen Papyri*, 1958; 'Vertragsinhalt und Rechtsnatur der didaskalikai', *Journal of Juristic Papyrology*, 1958, pp. 119 ff.; B. ADAMS, *Paramoné und verwandte Texte, Studien zum Dienstvertrag im Rechte der Papyri*, 1964. The nature of purchase as a strictly cash transaction was first worked out by J. PARTSCH, *Göttinger Gelehrten Anzeigen*, 1911, pp. 713 ff. (*Aus nachgelassenen und kleineren verstreuten Schriften*, 1931, pp. 262 ff.) and fully set forth by PRINGSHEIM in his *Greek Law of Sale*.

On the free disposability of the right to *praxis*, see WOLFF, 'Die Praxisklausel in Papyrusverträgen', *Beiträge zur Rechtsgeschichte Altgriechenlands und des hellenistisch-römischen Ägypten*, 1961, pp. 102 ff. The view still shared by some scholars that Hellenistic law recognized direct agency in the sense attributed to it by modern civil law, was argued by L. WENGER, *Die Stellvertretung im Rechte der Papyri*, 1906, but effectively refuted by E. RABEL, 'Die Stellvertretung in den hellenistischen Rechten und in Rom', *Atti del Congresso Internazionale di Diritto Romano* I, 1934, pp. 235 ff., and on 'Systasis' in *Archives d' Hist. du Droit Oriental* I, pp. 213 ff. (*Gesammelte Aufsätze* IV, pp. 491 ff., 607 ff).

The authoritative work on the Graeco-Hellenistic law of suretyship remains J. PARTSCH's *Griechisches Bürgschaftsrecht I. Teil: Das Recht des altgriechischen Gemeindestaats*, 1909, with supplements in K. SETHE and J. PARTSCH, *Demotische Urkunden zum ägyptischen Bürgschaftsrechte vorzüglich der Ptolemäerzeit*, 1920; a recent discussion of the institution is found in H. W. VAN SOEST, *De civielrechtelijke engye* (*garantieovereenkomst*) *in de griekse papyri uit het ptolemaeische tijdvak*, 1963.

Elucidation of the principles governing real securities is due mainly to L. RAAPE, *Der Verfall des griechischen Pfandes, besonders des griechisch-ägyptischen*, 1912, and A. B. SCHWARZ, *Hypothek und Hypallagma. Beitrag zum Pfand- und Vollstreckungsrecht der griechischen Papyri*, 1911, and 'Sicherungsübereignung und Zwangsvollstreckung in den Papyri', in *Aegyptus*, 1937, pp. 241 ff.

The subject of torts has been very little worked on so far. Mention may be made of the relevant chapters in TAUBENSCHLAG, *Das Strafrecht im Rechte der Papyri*, 1916, and of section IV ('Das Injurienrecht') in PARTSCH's article on the Alexandrian *dikaiomata* in *Archiv für Papyrusforschung*, 1920, pp. 34 ff. (54 ff.).